Stephen Parker

Peter Huchel

A Literary Life in 20th-Century Germany

PETER LANG

Bern · Berlin · Frankfurt /M. · New York · Paris · Wien

Die Deutsche Bibliothek – CIP-Einheitsaufnahme

Parker, Stephen:
Peter Huchel : a literary life in the 20th-century Germany / Stephen
Parker. – Bern ; Berlin ; Frankfurt/M. ; New York ; Paris ; Wien :
Lang, 1998
(British and Irish studies in German language and literature ; Bd. 15)
ISBN 3-906760-55-3

ISSN 0171-6662
ISBN 3-906760-55-3
US-ISBN 0-8204-4202-X

T

© Peter Lang AG, European Academic Publishers, Berne 1998

Printed in Germany

1001367880

A l'ami inconnu et anonyme
connu et nommé Huchel et son
ombre, et son silence.
Cheng Tcheng
Paris, le 9 Juillet 1928[1]

Acknowledgements

Work on this book has taken more years than I care to remember. I have incurred many debts on the way and should like to acknowledge at least some of them here. I was introduced to Huchel's poetry as an undergraduate by Raymond Hargreaves at the University of Leeds. As a research student at the University of Manchester, I had the good fortune to be supervised by Rhys Williams and to enjoy the excellent facilities of the John Rylands University Library as well as the support of its dedicated staff. During my spell as a lector at the University of Mannheim, a number of people encouraged me in my work, particularly Hermann Fischer.

While in Mannheim, I first made contact with Dora Huchel, Peter Huchel's first wife, and their daughter, Susanne Huchel, who kindly invited me to visit them at their home in Mora, Sweden. A mere doctoral student, I was unusually privileged in being given access by them to the family library, documents and their testimonies of their life with Peter Huchel. This visit in 1981 set my research on a trajectory which reaches its conclusion with the publication of the present study. Susanne Huchel contributed decisively to its development through her decision after her mother's death to release the material at her disposal, which was acquired by the John Rylands University Library of Manchester. The acquisition would not have taken place without the efforts of David Miller, John Tuck and Roger Paulin. Thereafter, the John Rylands Research Institute awarded me a Research Fellowship and a Bursary, which enabled me to write a book of the scope that my material demanded. The Research Institute joined with the Research and Graduate School in the Faculty of Arts to provide generous subventions for its publication. I am particularly grateful to Richard Hogg, Research and Graduate Dean, and Peter McNiven of the Research Institute.

The final manuscript emerged from a number of preliminary studies. I should like to thank the editors of the following journals and books for permission to reproduce material that was first published in them: *German Life and Letters*; *Internationales Archiv für Sozialgeschichte der deutschen Literatur*; *Bulletin of the John Rylands University Library of Manchester*; *Rundfunk und Fernsehen*; *German Monitor*; *German Writers and the Cold War*; *Sinn und Form*; *Aliens – Uneingebürgerte*; and *Neophilologus*. My colleagues in the Manchester German Department were patient and discerning in their comments on a number of papers, while special thanks are due to Ricarda Schmidt for her scrupulous and perceptive reading of the manuscript. My other readers include Ian Wallace, without whose support the manuscript might never have seen the light of day, and my friend, Justus Fetscher, whose knowledge and acumen have long been an enormous boon.

After the collapse of the GDR, Justus encouraged me to visit Berlin and Potsdam archives that might contain information about Huchel. Short trips were funded by the University of Manchester, during which I met the editorial staff of *Sinn und Form*. The chapters on Huchel's GDR years would have been unthinkable without Sebastian Kleinschmidt, Gisela Schöne and, above all, Heide Lipecky. Our mutual interest in the journal's history during Huchel's editorship became the focus for an extremely productive exchange and collaboration, which grew into a parallel project in its own right. A year in Berlin to conduct the necessary archival research was generously funded by the Alexander von Humboldt-Stiftung and sponsored by Eberhard Lämmert of the Free University's Institut für Allgemeine und Vergleichende Literaturwissenschaft. During that year, I discovered additional material which has been incorporated in the present study. Then and earlier, I had access to a number of Berlin's excellent libraries, principally the Staatsbibliothek and those of the Free University, as well as to archives located in institutions that I list below, together with others which I consulted from the early 1980s until the mid-1990s: Aufbau Verlag, Berlin; Bundesarchiv, Berlin, Koblenz and Potsdam; Bezirksamt Steglitz; Brandenburgisches Landeshauptarchiv, Potsdam; Der Bundesbeauftragte für die Unterlagen des Staatssicherheitsdienstes der ehemaligen Deutschen Demokratischen Republik, Berlin; Deutsches Literaturarchiv, Marbach; Deutsches Rundfunkarchiv, Frankfurt am Main and Berlin; Geheimes Staatsarchiv Preußischer Kulturbesitz, Berlin; Hermann-Ehlers-Oberschule, Berlin; Hessischer Rundfunk, Frankfurt am Main; Humboldt-Gymnasium, Potsdam; Humboldt-University, Berlin; John Rylands University Library of Manchester; Kulturbund, Berlin; Magistrat der Stadt Wien; Norddeutscher Rundfunk, Hamburg; Pädagogisches Zentrum, Berlin; Polizeipräsident, Berlin; Sächsische Landesbibliothek, Dresden; Staats- und Universitätsbibliothek, Hamburg; Stiftung Archiv der Akademie der Künste Berlin-Brandenburg, Berlin; Stiftung Archiv der Parteien und Massenorganisationen der DDR (now in the Bundesarchiv), Berlin; Schloß Elmau, Mittenwald; Stadtarchiv, Potsdam; Süddeutscher Rundfunk, Stuttgart; University of Freiburg; and University of Vienna. The following individuals were particularly helpful in my searches and in correspondence: Ruth Dinesen; Brigitte Fischer; Doris Fürstenberg; Rolf Harder; Barbara Heinze; Carla Krüger; Ludvík Kundera; Herr Lange; Gesine von Prittwitz; Dietmar Röhl; Frau Rogalla; Petra Uhlmann; Manfred Voigts; Joachim Walther; Frau Weber; and Carsten Wurm. I also benefited from conversations with Wolfram Wessels and Hans Dieter Zimmermann. Although this is not an 'official' biography, I should like to thank Huchel's widow, Monica, for agreeing to see me.

Above all, however, I owe an immense debt to Chris Banerji, who improved countless drafts and helped in so many other ways. It is to Chris that this book is dedicated.

Manchester, March 1998

Contents

Introduction

Those who met Peter Huchel remember a man who was physically attractive in a quite unusual way, an unassuming man with a capacity to remain wholly silent and still for lengthy periods, as if completely self-absorbed, yet whose presence in any company was unmistakable simply because he exuded an extraordinary charisma. He was a big man, whose movements were, however, quite understated; they were informed by an ease and grace that blended in a most pleasing, winning fashion with a conversational manner that was coloured by a gentle, self-deprecating irony. Before they filled out and dropped in old age, his facial features were drawn so finely as to suggest a delicate fragility barely in keeping with his size, while his dark brown eyes, warm yet always tinged with melancholy, conveyed a sensibility easily wounded.

Throughout his life, fellow writers attested to his fascinating appearance. Shortly after the war, Elisabeth Langgässer wrote to Oda Schaefer, a mutual friend and an admirer of Huchel's from the Berlin *Kolonne* Circle of the 1930s, telling her of her recent meetings with him. Langgässer confided to Schaefer, 'Beim Anschauen H.s geht es mir ähnlich, Odalein, wie bei Dir – ich könnte ihn stundenlang betrachten ohne eine Spur von Sexualität'.[1] Willy Haas, the influential editor of the Berlin journal *Die literarische Welt*, who discovered Huchel in 1930, was captivated by the young poet, when he first visited Haas' house in the Plötzensee area of Berlin, 'Er war sehr jung und so, wie ich ihn mir vorgestellt hatte – ein schöner, muskulöser Mann mit den Augen eines Dichters'.[2] Haas' secretary and librarian, Rolf Italiaander, painted a vivid picture of Huchel at that first meeting, 'Huchel überraschte durch seine Erscheinung. Er trug an nackten Füßen Ledersandalen, war rustikal angezogen wie ein Waldarbeiter – eine absolut unliterarische Erscheinung. Was er sagte, gefiel auch mir. Er sprach über Naturerlebnisse und Mythologisches'.[3] Even in old age, Huchel lost nothing of his rather exotic appeal, despite a bitterness born of experience that he made little attempt to conceal. Günter Herburger recalled an encounter in Rome, 'Huchel sah wie ein Indianer aus: viel graue Haare, große Lippen, im Gesicht längs- und querverlaufende Runzeln. Es war faszinierend. Entweder stammte er aus Kanada oder aus Kamtschatka'.[4] His fellow septuagenarian poet Marie Luise Kaschnitz fell for his singular charm, and at that late stage in their lives they enjoyed a flowering of love. Kaschnitz's biographer, Dagmar von Gersdorff, remarks of his attraction for her in contrast with other men she had known, 'Weder verfügte er über die ubiquitäre Eloquenz des geistvollen Dolf Sternberger, noch über die bestechend scharfe analytische Intelligenz Adornos, er war vielmehr eher schweigsam, ein eigensinniger und grüblerischer Einzelgänger'.[5] Huchel's was much less a 'schooled' intelligence. With characteristic self-irony, he described his 'geistige Mitgift' as a 'Mischung aus Halbbildung und Vulgäraufklärung'.[6] Huchel relied on his poetic talent and upon a native wit, in which Walter Jens, recalling his conversations with Huchel about the figure of Odysseus, highlighted Huchel's very cunning.[7] The poet was, in truth, much less interested in the establishment of analytical categories than in the creative manipulation of language in keeping with a mix of emotional needs and ethical concerns. Kaschnitz was drawn to him not least because she, like many other writers, knew that he was in a very real sense a poet's poet.

When in 1971, exhausted and embittered after a decade of struggle with the SED, Huchel was finally permitted to move from East to West, many commented upon how lightly, despite his tribulations, he carried his formidable reputation as a poet, whose experience of history had left its indelible mark on his vision of nature. Nor could they fail to be impressed by the enormous moral authority that he had acquired as the deposed editor of the legendary, all-German creation of Cold War cultural diplomacy, *Sinn und Form*. The dissident's hardships endowed him with an aura redolent of saintliness, and in the press and critical writing the correlation was established between his martyrdom in the GDR and his principled opposition to the earlier German totalitarianism of National Socialism.[8] He was held to embody an integrity otherwise so frequently absent in twentieth-century cultural life in Germany, characterised as it is by stories of complicity with corrupt power in situations themselves loaded towards compromise. One critic claimed, not untypically, albeit for the uninitiated quite astonishingly, 'Wenn jemand, dann hatte er Grund, sich immer wieder als Opfer der Geschichte zu empfinden'.[9] His moral resoluteness was thus imbued with a continuity of purpose and, inevitably, of suffering well nigh unique among writers who pursued their careers within Germany in the twentieth century.

The steady stream of prizes that – without parallel for a GDR writer at that time – he had won in the West since 1959, turned into a flood after 1971, when he was buoyed upon a wave of sympathy. It mattered little that by the age of 68 the poet had published only two collections of verse and that his life and work had been the subject of only limited critical scrutiny. The awards culminated in the Federal Republic's most prestigious distinction, *pour le mérite*, and by the time of his death in 1981 Huchel had become the most decorated of all writers in the history of the Federal Republic. Interest abated somewhat in the 1980s, yet after 1989 his singular fate assumed fresh significance as an integrative symbol for German unity. This, in turn, prompted renewed interest in the German media and in an academic community whose inquiries, conducted in the climate of crisis in cultural life sparked by unification, have generally been limited to the re-affirmation of an established image. One critic, commenting on the unseemly and protracted quarrel that informed the merger of the East and West Berlin Academies of Arts, suggested that Huchel would have known what to do: he would simply have resigned.[10] In this way, as the century draws to a close, Huchel, born at its beginning in 1903, has his place as a quite phenomenal presence that spans twentieth century German culture.

On that basis alone, Huchel's life in German literature merits the scrutiny of a critical biography. Yet, there is much to complicate what, on the face of it, might look like a reasonably straightforward undertaking. In the 1970s, westerners who had sympathised with Huchel from afar at last had an opportunity to enter into a dialogue with him. In January 1973, Michael Hamburger, his English translator, met him for the first time when Huchel travelled to London, where he represented the Federal Republic at the Fanfare for Europe reading. Hamburger recalls that during his visit Huchel was sociable and took an interest in issues and events, yet the realm of personal experience was shrouded in a discretion and reticence that excluded any real intimacy. Hamburger observed, 'Mehrdeutigkeiten, Verschwiegenheiten, Geheimnisse gehören zum Wesen der Lyrik Huchels – wie auch zum Wesen des Mannes, den ich "kennenlernte"'.[11]

For all Huchel's friendly, engaging manner, Hamburger could not penetrate the spell of silence that he cast. Like others before him, Hamburger was left to ponder Huchel's enigmatic presence. A number of people who came to know Huchel during his years of isolation in the GDR in the 1960s have published their memories of him. Wolf Biermann, for example, who, like Huchel, had been ostracised by the SED, was a frequent visitor at Huchel's house in Wilhelmshorst near Potsdam. Yet Biermann was forced to conclude, 'Ich weiß ja nicht mal was von Peter Huchel, obwohl wir uns so oft sahn und uns so nah waren'.[12] It was precisely 'das Schweigen zwischen den Worten'[13] that Biermann learnt from Huchel. One of Huchel's closest friendships in the Eastern Bloc was established in the mid-1950s with Ludvík Kundera, who became his Czech translator. At the turn of the 1960s, Kundera was commissioned by the East Berlin Academy of Arts, of which Huchel was a member, to write a study of his friend's life and work. Although Kundera believed that the latter aspect could be readily accommodated since it was 'damals sehr schmal', the undertaking rapidly proved to be much more demanding since 'die Lebensgeschichte bestand ... meistens nur aus weißen Flecken'.[14] Huchel invited Kundera to stay with him on a number of occasions so that he could better answer his questions. The notes that Kundera made of their conversations are intriguing in their, as Kundera writes, fragmentary nature. Beyond the expected references to places and dates, the notes are punctuated by vignettes, behind which one immediately senses the presence of a born raconteur. The at times quite improbable detail recorded by Kundera in his jottings was evidently conveyed to the listener in such a beguiling manner that there could be no question but that disbelief had to be suspended. One such vignette describes Huchel's life in the South of France in the 1920s,

In Nizza lebte er mit dem halbwahnsinnigen Lyriker Ernst Reissig. Homosexuell, er hatte als Besitz nur einen Benn-Band. Verlorener Sohn eines Berliner Hoteliers. In Nizza lebte er auch bei einem alten Schauspieler von der Comédie Française. Als Reissig seine Monatsrente 800 RM bekam, fuhren beide nach Monte Carlo. Spiel! Abwechselnd hatten sie so viel Geld – und dann nichts. Reissigs Vater schickte dann nichts, so lebten sie in

einem Pferdestall. Dann arbeitete PH als Hafenarbeiter, schleppte Kisten und schlief auch
zwischen Kisten in einem Magazin.[15]

What for Hamburger was the spell of silence was for Kundera the spellbinding
anecdote. In the event, Kundera's book was never written. Colourful episodes such
as Huchel's exploits on the Côte d'Azur might have fleshed out some of the 'weiße
Flecken' that Kundera encountered when he began his research, yet in truth the
stories that he heard did not equip him to write an authoritative, biographically-based
study.

Kundera's notes echo the accounts of other friends who, rather surprisingly
for a reading public that knew him only through the high seriousness of his poetry
and his spare public statements, remember Huchel as an incredibly humorous
raconteur. Günter Kunert has written of 'seine ihn selber amüsierende, witzige
Eloquenz'.[16] Kunert's fear that this little appreciated side of Huchel would in time
be lost sight of, since his stories had not been written down, is to some degree at
least alleviated by Kundera's jottings. Yet, as Uwe Grüning, another friend from the
1960s, points out, anecdotes do not always stand up well to the translation from the
fluidity of the oral form into the fixedness of the written.[17] Like Huchel's other
regular visitors, Grüning was treated to an endless round of stories drawn from
Huchel's rich and colourful life. Grüning was under no illusion that he was a guest
at a performance, whose success depended on the willingness of the listener to enter
into the play of the raconteur's imagination, sparked as it was by the 'Genius des
Ortes und der Genius des Augenblicks'.[18] Grüning observes, 'Ich habe die gleichen
Begebenheiten aus dem Mund Peter Huchels in den unterschiedlichsten Versionen
gehört, und immer waren sie in einem höheren Sinn wahr und immer in ihrer
Bildhaftigkeit glaubhaft'.[19] While Hamburger was left with enigmatic silence,
Grüning was left with a multiplicity of possible meanings to choose from if he
wished to distil the 'truth' from Huchel's imaginative constructions. Yet, for Grüning
the stories were less to be believed in any literal sense than to be enjoyed. He
recalled one particular version of a story related by Huchel in front of his wife
Monica and son Stephan. It concerned a publication for *Die literarische Welt*,

> wo er, mit gezogener Pistole bis zum Schreibtisch des kaufmännischen Leiters vorgedrung-
> en, die ihm geschuldeten fünf Mark von dem zitternden Mann eingefordert habe: 'Sie
> ahnen gar nicht, wieviel trockene Schrippen und Milch man damals für fünf Mark kaufen
> und wie lange ich davon leben konnte'.
> 'Das hast Du getan?' fragte Stephan verblüfft. 'Natürlich', entgegnete Huchel, und Monica
> wandte sich kommentierend an ihren Sohn: 'Du kennst wohl die Wutanfälle deines Vaters
> noch nicht?!'[20]

The episode was part of the Huchel repertoire. When I visited his first wife Dora in 1981, she recollected how Huchel had rehearsed his threats to punch Artur Rosen, the man responsible for the journal's finances, and that Huchel had in the event got his money.[21] Over the years, the story underwent a pretty drastic embellishment with the introduction of the pistol, yet, as Grüning's account makes clear, that detail was calculated to trigger a frisson of aesthetic pleasure among Huchel's audience, who, the adults at least, were aware of the game they were playing in his charmed circle.

Given this playful conversational manner, it is on the face of it surprising, as far as Huchel's poetry is concerned, that, in Grüning's words, 'suchte und ertrug er bei den eigenen Texten keine Form von Distanz, heiße sie nun Imitation, Parodie, Selbstkommentar oder Satire'.[22] In the composition of his poetry, Huchel was engaged in an act of deep existential earnest that was no mere creative activity. Grüning could not have known that in radio play adaptations in the 1930s such as his version of Alphonse Daudet's *Tartarin de Tarascon* Huchel had ventured into such areas. That adaptation, like the vast majority of Huchel's radio plays, has remained unpublished. *Tartarin de Tarascon* is particularly interesting, however, since in choosing that material Huchel opted for a work that depicts the play between reality and heightened illusion through the ironic portrayal of the lovable, if self-deluding Tartarin. It is not difficult to see the attraction of Tartarin for Huchel the raconteur. The poet, however, operated on a quite different plane, and we shall have occasion to probe the high seriousness of his verse, founded as it is on the apparently seamless unity between autobiographical experience and poetic expression. Certainly, he did not wish to deflect attention from that project, and that was one reason – though there are others – why, during his lifetime, he ensured that only the poetry was permitted to count in public.

Nor, despite Huchel's anecdotal talents and rich store of experience, was autobiography foregrounded in the way that his publisher hoped in the 1970s. The raconteur's generation of multiple versions of any given event might, in the hands of an astute editor, have resulted in a highly readable book of mémoirs. Yet Huchel could not move beyond the vignette recounted as anecdote. He was never really interested in subjecting himself to the discipline of sequential narration that underlies conventional prose writing. The autobiography remained unwritten. It is telling that the one autobiographical piece of any length that he published in the mid-1970s moves quickly into the realm of fantasy and that a much earlier piece from 1931 was both written in the third person and its authenticity later called into question by the author himself.[23]

We see here evidence of what one perceptive critic, actually writing about the poetry, has described as Huchel's 'Rückzug aus dem Ich statt Konzentration in einem Ego'.[24] Both Grüning and Hamburger were well aware that the Huchel that presented himself to them was intent on concealment of his 'real' self. Grüning understood that, on one level at least, Huchel's sociability was a device to guard his 'Wesen aus Furcht vor Verletzungen'.[25] Hamburger identified less an essential sensibility than the circumstances of Huchel's life as the source of Huchel's evident 'wunde ... Stellen',[26] his pronounced sensitivity, which had left Hamburger himself rather at a loss. He later concluded, 'Daß sich das Leiden an der Geschichte mit der persönlichen und künstlerischen Eitelkeit schlecht verträgt, wußte ich schon. Im menschlichen Umgang, wenn nicht in Gedichten, kann also auch die Verschwiegenheit auf Mißverständnissen beruhen, zu Versäumnissen führen'.[27]

Both the spell of silence and spellbinding story-telling left vast space for misunderstandings and omissions, for projection into that space of the unwary listener's preconceptions. There were many such listeners. Just what had the 'victim' of history to conceal from friends and acquaintances? German history has set severe tests this century, and Huchel certainly emerged unbowed from one such test in 1971. Yet, is it appropriate to extrapolate from the events of the 1960s an image of moral authority which then serves as a template to assess earlier phases of a long life about which, until very recently, little was actually known with any certainty? Writing about Huchel has hitherto proceeded on such a basis, and there has been a signal failure to appreciate the very complexity of the life of an artist acting within a notoriously volatile historical context.

I must say that it is the progression of this complex artist figure within that historical period which has proved quite compelling for me during my researches. The schoolboy's earliest compositions date from the final stages of the Wilhelmine Empire. His participation in German literary life took him from the Weimar to the Federal Republic via the Third Reich, Berlin of the period 1945-49 and the GDR. Conventionally, German literary historiography of the twentieth century proceeds on the basis of discontinuities marked by the key dates of political history. Yet Huchel's life in literature represents a rare thread of continuity, the charting of which in this study provides a challenge of some magnitude, especially with regard to his path through the mid-decades of the century, spent in the highly repressive, ideologically antagonistic Third Reich and GDR. Both regimes were keen to promote nature poetry which would support their ideological views. Could he, a nature poet, survive merely as a foreign body victimised in both regimes? The challenge of exploring Huchel's development is potentially all the more rewarding now that much more archival material is available, which relates principally, though not exclusively to those years. At last, the study of source material can replace the speculation and often feverish construction of legends that so frequently surrounds non-conformist figures in totalitarian states.

Given the spell that Huchel cast over his own life, it has been necessary to advance, wherever possible, evidence from sources which can be juxtaposed with the various versions of events that emanate from Huchel himself or from the elaborations undertaken by journalists and critics on the basis of his often elliptical comments. In that way, the 'higher' truth of the poet's imagination might be read alongside the biographer's own findings. An inevitable consequence of this necessarily somewhat laborious method is the erosion at many points in the Huchel story of the moral certainties invested in him. If previous experience is any guide, this will not go down well in certain circles in Germany, where literary debate, once more since 1989, tends so often to be conducted on the basis of a crude extrapolation of political causalities and moral judgments. Nor will it find favour among those germanists who take their cue from the Huchel legend cultivated in that specific environment.[28] The present study will, rather, take seriously Horst Piontek's observation, 'Freilich, tatkräftig springt dem Werk die Person seines Urhebers bei. Denn niemand wird Huchel sein Charisma absprechen wollen'.[29] What I hope will emerge is a much more colourful, unpredictable and unreliable artist figure, in some ways a brilliant chameleon, someone who was certainly concerned with ethical issues and social justice, but whose supreme achievement consisted in creating himself in a particular image, which he used as an anchor-point both in his verse and his life, on the basis of which he re-invented himself as circumstances dictated. Like the figure of Odysseus that Huchel discussed with Jens and whose fate he captured in his poetry, Huchel, a hero to some, was a great survivor, who used his intelligence, charm and native wit, together with his poetic gift, to overcome those obstacles that life put in his way from childhood onwards.

Part 1
The Search for the Self

1
Origins

The Silence and the Song of Childhood

In the late poem 'Unter der blanken Hacke des Monds', (i,211) Huchel, as he so frequently did in the 1970s, returned to the site of childhood, the favoured subject matter of the verse with which he had made his name in the early 1930s. He reflected upon the impossibility of acquiring substantial knowledge about the world, and specifically about the childhood world of memory. The poem's middle stanza reads, 'Im Wasserzeichen der Nacht / die Kindheit der Mythen,/ nicht zu entziffern'. These lines acquire a particular resonance in the light of the spell of silence that Huchel had long cast over his immediate family background. Beyond the fact of his birth as Helmut Huchel[1] on 3 April 1903 in the suburbs of Berlin, readers will search in vain among his writings and public statements for any mention whatsoever of his childhood years spent with his parents, Fritz and Marie, and his elder brother, also Fritz. The family lived at various addresses in Groß-Lichterfelde and the neighbouring suburb of Steglitz to the south-west of Berlin.[2] Only in his depiction of adolescent years in Potsdam, where the family moved in the autumn of 1915, does the reader gain any insight whatsoever into the poet's immediate background and the formative years that he spent with his parents and brother. The childhood years in Groß-Lichterfelde and Steglitz constitute the first and the most significant of the many 'weiße Flecken' that Kundera, or perhaps better, the 'wunde ... Stellen' that Hamburger identified in the poet's biography.

Huchel told Kundera nothing about his immediate family. How can the void be filled and explained? Huchel's was not a literate family, and though both parents lived to witness some of their younger son's achievements, neither of them left any written testimony. Nor did his brother, who was killed in the First World War. Huchel's was, however, a modern biography, in the sense that throughout our lives public records are kept of our whereabouts and activities. We shall be able to draw upon such records, as well as material from other archives, which help to paint a picture of Huchel's boyhood. Not only that, Huchel was close enough in time to us to ensure that at least some reliable testimony can be drawn upon. A key source is his first wife, Dora (née Lassel), whom he got to know in Vienna in late 1925.[3] In 1981, she recollected how, after they met, the elegant young poet was at first playfully evasive about his background, before becoming forthrightly earnest and making the statement, 'Meine Mutter stelle ich Dir nie vor'. Nonetheless, the following year Dora Lassel travelled to Potsdam where she met Huchel's parents and his maternal grandmother, Emilie Zimmermann, who lived with his parents after her husband's death. Over the next twenty years Dora was treated by them and her husband to the family folklore, which she recounted to me in 1981 and set down in the account of her life with Huchel that she wrote shortly before her death in 1985.[4]

For Dora Huchel, it was 'wirklich wunderlich, daß Peter Huchel der Sohn solcher Eltern war'. She could not begin to understand how he could possibly belong to them. She came from a long-established Transylvanian-Saxon family of clergymen, academics and factory owners, and – the daughter of her class – the only word that she could find to describe Fritz and Marie Huchel was 'primitiv'. Not only were their intellectual horizons in her view far too limited to appreciate their son's gift; their antagonisms and mutual incomprehension made for an acrimonious atmosphere that gripped the Huchel household. Exceptionally, in the first published version of the poem 'Die Kammer' in 1930, the angry exchanges of the Huchel household come through in the lines, 'die Kammer brannte weiß in Scham,/ wenn lauter Hader sie durchschrie'. (i,374) Yet these lines were replaced in later publications. Alluding from the child's perspective to the evil of the adult world and to the meagreness of his childhood, the poet also wrote in 'Die Kammer', 'Ich war allein, bis ich ins Böse wuchs,/ mein eigner Tisch war schlechter Napf'. (i,26) The poem's content is diametrically opposed to what Huchel subsequently said and wrote about his childhood. Dora Huchel's wholly plausible view, supported by what her husband told her and wrote in 'Die Kammer', was that his home life had been blighted by a lack of emotional support. This produced in the talented and sensitive boy a deep sense of hurt, which in time gained expression in his rejection of his parents and his establishment through poetry of an identity quite independent of them.

Nor can Huchel's early development and his later response to it be accounted for without consideration of the shattered values of his generation. The boy's father, a Prussian NCO who gained a minor civil service post, was eagerly supportive when it came to the propagation of Prussian militarist values and the cult of the Kaiser, which Helmut Huchel's schools in Steglitz and Potsdam loyally inculcated immediately before and during the First World War. Yet all the talk was exposed as an awful lie and his father as a dupe, following wartime deprivation, his brother's death on the Western Front and the humiliation of defeat for the Hohenzollerns and the Prussian Establishment. In the chaos that followed defeat, the young Huchel was prey to the bewilderment and disorientation that constituted the typical experience of the generation born just after the turn of the century. The confusion was, arguably, nowhere greater than in Potsdam.

The attractions of politically radical solutions for Huchel's generation have been exhaustively documented. The gifted Huchel found his own very personal solution to the problems of his early years through the radical re-casting of his background. It is an index of his deep disorientation and, by the same token, of the poet's craving for a secure identity amid the debris of his upbringing that over a period of some fifty years Huchel obsessively reiterated and embellished in public the story of his upbringing on his grandfather's farm in Alt-Langerwisch. The silence cast over the suburban childhood was lost in the song of the rich, rural upbringing. Yet, as Dora Huchel pointed out to me in 1981, this story was never recounted in the family. It was an essential element of a poetic persona, a projection of the self for public consumption, untenable in a private context yet indicative of deep needs deriving from the insufficiencies of that context and from his awareness of an attractive alternative. In publications and broadcasts from the early 1930s to the late 1970s, he presented a version of his life through autobiographical and lyrical modes, which inflated and embellished one element of experience – a stay of just a few months with grandfather and grandmother Zimmermann while his mother was treated for a lung complaint in the sanatorium at nearby Beelitz – to the exclusion of his actual suburban childhood with his parents and brother.

During an interview in the 1970s, Huchel claimed that he was given to his grandparents during the first year of his life and stayed with them for a number of years,

> Ja, ich bin in Berlin geboren, kam aber schon im ersten Lebensjahr, weil meine Mutter lungenkrank war und für Jahre ein Sanatorium aufsuchen mußte, zu meinem Großvater in Alt-Langerwisch, wo er ein Bauerngut besaß. Dort wurde ich aufgezogen von einer Magd, die ich in dem Gedicht 'Die Magd' beschrieben habe.[5]

Similarly, Kundera noted, 'Bis zum zehnten Lebensjahr ausschließlich auf dem Lande. Dorfleben. Insgesamt 14 Jahre'.[6] Much earlier, in a radio talk delivered in 1932, he had suggested a somewhat later beginning to his rural upbringing. He introduced himself through reference to the village 'in dem meine Mutter groß wurde – und in dem ich später aufwuchs', (ii,242) adding,

> Dort, in Alt-Langerwisch/Mark, bin ich zwar nicht geboren, aber dort bin ich schon als Kind hingekommen. Mit vier Jahren, als meine Mutter erkrankte, gab man mich zu den Großeltern aufs Land. Dort verlebte ich einen Teil meiner Kindheit; dort war ich auch in den späteren Jahren, jeden Sommer, jeden Herbst. (ii,242)

According to the more modest, early claims, then, the rural childhood began during the boy's fifth year and continued for a period of time unspecified by the poet. Afterwards he paid regular visits to his grandparents. Yet the degree of circumspection in evidence here was lost sight of in the growth of the Langerwisch legend. The reference to the boy's fifth year occurs elsewhere,[7] and available evidence points to the fact that it was indeed at that age that he went to stay with the Zimmermanns, while his mother was being treated at nearby Beelitz. Dora Huchel recalled that the episode was recounted in such terms in the Huchel family. Marie Huchel's complaint proved to be not serious. It was nothing more than many people suffered when they moved to low-lying Berlin with its slightly damper climate from the somewhat higher rural areas. When her treatment at Beelitz was completed, she returned with her child to rejoin her husband in Steglitz. She went on to live until the age of eighty-five.

In 1981, Dora Huchel made the following carefully considered statement, which is supported by available documentation,

> Er kann nicht dort aufgewachsen sein. Er erwähnt keine Schule dort in Alt-Langerwisch. Er hat die Volksschule in Steglitz besucht, weil er in der Stadt gewohnt hat. Er hat einige Monate bei seinen Großeltern in Alt-Langerwisch verbracht, während seine Mutter in Beelitz-Heilstätten wegen einer Lungenkrankheit war. Daß er von seinem Großvater großgezogen worden ist, kann keine Rede sein ... Diese ganze Geschichte hat er nie privat verbreitet, erst in 'Europa neunzehnhunderttraurig' und im Rundfunkvortrag. Er hat erst gegen 1930 die Kindheitsgedichte geschrieben und damit den Mythos erfunden.

As she explained, he had, of course, paid visits to his grandparents both before and after the lengthy stay. Yet he had constructed out of the various visits a continuum of experience which totally eclipsed his suburban childhood. The biographical and poetic selves which he presented conveyed a seamless unity, in keeping with which critics have interpreted his poetry of his rural childhood against a background of experience gained far from the suburban world of Groß-Lichterfelde and Steglitz. Remarkably for someone who achieved such prominence, Huchel's story was never properly investigated, let alone seriously questioned during his lifetime.

The boy was given the nickname Piese in the family and was known as such by close friends in adult years. It was when he began to publish the poetry of childhood in the early 1930s that he took the pen-name Peter to replace Helmut, the name with which he had been christened and with which he had signed poems in the mid-1920s. The name Peter was adopted from his maternal great-great-grandfather and great-grandfather, both called Peter Zimmermann and both Brandenburg farmers from Michendorf.[8] In the early nineteenth century, the first Peter Zimmermann had come to enjoy freedom from allegiance to the lord of the manor and had been a pillar of the village community through his work as church superintendent. The poet chose to align himself closely with the first free Zimmermann and his son through his poetry of rural Brandenburg life. In 1926, in what is the earliest example of what I shall call Huchel's distinctive mythologising imagination, if not of his nature poetry as such, he celebrated his childhood experiences in the rural world of his ancestors in his composition of 'Die Magd'. (i,52). In this poem, a maidservant, a surrogate mother who cares for the child ('Die Magd ist mehr als Mutter noch') and who was later identified by him as Anna, is depicted as rooted in the rural world and endowed with supernatural powers. Her knitting links her with the Three Fates of the classical tradition, which – as frequently occurs in Huchel's poetry – is integrated within folkloric Brandenburg, 'Sie wärmt mein Hemd, küßt mein Gesicht/ und strickt weiß im Petroleumlicht./ Ihr Strickzeug klirrt und blitzt dabei,/ sie murmelt leis Wahrsagerei'. In this way, the rural world experienced by the child is imbued with a numinous quality, which leaves behind mundane reality, transporting the child into the magical realm of prophecy evoked by the maidservant, the mythically heightened site of 'Naturerlebnisse' and 'Mythologisches', about which Huchel talked to Haas and Italiaander.

The *Naturmagie* of 'Die Magd' is replicated in other publications from the early to mid-1930s such as 'Die wendische Haide' (i,276), 'Kindheit in Alt-Langerwisch' (i,51) and 'Am Beifußhang'. (i,57) Near the end of his life in the Federal Republic of the 1970s, where such concerns seemed at best remote, Huchel would, one last time, revisit the scene of rural childhood prophecy, this time under the aegis of his grandfather, the farmer Friedrich Zimmermann, who himself had written verse. In 'Mein Großvater', (i,243) which he included in his final collection, *Die neunte Stunde*, the grandfather figure is viewed by the onlooking, adoring grandson, as he pursues his favourite pastimes, shooting and trapping game. In the lines 'Prophetisch begann die Nacht,/ messianisch die erste Stunde', their relationship is endowed with properties not without echoes of God the Father and God the Son in a collection whose title alludes to Christ's cry of despair during the crucifixion. Yet the child, having inherited the grandfather's mantle, dedicates himself in his verse to the evocation of a magic world through the mystery of poetry and avers his unbroken attachment to the grandfather's legacy in the line, 'Ich ging nicht über die sieben Seen'. Presently, we shall explore further 'Mein Großvater' and the rural poet Friedrich Zimmermann, considering the latter's great significance for Huchel's poetic identity.

The Huchels

From the composition of 'Die Magd' in the mid-1920s to 'Mein Großvater' in the 1970s, Huchel consistently articulated in his verse and in autobiographical statements a sense of self defined in opposition to a paternal influence rooted in the Prussian army and bureaucracy and located in the modern urban centres of Berlin and Potsdam. He looked instead to the magical memory of early rural experiences with his mother's side of the family, the Zimmermanns, and with that to the traditional life of the Brandenburg village communities. There was no place for the father in the account of the boy's rural upbringing, though in a questionnaire that Huchel filled in after the war in East Berlin he went so far as to claim that his father, too, had been a peasant farmer.[9] Fritz Huchel's career as a Prussian soldier and minor civil servant was made of much less promising stuff. Indeed, his son from quite an early age grew to detest both the grandeur of Prussian pretension and the pettiness as well as the rigidity of Prussian officialdom that his father represented. Spare public statements about his father are framed in such a way as to convey the impression that Fritz's son regarded his father's life as a kind of deviation from a family background which – so he led readers of *Die literarische Welt* to believe – was not really so different from the Zimmermanns'. With the help of his friend, Hans A. Joachim, in 1931 Huchel wrote of his immediate background,

> Peter H., Potsdam, ist als Kind einer Bäuerin und eines Soldaten auf die Welt gekommen.
> Sein Vater, entstammend einer sächsischen Schäferfamilie, die 1546 bei der Kirchenvisitation in Harbke für einen Altar lehnspflichtig genannt wird und die im 19. Jahrhundert auf dunklem Prozeßweg Haus und Mühle an das gräfliche Stammgut verloren hat, hat als Ulanenwachtmeister im Sommermanöver bei Alt-Langerwisch eine wohlhabende Bauerntochter zur Frau genommen. (ii,213)

The reason for his father's deviation is thus located in social injustice which had deprived Fritz Huchel's family of its birthright as shepherds, millers and farmers. Fritz, or so his son leads us to believe, had at least re-established the link with farming stock through his marriage to a 'Bäuerin', who was, moreover, a 'wohlhabende Bauerntochter'. Yet the depiction of Fritz's family background is so deliberately over the top that the reader can surely scarcely take it at face value?

Fritz Huchel's family background was in almost every detail at variance with his son's imaginative construction. He came from the village of Laasau, near Striegau in Silesia, where he was born on 15 August 1867, the younger son of Friedrich Wilhelm *Karl* Huchel and his wife Ernestine Pauline (née Anders).[10] The family later moved to the town of Reichenbach, also in Silesia. Karl Huchel was employed as an overseer, which meant that he was required to keep migrant labourers, usually Poles and Slavs, in check. By all accounts, the brutality required of the overseer was matched only by the wretchedness of the conditions in which he and his charges lived. The overseer was frequently armed with a revolver and supported by a fierce dog. He could be required to share the migrant labourers' quarters to ensure that there were no escapes in the night. The information about the occupation of Huchel's paternal grandfather provides an unexpected gloss for the early post-war publication 'Der polnische Schnitter', (i,54) in which the migrant worker's lament over his poor rewards for long hours of toil is transformed in the red dawn of the revolution, 'kehre ich heim ins östliche Land,/ in die Röte des Morgens'.

One detail in Huchel's account of his father's family that can be authenticated is his reference to the Saxon background. Karl, the poet's paternal grandfather, whom he probably never knew, had moved to Silesia from the Altmark area now in Saxony-Anhalt, where he had been born in the tiny village of Wieglitz on 30 March 1834. The Huchel family, whose descendants still live in the village today, were not landowners. According to local records, Karl Huchel was the son of Johann Wilhelm Huchel, an innkeeper in Wieglitz.[11] His father in turn was Johann Christoph Huchel, who was a linen weaver in the village. There is no record of the Huchels' ever having lived in Harbke. Peter Huchel, at the time perhaps only vaguely aware of a Saxon dimension to his father's immediate Silesian background, may well have simply selected a place on the map, upon which he could hang the fiction of his father's peasant farming background and the injustice perpetrated on the family by the local gentry.

Fritz Huchel frequently referred to Görlitz in stories which he told within the family about his early adult years, and it can be safely assumed that he spent some years there. However, like many other young men in the late nineteenth century who left the eastern provinces for the Prussian capital in the hope of a better life, Fritz Huchel and his elder brother Carl left Silesia for Berlin/ Potsdam.[12] In the burgeoning centre of imperial power the brothers achieved a degree of social advance, both gaining modest, though secure employment in Prussian service. This was probably the most they could expect in a rigidly stratified society, in which only the most exceptional talents could achieve any dramatic advance out of the lower classes. Neither of the brothers was made of such stuff. Carl Huchel was employed as a minor official in the postal service in Berlin, where, until his death in the early 1920s, he lived in the Schöneberg area with his wife Auguste and their daughter Erna.

Fritz, meanwhile, chose the more glamorous life of a career soldier in Potsdam. He followed the conventional route through the Prussian system for someone from the lower classes, especially the rural poor in search of some social advancement and security, namely the system of military candidates. Following twelve years' service as NCOs, the candidates were taken over to man the lower ranks of the Prussian civil service. Despite objections from the civil service regarding the quality and suitability of former NCOs for administrative tasks and for dealing with the general public, such was the power of the military in Wilhelmine Germany that it was able to ensure that all the lower and as many as half the middle-ranking positions in the civil service were reserved for former NCOs. Fritz Huchel entered the army as a nineteen-year-old on 1 October 1886.[13] Beyond general soldierly skills, the three years' training that he and other candidates received focused on taking dictation in an elegant hand and basic maths. They were thus prepared both for their role as teachers of the lower ranks in the army and for their subsequent civil service careers. They were encouraged to view themselves as role models for the lower ranks, and in this way as a group they came to be known as bulwarks of the system, exhibiting undivided loyalty to the Kaiser as well as unquestioning belief in the Prussian army ethos and its key role in the state.

Fritz Huchel joined the crack First Lancer Guards Regiment, known as the Red Uhlans, which was stationed not far from Sanssouci, at the Uhlans' Barracks near the Ruinenberg, which after 1945 until the early 1990s housed the Soviet barracks to the north of Potsdam's centre just off Voltaireweg. This light cavalry regiment was one of the most prestigious in the Prussian army, the officer corps made up almost entirely of sons of the nobility. Meanwhile, the ranks were recruited from the rather backward lower classes from the countryside, particular emphasis being placed on recruitment from the eastern provinces, especially the Grand Duchy of Posen, as a means of binding those subjects into the Prussian state system. In terms of his social background, Fritz Huchel was a typical recruit. He pursued his career as a professional soldier with some success and reached the highest NCO position, 'Vice-Wachtmeister'. A photograph of him in uniform shows him sporting the conventional Wilhelmine moustache in imitation of the Kaiser.[14] As one of four sergeants in the regiment, he occupied the key mediating position in the hierarchy between the officer corps and the ranks. Such was the Wilhelmine system, with the army's budget outside any real parliamentary control, that its first loyalty was always to the Kaiser, who virtually exercised a form of direct rule over an institution that was a state within the state. This relationship between monarch and army made for that almost slavish loyalty and quasi-feudal allegiance that was a feature of institutionalised Prussian life in the Wilhelmine period. Fritz Huchel firmly supported the social and political hierarchies of Wilhelmine Germany: until his death in 1945 he continued to uphold the Kaiser and the Wilhelmine system as an ideal, the passing of which he deeply regretted.

Fritz Huchel remained a bachelor until he was thirty and during these years became used to the rituals and routine of life in barracks. The sheer brutality of army discipline and the unstinting emphasis on physical training were offset by the pleasures afforded by alcohol. Throughout his adult life, Fritz Huchel was quite a heavy drinker, a habit which he nevertheless managed to combine with a thoroughly conscientious attitude towards work. In that respect and in certain others he shares characteristics with Herr Steuersekretär Karl August W., the subject of Huchel's satirical portrait, again co-authored with Joachim, in the prose piece 'Im Jahre 1930', published in *Die literarische Welt* in 1931. Like Fritz Huchel, Karl August W. is a minor Prussian civil servant following an army career of 'die zwölf strammen Jahre, vom Gefreitenknopf bis zur Feldwebellitze', (ii,223) which is to say that he, too, came through the system of military candidates. In the evening he tries to relax with beer, 'das er aus vielen Flaschen trinkt'. (ii,225) Unlike Fritz Huchel, Karl August W. in the early 1930s supports the Nazis. Nazism held no attractions for Fritz Huchel, though the same could not be said of his wife. We shall return to Huchel's portrayal of the petty official later.

It was as the drinker that Huchel chose to portray his father in the poem 'M.V.', (i,190) which is a late treatment of Fritz Huchel's death, written in Rome in 1971. It was published the following year in the collection *Gezählte Tage*. The first section reads,

Er ging fort,

das Zimmer ist leer,

der Ofen kalt,

die Flaschen recken die Hälse.

Er ließ nichts zurück

als eine Fußspur im Sand,

vom Eis des Winters ausgegossen.

The chilling final image sets the seal on this disarmingly bald statement of the son's profound alienation from his father. In sharp contrast to the intense identification with Friedrich Zimmermann, the poet could find nothing in his father's life to take over for his own. That very absence, of course, determined the son's search for an identity located elsewhere. Although other members of the family did not share such an unreservedly negative view of Fritz Huchel, for his gifted son his father's life did, indeed, represent a wasted existence, which had threatened to cripple his own life. Even in 1971, some 25 years after his father's death, the poet could do no other than record his alienation.

As early as 1934, Huchel wrote a poem that anticipated his father's death in 1945. The poem in question is 'Letzte Fahrt', (i,62) which was published in *Das innere Reich*. Here the son, exceptionally, presents himself as following the path through life taken by the father, who is depicted as the angler that Fritz Huchel was. The father's death, though, is described as a death in life. The dreams he had cherished ebbed away, 'er sah die toten Träume ziehn/ als Fische auf dem Grund'; and in the next stanza, 'sein Traum und auch sein Leben fuhr/ durch Binsen hin und Sand'. The final stanza is the son's,

Ich lausch dem Hall am Grabgebüsch,

der Tote sitzt am Steg.

In meiner Kanne springt der Fisch.

Ich geh den Binsenweg.

It makes sense to read these lines in the context of the mid-1930s, when the despair and melancholy felt by the poet living in Nazi Germany, articulated more fully shortly afterwards in the cycle 'Strophen aus einem Herbst', invited comparison with the, in the son's eyes, failed existence of the father, the dupe of Prussian authoritarian values. The sympathetic view of the father's failure held out by the poet chastened during that critical period of his own death in life, however, later gave way once more to the chilling sentiments of 'M.V.'.[15]

The young Fritz Huchel had, understandably enough, viewed the Prussian system as his best chance of making a career for himself. And in 1897, during an evening off duty while participating in an exercise – probably in the winter rather than the summer months to which his son later referred – in the countryside south of Potsdam, the Lancers' sergeant met his wife to be, the twenty-one year-old Martha Maria Emilia Zimmermann. The story passed down in the family is that a dance took place at the local inn and it was soon the talk of the village that 'Mariechen' had danced with a soldier, 'Kiek mal, Timmermanns Mariechen tanzt mit'm Unteroffissier!'[16] An allusion to the event that the poet evidently regarded as an unmitigated disaster comes in the late poem 'Brandenburg', (i,245) which plays off the Brandenburg of the Zimmermanns against the Prussia of Fritz Huchel. The poem's treatment of the disabusing of cherished dreams of love and honour is introduced, in ironic counterpoint, by Kleist's famous line from *Prinz Friedrich von Homburg*, 'Ach, wie die Nachtviole lieblich duftet!' The central section of the poem reads, 'Noch immer tanzt abends/ der rote Ulan/ mit Bauerntöchtern auf der Tenne des Nebels,/ die Ulanka durchweht/ von Mückenschwärmen über dem Moor'. The reference to the Red Uhlan engaged in this rustic dance of death introduces a further exact biographical detail to the traumatic scene of courtship in a relationship blighted from the outset. The final section, which follows immediately, reads simply, 'Im Wasserschierling/ versunken/ die preußische Kalesche'. The demise of Prussia is thus linked to that of the Huchel family. Just as Prussia dragged Brandenburg down with it, so too Fritz Huchel dragged down the Zimmermanns' daughter through his attentions.

The extent of the damage incurred during the meeting of Fritz Huchel and Marie Zimmermann was presently established and arrangements made accordingly. Marie Zimmermann married Fritz Huchel at Bornstedt, Potsdam, on 14 August 1897.[17] A son, Fritz Carl Hans, was born soon afterwards on 6 October 1897 in the flat at Große Weinmeisterstraße 73, which the couple rented following their marriage. The flat was convenient for the Uhlans' Barracks and was situated in an attractive location near the eastern edge of Potsdam between the Neuer Garten and Pfingstberg. The nearby lakes, the Heiliger See and Jungfernsee, separated Potsdam from the south-western suburbs that stretched out beyond the city of Berlin. Große Weinmeisterstraße accommodated a varied social mix, with residents ranging across the social spectrum from servants, coachmen and other workers to civil servants and army officers, retired and serving. Fritz and Marie Huchel would stay there with their first son for some three years before moving to Lichterfelde. This removal followed the completion of twelve years of service on 31 March 1899.

The Zimmermanns

Despite physical proximity to Alt-Langerwisch, life in the Prussian residence and garrison town of Potsdam, with its historical and royal splendours, was a far cry from the closed Brandenburg village community from which Marie Huchel had come. She was born, a first child, on 2 January 1876 in Michendorf, a village only two kilometres from Langerwisch. Her father Friedrich Zimmermann was a farmer, who had married Pauline Emilia Siebecke, herself a farmer's daughter from nearby Trebbin, on 11 December 1873. The Zimmermanns had settled in Michendorf in the eighteenth century. At that time the village was still slowly recovering from the devastation that it had suffered during the Thirty Years' War, when it was totally destroyed and the population dispersed. The first Zimmermann to be mentioned in local records is a Christoph, who in the mid-eighteenth century lived in nearby Caputh, a village situated on the Havel to the west of Potsdam, which gave its name to Huchel's poem 'Caputher Heuweg'. (i,138) The first Zimmermann in Michendorf was Georg, a 'Hufner' (or 'Hufenbauer'), whose name appears in local records in 1746, 1750 and 1765. He enjoyed the status of 'full peasant', which meant that while he was subject to the local lord, he could with his approval bequeath, mortgage or even sell his property.[18] Full peasants, in fact, formed the nucleus of peasant life in the villages east of the Elbe. Their holdings were between about 20 to 70 hectares each and they could also use common pastures for grazing. Hartmut Harnisch points out that, 'Depending on the amount of land actually cultivated, and on the number of children able to work, these peasants employed about two to five farmhands from outside the family to maintain their farmsteads and to fulfil their feudal duties'.[19] For a full peasant, these duties normally amounted to not more than two to three days enforced serf labour and a percentage of their crop. Yet such were the burdens placed on peasants by the lords and by the government through taxation that their financial position was always precarious until the final third of the eighteenth century. From then on, the increase in the demand for grain for export to Great Britain and in order to satisfy burgeoning domestic needs as the urban population expanded, led to constant price rises. Above all those producers benefited who, like Zimmermann, were close to major markets such as Potsdam and Berlin. In this way, in the decades leading up to the agrarian reforms initiated in 1799 and 1807 agriculture became profitable and full peasants began to break the cycle of near destitution.

Peter, Georg Zimmermann's son, inherited the farm and was able to enjoy the benefits of emancipation from feudalism after 1807. As church superintendent in Michendorf, Peter Zimmermann enjoyed a position of some standing in the village. His son, Peter Wilhelm, was born on 10 June 1815. As we have seen, in his adoption of the name Peter, the poet established a link with his maternal ancestors, who had first enjoyed the family's independence. Peter Wilhelm, who inherited his father's property, was married on 8 September 1843 to Maria Dorothea Kroop, the eldest daughter of Gottfried Kroop, a farmer from Langerwisch. They had two children, a son and a daughter. Maria Zimmermann died of pneumonia on 11 November 1876, while her husband survived until 18 June 1896. Their son, Johann Friedrich Wilhelm Zimmermann, the poet's grandfather, was born on 9 December 1844. Following his father's retirement, he assumed control of a farm of some 130 'Morgen', between 30 and 40 hectares.

In a Michendorf chronicle, Friedrich Zimmermann is described as a person of lively intelligence with a wide range of interests stretching well beyond farming. A photograph taken of him in the early 1890s, together with his wife and daughter, conveys a warmth in his eyes of similar quality to his grandson's,[20] who offered his own depiction of the unconventional countryman-poet in 1931 in *Die literarische Welt*. He (and Joachim) wrote,

> Der Großvater hat Heide, Acker, Wiese. Leider ist er kein Bauer darauf. Er überläßt die Bewirtschaftung seiner Frau, dressiert den Hund, legt heimlich eine Bibliothek auf dem Heuboden an und schreibt Verse in ein blaues Heft, die Napoleon und Garibaldi verherrlichen und dem Dorfpastor ans Leder gehen. Er glaubt nicht an Gott; eher an die Macht von Kuhbeschwörungen. (ii,213)

However attractive a figure he cut for his grandson, Friedrich Zimmermann's lifestyle had a ruinous effect on the family's financial circumstances. Huchel acknowledged this in an interview in the 1970s, when he spoke of the 'Warnendes Beispiel: der märkische Großvater. Der hat hundertstrophige Balladen geschrieben und den Bauernhof verfallen lassen. "Wenn ein Ast am Obstbaum zuviel Früchte trug, hat er nicht eine Gabel daruntergestellt, sondern ein Gedicht darüber gemacht"'. (ii,394) He was, like his grandson, a difficult customer for neighbours and authorities. In 1974 Huchel recalled,

> wie mich mein Großvater nachts aus dem Bett holte, um wenigstens die paar dünnen Erlen abzusägen, die auf dem verlorengegangenen Streifen standen. Wir krochen übers Eis, blieben reglos liegen, ein spätes Fuhrwerk ratterte vorbei, dann sägten wir die Bäume ab. Die Prozeßsucht meines Großvaters war schon manisch, es ging um einen Grenzstein, der vom Nachbarn heimlich verrückt worden sein sollte, oder um einen Scheunenbrand, die Versicherung wollte nicht zahlen, weil die Agenten ein Petroleumfaß in der Asche gefunden hatten.[21]

Monica Huchel remembered her late husband telling her that Friedrich Zimmermann, the descendant of the full peasant Georg Zimmermann, had cultivated the lifestyle of a *grand seigneur*, living in a manner unheard of among the other local farmers.[22] The barber came at nine o'clock every morning to shave him. He spent his time shooting and trapping wildlife, reading the books in his library and composing verse, activities celebrated by Huchel in 'Mein Großvater'. Friedrich Zimmermann's wife Emilie, who generally figures only marginally in Huchel's accounts though quite prominently in one piece from 1931, 'Frau', (ii,226-8) could call upon a male and female farm servant, later identified by Huchel as Ziegener and Anna. She evidently had to do much work on her own or, in time, with the help of her daughter. With a sturdy physique like her mother, Marie was well suited to helping out on the farm. The same was not required of her younger brother Carl Otto Friedrich, who was born on 5 May 1879 and was later the local government official in Langerwisch. While he was permitted a reasonable education, Marie had no schooling beyond the basics. Farm work and village life remained the extent of her horizons until her marriage to Fritz Huchel.

The Michendorf chronicler writes that for all his intelligence Friedrich Zimmermann was rather easily manipulated into abandoning his quite valuable property in Michendorf, whose stock was rising through the rail link with Berlin established in 1879, for another in the less fashionable Alt-Langerwisch. According to the chronicle, in 1888 the local estate agent Markus, who was having difficulty in disposing of property in Alt-Langerwisch, proposed a deal which probably appealed to Friedrich Zimmermann's vanity but was almost certainly much less to the liking of his elderly father. Zimmermann agreed to swap his farm for the same amount of land in Alt-Langerwisch. The latter holding, however, was the core of the local Alt-Langerwisch manorial estate, which included a portion of Seddin Lake and, more important still, the rather impressive manor house situated in the centre of the village. The manor house, which still stands today, a listed building used as a restaurant, 'Zum alten Schloß', is a sturdy, two-storey building with a mansard roof, built in the Berlin style for rural agricultural buildings.[23] Friedrich Zimmermann was, no doubt, taken by the fact that the house had been built, it is estimated, in 1779 by Frederick The Great and that the estate on which it stood was in the Hohenzollerns' possession until it was sold by Frederick William III in 1811 to a Herr Kühne, who was a senior official and head forester of Cunersdorf. The house and land remained with the Kühnes until 1870 or so when they were sold first to a Herr Claude and then to a Max Orenstein. Herr Markus acted as his agent in the sale of the house and some of the land to Friedrich Zimmermann.

At the turn of the century, following his father's death, Zimmermann demonstrated his ambitions by erecting new buildings and a 'Landschlößchen' not far from the manor house near the road to Saarmund, the next village to the East. These were intended for his son and heir, Carl Otto Friedrich. Yet Friedrich Zimmermann's grand and expensive gesture in setting up his son was quite misplaced: his interests lay elsewhere. Following his father's death on 9 November 1913, which that same day he recorded in the register of deaths together with his sister, he gradually sold off all the property to clear the financial mess that his father had left behind. He then lived as a respected and quite well-off local official. Yet the fact that Carl Otto Friedrich excluded his elder sister from the property dealings which he conducted on his mother's behalf soured relations with his sister, to whom he was in any case not close. Matters would come to a head much later following the death of their mother in 1939.

Groß-Lichterfelde and Steglitz

The Huchels' move to Groß-Lichterfelde coincided with Fritz Huchel's switch from the army to the civil service. Entry to the civil service, even at the lowest level, was subject to close political control and candidates were required to demonstrate the soundest monarchist and nationalist convictions. Through his military service, Fritz's credentials were beyond reproach, even if his limited education and the level of skills acquired in the army meant that he was capable of performing only routine clerical work. His appointment, initially for a six-month probationary period, began on 1 January 1901.[24] From 1 July 1901 until 31 March 1906, he was employed at the bottom of the hierarchy as a 'Kanzlei Diätar' at the Royal Provincial School Department for the Province of Brandenburg. It was a branch of the Prussian Ministry of Education and was situated at Linkstraße 42, Berlin W9, in the centre of the city near the Potsdamer Bahnhof. He was in effect a scrivener or copying clerk, whose duties were restricted – as had been intended in his military training – to producing clean drafts of documents and correspondence in an elegant hand. The poet's father was thus required to do no more than reproduce the words of others. It was a skill that later, following his retirement in the early 1930s, he would be happy to perform for his son as he produced drafts of his radio plays.

Huchel's satirical portrait of Karl August W. – like Fritz Huchel, as we have seen, a minor civil servant and former soldier – suggests that he saw his father's modest achievements during his career only in terms of a rather squalid pettiness and servility. Like Fritz Huchel, Karl August W. travels by train from the suburbs to the Potsdamer Bahnhof, where 'Er tritt auf den Potsdamer Platz hinaus'. (ii,223) From there, he makes his way to the Ministry where he works,

> Fünf vor acht schnauft der Herr Steuersekretär die Treppe hinauf, auf der er in zwanzig
> Dienstjahren von Gehaltstufe IV bis Gehaltstufe VII aufgestiegen ist ... Mit genießerischer
> Würde sitzt er dann vor seinem Pult, reißt das Kalenderblatt ab, spitzt den Rotstift, notiert,
> erledigt, was sein muß, und setzt nicht ohne Feierlichkeit seinen Stempel unter eine Akte,
> die der Minister persönlich unterzeichnet hat. (ii,224)

It is fair to say that Fritz Huchel shared the pride evidently felt by Karl August W. in belonging to the Prussian hierarchy.

In order to be closer to Fritz's work in the centre of Berlin than their Potsdam flat permitted, the family moved not into the city proper but to the south-western suburb of Groß-Lichterfelde. Development of Groß-Lichterfelde as a residential area equi-distant between Potsdam and Berlin had been progressing since the mid-nineteenth century, following the merging of the villages of Lichterfelde and Giesendorf. By the turn of the century, despite setbacks during the frequent economic slumps, some 16,000 people had moved to the area. By 1910 this number had swelled to over 40,000. As with the even larger suburb of neighbouring Steglitz, people were attracted by pleasant housing and by the woodland and lakes immediately to the west. The suburban environment was further enhanced by the 100 acre Botanical Garden, the re-location of which from Schöneberg was completed in 1903. For the rapidly growing ranks of commuters like Fritz Huchel, the suburban railway system provided ready access to the city.

The Huchels' choice of Groß-Lichterfelde indicates a degree of ambition which matches Fritz Huchel's career advances, however unspectacular they may seem when measured against late twentieth century social mobility, not to mention his younger son's own life. There were certainly quite severe limits to what could be sustained materially with a young family in a relatively high cost area, especially in the early years of low-ranking civil service employment. The Huchels took a flat at Chausseestraße 45, nowadays a main thoroughfare named Hindenburgdamm. Not long afterwards, they moved down the road to a first-floor flat at number 32. Unlike the Potsdam flat and other Groß-Lichterfelde and Steglitz addresses where the Huchels lived in the early years of the century, Chausseestraße 32 has survived. Since July 1994 it has borne a plaque commemorating Huchel's birth there. It is distinguished from surrounding properties through an internal architectural style with low ceilings and narrow staircases reminiscent of earlier rural design rather than the more typical late nineteenth and early twentieth century Berlin housing. At the same time, it shares with the Huchels' other addresses the rather cramped living conditions that were a feature of life for so many urban dwellers in Germany at the turn of the century. It was at Chausseestraße 32 that the Huchels' second son Helmut was born on 3 April 1903. He himself later celebrated the event in the poem 'Die dritte Nacht April', (i,70) which echoes Goethe's description of the circumstances surrounding his birth in *Dichtung und Wahrheit*. Significantly, Huchel casts the event under the aegis of nature, represented by the River Havel and its lakes a little to the west rather than in terms of his immediate suburban environment. As so often, it is the apparently incidental detail which supplies a clue to biographical circumstance. The second stanza contains the line 'Der Birkbusch wuchs, ich blieb nicht jung'. 'Birkbusch' is surely an allusion to Birkbuschstraße, the thoroughfare in Steglitz between Chausseestraße/Hindenburgdamm and the addresses where the Huchels subsequently lived.

The Huchels experienced unsettled years during the first decade or so of the century. And it was these years until 1907 of which Huchel later stated that he had no memory. The years from 1907, or even earlier as he would on occasion claim, had, he said, been spent far away on his grandfather's farm. In the examination of these early years and, indeed, those after his stay with his grandparents, it is possible to identify external pressures, social and financial, as well as domestic difficulties and weaknesses on the part of both parents, which surely contributed to the unhappiness of the boy's early years, from the memories of which he later sought release.

An index of the Huchels' unsettled existence is the frequency with which they changed flats in these years, as they sought accommodation which matched Fritz Huchel's modest progression up the civil service ladder. By 1906 the 'Kanzlei Diätar' and his family had left Groß-Lichterfelde for nearby Steglitz, where they occupied a ground-floor flat at Adolfstraße 18, moving to a first-floor flat in the same house not long afterwards. Though the poet's upbringing was far away from the poverty and wretched conditions to be found in the typical Berlin tenements in the north and north-east of the city, the family did not enjoy the affluence associated then as now with the south-western suburbs. In addition to the Huchels, Adolfstraße 18 was inhabited by nine other families, all of whom were working-class. They included a building worker, a cook, two fitters, a metal worker and four others described simply as 'workers'. A picture of slight social advance emerges in details of the Huchels' next Steglitz address, a third-floor flat at Marksteinstraße 7, today's Suchlandstraße. On 1 April 1906, Fritz Huchel was promoted one rung up the ladder to 'Kanzlei-Sekretär', and this promotion preceded their move. Neighbours at Marksteinstraße included other minor officials as well as skilled and unskilled workers. A similar social distribution obtained at their final Steglitz address, a second-floor flat at Jeverstraße 18. They moved there following Fritz Huchel's promotion to 'Geheimer Kanzlei-Sekretär' and his transfer on 1 May 1912 to the Ministry of Education at Unter den Linden 4, where the minister in charge was von Trott zu Solz, whose son Werner Peter Huchel later got to know at school in Potsdam, where the family would move in the autumn of 1915. Werner's brother was the more famous Adam von Trott zu Solz, who plotted against Hitler and was executed in August 1944.

The evidence of such frequent removals – on average once every three years with only marginal improvement in the family's situation – suggests that the family could achieve the desired social advance only with some difficulty in an area with escalating rents, in which they could in any case only just afford to live. It was certainly an advantage that as a civil servant Fritz Huchel enjoyed the perk of a housing allowance, since his income in the early years of civil service employment, though higher than that of an average worker, was quite modest. In 1908, for example, his salary was 1,850 marks, against an average for a worker of around 1,000 marks, yet much lower than other state employees such as postal assistants and engine drivers. In 1908, the Huchels' housing allowance was raised from 540 to 720 marks.

Beyond social and financial considerations, the evidence of repeated domestic upheavals points to an instability within the family, an impression which certainly fits in with information concerning the acrimonious atmosphere of Fritz and Marie Huchel's marriage. Members of the family remember them as a couple who shared few interests. There was little communication and little emotional attachment in evidence. Fritz had been schooled in the unquestioning obedience of military life and he expected to preside over a household maintained in orderly fashion by his wife. She, however, was her father's daughter, disinclined to submit to her husband's authority and unwilling to devote herself to the care of the home and family. A latent antagonism in such exchanges as they had frequently erupted into violent arguments of the sort Huchel testified to in 'Die Kammer'. The sensitive Helmut recoiled at the shock of what he came to regard as the sheer awfulness of this thoroughly unpleasant atmosphere. At the age of eight he was further isolated, when in October 1911 his elder brother, aged fourteen, left home to take up a place at the seminary for elementary teachers at Oranienburg. 'Die Kammer' supplies a rare and telling commentary on the poet's lonely and meagre early years, which runs counter to, and as such helps to explain, the Alt-Langerwisch idyll.

Nor did the Huchel household offer the boy any compensation for the prevailing acrimony through intellectual stimulus. Although Fritz Huchel's taste in reading extended as far as Fritz Reuter, pride of place was reserved by him for his album containing photographs of the Kaiser and his family, which he kept until his death, showing it off to anyone he could find to take an interest and regaling them with stories of past glories. For her part, Marie Huchel enjoyed serial stories written for domestic servants. She was also a notorious gossip, which prompted her son's later uncomplimentary reference to his mother's 'Mundfunk'.[25] They pursued pastimes outside the home, away from each other and away from their children. Fritz was a keen angler and drinker. Then as later, Marie belonged to a number of clubs and ladies' circles, activities which she viewed as appropriate for a civil servant's wife. She would promptly join those women's circles which were set up in Nazi Germany and the GDR. When she came to know Marie Huchel in the 1920s, Dora Huchel saw her as someone who had 'Eitelkeiten angenommen als Beamtenfrau'. In Dora Huchel's highly critical view, her petty snobbish behaviour, clashing with her deeply ingrained, uncouth peasant manners, highlighted an essential eccentricity. For Dora, she was an unpredictable and moody person of shifting loyalties, who throughout her life remained a difficult person to live with. In Dora Huchel's estimation, Fritz was a much more honest person than his wife, yet his horizons, too, were strictly limited. Neither parent could act as a suitable role model for their gifted younger child. The Huchel boys assimilated certain conventional conservative and patriotic attitudes, which were inculcated at home and at school. Both boys displayed sufficient intelligence to ensure progression in the school system, and, with their parents' material support, to maintain the family's steady, if unspectacular social advance. In this way, the boys were gradually introduced to the knowledge and values of the educated middle classes, which had remained a closed book to their parents. Helmut's education would, in time, set him apart from his parents, endowing him not only with knowledge but also the sense of superiority over them which he needed in order to forge his own identity.

Yet even before education made its impact, for Helmut another world, the one from which his mother had come, began to exercise a fascination and an emotional appeal, which contrasted starkly with the rather bleak suburban life he had come to know with his parents. This fascination and emotional appeal were, moreover, bound up with the magical use of language in poetry. In time, the Alt-Langerwisch world would totally eclipse his suburban childhood as Huchel undertook what Michael Hamburger has called his 'thorough-going transference of allegiance and affection to the rural environment'.[26] Life with his parents would later figure only on the periphery of the construction of the poetic myth.

Alt-Langerwisch

Neither Marie nor Fritz Huchel were greatly concerned to cultivate relations with their respective families. Marie had little in common with her brother, but somewhat closer contact was maintained with Fritz's brother Carl and his wife Auguste, (their names were perhaps Huchel's source in his invention of Karl August W.) who lived together with their daughter Erna in nearby Schöneberg. Erna, later a department manageress for Wertheim, shared some of her cousin's literary interests, and they stayed in touch through the 1930s. After her early death, Huchel acquired her small collection of classics of German literature, which are now among the Peter Huchel Collection in the John Rylands University Library.

Of immeasurably greater importance for Helmut's development and later life were, however, his visits to his grandparents in Alt-Langerwisch. The journey by train took the boy out of the suburbs, through the woods and lakes separating Berlin and Potsdam before crossing the Nuthe, beyond which the flat terrain gave way to somewhat hilly ground, where woodland alternates with fields and meadows. In addition to pastureland for grazing and for the cultivation of a variety of crops and vegetables, fruit trees do well in the fertile, sandy ground. Just beyond Michendorf and Langerwisch there is a group of lakes. Part of one of them, Seddin Lake, belonged to the Zimmermanns. Smaller than the Havel lakes, they are nonetheless an important ingredient in a landscape generally acknowledged to be attractive, if not spectacularly and captivatingly beautiful in the manner of Wordsworth's or Goethe's sites of poetic inspiration. Huchel's deep emotional attachment to this Brandenburg landscape, however, gave rise to verse, whose beauty captures the area's natural charms.

In 1932, he wrote a short piece about Seddin Lake and the surrounding area. It was commissioned by Haas for a series dealing with local history and landscape. It is one of Huchel's best pieces of prose writing. Its opening contains the descriptive and visionary qualities that inform Huchel's verse,

Wo der karge, von Roggen, Kartoffeln, und Lupinen bestandene Boden seinen schlafenden

Ackerweg ganz in der krautigen Brache versanden läßt, wächst nichts als der wilde Hafer und dürre Kiefernheide: watet man aber durch Wellen von Farn die Föhrenhügel hinauf und sieht plötzlich, im blauen Feuer des Mittags, einen von Algen verschleierten See unter sich – dann nimmt das Land eine sanfte Gewalt an. Noch steht man in der brandigen Luft von Harz und Borke, auf einem moosarmen, nur von Kiennadeln überknisterten Grund, doch man blickt hinab und fühlt, wie schön dort unten, im Zauber der Zauche, Wald, Schilf und Wasser beieinander liegen. – Ganz in dieser Stille, an Wald und Hügel hingelagert, schläft das kleine Kähnsdorf, auf der Südseite des großen Seddiner Sees. (ii,234)

The passage conveys well Huchel's gentle vision of a natural world ultimately in harmony, though containing hints of eruptive elemental forces. The Zauche is the name of the area south of Potsdam that includes Alt-Langerwisch, which is only a short distance from Seddin Lake. The manor house owned by the boy's grandparents was located by the crossroads at the centre of the otherwise quite unremarkable, traditional Brandenburg village, which is to say that it consisted essentially of one main street.

The focus of Huchel's memories was the farm and the figures who lived and worked there. In 1931, he referred to 'damals, als man mich zu den Scheunen, Kühen und Wiesen klein und staunend aufs Land gegeben hatte'. (ii,226) The rural world evidently meant a release from the constraints of time, space and convention which a suburban childhood necessarily imposes. Hence he wrote, too, of the time 'da ich, barfuß und zehnjährig, durch den präriehohen Beifuß zigeunerte, Akazienblüte kaute und lange über Mittag, am Teich Kalmus blasend, ausblieb'. (ii,226)

Huchel's writings bear witness above all to the extraordinary spell that Friedrich Zimmermann cast over his grandson, whose fascination with his grandfather continued undiminished to the end of his life. Friedrich Zimmermann, poet and lord of his Langerwisch kingdom, offered the boy a focus of identity altogether more appealing than the meagre and acrimonious life that he had come to know with his parents. The very unconventional manner of the countryman's way of life was deeply attractive to the boy, when in the first decade of the century he came to know him at his farm in Alt-Langerwisch. The poet-farmer became a role model for the aspiring poet in a way that his own father could never be. In 1931 Huchel wrote of his grandfather's influence, 'So hat er den Knaben bald soweit, daß es sich auch in ihm nur innerlich regt. Er fängt früh damit an, lebensuntüchtig zu denken. Einige Jahre später schreibt auch er in ein blaues Heft'. (ii,213-4) In 1962, Huchel returned to his grandfather's house – in the meantime converted into the village inn at Alt-Langerwisch – and said, 'Hier hörte ich zum erstenmal in meinem Leben Verse, lange Balladen über den Räuber Rinaldo Rinaldini, über den unglücklichen Kaiser auf Sanct Helena, Spottverse auf Landräte und Pastoren. Der sie mir vortrug, abends am Küchenfeuer, war auch ihr Dichter, es war mein kauziger Großvater'.[27]

As far as can be ascertained, none of Friedrich Zimmermann's verse has survived. At quite an early stage in his life, probably in early adolescence not long after his grandfather's death in 1913, Huchel shifted his focus of emotional identification irrevocably from his father to his grandfather, whose memory he cultivated as an alternative source of values and identity. The image which he fostered of him thus certainly owes something to the accounts of Friedrich Zimmermann's exploits and practices passed on in the family by his mother and grandmother. As we have seen, Emilie Zimmermann came to live with her daughter's family in the 1920s. These two survivors of the lost Alt-Langerwisch kingdom were in their story-telling also a source for some of the colourful regional expressions which found their way into Huchel's poetry. A further stimulus to the grandson's imaginative identification with Zimmermann is the material that Huchel rescued from his grandfather's library and made use of in his own writing. On a number of occasions his grandson briefly characterised the library, explaining that it contained early reading material of seminal importance for him. In 1959, for example, he said,

> bin ich doch mit der recht seltsamen Bibliothek meines kauzigen bäuerlichen Großvaters aufgewachsen, in der neben englischen Gespensterromanen die "Volksschriften zur Umwälzung der Geister" standen, eine Sammlung sich kontinuierlich fortsetzender Heftchen, wie etwa: "Die Schöpfung nach biblischer Auffassung" oder "Haben wir Willensfreiheit? Ein Kapitel für ernsthafte Leser. 20 Pfennig". (ii,300)

In similar vein he said in 1974,

> Meine geistige Mitgift, eine Mischung aus Halbbildung und Vulgäraufklärung, fand ich im Bücherschrank meines Großvaters. Neben englischen Gespensterromanen standen dort die grünen Bände des *Forst- und Jagd-Archivs von und für Preußen*, die *Volksschriften zur Umwälzung der Geister*, *Schriften der freireligiösen Gemeinde*, ferner *Meyers Groschenbibliothek der deutschen Classiker für alle Stände (Bildung macht frei)*, handgeschriebene Kuhbeschwörungen lagen vergilbt zwischen den Büchern.[28]

Through these motley references to popular religious tracts and editions of the classics, English ghost stories, folkloric superstition and forestry references works, (left behind by head forester Kühne?) the poet places his early reading development well outside any conventional academic mainstream. This self-characterisation, of course, fits in with the established self-image. And while there can be no doubting that such reading matter had very special associations, Huchel can be seen here, as so often, to be diverting his readership's attention away from the rather more conventional path that much of his upbringing took. We shall presently examine some of the detail of the boy's middle-class education in the Prussian state system, which for all its flaws introduced a gifted pupil to a wide range of literature from German high culture. This 'geistige Mitgift' was every bit as important as the less conventional material to which he later drew attention.

In addition to common character traits already mentioned, Huchel later adopted certain intellectual attitudes which he attributed to his grandfather and his influence. For both, it seems, rejection of the God of Christianity was not incompatible with a lively interest in popular mysticism. In Huchel's case, this interest would lead to his fascination with mystics such as Jakob Böhme and with the living 'seer', Oskar Goldberg. These encounters would, in turn, have a profound effect on the development of his own mythologising mind. Huchel took over, too, a belief in the value of folkloric traditions and superstition, which Friedrich Zimmermann cultivated in the form of what his grandson described as 'handgeschriebene Kuhbeschwörungen'. Until the end of his life Huchel kept a document rescued from his grandfather's cupboard and apparently in the hand of his grandfather's male servant, Ziegener, which he took to contain such spells but which are probably recipes for popular medicines. They are reproduced in the 1984 edition. (ii,425) One of them is referred to in 'Kindheit in Alt-Langerwisch' (i,51) in the lines, 'Hörten den Knecht beschwören die Kuh,/ Kranke von Schierling und Klee:/ Milch, blaue Milch, Satansmilch du,/ im Namen des Vaters vergeh!' In this way, an authentic link is established between Huchel's evocation of the magical world of childhood and the customs and practices of the Alt-Langerwisch world presided over by his grandfather. The inclusion of such talismanic relics representing popular wisdom and magic lends Huchel's early poems on occasion, it must be said, a quite astonishing naivety when they are set alongside other modern poetry.

In one of his vignettes of his grandfather, which was published in 1975, Huchel recalled him showing visitors around his property,

"Ein Barockbau aus dem Anfang des achtzehnten Jahrhunderts," höre ich meinen Großvater zu den Besuchern sagen, "siebenachsige Fassade, Mansardwalmdach". Die Besucher standen im Hühnerdreck auf dem Hof und staunten die siebenachsige Fassade an, in breiten Strängen bröckelte der Verputz ab, sie sahen das von Stürmen und Vereisungen angebissene Mansardwalmdach. (ii,319)

'Kindheit in Alt-Langerwisch' depicts the boy at play on the farm as, entranced in a manner that only an urban child could be, he undertakes a voyage of discovery with another child, whom the reader may choose to identify as Huchel's elder brother. The poem begins,

Kindheit, o blühende Zauch,

wo wir im nußweißen Tag,

klein im Holunderrauch

waren den Hummeln nach.

The day's adventures draw to a close with the following lines,

Seufzte am Maul der Kühe das Heu,

Gott, wie schliefen im Schlafe wir treu,

nachts im strohwarmen Bette.

Und die Träume flogen wie Spreu,

warfen ins Haar die duftende Klette.

The subjective truth of the poem emerges in the absolute contrast between the tender memories of Alt-Langerwisch – which present themselves to the poetic imagination as idyll, a haven of peace – and the bleakness of the central stanzas of 'Die Kammer'. Viewed in the light of this contrast, 'Kindheit in Alt-Langerwisch' and related poems such as 'Am Beifußhang' demonstrate that at the heart of Huchel's creativity was what Walter Jens, writing about the war poetry and other later work, has called the production of 'zarte Gegenbilder' in contrast to the scenes of destruction witnessed by the poet.[29] Huchel's poems of childhood demonstrate not least his early preference for the idyll, a preference to be understood in the light of his background and early experiences. The compensatory function of the idyll as a natural outgrowth of the myth scarcely requires further elucidation in terms of the poet's psychology. Within the mythologising pattern of Huchel's poetic imagination the idyll also attracted its own opposite, the elegy, and these two traditional forms of lyrical expression, which occupy such a central position in Schiller's aesthetics, co-exist in Huchel's verse. The manner in which he combines them makes for much of the distinctive quality of his verse. In the poetry of the mid-1920s and early 1930s, the elegiac tone is struck in the awareness of the transience of the childhood idyll.

It is surely as a monument to his personal identification with the manor house, its owner and figures associated with it that Huchel produced the poem 'Herkunft'. (i,49) The poem came to enjoy a prominent position in Huchel's oeuvre. He chose it to introduce his first published collection *Gedichte* in 1948, whose opening section, charting Huchel's poetic biography, was also called 'Herkunft'. With its echoes of Friedrich Hebbel's verse, the poem illustrates Dora Huchel's recollection that Hebbel was a key influence in the early 1930s.[30] The version collected in *Gedichte* contains a portrait of the figure of the male farm servant Ziegener, a favourite figure in Huchel's verse. He is portrayed in 'Herkunft' as possessing the power to prophesy the weather through his observation of a spider: 'Und der Knecht, der grübelnd sann,/ war der Tag kaum hell,/ forschend, was die Spinne spann,/ lief im Netz sie schnell,/ seilte sie die Fäden fest,/ zog ein Sturm herauf,/ Regen blieb lang im Geäst,/ war sie träg im Lauf'. The intuitive knowledge of the male servant also provided subject matter for the radio play 'Der letzte Knecht' broadcast in 1936, (ii,414) and Huchel returned to the figure of Ziegener in a speech in 1974,

> Ich erinnere mich noch ganz deutlich des alten Knechtes, er hinkte, war bartlos, mit grämlich zerfurchten Gesichtszügen, der aus dem Bau der Spinnen am Netz das Wetter voraussagte. Damals gab es noch keine Verhaltensforschung, kein staatliches Institut für Spinnenforschung, er wurde von den Dorfbewohnern mitleidig verspottet, aber seine Wetterprognosen stimmten. In seinen Beobachtungen, so denke ich manchmal, schien mir mehr Kenntnis zu stecken, als in den Berichten der Meteorologen heute.[31]

'Herkunft' also contains the lines, 'Nachtgeläut umweht das Haus./ Und durchs kalte Tor/ gehn die Freunde still hinaus,/ die ich längst verlor'. These lines in commemoration of figures now dead may be readily linked to the death of the poet's grandfather in 1913 and to the Zimmermann family's subsequent sale of the property. For it was against this background of loss that the poet, employing the elegiac mode, sought to preserve his memories and hence sense of identification with the Alt-Langerwisch world that he had known as a child. The final stanza, indeed, conveys the poet's sacramental sense of continuing allegiance with the community of the household, beneath whose protective powers he lives, 'Alle leben noch im Haus:/ Freunde, wer ist tot?/ Euern Krug trink ich noch aus,/ esse euer Brot./ Und durch Frost und Dunkelheit/ geht ihr schützend mit./ Wenn es auf die Steine schneit,/ hör ich euern Schritt'.

The re-creation of the childhood state evoked in 'Kindheit in Alt-Langerwisch' and the monument to that world in 'Herkunft' yield to the uncertainty of *mémoire involontaire* in 'Der glückliche Garten'. (i,74) This poem concluded the first section in *Gedichte*. Like 'Kindheit in Alt-Langerwisch', 'Der glückliche Garten' uses the first person plural form. It begins, 'Einst waren wir alle im glücklichen Garten,/ ich weiß nicht mehr, vor welchem Haus,/ wo wir die kindliche Stimme sparten/ für Gras und Amsel, Kamille und Strauß'. It ends with the familiar scene in Huchel's Alt-Langerwisch verse of the maidservant caring for the children at the end of the day, 'Und wenn dann die Mägde uns holen kamen,/ umfing uns das Tuch, in dem man gleich schlief'. Yet the seemingly effortless recall of 'Kindheit in Alt-Langerwisch' contrasts with a composition in which the vagaries of memory threaten the poet's identification with the site of childhood happiness. The poem has, indeed, hitherto been read in precisely this way, yet the threat may be understood not only in terms of the ravages of time but also against the background of the unspoken co-presence in the mind of decidedly less appealing images of childhood. The poem's tension is resolved in the image of the maidservant, which in 1932 Huchel interpreted as 'das rettende Bild der Magd'. (ii,246) Like the figure of the grandfather and his material goods, the maidservant enjoys a talismanic status in Huchel's imagination, banishing the threatening forces of evil that might so easily assail him.

Anna and Marie

As we have seen, Huchel used the phrase 'das rettende Bild der Magd' of the maidservant Anna. Yet what precisely did the boy need saving from in the poet's evocation of the Alt-Langerwisch world? The prose piece 'Frau' ends with the memory of the boy, yearning rather forlornly for comfort, confused as he is by the attentions of his grandmother – viewed as 'eine böse Alte' – and the girls at the village dance, 'Weil ich fror, kauerte ich mich in die Wärme des Schultertuchs hinein; aber ich sehnte mich weit weg, irgendwohin; mitten in mir drin war eine dunkle Sehnsucht; vielleicht nach meiner Mutter, die ich damals lange nicht gesehen hatte'. (ii,228) As the adverb 'vielleicht' indicates, the poet cannot identify the object of his yearning unequivocally with the mother figure, whom the boy, therefore, did not feel he could love unconditionally. Abandoned by the mother, the poet is 'rescued' by the maidservant, who in 'Die Magd' assumes the role of surrogate mother.

Yet, it was not possible for Huchel completely to exclude his mother from his poetic universe as he did his father. Marie Huchel was, after all, a Zimmermann, who had been removed from her natural home by Fritz Huchel for a life of strife and unhappiness in the city. Huchel 'solved' her problems and his with her by 'rescuing' her, by transporting her back in his imagination to the world in which she rightly belonged. Like her father, Marie Huchel was a considerable, if difficult presence in her family. When she was portrayed by her son in a poem late in her life, it was not as the civil servant's wife that she had been throughout the poet's life. Instead, he chose to see her in the role of maidservant that she had occupied before her fateful meeting with Fritz Huchel at the dance. As with his father, thoughts of the parent's death triggered Huchel's portrayal of his mother. In 1953, shortly after his mother had suffered a stroke, he published 'Erinnerung'. (i,297) It contains lines such as the following, '... Durch diesen Wald,/ vom unbeweglichen Licht/ des hohen Sommers erhellt,/ ging meine Mutter mit jungem Gesicht/den Hügel hinab ins tauige Feld'. The poem ends with lines that convey his anguish at the prospect of her loss, 'meine Mutter geht nicht mehr ackerwärts./ Aber aus ihren Schuhen der Sand/ weht brennend über mein Herz'.

At what promised to be the last, then, Huchel re-claimed his mother both for himself and for her rural heritage. What is more, the figures of Marie and Anna merge in the imagery of 'Erinnerung' and 'Die Magd'. The latter poem, for example, contains the lines, 'Klaubholz hat sie im Wald geknackt,/ die Kiepe mit Kienzapf gepackt'. In 'Erinnerung', one can read, 'ehe sie schritt mit Kiepe und Hacke den Höfen zu'. The wish fulfilment in 'Die Magd' can thus be clearly identified with Marie as well as Anna. In this way, Huchel's poetry of the maidservant figure can be seen to operate on the level of doubling as a means to accommodate the emotional problems that he experienced with his mother. The love that the child was denied in the world occupied by Fritz and Marie Huchel would surely have been forthcoming had his mother remained in her 'natural' environment. Instead, it was left to the maidservant, which Marie herself had earlier herself been, to perform the mother's role. The transporting back of Marie into the rural world, where she can be all the child's, is enacted in the poem originally entitled 'Marie', (i,389) which Huchel published in a number of places in 1933 and 1934.[32] The opening and closing stanzas read,

> Fliegen im Juni auf weißer Bahn,
>
> flimmernde Monde vom Löwenzahn,
>
> liegst du, Marie, im Wiesenschaum,
>
> löschend der Monde flockenden Flaum.
>
> ...
>
> Wenn es so weiß im Juni schneit,
>
> denkst du, Marie, an die Zittergraszeit,
>
> da ich von deinem Gesicht nicht ließ,
>
> als sich der Löwenzahn weiß zerblies?

The poem was collected after the war, but the title was altered to 'Löwenzahn' (i,80) and the references to Marie were removed. Yet Marie's name is incorporated in intriguing neologisms in a number of other poems about childhood, invariably within a rural scene featuring the child and maidservant. A case in point is 'Damals', (i,137) 'ich lauschte lange/ Den Stimmen im Sturm und lehnte am Knie/ Der schweigsam hockenden Klettenmarie,/ Die in der Küche Wolle knäulte'. As Axel Vieregg has pointed out,[33] like the maidservant in 'Die Magd' and in other poems, the 'Klettenmarie' is depicted in the manner of the three Fates. The thread spun, measured and cut by them determines the life span of those under their influence. Asked by his Czech translator Ludvík Kundera to explain the image, Huchel replied, 'eine alte Magd, die stets Kletten (botan. Arctium L.) am Rock hatte; nicht spöttisch gemeint, sondern im Gegenteil: zärtlich, märchenhaft vom Kind gesehen. "Alte Marie" ginge notfalls'. (ii,341)

The female, as mother or maidservant, comes to occupy a crucial, if highly ambivalent role in Huchel's poetic universe. In similar vein to the above poems,

'Heimkehr', (i,109) the final poem in his first collection, which depicts his return to his Brandenburg village of Michendorf after captivity at the end of the war, celebrates 'eine Frau aus wendischem Wald'. All hopes of re-construction are invested in this figure who emerges from the mists of early modern history in the Brandenburg landscape. Her depiction is further mythically heightened in the final section, with a pathos that would have appealed to the Soviet cultural officers with whom Huchel collaborated in East Berlin,

> Da war es die Mutter der Frühe,
>
> unter dem alten Himmel
>
> die Mutter der Völker.
>
> Sie ging durch Nebel und Wind.
>
> Pflügend den steinigen Acker,
>
> trieb sie das schwarzgefleckte
>
> sichelhörnige Rind.

This poem sees the apotheosis of the maidservant, and in general the maidservant emerges as the benevolent, loving double, by means of which the poet could re-integrate his mother within the world she had abandoned, 'saving' her from Fritz Huchel – and herself.

Yet the psychological truth could not be denied that the benevolent double of the maidservant in Huchel's early poetry occluded its opposite, the terrifying image of the murderous old hag, which, as Axel Vieregg has pointed out, becomes an ever more ominous presence in Huchel's later verse.[34] The double of benevolent maidservant is reversed in 'Ölbaum und Weide'. Written in Argentario in September 1971 and collected the following year in *Gezählte Tage*, the poem enacts the familiar configuration in Huchel's later work of the Mediterranean and North German worlds. The movement of the poem is, however, from evocation of the South to memories of sinister figures from the North, which come flooding into the Mediterranean space. The final stanza, prefaced by the line 'Es ankern Schatten in der Bucht', reads,

> Sie kommen wieder,verschwimmend im Nebel,
>
> durchtränkt
>
> vom Schilfdunst märkischer Wiesen,
>
> die wendischen Weidenmütter,
>
> die warzigen Alten
>
> mit klaffender Brust,
>
> am Rand der Teiche,

der dunkeläugig verschlossenen Wasser,

die Füße in die Erde grabend,

die mein Gedächtnis ist.

The ominous counterpoint to the rich, teeming images of childhood is named and emerges as those deeply disturbing figures and elements of experience blocked out by the memories of life with grandfather Zimmermann and Anna. Axel Vieregg writes of the poem that Huchel 'der mythisierten Erde, die ihn jetzt bedroht, nicht entkommen kann: sie ist identisch mit ihm, sie ist sein "Gedächtnis" ... Schöpfung und Schöpfer sind eins, die Privatmythologie ist zur Privatreligion geworden, die auf ihren Stifter zurückschlägt'.[35] Vieregg confirms the importance of exploring the biographical ramifications of his findings when he writes,

> Wir setzten den Begriff der Privatreligion mit Bedacht, denn es handelt sich ... um mehr als eine sich nur im Literarischen vollziehende mythologische Spiegelung von Huchels Gedankenwelt, die er etwa in andere oder wechselnde Formen hätte gießen können. Dafür sprechen die Insistenz, mit der Huchel auf dieser Figur verweilt und die Ausschließlichkeit, mit der er alle Lebensstufen- und Vorgänge auf sie bezieht.[36]

One might accordingly speak of 'Ölbaum und Weide' as Marie Huchel's revenge.

The Steglitz Schoolboy

Friedrich Zimmermann died on 9 November 1913. His grandson set an autobiographical piece composed in the mid-1970s at the beginning of 1913, in early January. Near the end of the story we can read, 'Am letzten Ferientag war ich bis zum Anbruch der Dunkelheit damit beschäftigt, lustlos die Mappe zu packen, morgen ging es nach Potsdam in die Schule zurück, ein elendes Gefühl'. (ii,324) Yet in January 1913 there could have been no question of him packing his bag before starting back at school in Potsdam. Indeed, nowhere did Huchel ever refer to the six and a half years' schooling in Steglitz where he lived with his family prior to their removal to Potsdam. Within the indeterminate period of time that embraces the myth of the Alt-Langerwisch childhood there is no mention of anything quite so prosaic as schooling. Contact with nature and with the figures who populated the rural community apparently equipped the child with the insights and sensibility vital for the moulding of the lyrical temperament. Huchel himself in fact only ever referred in public to his schooling in Potsdam, yet in his family it was self-evident that his upbringing in Groß-Lichterfelde and Steglitz had been accompanied by schooling there until the family moved to Potsdam in the autumn of 1915. This omission followed quite naturally from the more general suppression of his suburban upbringing. By the same token, it obscured the formative influence that school, like his family, had exercised on him.

When in 1931 he referred to his Potsdam schooldays, Huchel adopted a left-wing attitude towards the conservative nationalism and the cult of the Kaiser that had loomed so large during his schooling. These things were now obvious enough targets of criticism, and retrospectively it might, indeed, have appeared that school had consisted of little else,

> Die Schule lehrt ihn die Fragen des Tages geringschätzen, den Arbeiter, das Hinterhaus. So eignet er sich frühzeitig die allgemeine Kenntnis an, mehr auf die wöchentliche Zeitungsphotographie seines Kaisers zu achten als auf den Belag seiner Butterstullen, die oft darin eingewickelt sind. (ii,214)

This imperial diet was standard fare for all young Prussians of his generation, as it was for millions of other young people in Europe immediately before and during the First World War. As the story of Fritz Huchel's photo album illustrates, school and home were at one in the glorification of the state's military prowess and of the Kaiser's charismatic leadership.

Similarly, during his Oranienburg seminary's celebrations to commemorate the 200th anniversary of the birth of Frederick the Great, the fourteen-year-old Fritz Huchel was the fortunate recipient on 27 January 1912 of Reinhold Koser's *Aus dem Leben Friedrichs des Großen. Denkwürdige Worte des Königs mit kurzer Erzählung seiner Taten*, (Stuttgart and Berlin, 1912). The volume is now in the Peter Huchel Collection. Like so many others of his generation, the young Fritz Huchel would perish fighting for his country only a few years later. His brother, who never subsequently mentioned Fritz in public, would soon have become aware that only the accident of birth had saved him from that fate. And surely the link between the inculcation of militarist ideology and the senseless death of his brother as well as that of many others, whose 'sacrifice' was regularly the subject of discussion at school, fuelled Huchel's emotional flight to the countryside. Without any doubt, these experiences were also determining factors in the anti-militarist position that Huchel adopted throughout his adult life.

Yet, as his brief sketch of schooldays suggests, the child was initially defenceless. Against this background, his involvement in 1920 as a sixteen-year-old in the Kapp Putsch on the side of the anti-democratic right-wing putschists becomes more readily comprehensible. Nor did this involvement merely amount to the harmless escapade that it might initially have seemed: the boy suffered a quite serious thigh wound and was, by his own account, lucky to escape death. By the early 1930s he had come to regard this as a turning-point in his life. Yet the interpolation in his experience of the Alt-Langerwisch idyll has hitherto obscured the prevailing pattern of experience, in which the emotional poverty of home life was compounded by a schooling in the harrowing period around the First World War.

Records of Helmut's schooling in Steglitz from the age of six, when his formal education began, to twelve and a half, when the family moved to Potsdam, are deposited in the archive of the Hermann-Ehlers-Oberschule, Elisenstraße 3-4, formerly the Oberrealschule zu Berlin-Steglitz, which the boy attended from 1913.[37] These records corroborate the statements about Huchel's schooling made to me by Dora Huchel in 1981 and repeated in her mémoirs. His elementary schooling began after Easter 1909, following his sixth birthday, at the elementary school, the Gemeindeschule 1 in Steglitz. Records include no mention of any attendance at the Alt-Langerwisch village school, which his version of his upbringing would require. He enjoyed his pre-secondary education at the boys' elementary school, which was situated on the same site at Ringstraße 54-5 as the girls' elementary school. The site was just round the corner from the Oberrealschule.[38] During the years of his Steglitz schooling Huchel never lived more than a few streets away from his school.

At his elementary school, Helmut Huchel was introduced to the standard fare of the three Rs. In a curriculum of some 20 hours, initially nearly half were devoted to Reading and related skills, a quarter to Arithmetic, three to Writing, two to Religion and one to Physical Exercise. In time, an hour was devoted to Singing and to History and Geography.[39] The boy evidently progressed well in a system which devoted so much attention at that stage to the development of language competence. He was able to proceed to a secondary school with a decidedly academic approach, a step which was at the time by no means the norm for a child of his background. The Huchels were in a position to choose for their younger boy a school at which progress to *Abitur* was possible, and from there access to a place at university. Expectations were thus higher for the younger boy than for his elder brother, who could expect only modest social advance as an elementary schoolteacher. For his part, Fritz, following a year at the elementary school in Groß-Lichterfelde and six and a half years in Steglitz, progressed in October 1911 to the first stage of the seminary for elementary schoolteachers in Oranienburg.[40] From this point onwards, the Huchel boys were separated during Fritz's terms, when he lived in Oranienburg.

All that we know about Peter Huchel's later development demonstrates that he would have certainly benefited more from the literary, if not necessarily the specifically philological orientation of a traditional humanist Gymnasium than from the emphasis on science in the Oberrealschule, the new model for secondary education which enjoyed the Kaiser's seal of approval. In elements of the later man-of-letters' work there is at times some evidence of compensation for early omissions that could never be fully made up for. At least one publication that enjoyed Huchel's blessing, *Über Peter Huchel*, refers to Huchel's schooldays at a Potsdam Gymnasium.[41] The Gymnasium, of course, enjoyed greater social prestige than the Oberrealschule.

Fritz and Marie Huchel could scarcely have been aware near the end of Helmut's elementary education of the direction in which their younger son's gifts lay; and had they been, it is highly unlikely that they would have taken steps to foster his literary talent. Marie was only too aware of the problems for the Zimmermann family which had come about through her father's lifestyle as a poet and lord of the manor, whom her younger son would come to resemble to a worrying degree. A time would, however, come in Helmut's adolescence when she would accept her son's literary leanings. Fritz, meanwhile, saw Helmut's future as lying in the professional classes, after a modern scientific training. At one stage Fritz even entertained hopes that there would be a doctor in the family.

Through his post with the Ministry of Education, Fritz was sufficiently acquainted with the school system to follow the Kaiser in identifying an institution which matched his aspirations for his younger son. The Oberrealschule in Steglitz enjoyed a very good reputation as an institution which, in its own estimation, provided an education designed to prepare its pupils for the practical application of knowledge in their future careers.[42] It was a recent foundation, having emerged from the former Realschule in 1906 following the success of the latter in presenting an alternative to the traditional Steglitz Gymnasium, which had itself been founded in 1886. The upgrading of the Realschule into an institution permitted to award *Abitur* coincided with the opening of the impressive new buildings at Elisenstraße. The school, popular with parents well beyond the Steglitz boundaries, came to be regarded as the best in the area. By the outbreak of the war it had over 570 pupils. Its major academic strengths lay in Mathematics and the Natural Sciences, but another attraction was the teaching of Philology and the Humanities not through the traditional medium of Greek and Latin but instead through the first modern European language, French, and the second, English. The school's academic standing was underpinned by a fine record in Physical Education, something surely not lost on the former lancers' NCO,

> In Turnwettkämpfen, bei den Preußen- und Bismarckspielen gehörten ihre Mannschaften stets zu den führenden, und zahlreiche Siegerurkunden und Ehrenplaketten, die sie im Geräteturnen, in der Leichtathletik, im Barlauf und beim Schlagballspiel davongetragen hatten, schmückten die Flure und Hallen des Schulgebäudes. Der Zusammenhang der dem TOS angehörenden Schüler war so nachhaltig, daß er im *Oktober 1909* zur Gründung des *Altherrenverbandes des Turnvereins der Oberrealschule (ATOS)* führte.

As in other schools, physical exercise occupied a prominent place on the timetable. Three hours a week were devoted to exercises which were performed with quasi-military discipline. Their description sounds like everyone's caricature of schooling in Wilhelmine Germany,

Jede Turnstunde begann mit Ordnungsübungen nach Kommando. Zackige Freiübungen, anstrengende Übungen mit Eisenstäben oder Stützhanteln schlossen sich an. Seufzer der Erlösung wanderten durch die Klasse, wenn diese Disziplinierungswerkzeuge abgelegt werden durften.

Such training was prescribed for all pupils, very few escaping its rigours. Helmut Huchel was admitted to the Steglitz Oberrealschule on 3 April 1913, by coincidence his tenth birthday.[43] He embarked on the Johannes or summer term in class Sexta B, whose form teacher was Dr Fiedler.[44] In the lower classes much of the earlier emphasis on the three Rs remained, with five hours devoted to Reading and related skills, two hours to Writing and five to Arithmetic.[45] Some considerable importance was attached to rapid progress in French, which was taught six hours a week. The Natural Sciences, so important in the higher classes, were introduced only slowly, in the form of two hours' Nature Studies, with a focus on Botany and Zoology. This subject, like German and French, was taught by the form teacher. The curriculum was completed by two hours of History and Geography, two hours of Singing and three hours of Religious Studies. Some of these classes were taught by teachers from the elementary school attached to the Oberrealschule. The reading matter prescribed for each year was purchased by parents, who were responsible for the provision of other materials as well as the payment of school fees. They were collected quarterly and amounted to 160 marks annually. The sums involved were not inconsiderable, especially when set alongside those for the Oranienburg seminary. At the outset of a boy's education at the seminary, the boy's father had to declare that he could cover annual costs of some 650-700 marks. This included board and lodging as well as fees. There was some possibility of remission for the son of a civil servant. Nonetheless, education beyond the basics was a great commitment, not to be entered into lightly.

A vivid impression of the activities carried out in the course of the school year at the Steglitz Oberrealschule is conveyed in the annual reports of the headmaster Dr Lüdecke. Among the directives for the school year 1913-4, which emanated from the Royal Provincial School Department, where Fritz Huchel served from the turn of the century until 1912, were instructions for the celebration of the Kaiser's jubilee after 25 years on the throne. All pupils and teachers attended a festival service on 15 June, followed the next morning by separate celebrations for upper and lower school classes. A senior teacher, Professor Dr Handke, spoke to the younger boys about the Kaiser's early years. The talk was accompanied by songs and poems, presumably of a patriotic nature, presented by the pupils. The celebrations continued in the afternoon with the Berlin schools' athletics championships, 'Am Nachmittage beteiligten wir uns an den Bismarckspielen im Barlauf um den Bismarckschild und gewannen mit einer Mannschaft die "Kaiserstafette", für die ein gerahmtes Hohenzollernbild als Preis gestiftet wurde'.[46] The Kaiser's birthday on 27 January provided a further opportunity for festivities. Celebrations included the pupils' choral recitations and singing, and speeches by teachers. The speech to the lower classes was delivered by Dr Fiedler, Helmut's form teacher. Prussian military prowess was also deemed a suitable subject for commemoration. As with the celebration of the Kaiser's jubilee, sports were an integral part of the day's events in the festivities marking the anniversary of the victory over the French at Sedan. Dr Lüdecke reported that the anniversary on 2 September was celebrated together with other schools in an athletics competition in Zehlendorf. The Oberrealschule won the competition. Greater pomp was reserved for the centenary of the Battle of the Three Nations which had taken place at Leipzig on 18 October 1813, when the crucial victory had been won over the arch-enemy Napoleon. Speeches to upper and lower schools by senior teachers were accompanied by choral singing and the recitation of poems. That evening a torch-lit parade was organised in Steglitz attended by thousands of citizens and some 220 pupils from the Oberrealschule. Given Fritz Huchel's loyalties and enthusiasms, it is quite conceivable that he took his younger son along.

For all the emphasis on the monarchy and Prussian military successes, Lutheran traditions were also cultivated in an annual celebration of the Reformation. The children were told about Luther's marriage and family life. At the Christmas celebrations held on 19 December, the younger children and their parents were treated to words of introduction by Herr Maske, who was accompanied by the recitation of Christmas poems and songs. This was followed by the performance of the traditional Christmas story *Frau Holle* by Matzdorf.[47] The school's sporting calender included rowing, while a further feature of the school year was the short annual excursion for all classes. In keeping with rapidly improving standards of public health, it was obligatory for all new pupils to be examined by the school doctor Herr Wegener and the eye specialist Herr Enslin.[48] All pupils were given two rounds of vaccinations against serious diseases. Nevertheless, in the winter of 1913-4 there were outbreaks of scarlet fever. In addition a boy in the Sexta, Kurt Rottstädt, died of a heart attack on 15 June 1913. The boy was in the same year as Helmut. Taken on its own, this death might not have merited comment. Though it must have cast a shadow over the school, Helmut in all probability scarcely knew him personally, since he was in a different class. Yet this death initiated a period in which death was never far away. Friedrich Zimmermann passed away in November 1913, while the onset of the First World War brought regular reports at school of the heroic deaths of former pupils and of teachers. In time, Helmut's own brother would join them. In the elegiac tone of Huchel's poetry from the late 1920s and early 1930s, there is the sense of an 'intact' community now lost which may be identified with the pre-1914 world.

The Outbreak of War

When in 1931 Huchel recounted his memories of how the First World War had begun, he used what looks like a sequence of implausible clichés drawn from literary and popular culture, which – rather in the manner of his depiction of his father's background in the same piece – call the credibility of his account into doubt, while serving to divert attention from the pain of those years,

> *Der Krieg* fängt für ihn so an: Er hämmert auf dem Klavier, mit paukendem Anschlag, die Pedale als Steigbügel, das Reitersterbelied 'Morgenrot, Morgenrot' und hört das Schluchzen der Zahlmeistersgattin im unteren Stockwerk immer lauter werden. Das versetzt ihn in Kriegsrausch. (ii,214)

For Huchel, reflection on his childhood during the First World War by means of Wilhelm Hauff's popular 'Reiters Morgengesang' would have had decidedly more mixed associations than he was able openly to acknowledge. The poem was among the canonical texts that Huchel was required to learn off by heart in the Quinta, the second year of his Oberrealschule education, to which he progressed in April 1914. 'Reiters Morgengesang' was included in the boy's German reader, *Deutsches Lesebuch für Quinta* and again in *Deutsches Lesebuch für Quarta*.[49] It was one of those texts that the boys practised for recitation before the war in commemoration of Prussian victories and during the war in order to remember the school's dead. With lines such as 'Gestern noch auf stolzen Rossen,/ Heute durch die Brust geschossen' and 'Ach, wie bald/ Schwindet Schönheit und Gestalt!', this poem would surely have assumed the most dreadful poignancy following his brother's death later in the war. If his father's earlier career as a cavalryman was for him an inescapable allusion, then the pain of his brother's fate in a war supported by his father was also captured in Hauff's lines.

Echoes of Hauff's poem can be found in Huchel's poem 'Sommerabend', (i,58) in which he adopts an altogether different register from the prose passage above. Moreover, in a letter to his wife dated 19 April 1945, the last before he was taken prisoner by the Soviets, Huchel asked her to make a copy of 'Sommerabend', which was then unpublished, and to ensure that it was kept in trustworthy hands.[50] On the face of it 'Sommerabend', a poem to which Huchel's second wife objected with some justification on account of elements of kitsch,[51] is an unlikely composition to be singled out for special care. Yet it was also selected by Huchel as one of his earliest publications after 1945.[52] It would appear that the poem's subject matter, the threatened idyll of boys riding horses to water, had a particular autobiographical resonance. With its *memento mori* in the closing line, 'Bald ist der Sommer vorbei', it might easily have come to act as an epitaph for both Huchel boys lost at war. It is quite in keeping with Huchel's general, very guarded attitude towards his background and the allusive quality of his poetry that such a meaning would almost certainly have been lost on readers. The biographical significance can be traced through the imagery of the poem with its description of 'Reiter mit jungen Stimmen'. Through thematic counterpointing with Hauff's composition, apparent already in the title as well as in the idyllic setting, Huchel recasts the imagery of the young horsemen, 'Wenn sie reiten zur Schwemme'. As the poem draws to a close, the poet addresses them as follows: 'Knaben, schön ist das Leben,/ wenn es noch stark ist und gut'. The 'noch' hints at the threat to existence which becomes explicit in the final line.

Huchel's two very different responses to Hauff's verse reveal, precisely in their very difference, his difficulties in coming to grips with the traumas of these early years. Indeed, for all the efforts to maintain business as usual, school life was inevitably disrupted by the war. The Minister of Education von Trott zu Solz proclaimed in August 1914, 'Wir vertrauen zu (sic) dem vaterländischen Sinne unserer Direktoren und Lehrer, daß sie in dieser großen Zeit auch im Unterricht jede Gelegenheit zur Stärkung des Vaterlandsgefühls der ihnen anvertrauten Jugend wahrnehmen werden'.[53] Especially in German and History lessons, there was an opportunity for the treatment of patriotic writing and of the great Prussian and German victories in the wars of the eighteenth and nineteenth centuries. In this way the 'needs' of pupils could be addressed and their confidence in a coming victory strengthened. Unsurprisingly, the annual round of celebrations of Prussian history and the monarchy was strongly coloured by the atmosphere of war. Among those teachers who went off to war was Helmut's form teacher, Dr Fiedler. He returned to the school not long afterwards as a war hero, when in a scene of the type later immortalised in Grass' *Katz und Maus*, he addressed the assembled pupils and teachers,

Herr Dr. Fiedler, der als Leutnant d. R. beim Grenadier-Regiment No. 5 einberufen war, wurde am 30. September in Frankreich durch einen Schulterschuß schwer verwundet und erhielt am 15. Oktober das Eiserne Kreuz. Am 22. Dezember gab er, obwohl noch nicht geheilt, den versammelten Schülern und Lehrern in 1½-stündigem Vortrag eine anschauliche und fesselnde Schilderung seiner Erlebnisse. Nach vollständiger Herstellung hofft er demnächst wieder in's Feld rücken zu können.[54]

There is nothing to suggest that the boy did not succumb to the propaganda bombardment to which all the pupils were subjected in Germany as in the rest of Europe. Nor were things any different at home thanks to his father. Yet for all the efforts to justify the carnage as patriotic sacrifice and to maintain the illusion of business as usual, the early wartime years were deeply unsettling, even before the material deprivations and upheavals of the later war years and its immediate aftermath set in.

The records for Helmut's two years of completed schooling at the Oberrealschule in Steglitz indicate only a modest academic performance. While in Sexta B, in the Michaelmas 1913 term he was ranked 15th among 38 pupils and was given a 3. He progressed to Quinta B the following year, but in the Lent term he slipped to 27th of 36, again with a 3. Easter term, when he was 26th with a 3, saw little improvement. He was nevertheless permitted to join Quarta B at Easter 1915. Before he left the school in the autumn of 1915,[55] he spectacularly bucked the trend in his performance to date, when he was the only boy to achieve a 1. Curiously, though, the record indicates that he was ranked only 5th in the class in spite of this outstanding performance. There is no indication from what work this mark was derived. It is quite possible, however, that it was awarded for German: this was the one subject at which he really excelled during his later schooling in Potsdam, and it was not long before he realised that his vocation lay with the German language.

Adolescence

Potsdam and the Oberrealschule

By the time the Huchels moved to Potsdam in the autumn of 1915, the south-western suburbs of Berlin, which had continued to grow at a prodigious pace, could scarcely be distinguished from the city proper, into which they were formally integrated in 1920. The much smaller Potsdam, with its population of 60,000 (excluding the garrison of some 7,000 in peacetime) and with its natural beauties, dynastic and military splendours, provided an attractive environment, which was, of course, well-known to the Huchels from Fritz's days with his regiment and from the early years of their marriage spent at Große Weinmeisterstraße.

Fritz Huchel, the keen angler, was also attracted back to Potsdam by the excellent fishing to be had in the Havel and Nuthe rivers, as well as the adjoining lakes. He would in later years disappear for days on end on fishing expeditions along the Nuthe. Despite the erosion of his salary during the war years, he was prepared to undertake the somewhat longer and more expensive journey to work in the centre. They found accommodation on the less glamorous side of town, south of the Havel on a quite modern development in the Teltower Vorstadt.[1] As before in Groß-Lichterfelde and Steglitz, the Huchels lived in a house populated by a mix of lower-middle-class, skilled and working-class families. They lived first at Teltowerstraße 16, but by 1917 had moved to number 9 on the same street. Records show that they were still living there in 1922. However, by the time their son entered university in the autumn of 1923 they had moved next door to Teltowerstraße 8.[2] Dora Huchel, who got to know that house in 1926, recalled Teltowerstraße quite accurately as gloomy and slightly forbidding. The proximity of the main Potsdam railway station was convenient for Fritz but provided a constant backdrop of noise. The Huchels would stay at number 8, where they had a flat with three rooms and a kitchen on the third floor, until Fritz Huchel's retirement in the early 1930s. They would then move out to the area where Marie Huchel had grown up, living first in Alt-Langerwisch, Am Wolkenberg, and then in Michendorf at Waldstraße 31, next door to their son's family.

Teltower Vorstadt was not without natural advantages. Teltowerstraße was close to open meadows giving on to the banks of the Havel and the Nuthe; just beyond the nearby district of Nowawes, where Peter Weiss was born in 1916 and which would constitute an isolated working-class stronghold in the Kapp Putsch, was Babelsberg with its nineteenth-century park and Schloß; finally, the wooded Brandenburg countryside leading to the outlying villages to the south began as the ground rose quite sharply at the edge of the Teltower Vorstadt. In the early 1920s, the hill to the south of Potsdam, the Brauhausberg, became the site of the modernist Einstein Tower. The great man himself later came to live in the outlying lakeside village of Caputh. Again, the Huchels chose a place to live in which the limitations of affordable housing were offset by a quite pleasant environment. This was the world which their younger son would explore during his adolescence and which, as he acknowledged in his 1932 radio talk, provided the setting for much of his poetry from schooldays onwards. He said, 'Es ist die Gegend, die mir am vertrautesten ist, die Gegend um Potsdam, wo Wald, Schilf und Wasser beieinander liegen'. (ii,248) In 1931, he wrote about the Nuthe river valley for Haas, describing it in particularly evocative terms as

> eine einzige riesige Wiese, die von Rehbrücke bis weit über Trebbin hinaus in unberührter Einsamkeit daliegt. Die Nuthe fließt flach und schnell, kaum breiter als ein Bach, zwischen Schilf und Gras hin ... Hier, unter diesem Himmel, zeigt die Mark ihre traumhafte Weite. (ii,234)

He continued in similar vein to describe the river valley further south near the Wendish village of Schiaß,

> Nirgends ist die Mark einsamer als hier. Als ich vor Jahren dort war, erblickte ich nur einen alten Kauz von Mann. Er stand am schilpenden Schilf und starrte, in der leicht vorgeneigten Haltung des Anglers, auf den in der Abendsonne brennenden Kork seiner Hechtrute. Er sah und hörte mich nicht. (ii,235)

The reader is inevitably reminded of 'Letzte Fahrt', and a further association with Fritz comes in a later reference to 'Mückenschwärme', an image which, as we have seen, is employed in 'Brandenburg' in conjunction with the depiction of the Red Uhlan and his bride-to-be, engaged in their death dance.

A further factor in the Huchels' return to Potsdam was also surely the desire to be closer to Marie's widowed mother, Emilie Zimmermann. No doubt Marie wished to be in a position to help her ageing mother. However, a further concern for Marie Huchel was Friedrich Zimmermann's estate. After his death, Emilie Zimmermann initially stayed on in the manor house. Soon afterwards, Carl Otto Friedrich began to dispose of the family's property. As we have seen, he was quite capable of performing such a task: he possessed a finer intelligence than his sister and was employed as a local government official in Langerwisch. As a result, he had some knowledge of property and inheritance laws. Carl Otto Friedrich and his sister did not get on, and as a result they at no stage sat down to talk things through. Local records clearly identify Carl Otto Friedrich as Friedrich Zimmermann's heir, yet until his mother's death in 1939 his sister and her son had expectations of a sizeable inheritance. Their expectations were quite legitimate, since it was the practice for the daughter of the family in a farming community to receive a settlement, while the son inherited the majority share. Yet the Huchels were deceived by Carl Otto Friedrich. Clearly, Marie's brother initially had no choice but to dispose of some of the property. His father had behaved in a cavalier fashion: through his unwise transactions, building projects and lord-of-the-manor lifestyle he had seriously undermined the family's finances. The Langerwisch chronicle explains, 'Zuerst mußte der Gutshof mit einigen Morgen Land daran glauben'. Transactions were completed when, in 1919, the manor house and remaining land attached to it were purchased by Heinrich Weber, a local mill-owner, for his son, also Heinrich, who opened the restaurant 'Zum alten Schloß' on the ground-floor of the house. The following year, the 'Landschlößchen' which Friedrich Zimmermann had built for his son was sold. It later passed from the Funke to the Körwer family, who fled to the West in 1945. The building was then demolished on Soviet orders. By the end of the 1910s, all the property had been sold off by Carl Otto Friedrich, who was able to clear the debts and enjoy a comfortable life, while his mother received a regular income.

The sale of the manor house to the Webers was arranged in such a way that Emilie Zimmermann was permitted to stay on in the house. However, in the 1920s she went to live with her daughter's family in Potsdam, and she remained with them until her death. The fact that Marie Zimmermann and her family cared for Emilie Zimmermann throughout this period served to foster the illusion that some of the inheritance would pass to them. It is more than likely that the old lady was unaware of the arrangements that her son had made on her behalf. Certainly, the sight of Emilie Zimmermann's income encouraged Marie and her family in their expectation of a legacy. Yet in the event they would not receive a penny.

The Huchels' move to Potsdam caused minimal disruption to their boys' education. Fritz had progressed satisfactorily in his three years in the lower school of the seminary and in the autumn of 1914 passed the entrance examination for the upper school. It was, however, only a matter of time before Fritz, like many of his fellow pupils, would be conscripted to fight in the war. His turn would come on 2 March 1916, when he was recruited to the 11th Company of the 2nd Regiment of Foot Guards and went off to fight on the Western Front.

Meanwhile, in the Potsdam Oberrealsschule, situated in the city centre by the canal, the Huchels found for their younger boy a school of the same type as he had attended in Steglitz. It had some 600 pupils in twenty classes, who were taught in peacetime by over thirty teachers. Along with so much else in the heart of imperial Potsdam, the school was destroyed by allied bombing in April 1945. Unlike the Steglitz Oberrealschule, the Potsdam school was quartered in rather cramped buildings, which had been scheduled for replacement in 1914.[3] The project was delayed indefinitely and everyone simply had to make do in the dire material conditions that prevailed for the rest of Helmut's schooldays. Helmut's journey to school from the Teltower Vorstadt took him past the main station and over the Lange Brücke (or Kaiser-Wilhelm-Brücke). Upon it as well as below on the

Freundschaftsinsel, there were statues commemorating Prussia's great military past. He walked on past the Stadtschloß and parade ground. Other landmarks close by were the Garnisonkirche, where he was confirmed, and the Nikolaikirche, which was between the Stadtschloß and the school. Another pupil, Gerhard Heller, who later gained a remarkably good reputation as the German censor in Paris during the Second World War, provides confirmation in his brief description of the school that it was very similar to the one Helmut had left in Steglitz,

> 1920 war ich in die höhere Schule gekommen, die zu meinem Leidwesen überwiegend naturwissenschaftlich und mathematisch ausgerichtet war; und in diesen Fächern war ich wie eine Niete. Zum Glück konnte ich diese Mängel durch gute Noten in Deutsch, Französisch und Musik wettmachen und somit später in Berlin mein Hochschulstudium beginnen.[4]

Heller later became a good friend of Huchel's. However, as Heller wrote to me, he knew Huchel only by sight as a schoolboy.[5] Six years younger than Huchel, he recalled how a friend had pointed out the schoolboy poet – as which Huchel was already known – to him across the playground.

Heller's difficulties at school resembled Huchel's own in an institution where only a relatively small portion of the curriculum stimulated literary interests and artistic talents. Pride of place was reserved for natural sciences, as headmaster Schulz wrote in the *Festschrift* for the school's centenary in 1922,

> Neben den physikalischen und chemischen Übungen, an denen sich alle Schüler von Untersekunda ab beteiligen, haben wir besondere biologische für die Prima. Wir führen unsere Schüler an die Stätten der Industrie und Technik und machen mit ihnen geologische und biologische Studienfahrten. Wir haben wertvolle Instrumente, und unser Naturalienzimmer enthält manch schönes Stück.

During peace time extra-curricular activities such as literary evenings had been organised by the German teacher, Naumann, while an introduction to the appreciation of art was offered by Dr Schulze. Visits to the theatre and concert trips were also on the agenda. Yet the war curtailed such activities, when the school had to struggle on with a skeleton staff. The boys were commandeered to undertake menial duties around the town and in the nearby countryside in order to help keep things running.

Huchel's base for academic success in this environment was even narrower than Heller's. Following the two-and-a-half years at the Steglitz Oberrealschule, it took a further eight years of schooling in Potsdam before, in the autumn of 1923, he was awarded Abitur at the age of twenty. Ewald Fritsch, a schoolfriend, fellow fledgling Bohemian and neighbour, who lived with his widowed mother at Teltowerstraße 8 and who is featured on a photograph with Huchel from the early 1920s,[6] later wrote to Dora Huchel that Huchel had been a very weak pupil and had once been asked to leave. This was in the upper school, he remembered. His weakness related directly to his academic performance in a range of subjects where he could muster little interest. School reports identify this and a resulting lack of application as the source of his mediocre performance rather than any discipline problems.[7]

In addition to the subjects studied in the lower classes in Steglitz, English was introduced as the second foreign language in the Untertertia (1916), while the following year saw the introduction of the major sciences, physics and chemistry. Records indicate that although he had already completed half the Quarta in Steglitz, it took four years from the autumn of 1915 for him to progress to the point where he was deemed ready for the Obersekunda. The *Festschrift* lists him as one of the pupils permitted to progress to Obersekunda in 1919. This tallies with Huchel's own account of involvement in the Kapp Putsch in March 1920 as a Sekundaner. Yet, as Fritsch reported to Dora Huchel, his real difficulties set in during the Prima and Oberprima, in each of which – as was possible at the time – he spent one and a half years.

One particular event surely contributed to the adolescent's lack of motivation in the debilitating wartime atmosphere. After a year at the front, Fritz Huchel was reported missing at Hurtebise on 25 April 1917.[8] The family was notified of what was almost certainly their elder son's death. The awful truth had gradually to be accepted as no further news was forthcoming. It is not fanciful to relate this grievous loss to Huchel's awakening as a poet: the earliest dated poems are from the following year, 1918, which saw a veritable outpouring. One poem in particular, 'Erster Aufbruch', (i,24) which is actually undated but which was selected for the abortive collection *Der Knabenteich* in 1932 and finally published in the 1984 edition, articulates the family's grief and the younger brother's traumatised response. The opening stanza evokes this grim reality in decidedly nightmarish fashion, 'Nachts hing tot der Bruder im Gebälk./ Fremder Mann, pochst du ans Tor?/ Ach wie war im Schlaf die Mutter welk./ Vater schrak in Nacht empor'. The closing lines, convey the boy's anguish, 'Brach ich weinend Schloß und Angel auf./ Fremder Mann hielt hart das Tor./ Auf der Schwelle stand der Lauf'.The profound and enduring impact that his brother's death had on the poet is acknowledged in the line 'Schlug ein dunkler Vogel meine Stirn'. This loss, compounding that of Friedrich Zimmermann and the gradual disposal of the Langerwisch kingdom, coloured Huchel's response to what he came to regard as a hostile, cruel world. From the very beginning, melancholy, anguish and helplessness inform his poetry: in this way, the elegiac mode asserts itself and he creates 'zarte Gegenbilder' as an idyllic counterpoint.

A second early poem, 'Klage', (i,13) again undated, intended for *Der Knabenteich* but published only in 1984, is also highly illuminating in its description of early years plagued by loss and deprivation, emotional as well as material. It begins and ends with the lines, 'Weiß ich denn, wohin ich fahre/ auf dem finsteren Geleis?/ Hungerjahre, Betteljahre/ heißt nur alles, was ich weiß'. Characteristically employing biblical imagery, though here to deliberate blasphemous effect, he describes the meagreness and unhappiness of childhood, 'Nur die mutternackte Frühe/ gab mir ganz die weiße Brust./ Jahre wie die magern Kühe/ kamen ohne Milch und Lust'. His hopes of drawing into himself the splendour of existence have come to nothing, since such a rich world has been irretrievably lost, 'Wo die Holzglut raucht aus Spänen,/ weit zurück ließ ich das Haus./ Nur das Echo seiner Tränen/ füllt die zweite Heimat aus'. Memories of the manor house, which he would later describe in 'Herkunft', thus remain with the poet in the world into which he has been cast out, yet these memories are filled with unremitting grief, not the magical identification which the poet would later find in his lyrical recollections.

Both 'Erster Aufbruch' and 'Klage' contain a high degree of biographical authenticity. The experiences of adolescence are rendered with a directness and ingenuousness that would later be transformed into the poetry and autobiographical accounts of the Alt-Langerwisch childhood. In 'Klage', we encounter as key experiences the wretchedness of an emotionally deprived childhood as well as the bitter loss of the rural world. As we shall see presently, for all its rawness some of the early verse appeals to the reader through its very lack of artifice. It was only in the mid-1920s that Huchel became the master of the design that has hitherto so misled critics. While something of that design can be traced back to other early poems, the juvenilia reveal, too, a range of the adolescent's concerns, on the basis of which we can sketch his poetic and intellectual development from the final stages of the war onwards. We shall do that following consideration of the friendships that he formed in these years.

Friendships

During adolescence interests were awoken in the schoolboy, which neither school nor home could satisfy and which brought him into a state of latent, if not open conflict with his teachers' and parents' authority. The discovery within himself of the gift of poetry was accompanied by the cultivation of a circle of friends, boys and girls, who shared his interests. Among them were his neighbour and schoolfriend, Ewald Fritsch, and others such as Kurt Eckert and Herbert Lobbes. Lobbes' sister, Gertrud Zappe, later recalled that Huchel was given the nickname 'Pfaff', presumably because of his keen interest in religious matters.[9] Already in these years he became a focus of attention, as Heller's account attests, and it would certainly not be misplaced to view in Heller and in Rudolf Elter, another friend from adult years, admirers of the talented and physically attractive older boy. In these years, those charismatic qualities emerged which would help Huchel to negotiate the difficult path that his life would be. For all the plaintive cry of 'Klage', Huchel developed, though not in any straightforward way, a strength of personality, through a quiet confidence in his special gifts, which could act as a counterweight to what he felt to be the debilitating effects of home and school life. An early lesson learnt by him was the wisdom of not becoming embroiled in the violent conflict that characterised his parents' relationship. Rather than engaging in any demonstrative confrontation, the phlegmatic and sensitive Huchel tended to withdraw quietly to the sidelines. Schwejk-like, he sought to evade unacceptable authority by heeding it as little as possible, while doing enough in a reasonably conscientious fashion to get by. In this way, he could save his energies for things that really mattered to him personally. This would, in fact, be Huchel's characteristic response in the face of the authoritarianism which he encountered as a writer in the Third Reich and the GDR, and as a soldier during the Second World War. As a strategy for survival which left some space for individual creativity through the adoption when necessary of the mask of conformism, it worked reasonably well. Despite the prevailing hostile climate to individual creativity, Huchel was generally left alone to pursue his literary projects and, as we know, his achievements were considerable. Yet the limitations of this strategy emerged at times of greater pressure and repression. Neither in the Third Reich nor in the GDR would Huchel escape the attentions of cultural politicians. Nor would he ultimately be able to resist pressure to conform in the Third Reich, though the story of the post-war years – and this an index of resoluteness acquired through bitter experience – is rather the reverse.

It is of some significance for our appraisal of Huchel's development and for the growth of his interests outside the home and school that his teenage years coincided with the growth of the Youth Movement, that uniquely German phenomenon of the early decades of the century. There is no indication that Huchel actually became a member of 'Wandervogel E.V.' or of any of the other organisations of which boys from the Oberrealschule were members. The list of such organisations, supplied by the headmaster to his ministry in his report on 1923-4, reads,

Turnerschaft, K.Y.C., T.V.P., Neudeutschland, Ruderverein, Wandervogel E.V., Turnerschaft J.Jahn, Bismarckbund, Potsdamer Schwimmklub, Christlicher Verein junger Männer, Potsdamer Sportfreunde, Potsdamer Sportunion, Bund deutscher Neupfadfinder, Madrigalchor, Deutscher Pfadfinderbund, Verein für Leibesübungen, Jungsturm E.V., Deutschnationaler Jugendbund.[10]

There can be little doubt that, like the rest of his generation, Helmut was influenced by a climate in which young people were asserting their right to an identity of their own in the face of traditional forms of authority which were losing their grip and would collapse spectacularly in the crisis of defeat in the autumn of 1918. It is probably fair to say that, even at that age, Huchel felt little need for large group activity in organised form, since, increasingly confident of his own gifts, he himself became a focus of attention. Beyond friendships mentioned above, he also became aware of the intriguing possibilities afforded by female companionship. Handsome in his youth as he would be throughout his manhood, it was not lost on Helmut Huchel that many females found him deeply attractive. He would have the same effect on many men, including Italiaander, Heller and Hans Mayer.

In the autobiographical piece of 1931, using the familiar technique of foregrounding cliché, he subverted any serious message of what the First World War had meant for him by describing an adolescent sexual encounter as a fourteen- year-old, in which carnal knowledge was bartered for that most valuable commodity, bread,

> *Kriegsjahre*. Die werden auch für ihn mehr die Bitte um das tägliche K-Brot aus Kartoffel und Häcksel. Sie wird erhört von der Tochter eines Landbrotbäckers, die zweimal wöchentlich in die Stadt kommt. Er hilft ihr den Planwagen durch die Straßen kutschieren und auf der Heimfahrt durch den mondverwachsenen Wald über die ersten Gefühle der Pubertät hinwegkommen. Dafür erhält er allemal Brot. Und ihrem Hunger, seinem Hunger und dem Hunger seiner Eltern ist für drei weitere Tage geholfen. November 1917 endet die Zeit der ersten broteinbringenden Liebe. Der Gendarm steht vor der Bäckerei. Sie ist wegen Brotmarkenunterschleifs geschlossen. (ii,214)

For all the blatancy of the story, a similar image of Huchel as the adolescent sexual adventurer found its way into an essay by Karl Alfred Wolken, written after conversations with Huchel at the Villa Massimo in Rome, where Huchel stayed in 1971-2 following his departure from the GDR. Wolken writes, 'So brennt der junge Huchel sechzehnjährig mit seiner Klavierlehrerin durch'.[11] On the basis of this episode, Huchel's involvement in the Kapp Putsch and his later adventures in France and Romania, Wolken constructs an image of Huchel's personality which takes Huchel's charismatic qualities wholly at face value. The stories surrounding Huchel's stays in France and Romania will be examined at the appropriate points. The story of the 'Klavierlehrerin', in the view of Dora Huchel, echoed a story told in the Huchel household of his adolescent relationship around 1920 not with a piano teacher but with a girl from the neighbourhood. The girl in question, Erna Kretschmar, was two years younger than him. She remained a family friend until after the Second World War and shared with the Huchels the humour of the memory. She could indeed play the piano and invited the boy to her parents' home while they were out. Unexpectedly, her father returned and they were found alone. She and Huchel fled the angry Herr Kretschmar and stayed out of the way until late in the evening, when she plucked up the courage to return home. All was soon forgiven, and there remained a story to be told. As usual, Huchel could later not resist embellishing it for an eager audience.

There was, though, one significant legacy of Huchel's first love, the hand-written collection of verse, *Für das Tausendschönchen*, which he dedicated to Erna. In all probability Huchel's first collection, *Für das Tausendschönchen* was referred to by Huchel much later, in a letter to his first wife in November 1941, in which he reported that Erna Kretschmar had returned the poems to him.[12] Dora Huchel remembered him removing the collection from the family home in 1947 following their separation. The poems seem in the meantime to have been lost: there is no mention of them in the 1984 edition.

There was, as we have already seen, another side to the war years and their immediate aftermath. Something of the wretchedness and deprivation of 1917-8, if not of personal loss, in a country on starvation rations, emerges in the wry tone of the five-line ditty published under the heading *Kriegsweihnachten* in the same autobiographical piece of 1931, 'Einen halben Meter "Stacheldraht" quer durch den Bauch/ drei Pfund Kriegsmus in die Haare/ einen blauen Spucknapf auch/ so bescherte im Kohlrübenjahre/ ihn der bittre Weihnachtsrauch'. (ii,214) His account of his father's response to the German defeat and the Kaiser's abdication contained in the short section *November 1918* of the same piece certainly has an authentic ring about it and tallies with the story passed down in the family, (even if the son's recitation of the 'Lied der revolutionären Straße' may be another matter),

Da nach der Auffassung seines Vaters der Kaiser an der Spitze der Truppe hätte fallen müssen, darf der Sohn das Lied der revolutionären Straße am abendlichen Familientisch hersagen:

Der Kaiser hat in Doorn

den Sack gehaun vor Zorn

Auguste muß nach Butter stehn

der Kronprinz muß Granaten drehn. (ii,215)

Like other Prussian patriots, who were conditioned to believe in a military destiny for the country akin to that of Rome, Fritz Huchel fully expected such an act of 'heroism' from his monarch. After all, like so many others, he had continued to believe unquestioningly until the abrupt and bitter end in the certainty of a victory which, he had repeatedly been promised, would be secured by the superior German forces. As the wave of strikes gave way to mutiny in Kiel and revolution throughout the major centres of the Reich, the Hohenzollerns abandoned their seat in imperial Potsdam. With that, Fritz Huchel's world collapsed. His fifteen-year-old son witnessed the remarkable scenes of chaos and civil strife which spread even to normally sedate Potsdam, before the unholy alliance of SPD and Free Corps restored order. Just over a year later, in March 1920, the boy would join the ranks of the anti-republican Free Corps forces of the Kapp Putsch in the first concerted effort by the extreme Right to smash the republic. For a while the boy would be singing a tune radically different from the 'Lied der revolutionären Straße', as he became caught up in the turbulence and adventurism which swept the country as the counter-revolution gathered strength.

In the chaotic political situation, the adolescent's response could hardly be any other than a confused one. In the late 1910s he was, though, in the process of discovering within himself the lyrical gift, which would always be of immeasurably greater importance to him than anything else in his life. He discovered that through poetry – for all his early unalloyed outpourings of grief – he could also create the illusion of a world shaped according to the workings of his imagination. This unique power lent his existence an autonomy upon which external circumstances could impinge only to the extent that he himself permitted this to happen, be they school, family or the grim social and political reality of those years.

The Schoolboy Poet

Despite the domination of the town by its military traditions and dynastic splendours, the 'spirit of Potsdam' had long had a place, too, for the arts. For someone growing up there in the 1910s and 1920s, there was a keen sense that Potsdam had a place in the contemporary literary scene. A number of authors had been born and continued to live there, among them Bernhard Kellermann and Hermann Kasack. From 1919 to 1928 Potsdam was also the home of one of the foremost publishing houses for contemporary German and European literature, the Gustav Kiepenheuer Verlag. From 1920 to 1925 Kasack worked there as a reader. Hermann Kesten was employed there, too. Among prominent authors published by Kiepenheuer were Georg Kaiser, Yvan Goll, Max Hermann-Neiße, Carl Zuckmayer and Bertolt Brecht. While still at school Huchel, had he cared to walk to the publisher's premises and flat just south of Sanssouci, would have observed the famous as they came and went. His library shows that he acquired some of their books, as well as books by others such as Tolstoy and Turgenev who were at the time published by Kiepenheuer.[13] He also, of course, used the local bookshops. Adam Mickiewicz's *Sonette aus der Krim*, which was published in 1919 by Roland-Verlag in Munich in Ernst Rutra's translation, was bought from Karl Heidkamp's bookshop at Humboldtstraße 1. The copy in the Huchel Collection contains Heidkamp's label and is signed Helmut Huchel.

In 1981 Dora Huchel stated in conversation with me, 'Er hat ganz früh in der Schulzeit Gedichte geschrieben'. In characteristically self-deprecating fashion, Huchel had always maintained, she recalled, 'daß die Mutter Mariechen sein Schulbrot in Gedichtentwürfe eingewickelt hat'. We have another testimony which shows that Marie Huchel showed a greater acceptance of her son's poetry than her husband. Gertrud Zappe wrote to Huchel in the mid-1950s, recalling,

> Ich muß zurückdenken, da Sie als junger Mensch 'Pfaff' in der Kolonie Daheim, begünstigt von Ihrer lieben Frau Mutter, begonnen haben, Ihre Gedichte zu schreiben und im Freundeskreis vorzulesen. Auch Herbert hatte von Ihnen ein Büchlein mit selbstgeschriebenen Gedichten erhalten, und meine Schwägerin bewahrt es noch heute auf. So waren Sie schon früh berufen.

Huchel's poetry was, then, by no means a private adolescent affair. Instead, it became a point of focus for the circle of friends that 'Pfaff' gathered around him, including Ewald Fritsch, Herbert Lobbes and Kurt Eckert. At that stage, Gerhard Heller and Rudolf Elter admired the older boy and his friends from a discrete distance.

A large number of his early compositions have survived their use as wrapping paper for his school snack. They were published posthumously in the 1984 edition, where they were described as 'ein Konvolut von 112 mit der Maschine geschriebenen und 27 handgeschriebenen Blättern sowie ein Heft mit dem Titel: *Erste Gedichte 1918-1923 Auswahl, ungeordnet*, das 34 mit der Hand geschriebene Texte enthält'. (i,450) The date 1923 was relevant both on a personal and a public level: Huchel left school that autumn and the chaotic early years of the Weimar Republic came to an end.

These poems are of enormous value since they tell us a great deal about the early stages of the poet's emotional, intellectual and lyrical development. As we have already seen with 'Klage', they take us back beyond the articulation of the Alt-Langerwisch myth and the *Naturmagie*, which has hitherto been regarded as the style of Huchel's earliest poetry. These poems of the late 1910s and early 1920s demonstrate, too, that for all the emphasis at school on scientific subjects and on the inculcation of patriotic values, principally through classes in German literature and German history, the study of the German classics and of the Bible at school as well as at church played a significant role in stimulating his lyrical talent. His performance in German and Religious Studies stood out from the mediocrity of his marks in other subjects. Indeed, everything – not least his nickname 'Pfaff' – points to an early, serious engagement with Christianity. In 1959, Huchel drew attention to his early assimilation of the rhetoric of classical German literary and theological discourse, (though through his choice of illustrative material he proceeded to undermine this impression before an audience appreciative of a literary joke) when he recalled the teaching leading up to his Lutheran confirmation, presumably in 1917,

Und schließlich war es der preußische Konfirmandenunterrricht in der Potsdamer
Garnisonkirche bei Hofprediger Vogel, der mir später den streitbaren Lessing schmackhaft
machte, besonders die Stelle eines Briefes, den er 1774 an seinen Bruder geschrieben hatte:
'Was ist sie anders, unsere neumodische Theologie, als Mistjauche gegen unreines
Wasser'. (ii,300)

It has often been remarked that, for all Brecht's atheism, his poetry is unthinkable
without the Bible. Huchel's poetry, too, is imbued with biblical language, yet he
differs from Brecht in that his poetry retains a transcendent quality that was quite
explicitly rejected by Brecht. Huchel's formal instruction in Lutheran theology at
school and at church was enriched by his early reading of the popular tracts that his
grandfather had kept. On one occasion, Huchel drew attention to the significance of
'der recht seltsamen Bibliothek meines kauzigen bäuerlichen Großvaters'. (ii,300)
On another occasion, he went so far as to characterise his early literary education
under his grandfather's aegis as 'Meine geistige Mitgift, eine Mischung aus
Halbbildung und Vulgäraufklärung'.[14] To set these statements alongside the evidence
of his schooling is not to deny the powerful and abiding image of the grandfather and
his unconventional literary lifestyle. Rather, Friedrich Zimmermann's influence
emerges as all the stronger when contrasted with the intellectual void that he felt life
with his parents represented.

The early poems show intense adolescent belief, giving way to a questioning,
whose metaphysical darkness surely went far beyond Friedrich Zimmermann's
unorthodoxy, which irritated the local pastor. His grandson's adolescent experiences
were such as to culminate in metaphysical revolt. The early poems, as well as his
library, indicate an early acquaintance, not just with the canon as defined by school
readers, but with celebrated contemporary poets such as Richard Dehmel, Stefan
George, Rainer Maria Rilke and Georg Heym, the local legend whose memory was
fostered by figures from the *Neuer Club* whom Huchel would encounter soon after
as a student in Berlin. George and Rilke are both particularly well represented in
Huchel's library, yet he would later play down his affinities with them.[15] Of the poets
in the German tradition, in addition to Goethe, Heine and Schiller, it was Novalis,
revered as akin to a demi-god by the Youth Movement, to whom that generation
looked. Novalis was the key mediating figure in the constellation of poetry,
Christianity and mysticism, which Huchel would go on to develop in his own way.
Such reading matter took the adolescent beyond his parents' sphere of understanding
and probably beyond that of many of his teachers, though we can say with some
certainty that the German teacher, Naumann, came to recognise his interests and
gifts. Otherwise, his education at school and church provided a more conventional
foundation for his poetic practice than he would later acknowledge.

What we now know about Huchel's childhood and adolescence can profitably
be set alongside the juvenilia so as to shed light on both.[16] For all his insistence from

the early 1930s to the late 1970s that his early rural experiences constituted 'der eigentliche Urgrund des Schaffens',[17] they play only a modest role in the juvenilia, which I take to mean his verse produced before the mid-1920s. Where in such early poems as 'Die Magd Martha' (i,42), 'Blick aus dem Fenster' (i,323) and 'Die Wiege' (i,44) the Langerwisch world does figure, there is no focus on social issues, nor for that matter is the world magically transformed in the manner of 'Die Magd' and other later verse. Like the other two poems, 'Die Magd Martha' was included among *Erste Gedichte*. It is a bald, not to say crude statement of adolescent sexual desire, presenting a group of rural workers in the fields, including the 'ich' of the poem, lusting after a maidservant, who bears one of Huchel's mother's names. 'Blick aus dem Fenster', dated 1919, captures the scene of farm life and activity on a summer's day with lines such as 'Pusten pflockt weiß in die Haare/ einer Magd, die pflückt den Dill'. The alliteration on 'p' and 'pf' is early evidence of Huchel's skill in exploiting the musical qualities of language to animate a descriptive passage. With its neo-Romantic *Geborgenheit*, 'Die Wiege' – dated 1920 by Huchel – prefigures other compositions treating the Langerwisch idyll, 'Mit gemaltem Rosenlaube/ schaukelst du mich hoch und tief,/ Nest, wo ich als junge Taube warm und weich in Federn schlief'. We encounter here the tenderness of Huchel's later imagery, but 'Die Wiege' does not yet possess the evocative power that Huchel's somewhat later reading of the mystics and Bachofen as well as the teachings of Oskar Goldberg would bring to bear on some of his best compositions. If the Alt-Langerwisch world figures in a much less significant way in Huchel's earliest poetry than has hitherto been assumed, this is not to gainsay the abiding spiritual presence of the poet Friedrich Zimmermann in the mind of his grandson. In time, as in the mid- to late 1920s Huchel rejected his early verse and the terms of his poetic project crystallised, the compelling image of the mythical upbringing by his grandfather fell into place. Memories of an unhappy urban childhood with his parents, of whom he was ashamed, could finally be buried in the poetic myth.

The major themes in Huchel's *Erste Gedichte* are love, religion and metaphysical revolt, nature, death, and the encounter between the privileged, gifted young and the unenlightened urban poor. The selection also contains three poems, each of two stanzas, which celebrate the boy's discovery within himself of poetry, of what he would later call 'die drängende Bilderfülle in meinen frühen Versen'. (ii,300) The three poems are 'Gebet' (i,321), 'Alles spricht nun tief in mir' (i,321) and 'Manchmal, wenn der Abend weht'. (i.324) In them, the boy evokes the sensation, as much physical as emotional, of discovering within himself the gift of poetry, which transforms his existence and amounts to a re-birth in a purer state of being. However naive, the poems have an authenticity which demands that they be taken seriously as expressions of a crucial stage in the adolescent's development. Each of the poems inquires after the possible sources for this transformation into an inspired being. 'Gebet' and 'Manchmal, wenn der Abend weht' attribute it to the divine presence. The latter, for instance, conveys God's visitation to the young poet, who has sunk into a trance-like state,

> Manchmal, wenn der Abend weht,
>
> stehe ich an fremden Toren,
>
> bin Gesang und bin Gebet
>
> und im All verloren.

> Gott wird in mir laut und tief,
>
> alle Schalen brechen,
>
> was verdunkelt in mir schlief,
>
> kann erleuchtet zu mir sprechen.

The rather obvious alliteration of line three points in the first stanza is also a feature of 'Gebet', line two of which reads, 'in Gebet und in Gebärde'. and, in a slightly less obvious way, of 'Alles spricht nun tief in mir'. Its second stanza reads, 'Dämon, Harfe in der Brust,/ spiele, was rein in mir tönt:/ wer hat mich, o Leid und Lust,/ aufgebrochen – allversöhnt?' Here the creative force, identified as demonic in a Goethean sense, takes possession of the boy with a force amounting to physical violence. The imagery of the stanza conveys persuasively the radical transformation to which the adolescent feels himself to have been subjected, with the result that his life has been profoundly and irrevocably changed. Little can have prepared him for this invasion of the self by the creative power of language and song, through which he senses a purity and beauty which was surely far removed from the world of home and school. The poem concludes on a note of sublime confusion, as the boy transcends his previous existence through the power of his song.

Two further poems, 'Spruch' (i,323) and 'Widmung: Der Dichter', (i,333) postulate a development beyond the initial wonder at creativity. In the two-stanza 'Spruch' he uses the conceit of the gardener as the cultivator of his own poetic self, who tends the flower-bed and removes the weeds in himself in order to foster the growth of the seed within him.[18] In this way, the image of the poet as vessel for divine inspiration is complemented by a more self-conscious attitude: the budding poet must work to shape a self in which all the imperfections of the unreconstructed self are sloughed off and the purity of the poetic voice can prevail. 'Widmung: Der Dichter', probably written in 1922, sees the schoolboy proceed to make the remarkably confident assertion, 'Auch mein Wort wird ewig sein', assured as he is of his calling. In 'Widmung: Der Dichter' it is elemental nature that is identified as the source of the poetic inspiration. It is to the eternal breath of the winds that his own breath will return. With its slightly different emphasis from the other verse above, 'Widmung: Der Dichter' establishes a sense of the transcendent quality of poetic language rooted in the imagery of nature, which, for all the upheavals in Huchel's life and the crucibles of ideology through which he passed, would remain an article of faith.

Two very early poems illustrate the schoolboy's treatment of nature. The fifteen-year-old's five-line 'Der Morgen graut' (i,318) reads,

> Der Morgen graut.
>
> Noch liegen nasse Schatten
>
> den Bäumen um den Fuß als Matten.
>
> Im Osten will es tagen
>
> und graue Wolken jagen.

The poem was dated 13 December 1918, and it is by no means fanciful to read its simple imagery of daybreak as an expression of hope for a fresh start after the war. The sixteen-year-old's composition 'Mein Herz so bange lauscht' (i,326) contrasts his dreams with an awareness of the transience of earthly existence. He hears the scythe sweeping through the corn and the axe cutting down the tree. The poem concludes in the manner of the Heine of *Buch der Lieder*,

> Der Herbst ist da,
>
> die Sichel rauscht, der Wald erkracht
>
> nun fern und nah.
>
> Ade, was ich erträume!

If the dense and sustained patterning of nature imagery, symbols and metaphors was yet to be mastered, then this poem demonstrates the confidence which Huchel proclaims in 'Widmung: Der Dichter'. Yet, it would be only through the encounter as a student and afterwards with Trakl and nineteenth-century voices such as Mörike, Droste-Hülshoff, Hebbel, Rückert, Eichendorff and Lenau that Huchel, drawing on other influences such as Bachofen, would begin to forge his distinctive contribution to nature poetry. Verse such as 'Tief im Herbst' (i,329) is, for example, distinguished only by the rhetorical device of heavy alliteration on juxtaposed nouns in a short line, 'Flöte und Fest/ bekränzen den Tod'. There is quite a lot of that.

The gentle, playful tone of 'Sommer' (i,332) is more indicative of what the schoolboy could achieve through the use of nature imagery, however unconvincing the diction might finally be,

> Die Silberdisteln, Silberlocken,
>
> der Sommer geht ins Beifußjahr,

und über windgesträhntes Haar
schneit Pusten seine dichten Flocken.

Laß zu den Stämmen schlanker Birken
still lenken unsern Abendgang,
wo Winde, Moos und Blattgerank
uns einen bunten Teppich wirken.

The link between nature and the companion through the colour silver, which is developed in the first stanza, gives way in the second stanza to the portrayal of the destination of their evening walk, a parkland which shapes itself so as to receive the poet and his companion. The evening calm of the relationship gives way in 'Mondballade', (i,31) against the background of rivers and lakes which suggests the immediate Potsdam environment, to the eroticism of the lines 'bis dein Leib, der sanft entblößte,/ vor mir lag wie Mond im Meer', as the loved one succumbs to the pursuing lover. Both are given appropriate animal identities in a scene reminiscent of Ovidian myth,

Schritt ich Tiger auf der Fährte
nach dir, junges, blondes Reh,
aber du, die Nachtbescherte,
flohst in Birke, Gras und See.

'Verlassen' (i,326) echoes Goethe's 'Heidenröslein' in treating the theme of the tempestuous youth's seduction of the girl in quite conventional imagery but, interestingly, adopts the perspective of the distressed, abandoned girl. 'Birken' (i,30) operates with a similar constellation of imagery to 'Mondballade', drawing, like it, on the cult of nakedness so much in vogue in the alternative and youth scenes of the 1910s and 1920s,

Birken und nackte Mädchen am Wasser,
aber Birken sind schlanker und blasser.
Steigen die Mädchen weiß in den See,
bleiben Birken, Knabe und Reh.

The schoolboy's attraction to the cult of nakedness and to girls is celebrated in the uninhibited ecstasy of the vitalist dithyrambs in 'Die Begegnung am Meer', (i,270) which was amongst Huchel's earliest publications in 1925 in the Kiepenheuer journal *Das Kunstblatt*. The dialogue between the 'Jüngling' and the 'Mädchen' echoes *Zwei Menschen* by Richard Dehmel, a figure who exerted an extraordinary influence on the young early in the century. The couple strip off and delight in cosmic raptures on the beach, which reach their climax in the following exchange,

Jüngling ekstatisch:

Meer und Mond und Albatros-Gekreisch ...

Du nur nacktes steiles Flammen,

du nur Tanz und rotes Fleisch

flackerst riesig hoch am Horizont:

Wogen schlagen über mich zusammen,

Wollust rot und blond!

Ich kann mein Gefühl beenden ...

Mädchen schon Gefühl:

Gott bohrt seinen Speer durch meine Lenden ...

He wrote the following dedication on the copy of *Das Kunstblatt* that he gave to his wife-to-be, 'Lieber Titzho, solchen Blödsinn schrieb ich mit 17 Jahren. Der jetzt wissende Helmut'.[19] Some of the imagery and rhetorical effects of the love poetry already examined is included in 'Abend der Empfängnis', (i,25) published in 1926 in *Klingsor*. The mix of the cosmic and the sexual within a highly ritualised scene is tempered by the poet's awareness of his loved one's distress,

Am Abend unter grüner Birken-Demut,

da ich dir tief im Blut vergab,

wie pflücktest du die Blume Mond der Wehmut,

Gewölk und Stern in deinen Schoß hinab.

The poet goes on to assure his lover that they can draw comfort from the fact that their union is divinely blessed: 'Wer rief uns so? – Ein guter Mund schalmeite./ O Mutter unser du, Gebenedeite. Und gingen ein zu dir auf nacktem Knie'. As in 'Psalm' (i,319), the reference is to the Virgin Mary as the symbol of the divine.

'Abend der Empfängnis', like the other early love poem 'Mondballade', contains a reference to the loved one's fair hair. 'Liebesgedicht' (i,331) concludes with the same reference,

> Noch kann ich glücklich sein
>
> in der scheuen Landschaft deiner Worte,
>
> die Gärten blühn von deinem Blond,
>
> du hast viel Traum im Haar.

The fair-haired girl in question was called Lydia. She was from nearby Neu-Babelsberg and became Helmut's girlfriend at the earliest in 1920. If we take the evidence of verse such as 'Abend der Empfängnis' to reflect experience rather than wish-fulfilment, then we can conclude that what was prevented by the intervention of Herr Kretschmar took place not so long afterwards with Lydia. Dora Huchel met her later in the 1920s and remembered her as an attractive young woman, whom Huchel was together with until 1925, when he met her in Vienna. By the time he met Dora Lassel, he certainly sexually experienced. As far as can be ascertained, the only use of the name Lydia in Huchel's work is in two unpublished lines among his papers in Marbach, which read, 'Stärker als Tanz, stärker als Tod/ und Musik bist du (Lydia)'. The lines, written in Huchel's hand, appear, appropriately enough, below 'Liebesgedicht' on page 14 of *Erste Gedichte*.[20]

Love poetry of various tones and moods would remain a feature of his writing until the early 1930s, after which it would become much rarer. As a rule, it is the poetry of the successful lover. A rare example of the male's rejection by the female is provided by 'Deine Tore sind verschlossen'. (i,317) The poem is of further interest in its depiction of poverty and deprivation. Following his rejection, the boy wanders aimlessly through the streets until,

> Plötzlich sah ich mich in einer Gasse.
>
> Aus den Kneipen scholl Gezänk ...
>
> Arme, bleiche Kinder
>
> greisenhaft und abgehärmt,
>
> bettelten mich hungrig an!

The scene is one of sudden confrontation with another world normally out of sight, which symbolises the abyss into which the lover himself might fall following his rejection. Similarly, the poor in 'Die Versöhnung' (i,320) are presented in Rilkean manner as cowering creatures, who will be spiritually transformed within an all-embracing brotherhood of beings created by the awe-inspiring power of the gifted young,

Als wir jung auferstanden und zu uns gelangten,
durch Gassen schritten voller Schrei und Qualen,
da ahnten wir, wie arme Menschen bangten
vor diesem Überfluß in unsern Schalen.

Die Brüder fühlten dunkel sich verloren
und weinten, als aus unserer Gebärde
Versöhnung strahlte, tief in uns geboren.
Verzückte knieten sie hin auf die Erde!

Wir aber gossen Licht aus unsern Händen
auf jene aus, die nur sich scheu verschwiegen.
Da schrie Gott auf, es bebten seine Lenden:
er sah sich selbst auf allen Knien liegen!

Verbrüdert waren wir und nicht mehr einsam.
Wir fanden uns tief wieder und zerbrachen.
An ein versöhntes Ufer schwammen wir gemeinsam,
die Wälder blühten und die Tiere sprachen.

More clearly than any other of the schoolboy poet's compositions, 'Die Versöhnung' demonstrates to what extent his consciousness was shaped by his education, his reading of contemporary literature, principally Rilke and Expressionism and by contact with the ideas associated with the predominantly middle-class Youth Movement. In the third stanza, the glorious, gifted young usurp the position of an impotent God in an act which transforms the world and the wretched poor within it. Culminating in the Utopian imagery of universal brotherhood within a magically transformed natural world, it is the composition of the young ethical idealist that Helmut was becoming.

The poem is a particularly good early example of the young Huchel's questioning of religious orthodoxy and of his perspective on the urban misery after 1918, which was as visible in Potsdam as in all other German cities. The questioning of God is undertaken in a variety of ways. 'Du Name Gott' (i,265) echoes Rilke's 'Du Nachbar Gott' in *Das Stundenbuch*. The questioning ends not in the certainty, but in the hope of salvation through God. Other poems such as 'Der Pilger' (i,269) and 'Kniee, weine, bete' (i,266) provide such certainty. The latter, which Huchel chose for his first publication in 1924, links the faith of the individual and the salvation of all those, including the poor, who choose to embrace God. The poem's final lines read, 'Leben ist nur Gottes in dem Bunde,/ der verbrüdert lächelt hohe Kunde:/ daß Versöhnung schläft im Wir'. As such it represents a counterpoint to the irreligious 'Die Versöhnung'.

Like Rilke and earlier Novalis, Huchel's religious questing includes not just God the Father, but also Mary, the mother of Jesus, in a form of veneration normally associated with Catholic rather than Protestant traditions. Huchel takes this over in a number of early poems such as 'Der Abschied' (i,265) and 'Psalm', (i,319) in which she is depicted as the 'Göttin der Barmherzigkeit' and appears as follows, 'Da wir Wein und Speise teilen/ mit dem armen Bruder, erscheint sie uns/ in der stillen Dankbarkeit seiner Hände, die nach unserm Herzen tasten'. In this way, as in 'Kniee, weine, bete', the poor are integrated within a vision of a religious community.

Yet, as we saw in 'Die Versöhnung', that vision cannot always be sustained. Indeed, just as the Prussian patriarchy collapsed before the young Huchel's eyes, so, too, do we see him rejecting the divine patriarchy. A much darker vision informs 'Litanei', (i,330) which with its violence and blasphemies echoes 'Abraham', (i,110) who challenges God, with the result that 'Da fiel auf Gott die Angst'. Yet, Huchel takes things further than Abraham's disputation or God's quaking in 'Die Versöhnung'. As we have seen in 'Die Kammer', Huchel could conceive of the adult world as 'das Böse'. His early verse such as 'Hängt dein Herz am Galgen' (i,23) depicts Satan as a real presence in the world, which, as in 'Die Sichel Satans', (i,32) is the site for the competing powers of good and evil, and where the destructive capacity of the latter might easily gain the upper hand. Early experience, especially during the war and its aftermath, did little to dispel that possibility for Huchel.

Thus, on occasion he adopted a quite deliberately cynical voice that we might associate more readily with Georg Heym. The reference to Heym is appropriate in interpreting the disturbing portrayal of urban misery and turmoil in 'Ihr, die ihr übrigbleibt'. (i,43) It may have been composed as late as 1925 but is conceivably somewhat earlier. In its depiction of the aftermath of destruction 'in einer Stadt voll rotem Rauch', the poem's opening echoes Heym's uncanny prophecies of impending disaster in war. With heavy irony, an attitude of help-yourself cynicism is recommended to those who have survived 'im Hungerhemd', presumably soldiers who, like Brecht's Andreas Kragler, returned to a country in the turmoil of defeat. As a sixteen- year-old, Huchel came into direct contact with such figures when in March 1920 he joined the Freebooters of the Kapp Putsch. He recommends to the survivors of the war,

> Geht in das Haus, deckt euch den Tisch,
>
> er steht für euch bereit,
>
> und werdet nicht dran träumerisch,
>
> sonst wird euch manches Leid!

Und steht nicht auf und geht nicht mit,

wenn jemand euer Herz berührt,

und tröstet nicht, wenn jemand litt,

bei dem ihr nie ein Herz gespürt.

The young poet was well aware just how attractive the deadening of sensibility was in the struggle for survival. In March 1920, he himself became a victim of the brutality that the violent chaos of post-war Germany bred.

The Kapp Putsch

By the time when in 1931 he wrote his quite detailed, if somewhat ironic account of his involvement in the Kapp Putsch, Huchel had come to regard his schoolboy flirtation with the activist politics of the counter-revolution as a seminal experience, which underlay his later conversion to the politics of the Left. His account of the events in March 1920, under the heading *Eintagssoldat*, begins as follows,

> Der Krieg unter Kapp dauert einen Tag. Am Vormittag meldet sich der Sechzehnjährige von der Schulbank in die Reihen der Potsdamer Freikorps, stülpt der Sekundaner den Stahlhelm auf. Sein Zug, Dilettanten am Gewehr, Angestellte, Studenten, Schüler, wird unter dem Decknamen der Einwohnerwehr zum Schutz des Wasserwerks eingesetzt. Stacheldraht sperrt die Straße. Passanten, Autos werden aus Mangel an kriegerischer Betätigung angehalten und streng militärisch befragt. Auch sonst ist die Stimmung gehoben, ihre Grundlage gesund, hohe Tageslöhnung, Freibier, Zigaretten. (ii,215)

Predictably, the garrison town of Potsdam was a stronghold of the counter-revolutionary forces. During the Spartacist Uprising in January 1919 the Potsdam Free Corps, formed the previous December from the remnants of the First Regiment of Foot Guards and the Imperial Potsdam Regiment, had been in the forefront of the action in Berlin. On the orders of the SPD-led government, they had attacked and murdered the Spartacists occupying the newspaper quarter around the Belle-Alliance-Platz. By March 1920, the Freebooters had turned against the republican government, which, in compliance with the Versailles Treaty, was moving to disband them. The Ehrhardt Brigade's march on Berlin in the night of 12-13 March was a desperate attempt to preempt the government. The initial success of the putschists was made possible by the refusal of the army high command in Berlin to support the government against them. The putschists managed to hold on to power for only five days until 17 March. The fleeing republican government called for a general strike.

The response in the capital was so solid that the city ground to a halt. The putschists' support rapidly disintegrated and they were forced to flee under assumed identities. Potsdam was somewhat different from Berlin. An account of the putsch produced by GDR historians describes events in Potsdam in terms that to some extent echo Huchel's own,

> In der alten preußischen Garnisonstadt Potsdam, dem Sitz der Reichswehrbrigade 3, errichteten die Militaristen ein Terrorregiment. Sie verbarrikadierten die Stadt festungsartig; Brücken und Zufahrtsstraßen sperrten sie durch Stacheldrahrverhaue und Posten, Einwohnerwehren, Sicherheitspolizei und Technische Nothilfe wurden mobilisiert. Trotzdem kam es zum Generalstreik. Der Potsdamer Aktionsausschuß rief am 16. März zu einer Demonstration gegen die Putschisten auf. Die Reichswehr schoß rücksichtslos in die unbewaffnete Menge; vier Tote und elf Verwundete blieben im Feuer liegen.[21]

Huchel's account describes how he came to be one of the eleven wounded, when he was the victim of the mercilessness of his own forces. He was shot in the left thigh and later bore quite a large oval scar. It would appear that the 'Eintagssoldat' joined the putschists only on the 16th, opting for what at the time he saw as the right side, as, on the other, the working class mobilised to resist the overthrow of the republic. Undoubtedly, his father supported the aim of the putsch but it is unlikely that he would have sent his son into battle. The boy probably seized the opportunity to skip school and went looking for the action amid the general excitement and turmoil. From the headquarters of the civil guard in the NCO school on Jägerallee, he was deployed in a support role at the water works on Leipzigerstraße. From there, he was sent into town to fetch supplies. On the way, he claimed, he became caught up in the mass of demonstrating workers, who did not take the schoolboy seriously and let him go. At this point and later in his account Huchel, from his 1931 perspective, makes propagandist points in his depiction of the masses and their power, 'An der Bahnüberführung stauen sich ihre Massen, sie strömen aus der Versammlung'. (ii,215)

That evening, 'gewarnt und in Zivil', (ii,215) he set off for a meeting called by the Kapp government to inform the population about the measures being taken to protect them. The meeting was due to take place at the Wirtshaus Sanssouci but the officer in charge of the garrison, Major General von der Hardt, banned the meeting as it was about to begin. Predictably, chaos ensued. Von der Hardt's report states,

> Die radaulustigen und hetzerischen Elemente vereinigten sich dann und zogen trotz des ausdrücklichen Verbots von Umzügen in einem etwa tausendköpfigen, geschlossenen Zuge

durch die Straßen mit ausgegebener Losung 'Lustgarten'. Im Zuge wurde geschrien, gejohlt, mit Hetzrufen gearbeitet. (Hoch Rosa Luxemburg, Nieder mit Hindenburg).[22]

Von der Hardt believed that the demonstration was orchestrated by self-styled, working-class leaders from nearby Nowawes. Huchel's account indicates that he became caught up among the demonstrators, whose goal became the town hall near the Stadtschloß, 'Ihre Masse, unabsehbar, schwärzt die Straßen'. (ii,215) According to von der Hardt's account, 'Etwa 8 Uhr 45 abends drängte diese Masse auf das Stadtschloß zu. Trotz dreifacher Aufforderung des Führers der Stadtschloßwache zum Auseinandergehen drang die Menge unter Schimpfworten weiter vor'. The boy was swept along in the throng until 'der Posten vom Stadtschloß her das erste Feuer in die Menschenmauer jagt. Vom Pflaster abprallend, haut ihn ein Querschläger hin'. (ii,216) Lying wounded on the tram lines, shot by his own side, the boy witnessed around him the scene of carnage including the shooting of a woman, 'da sackt die Frau knochig vornüber, mit klaffender Schläfe, drei Schritt vor ihm, aufs Pflaster'. (ii,216). One of four dead and eleven wounded among the civilian population, he fell unconscious and woke up in hospital surrounded by the dead and wounded workers. After an operation he was placed in a ward together with the other wounded, where he stayed for two months, 'Erst spät kommt es zu Debatten von Bett zu Bett: Politik. Der Nachbar, ein Metalldreher, macht ihm immer wieder die einfachsten Begriffe klar. Mit einem Heizer, der seine Lokomotive Lotte nennt, schließt er Freundschaft'. (ii,217)

It was not that during his two months in hospital Huchel encountered members of the urban working class for the first time. As we have seen, the addresses at which he had lived with his family generally housed a mix of the working class and lower middle class. Huchel's development to that point and, indeed, later enabled him to rise out of a milieu with whose limitations he was all too familiar. Knowing the proletariat from that perspective, he would always be sceptical about leftist claims concerning that 'rising class'. What was probably new, however, was to talk to working class men who were sufficiently opposed to the forces of reaction to risk their lives by taking to the streets in defiance of the putschists. The Nowawes workers had developed a solidarity and awareness not to be found elsewhere in Potsdam. In 1971, Huchel explained that he had shared the ward with four workers, and 'Sie gaben mir linke Literatur zu lesen, und von da an war ich vollkommen rot'. (ii,370-1) He later told Dora Lassel that the key text in his conversion was Henri Barbusse's *Le feu*. The socialist Barbusse's account of the barbarity of trench warfare would have struck a chord. Yet it would be a mistake to assume either that Huchel's political consciousness was immediately transformed through the experience into support for the politics of working class victory or that he could ever bring himself to believe unreservedly in the rhetoric of the rising working class. Indeed, he concluded his account of his political initiation with the following words,

'Ein Schuß hat genügt, um in ein neues Leben zu humpeln. Aber das ist auch danach; es geht im Zickzack vor sich'. (ii,217)

The events of 16 March 1920 must surely have triggered a profound shock in the boy, who had been just a few inches away from the death that had befallen others that evening in Potsdam. The experience can only have contributed to his subsequent rejection of militarism and to his alienation from home and school, where the values of the old order to some extent continued to be proclaimed. However erratic the course of Huchel's development between 1920 and 1931, when he wrote his account, the key choices he made were consistently at odds with what the old order had stood for, let alone with what the new radical Right was proposing. For Huchel and those with whom he associated, the exciting, new political ideas came from the Left, yet he would not be sufficiently convinced by those ideas to throw in his lot with the Left before 1933, as the Right in any case increasingly set the agenda.

As a student the aspiring poet, increasingly confident of his calling, would escape the stifling confines of his parents' petty bourgeois world and immerse himself in the limitless opportunities afforded by the Bohemian world of Berlin, Freiburg, Vienna and Paris. If the attractions of that world were irresistible for someone of his talent and temperament, and equally he too for members of that world, it cannot be said that Huchel enjoyed a comfortable passage. Social, cultural and financial limitations of his background made for very real problems, material and emotional, at a time when it was still the exception for someone from his social position to study. His modest academic achievements at school might well have stopped in his tracks someone less assured of his very special talents. Poems such as 'Klage' (i,13) and 'Die Einsamen', (i,331) the latter composed in 1922, convey his uncertainties, helplessness and self-doubt. 'Die Einsamen', for example, begins, 'Wir klagen in uns an und weinen stumm./ Im Auge steht ein trauriges Warum'. Yet he was able to move forward, carrying with him his melancholy and distress. Indeed, the mid- to late 1920s would prove the decisive years in the poet's personal development, which would bear fruit in the early 1930s.

Abitur

Having escaped from near-disaster in the Kapp Putsch, Huchel resumed his schooling after convalescence. In the autumn of 1920 he was permitted to proceed from Obersekunda to Prima. Yet, as Ewald Fritsch later told Dora Huchel, in the upper school Huchel's devotion to literature was still not matched by any similar level of commitment to his schoolwork. It must be said that conditions were far from ideal. If the crass militarism and jingoism were no longer being pushed, the school and its pupils had to cope with the aftermath of war, which had seen the death of no less than 160 former pupils. In his annual report to the Ministry of Education for 1921-2, the headmaster Schulz complained about the chronic lack of space and the fact that five different sites had to be used.[23] A shortage of coal forced the school to close between 8 and 19 February 1922, while a heatwave prompted a further four days closure in May and June. There were no classes on 19 April, the day on which the former *Kaiserin*, Auguste-Viktoria, was buried, with the majority of teachers and pupils in attendance. The previous day had seen the celebration of the 400th jubilee of 'Luther vor dem Reichstage zu Worms'. A 'Feier des Reformationsfestes' took place on 31 October. The school's own jubilee was celebrated by the publication of the *Festschrift*, by a performance on 5 January 1922 in the State Theatre of scenes from acts one and two from *Wilhelm Tell* given by senior boys, and on 7 January by a gymnastic display by the boys in the gymnasium on Türkstraße. The headmaster did not conceal other difficulties,

> Bei den Schülern sind im großen Ganzen, wenigstens was den Unterricht betrifft, die Nachwehen des Krieges so ziemlich überwunden. Hier treten die Erfolge sichtlich hervor. Dagegen ist die Unterernährung bei einem Teil der Kinder immer noch groß. In dankenswerter Weise haben es uns wieder wie im vorigen Jahre die amerikanischen Quäker ermöglicht, eine große Zahl von Kindern – zuletzt 81 – zu ernähren. Ebenso konnten Kinder nach Ostpreußen und der Neumark auf das Land geschickt werden, auch nach Schweden und Holland.

There is little evidence that Helmut could muster sufficient enthusiasm to make a success of his school career in these conditions. After taking one and a half years in both Prima and Oberprima, he did nevertheless finally scrape through Abitur aged twenty-and-a-half on 20 September 1923.[24] He cuts a particularly handsome figure in the 'Abitur' photograph which features him with four others who passed at that sitting.[25] In conversation with me in 1981, Dora Huchel recalled him saying that he had passed 'Mit Hängen und Würgen. Physik mit Hilfe von Zeichensprache'. Records show that he, along with four other pupils from a group of sixteen, was withdrawn from the Abitur exam at Easter 1923 by the school authorities. A report on him, entitled 'Gutachten über die Reife', reads,

> Von Quarta an Schüler der Anstalt. *Sittlich nicht gefestigt genug.* Zwar nach der literarischen Seite hin besser beanlagt (sic), aber ohne das nötige Interesse für sonstige Lehrgegenstände der Schule und ohne den erforderlichen Fleiß, hat er in drei Hauptfächern (Französisch, Englisch, Mathematik) nicht genügende Leistungen aufzuweisen. Die Kommission hat einstimmig beschlossen, ihn von der Prüfung *zurückzuweisen*.

This decision virtually amounted to the recommendation that he should leave without Abitur. It was surely to this episode that Ewald Fritsch was later referring when he told Dora Huchel that Huchel had once been thrown out of the upper school. One can assume that both the boy and his parents had to demonstrate their commitment to his resumption of his schooling with a view to securing a successful outcome. The report which was produced later that year when he was entered for the September sitting reads,

> Von Quarta an Schüler der Anstalt. Ostern 1923 von der Prüfung zurückgestellt. *Sittlich*
>
> *reif.* Durchschnittlich begabt, einseitig interessiert und darum nicht gleichmäßig fleißig.
>
> Seine Leistungen sind in der Mathematik mangelhaft, in Französisch, Englisch, Geschichte
>
> und Physik nur schwach genügend, in Deutsch und Religion gut, im übrigen genügend.
>
> Das Bestehen der Prüfung ist *nicht zweifellos*.

Written papers began on Tuesday 4 September 1923 with the French essay. The boys were expected to write for five and a half hours, beginning at 8.10 am., on 'Louis XIV et Fréderic le Grand. (Tracez les traits caractéristiques et distinctifs dans la manière de penser et d'agir des deux rois.)'. Huchel, the record tells us, left the room between 12.08 and 12.10. He was awarded a 3. The same amount of time was allowed the next day for the German essay, 'Macht die Technik den Menschen frei?' Naumann awarded Huchel the truly outstanding mark of a straight 1, the only such mark achieved by any of the candidates in any subject. It is a great shame that the Abitur essays from that particular year have not survived. Given what we know of Huchel's development before and after we would expect a decidedly sceptical answer to this question, informed by ethical and religious considerations. Maths was sat on 6 September. Huchel's result was a weak four. With the help of 'Zeichensprache', Physics the following day yielded a surprisingly respectable 3. The written exams concluded on 8 September with English, for which he was awarded a 3. He was required to sit a viva in French and English as well as History and Chemistry. A mark of 4 was returned for a poor performance in French. His English pronunciation rescued him from oblivion in that subject, although he was not able to answer any questions on *Beowulf*, including 'What is alliteration?' He was given a 3, as he was in History, though he fell back to a 4 in Chemistry.

He excelled only in German, and with the exception of Religious Studies, in which his performance throughout the year was good, all his marks were quite mediocre. He was fortunate to pass against a background of earlier failure and question marks against his application and motivation. His performance scarcely indicated the potential for further study. It was not uncommon in such cases for Oberrealschule leavers to pursue a career in commerce. This was especially the case for someone of his lower middle-class background, for whom progression to higher education was still the exception. Indeed, Huchel's school leaving certificate dated 3 November 1923 contains the statement that he was leaving school 'um Kaufmann zu werden'.

Student Years

Berlin, and Europe

Whatever the views of teachers and parents, Huchel clearly never had any intention whatsoever of becoming a salesman. His parents were not inclined to stand in the way of their surviving son's wishes, and with their financial support he entered university. It was, though, more with a view to pursuing his vocation as a poet than any systematic programme of study that on 19 October 1923 he registered as a student of German and Philosophy at the Friedrich Wilhelm University in Berlin.[1] From the information he gave at registration, it would appear that at the beginning of his studies he continued to live at home, travelling in to classes by train. Certainly, Potsdam friends remained important to him during this period, when he was still seeing Lydia. Though one cannot say so with any certainty due to the quite meagre information available about the years immediately after he left school and before he met Dora Lassel, one would expect that he spent more and more time in Berlin as he began to move in new circles during the three semesters he spent there.

In 1931 he characterised his life as a student and the divergence of his path from that of many of his Potsdam contemporaries,

> Als Student versucht er in die Zeit zu horchen. Er besucht Meetings, liest Broschüren, debattiert. Die Inflation bricht aus. Und das Schicksal seiner Generation wird vollends Lotterie. Im Kriege hatte dem einen der große Treffer den Ernährer genommen, den anderen hatte er zum Kriegsgewinnlersohn gemacht. Jetzt sind seine Freunde Banklehrlinge; sie haben Vermögen aufzuweisen. Ihr Motorrad ist eine Sache, ihr Likörlager, ihre Stoffballen. Heut sieht er sie meist gedrückt, arbeitslos, schlecht angezogen. Es sind dieselben, die es sich nicht abgewöhnen werden zu spekulieren. Hier und dort erkennt er sie wieder. Und meist setzen sie auf das Hakenkreuz. (ii,217)

He succeeded in breaking with what, retrospectively, must have looked like the almost inevitable progression from a conservative, petty bourgeois background, into the brief and relative affluence of a minor post during the stable years of the mid-1920s, followed after 1929 by unemployment and support for the solutions of the radical Right. And certainly, whatever compromises Huchel later made in the bleak cultural climate of the 1930s and early 1940s, he never became a supporter of the Nazis.

It was the decision to become a student that lifted him for good out of the confines of the petty bourgeois milieu. No longer subject to the rules and regulations of school, he embarked on a steep learning curve, which propelled him through the rest of the decade and took him across continental Europe from West to East, from the island of Bréhat in Brittany to Istanbul, before he settled in Berlin. Though he was ostensibly a student for most of these years in Berlin, Freiburg, Vienna and Paris, the most exciting discoveries were made outside any strictly academic environment. Key friendships developed with the sons and daughters of the educated middle classes and with others who, like him, had risen thanks to their talents. He gravitated to the company of people, many of a Jewish background, who were cultivating a Bohemian lifestyle on the margins of bourgeois society, where they pursued their literary and artistic interests. His lyrical gift and personal charm guaranteed his ready acceptance by them. In his three semesters in Berlin he got to know Harry Landry, an eternal Bohemian, and Karola Piotrkowska, who later married Ernst Bloch. In 1925 he formed a close friendship with Hans A. Joachim in Freiburg, who knew Landry and Piotrkowska from Berlin. When he moved on to Vienna, he shared a flat for a while with a Berlin friend, the violinist Wilhelm Blaß, and became close to the dramatist Franz Theodor Csokor. In Paris he got to know the Berliner, Alfred Kantorowicz, through their mutual friend Joachim. Cosmopolitan Paris also saw friendship with the Chinese poet and revolutionary Cheng Cheng and the acquaintance of the Japanese painter Foujita, as well as Claire and Yvan Goll. These and other contacts contributed to the broadening of horizons, social and artistic, to which Huchel was extremely open in these years, as he and the others sought to find their way in the, as it turned out, fatally flawed new order that had emerged from Versailles. Some of the contacts that Huchel established in these years would be of lasting importance, joining those older friendships with figures such as Rudi Elter and Ewald Fritsch in Potsdam.

The fundamental achievement of those years was, however, the transformation of Huchel's lyrical voice that began in the mid-1920s, when, in the post-Expressionist literary world receptive to myth-making and nature poetry, he forged the distinctive tone of the poetry of the Alt-Langerwisch childhood that characterises his publications from the early 1930s. The fact that in 1948 Huchel included only those poems in *Gedichte* which had been composed from 1925 onwards indicates that he himself came to view the mid-1920s as a turning-point. A number of personalities and books had a great impact on him, as he, in turn, gradually defined himself among his friends and acquaintances in such a way that lent him a standing as someone whose existence had not been wholly determined by modern urban life. Equally, the emerging myth of the Alt-Langerwisch upbringing provided a means of escape from the shadow that his parents cast over him.

Mythology and Mysticism: the Goldberg Circle

As his juvenilia amply testifies, Huchel had enjoyed a conventional Lutheran education. That is reflected in his first publication, 'Kniee, weine, bete', which was included in the *Dürer Kalender* for 1924 on the tear-off sheet for 18 July. As the

1920s progressed, he left religious orthodoxy behind but the religious impulse remained a vital component in the poet's spiritual quest. On more than one occasion in the final years of his life, Huchel explained that his poetry could only be understood through reference to the mystics. 'Der Herbst', for instance, a poem composed in the late 1920s, contains lines in which the seasonal change of nature is depicted quite explicitly in terms of an alchemical transformation, viewed by the mystics as an allegory for the spiritual metamorphosis of the world, 'Herbst, dunkler Herbst, voller Gerüche,/ wo Wind dein Feuer groß beschrie,/ wo Laub zu Gold kocht, dunkle Küche/ der erddurchflammten Alchimie'. (i,80) In a letter to Axel Vieregg in 1974, Huchel cited quite specific influences in his student years, writing, 'Als ich aber 1923 die Humboldt-Universität bezog und mich dort in den Bibliotheken umsah, entdeckte ich die Mystik. Neben Meister Eckehardt, Seuse, Swedenborg, Paracelsus, Baader, Theophrast von Hohenheim u.a. war es vor allem Jakob Böhme, der mich fesselte, nicht nur "Aurora", auch seine anderen Schriften'. (ii,359)

Vieregg has argued for the centrality of Böhme's writings, together with J.J.Bachofen's exploration of pre-Christian myth in *Das Mutterrecht*, for an understanding of the network of imagery which constitutes what Vieregg calls the private mythology which Huchel developed in his poetry from the mid-1920s onwards. Yet, as we have seen, the workings of Huchel's mythologising imagination can be traced back to much more private, that is to say biographical sources, which is not to say that literary influences did not decisively colour the manner in which he presented his life. Despite access to only quite limited biographical information, in his interpretation of 'Brandenburg' Gerhard Schmidt-Henkel argues persuasively that biographical details 'liefern dem Verständnis der Privatmythologie Huchels eine festere Basis als die Suche nach literarischen Einflüssen oder Sagenstoffen'.[2] That said, there can be little doubt that Huchel's reading of Bachofen's work contributed towards a qualitative change in his imagery, which, from the composition of 'Die Magd' onwards, became much more precise and redolent of the transcendent order that he sought to evoke. Vieregg highlights in Böhme's writings his depiction of the inter-relations between inner and outer worlds in the seer's contemplation of matter, arguing that this provided the framework for Huchel's private mythology. Yet Böhme's writings describe an operation common to virtually all mysticism, Christian as well as non-Christian, and found, too, in much visionary poetry. Whilst not seeking to deny Böhme's attraction for Huchel, the terms of inquiry can be profitably extended beyond a rather exclusive focus to include other intellectual and artistic influences as well as consideration of the poet's emotional and psychological make-up, which made him receptive to such influences.

Huchel drew attention on more than one occasion in later years to a vital formative influence of the 1920s, yet so obscure was his reference, characteristically enough, that its significance has hitherto not been considered. In a slightly earlier letter to Axel Vieregg dated 3 January 1974, (ii,358) Huchel distinguished between his own artistic background and that of other prominent contemporaries or near-contemporaries among German nature poets, Wilhelm Lehmann, Johannes Bobrowski and Günter Eich, as well as other members of the *Kolonne* Circle. He explained that in addition to the paternal influence of Ernst Bloch – which in fact dates from the early 1930s when Bloch's *Spuren* was published and Huchel got to know him – , 'im Berliner Goldberg-Kreis – *Die Wirklichkeit der Hebräer* – war ich ein Jahr lang der Schabbesgoi'. Whatever we might make of this self-characterisation as the shabbes goy, the Gentile servant on the Sabbath – and here surely is an example of Huchel's propensity to tease his readers, just as he, it seems, was teased with this name by his friend Hans A. Joachim in 1925 [3] – , there can be no denying the impact of his encounter in 1924 with the thinkers and artists of the Goldberg Circle that gathered around its leader, the speculative private scholar Oskar Goldberg, whose teachings were based on the text of his major work, *Die Wirklichkeit der Hebräer*, which appeared in 1925.

It was surely partly to the meetings and publications of the eclectic Goldberg Circle that Huchel was alluding when in 1931 he wrote of attending meetings, reading brochures and engaging in debate during those student years in Berlin. Philosophical and literary matters were at the core of the wide range of intellectual interests represented by the Circle and its speakers at its meetings. The Goldberg Circle's was an esoteric fame, and until recently Goldberg himself (1885-1952) was a forgotten figure of German-Jewish intellectual life. Through the painstaking research of Richard Sheppard[4] and Manfred Voigts[5] it has become possible to flesh out something of the life and ideas of a man who, as we shall see, exercised an enormous influence over his followers, yet excited, too, the strongest of aversions, a figure charismatic to some, physically and morally repulsive to others.

Following Goldberg's own pre-occupations, consideration of myth, revelation and mysticism was of central importance in the Circle's activities. With little hesitation, we can locate the stimulus for Huchel's reading of the mystics less in the seminar rooms of Berlin University than in discussions of the sort cultivated by the Goldberg Circle. It is no exaggeration to say that the Circle of predominantly Jewish figures attracted some of the most original thinkers in Berlin intellectual life. Among them were Werner Kraft, Gottfried Salomon, Simon Guttmann, Hans Reichenbach, Karl Korsch, Arthur Rosenberg, Alfred Döblin and Robert Musil. At the very outset of his literary endeavours, then, Huchel found himself in decidedly interesting, highly unconventional company. That is the way things would stay. Voigts' findings indicate that Huchel did not belong to Goldberg's inner circle, which included Erich Unger, Adolf Caspary, Joseph Markus and Ernst Fraenkel, but for a year or so was part of the broader grouping that included Te Fuchs, Olga Katunal and, for a while, Hans G.Adler, as well as the participants at meetings mentioned earlier.[6]

However, Huchel's statements point to an association that had considerable bearing on his development, both in terms of his wider intellectual interests and his poetic calling. Given Huchel's own reference to Goldberg, it is certainly an omission, though an understandable one given the Goldberg Circle's obscurity, that the Circle and Goldberg's book figure nowhere in Axel Vieregg's exploration of the roots of Huchel's integration of mysticism and mythology in his poetry from the mid-1920s. Mysticism and mythology were *the* subjects that Goldberg himself treated, even though the Circle's interests were more broadly based. It was surely no accident that Huchel developed his own distinctive brand of *Naturmagie* shortly after he began his association with the Goldberg Circle. Not only Goldberg's writings but also his self-proclaimed status as a seer certainly had a seminal influence on Huchel, including the manner in which he chose to cultivate the Alt-Langerwisch myth.

If Goldberg's name is known to few people today, then it must be said that he provoked the most violent responses in those who encountered him. These responses range from adulation to utter rejection. A number of leading intellectuals, among them Thomas Mann, took Goldberg extremely seriously, and some of the same people, including Thomas Mann, were also very rude about him. Gershom Scholem was more consistent than Mann. Scholem encountered the Goldberg Circle in Berlin just before Huchel, in the years 1921-23. Photos bear out Scholem's description of Goldberg as a 'small, fat man who looked like a stuffed dummy'.[7] Nevertheless, he

> exerted an uncanny magnetic power over the group of Jewish intellectuals who gathered around him ... Above all, however, it was the visions which he had over a long period of time in schizoid twilight states before awakening and the revelations about the Torah to which he laid claim that had made him an absolute authority for the initiates of this circle ... Goldberg disseminated his teachings in private courses, and if one of his adherents was asked about his observance or non-observance of some aspect of the Jewish ritual, the answer was: 'That is what Oskar told us to do'. No questions could be directed to Oskar, for he was in the enlightened possession of revelation.[8]

Sheppard has described Goldberg as 'eine zur Schizophrenie neigende und höchst autoritäre Persönlichkeit', who could bear 'keinen Widerspruch innerhalb seines Kreises. Den empirischen Zionismus ablehnend, betrachtete er sich als einen prophetischen Mittler zwischen Gott und dem neu zu gründenden Israel'.[9] Papers recently published by Voigts show that Goldberg made many claims for himself, some more plausible than others, and that Scholem's view that he was a charlatan was shared by others and was not without foundation. Attempting a more charitable view, Voigts acknowledges that Goldberg was 'zweifellos eine der problematisch-sten Persönlichkeiten' in twentieth century Jewish intellectual history, yet he stresses that he was a 'gelehrter und außergewöhnlich engagierter Jude und gleichzeitig ein ebenso engagierter Kritiker der Juden. Er war ... ein intensiver "Zeitgenosse", fortwährend tätig, Verbindungen herstellend und bekannt mit einem großen Teil der kritischen Intelligenz der Weimarer Republik'.[10]

Before the First World War, Goldberg had been loosely associated with the artists and intellectuals of the *Neuer Club*, whose most famous representatives were Kurt Hiller, Georg Heym and Jakob van Hoddis. After the war, he placed himself at the head of a revamped literary and intellectual grouping. Walter Benjamin resumed contact with members of the group such as Erich Unger. Walter and Dora Benjamin sometimes met up with Unger, Goldberg and others at the Lichterfelde home of Elisabeth Richter-Gabo, a close friend of Dora's and a patron of the Goldberg group.[11] Unger's flat on Uhlandstraße, on the corner with the Kurfürstendamm, was also used for meetings. Like Scholem, Voigts distinguishes between Benjamin's close relationship with Unger and his utter and complete rejection of Goldberg, testified in Benjamin's letters to Scholem, which contain some of the rudest statements about Goldberg in print. In January 1921 he referred to Goldberg, 'von dem ich zwar wenig weiß, durch dessen unreinliche Aura ich mich aber so oft ich ihn sehen mußte aufs entschiedenste, bis zur Unmöglichkeit ihm die Hand zu geben, abgestoßen fühlte'.[12] Nor could Benjamin later overcome his revulsion. On 26 December 1934, he wrote to Scholem from San Remo,

> daß ich ins Hauptquartier der wirklichen Zauberjuden gefallen bin. Es hat nämlich (Oskar) Goldberg sich hier ansässig gemacht und seinen Schüler Caspary in die Cafés, die *Wirklichkeit der Hebräer* in den hiesigen Zeitungskiosk delegiert, während er selbst – wer weiß – im Casino die Probe auf seine Zahlenmystik anstellt. Überflüssig zu sagen, daß ich nach dieser Seite keine Kommunikation aufgenommen habe.[13]

Scholem was personally far from convinced by Goldberg, and in his mémoirs he wrote, not without a certain mischief, 'I used to define the three groups around the Warburg library, Max Horkheimer's Institut für Sozialforschung ... and the metaphysical magicians around Oskar Goldberg as the most remarkable "Jewish sects" that German Jewry produced. Not all of them liked to hear this'.[14] For all his reservations, Scholem, in his mémoir of his friendship with Benjamin, describes the powerful effect that Goldberg's *Die Wirklichkeit der Hebräer* had on figures such as the paleontologist Edgar Dacqué and Thomas Mann following its publication in 1925. Goldberg's radical interpretation of cultural history conceived in metaphysical terms commended itself particularly to those intellectuals who were searching for an understanding of the crisis of German and European culture that was based on more than a materialist analysis. According to Scholem, the metaphysical sections of the first of Mann's *Joseph* novels were based entirely on Goldberg's book. Goldberg later contributed to Mann's exile journal *Maß und Wert*, and Mann recommended Goldberg's project for a sequel to *Die Wirklichkeit der Hebräer* to the Guggenheim Foundation. Yet Mann's attitude changed radically in the light of the Holocaust and what Manfred Voigts calls 'Goldbergs immer schärfere Kritik am Judentum'.[15] In fact, Mann made Goldberg the target of his irony a few years later in a chapter of

Doktor Faustus. There Goldberg appears as the scholar Dr Chaim Breisacher, 'a kind of metaphysical super-Nazi who presents his magical racial theory largely in Goldberg's own words'.[16] By the later 1940s, Mann had come to regard *Die Wirklichkeit der Hebräer* as 'das Werk eines typischen jüdischen Faschisten'.[17] In Mann's view Goldberg belonged 'zur Bewegung: antihumanistisch, anti-universalistisch, nationalistisch, religiös-technizistisch'.[18] For his part, Huchel continued to acknowledge in private his indebtedness to Goldberg's intellectual stimulus. Monica Huchel remembered her husband's 'vehement vorgetragene Wut auf Thomas Mann, der die *Wirklichkeit der Hebräer* geradezu ausgeschlachtet habe bis zum letzten, ohne Goldberg auch nur eines anerkennenden Wortes zu würdigen, ihn im Gegenteil noch karikiert habe'.[19]

We know enough about the schoolboy poet to see why he should have been attracted to Goldberg and his Circle, and they to him. From his interest in biblical stories and through the awesome sense of the self as the receptacle for the flood of divine inspiration, Huchel's adolescent development disposed him to become a disciple of Goldberg's. For Huchel, it represented the first sustained encounter with the marginal Bohemia of Berlin intellectual life. Goldberg's immersion in Jewish history and mysticism, in the irrational, in magic and mythology was a far cry from life with Fritz and Marie at Teltowerstraße, as indeed were the group's wider intellectual concerns. Through the meetings of the Circle he in all likelihood had his first dealings, if only from a distance, with figures such as Döblin and Benjamin, whom he would get to know personally in the years to come and whose work he would publish in *Sinn und Form* after the war. In this way, though neither he nor anyone else at the time could have suspected it, the ground was being prepared in the mid-1920s for what, beyond his poetry, would be Huchel's greatest contribution to German literary life.

The Goldberg Circle opened itself to the public in 1925 as the Berlin Philosophical Group, advertising its activities through the *Vossische Zeitung*, which occasionally carried reports of its meetings that saw the discussion of a wide range of contemporary intellectual issues and, as we have seen, attracted some of Berlin's most original thinkers. On 11 December 1927, for example, the *Vossische Zeitung* reported on Unger's critical exploration of theoretical Marxism in a public lecture, at which Karl Korsch also spoke, representing the Marxist point-of-view.[20] The Philosophical Group continued to meet until the early 1930s as, in Voigts words, 'eines der wichtigsten Diskussionszentren in der ungeheuer lebendigen und intensiven Kulturszene der Reichshauptstadt Berlin'.[21] In 1981, Dora Huchel told me that Huchel's link with the group and with figures loosely associated with it was maintained throughout the 1920s and early 1930s whenever he was in Berlin. Yet, as he acknowledged when he met Joachim in 1925, it was the ideas that Goldberg published in *Die Wirklichkeit der Hebräer* that had the greatest impact on him.[22]

Die Wirklichkeit der Hebräer:
a Metaphysic of Cultural History

The language of German nature poetry is unthinkable without Jakob Böhme, and Huchel's poetry is no exception. It was as a seer and nature mystic that Huchel, like so many generations of German poets before him, came to value Böhme. As legend has it through Franckenberg, Böhme was a simple, self-taught cobbler, whose natural gifts had been sparked by divine inspiration. It was surely a sense of affinity with such a figure rather than with the specifically Christian quality of Böhme's thought that, by the mid-1920s, must have appealed to Huchel. Not unlike Friedrich Zimmermann, Huchel developed a decided antipathy towards the Christian message conveyed by the Church, without by any means abandoning his own aspirations to metaphysical insight as poet-seer. In an interview in 1971, Huchel suggested such a distinction when he stated the following,

> Ich gehöre keiner Kirche an, bin aber im Grunde genommen gläubig – immer im Widerstand gegen die "Hofkirche". Ich glaube nicht an die Auferstehung des Fleisches, doch an eine höhere Ordnung. Und Sie werden auch bemerkt haben – vor allem in meinen neueren n – daß die Bibel zu meinen Lieblingsbüchern gehört. Außerdem verehre ich die Mystiker, vor allem Jakob Böhme. (ii,370)

With his rejection of the Resurrection and his belief in a higher order underpinned by the stories of the Bible, Huchel's religious beliefs might be said to be closer to Judaism than conventional Christian teachings. We have seen that some of the earliest poems contain a strand of conventional piety and an acceptance of the Christian path to salvation, but from the mid-1920s there is rejection of Christian teaching, while biblical stories, particularly from the Old Testament, remained a source of inspiration for him. Indeed, his late poetry testifies to his return to interests that he first developed in the 1920s. In a letter to Axel Vieregg in 1972, he commented as follows on his work composed in the 1960s, 'Ja, es stimmt, ich habe in manchen Nächten meiner Isolation das Alte Testament gelesen, vor allem Jesaja'. (ii,357) In the mid-1960s, in a letter to Ludvík Kundera, he drew attention to the relevance of the Book of Genesis for the interpretation of 'Die Engel', adding, 'In den altjüdischen Legenden wird unverblümt von der Hurerei zwischen Engeln und schamlosen Menschentöchtern gesprochen'. (ii,353) Huchel had long been acquainted with Jewish myths and legends: his library contains a copy of I.L.Perez's *Jüdische Geschichten*, number 204 in the Insel-Bücherei series. Well acquainted with Old Testament stories from school and church, in the mid-1920s Huchel, in his encounter with Oskar Goldberg, experienced a breathtaking re-interpretation of what must have appeared all too familiar through the teachings of church and school. Goldberg's teachings imbued these stories with the quality of a vibrant, living mythology, of vital significance for understanding the present and overcoming its inadequacies. In the light of the transformative power of biblical mythology, effected by the 'dynamic prophecy' of the seer, Huchel sharpened his understanding of his own life and poetic gift.

Goldberg's *Die Wirklichkeit der Hebräer* has been situated within the history of ideas as a text displaying Nietzschean attitudes and ideas, and employing a language of biological categories in keeping with the then fashionable popularisation of science, which today, however, sounds dangerously close to fascist jargon. One can readily appreciate how in the 1920s Thomas Mann might have been attracted to a book whose author by the late 1940s he was denouncing as a Jewish fascist. Indeed, the attraction of Goldberg's radical conservatism in his re-interpretation of the Hebrew Bible was real enough for many who came into contact with him at a time when the German-speaking world was in the grip of a crisis that invited bold, alternative visions. Goldberg's work draws upon and is echoed in patterns of thought found in the writings of many other people at the time, and Huchel's later references to Goldberg's *Die Wirklichkeit der Hebräer* may be taken to stand for his assimilation of intellectual currents of the mid-1920s which, in Huchel's case, crystallised around Goldberg. The sceptical Scholem writes of Goldberg's grand project,

> He had fashioned for himself a sort of biological Kabbalah which was intended to demonstrate the ritual of the Torah ... as a continuum of perfect magic. These ideas did not lack a demonic dimension, nor should one underestimate the fascination exerted by commentary which explained Judaism as a sort of theological state of decline of the ancient magical Hebraism and in doing so shrank from no conclusion and no absurdity. What Goldberg aimed at was the restoration of the magic bond between God and His people (of which he viewed himself as the biological center), and things that he did not deem capable of realisation in our time were shunted aside unconsidered. Goldberg's formulations were uncommonly incisive and presumptuous, and they had a certain Luciferian luster.[23]

Goldberg's book opens with a series of statements regarding 'philosophical and cosmological foundations', in other words, 'the concept of prophecy'.[24] He distinguishes between two forms of reality, 'manifest, finite reality' and 'latent, infinite reality'. Of the two, it is not the mundane world of normality that is of interest but the infinite potential that resides in the latter, which is no less a reality for not yet being fully manifest. Its realisation can be achieved through what Goldberg calls 'dynamic prophecy' or the 'application of appropriate metaphysical methods'. Reality is thus a phenomenon that can be shaped by the individual will if that will is itself sufficiently powerful. Such power is possessed by the 'transcendent organism', by which he means 'the principle that precedes and produces "biology". In the Pentateuch that is located in the Zelem Elohim'.

The second chapter, 'Die Gleichung: Völker = Götter = Welten', explains that the 'worlds' that constitute the 'latent, infinite reality' are linked to the present world in a manner which is to be conceived in the first instance 'mythologically'. Goldberg maintains that our world is the only one where the gulf between spirit and material is already so great that spirit can no longer align itself with material as a 'person' in the shape of a 'world'. What Goldberg calls 'biological centres', on the other hand, are 'persons on a higher plane' that are at the same time 'worlds': they are the real 'world powers'. He goes on to maintain that the key to the whole mythology derives from the insight that the biological centres are the gods of the various peoples. The god of each people is specific to that people because its biological centre, i.e. the centre of its descent, is different from that of other peoples. God is, then, not a universal being for all peoples the world over but has an 'eminently biological meaning' for a specific people, provided that people constitutes what he calls a genuine, anthropological, racial stock. Goldberg then proceeds to a key statement,

> Der ganze Umkreis dieses Verhältnisses (von Volk zu Gott), das sich sowohl durch psychophysiologische als auch durch psychophysische Wechselwirkungen *experimentell* nachweisen läßt, ist die *Mythologie* des betreffenden Volkes. Damit tritt das, was hier unter Mythologie verstanden wird, in schroffen Gegensatz zu dem, was die mythologische Wissenschaft darunter versteht. Mythologie ist nicht eine Sammlung ethnologischer Phantasmagorien, sondern die Lehre vom Bestehen einer metaphysischen Volkswirklich-keit und einer vom Volkskörper getrennt vorhandenen metaphysischen Volkskraft, dem biologischen Zentrum oder dem Gott. Mythologie ist somit keine Altertumswissenschaft, sondern aktuelle transzendente Realitätsforschung, – die *Völker selbst* werden Gegenstand des wissenschaftlichen Versuchs: es ist die *ethnologische Experimentalwissenschaft.*[25]

This highly dynamic conception stresses the interdependence of a God and a given people. Without the dynamic engendered by a people, a God is rendered quite ineffectual, while for the God individuals represent potential for development, and the whole people is the instrument of his power.

On the basis of his philosophical statements, Goldberg undertakes his re-interpretation of the scriptures, arguing that the Pentateuch is to be regarded as *the* experiment integral to this theoretical perspective. He argues further that every genuine i.e. metaphysical people is the periphery of a system, in the transcendent centre of which there is the biological centre, the God of the people in question. Only 'metaphysical peoples', whose connection with their biological centre or God remains intact are capable of great historic feats. If a people becomes detached from its centre of descent and therefore its biological centre, this leads to the dissolution of that people. The reciprocal link between the people and the divine source of being is lost and the people's metaphysical standing gives way to a state of mundane normality. In Goldberg's view, the story of Cain and Abel, which Huchel alludes to in 'Die Engel' with his reference to the 'Töchter Kains', provides the first example of such decline, since in killing Abel Cain 'slays metaphysics'. For Goldberg, the scriptures catalogue the decline of the Jewish people: while the Pentateuch describes a metaphysical people, the Psalms present a people lost, in a mundane state with a weak and distant God. The God of Abraham, Job and Moses was by contrast a vigorous presence, with whom those leaders of the ancient Jewish tribes took issue in vehement disputation. The young Huchel certainly did what Goldberg urged his readers to do: he studied the ancient texts. He also composed the poem 'Abraham', (i,11) in which he depicted such a disputation with God, which ends with Abraham's words, 'So hau ich ab mein Fleisch, mein Stamm/ und fall, daß du drum bangst,/ sprach unterm Messer Abraham./ Da fiel auf Gott die Angst'. Through his poetry, the young Huchel demonstrated his allegiance to Goldberg, who argued that Abraham represented the watershed in Jewish history, since Abraham's Israeli people were a new foundation, which signalled a break with the centre of descent. The Jewish people thus lost their status as a genuine metaphysical people, which they had possessed as the Hebrew people before the foundation of the Israeli people, and were threatened with the Diaspora. Jaweh is the substitute God worshipped after the Jewish people lost their intimate connection with their original biological centre. They come to depend on Jaweh as a means of survival, while they are actually pitted against their own nature. Goldberg thus calls upon all Jewish people to re-discover their original nature as a metaphysical people through a radical rejection of all that has reduced them to their present impoverished state. They should turn their attention instead to the fundamental teachings of the Pentateuch in the manner that Goldberg recommended, that is to say, as a source of revelation and dynamic prophecy.

Goldberg was, then, one of the many prophets with prescriptions for radical renewal that were spawned by the crisis of the early decades of the twentieth century. Like Nietzsche, he presented his ideas with a verve and vigour which appealed to the literary imagination. We have already noted that Thomas Mann based the metaphysical sections of the first of his *Joseph* novels on Goldberg's book. Although Goldberg was writing about Jewish cultural history, his project to rescue an authentic culture from decline and dispersal was bound to exercise a great fascination upon someone of Huchel's temperament, background and gifts, who was seeking to find his way in the 1920s. The structure of Goldberg's thought must have struck a very personal chord in someone who was trying to free himself from an immediate background that filled him with shame and guilt yet felt a profound emotional attachment to the deeper past of his mother's family.

In Huchel, Goldberg found an eager listener, whose creativity was sparked by the master's potent re-evaluation of biblical legend. We can look beyond 'Die Engel'

and 'Abraham' to see how Huchel seized upon Goldberg's teachings in order to re-
interpret his own background and identity in terms of a metaphysic of cultural
history. It is not difficult to see how Huchel could readily read Goldberg's ideas for
the reversal of cultural decline in terms of his own situation. We have explored how
he saw the mediocre Fritz Huchel, the Prussian NCO and minor civil servant, as
blighting the Zimmermann family, ethnic Brandenburg stock, representing an
authentic rural culture trapped in a relentless decline effected by modern Prussia.
Both 'Die Magd' and 'Mein Großvater' enact Goldberg's idea of dynamic prophecy.
The spiritually charged figures reveal an awareness of a transcendent reality to the
adoring boy, to whom they pass on their magical power. In his poetry, Huchel
depicts the Alt-Langerwisch world as embodying the unity of spirit and material,
which is otherwise lacking in the modern world. The Alt-Langerwisch figures
represent a metaphysical people intimately connected to a biological centre, of which
the boy is part in a way that his father never could be. In his poetry of rural
Brandenburg, Huchel was more completely a practitioner of *Naturmagie* than has
hitherto been acknowledged. Through his verse, he created a Utopian vision to hold
up against the insufficient reality of contemporary life. 'Herkunft', for instance, can
be read as a celebration of the poet's knowledge that he belongs to that rural centre
of descent, marginalised yet the source of a rare, dynamic metaphysic. Its final
stanza reads, 'Alle leben noch im Haus:/ Freunde, wer ist tot?/ Euern Krug trink ich
noch aus,/ esse euer Brot./ Und durch Frost und Dunkelheit/ geht ihr schützend mit./
Wenn es auf die Steine schneit,/ hör ich euern Schritt'.

By assuming the prophet's mantle from the Brandenburg patriarch, Friedrich
Zimmermann, the poet contributes to the reversal of cultural decline symbolised by
Fritz Huchel. His rejection of his father, and with that of the Prussian patriarchy of
militarism and authoritarianism, certainly made him receptive to the symbols and
images of Bachofen's matriarchy, though there is nothing to suggest that he followed
Bachofen in evaluating matriarchy as a primitive stage to be overcome by a more
spiritual patriarchy. Axel Vieregg has drawn attention to numerous poems in which
matriarchy figures prominently as a power informing nature. It is, however, advisable
to read such poems, too, against the background of the Anna-Marie double, that is
to say not merely on the level of ideas. It is also necessary to guard against the
assumption that rejection of the Prussian patriarchy implies rejection of patriarchy
per se in Huchel's poetic world. Like Goldberg's metaphysic of cultural history,
Bachofen's matriarchy was attractive to Huchel as a myth by means of which he
could re-create an image of a culture lost from sight following decline. The
unconventional Friedrich Zimmermann represented an alternative patriarchal
presence in that world, which gains its most telling expression in the poem 'Die
wendische Haide', (i,276) first published in the mid-1930s.[26] The second stanza
contains the following lines,

Grellsandig wars, die Grille schrillte scheuer.

Und vor mir stand ein Hirt im Mittagsspuk,

der lautlos mit dem Stock die weißen Feuer

der Haide aus den Steinen schlug!

The shepherd's magical action of releasing the white fires echoes Goldberg's description of the patriarch Moses, who strikes the rock with the staff, 'which is necessary for particular metaphysical actions'. In this way, Huchel assimilates Goldberg's interpretation of biblical mythology within his own mythology of rural Brandenburg. Huchel's use in the title – and frequently elsewhere – in his poetry of the term 'wendisch' acquires a much clearer significance in the light of his reading of Goldberg. The Wends were the Slavonic people who populated parts of North Germany, including Brandenburg, in pre-Christian times, traces of whose culture can still be found. We have already seen Huchel's use of the term in 'Heimkehr', which contains the line 'kam eine Frau aus wendischem Wald'. He told Kundera that he could only conceive of the woman in the poem as Wendish and that he viewed his mother's family as descendants of that Slavonic people.[27] Huchel's invocation of the Wendish patriarch in 'Die wendische Haide' thus expresses his rejection of both a Christian and a Prussian culture and affirms instead his allegiance to a seemingly authentic, metaphysical people marginalised by Prusso-Christian culture yet whose most significant representatives maintain their magical powers. Remnants of a magical vitality were deposited in special places and with divinely-inspired individuals, who maintained contact with the unseen sources of metaphysical power deposited in the worlds of latent reality. Poets like Friedrich Zimmermann and his grandson were such individuals, not to mention Goldberg himself.

The allusions to Goldberg's teachings are more striking still in the post-war version of 'Die wendische Haide', where the archaic spelling was, however, changed in the title 'Wendische Heide'. The final stanza of the poem depicts the shepherd and his flock – characterised as his 'Volk' – as follows,

Verstreutes Volk in großer Helle,

erscholl nicht geisterhaft Gesang?

Umklirrt von leiser Widderschelle

stand einsam dort der Hirt am Hang.

Like the ancient Hebrew people, the Wendish 'Volk' have experienced violent dispersal yet they retain a metaphysical potential. Vieregg rightly points out that in this depiction of Wendish culture, Huchel intimates that they are 'einer Wahrheit näher, die den schon früher christianisierten Nicht-Wenden verlorenging, und

[Huchel] glaubt, "geisterhaft Gesang" bei ihnen wahrzunehmen, der sie mit einer sakralen Weihe umgibt'.[28]

The references to ethereal music and the gentle ringing of the rams' bells are susceptible to further explication. The earlier version of the poem features the 'Widderschelle' in conjunction with the patriarchal shepherd's wielding of the staff,

> Doch leise tönte eine Widderschelle,
>
> als er den Stock wie hütend schwang
>
> und langsam treibend nur die Helle
>
> am Rand der Haide ging entlang.

It comes as no surprise to discover that at two points in his book Goldberg treats the metaphysical properties of the ram, nor that Huchel made use in his poetry of the fact that his birth sign was Aries. Vieregg reports a conversation in which Huchel told him, 'ist ihm, dem an einem 3. April unter dem Sternbild des Widder Geborenen, der Widder das persönlichste Zeichen'.[29] The use to which Huchel put the image of the ram demonstrates that he intended it to have a range of associations beyond the merely astrological. Goldberg first refers to the ram in the context of Abraham's sacrifice, writing that the ram 'ist kein gewöhnliches Tier, sondern – wie die Überlieferung richtig sagt – der Vertreter des himmlischen sive Urwidders, "der seit den sechs Schöpfungstagen da war": es ist der Repräsentant des Abstammungszentrums der Hebräer und somit desjenigen des Abrahams'.[30] In Genesis 22, xiii, one can read, 'Da hob Abraham seine Augen auf und sah einen Widder hinter sich in der Hecke mit seinen Hörnern hängen und ging hin und nahm den Widder und opferte ihn zum Brandopfer an seines Sohnes statt'. This information permits a more intriguingly allusive reading of Huchel's 'Abraham'. The sacrifice of the ram, and hence of the self as the suffering victim, occurs elsewhere in Huchel's poetry. For example, a late poem, entitled significantly 'Abschied von den Hirten', (i,209) contains the lines 'vergiß die Hirten,/ sie bogen dem Widder den Hals zurück/ und eine graubehaarte Hand/ stieß ihm das Messer in die Kehle'. Even without Goldberg's reference to the biblical story, the allusion would have been clear enough, especially as the second stanza of the poem opens 'Im Nebelgewoge/ schwimmt wieder das Licht/ der ersten Schöpfung'. The ram figures, too, in 'Das Zeichen', (i,113) which captures the poet's disillusion with village life after the collectivisation of agriculture in the GDR. There the ram figures not as an animal sacrificed but as reduced to a suffering, limping state, 'Ich ging durchs Dorf/ und sah das Gewohnte./ Der Schäfer hielt den Widder/ Gefesselt zwischen den Knien./ Er schnitt die Klaue,/ Er teerte die Stoppelhinke'.

The ram is discussed for a second time near the very end of Goldberg's book in the section dealing with revelations. Goldberg writes, 'Die akustische Begleiterscheinung des "Offenbarungs"vorgangs ist ein Tönen, das nur dem Laut eines einzigen Instrumentes – nämlich dem Blasen des Widderhorns, des Schofar oder Jobel – entspricht'.[31] Both versions of 'Wendische Heide' contain references to music and song, to the 'Widderschelle', which accompany the magical transformation of the 'Heide', as it becomes a site for revelation of the Wendish people's intimate connection with latent, infinite reality.

Like the patriarchal shepherd, the poet born beneath the sign of Aries was singled out for a special fate on behalf of the Wendish people: to sing and to suffer for them. Huchel's calling as a poet came into focus in the mid-1920s as he forged a spiritual link between his own personal situation – as the descendent of the Zimmermanns who was called a Huchel – and that of Brandenburg, whose Wendish culture had been all but extinguished by the relentless march of the Prusso-Christian state. This was the way in which Huchel came to conceive his poetry, as a mission of cultural regeneration through a mythologisation that embraced both himself and rural Brandenburg. That is the full sense of Uwe Grüning's view that Huchel's poetry represents something more than a mere creative activity. His image of the self became bound up with a Utopian vision of a culture anterior to, and untainted by the ravages of history. For all Goldberg's radicalism, Huchel's vision was in keeping with the humanism of the German literary tradition. His attachment to that vision was driven by deep emotional currents which, he knew, rested uneasily with the material circumstances of his life in the 1920s. Those currents meant that Huchel was predisposed to a creative assimilation of Goldberg's metaphysic of cultural history, as well as Bachofen's pre-Christian symbols and imagery. Neither thinker was in any sense a materialist, nor at its deepest level is Huchel's poetry informed by the dialectical materialism which, as a set of politically untested new ideas, was nonetheless intellectually attractive to Huchel in the 1920s, as it was to a whole generation that was seeking to establish a new politics after the debacle of the First World War. Huchel's sympathy with these ideas came to inform his poetic vision only to a limited degree in the 1920s and early 1930s, to the extent that his magical, humanist vision was an inclusive one for all members of the rural community, and that all those such as beggars, who were excluded from that community, were objects of his sympathy. And yet, Huchel's cultivation of a mythology of a pre-Christian rural region would prove to be not without its pitfalls in a German context that was notoriously volatile and in which the radical Right was increasingly eager to cannibalise all creative visions of a German culture.

Freiburg: Hans Arno Joachim

Having agreed to finance their son's studies, Huchel's parents expected that he would work assiduously and in time embark on an appropriate career. Given the German system and Huchel's choice of German and Philosophy, this probably meant teaching. Yet the balance of evidence was already running strongly against such expectations. His track record at school did not bode well. Even more worrying than the fact that study had not produced any tangible results was the fact that poetry had come to dominate his life. Fritz Huchel could not begin to comprehend his son's literary aspirations, which he inevitably saw as a grave distraction from the central issue of how his son was going to earn a living.

Huchel's parents had only a limited understanding, too, of his need to forge an identity independent of their own. In the mid-1920s, this meant moving away from the all too familiar and constricting environment of Potsdam. After three semesters in Berlin, Huchel looked to South Germany and the University of Freiburg for the summer semester 1925. It was to that area that Huchel would return, when in 1972 he settled in Staufen for the final decade of his life. In Freiburg, he chose one of Germany's most attractive and highly regarded university towns. South Baden with its liberal traditions and francophone influences was a marked contrast to his Prussian background. It was surely not altogether chance that its location near the junction of the French, German and Swiss borders was as far away from his parents as he could possibly get without actually leaving the country. That would be his next step when he moved on to Vienna.

Huchel had no personal contacts in Freiburg prior to his arrival. He was, however, fortunate that a Berlin friend (unnamed but possibly a figure from Jewish intellectual circles such as Harry Landry or Karola Piotrkowska) knew in Alfred Kantorowicz someone who had recently studied in Freiburg. Kantorowicz, who was working on the arts pages of the flagship of the Ullstein empire, the *Vossische Zeitung*, agreed to write a letter of introduction on Huchel's behalf – though he did not yet actually know him personally – to his Freiburg friend, Hans Arno Joachim, with whom he had earlier shared a flat on Kantstraße in Berlin.[32] It was actually through Joachim that Kantorowicz would finally get to know Huchel in Paris in 1928. In this rather roundabout way, Huchel established contact with two Jewish intellectuals, who would become close friends in the years leading up to 1933, when both left Germany for exile in Paris.

Kantorowicz developed into a more decisive and politically active figure than either Huchel or Joachim. Joachim remained on the periphery of literary life during the Weimar Republic and in exile, never achieving the breakthrough of the more adept publicist Kantorowicz or of the gifted poet Huchel. Documents recently published along with a collection of Joachim's writings catalogue the hardship of his life in French exile with his wife Gerta.[33] Unlike Kantorowicz, the Joachims failed in their attempts to escape from France to the USA. In the early 1940s, Joachim searched in vain for his wife, from whom he had been parted. While Gerta Joachim survived, in February 1944 he fell into the hands of the authorities. He was taken to Auschwitz in March 1944, where he was murdered in the gas chambers.

Huchel remembered his friend in the poems 'Cap d'Antibes' and 'Klage', which he published under the heading 'In memoriam Hans A. Joachim' in *Gedichte*. Also, in 1952 he published Joachim's radio play 'Die Stimme Victor Hugos' in *Sinn und Form*. In a later prose piece, 'Der jüdische Friedhof von Sulzburg', he recalled the beginning of their friendship in Freiburg in 1925.[34] He referred to Joachim as the 'Sohn eines jüdischen Sanitätsrates zu Freiburg', though his father was actually a gynaecologist. Joachim, just a year older than Huchel, adopted an approach to his studies which, like Huchel's own, was determined more by his personal interests and literary aspirations than by the distant prospect of examinations and a conventional career. He devoted much energy to studying the life and work of the local Allemannic writer, Emil Gött. Gött, who combined his literary interests with farming, would later be claimed by the Nazis as one of their own. There is an obvious parallel with Friedrich Zimmermann and with Huchel's own later self-image. For his first major publication, Joachim succeeded in placing an essay celebrating Gött's sixtieth birthday in the prestigious *Frankfurter Zeitung* on 28 July 1924. As Joachim's choice of Gött suggests, he was at the time 'eher von konservativer Gesinnung', [35] though not a person who held particularly strong political views. Essays published in the early 1930s saw him, like Huchel in his prose work for *Die literarische Welt*, showing leftist sympathies, though not the commitment to the KPD espoused by Kantorowicz from the autumn of 1931.

Joachim was, by all accounts, good company. Like Huchel, he possessed a well-developed sense of irony. He was eager to engage in literary discussion, where he could demonstrate his great breadth of reading. Again like Huchel, he greatly enjoyed the company of women. He came to enjoy a certain standing in Freiburg cafe life, and figures such as the local poet Walter Gutkelch valued his advice and friendship.

In Joachim, then, Huchel hit upon a kindred spirit. His portrait of Joachim in 'Der jüdische Friedhof von Sulzburg', where he distinguishes Joachim's Jewish background from that of the Goldberg Circle, captures something of his friend's wit and teasing good humour, traits which emerge, too, in the recently published letters and cards which Joachim sent to Huchel in the late 1920s and survived in the latter's possession until his death. Huchel wrote,

> Joachim war kein orthodoxer Jude. Das Traumhafte, Mystische, Irreale war nicht seine Sache. Auf seinem Gesicht lag ein leiser Anflug von Spott, wenn er von russischen und polnischen Juden sprach, er zählte sich zu den spanischen Juden, den Sephardim. Und da er wußte, daß ich in Berlin einem Kreis von Ostjuden, dem Goldberg-Kreis, angehörte und für Goldbergs Buch *Die Wirklichkeit der Hebräer* schwärmte, nannte er mich den kleinen 'Schabbesgoi' und lachte jedesmal herzhaft, wenn er mich damit in Wut brachte.

During his semester in Freiburg Huchel lived at Eschholzstraße 21.[36] He registered for three lecture courses. They were Witkop's 'Goethe und seine Zeit' and 'Die deutsche Dichtung im 17. Jahrhundert', and Friedländer's 'Die Malerei des 17. Jahrhunderts in den romanischen Ländern'. Yet then as later, there was much time

for activities beyond formal study. Huchel's prose piece recalls his trip on foot with
Joachim from Staufen to Sulzburg in the summer of 1925 to visit the cemetery of the
long-established Jewish community, which would be decimated by the Nazis, 'Es
war ein heißer Augusttag, die Jacken über die Schultern gehängt, hielten wir uns im
Schatten der Weinberge und Bäume'. He would, he wrote, visit the cemetery alone
one evening some six months later, before returning to the scene nearly half a
century later in 1973.[37] His visit alone in 1925 would remain with him. He recalled,
'Regen setzte ein, und ich suchte Schutz unter einem Baum. Ein Geruch von
faulendem Laub, von nassem Moos überfiel mich, der Regen schlug gegen die
Steine, durchdrang die Wurzeln, das Erdreich, Nebel hing zwischen den Gräbern'.
In this atmosphere, he entered into a sense of communion with the dead and their
centuries of suffering. As was Huchel's way, he would turn this episode over in his
mind in the years to come. During his stay in France in the later 1920s he composed
'Novemberstimme'. (i,388) It begins, 'Wär nicht der Sturm so am Gemäuer,/ gern
trüg ich hinaus ein Feuer,/ zu wärmen, wenn die Wasser waschen,/ die armen Seelen,
armen Aschen'. The poem underwent some modification before first publication as
'Totennacht' in 1935 in the *Almanach der Dame*. The immediate occasion for the
composition of this lament for the dead of the Jewish cemetery of Sulzburg is not
signalled in the poem. Yet this information is germane to the consideration of the
verse within the context of its first publication in Nazi Germany. By virtue of this
association, of which possibly only the poet himself was aware, 'Totennacht' comes
to occupy a particularly poignant place in his work alongside other laments such as
'Letzte Fahrt' and 'Strophen aus einem Herbst' which were published in the mid-
1930s, that period of death in life for Huchel himself.

During his Freiburg semester Huchel, as was his habit, worked away at his
verse. On numerous public occasions he would later explain how it often took
weeks, months or even years for him to settle on a final draft. Joachim was one of
the select few – his two wives were others – who were permitted to share the long
process of creation with him. Kantorowicz went so far as to suggest that Joachim
had been Huchel's early mentor, a view that Huchel himself echoed in an interview
with Ekkehart Rudolph in the 1970s. Kantorowicz perhaps overstates the extent of
Joachim's influence when he writes,

> Joachim ... blieb der intellektuell Führende. Er erkannte die seltene lyrische Begabung von
> Huchel, und er forderte viel von ihm. Er forderte unerbittlich, er ließ nichts durch. Was
> anderen gefällig erschien, verwarf er. Huchel weiß ein Klagelied davon zu singen; er hat
> wohl oft rebelliert, aber er weiß, was er dem Freund zu danken hat.[38]

In 1953, Huchel presented himself as the raw, untutored natural talent, who had been
introduced to the discussion of methods of composition by his friend,

Als mich 1925 Hans A.Joachim nach meiner Arbeitsmethode fragte, war ich um eine Antwort verlegen. Ich hatte keine. Schließlich sagte ich: Ich raune so lange meine Verse, bis die notwendigen – die hellen und die dunklen – Vokale die Grundstimmung der Seele ausdrücken. Die strengen, fast mathematischen Gesetze, die im geistig-sinnlichen Raum der Sprache aufzufinden sind, waren mir damals noch unbekannt. Ich wußte nicht einmal, in welchen Fällen es erlaubt war, eine Verszeile aus *nur* einsilbigen Worten 'schwingen' zu lassen. Nur das Ohr als Kontrollorgan für die feinsten Abstufungen der Vokalklänge – das war wenig, doch immerhin ein Anfang. (ii,295)

According to Kantorowicz's account,[39] it was Joachim who was responsible for mediating Huchel's publications in 1925 in *Das Kunstblatt* and in 1926 in *Neue Badische Landes-Zeitung*. Then as later, Huchel continually modified his verse and was extremely reluctant to release for publication what he regarded as work in progress. Kantorowicz was employed as arts editor on the Mannheim newspaper following his first spell with the *Vossische Zeitung*. He recalled, 'Leicht ließ sich erkennen, daß die Verse, die mir da auf meinen mit so vielen mediokren Einsendungen überhäuften Redaktionstisch kamen, einen nahezu einsamen Rang hatten'.[40] It can be safely assumed that Joachim's influence was also at work in the publication of five poems in 1925 in the local weekly for the arts, *Der Freiburger Figaro*. The paper was edited at Zasunstraße 3 by Franz Scheller, a friend of René Schickele. With one exception, the publications from the mid-1920s were schoolboy compositions, which Wolfgang Heidenreich has aptly characterised in terms of their religious zeal and neo-Romantic yearning expressed in quite conventional imagery.[41] The somewhat later Viennese poem published in Kantorowicz's newspaper in 1926 as 'Stadtpark im Frühling' (i,373) (and which was also called 'Wiener Stadtpark' in manuscript), contains much that is rather similar within an evocation of an urban environment that is in itself unusual in Huchel. The final lines read, 'Des Parkes Buch liest sich hinan zu Gott:/ da schwebt des Maimarkts roter Luftballon,/ ach, über Autotier und Straßenentrott/ zigeunert unsrer Kindheit Lampion'.

In truth, then, the taste of the three of them at the time contained much that was quite conventional. Huchel, however, following his encounter in Berlin with Goldberg, the mystics and Bachofen, was on the point of breaking with some of those conventions. In 1981 Dora Huchel, who got to know him shortly after Joachim, would question the description of Joachim as Huchel's mentor. Joachim was certainly widely read, and he was eager, too, to forge contacts in order to promote himself and his somewhat reluctant friend. Nor, in the mid-1920s, was he short of suggestions as to how Huchel might improve his compositions. Yet it was Huchel who possessed the lyrical gift, and, as Dora Huchel recalled, he generally found Joachim's suggestions too contrived. Joachim had a particular penchant for neologisms. Much later, in a letter to his wife written during the war, in November

1941, Huchel remembered their friend, wondering what had become of him and recalling with wry amusement his 'Expressionist phase'.[42] Huchel went on to refer specifically to the neologism 'Einsamkammer', which appears in the poem 'Der Totenherbst' in combination with the phrase 'ohne Licht und Frau'. (i,15) The poem, first published in 1930 in *Die literarische Welt* but collected only posthumously, draws on Expressionist imagery and stylistic devices found in Trakl and Heym. It contains lines such as the following: 'Im Laub die Engel wehn, grabend ein Schwarzes/ am Abhang längst erloschnen Mondes ein,/ ihr Flügelschlag trägt Rauch verflackten Harzes/ aus Stumpf und Schneeloch über Flachfeldschein'. The poem came to occupy a particular place in Huchel's oeuvre due to its associations with Joachim. In 1953, Huchel made the following statement about the composition of the poem, drawing attention to another neologism, though not to Joachim's hand in it,

> Gedichte, die den stärksten Atem haben, leben von der einfachen Sprache! Dennoch konnte ich in einem Fall nicht umhin, ein neues Verbum zu prägen. Die Verben mähen und sicheln klangen mir in dem Gedicht 'Der Totenherbst' zu weich, so bildete ich aus dem Hauptwort Sense das Tätigkeitswort 'sensen'; es war härter, es gab treffender die frostige Stimmung wieder, die ich brauchte. (ii,295)

He could, in fact, have proceeded to list further examples such as 'wölkt' and 'im Nachtanbrausenden'. Huchel continued to make use of neologisms in his poetry, but was more sparing than in 'Der Totenherbst', which may, perhaps, be regarded as a high point in his 'Expressionist phase', in which Joachim's influence can be detected.

For all the richness of Huchel's imagery, he generally aspired to a blend of descriptive precision and spiritual evocation, seeking to avoid the impression of contrivance which the excessive use of neologisms can create. Joachim's role in Huchel's development in the mid-1920s might be viewed more accurately as a close friend's encouragement and his promotion of someone not inclined to put himself forward to editors. Letters and cards from Joachim to Huchel in the late 1920s testify to the mediating role which the enthusiastic Joachim wished to adopt on his friend's behalf. Yet Joachim's efforts probably came to be viewed by Huchel as a mixed blessing: after the publication of ten poems between 1924 and 1926, in nearly all of which Joachim acted as a mediator, Huchel, as far as has been established, released nothing further until 1930. The period of experimentation and gestation upon which he embarked was generally spent away from Joachim, whose influence on the key stage of Huchel's development can easily be overstated. In the second half of the 1920s, he subjected his verse to a fundamental re-appraisal, sloughing off many of the adolescent dependencies still in evidence in his publications from the mid-decade. The style which he developed owed much to a deepening understanding of the nineteenth-century German lyric tradition as well as to the intellectual influences already identified. These things crystallised in his treatment of the Langerwisch material in accordance with his emotional needs and spiritual ambitions.

Schloß Elmau: Johannes Müller

After the Freiburg interlude, Huchel moved further afield, to Vienna, which, alongside Berlin, was the second major cultural and political centre of the German-speaking world. Through his publications in 1925 in *Das Kunstblatt* he had developed links with Gustav Kiepenheuer Verlag, and the recommendation of the Potsdam publishing house could act as an introduction to figures in Viennese intellectual life. Armed with his letter of recommendation, he set off in late September 1925, travelling, as he later told Ludvík Kundera, through Bavaria and on to Vienna.[43] On the Bavarian leg of his trip, he was joined by Joachim. Their destination was Schloß Elmau, situated near Mittenwald in Upper Bavaria.[44] The visitors' book shows that they arrived at Schloß Elmau on 27 September and stayed for four weeks, leaving on 24 October. Other guests were generally students and more or less the same age as Huchel and Joachim.

At Schloß Elmau, they were the paying guests of Johannes Müller, who had gathered around him a group of people who broadly shared his spiritual quest. Like Goldberg, Müller was a self-styled seer and man of wisdom, another among that proliferation of prophets, as Michael Hamburger aptly put it, that populate the German cultural scene after Nietzsche's Zarathustra. Müller had achieved a certain fame already by the turn of the century. He had embarked on the study of theology and philosophy but rejected the world of scholarship and Christian orthodoxy for the world of experience through nature and a personal, spontaneous understanding of Christ's teachings. He made a name through his unscripted performances on lecture tours before he founded his journal, the *Grüne Blätter*, and his 'Freistatt persönlichen Lebens' at Schloß Mainberg. Mainberg was made possible by the generosity of his friend, Alexander Erbslöh. It was staffed by female 'helpers', whom Müller viewed as central to the development of a true community of residents and guests, who were subject to no formal programme of activity in their quest for spiritual growth. Müller himself was, however, very much the presiding spirit, a man who was ready to convey the visions and revelations that he personally experienced. He was critical of an excessively cerebral 'Bewußtseinskultur' and promoted instead a holistic 'Wesenskultur'.

Müller succeeded in appealing to both rich and intelligent people. He met with Adolf von Harnack, enjoyed friendships with Wilhelm Langewiesche and Max von Baden, while Elsa Gräfin Waldersee was so captivated by her visits that she agreed to finance a new and larger centre in the German Alps at Elmau. Schloß Elmau opened in 1916. There, Müller continued to attract the well-heeled, but in the off-season of the spring and autumn cut-price 'academic weeks' were offered to interested students. It would appear that Huchel and Joachim attended such 'academic weeks'.

Müller was particularly enthusiastic about the arts, which he regarded as a vehicle for divine revelation. Above all, he believed that the combination of music and dance opened the way to the divine. One can imagine that the young Potsdam poet, who had recently published 'Du Name Gott' and 'Die Begegnung am Meer', would have received a warm welcome from Elmau's presiding spirit. Yet, beyond his mention to Kundera of the journey to Vienna via Upper Bavaria, Huchel did not choose to comment on this episode. Müller's later enthusiasm for Hitler can only have placed Huchel's memories of Müller in a somewhat questionable light. Even though there is no direct evidence of an intellectual legacy as with Goldberg, we can see in his visit to Müller further evidence of Huchel's great attraction in the mid-1920s to personalities whose unorthodox religious visions might stimulate his own poetic quest.

In the mid-1920s, Huchel, in his rejection of the Prussian patriarchy, was motivated primarily by spiritual concerns, as he embarked on the mythologization of the self within the magic Alt-Langerwisch world. In the early 1950s, however, he would posit a unity shaped by political considerations in the poetry that he wrote from the mid-1920s, arguing, 'Ich wollte eine bewußt übersehene, unterdrückte Klasse im Gedicht sichtbar machen, die Volksschicht, Mägde und Kutscher'.[45] By the early 1950s, the experience of Nazism had forced on the artist an acute sense of social responsibility, while the primacy of Marxism-Leninism in the GDR had its effect on Huchel in his espousal here of the rhetoric of class struggle. In comparison with the ideology-riven world of literary politics that emerged after 1933, the 1920s were almost virgin territory. Indeed, Peter Gay has written of the unpolitical socialists among German artists and intellectuals during the Weimar Republic.[46] In his rejection of the Prussian patriarchy, Huchel assumed a broadly progressive political stance, generally in sympathy with the ideas of the Left. It went without saying that Huchel was a socialist; that was the mood in the mid-1920s of the generation born at the turn of the century. Any cultivation of alternative visions and lifestyles could be squared with a notoriously elastic term, only one of whose possible meanings was specifically the materialism and class struggle of Marxism-Leninism. Yet, as we have seen, Huchel's development was more that of an ethical idealist, whose creativity was becoming rooted in spiritual transformation. The unity of his poetry was hence posited on a quite different basis from the politics of working-class victory.

Vienna: Dora Lassel

Huchel completed his sojourn at Schloß Elmau on 24 October. He and Joachim said their farewells but both knew that they would stay in close contact. Joachim returned to Freiburg, while Huchel went on his way to Vienna. After his one semester in

Freiburg, he spent a whole academic year in Vienna and lived at three addresses. From 16 November until 19 December 1925 he was registered as living as a student at Servitengasse 15/4, from 23 December 1925 until 4 February 1926 at Florianigasse 58/12 and from 4 February 1926 until 13 July 1926 at Burggasse 44/12.[47] He did not, however, register at the University of Vienna during the Winter Semester 1925-6.[48] When he came to register for the Summer Semester, he described himself as in his fifth semester of study. This is consistent with his non-registration for the Winter Semester, which itself reveals the extent to which the young poet was driven to write rather than to study.

Looking back on his stay in Vienna when in 1972 he returned to the city to receive the Austrian State Prize for European Literature, Huchel recalled that the Kiepenheuer letter served as an introduction to Dr Rudolf Beer, who was 'Intendant am Volkstheater'. (ii,312) He also soon got to know the 'Dramaturgen und Dichter Franz Theodor Csokor' (ii,312), who was engaged at the Raimund Theater and the Volkstheater. He recalled premieres with Elisabeth Bergner and Moissi and how, just twenty-three, he had immersed himself in Vienna's rich cultural life. He admired the work of Hofmannsthal, whose books were well represented in his library,[49] Musil and Alexander Lernet-Holenia's *Saul*. Above all, he revered the great Austrian poet Georg Trakl, 'Ich las nachts Trakl, immer Trakl'. (ii,313) He acknowledged Trakl's importance in a speech in 1974, too, and Dora Huchel confirmed the role that Trakl played in that year. One might be tempted to make quite a lot of the Trakl connection. There would, of course, be a neat congruence between Huchel's reading of Trakl and his year in the Austrian capital, which, it might be argued, left their indelible imprint on Huchel's poetry. Traces of Trakl can certainly be isolated in a poem such as 'An den Herbst', (i,341) notably in the the diction and cadence,

> wir fühlen die Trauer der Landschaft,
>
> das zerbrochene Lächeln
>
> der abgemähten Wiesen,
>
> den müden Vogelflug
>
> in die Wolken des Abends ...

Yet Huchel cautioned against reading too much Trakl into his poetry, writing to Axel Vieregg, 'ich glaube kaum, daß es eine "Vielzahl" von Einflüssen Trakls gibt'. (ii,359) Neither 'An den Herbst' nor other poems identified by Vieregg as echoing Trakl such as 'Sommerabend' (i,342) and 'Lied am Abend' (i,343) were later collected by Huchel. Set against a broad appreciation of Huchel's development in the 1920s, we can see Trakl's dark melancholy as a means of moving beyond the adolescent religious fervour present in such poems as those published in *Der Freiburger Figaro*. Yet Trakl did not directly prepare the ground for the decisive shift in Huchel's work inaugurated by 'Die Magd' in 1926. As a result, the significance of Trakl was, indeed, limited to a quite specific period and without fundamental consequences.

On Huchel's return to Vienna in 1972, he could not resist the temptation, to which he frequently succumbed on public occasions, especially in his later years, to stylise himself as the farm boy, who had brought with him to the city's sophisticated metropolitan culture his untutored rural mode of perception,

> Ich kam aus der preußischen Provinz, aus der Mark Brandenburg, es war meine erste Reise ins Ausland, ich kam vom Lande. Gleich nach meiner Ankunft, im Ohr noch das leise Drämmern der Milchkannen, die man abends bei uns auf die Rampe stellte, erlebte ich die Uraufführung von Strawinskys *Feuervogel*, vom Komponisten selbst dirigiert. Zu meinem fassungslosen Staunen sprang Strawinsky, kaum hatte er den Taktstock aus der Hand gelegt, von einem etwa anderthalb Meter hohen Podest, sprang wie in einen Heuhaufen, stand aber fest auf dem Parkett und verbeugte sich vor dem Publikum, das ihn stürmisch feierte. (ii,313)

Huchel was, indeed, abroad for the first time. Otherwise his self-characterisation cannot be said in any literal sense to correspond to the reality of his situation in the mid-1920s. His grandparents' property had been sold off some years previously, and the only sound he could expect to hear regularly in the vicinity of his parents' flat in Teltowerstraße was of trains from the nearby Potsdam railway station. Here we find, as so often, an example of the poetically created public self, behind which he hid other reminiscences of the private self, which had in the meantime become unwelcome to him.

There was one constant presence in particular in his life from late 1925 in Vienna, which remained unmentioned in his post-war accounts of earlier stages of his life. Shortly after arriving in Vienna, he met Dora Lassel, the woman who would share his life for the next twenty years. She left her account of her life with Huchel which can be juxtaposed with his own and with other documents in charting the poet's life and work in the years until they separated in 1946. In 1981, she described to me how she met Huchel in the buildings of the University shortly before Christmas in 1925,

> Ich habe ihn in der Jausenstube kennengelernt. Irgendein komischer Kauz hat mich verfolgt. Eines Tages hat er gesagt: 'Heute stelle ich Ihnen einen großen Dichter und einen großen Geiger vor'. Er schleppte mich in die Jausenstube, da waren Peter Huchel und Wilhelm Blaß. Huchel gefiel mir sofort am besten: er war ganz verträumt. Ich tat so, als ob der Blaß mich mehr interessierte.

The three of them became close friends, spending much time together. She was fascinated by the figure cut by the handsome young poet, by his manner and by his enthusiasms. He dedicated to her his copy of *Das Kunstblatt* with his two poems from the previous summer. That Christmas she gave him the fine 1923 Insel edition of Hans Bethge's *Chinesische Flöte*. The volume, now in the Peter Huchel Collection like the copy of *Das Kunstblatt*, contains the dedication, 'Für Dich Weihnacht 1925 Dora'. Though new to Vienna, he already had friends who could open the doors of the city's theatres for them free of charge. He could talk, too, of life in the German capital and of his links with Kiepenheuer and with Berlin figures who had known Franz Kafka, who had died in 1924 and whose genius was now beginning to be widely acknowledged. In 1974, Huchel recalled reading Kafka at the same time as Trakl.[50] It was quite consistent with the pathos which he cultivated that he should have been attracted to these two geniuses, who died young. Huchel possessed some of Kafka's earliest stories published in Kurt Wolff's series *Der jüngste Tag*, and shortly afterwards he would make a present of *Die Verwandlung* to his new companion. The dedication reads, 'Für Dora Ostern 1926 Helmut'.[51]

Helmut was not only aware of the latest literary trends, he could also tell her what he had learned from the years of upheaval in Germany that had left their indelible impression on his thigh. By the mid-1920s, he had come to regard the Kapp Putsch as the turning-point in his life. He showed her his scar and talked of the workers from Nowawes who had given him *Le feu*. He wore a red carnation in his lapel as a token of support for the Viennese workers in their struggle to sweep away the remnants of the old order. He recalled in 1972, 'Wien war arm, hatte wirtschaftlich zu kämpfen, die Arbeiter demonstrierten am Großen Ring'. (ii,312-3) Yet, Dora Huchel observed, it would not have occurred to him to join in with them. He added, 'Ich war jung, 23 Jahre, hatte einseitig literarische Interessen'. (ii,312) On another occasion, he commented, 'Wir sind in den zwanziger Jahren durch Kunsterlebnisse zur Linken gestoßen – der große sowjetische Film, die große sowjetische Lyrik haben uns begeistert'. (ii,369) The early aftermath of the October Revolution seemed to promise a symbiosis between the new revolutionary politics and an artistic avant-garde. This fired the enthusiasm of the young poet, just as it captivated a whole generation of young Europeans who were searching for a genuinely new alternative. Yet this enthusiasm did not filter through to either political commitment or, in any sustained way, to Huchel's poetic imagination. For Huchel, the 1920s were a period of eclecticism and experimentation, when little was yet fixed as he was in the process of re-creating himself at one remove from the influence of his immediate family background. Looking back in 1981, Dora Huchel took her husband's mid-1920s enthusiasms with a pinch of salt. They were larded with a pathos of *Weltschmerz* that she could not altogether trust. In her account she wrote, 'Nicht ohne einen Anflug von Zynismus trug Peter Huchel Weltschmerz, vermutlich auch nicht ganz ohne Eitelkeit!' By 1930 he had moved on from the experimentation of the mid- to late 1920s, distilling a poetic vision quite deliberately at variance with any notion of political commitment.

In late 1925 in Vienna, he was keen to make an impact on his new friend and was increasingly aware of the power he could exercise over others, a power quite at odds with the debilitating sense of inadequacy that thoughts of his parents triggered in him. His friend Wilhelm Blaß' hopes were dashed when Dora Lassel and Helmut Huchel began their relationship. Blaß had to play second fiddle to the dreamy good looks of the young poet. Consequently, as Dora Huchel explained, 'Ich durfte seine Geige nicht anfassen (kurz)'. Dora Lassel was invited to the flat in Florianigasse which Huchel shared with Blaß, and of which he recalled in 1972, 'Ich mußte von 60 Mark in einer kleinen Kammer mein Leben bestreiten'. (ii,313) In her account Dora Huchel, too, recalled the 'Kammer', linking it with the poem 'Die Kammer'. According to her, it was written shortly after they had consummated their relationship in that room. The poem, in the version published in *Die literarische Welt* in 1930, the year of their marriage, is informed by the contrast between the bleak central stanzas charting the poet's growth, which have already been examined ('Ich war allein, bis ich ins Böse wuchs,/ ... Die Kammer brannte weiß in Scham,/ wenn lauter Hader sie durchschrie') and the final stanza, 'Du kamst und schürtest Küchenrauch./ Du spannst Mariengarn aus Wegerich./ Dein Licht glomm auf im Abendhauch./ Dein Brot und Bett waren für mich'. The loved one, endowed by the poet with the attributes of the benevolent maidservant, even down to the neologism 'Mariengarn', in effect 'saves' the poet through her care and affection from the isolation and acrimony of his background and early experiences.

At the start of their relationship, Huchel deflected questions about his background through a teasing playfulness and irony, using his charm to mount a successful defence against, at that time, unwanted intrusion. Somewhat later during the period in Vienna, he revealed a major reason for his sense of shame about his background when he said, 'Meine Mutter stelle ich dir nie vor'. Though such a meeting could not ultimately be avoided, Huchel's attitude towards his parents, and to his mother in particular, testifies to the great barriers he had to overcome before he could establish trust and intimacy in relationships. His problem was certainly in no way diminished by the fact that his companion's family background contrasted markedly with his own. A year younger than Huchel, Dora Lassel (1904-85) was a student of French, German and English. She was the daughter of an upper-middle-class Transylvanian-Saxon family of academics, clergymen and factory owners long-established in Kronstadt (now Braşov), Transylvania, where her father was vicar of St. Bartholomew's. In his own writings, Eugen Lassel (1867-1932) presents himself within a tradition established by the humanist scholar Honterus, who was born in Kronstadt and brought the Reformation to Transylvania.[52] Eugen Lassel studied theology, philology, history and philosophy at Marburg, Budapest and Berlin. Among his teachers were von Harnack, Hermann, Dilthey, Paulsen, Curtius and Treitschke. After four years of study, he returned to Marburg, where he was awarded his doctorate on 5 August 1890 for a study entitled *De fortunae in Plutarchi operibus notione*. He went home and, like his father before him, taught at the Kronstadt Gymnasium before he entered the ministry in 1905. In 1893 he had married Josefine Arzt (1872-1944), daughter of a wealthy family of Kronstadt factory owners. In 1895 they had a son, Konrad, who became an architect, followed in 1904 by Dorothea and later by Helmut. Throughout his life Eugen Lassel maintained a great interest in literature and in 1905 he referred to 'meine ganz geringfügige literarische Tätigkeit'. His daughter would share this passion. As she wrote shortly before her death, her interest in literature and especially poetry was one of the things that brought her together with Huchel. Similarly, in early 1930 her father would be won over by the young poet.

On the one hand, Huchel represented a potentially dangerous deviation from the safe middle-class Kronstadt world, to which, it was assumed, Dora Lassel would return after her studies. On the other, he possessed the most precious of creative talents, which the Lassel family valued greatly. Not only that, the handsome Huchel was the very romantic image of what a young poet should be. Dora Lassel could, thanks to her family, take for granted things which he could only discover through distancing himself from his own family. For Huchel, the Lassels represented that more refined world of the educated and moneyed middle classes, which was so singularly absent from his own background. His shame regarding the inadequacies of his parents was thrown into stark relief in his encounter with the Lassels' daughter. There is no doubt that he was drawn to the intellectual and material advantages that her background offered. It represented not only a stability and solidity missing from his world, but also the possibility of freedom to pursue his spiritual quest through poetry. The psychological tension created through this 'clash' between the Lassels and the Huchels undoubtedly contributed to his presentation of his background in what he perceived as more acceptable terms. To some extent, the cultivation of the Alt-Langerwisch myth, with its property and authentic rural culture, can be explained against this backcloth, as Huchel sought to compensate for the deeply ingrained feelings of inadequacy with which Fritz and Marie had left him.

In the second draft of her account written just before her death, Dora Huchel presented other details from the early stages of their relationship,

Ich studierte damals äußerst fleißig an der Alma Mater, und 'Helmut' versuchte sträflicherweise, mir die Notwendigkeit dieser oder jener Vorlesung auszureden, um für sich mehr Zeit herauszuschlagen. Doch ich ließ mich – wenigstens in dieser Hinsicht – nicht verführen. Dennoch konnte er sich über Vernachlässigung seiner Person nicht beklagen. Ich war von jeher literaturinteressiert und liebte ganz besonders Lyrik, so daß auch dadurch die Beziehung einen wichtigen Inhalt erhielt. Konsequent besuchte Peter Huchel niemals Vorlesungen, es gab darüber auch niemals Nachweise. Ich erinnere mich nur, daß wir zusammen in einer Vorlesung über 'Nietzsche als Philosoph' saßen, die ich belegt hatte. Noch bevor ich Huchel kennengelernt hatte, hörte ich ab Okt[ober] 1925 eine Vorlesung über 'Grundriß der Poetik', die Huchel aber als völlig überflüssig abtat und meinte, er könne mir darüber viel Interessanteres erzählen. In den Vorlesungslücken trafen wir uns oft in der schon erwähnten Jausenstube, lehnten am Galeriegeländer und blickten in den Universitätshof oder schleuderten in Universitätsnähe herum, wenn es die Witterung zuließ. Ich wohnte damals bei einer Freundin meiner Mutter in der Reißnergasse.[53] Mein Weg zur Universität, den ich natürlich zu Fuß zurücklegte, führte über den Schwarzenbergplatz. Hatte ich nicht gerade eine sehr frühe Vorlesung, so erwartete mich 'Helmut' im Schwarzenbergpark, denn er hatte mein Vorlesungsverzeichnis. Nachmittags gab es nur vereinzelt eine Vorlesung, da arbeitete ich meist in der Universitätsbibliothek die Anmerkungen aus, die ich mir in den Vorlesungen gemacht hatte, und bereitete mich auf Colloquien vor. Die restliche Zeit gehörte aber ausschließlich meinem neuen 'Freund', ein Wort, das bei meiner Wirtin nur die schlimmsten moralischen Bedenken hervorgerufen hätte. Das also war Tabu, und ich mußte, wenn ich gefragt wurde, meine Phantasie wegen der fraglichen Zeiten spielen lassen, was in Wien hinsichtlich des Zeitverbringens ohnehin sehr leicht ist. Was Ausreden anlangt, brauchte ich sie ja nur für Stunden, die ich in Huchels Wohnung zubrachte, die er mit dem Geiger Wilhelm Blaß teilte. Huchel hatte dort eine schmale Schlafkammer, die im Gedicht 'Die Kammer' gemeint ist, das eben 1926 entstand und keineswegs 1922, dies letzte wohl eine bewußte Fälschung. Der Besuch eines 'Freundes' in der Wohnung meiner Wirtin war ja ein Ding der Unmöglichkeit. Nur Telefonanrufe wurden mir nicht ganz verwehrt, man mußte begreifen, daß es notwendige Verständigungen mit Kommilitonen (übrigens auch weiblichen) gab. Nach Theater-, auch Opernabenden konnte ich sogar Einlaßkarten vorzeigen. Soviel ich mich erinnere, hatte Peter Huchel eine Empfehlung an einen Menschen mit Bühnenbeziehung, (war es Csokor?). Jedenfalls kamen wir auf solche Weise oft zu Freikarten, besonders für's 'Theater in der Josephstadt'. Wir sahen z.B. Moissi als Hamlet und in der Titelrolle des 'Lebenden Leichnams' und zahlreiche neue Bühnenstücke. Wir besuchten viele Vorträge, Freud, den Huchel gehört haben will, scheint mir da entgangen zu sein.

Wir waren bei vielen Sternguckernächten des Professor Thomas (eines Siebenbürgers) dabei, die in die Wiener Umgebung führten, ein durchaus von meiner besorgten Wirtin gebilligtes Unternehmen.

Beyond its significance in capturing something of a female student's life in Vienna in the mid-1920s, Dora Huchel's account provides valuable insights into Huchel's lifestyle during the early stages of their relationship. She enlarged in the second draft upon her participation in their shared passion, poetry, 'Ich lernte kennen, was bis dahin an Gedichten entstanden war, was er änderte, was im Entstehen war. Ein wichtiger Inhalt unserer Beziehung entstand'. And regarding the use to which he put his time, she added in the first draft, 'Er selbst fühlte sich weniger von der Wissenschaft als vielmehr fast ausschließlich von Euterpe angezogen'.

The records of the University of Vienna indicate that during the summer semester 1926 Huchel registered for four courses, among them two mentioned above by his first wife. The four courses were, 'Grundriß der Poetik', taught by Professor Robert Franz Arnold; 'Nietzsche als Philosoph', taught by Professor Robert Reininger; 'Soziologie des modernen Dramas (erläutert an Ibsen)', taught by Professor Emil Reich; and 'Platons Ideenlehre', taught by Professor Heinrich Gomperz.[54] Yet, as Dora Huchel writes above, he was more concerned with his own compositions than with formal study, and like his friend he was eager to explore the cultural life of the city and the surrounding area. A rare city poem was 'Stadtpark im Frühling' (i,373), which, as we have seen, he sent to Joachim, who forwarded it to Kantorowicz im Mannheim. Kantorowicz published it in his paper on 10 May 1926.

In her third draft, Dora Huchel recalls the spring that they spent together in Vienna,

> Der Frühling kam und mit ihm die Entdeckung der näheren und weiteren Wiener Umgebung, die Donauauen, natürlich auch Prater, Schönbrunn, berühmte Gräber, Wienerwald, die 'Heurigen'-Orte, Nachtwanderungen in Astronomie unter fachkundiger Führung. Der Höhepunkt allen Glücks aber war eine etwa zehntägige Wanderung durch die Wachau, die dann den Dichter zu 'Holunder' und 'Mädchen im Mond' inspirierte und eine nostalgische Erinnerung blieb.[55]

The love poems written during the early stages of Huchel's relationship with Dora Lassel, including 'Die Kammer', were only collected posthumously, having first appeared in journals and anthologies in the early 1930s, although all had been intended for publication in *Der Knabenteich*. 'Holunder' (i,11) appeared in the anthology *Mit allen Sinnen* in 1932 and was chosen to introduce *Der Knabenteich*.[56] In its earliest published form, the third and fourth stanzas read,

> Blätterstark im Niederwehen
> Der Holunder uns umschlang,
> Daß es deine nackten Zehen
> Feucht und wiesiger durchdrang.

> Und der Strauch kam auf uns nieder,
> daß der Halm am Boden klang,

schlug um uns das Laubgefieder,

saß in unserm Schlaf und sang.

After the earlier erotic verse of 'Die Begegnung am Meer' and 'Abend der Empfängnis', 'Holunder' strikes a fresh note of tenderness and sensual pleasure in a natural environment that is defined much more closely and is in tune with the lovers' feelings. In 1932, Huchel provided his own brief commentary on his poem, viewing stanzas three and four as illustrating 'Das Verbindende von Mensch und Landschaft: unser Gesicht, unser Gefühl verschmilzt mit ihr'. (ii,249) Here, Huchel begins to explore a vision of the sensual interaction between humans and nature in the style of *Naturmagie*. 'Holunder' shares this quality with 'Mädchen im Mond', (i,17) which appeared first in *Die literarische Welt* in 1932,

Dort wo das Schilf im Winde lebt

und stiller an die Sterne schwebt,

gehst du vorbei mit weißem Schuh,

du blühst wie Schilf dem Monde zu.

Auf dein mongolisches Gesicht

von gelben Gräsern fällt ein Licht,

auf deine Wimpern, deine grauen,

auf deine gräserdünnen Brauen.

In deinen schrägen Augen wohnt

die Katze mit dem Fell aus Mond.--

Du stehst ganz still, wenn im Geäst

der Vogelgeist singt aus dem Nest,

das Lied hält deine Füße fest.

Doch wenn vom Mond das Feuer raucht,

dein Schatten in die Nacht eintaucht.

Du legst dich in den Wind hinein

und bist im Fluß der tiefste Stein.

Der Fluß in deinen Haaren wühlt,

der Mond die grauen Augen kühlt, -

bis dir der Schritt im Schlaf hinstirbt,

wo gräsern eine Grille zirpt.

In its for Huchel quite unusually detailed depiction of facial features, the poem is unmistakably his tribute to Dora Lassel. Like 'Holunder', it offers a blend of the visionary and realistic through the depiction of the loved one in nature. Ending with the chirping of the cricket, the poem echoes a motif found already in 'Holunder' to herald love. The poem evokes, too, the sense in which the poet regards his friend as a steadfast character, 'Du legst dich in den Wind hinein/ und bist im Fluß der tiefste Stein'. As we have seen, a similar message is conveyed in the final stanza of the earliest published version of 'Die Kammer'. After the despair, ravages and isolation of his upbringing and adolescence expressed in poems such as 'Klage', Dora Lassel's arrival in his life offered the prospect of love, warmth, peace and security.

As Dora Huchel writes, they were inseparable during the time in Vienna. She recalled them leaving the city at the beginning of August 1926, 'Schließlich schwerer Abschied in verschiedene Richtungen, Huchel nach Potsdam, wo seine Eltern damals wohnten, ich nach Kronstadt zu Eltern und Bruder. Unzählige Briefe und die Gewißheit des Wiedersehens im Herbst trösteten uns'.[57]

Berlin again

It has been assumed hitherto, on the basis of Huchel's own statements, that after the Viennese sojourn he abandoned his studies and went to Paris, thus embarking on the *Wanderjahre* which, in the second half of the decade, took him across the continent from its westerly to its easterly extremity. In 1931, adopting a studiedly world-weary tone of *Weltschmerz*, he wrote,

Nach sechs Semestern Berlin, Freiburg, Wien liegt es näher, Reisen zu machen als auf der Universität zu bleiben. Die Städte: Paris, Marseille, Bordeaux, Prag, Budapest, Kronstadt, Konstanza, Konstantinopel kennt er. Seine Hotelzimmer sind billig. Ob er in Balzik am Schwarzen Meer lebt oder in Bayonne am Atlantischen, da gibt es wenig Unterschied. Denn das europäische Gesicht hat überall die eine Müdigkeit für den, der zwischenzeitig geboren ist und im Jahre neunzehnhunderttraurig. Er ist schon zu spät auf die Welt gekommen: er wird nie zur Zeit kommen. (ii,217)

In later years he returned to the experiences of the mid-1920s, referring in the 1972 Vienna speech, for instance, to Paris 'wohin ich dann für einige Jahre ging' (ii,313) after Vienna. In 1977, he once again gave this impression, when he enlarged upon his stay in France as follows,

Europa hat sich mir früh erschlossen, ich habe es als Student durchwandert, war in Paris
1925, 1926 in einem Übersetzungsverlag tätig und blieb, angesichts des heraufziehenden
Nazismus, für mehrere Jahre in Südfrankreich, wo ich in Corenc als Landarbeiter mein
Brot verdiente. (ii,331)

Here as elsewhere Huchel was careless with dates, yet his inflation of certain periods
of time and activities to the exclusion of others clearly adds up to something a little
more deliberate in shaping elements of his autobiography. As we shall see, the length
of his stay in France was in fact somewhat more modest than he suggested, nor were
his activities in those years quite as he presented them in public after the war.

He was more exact in an unpublished account of his life written in 1948 when
he was applying formally for the editorship of *Sinn und Form*.[58] There he referred
to 1927 as the year he went to Paris. This leaves a year to be accounted for, 1926-7.
Dora Huchel deals with this period in the short section 'Berlin 1926/27' in the first
draft of her account.[59] The section reads as follows,

Oktober 1926 Universität Berlin. Ich wohne zunächst in Universitätsnähe, später in
Potsdam bei Huchels, mit der S-Bahn hin und zurück. Landschaft um Potsdam, Huchels
Freunde. Huchels Eltern: Fritze und Marie, Huchel redet sie mit Vornamen an. Im
Sommersemester im Segelboot eines Freundes viel auf den Havelseen. Mein Vater besucht
mich im August, wird nicht in meine Beziehung zu Huchel eingeweiht, besucht mit mir
seinen Lehrer Adolf von Harnack, geht mit mir auf Reisen: Rügen, in Göttingen, Marburg,
Fritzlar ehemalige Studienfreunde. Bekomme nachher vom Sohn eines Freundes einen
Heiratsantrag. Huchel formuliert die freundliche Ablehnung. Ich lande wieder in Potsdam,
wie das möglich war, nicht mehr erinnerlich.

It is possible that Huchel neglected to mention this year in Berlin/Potsdam because
it added little in terms of fresh experience to what came immediately before and
after. The impression is that he was marking time. His omission may also be related
to the fact that Huchel's *amour propre* was wounded by the treatment accorded to
him by the university authorities in Berlin. Records indicate that he re-registered at
the Friedrich Wilhelm University on 4 November 1926.[60] This would have been the
sixth semester, to which he referred in 1931. In this way, the pretence could be kept
up with his parents that he was still studying. The authorities, however, terminated
his registration on 24 January 1927 'wegen Unfleiß'. It appears that he managed to
keep this news from his parents, who continued to finance his 'studies' when he later
went to Paris. This in effect meant that he was able to continue writing at leisure and
to frequent the company of figures in Berlin around the Goldberg Circle, whom Dora
Lassel met, and of friends in Potsdam such as Ewald Fritsch and Rudi Elter.

The return to Berlin/Potsdam marked one significant advance in personal relations. Despite Huchel's avowal to Dora Lassel in Vienna, 'Meine Mutter stelle ich dir nie vor', the meeting none the less took place in the autumn of 1926 in Potsdam. In 1981, Dora Huchel conveyed her undiminished sense of wonderment that Huchel could possibly have been the child of such parents. She recalled being struck then as later by the total absence of any physical contact between Huchel and his mother. The lack of emotional warmth in that relationship was mirrored in that with his father, whose company Huchel felt he had no need of. By this time he had developed interests quite beyond them and was forging an identity which seemed not to depend at all on them. Knowledge of the difficulties in his relationship with his parents casts fresh light on a number of his statements. In 1931, for example, the poet drew attention to his relationship with the German language and referred to the void beyond, 'Er liebt die deutsche Sprache; sie ist das einzige, was er geerbt hat'. (ii,218) As we have seen, the late poem 'M.V.' (i,190), which treats his father's death, is more specific in identifying the emptiness of the son's inheritance, 'Er ließ nichts zurück/ als eine Fußspur im Sand,/ vom Eis des Winters ausgegossen'. Beyond the bitterness, in both cases one is struck by the regret at the absence of any substantial inheritance, of any tradition upon which to build. And, as we have seen, the lack of any such background contrasted sharply with his companion's situation.

The fact that Huchel felt that he could after all bring his old and new worlds together through returning to Berlin/Potsdam with Dora Lassel testifies to the strength and trust that he had developed in his relationship with her. For Fritz and Marie, as Huchel called his parents with barely concealed contempt, Dora Lassel was a 'feines Mädchen', someone from a higher social class to whom they always showed due deference. They could not understand her tastes nor begin to grasp how their son had come to be with her. It was for them merely to accept the situation. The clergyman's daughter, meanwhile, displayed on the one hand the openness to people of all walks of life that her father's Christian teaching and her student lifestyle had encouraged, on the other the prejudice of her class, which had taught her to distinguish sharply between people who pursued worthwhile activity of a professional, academic or business nature and other 'primitive' types whose lives could never rise above the drudgery of their menial work. Fritz and Marie belonged without any doubt to the latter category, yet for all that, the adventure of student life with her poet now meant, too, living with the Huchels and Emile Zimmermann at Teltowerstraße.

Dora Lassel continued her studies in German, French and English in Berlin, while Helmut drifted around, apparently not achieving a great deal during the incubation period of the mid- to late 1920s when, despite encouragement from Joachim, he released no further poems for publication. He was now prepared to wait, instead of releasing poems with which he might soon become dissatisfied. As for Dora, it had always been assumed that when she had completed her studies she would take up a teaching post in Kronstadt. Yet she managed to persuade her parents that after Vienna and Berlin a period of study in France was necessary preparation for examinations to be taken in Bucharest. Thus, it was Dora Lassel's studies that took the couple to Paris in the autumn of 1927, which in the event turned into a stay of two academic years.

Paris 1927-8

Some of the most extraordinary claims circulating about Huchel's life in the late 1920s and early 1930s concern his sojourn in France. We have seen how he described the *Wanderjahre* of these years, when he crossed Europe from West to East. Commentators have generally followed Huchel's own statements concerning the *Wanderjahre*, portraying him as the young Bohemian adventurer. Karl Alfred Wolken, apparently relying on conversations with Huchel at the Villa Massimo in Rome, has gone furthest down this road, describing his life in France as follows, 'Um die Mitte der Zwanzigerjahre streunt Huchel viereinhalb Jahre durch Frankreich als ein der Polizei durchaus verdächtiges Subjekt, einmal Land-, einmal Hafenarbeiter, ständig ausweisungsbedroht'.[61] Huchel told a similar story to Kundera at the turn of the 1960s. His account of 1931, studded with improbable clichés though it is, suggests that his difficulties were of more modest proportions, 'Ein Land, das er sich fast zu lieben erlaubt, ist Frankreich. Dort läßt es sich leben, gesetzt, daß die Carte d'identité in Ordnung ist. "La douce France", seine Einwohner sind jeden Tag liebenswürdig, Privatleben ist gestattet'. (ii,218) As we shall see, the young Prussian, who shows here his appreciation of French culture, did have a minor brush with the authorities, but the raconteur later inflated it in keeping with the image of youthful adventurer, which critics like Wolken eagerly propagated.

In addition to the depiction of the young poet living on the margin of legality rather in the manner of Verlaine and Rimbaud in Huchel's 'Gedicht', (i,334) Wolken's account repeats a story put into circulation by Huchel after the war in East Berlin. In the late 1940s, primarily through his friends Horst Lommer and Alfred Kantorowicz, Huchel maintained that during the years in France he had worked as a manual labourer. Most frequently, it was stated that he had been a farm servant, but on other occasions he was said to have been a shepherd or even a dockworker. In 1947, for example, in a piece of which Huchel at the time evidently approved, Lommer wrote that in the 1920s and 1930s Huchel had gained employment 'als Hirt, als Knecht, als Gelegenheitsarbeiter'.[62] Much later, in 1977, Huchel himself referred to the most frequently repeated story that while in France he worked on a farm in the village of Corenc near Grenoble, though similar stories of the shepherd exist in relation to Huchel's later stays in Romania. Yet the stories were strenuously denied by Dora Huchel, who spent the period in question with Huchel and shared an autumn holiday with him at Corenc, not to mention their lengthy stays later in the 1930s with the Lassel family in Romania.

The available evidence points quite unequivocally to the continuation in Paris and later of the poet's Bohemian lifestyle. Moreover, despite his own statements to the effect that he abandoned his studies after Vienna and embarked on a life of travel and adventure, in Paris he remained as much and as little a student as he had been previously in Berlin, Freiburg and Vienna. As before, he attended any lectures that interested him without doing any formal academic work by way of preparation for eventual exams. The post-war re-casting of the adult self as rural worker can be readily understood as an extension of the childhood myth, though, as we shall see in greater detail later, the particular emphases that Huchel lent his self-image in the immediate post-war period also need to be set in the context of East Berlin cultural politics, where it did not go amiss to beef up his peasant farming credentials. If critics have hitherto been disposed to accept this self-image at face value, then this can be attributed in part to the very acceptability of such an image in the immediate post-war years. Yet, the crucial factor was surely the persuasive manner in which the charismatic Huchel succeeded in presenting himself as the authentic embodiment of that image. The reality of his life in the late 1920s and early 1930s was, however, quite different from what the Huchel legend suggests.

His decision to go to Paris was prompted by Dora Lassel's studies and, with nothing keeping him in Potsdam, he followed her. Before doing so, he obtained a leaving certificate from the Friedrich Wilhelm University, which he could use, if necessary, to persuade his parents to continue financing his 'studies'.[63] He was able to draw on the French he had learned until *Abitur*, upon which he would improve during the eighteen or so months that he spent in France. By late 1929, he and Dora Lassel were in fact corresponding in a French that his surviving letters reveal to be quite simple but generally correct.

In her first draft, Dora Huchel describes how she travelled to Paris and how she and Huchel settled into the exciting life of the French capital, where he followed her some weeks later,

Anfang Oktober von Berlin nach Hamburg, mit dem Schiff nach Le Havre, mit Bahn nach Paris. Zimmer in einem Studentenhotel, in Paris übliche Unterkunft. Immatrikulation an der Sorbonne. Huchel kommt einige Wochen später nach und wohnt ebenfalls in einem Studentenhotel. Sowohl die vergangenen Jahre als auch die Pariser Zeit wurden von seinen Eltern finanziert. Keine Spur von Land-, Hafenarbeiter, Knecht und dgl. während des gesamten Frankreichaufenthaltes. Er lebt völlig ohne Sorgen und genießt Paris in vollen Zügen.

In 1981, she recalled that Huchel travelled to Paris from Potsdam by train. It is possible that he visited Joachim in Freiburg on the way, though the latter's exact whereabouts at the time are unclear. Two undated letters from Joachim were probably written immediately before Huchel's trip to Paris. In the first, Joachim inquires about his friend's 'Pariser Pläne' and in the second he invites Huchel to come and stay.[64] The likelihood of his having done so is increased by information imparted by Huchel that in 1927 he wrote the poem 'Lenz' in Strasbourg and Paris.[65] Strasbourg would have been a natural stopping-off point for Huchel after Freiburg on his way to Paris. Strasbourg has a particular place in German culture. It was there that Goethe, Lenz and other *Stürmer und Dränger* met in the 1770s. Huchel was drawn to Georg Büchner's fictional recreation of Lenz's descent into madness, which was set in the nearby Vosges mountains, where he was cared for by Pastor Oberlin. Indeed, Huchel later referred to his poem's exemplary status in representing a particular stage in his intellectual development.[66] In addition, in 1933 he published a short piece in *Die literarische Welt*, in which he acknowledged the great importance of Büchner's story for him. (ii,252-3) Yet, it is surely equally significant that it was only in 1957 that Huchel actually published his 'Lenz'. He deemed neither the early 1930s nor the immediate post-war period, not to mention the Nazi years themselves, as appropriate for the publication of such a poem. We shall have occasion at the relevant point to focus further on the import of that 1957 date for a poem that is now acknowledged as a classic re-working of Büchner's text.

The poem's original title on the manuscript now deposited at the Deutsches Literaturarchiv Marbach was 'Lenz bei Oberlin. Zwei Uhr nachts'.[67] The poem employs the, for Huchel, quite unusual ballad form, which is, though, found in other compositions from the late 1920s such as 'Der Tod des Büdners'. (i,272)[68] The narrative voice in the poem alternates between the description of unjust suffering in the world and the urgent second-person address to the acutely distressed Lenz, 'Lenz, dich ließ die Welt allein!/ Und du weißt es und dir graut'. The narrative voice identifies crass social inequality as one source of suffering, which is compounded by the cruelty of those who wield power, 'Landesherren, Fürstenfrauen,/ doch kein Wappen zeigt die Taten:/ Hoffart, Pracht und Üppigkeit,/ nicht den hinkenden Soldaten,/ armes Volk der Christenheit'. The other source of suffering is the apparent indifference of God to the trials of the innocent, which is treated in the poem, as in the original story, through the death of the girl at Fouday. At its conclusion, the poem returns to Lenz's tormented sensibility, 'Gott hat dich zu arm bekleidet/ mit der staubgebornen Haut./ Und der Mensch am Menschen leidet'. Through this broadening of the perspective to make the anguished artist Lenz the vehicle for the awareness of the tragedy of human suffering, Huchel conveys a much more compelling message than was achieved earlier in more narrowly subjective compositions such as the self-pitying 'Klage'. In general, however, Huchel did not in his compositions of the late 1920s and 1930s adopt the mask of historical figures. That is a feature of his later poetry and the publication of 'Lenz' in 1957 can be said to herald that development.

The original manuscript of 1927 bears the name Peter Huchel, the earliest recorded use of Peter at a time when he continued to sign himself Helmut on letters and to be known as Helmut or Piese by friends. The manuscript bears an address, rue Rollin 13, Paris, which can also be found on a postcard from Joachim to Huchel from the following September, 26.9.1928.[69] As the postcard further indicates, this was Huchel's address at Hôtel Liberty, where he stayed during his Paris sojourn. Initially, he and Dora Lassel had separate accommodation but moved in together at a later stage. His address shows that he lost no time in finding his way to the Left Bank and to the city's Bohemian life of artists and students. Situated between the Jardin des Plantes and the Jardin du Luxembourg, rue Rollin was just a short walk from the Sorbonne. It was also around the corner from rue Mouffetard, along which Dora Lassel passed on her way to the Sorbonne. Huchel, too, recalled the area in conversation with his second wife, Monica. She would later write of her husband's time in 'Paris, in der rue Mouffetard, wo er einmal in einem kleinen Hotel garni gelebt hatte'.[70]

The basic pattern of life remained much as it had been in Vienna and Berlin: Dora Lassel pursued her studies and Huchel devoted his energies to writing, while together they explored the city and its incomparable cultural and night life. Huchel's parents' unease at their son's attitude towards his 'studies' soon, however, became so acute that they took the step of writing to his friend, asking her to persuade him to apply himself to his academic work. They had been supporting him for five years and, as far as they were concerned, there was nothing to show for it. Paris was probably the last place where their plea might have had the remotest chance of success, though it can scarcely be said that Huchel was actually wasting his time. He regularly attended talks and lectures on literary themes and took in many other events as well as constantly updating his stock of literature from the city's excellent second-hand book stalls and shops. A number of these books are now in the Peter Huchel Collection in the John Rylands University Library.

As Dora Huchel writes above, the young Prussian enjoyed to the full the city's casual moral attitudes. In 1981, she recalled that one day when they returned to his hotel the concierge passed a note to him from a mutual friend, Georgette. Georgette asked him not to be annoyed to find her in his bed when he came to his room ... Something of the city's emancipated mood finds its way into the poetry composed there. In a letter of 31 January 1958 to his Czech translator Ludvík Kundera Huchel mentioned 'Hotel Liberty' as one of three 'Jugendgedichte' which he was contemplating sending Kundera. (ii,343) Though no poem bearing that title could be found among Huchel's papers (i,451), it seems quite plausible that Huchel was referring to the poem 'Frühling im Quartier', which was written from the perspective of someone living in a hotel in the Latin Quarter. 'Frühling im Quartier' was published in 1931 in *Die literarische Welt*. The poem is one of a small number of texts from the mid-1920s which treat city life in a manner that is not always wholly convincing. Huchel was never at home as a poet of the city. Its opening stanza, for instance, reads,

Der Mai steckt weiß die Kerzen ins Kastanienhaar,

nach Teer und Frühling riecht der Boulevard.

Die alte Apotheke öffnet ihre Türen,

du kannst die Lindenblüte ihrer Gläser spüren.

It closes with lines expressing the poet's sense of freedom and satisfaction with life, 'Du liegst im offnen Hemd zur Nacht im Lauen,/ nackt im Geruch von Mond und Frauen'. Life abroad in the city had its attractions for the young Prussian looking to strike out on his own.

A further poem which in its playful and mildly erotic tone conveys something of the city's sexually liberating atmosphere is 'Die Knäbin' (i,30), originally called 'Die Knäbin der Städte' and described by Huchel on the manuscript as a 'Chanson' written in Montparnasse in 1927. (i,375) Huchel later gave a copy of the poem to Joachim, who was seeking to place his friend's work through a publishing contact, Laven, and who wrote to him in the autumn of 1929, 'Laß ihn nur machen und quartiere Dich indessen bei Lotte Fink, Gartenstraße 8a ein, die von Deiner "Knäbin der Städte" in helle Begeisterungsflammen versetzt ist und von mir warmherzig präpariert'.[71]

The creation of the feminine form 'Knäbin' is possibly on the analogy of Trakl's 'Mönchin'. Its first stanza was composed as early as 1921 and shows the schoolboy's enthusiasm for naturism. The three stanzas that follow provide a sort of fashion update, both in terms of what the 'Knäbin der Städte' is wearing in Montparnasse in 1927 and of the poet's own style, which, quite unusually for Huchel, sees him as a practitioner of *Neue Sachlichkeit*. He actually distanced himself from the poem soon after its publication in 1932. (i,375) The 'Knäbin' is described as a

Zopfiges Mädchen der Wälderjahre,

Knäbin der Städte heut, du kürztest die Haare,

äugig und Reh der Untergrundbahn,

katzig und samtig in Pelz getan.

Quite apart from its evocation of the speed and modern fashions of city life, 'Die Knäbin' is a celebration of the type of female that Huchel found most attractive: slender and pretty in an almost boyish way, that is to say, quite the opposite of his sturdy mother but wholly in keeping with both his wives.

Casual Parisian morality also finds its way into 'Desdemona' (ii,219-22), another short prose piece published in *Die literarische Welt* in the early 1930s. 'Desdemona' is set in the cafés and hotels of the Latin Quarter, as well as at the 'bal nègre, rue Blomet'.[72] Huchel's choice of the name Yvonne Le Gall for one of the protagonists in 'Desdemona' would have struck a chord among the *habitués* of the Left Bank, echoing as it did not only the names of Claire and Yvan Goll, but also of Gwen Le Gallienne, a French-American painter, who was one of the best-known characters in the cafés of the Boulevard du Montparnasse. She is portrayed along with others in Wambly Bald's column 'La Vie de Bohème (As Lived on the Left Bank)', which appeared in the *Chicago Tribune* between 1929 and 1933.[73] As Huchel himself would, she took holidays in Brittany and Corsica and played the gaming tables at Monte Carlo. Kantorowicz, who in 1928 went to Paris, where he took over some of Tucholsky's work for the *Vossische Zeitung* and got to know the Huchels, noted his own sense of exhilaration at the opportunities for adventure that Paris offered,

> Aber im Grunde blieb man als Mittzwanziger in Paris eher auf der Jagd nach seinem Vexierbild seiner 'Lottchens' und 'Lydias' als nach dem Urbild von 'Mutterns Hände' und dachte nicht daran, daß er (Tucholsky – SP), wie es in einem Brief an seinen Verleger Rowohlt heißt, im Grunde jede Frau mit seiner Schreibmaschine 'betrog'. Da mußten nach dem leichtlebigen Lustrum erst die Wehen der aufbrechenden Barbarei einsetzen, um einen zu seiner Moralität, seinem sozialen Verantwortungsgefühl, seiner Passion aufzuwecken.[74]

For Huchel as much as for Kantorowicz, the carefree life in Paris of the late 1920s contrasted starkly with the conservative Prussian upbringing that had gone before and with what would come soon afterwards in Germany. With Dora Lassel, Huchel went to the bars and cafés of the Latin Quarter. They became regulars, she said in 1981, at La Coupole and Le Dôme, cafés on the Boulevard du Montparnasse frequented by the international artistic community that gathered on the Left Bank, including figures such as the Golls. She wrote in the third draft of her account, 'Oft treffen wir uns mit im Quartier Latin ganz und gar nicht zu übersehenden verwandten Geistern auf der jeweiligen Bude oder im Café Le Dôme und verschiedenen bistros'.

Cheng Cheng

Among the friends they made was the Chinese writer Cheng Cheng. When I visited her in 1981, Dora Huchel showed me a memento of that friendship. On 9 July 1928, Cheng Cheng presented Huchel with a copy of his recently published book of verse *Ma mère* (Paris and Neuchâtel, 1928). The author's dedication reads, 'A l'ami inconnu et anonyme connu et nommé Huchel et son ombre, et son silence'.[75] Cheng Cheng's words capture well the intriguing enigma that Huchel was for so many friends and acquaintances. Two further sources, Lommer and Kantorowicz, refer to Cheng Cheng, and his friendship with Huchel and his immediate circle. In 1947,

Lommer made the following claims, having mistakenly asserted that it was in France that Huchel got to know Joachim and Ernst Bloch,

> In Frankreich lernt Peter Huchel auch den chinesischen Revolutionär Cheng-Cheng, den Verfasser des bekannten Buches *Ma mère* kennen. Cheng-Cheng machte Peter Huchel mit dem russischen Dichter Jessenin bekannt, dessen Verse er ins Französische übertrug. Und es ist ein schönes Beispiel für eine geistige Zusammenarbeit von Menschen verschiedener Sprache, daß der russische Lyriker Sergej Jessenin, durch Vermittlung des Chinesen Cheng-Cheng, den deutschen Dichter Peter Huchel anregte.[76]

The constellation of nationals could, of course, scarcely have been bettered in early post-war East Berlin, demonstrating as it was clearly intended to, Huchel's early membership of the community of progressive internationalist poets! And in fact, if Lommer is suggesting a personal acquaintance between Huchel and Esenin, as appears to be the case, then he could not be more misleading. The Russian poet was last in Paris in April 1923 and hanged himself in a Leningrad hotel room in December 1925.[77] It remains unclear whether Cheng Cheng had known Esenin but it is quite plausible that the Chinese and German poet together read and translated the Russian. It must be said, however, that on his own Huchel would have been able to make no headway with the Russian language and that the range of his French remained quite limited.

Kantorowicz portrays Cheng Cheng in his *roman à clef Der Sohn des Bürgers*. Kantorowicz, who got to know Huchel and Dora Lassel in the spring of 1928, depicted himself as Martin Freimuth, Huchel as Peter Hügelin and Joachim as Georg Samuel. In reply to Samuel's question whether he had discovered anyone in Paris 'außer Bohemiens und Karrieristen', Freimuth replies, 'Oh doch! Da war ein junger chinesischer Schriftsteller, Cheng Tscheng mit Namen, der im gleichen Hotel wohnte und in dessen Gesellschaft ich mich wohl gefühlt habe. Er hat mir viel von den sozialen Bedingungen in seinem Vaterland erzählt'.[78]

It can be safely assumed that social issues formed the substance of some of Cheng Cheng's conversations with Huchel, who in 1966 told Norbert Randow of how he got to know his Chinese friend.[79] Huchel's account as told to Randow, larded though it is at points with the raconteur's outlandish pathos, places Wolken's picture of the poet on the margin of legality in a more realistic light. Huchel told Randow that in the autumn of 1927 he went walking on the Brittany coast.[80] He was stopped by a French coastal patrol and was apparently suspected of being a German spy because his papers were no longer valid. (One might object that no self-respecting spy would be without valid papers. No matter.) He told Randow that he was subjected to an unpleasant round of questioning and then let go, aber der Schock, als deutscher Spion womöglich in Paris oder an der französisch-deutschen Grenze noch einmal festgehalten zu werden, saß ihm in den Gliedern. So traute er sich, nach Paris zurückgekehrt, tagelang nicht aus seinem Zimmer. Als er es schließlich vor Hunger nicht mehr aushielt, ging er auf die Straße, fiel jedoch sogleich unter dem Anprall der frischen Luft und vor Entkräftung in Ohnmacht. Als er die Augen wieder aufschlug, sah er das fremdartige Gesicht eines Chinesen über sich gebeugt, der sich teilnahmsvoll um ihn bemühte. Er begriff sehr schnell, wie es um Huchel stand, nahm ihn mit und setzte ihm eine kräftige Hühnersuppe vor, die Huchel jedoch nach seinem tagelangen Fasten überhaupt nicht bekam.

The story is a classic from the Huchel repertoire. One can surely take the story of exposure to acute, life-threatening hunger to be an expression of the anxiety that the young Prussian abroad experienced during and following his arrest. As Randow writes, the anxiety stayed with him after he returned to Paris, and, seen in that light, it is surely advisable to consider the story of near-starvation as an example of the 'higher' poetic truth of his imagination.

Interestingly, Kundera noted the episode as follows, 'Bretagne-Erlebnisse. Die traurigste Zeit. Schwierigkeiten, Polizei. Verhör in Paris: "In 24 Stunden Paris verlassen!" Aber nach einer Intervention des Briand-Sohnes Frist 14 Tage'.[81] According to the version told to Kundera, he then left Paris for Grenoble. Things turned out quite differently in conversation with Randow. Cheng Cheng knew the son of the French Foreign Minister and Nobel Prize winner, Aristide Briand. This connection meant that Huchel's residence permit could be extended without further difficulty and there was no obstacle to his remaining in France. The reality is disappointingly trite; the stories of adventure, danger, confrontation with the authorities and near-starvation were undoubtedly much more thrilling for the captivated listener!

Huchel generally told his listeners stories about himself, yet there were equally interesting ones that could have been told about Cheng Cheng. Randow writes that a few months after visiting Huchel he chanced upon a German translation of Cheng Cheng's book. It had been published in 1929 by Kiepenheuer. We know of Huchel's link with Kiepenheuer. Might he have been the person who recommended Cheng Cheng? Like Huchel, as a teenager Cheng Cheng had a revolutionary past, though his was on the Left, not the Right. According to Paul Valéry, who wrote the foreword to *Ma mère*, he was one of the leaders of the Shanghai Revolution in 1917, when he was aged just 19. He was subsequently employed in the trade union movement and two years later he went to France as a student, where he stayed on in Paris, joining the company of its international community.

This brief portrait of the young Chinese writer and revolutionary enables us to appreciate better how, later, Huchel could come to speak of his 'Lenz' as the product of a specific point in his development. It was a time when the encounter with Cheng Cheng and with Paris' own revolutionary traditions sharpened Huchel's social and political awareness. Like 'Lenz', other Parisian poems treat suffering and death as, to some extent, a social matter. They mark a significant advance upon earlier compositions such as 'Die Versöhnung' or 'Kniee, weine, bete'. In 'Cimetière',(i,75) for example, (not to mention 'Totenregen' and 'Friedhof Montparnasse' (i,22)) he laments the lot of the poor in 'Mont-de-piété', in other words, those urban poor who through force of circumstance frequented Paris' pawnbroking area. The poem ends with the following lines, 'Manche hörten der Freiheit Schüsse,/ ehe sie fanden das späte Asyl'. This reference to the Parisian revolutionary tradition echoes Heine and Heym, and complements the use of Büchner as a literary model. Yet Huchel chose to publish neither 'Cimetière' nor 'Lenz' until after the war, the former in 1948, the latter, as we have seen, in 1957. He apparently did not wish to present himself to the reading public of the early 1930s as the author of such socially engaged verse. As a result, Huchel's sympathies with the Left did not emerge strongly and consistently in his pre-1945 publications. The verse that he selected for publication in the early 1930s testifies to more personal concerns and visions.

Indeed, a poem such as 'Der Herbst' (i,79), also dating from 1927-8 and suffused in its final stanzas with the language of alchemy and mysticism in its evocation of the grape harvest, illustrates a fertile line of development in Huchel's nature poetry independent of the Alt-Langerwisch myth, whose poetic possibilities were, after all, not unlimited. Autumnal nature would represent a rich seam for Huchel to work in the early 1930s with a poem such as 'Oktoberlicht' and the cycle 'Strophen aus einem Herbst'. The Paris years were then certainly ones of experiment as various influences and styles were being tried out, although not long afterwards, in Berlin of the early 1930s, Huchel would, through the careful choice of material he released for publication, be defining quite closely the sort of poet he wished to be regarded as in the specific climate of those years.

German Visitors

That was all still a way off in Paris in 1928. In the first few months of that year, Dora and Helmut were joined by German friends, with whom they continued their discovery of life in the French capital. Dora Huchel wrote of this time in her third draft, 'Des Entdeckens in der Stadt und Umgebung kein Ende. Spätestens im Vorfrühling tauchten Kantorowicz, Joachim und Wilma Papst auf, in die sich Cheng Tcheng (*Ma mère*) verliebte, den wir schon kannten'. Wilma Papst was a Berlin student friend, whom Huchel and Dora Lassel had introduced to Joachim. The group, excluding Cheng Cheng, would in early 1931 share a flat in Berlin. In Paris Kantorowicz finally got to know the poet personally. In the meantime, Kantorowicz's star had been rising. He may have lost his girlfriend Karola Piotrkowka to his friend Ernst Bloch but his new role supporting Kurt Tucholsky's work in Paris for the *Vossische Zeitung* was a plum job for any budding writer.

In post-war accounts of their friendship in Paris, Kantorowicz wrote that when they met, 'Huchel schlug sich teils mit Übersetzungen durch und teils mit Hilfe literarischer Stipendien, die ihm der gütige Feuilleton-Redakteur der *Vossischen Zeitung*, Dr. Monty Jacobs, verschaffte'.[82] In the 1984 edition, the translation work is also attributed to the *Vossische Zeitung*. (i,459) And certainly, in an early post-war account of his life that has remained unpublished, he went so far as to write that he went to Paris as a freelance writer and collaborator on the *Vossische Zeitung*.[83] In 1981, Dora Huchel knew nothing of such claims. She expressed her most profound scepticism about Huchel's supposed receipt of 'literarischer Stipendien' and about translation work undertaken by him. She had known nothing about such things at a time when, as she was well aware, he was still being financed by his parents. Dora Huchel told me that she wrote to Kantorowicz after the publication of his essay in 1964, inquiring where he had got his information from. Kantorowicz, who wrote his essay in 1948 shortly after returning to Berlin from US exile, replied that he had simply included biographical details conveyed to him by Huchel while he was preparing his essay. The temporal proximity of Kantorowicz's essay and Huchel's own account offers some explanation for the convergence of the two. That said, it is conceivable that chronologies were simply lost sight of. If Dora Huchel could remember no support from the *Vossische Zeitung*, then Huchel possibly received something at an earlier stage, before she got to know him. Although Huchel placed poems with the paper only from 1930, there were much earlier links between it and the Goldberg Circle. Huchel's friend Harry Landry, for example, played a mediating role. Support for the young poet may well have been forthcoming sometime between 1923 and 1925 in Berlin or Freiburg. Huchel had been published by then, not only in the *Dürer Kalender* and *Der Freiburger Figaro*, but in the much more prestigious *Kunstblatt* edited by Paul Westheim for Kiepenheuer in Potsdam. A fee would obviously have been payable, and, indeed, after the war in a publication which again drew on the author's own testimony, Franz Lennartz stated that in the 1920s Huchel had been supported by Westheim among others.[84] Yet, as far as can be ascertained, after his initial publications between 1924 and 1926 no more work by Huchel appeared until 1930. It is perfectly plausible that during the first few years when Dora Huchel knew him Huchel received no support beyond fees for his lone poems in the *Neue Badische Landes-Zeitung* and in *Klingsor*. Regarding the translation work, in 1977 Huchel, as we have seen, went so far as to claim that in 1926 he had worked in an 'Übersetzungsverlag' (ii,331) in Paris. When asked about this by me in 1981, Dora Huchel recalled a translation operation in Paris run by a German Jew, Desiré Schwarz, whom she and Huchel got to know. They occasionally visited him at his office but neither she nor Huchel did any translation work there or, for that matter, anywhere else. Certainly, Dora Huchel's version of events is not inconsistent with the pattern of inflation and transformation of elements of experience undertaken by Huchel. What emerges in the various stories of translation work and stipends is that later Huchel preferred to suggest the hard-won financial independence of the struggling young poet rather than acknowledge his parents' continuing support for the student's Bohemian lifestyle.

Bréhat

Kantorowicz, Joachim, Wilma Papst, Cheng Cheng, Huchel and Dora Lassel stayed together in Paris during the early summer and joined in the celebrations of Bastille Day. Shortly afterwards, Dora Lassel returned home to Kronstadt for the summer, where she was joined by Wilma Papst. Meanwhile, Huchel, Kantorowicz and Joachim took off for a holiday in Brittany, a favoured destination for the Parisian artistic community. They chose the tiny, remote island of Bréhat, just off the north coast, which had been recommended by the Japanese painter Foujita, one of the best-known figures in the café life of the Boulevard du Montparnasse.[85] Huchel later recalled in conversation with Kundera that Foujita had given him the address before the painter himself went off for the summer there with his 'harem' of ballet dancers. Huchel and his two friends followed by train from the Gare du Nord. At midnight, the journey ended in disaster for many of their fellow passengers as the train left the track and caused one of France's most serious railway accidents. Huchel conveyed to Kundera the extent of his injuries, 'Mein Koffer mit den Gedichten fiel mir auf den Kopf'.[86] The story told to Kundera was corroborated by Dora Huchel in 1981. She received a telegram in Kronstadt from Huchel assuring her that he and his friends had survived unscathed. Once more, Huchel had been within a whisker of death. They were able to resume their journey to Bréhat, where they spent the summer together. This was the first of a sequence of such holidays in remote locations untouched by modern civilisation which Huchel would undertake. In his imagination, they were in certain cases transformed, by analogy with the country childhood, from holiday stays into a life spent in such places together with the indigenous population. Bréhat was not subjected to such a transformation. Kantorowicz described their summer as follows,

> Wir verlebten einen unvergeßlichen Sommer gemeinsam, erst in Paris und dann in der Bretagne auf der Insel Bréhat. Wir bewohnten alle drei einen Raum in einem kleinen Fischerhaus, und wir diskutierten die Nächte durch bis zum Morgengrauen, und oftmals, bis die Sonne zum Vorschein kam. Es war eine reiche Zeit für uns. Es wäre zu billig, zu sagen, daß es eine glückliche Jugendzeit war. Glücklich waren wir gar nicht. Wir rangen schwer und erbittert mit den literarischen, kulturellen, sozialen und persönlichen Problemen. Es war 1928 und wir drei waren in den zwanziger Jahren, Söhne bürgerlicher, oder richtiger, kleinbürgerlicher Eltern. Wir standen im Umbruch. Es wurde uns nicht

leicht, und wir machten es uns auch gar nicht leicht, mit den Problemen unserer Zeit fertig zu werden.[87]

The 1920s, indeed, offered no easy answers. For Kantorowicz, all three friends were still struggling to define themselves in a way that distinguished them from their background, though none of them were decided on a particular path. Certainly, it did not occur to Kantorowicz to portray Huchel at this time or indeed later as a Marxist. Karola Bloch recalled that in the 1920s Kantorowicz himself nurtured the hope that 'die bürgerliche Demokratie eine soziale Gerechtigkeit schaffen würde'.[88] Like her, by the early 1930s, Kantorowicz had come to regard that as an illusion and had opted for the KPD. By all accounts, Joachim did not represent strongly-held political opinions. As for Huchel, in a three-stanza poem dated 1927, which he incorporated in the cycle 'Deutschland' (i,165-6) in the 1967 collection *Die Sternenreuse*, he contrasted the misery of Germany ('Deutschland ist dunkel, Deutschland ist kalt') with the French national spirit, as embodied by Joan of Arc. The earliest version (i,414) ends, 'Niemals aber im Frühtau ging,/ Hell gerufen, von Stimmen stark,/ In den Augen gekreuzigte Glut/ Über die Heide eine Jeanne d'Arc'. The language of the ecstasy of self-sacrifice for the sake of the nation was the preserve of the Right in France, among whom the myth of the national saviour was cultivated. It is true that Germany could not point to such an integrative figure in its history, but most people on the Left would have argued that Germany's problems could, in any case, not be solved by recourse to such a form of politics. Huchel himself could only have been all too aware of the pernicious effects of the cult of the Kaiser, to which his father had subscribed. For all his concern with social injustice in 'Lenz', Huchel clearly sets himself apart here from the Left's aim to pursue a rationally based politics. His verse is, rather, informed by the blend of pathos and myth-making, which lends substance to Kantorowicz's view that the three friends at the time shared an outlook which he described as 'weltschmerzlich',[89] which emerges as a characteristic strain in Huchel's writings of the time. Huchel's response to the deepening misery of Germany could only be an ever-darkening melancholy.

Paris, 1928-9

Kantorowicz's account of the summer of 1928 on Bréhat is followed by his information that Joachim returned to Germany, while 'Huchel verdingte sich als Bauernknecht, und ich blieb mit meinem Weltschmerz allein in Paris zurück'.[90] Drawing on his early post-war conversations with Huchel, Kantorowicz estimated that Huchel spent 'zehn Monate als Bauernknecht bei einem französischen Kleinbauern in der Nähe von Grenoble'.[91] As we have seen, in 1977 Huchel went so far as to claim that in the late 1920s he 'blieb, angesichts des heraufziehenden Nazismus, für mehrere Jahre in Südfrankreich, wo ich in Corenc als Landarbeiter mein Brot verdiente'. (ii,331) This represents quite an inflation on ten months. The editor of the 1984 edition, meanwhile, opts for a more modest period of time, writing of 'das Bergdorf Corenc in der Nähe von Grenoble, wo P.H. 1928 für einige Monate als Knecht bei einem Kleinbauern arbeitete'. (i,372) At another point the editor offers 1928-9 as the period Huchel spent as a farm labourer. (i,399) In conversation with Kundera, Huchel spoke of 'ein Vierteljahr in einem halbzerfallenen Haus Couronne (?)', but made no claims to have worked as a farm labourer.[92] As we have seen, Dora Huchel categorically denied the labouring story. According to her, they visited the remote village of Corenc together and spent an early autumn holiday there. Other documents, specifically the recently published letters and cards from Joachim to Huchel, indicate that the holiday must have been in the autumn of 1929.[93] Following his return to Germany, Joachim wrote to Huchel from Berlin on 26 September 1928 at Hôtel Liberty, where he had returned to from Bréhat.[94] Joachim's card reveals that he was trying to get hold of some money to help Huchel out of a difficult financial situation, although Joachim himself had been refused any further financial support from his father. The card continues,

> Ich habe genug Vorstellungskraft, um mir denken zu können, wie es Dir diese Tage in Paris ergangen ist. So konsequent ergeht es mir hier nicht. Aber ich weiß nicht was wird – Ich fliehe vor Freiburg mit drohenden Reden ohne hier etwas zu verdienen. Fica [*Hundename*] wird wohl bald bei Dir sein. So Vilma [*Pabst*] hat in Berlin gedroht, mich zu ohrfeigen. Wenn es einen Gott gibt, lebt sie nicht mehr lange. Keine Angst, es gibt keinen. Dein Achim.

Fica was not in fact the name of a dog, as the editor suggests, somewhat implausibly given the context, but a name that Huchel had given his girlfriend. Like her, the word is Romanian and, usually spelt fiica, it means daughter. It was frequently used by Huchel as an affectionate term of address in letters to his wife.[95] As Joachim and Huchel were aware, the Lassels had granted their daughter permission to study for a second year in Paris. Huchel was enjoying life there on his own before her return for the beginning of the new term in the autumn. In her third draft, Dora Huchel writes, 'Mitte Oktober beide wieder in Paris, Sorbonne, Huchel "raunt" alte und neue Verse, neue Bekanntschaften und Entdeckungen und Streifzüge. Daß wir zusammen bleiben wollten, stand fest'. Despite Kantorowicz's claim that he returned to Paris alone while Huchel went off to the remote Alpine village for the winter of 1928-9 to be a farm labourer, it seems highly likely that he continued to meet up with his friends in Paris. They were certainly there for him through the winter of 1928-29 if he wanted them. Again, the likelihood is that when Kantorowicz wrote his essay, twenty years on with all the traumas of exile just behind him, he merely relied upon the details supplied by his friend.

Both Huchel and Dora Lassel were aware that a second year in France would be as much as they could manage. For all the attractions of life in Paris, it could only remain an interlude. The Lassels expected their daughter to return home after her second year at the Sorbonne and there was little prospect that Huchel could continue much longer to draw on his parents' support. In 1931, ignoring such prosaic matters, he summarised the reasons for his return to Germany from France in the following terms,

> Denn in Deutschland hat er den Himmel zuerst gesehen, die Havel, die schilfige Nymphe, und das birkichte Flachfeldland. Er liebt die deutsche Sprache; sie ist das einzige, was er geerbt hat. Er liebt das Heimatland zum Trotz: wegen etlicher Bücher, einiger Freunde und Frauen, eines Hundes, die alle dort zur Welt gekommen sind. (ii,218)

Like so many other Germans of his own as well as of earlier and later generations, he could muster only strictly limited enthusiasm for his own country. Like so many others, too, France came to represent a substitute, since its proud, yet seemingly unforced national culture provided points of identification not available in the more complex and confusing German context.

The South of France and Corsica

Huchel and Dora Lassel made the most of their opportunities during their second year in France, in the city during the winter and spring, and in their discovery of the South of France and the Mediterranean in the summer of 1929. The trip to the south was Huchel's first encounter with the Mediterranean, a world that in his poetry came to act as a counterpoint to rural Brandenburg. This constellation can be found in his work from the late 1920s and, as he pointed out to Kundera, he took it up again in the late 1950s when he rediscovered the Mediterranean during holidays to Italy. Following the end of the academic year 1928-9, in late July 1929 they took off on their trip south, which is described by Dora Huchel in her third draft,

> Ende Juli noch einmal auf große Fahrt: 2 Tage Avignon, grandios, aber der Papstpalast häßlich. Weiter nach Arles bei van Gogh, Place du Croissière: immer noch Boule-Spêle ??. (= Spiele – S.P.) – Marseille, Huchel neugierig, besucht das Freudenviertel, wo ihm der Hut vom Kopf gerissen wird. Weiter Toulon und die ganze Côte bei Nizza. Dort auf verwachsenen Pfaden das hochgelegene Haus von Maeterlinck (war es Maeterlinck?) aufgespürt. Natürlich Monaco und in Monte Carlo geschenktes Geld eines Freundes verspielt. Am tollsten aber Überfahrt nach Korsika und das Durchstreifen der Insel, etwa zwei Wochen lang per pedes in vielen Richtungen, ein wunderbares 'Zigeunerleben', das

einzige entgegen der um Huchel zahlreich kursierenden Legende. Bis zuletzt blieb Huchel in 'La Douce France', ebenfalls entgegen aller Legende, ohne daß ihn jemals die Behörden dort verfolgt hätten.

After the war Huchel wrote a poem which he first called 'Avignon' (i,397) but which was subsequently modified and published under the title 'Verona'. (i,117) The opening lines of the earlier draft read,

> Zwischen uns fiel der Regen des Vergessens.
>
> Auf der Mauer die Katze,
>
> Sie dreht ihr Haupt ins Schweigen,
>
> (Das Haupt wendend ins Schweigen)
>
> Erkennt uns nicht.
>
> Das schwache Licht der Liebe
>
> Sinkt auf ihre Augensterne.

If we accept their common experience of Avignon as providing the occasion for the composition of these lines, then one can conclude that, despite the acrimony of their separation and divorce, on occasion Huchel, like his first wife, regretted the passing of the love that they had shared, which was preserved in memories of their travels of the late 1920s.[96]

Whatever curiosities Marseilles had to offer, it also inspired Huchel to compose the poem 'Marseille', to which he referred in the same letter of 31 January 1958 to Kundera in which he mentioned 'Hotel Liberty'. It has not proved possible to locate a poem whose content would point to a treatment of experiences in Marseilles. Dora Huchel, however, provided more details about Nice and the Monte Carlo gaming tables. In 1981, she recalled staying in a Nice hotel for a week and identified the rich friend in question as Ernst Reissig, who was on the Côte d'Azur with a girlfriend. Reissig was a young Berlin poet, whom Huchel already knew and who regularly received money from his father, a wealthy Berlin hotelier. For a short period of time Huchel and Dora Lassel enjoyed a taste of the good life with Reissig and his female friend, with whom they met up in Monte Carlo. Using Reissig's money, they lost once and won once at the casino.

In conversation with Kundera, Huchel embellished the story considerably, in quite familiar fashion. He told Kundera that he had lived together in Nice with Reissig, the half-insane, homosexual 'verlorener Sohn' of a Berlin hotelier. They travelled to Monte Carlo with Reissig's allowance of 800 marks and promptly lost all the money at the gaming tables. They were then forced to live in a stable. Huchel retrieved the situation for himself by working on the docks, where as a 'Hafenarbei-ter' he 'schleppte Kisten und schlief auch zwischen Kisten in einem Magazin.'[97]

Here then, we identify the source of Huchel's story of work on the docks, a claim which, as we have seen, was strenuously denied by his first wife. Huchel went on to explain to Kundera that with the money earned on the docks he was able to pay for his passage to Corsica, where he was able to live comfortably for a while.

Nowhere does Huchel mention his female companion on his travels. According to the account that she provided in 1981, they took the ferry from Nice to Ajaccio. In what was a 'besonders schöne Reise' of ten days or so, 'alles zu Fuß', they then hiked across the interior of the island from Ajaccio to Bastia. From there they took the ferry back to Nice. It was the type of holiday to a remote part of Europe almost untouched by modern urban and industrial development that appealed to Huchel and excited his poetic imagination. An early product of his exposure to this pristine Mediterranean world was 'Die Insel Aloe' (i,22), a poem described in the 1984 edition as written on Corsica in 1928. (i,372) The poem was first published in the *Vossische Zeitung* on 3 June 1931 and selected for *Der Knabenteich* but in the event collected only in 1984. Although it is not, due to its publishing history, one of Huchel's better-known compositions, a letter to Huchel from Dr H.A. Seelbach of 29 November 1949[98] indicates that this reader of the *Vossische Zeitung* was intensely disappointed that he had lost the newspaper cutting bearing the poem that he had carried round with him in his wallet for some twenty years and was anxious to receive another copy of this treasured possession. The poem does, indeed, convey a sublime, brilliant vision, and it is a little surprising that, despite obvious weaknesses ('Behext vom Licht, das traurig macht'), Huchel could not find any place for it in *Gedichte*. Conceivably, Huchel felt that the sheer dazzling richness of his vision in 'Die Insel Aloe' was not in keeping with the immediate post-war atmosphere.

The poem opens by offering a majestic, panoramic vision of the island rising above the sea and into the clouds and the burning sun of the Mediterranean sky. ('Im Feuerhimmel, Wolkenschnee/ schwamm blau die Insel Aloe./ Der blaue Fisch, der Fluß sang leis/ mit seiner Kieme silberweiß'.) This opening suggests the perspective of someone travelling towards or away from the island by boat, as the poet, of course, did. In addition to images of elemental power, the poem exhibits a dazzling array of colours, smells and sounds. ('Dort rochen Datteln, süß und mürb,/ die Spinnen hingen tot im Garn. Ein Quell am Weg kam wie Gezirp,/ wo Ziegen standen schwarz im Farn'.) These phenomena are blended in the evocation of the mystery of nature's creative sources.('O Hirtenpfad, der Traumwind stob!/ Behext vom Licht, das traurig macht,/ wahrsagend laut im Heliotrop/ des Himmels und der Palmennacht').

The aloe plant or African lily with its erect spikes of flowers, its juices traditionally used as a purgative and for their healing qualities, fits within this vision of a creative nature, of which the poet partakes. Indeed, as we have seen, the depiction of the seascape and the landscape of the island's interior in the first two stanzas gives way in the third to the heightened vision of an enchanted, dreamlike consciousness, the site of prophetic visions. We thus see Goldberg's disciple transplanted to the magic of the Mediterranean and adopting the stance of inspired visionary, conveying his unique insights and revelations into the workings of nature, which are heralded by the surreal quality of 'der Traumwind stob!'.The sublimity of his visionary consciousness informs the opening two lines of the final stanza, ('so zog ich durch des Mondes Schnee,/ durch Wind, durch Nacht und Aloe') before the seal is set on the enchanted scene in the repetition in the closing lines of the two final lines of the first stanza.

From the early to mid-1930s, Huchel's visionary gift was brought to bear much more intensely on the landscape and life of rural Brandenburg. It makes sense to read 'Die Insel Aloe' as a precursor of more mature compositions such as 'Oktoberlicht' and 'Havelnacht', in which Huchel did not treat the childhood myth, whose limitations must have become increasingly obvious to him. In these Brandenburg and Mediterranean poems Huchel places himself quite unmistakably within the tradition of poet as prophet, as seer mediating between his fellow humans and the forces of an infinitely rich and mystically charged natural world, through whose majesty and awe he is inspired. It is a matter of some regret that it would not be long before the time of grand poetic visions was past, as they were eclipsed by much more dangerous realities. It would be only later, in the late 1950s, 1960s and 1970s, that Huchel would once again feel disposed to exploit his capacity to evoke the splendours of the Mediterranean and South-East European landscapes.

Corenc

From the South of France, Helmut and Dora returned in September to Paris for what was essentially an opportunity to say goodbye to friends and to collect their things before returning together to Germany. Though their destination was now once more fixed as Berlin/Potsdam, there was nothing to speed their journey back to Fritz and Marie at Teltowerstraße. In 1981 Dora Huchel recalled that they took a final opportunity to discover more of the beauties of France, taking off for the mountains of Haute Savoie. They travelled there separately, meeting up in Grenoble. From there, they took a bus up to the mountain village of Corenc, where they rented a little house on the land of a farmer and wine-grower named Thomasset. They spent an early autumn holiday of some four weeks, again in the sort of place away from urban civilisation that appealed to their taste and fed Huchel's imagination. They helped out with the apple-picking and, as Dora Huchel writes in her third draft, 'Apfel-, Pflaumen- und Weinernte kam uns zugute'. They cooked 'Apfelreis' on an open fire and enjoyed walking amid the spectacular mountain scenery.

In conversation with Kundera, Huchel put quite a different spin on things, saying quite plausibly, as we shall see, that he went to Grenoble because of a love affair. He wanted to take his own life, he said, 'aber es regnete zuviel'.[99] He said that he had waited for a telephone call in Grenoble. Huchel went on to describe Corenc as 'Ein Dorf, das man vernachlässigt, wenn der Hang abrutscht. Erdrutsch. "In so einem Haus wohnte ich, die Trauben waren die einzige Kost"'. Though there was no mention of work as a farm labourer, he did go on to claim that the farmer and his idiot son attacked him with scythes, but somehow the situation was finally saved, 'Langes Verhandeln, dann Frieden'. Such details inform 'Corenc' (i,76), one of three poems relating to the holiday spent there. The poem begins,

> Zerfallnes Haus, Gehöft der Trauer,
> der Berg schob sein Geröll.
> Der Mörtel brach aus Tor und Mauer,
> von Eulen ein Gewöll.

This scene of desolation had, it seems, been caused by mysterious visitors, who had since departed. In 1981, Dora Huchel was at pains to stress that the scene described in the poem could in no way be taken to reflect the condition of the house they had stayed in. There were, it was true, rats in the attic but it was 'auf keinen Fall verfallen, schon in Ordnung. Inhalt hat nichts mit Überschrift zu tun'. This statement was in no way intended to detract from the poem, rather to preserve distinctions that her husband, in her view, tended to disregard. 'Corenc' in fact illustrates well Dora Huchel's point that he at the time 'gab sich pessimistisch, mit Weltschmerz, Pathos'. Yet, as Huchel's conversation with Kundera demonstrates, not to mention his stories of working in Corenc as a farm labourer, he subsequently went on to relate the content of his poetic construction back to his own experience, with the result that, in time, the poetic construction replaced the reality that he had shared with Dora Lassel. The Corenc episode is a particularly clear example of how in Huchel's mind poetic vision and experience were confused and how the former came to eclipse the latter. The replacement of the Steglitz childhood by the Alt-Langerwisch idyll was in the early post-war period parallelled by the transformation of an autumn holiday with Dora Lassel into months and, finally, years of manual labour on Monsieur Thomasset's farm.

Yet, there is more to the stay than Dora Huchel directly acknowledged. The stay prompted two further compositions, 'Ferme Thomasset' (i,124) and 'Wiese bei Corenc'. (i,19) The latter, collected only posthumously in the 1984 edition though first published in the *Vossische Zeitung* on 1 June 1930, is of considerable biographical interest, not least because, without knowledge of that edition and believing that the poem had remained unpublished throughout Huchel's life, Dora Huchel recalled the first stanza of the poem in the first draft of the account she wrote in the 1980s. She described the stanza as 'Dies Anfang eines dort entstandenen jedoch nie veröffentlichten Gedichtes'. 'Wiese bei Corenc' reads,

Fällt ein Hang,

weidenstrüppig, moorig,

Hund und Abend, tausendohrig,

horchen groß auf Grillensang.

Durch die mondverwachsenen Weiden

weht dein Haar.

Soll ich eine Rute schneiden

für das Mädchen, das mir untreu war?

Längst schläft schon der Vogel, der beim Namen

unsre Liebe nennt.

Krötenrufe kamen,

und des Sommers Herz verbrennt.

Huchel's mention to Kundera of a love affair and of thoughts of suicide in Corenc assumes a much clearer meaning in the light of the very direct second half of the poem, even though Huchel mentioned no names to Kundera. Nor did Dora Huchel do more than hint to me in 1981 that she had a relationship in those years with anyone other than Huchel, although he himself was never monogamous. Her almost perfect recollection of the first stanza of the poem over half a century later – and the omission of the ominous second and third stanzas – strongly suggests that there is a story half-concealed, its details probably lost for ever, of Dora's infidelity and Huchel's anger and anguish at his discovery of it. The traumatic scenes in Corenc that he later related to Kundera – not to mention the poem of the same name and the story of his employment there as a farm servant – were surely his way of dealing with his anguish. What remains, however, is the poet's revenge through the poem that was published in 1930 and was then lost sight of for over half a century before it was collected in 1984. The poem divides very clearly into two halves, the first setting the scene for romantic love heralded by the cricket's song, familiar from the Viennese love poems such as 'Holunder'. The second half, beginning in line three of stanza two, angrily breaks the romantic mood with thoughts of brutal beatings for the unfaithful female lover and the replacement of the cricket and the bird singing of love by 'Krötenrufe', by analogy with 'Unkenrufe' prophecies of doom, which accompany the consumption by flames of the tender heart of summer.

    The poet's lyrical response to female infidelity was both primitive and extreme, a response which demonstrates that for all his enjoyment of the relaxed morals of Bohemian Paris, Huchel was very much trapped in the delusions and insecurities deriving from a quite traditional view of male dominance and authority in sexual relations, where, due to his great charms, he could normally get his way. In time, he would put this affront to his masculinity behind him, blocking out the painful aspects of the stay in Corenc through the story of the farm servant. The farm servant's honest toil was, moreover, later presented as the poet's response to the growth of the Nazi threat, 'angesichts des heraufziehenden Nazismus'. In this way, the poet's myth-making took on fresh layers of meaning as he embellished it through time.

However serious the crisis in their relationship in Corenc, Huchel and Dora Lassel returned from there to Berlin/Potsdam in the autumn of 1929. This came to represent a re-affirmation of their earlier decision to stay together, though it appears that here as elsewhere the level of active commitment was greater on Dora Lassel's part, not least because she was giving up the career path planned for her and in doing so going against her parents' wishes, while for Huchel there was from his teens onwards never any question that he would do anything but simply *be* a poet. Those who wished to share their lives with him would simply have to organise their lives around that fact of his existence. He was content to accommodate a female companion on those terms, and in Dora Lassel he found someone who was appreciative of the particular needs of the poet. A corollary was, however, that then and later, he rarely felt the need to go out of his way to influence the course of personal relations but, rather passively, permitted himself to be carried along by events, relying on his charm and gifts to maintain a position that he was comfortable with.

His attitude towards the literary world of Berlin that he was about to re-enter was not dissimilar. He would be able to rely on the help of Joachim, who wrote to him in Corenc from Offenbach on 8 October 1929.[100] Joachim was looking forward to meeting up with him again soon in Berlin. There was no mention of any manual exertions undertaken by Huchel, only his literary projects, with which Joachim was eager to help. He urged Huchel to write to his friend Pyler at Reichart Verlag in Freiburg and to send him 'eine Gedichtauswahl für eine halbe Stunde, er wird sie für Dich einreichen. Schicke ihm zugleich das Material für das Chansonbuch, das im Frühjahr herauskommen soll. Sobald ich von Laven Bescheid weiß, schreib ich Dir'. Joachim's continuing efforts on his friend's behalf did not come to anything, and presently Huchel would be in a position to enlist the support of much more influential figures than Joachim could hope to muster on his friend's behalf.

Breakthrough

Back to a Country in Crisis

Huchel and Dora Lassel returned to a Germany thrown into turmoil by the disastrous repercussions of the Wall Street crash. At a stroke, this single event shattered the hard-won, temporary stability of the Weimar Republic, to which it delivered a blow that would prove terminal as any remaining consensus for parliamentary democracy crumbled. From now on, literary as well as political life in Berlin was characterised by the increasingly desperate search for solutions amidst an atmosphere of crisis that gripped public life.

The experience of the four years leading up to Hitler's accession to the Chancellorship in January 1933 affected deeply the attitudes of that whole generation of German intellectuals to which Huchel belonged. A fundamental conviction that these years left behind in many of them was that capitalism and the system of liberal democracy that supported it simply would not work. The crash of 1929 was the final nail in the coffin after the chaos of civil war during the Republic's founding years and the sense of bewilderment that had accompanied the inflation of 1923. For many Berlin avant-gardist artists, among them Bertolt Brecht, the process of modernisation was itself not thereby called into question. For them, Marx had argued convincingly that the capitalist system would be replaced by communism, which would place humanity on a higher plane of political, economic and cultural development. Belief in the communist revolution was the new humanism of the anti-fascist Left. Not that such a higher plane of development could, many of them acknowledged, be achieved without violent revolutionary struggle. The example of the Russian Revolution was close to hand, yet uncomfortably close, too, was the escalating violence in Berlin between the radical Left and Right. Indeed, National Socialism, viewed by the Left as the final mutation of capitalism, was promoted relentlessly as the only genuinely 'German' answer both to the threat of communism and to the debacle that the Republic had become.

Huchel's response to these events differed from the radicals. Temperamentally, he was not given to the aggressive proclamation of revolutionary politics. The sum of his experiences had left him with an altogether more sceptical attitude towards the supposed benefits of modernisation, let alone the possible attainment of a higher plane of political, economic and cultural development within a reality as it was configured in Germany. Capitalism had clearly failed, he mistrusted the 'scientific' claims of the Marxists, and the sheer barbarity of the Nazis was wholly anathema. Feeding on his acquaintance with the follies of the old Prussian order, the failure of the German Republic bred in him, as in many others, a degree of cynicism towards public life, which, again quite typically, co-existed uneasily with a Utopian belief in a just society, however hopeless the situation might be in practice. As we have seen, Huchel's was the belief of the ethical idealist, of the unpolitical socialist, one of the many paradoxical phenomena of the age.[1] The Weimar years saw the proliferation of this particular phenomenon among politically non-aligned artists and intellectuals. Their essentially humanist beliefs, however, shaded ever more into a despair akin to that felt by many progressive writers of the *Biedermeierzeit* such as Büchner, Lenau and Hebbel, as the gulf between aspiration and reality yawned all the more alarmingly in a post-revolutionary age of cultural conservatism. Huchel's verse would increasingly reflect his affinity with the poets of the *Biedermeierzeit*.

In an early post-war account of his life, Huchel referred to his receipt of 'marxistischen Unterricht durch Dr. Sternberg und Dr. Ernst Bloch' following his return to Berlin from France.[2] It is highly unlikely that Huchel pursued any systematic study of Marxism with them, and this statement is in any case misleading as an index of Huchel's position in the early 1930s. An examination of his actions and statements in these years shows him putting some distance between himself and the politically active Marxist Left. Through his verse he brought to Berlin literary life something quite different, which appealed in many quarters as an apposite response to the crisis.

Willy Haas

During the final months of 1929 and early 1930, Huchel established the links that were vital for his breakthrough. Kantorowicz had returned to Berlin from Paris to work on the liberal *Vossische Zeitung*, the flagship of the Ullstein empire. From mid-1930, the *Vossische Zeitung* became one of his two major outlets, the other being *Die literarische Welt*. It was with the latter journal that Huchel forged his closest links. It was first published by Ernst Rowohlt in the mid-1920s as a liberal weekly designed to cover the spectrum of literary life and subsequently taken over by Rowohlt's editor, Willy Haas. Haas belonged to that circle of Prague Jewish intellectuals that included Kafka and Max Brod. Later, both Haas and Huchel recalled the beginning of a friendship in which Haas assumed the role of a father figure. Dora Huchel remembered the early 1930s as the time of Huchel's 'große Freundschaft' with Haas, though Huchel was on less good terms with Haas' business partner, Artur Rosen, who, as we have seen, was a notoriously bad payer.[3] Huchel's friendship with Haas would survive, generally at a distance, Haas' years of emigration and the Cold War, which saw them on different sides of the German divide. In a letter to Rolf Italiaander of 5 November 1956, Huchel generously acknowledged the great debt he owed to Haas for his friendship and guidance during the early 1930s, to which he attached seminal importance for his development,

> Alles, was mit Willy Haas zusammenhängt, ist mehr für mich als eine Erinnerung an
> wichtige Jahre, in denen man versuchte, zu sich selber zu gelangen. Nichts ist mit dieser

Zeit zu vergleichen. Ich verdanke Haas viel, ohne seinen Zuspruch wäre wohl manches falsch gegangen.[4]

For his part, Haas recalled in an essay published in 1968,

Es war in der zweiten Hälfte der zwanziger Jahre, als mich in der Redaktion der *Literarischen Welt* ... ein Brief und eine Sendung eines Mannes namens Peter Huchel erreichten, die mich auf das höchste erstaunten und gefangennahmen. Die Verse, die mir Peter Huchel sandten, waren bemerkenswert durch ihre vollkommene Durchdringung von Geist und Materie ... Ich sagte zu mir, daß man angesichts dieser Verse entscheiden müsse, und beschloß, daß ich alles, was er etwa noch schreiben würde und mir anvertraute, veröffentlichen würde.[5]

Like many others, upon meeting Huchel shortly afterwards Haas was won over by the young poet's charm and handsome features. Haas wrote in 1968 how, when they met in Hamburg in the 1950s, Huchel had recalled that

er sei damals als völlig unerfahrener Dichter in die Stadt gekommen, und jemand habe ihm gesagt, die *Literarische Welt* drucke auch Gedichte junger, unbekannter Dichter gerne ab. Daraufhin habe er ein paar Gedichte ausgesucht und an mich abgeschickt. Und diese Gedichte erschienen bald darauf. Damit habe er, was die Publizierung seiner Werke betraf, einstweilen ausgesorgt gehabt.[6]

Huchel was invited to visit Haas at his house in the Plötzensee area of Berlin. As we have seen, the charismatic Huchel made a lasting impression on Haas, who wrote, 'Er war sehr jung und so, wie ich ihn mir vorgestellt hatte – ein schöner, muskulöser Mann mit den Augen eines Dichters'.[7] Italiaander, Haas' secretary and librarian, offered a memorable portrait of the young poet, 'Huchel überraschte durch seine Erscheinung. Er trug an nackten Füßen Ledersandalen, war rustikal angezogen wie ein Waldarbeiter – eine absolut unliterarische Erscheinung. Was er sagte, gefiel auch mir. Er sprach über Naturerlebnisse und Mythologisches'.[8]

Huchel, ever the consummate stylist beneath the nonchalant exterior, was aware of what was at stake in his first major sortie into Berlin's fast-moving literary scene: in Haas he was after all associating with a figure who, for all his own firmly established personal tastes, really mattered in spotting new trends and promoting fresh talent. Huchel's appearance certainly did go against the grain of fashionable literary Berlin, where the artist had become the intellectual worker of industrial society, generally impoverished except for the successful few. For most people, private means had been wiped out in the inflation of the early 1920s, and like all other walks of life, the arts were subjected to the effects of unpredictable, though relentless waves of rationalisation and financial upheaval. The avant-gardist response to the pressures of modernisation was to ride the tiger, rejecting the grand, traditional image of the poet as sage and seer in favour of the writer as critical commentator employing the style of *Neue Sachlichkeit*, even as journalist and purveyor of reportage about the urban, industrial world. True, there was a plebeian element in the carefully cultivated Huchel image, yet otherwise he was the very antithesis of the highly fashionable Brechtian persona, the tough-talking, aggressive urban animal, driving fast cars, sporting shiny leather and cigars, and preferring the company of the boxing fraternity to established literary coteries. And Huchel's point was, of course, precisely that he wished to represent something sharply different again from all that. He paid Brecht a visit with Joachim in late 1929 and saw the Brecht circle go about their business.[9] Huchel possessed a copy of Brecht's *Hauspostille*, the collection of verse in which Brecht set about debunking the grandiose pretensions and mystique surrounding the calling of the poet.[10] Brecht offered instructions for the use of his poems by the reader rather than, in the manner of the great seers George and Rilke, trusting in the intuitive powers of disciples to follow the visionary's lead. In his 'Weihnachtslied', (i,67) published by Haas, Huchel experimented with a re-working of 'Vom Brot und den Kindlein', the opening poem in Brecht's collection. Yet, as we shall see, in his published poetry in the early 1930s Huchel presented himself rather as the practitioner of a distinctive strain of *Naturmagie*, which was predicated on the search for the sublime, not the debunking thereof.

Huchel was an intriguing new literary presence for Haas, who found it increasingly difficult to conceal his impatience with the posturings of leftist writers and intellectuals, as well as with the urban-oriented discourse that had come to dominate the Berlin literary scene. Its limitations were, in his view, being ruthlessly exposed in the crisis that was gripping German culture. Indeed, in May 1930 Haas wrote in his magazine a programmatic article entitled 'Restauration?', which was sharply critical of the literary Left. He announced his desire to change the magazine's editorial direction in response to the sea change in the cultural and political climate. He proposed the withdrawal of support from previously fashionable leftist literature and the cultivation of more traditional, 'bourgeois' values that were actually more in keeping with his own tastes. Haas' article begins,

> Man spricht überall in Literatenkreisen von der kulturellen und literarischen Reaktion in der letzten Saison. Die radikale Berliner Literatur fühlt den Boden unter den Füßen schwinden. Die Theater wollen weder von dem sich revolutionär gebärenden Pubertätsgebrülle, noch von der forschen Sozialreportage in wilhelminischem Schnarrton weiterhin etwas wissen. Es ist vorbei ... Der Kredit ist einmal zu Ende.[11]

Recommending a cultural retrenchment to 1914, in the sense of a return not so much to Expressionism but to a period of perceived political and social stability pre-dating the upheavals that followed, Haas concluded,

> Wir sind für die Wiederherstellung der natürlichen Gegensätze und Zusammenhänge, der natürlichen Struktur ... Die Funktionen des sogenannten 'Bürgertums' sind in diesem Zusammenhang von unabsehbarer Wichtigkeit ... Nach einer gewissen Zeit kehrt man eben automatisch in die letzte sichere zurückliegende Stellung zurück und verschanzt sich dort. Also in das Jahr 1914. Das ist es, was geschehen ist und geschieht. Wir glauben nicht, daß diese gesellschaftliche Funktion, die wir hier als 'bourgeois' definieren, jemals verschwinden wird. Wir *hoffen*, daß sie nicht verschwinden wird. Eine bürgerliche Kunst-Restauration *mußte* unter solchen Umständen eintreten: als wichtige Korrektur.

Haas could not at the time have imagined quite what depths of reaction would be spawned from the general, restorative cultural trend that he sought to harness for his magazine, albeit, one must say, with only limited success.

The following month, he published 'Kindheit in Alt-Langerwisch', the first of Huchel's poems to appear in *Die literarische Welt*. As we have seen, some of his urban verse from the mid-1920s such as 'Frühling im Stadtpark' and 'Frühling im Quartier' appeared, too. Yet, he had moved on and the mood of the age had changed dramatically. It was for his nature poetry and the verse of the Alt-Langerwisch childhood that Huchel became known, especially as in early 1931 he made the autobiographical link with that verse in the journal. Between 1930 and the end of 1932, 'Kindheit in Alt-Langerwisch' was followed by verse such as 'Die Kammer', 'September', 'Der Totenherbst', 'Die dritte Nacht April', 'Der Osterhase', 'Die schilfige Nymphe', 'Die Magd', 'Der Knabenteich', 'Mädchen im Mond', 'Märkischer Herbst', and 'Am Beifußhang'. The most significant of these publications have, for the most part, already been commented upon. Huchel's work typifies a literary trend identified by Anton Kaes. Kaes argues, 'Im Literarischen setzte sich um 1930 ein im Formalen wie Thematischen rückwärtsgewandter Traditionalismus durch, der vor allem der Lyrik zugute kam'.[12] According to Kaes, within the new restorative cultural climate many politically non-aligned intellectuals withdrew from the realm of political discourse into a private realm in which more conventional attitudes were struck and more traditional stylistic influences cultivated. Mythology, religion and nature gained in currency over the depiction of political and social processes.

One should not underestimate the depth of the conservative mood that gripped Germany in the years immediately before the Nazis came to power. In his short prose pieces written for Haas' journal together with Joachim, Huchel satirised the politics of the Right. Yet in his poetry Huchel's interests were served much less by political considerations than by a quite traditional understanding of the lyric poet's calling to convey subjective impressions and feelings within a vision shaped by mythology, religion and nature. Huchel's sympathy with the Left became an increasingly remote issue, the more he followed the path recommended by Haas as he cultivated his poetic talent and vision. When confronted with the stark alternative of politics or poetry, there could be no question but that the poet would choose poetry. The adoption of this stance was, moreover, undoubtedly linked to the changes in his personal circumstances which took place following the return to Berlin.

Marriage

The return to Germany took Huchel to the threshold of fundamental choices about his private life as well as his vocation as a poet. After four years together with Dora Lassel, difficult decisions were looming, however much the couple, and particularly Huchel, were inclined to put off such thoughts. In addition, after eleven semesters of nominal study Huchel had nothing to show his parents. His father's hope that he would embark on a professional career was as remote from realisation as it had even been. For Huchel, however, the student lifestyle had now run its course.

For her part, Dora Lassel at the time intended to complete her studies in Berlin, while her family's wish was that she should take her exams in Bucharest. Although she and Huchel stayed with his parents at Teltowerstraße, she still wished to keep her relationship a secret from her parents. Accordingly, she used Wilma Papst's address at Sybelstraße when she wrote home and announced her intention to stay in Germany. The Lassels had surely long suspected that she was involved in a serious relationship and, faced with their unhappiness over a situation in which she was drifting right off the course mapped out for her (the second year in Paris was an indulgence they were prepared to sanction, but why then return to Berlin?), she travelled home in late November 1929 in an attempt to explain her situation. In 1981, she stated that she and Huchel had arranged that he should meanwhile write, informing her parents of their relationship and that they wished to stay together. The Lassels sought to dissuade their daughter from the course of action on which she was embarked, arguing that she had not thought things through. Huchel's earliest surviving letters to Dora Lassel, from December 1929 shortly after her departure from Potsdam, relate to this delicate situation.[13]

The letters, which were still at this stage signed Helmut, are written in a simple, generally correct French, perhaps in order to protect their content from prying eyes. They are informed by a playful tone not so far removed from Joachim's in his correspondence with Huchel. The first was written in Berlin, at the flat of their friend Wilhelm Blaß, with whom Huchel had shared in Vienna. He expressed his sorrow at the thought of Dora's room in Potsdam, in which they had said goodbye. He reported that together with Joachim he had paid a visit the previous evening to

Döblin and Brecht. He urged her to draw strength from the thought that in two weeks, after Christmas, they would, as arranged, be back together in Potsdam. In the second letter, signed, too, by Joachim and another person, who went by the name of Lala, he offered further words of comfort and encouragement. Clearly referring to the future of their relationship, he stated that he had not yet written to her parents; he was awaiting news from Dora and her father. They had to hope for the best. In this way, Huchel at this stage committed himself to nothing, leaving it up to Dora Lassel to deal with her parents alone.

Meanwhile, in Kronstadt Eugen Lassel, too, played for time. His daughter was not, however, prepared to accept her parents' advice. Without their agreement and using money that Huchel had borrowed from a friend, she fled Kronstadt and travelled back to Potsdam by train, returning more or less at the time they had agreed. There could be no more prevarication. Dora Huchel describes what then happened,

> Huchel schrieb an meine Eltern, worauf mein Vater ankam und die Situation sondierte, nicht ohne daß sich beim Kennenlernen von Huchels Eltern unbeschreiblich komische Situationen ergaben. Von 'Helmut' Huchel war mein Vater sehr angetan und unterhielt sich mit ihm sehr angeregt und erklärte sich außerdem bereit, uns auch nach Kräften finanziell zu unterstützen. Alles endete höchst friedlich. Im März 1930 Standesamt und zu Ostern in Kronstadt kirchliche Trauung.

Eugen Lassel travelled first to Berlin and went to Wilma Papst's, where he had been directed by his daughter, who was continuing to maintain the pretence that she was living at Sybelstraße. Wilma Papst sent a telegram Dora and Huchel in Potsdam and they took the next train into the city. Neither Huchel nor Dora Lassel set any great store by the convention of marriage and had certainly not made any such plans. However, Eugen Lassel's paternal authority introduced quite a new and indeed decisive factor, since he could not conceive any other course of action if they wished to share their lives. The offer of financial support was surely not at all unattractive, since it provided a basis upon which, without any financial pressure, his future son-in-law could pursue the literary career in which a breakthrough was now imminent. Marriage on those terms, however, also meant the end of plans for Dora to pursue a teaching career. It was almost as an afterthought that Huchel introduced his parents to Eugen Lassel. In 1981, Dora Huchel recalled that Fritz Huchel had not felt able to receive such a high-ranking guest without the aid of some libation but that this had done little to improve the quality of communication. It was none the less agreed that the civil ceremony should take place in Potsdam before the couple, but not Huchel's parents, travelled to Kronstadt for a ceremony to be conducted by Eugen Lassel in his church, St Bartholomew's. In the meantime, Dora Lassel did indeed go to live with Wilma Papst at Sybelstraße.[14]

A civil ceremony was arranged at the Potsdam registry office on 8 March 1930.[15] Dora Huchel described the occasion in 1981. None of her family attended, nor, indeed, did Huchel's father. Quite why Fritz Huchel was not present is unclear. It was only at the last minute that they considered the fact that they needed witnesses, and a female acquaintance was pressed into service alongside Marie Huchel. The Huchels' marriage certificate includes as first witness 'die Büroangestellte Alice Richter ... 23 Jahre alt, wohnhaft in Potsdam, im Bogen 22'. Dora Huchel is described as a student, while Huchel confidently stated his profession as 'Schriftsteller'. The only other creature present was, it seems, the Huchels' dog, which obliged with a sudden bark when the ceremony was over.

Kronstadt

Not long after the registry office wedding in Potsdam, the newly-weds set off for Kronstadt, travelling by train via Prague and Budapest. This was the beginning of a new adventure for Huchel as he got to know at first hand South Eastern Europe, of which he had heard from his wife. In the 1984 edition, the events of this period in Huchel's life, which, of course, includes his marriage and honeymoon, are summarised as follows, '1929-31 Reisen nach Ungarn, Rumänien, in die Türkei. 1930 Huchel heiratet in Potsdam Dorothea Lassel aus Kronstadt, Siebenbürgen'. (i,459) Through this manner of presentation, which also pre-dates events by a year, no connection is made between Huchel's travels and his marriage. Here as elsewhere when dealing with the circumstances of his life relating to his first marriage, the edition – which merely follows conventional wisdom – is highly misleading.

The journey to Kronstadt was the first of a number of visits to the Lassel family that Huchel would undertake with his wife in the 1930s, when they used Kronstadt as a base to explore Romania. It was, no doubt, a matter of some relief to him that none of his relatives undertook the journey to attend the church wedding, which took place at St Bartholomew's on 21 April 1930. Everything had been organised to give the Lassels' daughter the best possible send-off for her future life in Berlin. The whole congregation had assembled to see Reverend Lassel marry his daughter and to cast an eye over the groom. This time they had 'proper' witnesses, Dora Lassel's best friend and her husband. The service was followed by a reception at the Lassels' house, Am Roßmarkt 14. After a meal gramophone music was played and a professional photographer captured the occasion. A surviving wedding photo shows that the couple approached the occasion in a light-hearted fashion. Dora Huchel poked her tongue out at the grinning Huchel as the photo was being taken, while Huchel's clothing indicates a certain lack of regard for convention: he had borrowed a suit from Alfred Kantorowicz which was too short in the leg and not the best of fits at other points. A photograph from the following day shows the newly-weds having a meal with the Lassels and Dora's female witness.[16]

In addition to pledging their financial support for the marriage, the Lassels also paid for the honeymoon and a stay in Kronstadt, which lasted until September. The honeymoon – described in the 1984 edition simply as travel in Romania and Turkey! – is recalled by Dora Huchel as follows,

> Meine Eltern schenkten uns eine herrliche Reise mit Aufenthalt in Sinaia, Bukarest, Baltschik, Konstantinopel, dort im Hotel mit Schutzhimmel gegen allerlei Stechmücken. 'Hellmut' Wasserpfeife geraucht, im Schwarzen- und Marmarameer (Prinzeninseln) gebadet und natürlich die Touristenattraktionen die Heulenden und Tanzenden Derwische nicht versäumt – eine Traumreise. Zurück nach Kronstadt. Von Kronstadt aus Ausflüge nach allen Richtungen und natürlich tausend Einladungen. Zwischendurch mit Kleidungs-stücken ausgestattet und in den Koffern die tollsten Delikatessen des Landes, so gings im September zurück nach Berlin-Potsdam.

Dora Huchel's account of the honeymoon certainly contrasts sharply with the prevailing image of these *Wanderjahre* later cultivated by Huchel and reproduced by critics as a life of toil, adventure and some deprivation spent on the margin of legality.[17] For the duration of the honeymoon, the Bohemian lifestyle was replaced by the standards and style of the moneyed middle classes into which Huchel had married. In 1981 Dora Huchel recollected other details of their honeymoon. The short trip from Kronstadt to Sinaia took them to a prestigious spa and skiing resort in the southern Carpathian Mountains. They visited the sights, which included the summer seat of the Romanian monarchy. From there they travelled via Bucharest to Balçik on the Black Sea coast of Bulgaria. This place figures both in 'Europa neunzehnhunderttraurig' and in the title of the post-war poem 'Schlucht bei Baltschik', (i,125) which was composed following Huchel's return to the place with his second wife in 1957. From Balçik they travelled north to the larger port of Konstanta, also mentioned in 'Europa neunzehnhunderttraurig'. In Konstanta, they boarded the ferry for Istanbul, where they explored the intersection of European and Asian culture that the city represents. From there they returned directly to Kronstadt. In the summer months the town was ideal for the exploration of the mountainous regions that surround it.

While they were in Kronstadt, Huchel followed up Willy Haas' offer to publish in *Die literarische Welt* and also placed his first poem in the *Vossische Zeitung*. 'Wiese bei Corenc', which appeared in the *Vossische Zeitung* on 1 June 1930 without Dora's knowledge, is an intriguing choice, demonstrating that Huchel had not yet forgiven his wife. 'Kindheit in Alt-Langerwisch' followed almost immediately afterwards in *Die literarische Welt*, on 6 June 1930. These were

Huchel's first publications for over four years. With 'Kindheit in Alt-Langerwisch', Huchel released into the public sphere his first poem of childhood, which would provide the basis for the myth of his rural upbringing, upon which he would henceforth elaborate.

Berlin

Following their return to Germany in September 1930, the Huchels lived initially with his parents in Potsdam. They then rented a studio flat for a while on the Kurfürstendamm, 'acht Minuten zu Fuß, linke Seite von der Gedächniskirche aus, im Dachgeschoß mit lauter Glas', as Dora Huchel put it in 1981. It consisted of a 'Riesenraum, getrennt mit einem bessarabischen Teppich'. They had 'ganz primitive Möbel, Kisten als Schreibtisch. Teppiche hatten wir. Wir haben ein Fest gefeiert mit ganz primitiven aber attraktiven Mitteln. Joachim war auf dem Fest und eine siebenbürgische Pianistin'. They had arrived back in Bohemia. Yet the mood was darkening following the Nazis' election success on 14 September.

At the beginning of 1931, they moved into a large flat on the Bülowplatz, not far from the Alexanderplatz, which they shared with their close friends Kantorowicz, Joachim and Wilma Papst. All five were in their late twenties or early thirties. Wilma Papst was completing her doctorate on Frege at the Friedrich Wilhelm University,[18] while Dora Huchel had now abandoned her studies and career plans for a life as the poet's wife supported by her family. All three men were seeking to establish themselves in the literary life of the German capital. Kantorowicz, the most gregarious, had already done much to make a name for himself. He continued to work on the arts pages of the *Vossische Zeitung* and was instrumental in introducing Huchel to individuals and circles who would play roles in his literary development as well as in his private life. Meanwhile, Joachim had begun to publish essays of his literary criticism in the *Neue Rundschau*. Recalling their earlier conversations in Paris and on Bréhat, Kantorowicz later wrote of their development by the early 1930s, 'Die zwei Jahre hatten uns verändert, unsere Gespräche waren bewußter, gereifter, weniger weltschmerzlich als auf Bréhat'.[19] As Kantorowicz noted in his diary, the carefree Parisian lifestyle was a far cry from a Berlin in the grip of a protracted political crisis, the resolution of which many anticipated in the most apocalyptic terms.

While Huchel was living on the Bülowplatz, he began to place short prose texts in *Die literarische Welt*. These texts, a number of which have been examined above, are isolated examples of prose in Huchel's *oeuvre*. All were written in response to Haas' wish to have work from him. A number were produced for short, topical series run by the magazine. Huchel later recalled that these texts had been 'verbessert und umgearbeitet' (ii,405) by Joachim, and in conversation with Kundera he went so far as to state that they were not his prose.[20] It is impossible ultimately to determine how great Joachim's input was; at the very least he was involved in editing the work that Huchel produced. The prose pieces do nothing to undermine the accepted view that Huchel's gift lay with the lyric and, to some extent, with the dramatic dialogues of his radio plays. Their significance lies primarily in their presentation of autobiographical materials and in their distance from the politics of both the Nazis and the KPD. Indeed, it is difficult to countenance that Huchel would have permitted publication of the statement with which he concluded 'Europa neunzehnhunderttraurig' in January 1931 if it had been at variance with his political stance. The statement reads,

> Dieses wird nicht das beste sein. Denn er hat sich nicht an dem Start nach Unterschlupf beteiligt. Seine Altersgenossen sitzen im Parteibüro, und manchmal geben sie sogar zu, daß es aus irgendeiner Ecke her nicht gut riecht. Immerhin, sie haben ihr Dach über dem Kopf. Aber da ihm selbst die marxistische Würde nicht zu Gesicht steht, wird er sich unter aussichtslosem Himmel weiterhin einregnen lassen. Sie winken aus der Arche der Partei, und er versteht ihren Zuruf. Der lautet: 'Wir können dir an Hand des Unterbaues nachweisen, daß du absacken wirst, ohne eine Lücke zu hinterlassen'. Aber dagegen hat er nicht viel einzuwenden, nichts zu erwidern. Sie müssen es wissen; denn sie haben die Wissenschaft. Doch unterdessen schlägt sein Herz privat weiter. Und er lebt ohne Entschuldigung. (ii,218)

Both in what he said and in the manner in which he said it, Huchel put clear water between himself and the politics of the Marxist Left. Indeed, in the early 1930s Huchel gravitated increasingly towards what from a 1920s avant-gardist point of view looked like a rather traditional humanist position, in which he placed poetry above the chaos of politics. This would lead to a parting of ways with Kantorowicz before 1933. In the immediate post-war period such differences were forgotten or glossed over, at least for a while.

Kladow

After a number of months spent living in the centre of the city on the Bülowplatz, the Huchels and Kantorowicz opted to spend the summer beyond the city's western boundary at the village of Kladow on the west bank of the Havel. Kantorowicz later wrote, 'Dann folgte ein Sommer in einem kleinen Gärtnerhaus in Kladow am Wannsee bei Berlin, das Huchel mit seiner Frau Dora und ich gemeinsam bewohnten'.[21] Photos show Huchel working outside near outbuildings and walking on the woodland path in his swimming costume and leather sandals. The address was Waldvilla Kühn on Kirchweg.[22] Dora Huchel recalled visits from, among others, Joachim, who married Gerta Aufrichtig, a graphic artist, and Haas. A photograph shows Haas' car outside the Kladow house, which was a little more than the small 'Gärtnerhaus' of Kantorowicz's memory.[23]

As their friendship developed, Huchel, along with Joachim, was invited by Haas to help out in the editorial offices. Huchel later acknowledged that with Haas he had served the apprenticeship in editorial work which would stand him in such good stead when he came to edit *Sinn und Form*. It would be far from the truth, however, to suggest that Huchel entered into a 'eine feste Arbeitsverbindung'. (ii,405) In conversation with Kundera, when he used the term 'feste Verbindung', Huchel also pointed out that before 1945 he was never an employee.[24] In the early 1930s, he enjoyed a degree of financial independence which made employment as such unnecessary. In the offices of *Die literarische Welt* he did, however, learn the editorial ropes and come into contact with many figures who then and later played a prominent role in Berlin literary life. In this way, Huchel built up an extraordinary range of friends and acquaintances, upon whom he would be able to draw as a support network during the Third Reich, whom after the war he would exploit to such effect with Radio Berlin and *Sinn und Form* and upon whom he would, finally, be able to rely when the going got tough in the GDR and he left for the West.

In 1973, Huchel claimed that Ernst Bloch had shared the house in Kladow with them and at the time he also got to know Walter Benjamin and Arthur Koestler.[25] Bloch can be more aptly described as a visitor. Like Benjamin and Koestler, Bloch knew Kantorowicz and contributed to *Die literarische Welt*, where he would by now quite possibly have bumped into Huchel. Though the phlegmatic Huchel tended to wait for others to come to him rather than to seize the initiative himself, Haas was someone whose company he actively sought. In 1959, he recalled what his visits to Haas' house had meant for him. Haas had shown him his 'herrliche Bibliothek, und ich nun wußte, mit welcher Art von unsterblicher Literatur Sie sich beschäftigten'. (ii,299) And certainly, as we shall see, we can trace in Huchel's poetry an ever closer engagement with the German lyric tradition. Haas it was, too, who supplied Huchel with the motif for his poetry, which he took over from St Augustine, ' ... im großen Hof meines Gedächtnisses. Daselbst sind mir Himmel, Erde und Meer gegenwärtig ... '. (i,112) Huchel first made use of the phrase the following year in a radio talk, in which he introduced his poetry. In the post-war period he frequently returned to it, using it as a motto for *Chausseen Chausseen* as well as linking it quite explicitly with Friedrich Zimmermann's 'Hof' of his childhood memories.

Walter Benjamin's diary from the summer of 1931 records a visit to Haas' house, where he also found Artur Rosen and Huchel. Benjamin wrote of the occasion,

Am 16. August bei [Willy] Haas. Es ergab sich da in der kleinen, dem Hause vorgebauten Glasveranda – anwesend waren die Frau, Tritsch, [Artur] Rosen und [Peter] Huchel – ein

Gespräch, aus dem mir einiges des Festhaltens wert scheint. Indem ich von der Protestversammlung gegen die Zensur, die in den Schubertsälen am dreizehnten stattgefunden hatte, berichtete, ergab sich die naheliegende Aussprache über Marxismus und Kunst. Dabei konnte ich nun die Dialektik dieses Verhältnisses entwickeln. Ich stellte zwei Thesen auf, die seit jeher – genauer seit dem Aufgang des Kapitalismus – mit einander im Streit liegen:

die Kunst dem Volke die Kunst den Kennern.[26]

Huchel thus heard Benjamin expounding his ideas, as Benjamin argued first that, on the face of it, everything pointed towards the superiority of the latter thesis, since an art directed at the undifferentiated appetite of consumers instead of the critical participation of the well-informed very soon had a brutalizing effect. Employing imagery of culinary art in a similar manner to his friend Brecht, Benjamin illustrated the point with reference to the novel, arguing that the time had long gone when that food contained any nourishment and that the 'Volkstümlichkeit' of art, which was primarily represented by the popular novel, had long ago lost any productive or nourishing element. The Romantics' bold attempts to make the novel suitable reading for literary *cognoscenti* had robbed it of any 'Volkstümlichkeit'. Benjamin went on to argue that in any thriving literature there could be found a whole lot of different positions between the extremes of 'volkstümlich' and esoteric writing, which made for a inner continuity within a literary culture irrespective of sales figures and success. Yet such a situation, Benjamin argued, was wholly absent in Germany, so that work based on new forms of art with reference to the proletarian way of life and its linguistic forms posed an insoluble problem. He suggested that one might go so far as to say that the problem was no longer susceptible to formulation. This was, in Benjamin's view, the background to the present crisis in art and to calls on the Left for its abolition and replacement by journalism. Benjamin saw the remorseless assimilation of literature by the press as part of a dialectical process which represented the demise of writing within the existing social system and foreshadowed its re-establishment in a new system, features of which could already be discerned in what Benjamin viewed as the pre-revolutionary situation of Germany in mid-1931.

Benjamin's diary entry suggests less a conversation than that he expounded his ideas in order to seek a reaction from the others. Their responses are, unfortunately, not recorded. It would be hard to imagine Huchel, who was more a 'good listener', engaging in exhaustive theoretical debate with Benjamin. In addition, we know from other things written by Haas at that time that, while he was interested in the ideas of Benjamin and others on the Left – and indeed published them in his journal – he did not share their Marxist analysis. A similar point can be made about Huchel, as is demonstrated by the analysis of his published poetry and the poetics

that he espoused the following year on the radio. Through his encounters with
Benjamin and Bloch during the early 1930s, Huchel certainly became conversant
with the arguments of those Berlin intellectuals who were exploring the possible
interface between Marxist theory and aesthetic practice. If they had little bearing
upon his own practice as a poet at that time, he would not forget these conversations
and their writings when in the post-war period he had an opportunity to publish
Benjamin, Bloch and, indeed, Brecht, too, in *Sinn und Form*.

If in the early 1930s, Huchel's lyrical practice remained unaffected by the
ideas of Marxist theoreticians, then that was not least because he was enriching his
poetic voice through his immersion in the German lyrical tradition. Dora Huchel
recalled the summer in Kladow as an extremely productive period when many
compositions were begun, if not, as was Huchel's way, always completed. She and
Kantorowicz concur in their memory that it was in the village setting by the Havel
that Huchel wrote one of his finest poems 'Oktoberlicht', (i,60) which was
anthologised the following year in Ludwig Goldscheider's *Die schönsten deutschen
Gedichte*, as well as in Martin Raschke's *Neue lyrische Anthologie*.[27] In 1981, Dora
Huchel drew attention to the importance of Hebbel's famous 'Herbstbild' for
Huchel's composition. 'Herbstbild' reads,

> Dies ist ein Herbsttag, wie ich keinen sah!
>
> Die Luft ist still, als atmete man kaum,
>
> Und dennoch fallen raschelnd, fern und nah,
>
> Die schönsten Früchte ab von jedem Baum.
>
>
> O stört sie nicht, die Feier der Natur!
>
> Dies ist die Lese, die sie selber hält,
>
> Denn heute löst sich von den Zweigen nur,
>
> Was vor dem milden Strahl der Sonne fällt.

Huchel's response was a poem of three stanzas, each of eight lines, which elaborated
upon the autumnal scene with a richness of nature imagery and an eye for detail,
nuance and connections in a tableau 'frozen' in the last glorious sunlight of the
autumn. 'Oktoberlicht' is surely one of Huchel's lasting contributions to the German
lyric,

> Oktober, und die letzte Honigbirne
>
> hat nun zum Fallen ihr Gewicht,
>
> die Mücke im Altweiberzwirne
>
> schmeckt noch wie Blut das letzte Licht,

das langsam saugt das Grün des Ahorns aus,
als ob der Baum von Spinnen stürbe,
mit Blättern, zackig wie die Fledermaus,
gesiedet von der Sonne mürbe.

Durchsüßt ist jedes Sterben von der Luft,
vom roten Rauch der Gladiolen,
bis in den Schlaf der Schwalben wird der Duft
die Traurigkeit des Lichts einholen,
bis in den Schlaf der satten Ackermäuse
poltet die letzte Walnuß ein,
die braun aus schwarzgrünem Gehäuse
ans Licht sprang als ein süßer Stein.

Oktober, und den Bastkorb voll und pfündig
die Magd in Spind und Kammer trägt,
der Garten, nur von ihrem Pflücken windig,
hat sich ins müde Laub gelegt,
und was noch zuckt im weißen Spinnenzwirne,
es flöge gern zurück ins Licht,
das sich vom Ast die letzte Birne,
den süßen Gröps des Herbstes bricht.

Huchel takes over from Hebbel much of the imagery as well as the theme of the autumnal fruit harvest, and then extends and transforms them within his own vision. The intricate interweaving of the imagery of final light and life in the autumn scene, within a rhythmical pattern of sounds gently falling away to signal the onset of death, demonstrates that by now Huchel had acquired a voice to rank with those of past masters. 'Havelnacht', which we shall examine presently, was a composition of similar quality to 'Oktoberlicht', displaying the consummate creative vision that Huchel was now able to articulate. These poems no longer strain to achieve the sublime prophetic voice of 'Die Insel Aloe'. Instead, they represent a lyrical subjectivity at once more subdued and controlled, and with that they maintain a tone in keeping with Huchel's lyrical antecedents in the *Biedermeierzeit*. The mood and lyrical achievements of this earlier period of post-revolutionary authoritarianism would increasingly strike a chord with Huchel, who, like many others, saw the mood of his own time reflected in it. And this was certainly the way that Haas saw it when he reviewed Huchel's work along with that of other young poets the following year.

The *Kolonne* Prize

Through the publication of his poetry about childhood in *Die literarische Welt* and the *Vossische Zeitung*, Huchel struck a chord with a Berlin reading public that, as Haas had said, was looking for something other than literature as reportage. Almost overnight, his distinctive brand of *Naturmagie*, which evoked a world far removed from the chaos of contemporary life, became decidedly fashionable. Oda Schaefer recalled Huchel's sudden rise from obscurity in her mémoirs,

> Er wirkte damals ausgesprochen elegant, zu dieser Zeit wurde er von Berlin W hofiert, den
>
> Intellektuellen und den Snobs. Jedenfalls war er in Mode gekommen durch Willy Haas, der
>
> ihn entdeckt und in der 'Literarischen Welt' seine Mondgedichte gedruckt hatte. Huchel
>
> war schlagartig bekannt geworden.[28]

Schaefer met Huchel – 'ein junger Mann, männlich und schön, der uns aus seinen dunklen, unergründlichen Augen aufmerksam betrachtete'[29] – at Ludwig Meidner's apartment at Seesenstraße 30, near Halensee station. As ever, Huchel spoke very little. Like so many other Berlin artists and poets, Huchel was portrayed by Meidner. The portrait, which shows Huchel with rather full facial features, stayed in his possession until his death.

Schaefer and her husband Horst Lange both contributed to the journal *Die Kolonne*, which had been founded in 1929 by Lange's friend Martin Raschke and his co-editor, A.Artur Kuhnert. Published in Dresden by Wolfgang Jess, the journal had established a reputation as a forum for new verse by up-and-coming poets, among them Günter Eich, Elisabeth Langgässer, Georg von der Vring, Eberhard Meckel, W.E.Süskind, Willi Schäferdiek, Hermann Kasack and Jürgen Eggebrecht. Some of them would presently become Huchel's friends as he joined them among the contributors. Literary historians have attributed to *Die Kolonne* a key place in the regeneration of the German lyric.[30] There is little difficulty in integrating the journal within the climate of cultural restoration described by Haas in 1930, to which many politically non-aligned intellectuals had responded. The programmatic opening article of *Die Kolonne* from 1929, which was probably written by Raschke, states,

> Aber noch immer leben wir von Acker und Meer, und die Himmel, sie reichen auch über
>
> die Stadt. Noch immer lebt ein großer Teil der Menschheit in ländlichen Verhältnissen, und
>
> es entspringt nicht müßiger Traditionsfreude, wenn ihm Regen und Kälte wichtiger sind
>
> als ein Dynamo, der nie Korn reifte.[31]

The journal thus set itself firmly against the literary fashions of the 1920s in Berlin, which had seen the politicisation of the arts, as well as a focus on the city and the proletariat by writers who had come increasingly to view their calling in terms akin to journalism. Reportage was rejected by the editors of *Die Kolonne* as unworthy of a genuine poet, who should seek his company among the greats of the tradition. It would be a mistake, whatever became of the *Kolonne* Circle in Nazi Germany, to overlook the fact that the *Kolonne* programme distinguished the journal's position not only from the literary fashions of the Left but also from the 'völkisch' authors of the radical Right. Like Haas, the *Kolonne* was looking to re-establish the centrality of poetry written within a recognisably 'bourgeois' tradition that had been rather lost from sight since 1914. This involved the cultivation of the German lyric through its high points in the eighteenth and nineteenth centuries, a position towards which Huchel himself had been gravitating. The most recent point of orientation in such a post-Expressionist enterprise was provided by the neo-Romantic style of the turn of the century. This proved attractive for many young poets at the time, Huchel too, as verse such as 'Der glückliche Garten' attests, whose opening lines read, 'Einst waren wir alle im glücklichen Garten,/ ich weiß nicht mehr vor welchem Haus,/ wo wir die kindliche Stimme sparten/ für Gras und Amsel, Kamille und Strauß'. Such verse looked quite at home on the pages of *Die Kolonne*, where, indeed, 'Der glückliche Garten' was first published in 1932.

The prolific Raschke was the sort of writer who through his editorship sought to exert an influence on the direction of literary fashion. An instrument for doing this was the *Kolonne* prize for poetry, which was established in 1931. The first competition was won by the Austrian Guido Zernatto, whose work was selected from 566 entries. The second competition was announced in the fourth number of 1931 (July/August), with a closing date of 10 November, which was, however, put back to 10 December. In conjunction with Wolfgang Jess, *Die Kolonne* offered a first prize of 300 marks. The winner would be given further opportunities for publication with Jess: Raschke was to edit an anthology of new verse and a collection of the winner's poetry would appear in Jess' series 'Junge Reihe'. The series had been established in 1930 with Eich's *Gedichte* and Raschke's *Himmelfahrt zu Erde*. The outcome of the competition would be announced in the first number of 1932 (January/February).

In winning the second *Kolonne* prize for poetry, Huchel enjoyed his first great success. He was, of course, delighted at this achievement, yet he later almost totally obscured that delight by the manner in which he distanced himself from the *Kolonne* prize. He later played down any links with Raschke in particular and *Die Kolonne* in general. After the war, he was more comfortable with his links with *Die literarische Welt* than with *Die Kolonne*. This is partly due to the conservative associations of certain of the members of the *Kolonne* Circle. Potentially much more embarrassing was what became of the *Kolonne* Circle during the Third Reich, a story that has only in recent years begun to emerge. In an interview with Joseph

Dolan, Huchel dismissed Raschke as a snob.[32] In a letter to Vieregg, Huchel wrote, 'Zur *Kolonne* habe ich niemals gehört, es war ein reiner Zufall, daß ich den Preis erhielt'. (ii,358) He enlarged upon this statement in 1973,

> Das war eigentlich ein reiner Zufall. Hans A. Joachim, mein damaliger Mentor, er war zwei Jahre älter als ich, hatte ohne mein Wissen einige Gedichte für das erste Lyrikpreis-ausschreiben der *Kolonne* eingereicht und erhielt sie nach Wochen kommentarlos zurück. Ich wußte gar nichts davon. Joachim ärgerte sich aber so sehr darüber, daß er zum zweiten Preisausschreiben des Lyrikpreisausschreibens der *Kolonne* dieselben Gedichte nochmal einschickte, die diesmal mit dem ersten Preis ausgezeichnet wurden.[33]

Huchel told broadly the same story to Dolan. In 1981, Dora Huchel stated that she had no recollection of the role attributed to Joachim; Huchel had sent in the verse himself. In Dolan's opinion, Huchel was clearly at pains during their interview to distance himself from *Die Kolonne* and to align himself instead with Marxists such as Bloch, whom, in the same letter to Vieregg referred to above, Huchel described as 'mein väterlicher Freund'. (ii,358) In Dolan's view – and this is surely the case – Huchel was seeking through such statements 'to establish a certain continuity in his political attitudes which led him from the Weimar Republic, through the Third Reich and into the GDR'.[34]

Further light is shed on the issue by the recent discovery among Raschke's papers of Huchel's correspondence with him.[35] On 28 September 1931, Huchel sent a letter to Raschke from Kladow. He was deeply apologetic about his behaviour in not responding to Raschke's earlier letter. He explained his silence through reference to his uncertainty about his poetry. He assured Raschke that he intended to participate in the *Kolonne* competition. He asked Raschke to let him know what the closing date was for entries. He hoped that there would still be some time for him; he was in the process of moving to Berlin.

Whatever role Joachim may or may not have played in the earlier competition, in the autumn of 1931 Huchel dealt with the matter himself. As we have seen, later there was more at stake than false modesty. His success in winning the first prize of 300 marks (Horst Lange was second) from 547 entries was announced early in 1932. The news reached Eugen Lassel just before his death in January of that year. It was on that occasion that Huchel composed his poem 'Requiem' that was first published in 1984. (i,36) In 1981, Dora Huchel recalled that Huchel's success was her father's last moment of joy. Five poems that Huchel had submitted were published in the January/ February number of *Die Kolonne*. The poems were preceded by a brief biographical note, which drew on information supplied by Huchel. It included the statement 'Kindheit in der Mark', with which for the first time Huchel moved beyond the rather indeterminate expressions of 'Europa neunzehnhunderttraurig'.

Raschke took over the statement for his essay that accompanied the poems. They were typical products of his development since the mid-1920s: 'Der glückliche Garten'; 'Die dritte Nacht April'; 'Die Magd'; 'Oktoberlicht'; and 'Der Totenherbst'. 'Die Kammer' and 'Der Knabenteich' appeared in the next number and six poems were included in Raschke's *Neue lyrische Anthologie* of September 1932.[36] Dolan's analysis of Huchel's poems published in *Die Kolonne* concludes that his work was quite in keeping with the aims of the journal. He argues that within the historical context 'we find that Huchel has placed himself, wittingly or unwittingly, and in contrast to the idea of continuity Huchel apparently wishes to foster – in the company of conservatives'.[37] Dolan rightly cautions against grouping Huchel's wistful, elegiac verse with the outpourings of the radical Right, and one might here re-affirm that Huchel's lyrical project was rather of the order of a search for stability, for a cultural restoration of the centre in order to overcome a brittle sense of self and the chaos of the present. Yet, of course, there was little remaining of the centre, upon which to build, and it was fundamental to the attractiveness of Huchel's work that it subtly reflected this very uncertainty, too.

It was as an expression of the new restorative fashion, to which Raschke himself subscribed, that Raschke understood Huchel's verse in the 'Laudatio' which accompanied the news of Huchel's success. One critic, following Huchel's post-war statements, has suggested that Raschke excluded reference to the dimension of social concern to be found in Huchel's verse.[38] Yet the poems which Huchel submitted as representative of his best work do not contain such a dimension. The rural population is not depicted as oppressed and suffering but as part of an authentic community. By the same token, these poems are indeed representative of the poetry which Huchel selected for publication in the early 1930s. Raschke's appreciation focuses on the recovery of childhood memories in Huchel's verse and concludes,

> Unablässig ruft Huchel mit erinnerungsträchtigen Worten diese Zeit zurück, und sie ersteht bisweilen vor uns in gültigen Bildern, Trost über die endlose Individuation alles Werdenden. So ist die Welt Peter Huchels alles andere als gestrig, als ländlich in einem herkömmlichen Sinne, wenngleich er sich hergekommener Vokabeln bedient; sie ist von unserem Blute, à la recherche du temps perdu wie alles menschliche Bemühen von jeher.[39]

Yet, Raschke's piece itself is marked by certain reservations, which cannot altogether have pleased Huchel, not least because Raschke detected an artificiality about some of the poems which were purportedly an authentic expression of childhood memories. For Raschke, 'die Worte wurden zu Drogen. Sie erzeugen, richtig ausgesprochen, im Dichtenden und in dem gleichgestimmten Leser einen rauschartigen Zustand des Verbundenseins mit dem Urgrund aller Wesen, eingehüllt in einen dumpfen sinnlichen Geruch'. Yet the inducement of this state of mind requires ever greater doses, giving the impression that 'es sei nicht mehr von Natur, sondern eben nur von Drogen die Rede'. Although he acknowledges Huchel's rural upbringing as the basis for his poetry and thus, finally, absolves him of the charge of artificiality, Raschke comes perilously close here to seeing through Huchel and hence undermining the sense of self that the poet was cultivating in Berlin literary life. From January 1932, he had in his pocket an agreement with Wolfgang Jess to publish his first collection of verse.

The Artists' Colony

The house in Kladow was intended only as a temporary summer residence, though the Huchels stayed there well into the autumn. Kantorowicz writes, 'Im Herbst 1931 zogen Huchel und ich von Kladow aus in die sogenannte Künstlerkolonie am Laubenheimer Platz in Berlin-Wilmersdorf'.[40] Like Kantorowicz, the Huchels had applied for a flat in accommodation then under construction by the Bühnengenossen- schaft and the Schutzverband deutscher Schriftsteller (SDS), the writers' organisation that Huchel joined in the years immediately before 1933.[41] The three blocks of what came to be known as the artists' colony in Wilmersdorf were reserved for artists and intellectuals who were members of the associations or were not yet established in Berlin cultural life. The blocks were located near what was then the edge of the smart, middle-class West of the city and looked out over fields and allotments. The flats still stand today.

The Huchels occupied a first-floor flat at Kreuznacherstraße 52. It was quite adequate for their needs, consisting of a kitchen, bathroom, bedroom and living room. Their rent of eighty marks a month was met through their income from Kronstadt, which covered some of their other regular expenditure, too, though the amount had to be reduced somewhat following Eugen Lassel's death. Huchel compensated by publishing more poetry and signing on as unemployed. Kantorowicz occupied a flat nearby at Kreuznacherstraße 48 with his first wife Friedel. Among others, their old friends Wilma Papst and Wilhelm Blaß lived in the colony, which also housed figures such as Ernst Busch, Erich Weinert, Gustav Regler, Axel Eggebrecht and Werner von Trott zu Solz. Huchel knew the latter from Potsdam schooldays. Ernst Bloch, too, came to live at Kreuznacherstraße 52 with Karola Piotrkowska. These figures were instrumental in the rapid growth of the colony's reputation as a left-wing stronghold. It quickly became a focal point for Berlin artistic and intellectual life, with much coming and going and much scope for the development of fresh contacts and friendships. That autumn, the Huchels got to know Götz and Baila Kozuschek, and Hans and Edith Nowak. Kantorowicz introduced them to the Huchels, as he had Horst Lange and Oda Schaefer. All these new and older friends, such as Harry Landry and his wife Erika, who would later marry Sebastian Haffner, had no truck with the National Socialists and their supporters.

In that autumn of 1931, Kantorowicz overcame his previous reservations and joined the KPD. He proceeded to found a KPD cell in the artists' colony. In postwar essays, Kantorowicz on occasion linked Huchel with his own activism, in the interest of demonstrating his friend's anti-fascist credentials. Yet Kantorowicz was not consistent and at points at best ambiguous in his portrayals of Huchel. On one occasion, he wrote that 'die Zeit unseres gemeinsamen geistigen oder militant-politischen Widerstandes gegen die aufkommende Nazi-Bewegung begann'.[42] On other occasions, however, Kantorowicz described the limits of Huchel's political enthusiasms, 'Seiner versponnenen Natur liegt das politische Engagement nicht. Er hat nie in seinem Leben einer Partei angehört, er war kein Kommunist oder Sozialist, aber auch kein Anti-Kommunist'.[43] On another occasion still, Kantorowicz simply dropped altogether the idea that Huchel might have been involved in any anti-Nazi activity, writing that he

> hatte auf seine verschlafene, musisch-versponnene Weise mit unseren Kampfaktionen gegen die Nazis sympathisiert, ohne sich bei Freund oder Feind sonderlich bemerkbar zu machen. Unsere Verbindung hatte sich daher in den Jahren meines Aktivismus gelockert; zuvor waren wir seit etwa der Mitte der zwanziger Jahre durch gemeinsame Jugend-erlebnisse in vertraute Beziehung gekommen.[44]

Kantorowicz went on to write that while he himself opted for activism, 'zog sich Huchel in den Elfenbeinturm zurück'.[45] Kantorowicz is surely correct in stating that Huchel was temperamentally disinclined to political activism. Huchel sympathised with the goals of the Left but had little interest in practical involvement. Dora Huchel captured something of this position when she wrote, 'Kanto, im Nebenhaus, gründete kommunistische Zelle, seitens Huchel keine Beachtung, aber mit unseren zahlreichen Besuchen heftige politische Streitgespräche'. In 1981, she commented more controversially, 'Als Kantorowicz neben uns in der Kreuznacherstraße eine Zelle gründete, machte sich Huchel darüber wahnsinnig lustig. Ich ging aus Neugier aber fand es reichlich kindisch'. She added, 'Er war eigentlich ziemlich indifferent, liberal. Ich habe bei ihm ein Engagement vermißt. Es war ihm viel zu unbequem, das in eine Tat umzusetzen. Es war eine Modesache, auch in den Kreisen, wo er diese Ideen nur wiedergegeben hat. Die anderen waren überzeugt'. In truth, the Huchels were rather alike in their scepticism and disinclination to commit themselves to a cause with which they could not wholeheartedly agree.

Huchel's prime concern remained with his poetry, to which he devoted most of his energy. Karola Bloch, a close friend during those years, recalled her visits to the Huchels' flat where Huchel would read from his verse,

Es war lustig, die Lebensgewohnheiten der einzelnen Nachbarn kennenzulernen. Huchels zum Beispiel (seine damalige Frau Dora war eine deutsche Rumänin aus Siebenbürgen) verwandelten den Tag zur Nacht. Das Leben begann mit der Abenddämmerung. Wenn ihre Katze miaute, wußte ich, die Huchels waren auf. Dora selbst glich einer Katze mit ihren großen Augen und grazilen Bewegungen. Wann immer die Zeit es zuließ, ging ich zu Huchels. Ernst kam manchmal mit, er schätzte die Bohème-Atmosphäre. Peter oder Piese, wie ihn seine Freunde nannten, las dann oft ein neues Gedicht vor, mit seiner schönen ruhigen Stimme. Ich liebte seine Gedichte, die Natur, die Landschaft in ihnen. Oft kamen agronomische Ausdrücke vor, altertümlich und wohlklingend. Die mußte ich mir erst erklären lassen.[46]

From her KPD perspective, Karola Bloch described Huchel as unpolitical, as someone who was valued as a friend and as a lyric poet. His distance from the political activism of friends such as Kantorowicz and Karola Bloch emerges in her characterisation of his response to Nazi election gains, 'Piese, der in keiner Partei war, wollte von mir wissen, was wir "Roten" gegen die braune Pest unternähmen'.[47] Her own response was to join Kantorowicz's cell, of which she writes,

Wir trafen uns, etwa zehn Genossen, einmal wöchentlich. Der politische Leiter war Kanto, der organisatorische Leiter Gustav Regler. Ein Genosse regelte die Finanzen (wir zahlten Beiträge, je nach den Möglichkeiten des einzelnen Mitglieds). Ich übernahm die Arbeit für die Rote Hilfe, eine Organisation, die sich um Arbeitslose kümmerte und um kommunistische Gefangene. [48]

Red Aid was a KPD 'front organisation', one of Willi Münzenberg's many initiatives on behalf of the Party though formally separate from it. The idea was to enlist regular donors among sympathisers to support the unemployed and victims of the judicial system. In 1981, Dora Huchel recalled that they had made such donations. They had in all probability been encouraged to do so by Karola Bloch. After the war in East Berlin, Huchel referred to his 'membership' of Red Aid between 1931 and 1933 in a questionnaire that he filled in for his employer, the German Academy of Arts.[49] He acknowledged that he had performed no duties for the organisation, yet his claim that his status as a donor constituted membership of a political party was somewhat wide of the mark. We see here, as so often in early post-war statements, the gentle boosting of anti-fascist credentials. Neither then nor later did Huchel ever belong to a political party. The Huchels' donations to Red Aid may best be viewed as part and parcel of the political culture that prevailed in the artists' colony.

Quite apart from his preoccupation with his poetry, Huchel's phlegmatic temperament made for a certain sceptical detachment and ironic distance. Not that he was in any way isolated from his neighbours. As Karola Bloch's depiction of the Huchels shows, their flat was a popular destination for neighbours, who sought out Huchel's company and enjoyed his readings. The award of the *Kolonne* prize and his fashionable success with *Die literarische Welt* demonstrate that through his dedication to perfecting his talent he was developing a distinctive reputation. Indeed, 1932 marked what initially looked as if it might turn into a decisive breakthrough. Yet, in the event, the profound changes in Berlin literary life that followed 30 January 1933 would mean that his opportunities to capitalise upon that breakthrough would be curtailed in a manner that no one could fully have countenanced.

Poetry and Cultural Renewal

Critical appreciation of Huchel's poetry began to appear following the *Kolonne* award. Raschke's article had been something of a mixed blessing, but in April Willy Haas was unreserved in his praise. By taste, Haas was more a traditionalist than an innovator, as is suggested by his great admiration for Hofmannsthal. In an editorial introduction, Haas singled out Huchel as a notable representative of the 'Junge Dichtung' to which he devoted a double number in April 1932. He wrote,

> Diese Jugend geht sogar tiefer unter das Maß des Artistischen zurück, als wir Älteren es im allgemeinen für möglich gehalten hätten ... Es wird hier noch sehr von alten Literatur- und Dichtungsvorstellungen zu konservieren versucht ... Man kann sogar, wenn man will, in der relativ konventionellen Wahl der Themen einen Vorzug finden: es ist der erste Ansatz zu einer mittleren Traditionsgebundenheit über Generationen hinweg, den wir in der deutschen Literatur seit Jahrzehnten erlebt haben ... Eine Erscheinung wie Peter Huchel aber ist schon, so jung er ist, eine Figur von Rang ... Gewiß ist bedauerlich, ... daß das Experimentative ... so ganz fehlt.[50]

Along with the poetry of Elisabeth Langgässer and Georg Britting, Huchel's verse for Haas represented an accomplished expression of the new restorative tendency, whose concerns were articulated most persuasively in *Die Kolonne*. In literature as elsewhere, the search was on for alternatives to the discredited republic, for vantage points from which to judge the chaos of the present, for enduring values to set against the all-pervasive instability. The literary tradition, flouted by the avant-gardists, seemed to Huchel and others to represent a source of such values and of great creative potential, by means of which better to understand the present. Shortly after the war, Huchel explained, quite plausibly, that in his poetry of the early 1930s he had sought to occupy 'die unbesetzten Provinzen des Geistes', (ii,262) which the

Left, with its rather supercilious attitude towards the countryside, had abandoned to the Nazis and their followers. Like the *Kolonne* poets, with whom Huchel was coming to associate more closely, he drew ever more on the German tradition from the early to mid-nineteenth century, from Romanticism to Poetic Realism. The post-revolutionary mood embodied in much of the finest poetry of that age of *Biedermeier* had a particular resonance for Huchel, as he lent expression in his verse to his search for a substantial grounding to his identity that memories of rural childhood experiences seemed to offer. As Haas suggests, Huchel's poetry, like that of other *Kolonne* poets, constitutes a break with recent experimental styles such as Expressionism and *Neue Sachlichkeit* in the attempt to establish a continuity within the German tradition at a deeper historical level. The regeneration of the lyric genre undertaken by Huchel, Langgässer and others was pitched quite deliberately in a different key from the anti-transcendent, urban idiom that had become the signature of 1920s Berlin.

Poets with shared concerns inevitably gravitated towards each other. Elisabeth Langgässer and Huchel got to know each other at this time. On 1 May 1932, she wrote the dedication 'Peter Huchel zu eigen von Elisabeth Langgässer' in a copy of her stories *Grenze: Besetztes Gebiet*, which was published that year by the Morgenland Verlag in Berlin.[51] In November of the same year, she presented him with her *Triptychon des Teufels*, which she had been able to place with Wolfgang Jess due to her *Kolonne* connection. As Langgässer wrote in a letter to Elisabeth Andre on 19 September 1932, she had recently invited Huchel, Joachim and Kantorowicz to dinner.[52] The two latter had recently published reviews of her work, while she and Huchel were rising stars of the new poetry. It is unfortunate that beyond details of the food and drink and of the cigarettes smoked, Langgässer's letter says nothing about their conversation that evening.

Der Knabenteich

Since the award of the *Kolonne* prize, Huchel had been in a position to consider what should go into the collection which Wolfgang Jess was committed to publishing. In the event, the collection did not appear. A surviving table of contents, on the basis of which the collection was re-constructed for the 1984 edition, indicates that at one stage Huchel intended to produce a wide-ranging selection of his verse, containing as many as 73 poems. This meant drawing on 39 poems which he later declined to publish, in addition to more recent compositions, most of which were collected after the war in *Gedichte*. Retrospectively, Huchel's selection of material for *Der Knabenteich*, including poems by the schoolboy as well as other weak pieces, can be seen to have been a mistake, and in fact when he came to assemble *Gedichte* in 1948 he included only such verse as had been composed since 1925. That collection, like later ones, is informed by a careful architecture which is, however, not discernible in the table of contents for *Der Knabenteich*.

Available sources indicate that in 1932 Huchel was unsure whether he should jettison his earlier work and could not decide upon a definitive arrangement of material. In the 1970s, he recalled, '*Der Knabenteich* wurde trotz Drängen des Verlages von mir aus selbstkritischen Gründen nur zögernd zusammengestellt'.[53] This statement tallies with what Huchel wrote to Raschke in the undated letter referred to already above, in which he acknowledged that Jess had every reason to be angry with him. This would be a familiar tale in the preparation of all Huchel's collections. He remained throughout his life loath to release material about which he might yet change his mind.

Despite the fact that, as far as can be ascertained, Huchel never got as far as finalising his selection for the collection, Haas had been busy on Huchel's behalf, using his contacts so that Huchel could introduce *Der Knabenteich* on the radio prior to publication.[54] Huchel went through with this arrangement, in which he delivered a text and read from his verse in the series 'Die Selbstanzeige', which was broadcast from Frankfurt am Main by Südwestdeutscher Rundfunk on 28 December 1932. The broadcast was Huchel's first taste of radio work, which over the coming sixteen years would assume central importance in his literary career. The talk is the longest and most informative commentary that Huchel ever produced about his poetological concerns. It is particularly instructive in that it provides a clear insight into how Huchel viewed his poetry on the eve of the Third Reich.

Both the commentary and the choice of poems indicate a movement away from the inclusive approach to the volume that characterises the table of contents. By late 1932, reflecting his development since the mid-1920s, he chose to foreground the poems about the Alt-Langerwisch childhood and their intimate link with his rural upbringing. This was, of course, only consistent with statements made by him in *Die literarische Welt* and to Raschke. The Alt-Langerwisch world was thus established as what he later called the 'Urgrund des Schaffens'.[55] In late 1932, Huchel was still quite circumspect in his claims regarding that element of his backgound, while as usual he passed over in silence his childhood years in Groß-Lichterfelde and Steglitz. He acknowledged the importance for his verse of 'die Gegend, die mir am vertrautesten ist, die Gegend um Potsdam, wo Wald, Schilf und Wasser beiander liegen'. (ii,248) However, he drew listeners' attention principally to the following,

Mit vier Jahren, als meine Mutter erkrankte, gab man mich zu den Großeltern aufs Land. Dort verlebte ich einen Teil meiner Kindhheit; dort war ich auch in den späteren Jahren, jeden Sommer, jeden Herbst. Dies muß gesagt werden, um das Buch: *Der Knabenteich. Gedichte*, das ich hier vor seinem Erscheinen (im Jess Verlag, Dresden) anzeige, deutlicher zu machen. Denn es ist die *Landschaft des Kindes*, es ist die *Landschaft der Mark*, aus der diese Verse ihr Leben ziehen. (ii,242)

Following a reading of 'Kindheit in Alt-Langerwisch' and other childhood poems, Huchel proceeded to distance himself and his poems from any *Tendenz*, arguing for their indifference towards contemporary events,

> Die erste Bedingung zum Verständnis dieser Verse wird darin bestehen, sich diesem Buch
> ohne jede Programmforderung zu nähern. Denn *zeitnah* sind diese Gedichte nur zum Teil,
> nämlich insofern es ihnen gelungen ist, die *vergangene Zeit wieder gegenwärtig zu*
> *machen.* (ii,243)

Huchel echoed this characterisation of his work in his recollection of the broadcast in 1959 in Hamburg and at the same time sketched in the profound uncertainties of German life at that moment in history,

> Die 'Selbstanzeige' ging 1932 über den Sender – zu einer Zeit also, da nichts mehr sicher
> war, da der Boden zu schwanken begann, jede dichterische Existenz fragwürdig wurde –
> und die Absicht, eine Poesie zu schreiben, die kein anderes Thema haben sollte als sich
> selbst, noch fragwürdiger. (ii,300)

Huchel's development had thus taken him to the point where he regarded his work as pure poetry in contrast to the chaos which threatened to envelop him and the rest of German society. This stance is of a piece with his introspective focus on the recovery of the mysteries of childhood generally lost to adult consciousness, the theme of poems such as 'Der glückliche Garten'. Following Raschke, Huchel described this process in terms reminiscent of Proust's 'mémoire involontaire',

> Etwas vom Geruch eines zerriebenen Nußblatts, und wir sehen in einen verschollenen
> Sommer hinein. Oder der Anblick einer grauen Steinschwelle, vor einem fremden Haus,
> läßt uns den vergessenen Platz wieder deutlich sehen, den ganzen Abend ahnen und was
> damals vorging, als wir auf einer gleichen grauen Steinschwelle saßen. (ii,246)

Raschke had drawn attention, too, to Huchel's metaphorical transformation of nature, which transcends any merely descriptive approach. Huchel again broadly agreed with Raschke's reading. He found the following words for his technique, which emphasise the sophistication to which he aspired through the exploitation of his visionary capacity as a poet and through the manner in which he portrayed people within the landscape,

Niemals wird die Landschaft photografisch gesehen, niemals wird sie naiv - als Lied zur Laute - besungen; mit Horizonten und Bäumen von innen her will sie über die bloße Idylle hinaus; und meist erscheint sie nur, wenn der Mensch in ihr auftaucht. Oft trägt dann der Mensch die Züge der Natur, und die Natur nimmt das Gesicht des Menschen an. (ii,248)

People and the landscape are thus perceived in a symbiotic relationship, each enriching the other within the transcendent poetic vision. Huchel's was a quite deliberately post-Expressionist statement, in that he takes issue explicitly with the relationship between people and landscape as set out by Kurt Pinthus in his foreword of 1919 to the famous anthology of Expressionist verse, *Menschheitsdämmerung*. Pinthus wrote, 'Weil der Mensch so ganz und gar Ausgangspunkt, Mittelpunkt, Zielpunkt dieser Dichtung ist, deshalb hat die Landschaft wenig Platz in ihr. Die Landschaft wird niemals hingemalt, geschildert, besungen; sondern sie ist ganz vermenscht'.[56] In keeping with his rejection of the excesses of the Expressionist avant-garde, which took people as the measure of all, Huchel argued for a much more nuanced perception of the relationship between man and his natural environment. Huchel illustrated his point that the two were mutually enriching through reference to a stanza from the poem published the following year as 'Marie' but collected in 1948 under the title 'Löwenzahn', 'Leise segelt das Löwenzahnlicht/ über dein weißes *Wiesengesicht,*/ segelt wie eine *Wimper blaß*/ in das zottig wogende Gras'. (ii,249) The italics are Huchel's own. His commentary is instructive, as he extends his argument from landscape to the greater concept of nature, 'Aber nicht so sehr das Hinfinden des Menschen zur Natur, nicht so sehr das Einfühlen oder die Rückkehr in die Natur will in den Gedichten zum Ausdruck kommen, mehr noch ist es die Natur als Handelnde, die auf den Menschen eindringt und ihn in sich hineinzieht'. (ii, 249) In this interpretation of the relationship between man and nature, it is in the final analysis the power of nature that is viewed as the dominant force, both greater than and beyond man, whom it shapes through virtue of its power. It is a view which opens the way for the vision of a transcendent nature, an idea which occupies a key place in Huchel's verse. In the last public statement made by Huchel in 1977 he re-affirmed this view, stating, 'Die Natur bleibt geheimnisvoll. Wir können in die Transzendenz, in jede visionäre Landschaft vorstoßen'. (ii,332) This idea of an essentially unknowable but infinitely rich natural world is quite in keeping with the influence of the mystics and, indeed, with Goldberg's metaphysical speculations. Together with the theme of childhood and the immersion in the rural way of life in a German region, however, it rests somewhat uneasily with the claims generally made by Huchel in the post-war period that his early poetry had been informed by Marxist concerns. As late as 1974 in the West he was claiming, 'Ich habe eine Kindheit auf dem Lande verlebt, und die Natur war für mich nicht mehr die heile, die absolute Natur, sondern es war für mich die vom Menschen veränderte Natur, in der er leben konnte'. (ii,393) This emphasis on man as a social being shaping his environment does not really tally with Huchel's poetological statements and, indeed, his practice in the early 1930s.[57] Nor were the figures who populated the natural world evoked by Huchel defined in terms of the exploitation of their labour. In his statement, Huchel acknowledged instead the very limitations of people in determining and shaping their world. His verse offered the consolation of a richer world, of a magically recovered childhood world and of the prospect of reward for sustained introspection untrammelled by socio-political concerns.

Like Raschke's statement, Huchel's presentation of his poetological concerns reveals a poet immersed in his personal vision. Huchel was responding to a cultural atmosphere in which an ever deepening pessimism left the fundamental optimism of many leftist attitudes looking decidedly naive. This situation needs to be borne in mind when evaluating the claims made in the post-war period regarding the non-appearance of *Der Knabenteich*. The 1984 edition rightly questions conventional wisdom, established in the immediate post-war period and accepted for decades to come, that Huchel withdrew the collection in early 1933 because a publication after Hitler came to power could have been interpreted as an affirmative statement vis-à-vis the regime. The editor's surmise that Huchel became aware of the uneven quality of the collection is supported by the poet's statement to Rudolph. Having made the point in that interview that the collection had been 'von mir aus selbstkritischen Gründen nur zögernd zusammengestellt', Huchel said, 'Dann kam das Jahr 1933' and then paused. Thereupon, Rudolph reproduced the conventional critical wisdom, 'Ja, und da haben Sie das Erscheinen verhindert'. On this occasion, one of Huchel's most informative interviews, he corrected this view with the words, 'Und da erübrigte sich eine Veröffentlichung von selbst'. Quite plausibly, Huchel here abandons the idea that he acted to withdraw the collection after 30 January 1933 as a protest against the Nazis. He casts events instead in terms of his very omission to act, leaving open the motivation for his inaction. This latter version of events certainly tallies quite closely with what Dora Huchel told me in 1981. She could not recall the withdrawal of a completed manuscript; the collection was not ready. It is therefore surely somewhat misleading, despite the scepticism noted above in the 1984 edition, for the editor to maintain the view that *Der Knabenteich* 'wurde aber kurz vor der Drucklegung von P.H. zurückgezogen'. (i,365) There is no mention in the edition of any archive material which would demonstrate that Huchel produced for Jess a more rigorous selection, which was subsequently withdrawn. Nor has any such material been identified since.

It is appropriate to point out here, too, that in contrast to the impression created in the immediate post-war period, Huchel did not withdraw from literary life in 1933. Such statements were of a piece with the putative withdrawal of *Der Knabenteich*. Yet the very fact that he continued to publish poems very regularly in 1933-4 gives the lie to the story that the non-appearance of *Der Knabenteich* was due to a decision on Huchel's part no longer to participate in German literary life under National Socialism. After the war in Berlin, Huchel was quite prepared to allow such a fiction to circulate along with others which demonstrated anti-fascist credentials and masked certain uncomfortable details from the twelve years of Nazi rule. Such was the stigma which in the early post-war period attached to involvement in the cultural life of the Third Reich that Huchel, like so many others, had little choice but to withhold information if, as was the case, he wished to be involved in the re-construction of German cultural life. In truth, the situation as it presented itself to Huchel and many others in 1933-4 was much less clear-cut than appears to be the case retrospectively. Equally, the legends which came to surround Huchel are to some extent typical products of the immediate post-war climate. As we shall see, however, the details provided by Huchel and his friends fit in with a particular biographical pattern already established.

It is surely fair to conclude about *Der Knabenteich* that Huchel had simply not completed the selection process in 1933. Nor, for that matter, was he inclined to put himself forward at a time when the Nazis were instigating their 'cultural revolution' and were identifying suitable writers and artists for the dubious honour of their support in order to bolster the regime's credibility. The fact that Huchel's name appeared on one such list is both a measure of the distance in his poetry from the politics of the Left and a most embarrassing misunderstanding of his aims in his verse.[58] As we have seen, he later explained that he had wished to occupy 'die unbesetzten Provinzen des Geistes', (ii,262) which the Left had abandoned for the Nazis and their followers. The Nazi 'occupation' of regional nature poetry duly took place and Huchel was left in the wholly ambivalent position of a non-Nazi nature poet working in a cultural environment in which such writing was appropriated by the Nazis quite indiscriminately beneath the slogan *Blut und Boden*. It was against that uncomfortable background that in the 1970s Huchel remarked, 'Ich kann verstehen, daß die jungen lieber die Expressionisten zu ihren Vätern haben wollen als uns. Denn wir werden ja, und zum Teil mit Recht, verantwortlich gemacht für die ganze Scheiße, die kam'.[59]

The Nazi Years

1933

As the German crisis deepened, Huchel was gripped by a pessimism that proved to be wholly justified. The Republic had forfeited its credibility in the eyes of the vast majority of the population and its collapse was imminent. Huchel's background was such that he had few illusions about the continuing attractions of the authoritarian Right. Like many others, he was resigned to the worst. In 1981, Dora Huchel recalled him saying on more than one occasion, 'Die Scheiße wird kommen, das ist vorauszusehen'. In adopting this stance, however, he once again differed from friends and acquaintances on the Left such as Kantorowicz, Max Schroeder and Axel Eggebrecht, who in July 1932 founded an 'antifaschistischen Schutzbund' and continued to combat the Nazi threat until it was too dangerous to stay.

In the weeks and months following 30 January 1933, many friends fled the country. Among them were Haas, Kantorowicz, Bloch and Joachim. Many abandoned the artists' colony, which had been identified as a stronghold of left-wing artists and intellectuals and was subjected to SA attacks and house searches. In her account, Dora Huchel describes how they were affected by these events, 'Unmittelbar nach dem 30. Januar Haussuchung auch bei uns, der marrokanische Dolch vom Pariser Flohmarkt, der offen als bloße Augenweide dalag, verschwand. Sonst blieben wir persönlich unbehelligt aber traurig zurück'. In 1981 she pointed out, 'Die engen Freunde sind alle weg. Für Huchel kam das nicht in Frage. Er war nicht richtig gefährdet. Im Nazi-Reich zu leben war widerlich'. Huchel never commented in public on why he himself had not followed his friends into exile. When on 10 May 1947 he delivered a speech on the anniversary of the burning of books he stated, 'ich entschied mich, in Deutschland zu bleiben'. (ii,262) He did not then proceed to give reasons for that decision but instead glossed his position in the Third Reich as follows,

> Meine Damen und Herren, ich gehöre zu den Schriftstellern, die 12 Jahre Hitlerdiktatur miterlebten. Zweimal war ich in dieser Zeit allerdings mehrere Monate lang im Ausland und hatte das Glück, von dort aus Verbindungen zu einigen emigrierten Freunden aufnehmen zu können. Und da ich bis zum Jahre 38 Besuch aus England bekam, war ich nicht ganz isoliert.

Beyond the fact that he did, indeed, stay, the reader here learns nothing of what the reality of those years in Germany meant for him beyond isolation, which, he says, was relieved only by trips abroad and by contact established with emigrants. We shall return to those trips and links at appropriate points. Clearly, it was not politic in 1947 to discuss more fully one's personal circumstances as a writer under Nazism, if one did not have the sort of evidence of persecution that Langgässer had. Huchel, legitimised by his collaboration with the Soviets at Berlin Radio, could enjoy some credibility with his brief self-portrait as a figure driven into isolation under Nazi rule. Early post-war statements should, however, be read with due caution, bearing in mind the climate that then prevailed, when it would have been tantamount to professional suicide to speak fully and frankly about the Nazi years. That implies the need for a certain degree of scepticism in the evaluation of such statements. Yet scepticism is frequently missing among critics, many of whom are inclined to accept established images, while others still are wholly dismissive. As a result of the former tendency, which has prevailed in Huchel criticism, legends were formed which continue to enjoy currency today. The recent edition of Huchel's correspondence with Johannes Bobrowski is a case in point. The editor takes over quite uncritically the view expressed by Huchel's friend Horst Lommer in June 1947 that from 1933 Huchel's life was one of 'äußerste Zurückhaltung' from cultural life, though Lommer himself was hardly the most reliable witness.[1] The distance from the stigmatised cultural life of the Third Reich required in 1947 is thus preserved in the 1990s, yet the reader is presented with a quite unrealistic and unhistorical view of what these years actually meant for Huchel.

An understanding of Huchel's response to the events of 1933 is to be gained less against the backcloth of the early post-war years than through an appreciation of the stance that he came to adopt in the early 1930s. Immediately after 1945, it would have been unthinkable for a writer with leftist sympathies to assume the explicitly private stance of the biographical sketch in 1931. It would have been equally unthinkable to draw attention to an indifference towards the sphere of contemporary relevance, as Huchel did on the radio in December 1932. Such has been the German cultural climate of the post-war era that only relatively recently has acceptance begun to filter through of the legitimacy in the early 1930s, in the wake of economic and social chaos, of a poetological position adopted in conscious opposition to that chaos. In 1947, Huchel could neither argue, nor would he have wanted to argue, for the legitimacy of that position in that earlier historical context, despite the fact that at that time he had set his life and his practice as a poet outside active involvement in social processes.

This position was quite similar to that of friends and acquaintances who stayed, such as the Langes and Eberhard Meckel. It was with these writers, associated with the *Kolonne* Circle, that the Huchels would now cultivate closer contacts. In March 1933, the Langes and Meckel, too, were subjected to house searches but not identified as the real enemy within. Meckel, who also lived in the artists' colony, noted on 15 March 1933, '8 Uhr. Polizeiabsperrung am Laubenheimerplatz. Haussuchung auch bei uns. Verhaftung von Kommunisten. Revolutionsstimmung'.[2] It was on the morning of 15 March that the police and SA launched their major attack on the artists' colony. They arrested fourteen residents suspected of communist activity, who were subjected to brutal treatment. The arrested included the Jewish editor, Walter Zadek, Günther Ruschin and Curt Trepte, who were members of the communist avant-garde theatre group 'Truppe 31'. Among the others were Theodor Balk, Peter Martin Lampel and Manès Sperber. Though Ernst Bloch had already fled, Karola Bloch remained for the time being at their flat in the same house as the Huchels. She recounts in her mémoirs how, following a tip-off from Johannes R. Becher, she removed all Marxist material from the flat and managed to place Bloch's manuscripts in the loft just before the search began. Nothing was found in the flat but the police and SA asked to see the loft. Her story, which she actually dates on 27 February, the day the Reichstag was set on fire, continues as follows,

> Nun werden sie dich verhaften, wenn sie die Manuskripte finden. Mein Gehirn arbeitete konzentriert: Wie kannst du dich retten? Da fiel mir ein, daß an meinem Schlüsselbund auch der Schlüssel zum Boden von Peter Huchel hing. Wir hatten bei ihm eine mittelalterliche Holzplastik, eine Madonna mit Kind, untergebracht, die auf unserem Boden keinen Platz mehr gefunden hatte. Ruhig öffnete ich das Vorhängeschloß an Pieses Bodentür. Ich wußte, daß er, unpolitisch wie er war, nichts Verdächtiges bei sich hatte – und die Madonna mit dem Kind lächelte uns heiter entgegen. Die Männer verabschiedeten sich sogleich, die Manuskripte waren zunächst gerettet, ich auch. 'Madonna hat geholfen', schrieb Ernst später in einem Aufsatz.[3]

In 1948, Huchel made two claims about the house search which are at variance with the accounts of Dora Huchel and Karola Bloch. In one document, he claimed that in the search of his flat undertaken by the SA and the Gestapo part of his library was confiscated.[4] In another document, he claimed that searches had been undertaken by the SA and the Gestapo because he was hiding illegal communist material from Kantorowicz's cell.[5] He had, he wrote, been interrogated but not arrested. Like much else that Huchel said in early post-war Berlin about his anti-Nazi activities, these statements are best taken with a pinch of salt. The Huchels, in fact, stored the Blochs' furniture following Karola Bloch's departure to join Ernst Bloch in Prague. In time the furniture was sent on to them.

That said, there can be no doubt that early 1933 was a period of extreme anxiety for the Huchels as it was for all marginal, non-conformist figures, who could not be sure how widely the Nazis would cast their net. The house searches were designed to intimidate and they had that effect. Members of the general public were encouraged to denounce 'unacceptable behaviour'. In her mémoirs Oda Schaefer reports that during that same March 1933 she and Horst Lange were the victims of such a denunciation, but through guile they managed to wriggle out of an unpleasant situation. Like their friends from the *Kolonne* Circle, the Huchels, for all their deep antipathy towards Nazi ideology, eschewed any idea of active opposition. This position is reflected in the writings of the *Kolonne* Circle, which Hans Dieter Schäfer chooses advisedly to describe as non-Nazi.[6] I shall generally follow him in this since the term non-Nazi provides a quite precise and appropriate analytical instrument for a nuanced appreciation of the contradictions in the reality experienced by some of these writers in those years. It was a reality of niches and compromises, expressions of dissent and of conformity, a reality much less clear cut than is suggested by other terms frequently deployed such as anti-Nazi or Inner Emigrant. While the former should surely be reserved for those who actively opposed the Nazis inside or outside the country, the latter term has long lost credibility and was, indeed, never claimed by Huchel for himself.

The Nazis engaged in a selective appropriation of elements of contemporary literature immediately after 30 January. It was undoubtedly embarrassing for Huchel at the time, not to mention later, to find his name in an official Nazi publication on a list of authors whose work merited promotion.[7] His name appears along with Blunck, Kolbenheyer, Carossa and Meckel, suggesting that the publication aimed to encourage quite sophisticated writing. Immediately after the war, Kantorowicz and Lommer both alluded to the list in their pieces on Huchel. It can be assumed that the allusion was agreed with Huchel so that, in the case of the discovery of the list, it could be pointed out that nothing had been hidden and the worst repercussions could thereby be avoided. Much later, in the 1970s, Huchel himself also alluded to that same list when he spoke of the 'Gefahr, als Landschaftslyriker von den Nazis in Beschlag genommen zu werden'. (ii,371) There is absolutely no evidence that Huchel sought to take advantage of the opportunity presented by the Nazis. Nor, however, did he act in the manner later described by many friends and critics, of whom Willy Haas is just one prominent example. In an essay published in 1968, Haas conveyed the impression that after January 1933 Huchel chose to withdraw from literary life. Haas wrote,

> Ich kehrte in meine Vaterstadt Prag zurück und gründete wiederum eine Zeitschrift, *Die Welt im Wort*. Unter anderen lud ich auch ihn zur Mitarbeit ein; aber er sagte ab. Er habe sich entschlossen, schrieb er, das Dichten bis auf weiteres ganz aufzugeben und durch die Arbeit seiner Hände zu leben.[8]

If we accept that Huchel himself was the source of Haas' information about his intentions, we can see how once more Huchel had recourse to the fiction of the manual labourer in order to deal with an awkward problem in his literary existence. In her account, Dora Huchel challenges the impression conveyed by Haas, seeking at the same time to point up the wholly ambivalent situation that Huchel found himself in as an artist, which was reflected in his work, 'Andere Töne, die nicht nach außen dringen konnten. Dagegen Entwürfe für "harmlose" Hörspiele'. This statement begins to flesh out something of the complexity of the position Huchel found himself in during 1933 when he remained with his wife at Kreuznacherstraße 52.

A Poet in the Third Reich

It is one of the great truisms that hindsight lends events a coherence, even an air of inevitability, that those who live through them could scarcely have grasped. This certainly holds good for the early phase of Nazi rule. In 1933, many people of quite different political persuasions were convinced that the Nazi regime would soon collapse. The atmosphere was one of great uncertainty. In 1932, Huchel had made the breakthrough that he had yearned for. In circumstances in which Nazism might prove to be only a brief interlude, it was reasonable to stay and build upon a developing reputation.

In 1933, Huchel continued to publish regularly. In the first half of the year, he looked to established links. He placed 'Das Haus', (i,380) with the *Vossische Zeitung* on 14 May 1933. Other work appeared in *Die literarische Welt*, which for a short period following Haas' departure was edited by Eberhard Meckel. Haas was evidently unaware that 'Alter Feuerkreis' appeared on 10 March, 'Havelnacht' on 21 April and the short prose piece 'Georg Büchners Lenz' on 12 May. The poem 'Der Herbst' was published later that year, simultaneously in *Die literarische Welt* and *Das Inselschiff*. Huchel's gloss on Büchner's *Lenz* indicates his continuing pre-occupation in the early to mid-1930s both with Büchner himself and with the writing of the *Biedermeier* period with its recurrent theme of extreme conflicts within the individual.

In 'Havelnacht', (i,88) Huchel presented the other side of that psychological coin. The poem is one of his most remarkable pieces of nature poetry, visionary with intimations of the sublime, which are beautifully focused through a manipulation of language of Goethean ease, which provides a gentle affirmation of the mystery of life. The abiding popularity of 'Havelnacht' is attested by its frequent inclusion in anthologies. The opening stanza of this night-time boat-ride on the Havel, with its echoes of Goethe's 'Auf dem See', reads, 'Hinter den ergrauten Schleusen,/ nur vom Sprung der Fische laut,/ schwimmen Sterne in die Reusen,/ lebt der Algen Dämmer-kraut'. A sense of cosmic plenitude is created in the wake of the poet's contemplation of the stars' reflection on the water's surface. He elaborates upon this in subsequent stanzas. We see here for the first time, too, the constellation of imagery that can be found in the later poem 'Die Sternenreuse', which in turn gave its name to the second section of *Gedichte* as well as providing the title for the revised edition of that collection in 1967. Through the gentle, even rhythm and the use of assonance, Huchel evokes the peace of the night-time scene, interrupted only by the occasional sounds of the fishes, of the birds, and the breeze in the bushes and reeds. Within the vision of the heavens and the waters meeting, the poet evokes 'das sanfte Sein im

Wasser', the principle of life which resides in this special place. He identifies, too, the proximity of a dynamic 'Geist', which 'nachtanbrausend/ noch in seinem Flusse taucht'. It will presently reveal itself in this place with the particular potency of its creativity. Assured of this, the poet turns to contemplate our existence, which is informed and sustained by the powers of nature. The poem ends,

> Duft aus wieviel alten Jahren
>
> neigt sich hier ins Wasser sacht.
>
> Wenn wir still hinunter fahren,
>
> weht durch uns der Trunk der Nacht.

> Die vergrünten Sterne schweben
>
> triefend unterm Ruder vor.
>
> Und der Wind wiegt unser Leben,
>
> wie er Weide wiegt und Rohr.

Together with 'Oktoberlicht', 'Havelnacht' arguably represents the consummate expression of what Huchel was striving to achieve in his nature poetry of the early 1930s.

Yet Huchel was exposed to distinctly more stormy weather, which would leave little room for the undisturbed continuation of such a self-possessed contemplation of matter and of existence. Indeed, in a short poem published only in 1948 as the first part of the cycle 'Deutschland' (i,98) but dated 1933 Huchel placed 'Geist' in a very different context. He wrote,

> Späteste Söhne, rühmet euch nicht.
>
> Einsame Söhne, hütet das Licht.
>
> Daß es von euch in Zeiten noch heißt,
>
> daß nicht klirret die Kette, die gleißt,
>
> leise umschmiedet, Söhne, den Geist.

The poem tells of those who, like Huchel, remain behind in isolation. He admonishes them to protect those traditional symbols of humanism under threat from the chains that Nazism would impose. These verses spell out clearly the nature of those 'andere Töne, die nicht nach außen dringen konnten', to which Dora Huchel referred. They characterise the position of the poet who, eschewing exile, urges himself and others in the same position to maintain artistic integrity in a barbaric age. This was a response in keeping with the artistic position that Huchel had assumed in the early

1930s. The contrast in the treatment of 'Geist' in this poem and 'Havelnacht' testifies, moreover, to the writer's well-nigh schizophrenic position in the dictatorship. As Schäfer points out, the Nazis explicitly guaranteed a 'politikfreie Sphäre' in the early years of their rule, which perpetuated the illusion of freedom of expression for accomplished literature which was not of a political nature.[9] Huchel made use of this continuing opportunity to place sophisticated work such as 'Havelnacht'. In time, this 'guarantee' would reveal itself to be a trap, from which, for many, it would be too late to escape.

Though the broadcast of a radio play by Huchel was still some time off, he built upon the experience of the presentation of December 1932 by reading from his poetry for two Berlin stations in the course of 1933. The readings were for the Berliner Funkstunde and the Deutschland Sender.[10] He also sought fresh outlets for his poems in journals. In doing this, he was able to rely on the help of friends such as the Langes, who were in a similar position. Gradually an informal network developed around the *Kolonne* Circle, through which contacts could be exploited to place poetry as well as radio plays. In this way Huchel became part of a grouping which continued to exist in a loose way following the demise of the magazine itself in the late summer of 1932. In the Berlin journal *Der weiße Rabe. Zeitschrift für Vers und Prosa* they found a publication with similar poetological concerns. Like *Die Kolonne*, it was a short-lived venture, launched in 1932 by the legendary V.O. Stomps and wound up in March 1934. Oda Schaefer recalls,

Es erschien auf dem Jahrmarkt der Eitelkeiten und der Literatur in jenen vergangenen, verschollenen Tagen eine neue Zeitschrift, *Der weiße Rabe*, die der eigensinnige Verleger Victor Otto Stomps, kurz als VAUO bezeichnet, herausgab. Es ist mir klar geworden, daß er uns in jenen Jahren manchmal wie in einem Zaubermantel geborgen hat, obwohl er selbst bedroht war. Stomps bot uns die Welt, nach der wir verlangt hatten, als wir nach Berlin gingen, ebenso wie Stomps danach verlangt hatte, junge Dichter zu drucken. Seine Behausung in der Stallschreiberstraße nahe dem Dönhoffplatz, in der auch seine eigene kleine Druckerei eingerichtet war, lag in einem düsteren zweiten oder dritten Hinterhof von fabrikartigem Charakter. Er liebte wie wir den vierten Stand und haßte den Bourgeois.[11]

Lange was invited to edit a special number devoted to 'Landschaftliche Dichtung'. In addition to a contribution under the pseudonym Konrad Ostendorfer, Lange wrote his 'Bemerkungen zum Inhalt dieses Heftes' and an editorial introduction. In the former, he explained the choice he had made. Interestingly, and in the light of Huchel's later reluctance to be bracketed with Wilhelm Lehmann as well as the *Kolonne* Circle, Lange explained that an excerpt from Lehmann's *Die Schmetterlingspuppe* had been chosen to introduce the issue 'weil diesem Dichter, der unbeirrt von allen Mode-Strömungen seinen eigenen ihm gemäßen Weg ging, seitens der jungen Generation Dank genug gebührt ... Damit sind erst die Wege freigelegt worden, die wir heute gehen'.[12] Among the 'Junge Generation' selected by Lange were Langgässer, Gertrud Kolmar, Meckel, Schaefer, Eich, Lange himself and Huchel. Of Huchel, Lange wrote,

> Die vorjährige Verleihung des Lyrik-Preises der Zeitschrift *Die Kolonne* lenkte mit vollem Recht die Aufmerksamkeit auf das eigenwillige und starke lyrische Talent Peter *Huchels*. In seine Gedichte ist das Leben der Havelniederung eingegangen. Der hier veröffentlichte Beitrag wurde dem leider noch ungedruckten Buch *Der Knabenteich* entnommen, dessen Erscheinen der Verlag Wolfgang Jess angekündigt hat.

At the time of the appearance of *Der weiße Rabe* in the summer of 1933, Lange, a good friend, had evidently not been informed of any decision by Huchel to withdraw the collection. His words may be construed as encouragement to his friend to complete the work on the collection. Huchel's contribution to the issue was 'Kinder im Herbst', (i,61) which had been included the previous year in Raschke's *Neue lyrische Anthologie*. The poem contains a number of features familiar in Huchel's published verse from the period. The depiction of village children in the autumnal landscape is imbued with suggestions of the magical dimension of which the children might partake.

Huchel's contribution is by no means out of step with the other material assembled by Lange. It is quite compatible, too, with the philosophical and poetological orientation of Lange's editorial introduction, even if in other statements relating to the spirit of the new age Lange articulated views with which Huchel surely did not agree and which Lange himself subsequently certainly regretted. Like Eich and others in the *Kolonne* Circle, in the months immediately after 30 January 1933 Lange looked to Gottfried Benn for a lead. The shape that Nazi cultural policy would assume after the removal of leftist and Jewish writers was still somewhat uncertain, and Benn was making a play for an influential role, pandering to Nazi ideology in such notorious pieces as 'Der neue Staat und die Intellektuellen' and 'Antwort an die literarischen Emigranten'. Lange's essay demonstrates that in the *Kolonne* Circle not only Eich showed early enthusiasm for the new regime.[13] Lange begins, with unmistakable echoes of Benn, by invoking the monumental importance of recent events in the history of the earth,

> Die geistigen Grundlagen unserer Zeit befinden sich im Zustand einer ungeheueren Umschichtung. Das kann nur mit jenen Epochen in der Geschichte der Erde verglichen werden, wo Gebirge einstürzten, wo im Meer sich das untergehende Land wälzte und riesige Schollen frischer, unbetretener Erde auftauchten.[14]

He polemicises against the 'democratic interregnum' and greets the fact

> daß wir, nach einer Zeit einer wahrhaft 'nihilistischen' Vernunft- und Aufklärungsliteratur, vor dem Aufkommen einer neuen Periode größerer, sittlicher und moralischer Dichtkunst stehen, die vielleicht alle Verheerungen wiedergutmacht, welche die circenischen Unterhaltungsgeschäfte eines entarteten Theaters, eines routinert-spekulativen Filmbetriebs und einer wankelmütigen Buch-Produktion angerichtet haben.

Lange looks forward to 'the appearance of the new German man', who will be created in a culture characterised as follows,

> Nachdem die rationalistischen Fortschritts-Lehren eines aus dem 18. Jahrhundert bis zu uns reichenden Bogens flacher, konstruktiver Weltauffassung gehört und geglaubt worden waren, mußte ein neues Bild vom Menschen werden, in dem *das Geheimnis* wieder Raum hat. Wir sind Zeugen seines Entstehens.

In his definition of 'mystery', Lange has recourse to categories of thought central both to Huchel's poetics and to those of other *Kolonne* figures. Lange, however, places them in the context of the 'New Germany',

> Es ist kein Zufall, daß in unseren Jahren Forscher sich um die Erkenntnis von Naturmagie und von Mythen bemühen, die Jahrtausende lang verschollen waren und jetzt eine neue Wirksamkeit erhalten, denn es gibt nichts, was für immer vergessen werden kann. Ein Zeitalter, in dem der Mensch vom Intellekt her die Welt zu beherrschen versuchte, in dem er sie von Zaubereien, Gespenstern und Fabelwesen reinigte, in dem er alle Spuren der Götter austilgte, geht unaufhaltsam in einer allmählichen Bewegung zu Ende.

In language redolent with Benn's appropriation of Spengler, Lange looks forward to a conservative revolution embracing all of existence. It will produce 'eine allgemeine neue Sinngebung ..., die die abendländischen Kulturen aus ihrer jetzigen Späte des Verfalls und der Beunruhigung hinüberführt in eine neue Wirklichkeit', in which the relationship between man and nature will be wholly re-cast. Lange offers up the new nature poetry of his generation as suitable material for the new culture of Nazi Germany. Lest there should be any doubts, he writes of this 'Hinkehr der deutschen Dichtung zur Natur' as being 'einer Wiederentdeckung Deutschlands gleich'. The idea of a national mission for nature poetry is brought to a conclusion, in which he draws upon ideas from Hofmannsthal's 'Schrifttum als geistiger Raum der Nation' to explain the national character of the German 'revolution',

Wenn die landschaftliche Dichtung überhaupt Aufgaben hat, die außerhalb des dichterisch

Werkgerechten liegen, so sind es die: im heutigen deutschen Menschen die Teile des

Seelischen wachzuhalten, die danach verlangen, Boden zu haben, auf dem die Füße stehen

können, Raum um sich und das Walten großer Gesetze in allem zu spüren.

Nicht ein Bauernmuseum, nicht ein Schrank für Altertümer ist zu füllen. Nein, es geht

darum, auch von dieser Seite her eine Einheit hervorzubringen, die, wenn sie besteht, mit

Recht Nation geheißen werden kann.

Lange was by no means alone in utterly failing to grasp what Nazism was about. It is difficult to measure the degree of opportunism and of actual belief in what Lange wrote here, though it must be said that later he would not repeat this error. Lange's piece, however, demonstrates the hysterical atmosphere that gripped Berlin literary life in the 'revolutionary' year of 1933. Whatever Huchel might have thought of his friend's statements at the time, he continued to submit poems to *Der weiße Rabe*. Lange's essay was not a typical product of Stomps' publishing house. 'Marie' appeared later that year and 'Die dritte Nacht April' in 1934.

Shortly after the appearance of the special number on 'Landschaftliche Dichtung', Stomps' Rabenpresse published Lange's collection of poems *Zwölf Gedichte*. He presented a copy to the Huchels as a sign of his friendship. It bears the dedication, 'Das tägliche Brot für meine lieben Huchels, Horst Lange, Berlin August 1933'. The dedication alludes to the title of the first of the twelve poems. Among other poets on Stomps' impressive list were Werner Bergengruen, Max Hermann-Neiße, Kurt Heynicke and Hermann Kasack. The Rabenpresse survived the demise of its journal and provided a meeting place for non-conformist Bohemian figures in the Berlin of the mid- to late 1930s. Christoph Meckel, Eberhard Meckel's son, writes, 'Die Verlags-Etage am Landwehrkanal war berühmt für Feste, Räusche und Leierkästen, die Atmosphäre genialisch und unzeitgemäß, eine heimliche Anarchie, die das Dritte Reich unterlief. Die NSDAP schien das nicht zu bemerken'.[15]

Oskar Loerke, 'der letzte Große, den man noch sah',[16] read at the Rabenpresse. In his diary, Loerke noted readings on 18 December 1932 and 28 January 1937.[17] Oda Schaefer recalls other readings organised by Stomps in the Humboldt villa on Fasanenstraße, which today is the home of the Literaturhaus. These occasions were 'leuchtende Abende mit dem Auditorium vieler prominenter oder ehedem prominenter Autoren, die dem Regime nicht genehm waren. Wir trafen dort Bergengruen, von dem wir wenige Häuser entfernt in Zehlendorf wohnten. Er wurde uns zum Freunde'.[18] The Huchels would presently get to know the Bergengruens through the Langes. In this way fresh contacts continued to be made during the dictatorship, however antagonistic the climate was to the development of literary life in a capital city that was just a shadow of its former self following the departure of such a large number of its most brilliant artists. Yet in the early years of the dictatorship an enterprise such as Stomps' was tolerated, since the Nazis were aware of the importance of maintaining the illusion of artistic freedom among figures who were not politically motivated. It was towards such undertakings as the Rabenpresse that Huchel, never a supporter of the Nazis, gravitated as he sought to continue his literary career as far away from the Nazi sphere of influence as was still possible. The breakthrough of 1932 was now stalled, as he embarked on a path which he clearly found distasteful but which he had chosen to follow in preference to emigration.

Some respite from the oppressive atmosphere of the new Germany was in prospect following an open invitation from the Lassels to come and spend time with them in Kronstadt as they had in 1930. It was three years since Josefine Lassel and her son Helmut had seen Dora and her husband: an extended stay was long overdue. The invitation was gladly accepted by the Huchels, who decided to give up the Berlin flat in the artists' colony, into which NSDAP members and sympathisers had moved. Huchel's parents, with Fritz now retired, had in the meantime moved from Potsdam to Alt-Langerwisch, a place where Marie and her mother, who continued to live with them and provided Huchel with a ready source of the regional idiom, felt at home. They moved to Am Wolkenberg 13. Peter and Dora Huchel stored their furniture with Huchel's parents with a view to finding a house in the area following their return from Kronstadt.

These were the arrangements for the Huchels' trip to stay with Dora's mother in Kronstadt. It was to this stay and a later one in 1939 that Huchel was referring in 1947 when he spoke of the two occasions after 1933 when he was 'mehrere Monate lang im Ausland'. (ii,262) In Kronstadt, he established contact with people whose interests were somewhat removed from the friends in exile, with whom he apparently resumed contact. After the war, it was scarcely politic to mention links with the Kronstadt literary magazine *Klingsor*, which was edited by the prominent Nazi supporter, Heinrich Zillich. Nor, for that matter, did Huchel make any reference to the fact that he had actually been visiting his wife's family. Yet such were the ties with the Lassels in the 1930s, that in a statement to the Reichsschrifttumskammer in 1939 Huchel suggested that since 1930, as a result of his marriage to a Kronstadt woman, he had been dividing his time between Germany and Transylvania.[19] At a time when close links were being encouraged between the Reich proper and ethnic German communities spread through Central and Eastern Europe, such a statement would have had a thoroughly positive ring in Germany. After the war, quite different stories circulated about Huchel's exploits in Romania, where, if we are to believe one critic, he emigrated.

Kronstadt 1934

On 29 December 1933 Huchel informed the Reichsverband Deutscher Schriftsteller, forerunner of the Reichsschrifttumskammer, that future correspondence should be sent to his wife's family in Kronstadt. Dora Huchel writes of the stay, all of which including the journey from and back to Berlin was paid for by her family,

> Dort in jeder Beziehung sehr verwöhnt. Zwischenfall Blinddarmoperation. Autofahrten mit Freunden in nähere und weitere Umgebung, im Hochsommer mehrere Wochen allein auf der sog. Magura in einem rumänischen Bauernhäuschen, wo wir die vielbestaunte Sensation der Gegend waren und eine rumänische Bauernhochzeit mitmachten. Im November lernte Peter Huchel dann auch noch in einer geliehenen Skiausrüstung die Anfangsgründe dieser gefährlichen Kunst. Mitte Dezember ging's leider wieder ins 'Dritte Reich' nach Langerwisch und zum 'Wolkenberg' zurück. Den Freunden war viel zu erzählen.

Once again, the Lassel family enabled the poet, when he chose, to adopt the lifestyle of the leisured classes. Karl Alfred Wolken, however, makes of Huchel's stay with his mother-in-law a tale of emigration from the Third Reich, which took him out of mainstream literary culture into a folkloric world populated by peasants, shepherds and gipsies. The story he tells is clearly linked to the Huchels' stay on the Magura,

> Kaum gebührend zur Kenntnis genommen wurde bisher, daß Huchel außerdem aus der politischen Unzucht der 'Welt der Wölfe, Welt der Ratten' nach Rumänien emigrierte – ein Schritt, der mehr wache, kritische Vernunft voraussetzt, als man heute noch darin wahrzunehmen geneigt ist. Und doch scheint dieses Schicksal bei ihm aus der Phantasie zu kommen. Wer damals, um Hitler aus dem Weg zu gehen, nach Rumänien ging, ging aus der Welt, der literarischen zumindest, ging zurück zu Bauern, Hirten und Zigeunern. Die Wahl des Dreißigjährigen führte ihn aus der Erwachsenen-Zweckwelt zurück in die Welt seiner Kindheit, gegen jede begründete Hoffnung auf Stellung und sicheres Einkommen. So kann es nicht wundernehmen, daß die Emigration scheiterte und Huchel zurückkehrte, auch wegen einer kranken Frau, die ärztlicher Behandlung bedurfte.[20]

This piece, written by Wolken after conversations with Huchel in 1971-2 at the Villa Massimo in Rome, teems with the unintended ironies which come to inform so many critics' accounts of Huchel's legendary life. In 1978 Heinrich Zillich, the prominent Nazi and editor of *Klingsor*, the Kronstadt literary magazine, challenged Wolken's depiction,

Welche Quelle hatte Wolken zu einer solchen Äußerung? Ich kann mir nicht vorstellen, daß Huchel selber ihm solche Unwahrheiten lieferte.

Die Wahrheit ist, Huchel hielt sich zweimal, am Anfang der dreißiger Jahre, wohl 1933/4 und dann 1937 länger in Rumänien auf, stets in meiner Heimatstadt Kronstadt in Siebenbürgen, wo er im Haus eines ehrenwerten, mir bekannten deutschen Pfarrers als Gast behaglich wohnte, weil er dessen Tochter Dora geheiratet hatte. Er verkehrte damals mit meinen Freunden, alle keine Zigeuner, Hirten und Bauern, sondern nach rötlichen Ansichten, denen Huchel nachher lange, obzwar eigenwillig diente: Kapitalisten, und bei denen fühlte er sich sichtbarlich wohl. Zigeuner, Hirten und Bauern erblickte er höchstens, wenn er in den Autos der Gastgeber, zum Beispiel mit meinem Schwager, den er zum Paten seines Kindes gewonnen hatte, auf die Jagd fuhr.

Das also war Huchels Flucht zu Zigeunern, Hirten und Bauern! Eine angenehme Einkehr bei Deutschen, deren Gastfreundlichkeit er reichlich genoß ... Auch hörte ich damals weder von Huchel noch von sonstjemandem, daß er gegen das Reich einen privaten Trotzkrieg führte.[21]

Zillich was apparently unaware that the Huchels' wedding had taken place in Kronstadt in 1930, and his choice of 1937 seems to have been determined by the year of a publication by Huchel in *Klingsor*. Supported by his wife's family in 1934, Huchel could enjoy the pastimes and leisure activities of Kronstadt's moneyed middle classes, shooting game, skiing and sightseeing. In 1981, Dora Huchel offered corroboration of Zillich's statement that on such outings Huchel often accompanied Zillich's brother-in-law, Hermann Scherk, a rich factory owner. Shortly after the 1934 visit, in July 1935 Scherk agreed to be one of the godfathers following the birth of the Huchels' daughter, Susanne. Just as they had in Corenc and on the Black Sea coast, during their stay in Kronstadt the Huchels sought out a rather remote village, where they could observe and to some extent participate in peasant life and folk customs. In Wolken's account this element of experience is inflated and transformed, until it conceals the surely embarrassing details of some relationships in Kronstadt. Life there mixing with the *Klingsor* circle is replaced by a pastoral world far removed from the viciousness of politics, German or, for that matter, Romanian.

During the stay in Kronstadt Huchel contributed on three occasions to *Klingsor*. 'Der Knabenteich', 'Der glückliche Garten' and 'Havelnacht' appeared in the May number. These were followed by 'Marie' in August and 'Oktoberlicht' in October. All were familiar work from the portfolio that Huchel had assembled. His choice of these particular poems indicates that he had come to recognise what were his most accomplished compositions. As a *Klingsor* author, the visiting Berlin poet and husband of the Lassels' daughter was very welcome in the social circle around the journal. The Huchels were invited to parties and at one of them, Dora

Huchel recalled in 1981, the Jewish wife of a Romanian teacher fell for Huchel. The couple repeatedly invited the Huchels to visit them, and when the Huchels went to stay in the remote village she turned up for a day, too. Huchel's behaviour towards the woman was ambivalent: while he did not discourage her attentions, he sought to persuade his wife that they should leave Kronstadt. She, however, wished to remain with her family and old friends. It was only when they had returned to Germany that Huchel revealed to his wife that he had met up with the woman alone. He reminded her that it was he who had been pressing to leave Kronstadt. The episode is not untypical of Huchel's interaction with women. Many found him deeply attractive and he was often happy to have their attentions, behaving in a rather passive manner and allowing things to take their course. As the one who had not made the running, he felt justified in rejecting any responsibility for emotional upheaval. His wife tended to accept such situations. In her moral code, the poet as genius was permitted to live by rules different from those of other mortals. This 'understanding' attitude not only sanctioned Huchel's encounters; it meant that he was able to continue to enjoy undisturbed the emotional and material support that his wife provided. This pattern of behaviour came to inform the Huchels' relationship as the years went by. Dora Huchel, like so many other wives, accepted her husband's behaviour, safe in the knowledge that he would return home.

During his absence from Germany, Huchel had not neglected the development of his profile as a poet within the country. One of the few new literary journals permitted in the period immediately after 1933 was *Das innere Reich*, which was edited by Karl Benno von Mechow and Paul Alverdes for the Munich publisher Langen/Müller. One can only assume, as Werner Volke has written, that it escaped the ban imposed on the founding of new journals because of the nature of the proposals made by the editors and publisher.[22] These aims were set out in a letter circulated to prospective contributors in January 1934. The letter contains the following description of the journal's aims,

> Sie will in erster Linie der lebendigen deutschen Dichtung dienen und den deutschen Autoren die Möglichkeit geben, ihre neuen Schriften schon vor Veröffentlichung in Buchform dem deutschen Publikum bekannt zu machen. Wir hoffen und vertrauen, auf diese Weise eine treue Gemeinschaft aller Freunde der gegenwärtigen deutschen Dichtung zu versammeln. Daneben und darüber hinaus soll versucht werden, mit Aufsätzen grundsätzlicher Art und mit Anmerkungen zum öffentlichen Leben unserer Gegenwart, dem neuen Reich nach bester Kraft und nach bestem Gewissen zu dienen. [23]

The aim to present quality contemporary German writing in the service of the new 'Reich' is elaborated upon in the journal's opening programme in its first number of April 1934, where one can read,

Aber nicht nur dem Leser in Deutschland soll unsere Arbeit gelten, sondern auch allen außerhalb unserer Grenzen, die bereit sind es aufzunehmen, daß mit den ins Ausland Geflüchteten keineswegs die guten deutschen Geister ihr Volk verlassen haben, sondern daß im Gegenteil im nationalsozialistischen Deutschland die Bahn erst recht frei geworden ist für die Entfaltung der Besten des 'Inneren Reiches' der Deutschen.[24]

The word 'inner' was meant in both a political and spiritual sense. The journal's ambitious programme attracted a great deal of interest. Among those who published in it were several figures from the *Kolonne* group. It has been said that Eich used his friendship with Alverdes to mediate the publications of friends.[25] That may have been the case for others in the group, but in early 1934 Huchel and Eich had not yet got to know each other. Huchel had two new poems in the first number, 'Nächtliches Eisfenster' (i,85) and 'Nachtlied'. (i,64) It would appear that he had responded to the editors' invitation to contribute. On 20 February 1934 Mechow wrote to Alverdes, 'Peter Huchel scheint mir nach flüchtigem Einblick schön'.[26] Yet the quotation from the opening programme illustrates the conflict in which Huchel now found himself as he contributed to a journal which had been established in order, among other things, to demonstrate that quality intellectual life had by no means departed from Germany. This legitimation was badly needed by the Nazis as the regime sought to establish its credentials abroad after the damage done by the bad press that had followed early acts of repression. A journal containing quality literature that would be read abroad in influential circles was clearly welcome. Huchel himself would later edit a journal where such considerations were of crucial importance.

Why did Huchel choose to contribute to this new venture? In 1934 he had no immediate material worries. After the departure of friends in 1933 and the initial anxieties, he sought to build upon the reputation that he had established. Here as elsewhere, he was guided more by his strong sense of his vocation as a poet writing in the German language than by the moral or political concerns that one would associate with a decidedly anti-fascist position. A journal which defined itself in terms of quality writing – and this was indeed the case – could not be merely the vehicle for ideology. In this way, though, Huchel slipped into company that was certainly far removed from the circles that he would frequent in the post-war years when he sought to convey a quite different impression of his literary background. Following his breakthrough with *Die literarische Welt* and the *Vossische Zeitung*, by 1934 Huchel had become an author of Alverdes' and von Mechow's *Das innere Reich* and of Zillich's *Klingsor*. Life with friends who had gone into exile must have seemed a long way away.

Huchel also contributed to Langen/Müller's almanac for 1934-5, *Ausritt*. Indeed, according to one account, Huchel edited the collection, which included his recent composition 'Die wendische Haide'.[27] Two further new poems appeared in the June issue of *Das innere Reich*, 'Frühe' (i,63) and 'Letzte Fahrt'. (i,62) Like the two earlier poems, these verses see Huchel as the practitioner of a *Naturmagie* by no means dissimilar to other accomplished non-Nazi poets. These poems move from the visionary celebration of the dawn ('Frühe'), to the commemoration of the mysterious figure of the 'Ziegelstreicher' ('Nachtlied') and on to the play of the imagination in 'Nächtliches Eisfester'. 'Letzte Fahrt', however, when taken together with other slightly later publications in the same journal, begins to strike a more sombre note, which testifies to the poet's uncomfortable awareness of the position he had come to occupy. In 'Letzte Fahrt', we will recall, the son presents himself following the path through life chosen by the father, who is depicted as the angler that Fritz Huchel was. The death described in the poem is, however, a death in life, as the dreams the father had cherished ebb away, 'er sah die toten Träume ziehn/ als Fische auf dem Grund'; and in the stanza that follows, 'sein Traum und auch sein Leben fuhr/ durch Binsen hin und Sand'. The son comes to the fore in the final lines, 'in meiner Kanne springt der Fisch./ Ich geh den Binsenweg'. The resignation and despair felt by the son would presently be articulated more fully in the cycle 'Strophen aus einem Herbst', which would appear in *Das innere Reich* in the autumn of 1935.

By then major changes would have occurred in Huchel's domestic and artistic life. The return to Germany in late 1934 would be followed by the beginning of Huchel's sustained involvement in radio, where he developed a career as an author of radio plays. As we have seen, the return had nothing to do with any collapse of any plans to emigrate, nor was it prompted by 'einer kranken Frau, die ärztlicher Behandlung bedurfte'. In fact, both Dora and Peter Huchel received medical treatment during their stay: Huchel had his appendix removed and in November his wife became pregnant.

A Niche in Radio, or a Pact with the Devil?

When the Huchels returned to Germany in late 1934, they drew on the hospitality of his parents in Alt-Langerwisch. Their stay with Fritz and Marie Huchel lasted some months while, in typically leisurely fashion, they looked for suitable accommodation in the area before their daughter's birth. As Dora Huchel writes, after their return they resumed contact with Berlin friends. Among them were Götz Kozuschek, Eberhard Meckel, Sebastian Haffner and the Langes, as well as Potsdam friends like Rudi Elter. In the later 1930s, Kozuschek and Haffner, both of whom were married to Jewish women, would flee Germany for England. In Cambridge, the brilliant Haffner would go on to produce work in which he sought to explain the phenomenon of Nazism to his host country and its allies. After the war, he would be an influential figure on the foreign affairs staff of *The Observer*.

It was the Langes who in late 1934 and 1935 introduced the Huchels to other writers in their circle, among them Werner Bergengruen and his wife Charlotte. Charlotte Bergengruen came to the rescue of the hopelessly impractical Huchels immediately before and after Susanne's birth, offering invaluable advice as well as baby clothes. In return, Charlotte Bergengruen was asked to be a godmother to the baby, who was given her name as a middle name. It was through the Langes that the Huchels, at the latest in early 1935, got to know Günter Eich, Huchel's friend and collaborator in the mid- to late 1930s. Eich had embarked with some opportunism on a lucrative radio career after 30 January 1933, making a name through radio plays broadcasts from major Berlin stations which operated from the building on the Masurenallee. For other *Kolonne* figures, too, such as the Langes, Meckel, Raschke, and Kuhnert, radio represented a good source of income. Following the exodus of talent after 30 January 1933, they seized their chance to establish considerable reputations in the medium.

It is surely no coincidence that Huchel's sustained involvement in radio began when he and his wife were looking to re-establish a household before the birth of their child. It clearly makes sense on one level to describe Huchel's radio plays as 'Brotarbeiten', (ii,405) though that term should not preclude further analysis. Over the years, Huchel derived a reasonable income from his radio work: in 1935 he earned an estimated 3,000 RM and a similar amount the following year. His earnings rose to 3,820 RM in 1937 and were 3,513 RM in 1938. In this way a financial dependency was established on the medium at a time when it was possible to make one's way within the terms of Nazi programming policy by writing a mixture of light entertainment and more ambitious literary work.

In his excellent study on the radio play in the Third Reich, which can be profitably read in conjunction with Hans Dieter Schäfer's essays, Wolfram Wessels has taken our appreciation of the medium well beyond the simple popular image of radio as a vehicle with the sole purpose of conveying the master propagandist Goebbels' totalitarian message. It was that, of course, but more, too. In April 1934, Goebbels summoned the heads of radio stations to Berlin and explained that the politicisation of radio had within it 'Die Gefahr der Einseitigkeit'. He continued,

> Erst die notwendige Auflockerung der Programme ergäbe eine fruchtbare Gesamtarbeit. Die nationalsozialistische Politik bilde selbstverständliche Grundlage jeder Programm-gestaltung im Rundfunk. Aber eben deshalb brauche die Politik nicht beständig zitiert werden. Musik, leichte Kunst, künstlerische Vielfältigkeit und dabei hohe Leistung müssen jedem Rundfunksender zu eigen werden.[28]

For the immediate future, this approach provided a framework for programming in which there was certainly room for non-Nazi work. Wessels identifies four phases of programming policy in all: 1933-4, primacy of overt propaganda and ambitious literary work celebrating traditional German life in the regions; 1935-6, primacy of entertainment; 1937-8, primacy of propaganda with the emphasis on the 'Volksgemeinschaft' rather than the regions, and not excluding more ambitious literary work; 1939-40, primacy of war propaganda, especially anti-British. During each phase emphasis was placed on a particular broad category or categories which was/were not, however, promoted to the total exclusion of others. As Goebbels explained, entertainment, too, belonged within the overall propagandist scheme, in that it provided a necessary release from the overt political message. At the same time, this approach created spaces which non-Nazi authors like Huchel sought to occupy. Yet such spaces were, of course, delimited by the Nazis, who would in time close them down. Indeed, during the two latter phases, after the Nazis had strengthened their grip on the radio network as they embarked on their expansionist policies, it became increasingly difficult to earmark airtime outside the explicit propaganda remit. As we shall see, much of Huchel's radio work can be readily accommodated within the categories established by Wessels.

There are aspects of Huchel's radio work which were certainly a source of acute embarrassment to him in the immediate post-war period. Had they become known, they would have been an obstacle to his rapid rise in the new cultural hierarchy and later could have been used to blackmail him when he came into conflict with SED cultural politicians. In early post-war Berlin, when he actually worked for the Soviets in the building on the Masurenallee from which much of his work was broadcast in the 1930s, Huchel's radio work was one of those aspects of his literary career over which he successfully drew a veil. As a result, until recently little was actually known about Huchel the radio play author, and critics were generally content to accept at face value an image of the poet who had withdrawn from literary life into the silence and suffering of a rural Inner Emigration. The tone was set by Kantorowicz, who in 1947 wrote, 'Während der Hitler-Zeit hat er geschwiegen'.[29] It was echoed as late as 1976 by Vieregg, who wrote of 'das Schweigen des Inneren Emigranten von 1933 bis 1945'.[30] In stating that the radio play manuscripts had disappeared Vieregg was merely following Huchel, who, according to his second wife, always maintained in public that they had been lost in the confusions of the war and its aftermath.[31] Indeed, in 1975 he went so far as to claim, 'Ich besitze überhaupt kaum Manuskripte'. (ii,391) As we shall see in greater detail later, after 1945 Kantorowicz and Lommer spread the story that all Huchel's personal papers had been destroyed in an Allied bombing raid.

Consequently, in portraits produced until the mid-1970s, when Hans Dieter Schäfer's research into non-Nazi literature began to appear, Huchel's radio work was generally mentioned only at the margin, if at all. Two not untypical statements from those who do mention the radio plays are Franz Schonauer's and Bernhard Gajek's. In 1968 Schonauer wrote, 'Nach 1933 zog sich Peter Huchel von der Literatur zurück; außer einigen unpolitischen Hörspielen veröffentlichte er nichts'.[32] Gajek explained, 'Da die Hörspiele nicht greifbar sind, ... ist eine Nachrechnung nicht möglich. Sie wäre auch unergiebig'.[33] Yet, as Schäfer pointed out, some archival material was available for scrutiny and accounts such as Franz Lennartz's of 1938, produced in collaboration with authors themselves, provided some basis for further investigation. Lennartz, for example, wrote of Huchel's radio plays, 'In seinen innerlich schönen Funkdichtungen erstrebt er unter Ausschaltung herkömmlicher Sentimentalität den volkstümlich Einklang von Gesprächen, Liedern und Gedichten. Seine Werke sind vielfach auf den Ton heimatlicher Volksweisen abgestimmt'.[34]

Critics seeking to penetrate the veil of secrecy did, however, have to negotiate smokescreens that Huchel put up such as when he told Gajek that 'er zwischen 1933 und 1939 mehrere Stücke unliebsamer Schriftstellerkollegen unter seinem Namen (zugunsten der wahren Autoren) habe senden lassen'.[35] This story and variations on it circulated during Huchel's lifetime but it was dropped without comment from the 1984 edition. The editor follows Huchel in conversation with Kundera when he writes that Huchel produced some thirty-five radio plays during the Third Reich.[36] Of them, more than twenty were broadcast. Just three of the extant sixteen manuscripts among Huchel's papers or in archives were included in the 1984 edition. Despite this difficulty, sufficient material can be advanced to support an informed analysis of Huchel's work as a radio author in the Third Reich.

It would certainly have been open to Huchel to emulate the opportunistic Eich in 1933 but there can be no doubt that such a course of action held no attraction for him. As we have seen, his radio work during the initial radical phase of Nazi radio in 1933 was restricted to two readings from his verse. Interestingly, however, in the questionnaire that he filled in for Reichsverband Deutscher Schriftsteller on 29 December 1933 he described himself principally as a radio author.[37] If by 1935 this would have been true, at the end of 1933 it signalled more an intention than a reality.

Following Huchel's return to the Berlin area, a key contact for him and for the *Kolonne* network in general was Langgässer's husband-to-be Wilhelm Hoffmann, who was the director of the Berlin Jugendfunk.[38] Huchel exploited the link with the right-wing radical Hoffmann in order to place his first piece, an adaptation 'Doktor Faustens Teufelspakt und Höllenfahrt', which bears the sub-title 'Nach alten Puppenspielen für die Jugend bearbeitet'. The broadcast took place on 16 December. Huchel took few risks with this adaptation, staying close to his sources in a piece of traditional entertainment for young people. It would be some months later, in the summer of 1935, that Huchel's career in radio would really take off. It is, however, heavily symbolic that the Faust legend should have provided the subject matter for Huchel's debut as a radio play author in the medium presided over by Goebbels,

Hört, ihr Leut, ich muß euch warnen,

Laßt euch nicht vom Teufel umgarnen.

Er hält nicht, was er euch verspricht,

Bis er euch gar den Hals zerbricht.

Zwölf ist die Glock ... Zwölf ist die Glock.[39]

Günter Eich

Huchel's most important literary encounter during this period was undoubtedly with Günter Eich. A number of critics have drawn attention to Eich's role in the early stages of Huchel's radio career. In the 1984 edition, for example, we can read, 'Er hatte Günter Eich kennengelernt, der bei der Vermittlung half'. (ii,405) The edition also contains Huchel's recollection of the time in the Third Reich 'Als ich mit Günter Eich zusammenlebte'. (ii,391) Similarly, in 1984 Hans Mayer observed, 'Gewiß ist richtig, daß Huchels Arbeiten für den Rundfunk seit 1935 wieder angeregt wurden durch die Freundschaft mit Günter Eich'.[40] Yet, in an episode all too familiar in the highly polemical and unstable world of German literary criticism, dealing as it does all too often with black-and-white images and knee-jerk responses, the discovery of the extent of Eich's opportunism in these years, which includes an application to join the Nazi party in 1933, was recently followed by the attempt to distance Huchel from his friend. In this way, Huchel might be 'saved' from any dangerous proximity to the damaged Eich.[41]

While, as has been established, Hoffmann provided the initial link with the Jugendfunk, in a letter of 13 April 1935 from his flat in Charlottenburg Eich encouraged Huchel to make an appointment to see Dr Werner Pleister at the Reichssender Berlin.[42] Pleister was interested in winning Huchel for radio work. In the event Huchel would collaborate from mid-1935 with Pleister's colleagues Harald Braun and Paula Knüpfer. None of these figures were Nazi supporters, unlike other figures at the Masurenallee with whom Eich collaborated such as Ottoheinz Jahn, Helmut Hansen and Gerd Fricke. Huchel steered clear of them as long as he could. In the meantime his relationship with Eich developed.

In 1981, Dora Huchel recalled that Eich invited them to visit him in June at his summer house at Poberow on the Pomeranian coast. Eich referred to the invitation in a letter from Poberow dated 25 May 1935. He explained that their friend Kuhnert's arrival had been delayed so there would be room for them only from Whitsuntide. He himself would be there until around the 20th. On 5 June, Eich sent Huchel directions from Berlin, adding that it would be nice if Huchel and his wife did decide to visit him. By 15 June, the Huchels were with Eich, and the Kuhnerts had departed. In a letter to Kuhnert on that day, which was also signed by Huchel, Eich said that he had persuaded Huchel to adapt 'Mein lieber Augustin' for the radio. Eich asked Kuhnert for details of the copy of the book that he had in his possession. Nothing appears to have come of that idea. Eich also asked Kuhnert to recommend Huchel to Veit Roßkopf. Roßkopf was an NSDAP member who was in charge of literary productions at the Reichssender Leipzig. Some of Huchel's work would be broadcast from there in the coming years. This letter and other documents show something of the workings of the informal *Kolonne* Circle as they extended their links in the radio network. Christoph Meckel's account of his father's life testifies to the fact that Poberow was a popular summer destination for the *Kolonne* Circle,

> Mehrmals verbrachte er ein paar Sommerwochen im Ferienhaus Günter Eichs an der Ostsee. Huchel, Eich und mein Vater in den Dünen von Prerow. (sic) Das Hafergras ging in die Verse ein, der Regen, die Sterne und was sie für zeitlos hielten. Sie arbeiteten gemeinsam, spielten Tischtennis und lasen sich abends neue Gedichte vor.[43]

For all that, in June 1935 relations between Eich and the Huchels were not altogether harmonious. Dora Huchel recalled, 'Mißstimmungen sind an der Ostsee aufgetaucht'. She would add only, 'Eich war Pedant'. Despite Dora Huchel's unwillingness to divulge the background to their differences, it appears safe to assume that the source of the disagreement was Eich's early enthusiasm for the Nazi regime, which was not shared by the Huchels nor for that matter now by the Langes, with whom Eich also quarrelled.[44] This would not be the last difference of opinion between Huchel and Eich. As we shall see, they disagreed violently at a meeting of the Gruppe 47 in 1954. Their old friendship would never be re-established after the war. In the 1930s, however, despite altercations and continuing tensions, the two poets – politically quite different – who were the most talented in their circle, recognised each other's gifts and continued to value personal friendship as their literary collaboration developed during the decade. Meckel writes,

> Mitte der Dreißiger Jahre machten Huchel, Eich und mein Vater eine Autotour nach Wiepersdorf. An den Ausläufern des Fläming, am Rand des märkischen Dorfs, liegt das Stammgut der Familie Arnim. Achim von Arnim und Bettina Brentano hatten dort vor hundert Jahren gelebt, ihre Gräber befinden sich auf dem Schloßgelände, ein schöner Schauplatz der deutschen Romantik mit Stallung, Orangerie und verwildertem Park. Es war ein heller, zeitloser Tag im Sommer. Jeder der drei versprach, ein Gedicht zu schreiben, das WIEPERSDORF heißen und den gemeinsamen Tag zum Gegenstand haben sollte. Das Gedicht meines Vaters ist nicht erhalten, die Gedichte von Eich und Huchel wurden berühmt: DEM LEBEN, WIE SIE'S LITTEN,/ AUFS GRAB DER BLUME LOHN:/ FÜR ACHIM MARGERITEN/ UND FÜR BETTINA MOHN! Und Huchel machte daraus ein Herbstgedicht mit dem herrlichen Anfang: WIE DU NUN GEHST IM SPÄTEN REGEN,/ DER MOND UND HIMMEL KÄLTER FLÖSST/ UND AUF DEN LAUBVERSCHWEMMTEN WEGEN/ DEN RISS IN DIE GESPINSTE STÖSST.[45]

Huchel's lines were, in fact, initially incorporated in the cycle 'Strophen aus einem Herbst', his most important publication from the mid-1930s, which he placed in *Das innere Reich* in the autumn of 1935. We shall deal with it presently.

Starting a family

The Huchels returned from the Baltic coast to Alt-Langerwisch with Dora Huchel's pregnancy at an advanced stage and with much work to be done on the flat at Jägerstraße 5 in nearby Michendorf, which they would move into after the birth of their child. The house was situated on the Willichslust development. Somewhat apart from the older village and its inhabitants, Willichslust was inhabited predominantly by middle-class professionals such as civil servants and teachers, some of them Potsdam and Berlin commuters. Willichslust also gave on to the property that Friedrich Zimmermann had sold to the Sydows in the 1890s. Following many years spent in cities, Huchel was returning to his ancestral roots. The progression of Huchel's literary career through the 1930s, however, shows that there is no reason to view residence in Willichslust as a withdrawal from literary life.

It was there, too, that he chose to bring up his child. Susanne Huchel was born on 21 July 1935 at the hospital at Hermannswerder, Potsdam. Huchel celebrated his daughter's birth with the composition of the tender poem 'Das Kinderfenster', which was published, with the dedication 'An Susanne', (i,277) in the second volume of the *Almanach der Dame* in 1935. Just a few days after their daughter's birth Huchel sent his wife a postcard, which bears the postmark 30 July 1935, showing the Herthasee in Michendorf.[46] The postcard was also signed by Götz Kozuschek, who was helping to decorate and move furniture. Huchel's description of their labours is informed by the gently ironic and self-deprecating tone typical of his correspondence with those close to him. The removal had been fraught with problems: the removal men had turned up at only eight in the evening and had worked until one in the morning to complete the job. Despite setbacks, he and Götz had almost finished painting the flat and varnishing furniture, which was now in place.

Huchel was particularly concerned that his daughter should enjoy the protection of a good number of godparents. Apart from Scherk in Kronstadt, they were drawn from Huchel's literary circle. Susanne Huchel recalled,

> Mein Vater, im Grunde ein sehr berechnender Mann, hat immer gesagt: 'So viele Paten wie möglich. Kann mal was passieren, dann ist das Kind versorgt' ... Ich nehme an, daß kaum ein anderes Kind so viele Paten hatte wie ich. Aus dem bewußten Kreis wurden jedenfalls Günter Eich, Götz Kozuschek, Oda Schaefer auserkoren, aber vor allem auch Charlotte Bergengruen. Letztere nahm ihre Aufgabe sehr ernst und hat sich um die Huchels, wie sie sagte, immer treu und regelmäßig gekümmert mit Geschenken, Geld-Gabe, Einladungen ... Mein 2. Vorname ist auch Charlotte.[47]

Paula Knüpfer, the head of children's radio in Berlin, also agreed to act as a god-mother.

Poetry in Die Dame – and elsewhere

The publication of 'Das Kinderfenster' in the *Almanach der Dame*, the almanac of the Berlin fashion magazine *Die Dame*, was one of a number by Huchel in these years. It was another of the outlets which Huchel shared with *Kolonne* friends. The common link was with Sebastian Haffner, who worked as an editor on *Die Dame*. In the first *Almanach der Dame* of the year 1935, Huchel placed two previously unpublished poems, 'Totennacht' (i,388) and 'Winter'. (i,384) The former was of older provenance, the latter a more recent composition. As we have seen, the communion with the dead in 'Totennacht' was later associated by Huchel with his visit to the Jewish cemetery at Sulzburg in 1925. It can, thus, be read as his own personal expression of solidarity with the Jewish people, who were subjected to increasing discrimination in Nazi Germany. Yet the uninitiated reader could scarcely have detected this association from a reading of the poem.

A much altered version of 'Winter' was published in *Gedichte* as 'Dezember'. (i,69) In 'Winter' the poet adopts the persona of the farmer in a narrative poem of ten four-line stanzas, following the model of the *Volkslied*. It is linked with 'Totennacht' through its pre-occupation with the dead. The final two stanzas depict the farmer as he hears sounds outside in the night, 'wer drämmert hart an meinem Tor?',

> Ich hör am Tor den Balken knarren,
> im Nebel läuten ein Gespann.
> Ich hör die Schattenhufe scharren
> und weiß, ein grober Knecht spannt an.
>
> Bang halt ich mich im Haus verborgen.
> Er aber weiß, wo nah ich bin.
> Und klirrend hinter Nacht und Morgen
> fährt er durch kalten Winter hin.

The farm servant remains a mysterious figure here, the tensions between him and the farmer unspoken, whilst the poem maintains the farmer's perspective. There is no social message: Huchel's affections extended to property owners as well as labourers in his depiction of rural Brandenburg.[48] Yet it is consistent with Huchel's development that the early post-war version of the poem should be much more pointed in its social comment. In 'Dezember', the farmer persona is abandoned and the lyrical subject assumes the role of observer of life in the rural community. The heightened realism of 'Winter' is maintained. Through the introduction of the new third, fourth and fifth stanzas the forces of nature come to be directed against the church and an unjust social order which has, however, by now been overcome. The new stanzas read,

> Das Licht der Tenne ist erloschen.
>
> Schnee drückt der kleinen Kirche Walm,
>
> im Klingelbeutel friert der Groschen
>
> und beizend schwelt der Kerzen Qualm.
>
> Der Wind umheult die Kirchhofsmauer.
>
> Des Todes karges Deputat
>
> ist ein vereister Blätterschauer
>
> der Eichen auf den letzten Pfad.
>
> Hier ruhn, die für das Gut einst mähten,
>
> die sich mit Weib und Kind geplagt,
>
> landlose Schnitter und Kossäten.
>
> im öden Schatten hockt die Magd.

In a letter to Kundera in 1958, Huchel offered a brief commentary on the poem, 'Es handelt sich um die toten Gutsarbeiter – noch im Tode sind sie heimatlos und arm'. (ii,344-5) Following the first stage of the land reform in the Soviet Zone, this poem had an immediate political relevance. It is, as we shall see, of a piece with other compositions from those years. Yet in the mid-1930s, it was the mysterious tensions in life rather than social justice to which Huchel drew attention in the poem.

Whatever Huchel later claimed, his poetry published in the early to mid-1930s which treats the rural community was not informed by any explicit references to social injustice, let alone the class struggle. This applies to the years immediately before 1933 as well as – it goes without saying – afterwards. Huchel's work continued to attract the attention of the custodians of the new official literature and in 1935 two poems, 'Die Magd' and 'Letzte Fahrt', were included in the anthology *Das Lied der Arbeit. Selbstzeugnisse der Schaffenden*, which was edited by Hans Mühle and published by the Leopold Klotz Verlag, Gotha in collaboration with the Deutsche Arbeitsfront. It was introduced by Robert Ley. Whatever his own personal views, Huchel's continued participation in the literary life of Nazi Germany entailed such embarrassing compromises. However sophisticated his writing was in comparison with other poets represented in the anthology such as Heinrich Anacker, and however sensitive in contrast to Anacker's crass aggressive chauvinism, his treatment of nature and rural life could be – and was on occasion – accommodated within the official *Blut und Boden* cult. After the war, the only line that he could take was a flat denial of any involvement in the stigmatised cultural life of the Third Reich.

There is ample evidence that Huchel tried to keep his distance from damaging compromise. The friends he kept testify to that as well as the contacts he maintained with producers in the radio world. Much depended on the relationship between author and producer. By no means all producers were Nazi supporters, especially in the early years, and they had some scope in the interpretation of their brief. Huchel sought out such figures as he moved to build on his first play.

The Radio Author: the Death of the Poet?

In 1935 light entertainment was high on the agenda in programming policy. Harald Braun was a producer at the Reichssender Berlin who worked in this particular sphere. Like Hoffmann, he was a figure with whom a number of *Kolonne* writers collaborated until he was forced to vacate his post. Braun produced four of Huchel's radio plays in 1935-6. The first was 'Ein Fahrstuhl ist nicht mehr zu halten. Ein Funkmärchen zu Himmelfahrt', which was broadcast on 30 June.1935. It was followed on 14 February 1936 by 'Ballade im Eisfenster. Ein Winterspiel', which was twice repeated; by 'Katzen auf allen Dächern. Ein Spiel um den Mond', which was broadcast on 15 June 1936 and repeated on three occasions; and by 'Der Fesselballon. Ein Funkkomödie', which was broadcast on 15 November 1936. With the exception of 'Der Fesselballon', these plays were broadcast in the series 'Das Funkmärchen'.

All exploit perennially popular themes of love and adventure through a blend of humorous dialogue, music and verse, some of which had already been published, the rest written for the occasion. As Wessels has argued and as Huchel's sub-titles indicate, in these plays Huchel draws extensively on traditional forms, which were popular in the 1930s, not least because they were broadly consistent with the anti-modernist thrust of official cultural policy. Huchel deploys musical forms to particular effect. His work is frequently reminiscent of the traditions of the 'Singspiel' and operetta; dialogue is often used as a bridge between songs. On occasion, too, his songs echo the style of the 1920s, most famous through Brecht's *Dreigroschenoper*. Furthermore, the plays show a side of Huchel as the purveyor of popular humour that does not figure in the serious project that was his poetry, yet which was well-known to those who entered the charmed circle of Huchel, the raconteur.

'Katzen auf allen Dächern', for example, tells the story of Monika and the mischievous 'Kunstpfeifer' Thomas. After quite understandable hesitation on the girl's part they fall for each other. The play ends with their duet rendering of

Huchel's poem 'Zunehmender Mond' (i,279) set to Rudolf Wagner-Regeny's music. The other three plays were written according to a formula, in which the protagonists escape from everyday life into a world of dreams and phantasies. For all the initial sense of wonder at the fairy-tale figures they encounter, the frightening aspect of the dream world is brought home to them through exposure to danger. This teaches them the value of the everyday world, to which they return. In 'Ballade im Eisfenster' the main character, Hans Sonnenburg, is accompanied by the comic 'Grenzwächter' into the realm of the 'Eiskönig' and 'Eiskönigin', who, tired of her elderly husband, falls for Hans. Hans is first feted by the 'Eiskönig' with 'Gletscherwein', then imprisoned for possessing matches, since with them he could destroy the ice kingdom. He escapes and as he awakens from his dream he remembers the final verse of the song sung by the 'Eiskönigin',

> Was bist du traurig ohne Grund?
>
> Mit jedem neuen Schnee
>
> Küß ich doch deinen heißen Mund
>
> Als Flocke und vergeh - -[49]

In 'Ein Fahrstuhl ist nicht mehr zu halten' two lovers, Paul and Franziska, are transported by a lift in a department store up into the clouds. There they meet the 'Wolkenhirtin', the 'Große Bärenjäger', the 'Marswesen' and the 'Himmlische Postillon'. As Schäfer writes, these encounters 'desillusionieren die Freiheitssehnsucht; schließlich wünschen sich Paul und Franziska ... die Rückkehr zur Erde'.[50] Huchel's formulaic pieces in fact conform to a pattern of the popular 'Funkmärchen' identified by Wessels, who writes that they

> orientierten ... sich am kleinbürgerlichen Alltag mit seinen Hoffnungen und Wünschen, die
> den Protagonisten im Traum oder einer Ausnahme-Situation als Realität vorgespielt
> wurden, um ihnen den augenblicklichen Zustand als vorteilhaft erscheinen zu lassen, und
> an die bürgerliche Tugend der Selbstbescheidung zu appelieren.[51]

Wessels regards 'Der Fesselballon' as a typical example of this 'Beschwichtigungsideologie des "arm aber glücklich"'.[52] This play, too, closes with a return to the everyday world after an excursion into a realm of dreams and adventures, in which, however, more serious themes are touched upon. The action hinges on the reversal of roles of the aspiring American writer, Jack Town, and the famous boxer, Bill Black. Town dreams of emulating Black's seemingly unlimited popular success. Having tasted it in his reveries, he dreams, too, of the problems of success in the shape of the attentions of managers, journalists and the public, who prevent him from writing. This restriction on his freedom of action is the price of fame. As Wessels has argued, this piece demonstrates Huchel's awareness of the nature of the dependencies he had entered into.[53] The critic in the play tells Town, 'Sie können nicht entwischen! Es wäre nur die Flucht eines Fesselballons! Sie schweben in den Wolken, wir aber halten die Seile!' The author asks why they will not let him go and receives the reply, 'Was sollen unsere Leser anfangen, wenn Sie plötzlich verschwinden? Sie kämen ja vor Langeweile um'. The writer is thus cast in the role of the harmless entertainer, engaged to distract the public. This was the position Huchel himself had come to occupy, as he himself was all too aware. Yet the play does not pursue this line of thought to its conclusion. Town awakens from his dream and comes to the realisation that, despite poverty and hardship, reality with his long-suffering wife Hester is preferable to the heights he had dreamt of. He is rewarded by a publisher's promise of financial support. The play provoked the following, scathing criticism from the editors of *Rundfunk und Fernsehen*, 'Daß Dichter auch an einem politischen Strick aufgehängt werden können, wußte Huchel damals wohl nicht'.[54] One is bound to say that Huchel knew that well enough and that by the mid-1930s his own aspirations as a poet had been all but destroyed in the cultural climate of the Third Reich.

As we have seen, critical discussion of these plays has progressed beyond their description in the 1984 edition as 'unterhaltsam-freundliche Spiele'. (ii,409) Indeed, as is hinted at in 'Der Fesselballon', Huchel himself surely did not construe them as wholly harmless, escapist works, since he was quite aware that they were in keeping with official policy. In considering the triviality of these plays and especially 'Ein Fahrstuhl ist nicht mehr zu halten', the editors of *Rundfunk und Fernsehen* conclude,

> Wie bei den drei anderen Hörspielen Huchels handelt es sich auch in diesem Fall wohl um eine Arbeit, die nur für den sofortigen Verbrauch bestimmt war. Die Möglichkeiten der Kunstform Hörspiel hat Huchel, der ohne Zweifel damals das Talent besaß, über den Tag hinaus zu schreiben, nicht erkannt.[55]

Material which was at the time not known to the editors demonstrates a greater degree of awareness of his situation on Huchel's part and also that he did deploy his talents as a poet to produce more accomplished work alongside the more banal and conformist pieces produced in conjunction with Braun. Oda Schaefer's account of the party that the Huchels held following the christening of their daughter shows, for all Schaefer's tendency to distort and exaggerate, the frustration that Huchel felt in his situation,

> Auf diesem Fest, das allmählich hitzig und turbulent wurde, setzten Günter Eich und der Komponist Götz Kosuczeck dem diesmal überaus mürrischen Poeten zu, er solle nun

endlich seine Gedichte aufschreiben, die er murmelnd zu memorieren pflege, er werde sie
sonst vergessen. Es war lange Zeit nichts mehr von ihm gedruckt worden. Die Freunde
wurden zudringlich wie Fliegen, wenn ein Gewitter kommt – und das Gewitter ließ nicht
lange auf sich warten. Aus dem unwirschen 'Piese', wie sein märkischer Spitzname lautete,
wurde unversehens ein wütender Berserker, er verlor gänzlich seinen Humor, den wir so
sehr liebten, riß Zinnteller von der Wand und schleuderte sie wie Wurfgeschosse nach uns;
wir mußten uns unter den Tisch ducken, dann brachen wir sehr schnell auf.[56]

Huchel in fact continued with poetry publications on a fairly regular basis until late
1935 but more lucrative radio work was starting to take precedence. It is to some
extent true that radio work was foregrounded out of financial necessity. Yet the more
significant point is that Huchel's hopes of building upon his reputation as a poet had
been all but dashed. In the mid-1930s Huchel, like the Langes, was approached by
Henry Goverts and Eugen Claassen, probably on Langgässer's recommendation, as
they sought to establish a list of young authors.[57] Yet he had not by this stage
developed his portfolio in any substantial way beyond the position he had reached
in late 1932. The major collection he wished to produce was still not ready and it
would in fact be more than a decade before he was ready to release such a volume.
The circumstances of the Nazi dictatorship militated against the untroubled
development of what he had achieved in the early 1930s. Yet amidst the frustrations
and unhappy compromises, there still emerged some work, both published verse and
writing for the radio, which is more accomplished. It includes in 'Die Magd und das
Kind' (ii,11-26) a play which is a continuation of the theme of the Alt-Langerwisch
childhood and in 'Die Herbstkantate' (ii,27-40) another which is a deeply serious
expression of the inner conflict into which involvement in the official literary world
of the Third Reich plunged him.

The greater accomplishment of these plays is linked to the fact that Huchel
constructed them around verse published during the early to mid-1930s. In the
former, the verse is interpolated within dialogue, while the latter, as the title
suggests, is a sequence of poems set to music. Huchel signalled the more
sophisticated nature of both pieces in his sub-title 'Eine Dichtung für den Rundfunk'.
'Die Magd und das Kind' was produced by Paula Knüpfer for the Reichssender
Berlin on 24 August 1935. By the end of May 1939 it had been repeated six times,
making it Huchel's most frequently broadcast play. Not only was this financially
attractive to the author, its incorporation in the repertoire of more ambitious literary
work ensured the growth of Huchel's reputation as 'einer der meistaufgeführten
Funkdichter' in the Third Reich.[58] This play, in Lennartz's view Huchel's most
successful, was less the tragedy of the elderly maidservant, which Lennartz
foregrounds, than a celebration through an act of remembrance of the tenderness and
affection shown to the adoring little boy by the otherwise uncouth old peasant

woman, Anna, of course, who speaks the dialect of the Brandenburg Marches. The boy replies in standard German,

> DIE MAGD erschrocken:
>
> Det Kind! Noa'm See! Joa, un du hest joa keene Strümpe nich an, barfbeenig biste ok!
>
> DAS KIND Bist du böse? Da – ich hab dir was mitgebracht. Maiglöckchen. Und wie es schon riecht im Garten, Anna, nach Flieder, grad wie deine Bluse am Sonntag.
>
> DIE MAGD Doa sall ick nich bös sin. Barfbeenig – un bibbern duste wie der Gras in 'n Wind. Man jut, det ick mein Duch hebbe. (ii,13-4)

The work thus elaborates upon Huchel's major poetic theme of the Alt-Langerwisch world of childhood. The dialogue, in four sections representing the seasons, is woven around poetry. By 1935, however, the treatment of regional themes and folkloric traditions had been consolidated within the *Blut und Boden* cult that was central to the official view of literature. Lennartz's characterisation of Huchel's radio work cited above makes it clear that Huchel's work could be understood in terms that were compatible with that cult, even though there was no trace of the aggressive chauvinism typical of 'hard-line' Nazi writing and however much 'Die Magd und das Kind' might reflect Huchel's own artistic and, indeed, emotional concerns. Involvement by a non-Nazi author in what was inescapably the official literature made such ambiguities inevitable.The second play identified above, 'Die Herbstkantate', also enjoyed success with listeners and critics. It was first broadcast on 14 October 1935 and twice repeated by May 1939. The first production was praised by Gerd Eckert in the following terms,

> Für den Nebenbeihörenden ein durcheinander von schwer verständlichen, zuweilen wiederholten Versen und Kammermusik. Dem lauschenden Hörer dagegen erschloß sich aus der Verbindung der klangreichen und lautmalenden Sprache Huchels mit der von Paul Hoeffer verständnisvoll geschriebenen Musik eine aus der Naturbeobachtung und der Tiefe des Gefühls eindringlich gestaltete Deutung des Herbsterlebnisses. (ii,412-3)

The depth of feeling articulated by Huchel in this sequence, which contains some of his finest autumnal verse, is not fully conveyed in Eckert's appreciation, despite its importance in stressing that here Huchel was making no concessions to easy listening. Huchel's cantata – a popular form in the official literature of the Third Reich – is structured around the cycle of poems, 'Strophen aus einem Herbst', which Huchel published virtually simultaneously in *Das innere Reich*. Through their common structure both works give expression to a progressively darkening vision of anguish and despair, as light yields to darkness, the poet's dream turns into a nightmare, creativity gives way to artistic barrenness and life is overtaken by death. Both works can be readily understood as expressing Huchel's deep distress over his position as an artist in Nazi Germany. The play's final section, 'November-Endlied' in the cycle, reads,

> MÄNNERSTIMME singt:
>
> Im Nebel nistet nun mein Traum.
>
> Ich pflanzte ein den Totenbaum.
>
> Auf roten Wolken fuhr die Nacht.
>
> Sie fuhr durch seine Zweige sacht.
>
> FRAUENSTIMME singt:
>
> Da rief ein Vogel – schlief ich schon?
>
> Wie dunkel stieg der Vogelton.
>
> O grauer Herbst, ich wünsch nichts mehr.
>
> Ach käme doch der Schatten her.
>
> MÄNNERSTIMME singt:
>
> Die Nacht auf roten Wolken zieht.
>
> Im Nebel nistet nun mein Lied.
>
> FRAUENSTIMME singt:
>
> Was rief der Vogel mich von fern?
>
> Ich läg im steingen Acker gern. (ii,39)

The profound sense of melancholy and inner conflict conveyed in the poetry, with its echoes of Lenau's autumnal verse of despair, points to the poet's torment and guilt at the compromises he was entering into.[59] The frequency of allusions to poets of the *Biedermeierzeit* indicates that Huchel, like many of his contemporaries, saw affinities between the two post-revolutionary ages and their repression of freedom. Operating in the mid-1930s in a voracious and politically instrumentalised medium, the nature poet was rapidly being stripped of his artistic identity and integrity, signified by the neo-Romantic 'Traum' and 'Lied' of the poem, which are now shrouded in mist as the poet longs for death as a release.

This work evidently struck a chord with another poet, Huchel's friend Eich. In a letter to Huchel written on 22 October 1935, Eich asked him to let him have a copy of 'Die Herbstkantate'. He would like to use material from it and any other material dealing with autumnal themes for the November number of his monthly broadcast, 'Der Königswusterhäuser Landbote', which he wrote in conjunction with Martin Raschke. That particular number had been advertised as a 'bunte Folge vom Beginn der langen Abende'. Eich hoped he would be able to visit the Huchels and their daughter soon. Eich incorporated 'November-Endlied', together with verse and prose by Heinrich E. Kromer, Georg von der Vring, Hans Friedrich Blunck and Georg Britting, in his broadcast on 1 November 1935.

Nor was that the end of the work's significance for Eich. It is illuminating to compare 'Die Herbstkantate' and what it tells us about Huchel's moral and artistic crisis in late 1935 with Axel Vieregg's interpretation of Eich's position just a few months later, in mid-1936.[60] Vieregg builds upon Glenn Cuomo's interpretation of Eich's play 'Radium', which depicts the poet Chabanais, who prostitutes himself by writing advertising copy for a corrupt organisation. Cuomo argues convincingly that Chabanais is Eich's self-portrait. Vieregg sets 'Radium' alongside the poem 'Der Tag im März', which he describes as one of Eich's most pessimistic pieces from the 1930s. It reads,

> Wo ist er nun der große Traum der Erde,
>
> der Traum von Vogelflug und Pflanzensein
>
> die Dinge blieben doch, ihr altes Werde,
>
> ihr alter Tod und ach, ihr altes Nein.
>
> Wo aus der Leere, wo sind da die Fluchten?
>
> Es endet keine mehr im Licht.
>
> Die Spuren wehen zu, die Felsen wuchten.
>
> Von Eis bewachsen Haar und Angesicht.
>
> So geht der Tag im März zu seinem Ende.
>
> Ein Rinnsal Glück reicht für ein ganzes Leben aus.
>
> Das Wasser dunkel, dunkeln Aug und Hände.
>
> Ist es genug? Es führt kein Wort hinaus.

Vieregg characterises the poem as a 'dunkler Abgesang auf das, was für ihn einmal Lyrik und die Existenz als Lyriker bedeutet hatte'. Like Huchel, Eich can no longer maintain an identity as a poet founded on an essentially Romantic idiom of nature poetry whose magic had been stripped of its integrity and credibility by the rapacious demands of the Nazi radio system. Vieregg concludes that Eich 'findet sich von der Macht des Faktischen so heftig bedrängt, daß seine innere Welt und damit seine lyrische Ausdrucksfähigkeit, so wie er sie bis dahin verstanden hatte, ersticken'. The publication of 'Strophen aus einem Herbst' signalled an end for Huchel, too: he virtually ceased to publish new poetry in the Third Reich. A new beginning as a poet was a long way off. It would be triggered by witnessing the horrific destruction in the final stages of the war. Yet the crisis of 1935 did not lead to any break with official Nazi culture in radio.

It is characteristic of Huchel's ambiguous position that, despite his evident intention to signal his despair, 'Die Herbstkantate' should have served to boost his reputation among critics. Not long after it was broadcast, Eckert singled him out together with Eich, Alfred Prugel and Ottoheinz Jahn as writers who 'überhaupt oder nur vorwiegend für den Rundfunk schaffen' and who were 'überhaupt literaturgeschichtlich unbeschriebene Blätter, obwohl ihr Publikum weit größer ist als die Leserschaft der meisten Romane'.[61] Eckert argued that the work of these authors demonstrated the unfairness of the inferior treatment of radio work and recommended the publication of their plays. Publication in fact remained very much the exception and none of Huchel's plays appeared in print in the Nazi period.

In that same autumn of 1935 half a dozen of Huchel's poems ('Zunehmender Mond', 'Frühe', 'Der Herbst', 'Havelnacht' 'Herbstabend' and 'Marie') already published in journals were included in an anthology representing the official literature. *Das Lied der Stille. Eine Auswahl neuer Lyrik*, was, as Hans Dieter Schäfer has pointed out, edited by Edgar Diehl in conjunction with the Reichsschrifttumskammer. Schäfer also points out that the anthology was launched on 13 November 1935 at a reception for the press. The main speaker was the head of the Reichsschrifttumsstelle, Dietz, who, according to a report in the *Berliner Tageblatt* of 14 November 1935 viewed it as 'eine besondere Aufgabe dieser Presseempfänge ... , auf die heranwachsende, teilweise noch unbekannte Generation aufmerksam zu machen'. He drew attention to 'das Wesentliche dieser Lyrik. Sie bewegte sich fern von allem Politischen und Kämpferischen'. The absence of the aggressive and overtly political tone to be found amongst 'alte Kämpfer' was excused on the grounds of age and experience, 'Diese Jungen haben andere Aufgaben'. The gentle tone of the verse was in keeping with the avoidance of explicit propaganda during this phase of 'stabilisation' of Nazi rule. The article was, however, not without a critical edge,

> Im übrigen bewegten sich die vorgelesenen Gedichte im rein Menschlichen, oft im allzu Persönlichen − Erlebnislyrik, die teilweise nicht zur dichterischen Gestaltung vorgedrungen war. Die alten Themen: Liebe (Hans Lenaerts, Arthur Max Luckdorf, Carola Schiel; Peter Huchel fiel auf mit einigen schlichten Versen; ...) und Natur überwogen.

In conversation with Kundera, Huchel later commented that he had at one time been of the view that 'die große Schlichtheit' was an appropriate response to his age but events had proved him wrong.[62] We see in this comment the earnestly held belief that the simple integrity of art should stand against the questionable world of politics, a belief consistent with Huchel's development during the early 1930s. While the critic of the *Berliner Tageblatt* certainly included Huchel in his criticism of the excessively personal and conventional character of much of the verse, Huchel's talent elicited a positive evaluation, a pattern by now familiar as the criterion of quality was balanced against that of overt ideological commitment. Quality was not ignored as Nazi cultural politicians continued in their efforts to use culture in the legitimation of the regime. Huchel's 'Havelnacht' was subsequently selected from the anthology for publication, as 'Nacht an der Havel' in the *Berliner Tageblatt* on 27 January 1936.

This episode, like the examination of the radio plays, demonstrates clearly how Huchel continued to cultivate his own poetic concerns without any trace of the Nazis' ideological trappings, yet how his work was assimilated within the official literature. As long as Huchel chose to pursue his calling as a professional writer through broadcasts and publications, it was impossible for him to escape from a system that would make ever greater demands. Even during the war, following conscription he continued to follow his vocation. The absence of any resolution to break with this system despite a clear awareness of its workings is the real wretchedness of the Huchel and, indeed, the Eich story. Financially dependent on the radio and unable to construe their lives in terms other than as writers, they continued to devote their energies to radio work, muddling through as best they could while conscious of the shabby compromises this entailed. The sense of inner conflict rose to the surface and abated as they responded to the fluctuating, yet in time ever greater pressures of the Nazi system, which bore upon a compromised sense of artistic and moral integrity. For all their clear political differences in the early period of Nazi rule, their experiences with the official culture of the Third Reich brought them together as the 1930s progressed and the Nazis tightened their grip on broadcasting.

The Established Radio Author

After 'Die Herbstkantate', Huchel maintained a quite prolific radio output. For all his profound misgivings, he had, like Eich, become part of a Berlin radio world, which offered ready and reasonably lucrative employment. The plays discussed above point up the unevenness in the quality of his output, a feature of Eich's output, too, throughout the 1930s. This can be accounted for in large measure by the dual pressures operating upon authors of programming requirements and financial need. In the mid- to late 1930s, they experienced these pressures as authors who frequently shared each other's company. On 3 November 1936, for example, Hermann Kasack noted in his diary that Huchel was going to stay with Eich at his house in Poberow.[63] Shortly after, on 15 February 1937, Huchel got to know Kasack, when the latter read his 'Archimedes' at the Potsdam Kant Gesellschaft.[64]

Between late 1935 and mid-1937, Huchel broadcast a further six plays, none of which have survived. They are 'Der Bernsteinwald. Funkspiel' (21.11.1935); 'Das Wunder am Wege' (5.1.1936); 'Der letzte Knecht. Funkballade' (20.2.1936); 'Gott im Ährenlicht. Kantate zum Erntedankfest' (4.10.1936); 'Putt, putt, putt, mein Hühnchen. Ein Spiel um alte Kinderlieder' (18.2.1937); and 'Reihe 3, Stand 10. Ein Funkspiel von Liebe und Wochenmarkt' (10.6.1937). Despite the loss of these plays, certain conclusions can be drawn from summaries of contents and other information. While 'Putt, putt, putt, mein Hühnchen' was evidently a piece for children, 'Reihe 3, Stand 10', produced by Paula Knüpfer, is described in the summary of contents in terms reminiscent of Huchel's other pieces designed for popular consumption. Like them it was not repeated. Though 'Das Wunder am Wege', too, was not repeated, the summary of its contents suggests scope for a more ambitious approach in keeping with his treatment of the rural world. The summary reads,

> In einer der zwölf Nächte zwischen Weihnachten und Dreikönigstag spielt Peter Huchels symbolische Dichtung, die der Reichssender Berlin uraufführt. An einem einfachen Begebnis der bäuerlichen Umwelt macht der Dichter seinen Hörern deutlich, daß auch der Alltag voller Wunder ist und daß in scheinbar belanglosen Begebnissen der Wirklichkeit Ewiges verborgen sein kann. (ii,413)

While the author ensured the acceptability of his work through the traditionalist message that the rural world was the source of eternal values, he refrained from developing any explicitly ideological perspective. A similar point can be made about 'Der letzte Knecht', Huchel's first play for the Reichssender Leipzig, which was produced by the head of production, Hans Zeise-Gött, who would produce two of Huchel's three others plays broadcast from Leipzig between 1937 and 1939. The list of characters and details of the setting shortly after the First World War – a time when the run-down farm of Huchel's grandparents was sold – suggests a re-working of the Alt-Langerwisch material, as does the summary of contents, which reads,

> Paul, der Pferdeknecht auf dem heruntergewirtschafteten Hof des Bauern Käthe, liegt im Sterben. Jahrzehntelang hat er mit seiner Gabe, das Wetter vorauszusagen, das Dorf beunruhigt und beherrscht. Jetzt, da dieses Geheimnis mit ihm begraben und vergessen werden könnte, kommen Dörfler, Landarzt und Wunderdoktor an sein Lager, um es zu erfahren. Aber der alte Peitschenpaul gibt das 'Geheimnis der Knechte' nur an den Bauernsohn weiter, in dem er schon den künftigen Knecht sieht. (ii,414)

The story of the transmission from generation to generation of the secrets of the rural world echoes the traditionalist message of 'Das Wunder am Wege'. It would appear that once more the author refrained from the adoption of any further ideological perspective in a story that reflects Huchel's own pre-occupation with his self-stylisation as a farm servant, who in the play is depicted as the source of authentic knowledge about the rural world.

If his treatment of the Alt-Langerwisch material distanced Huchel from mainstream Nazi propaganda, the circumstances surrounding the production of 'Der Bernsteinwald' suggest that through this play he was drawn a little further into the net. Lennartz describes the play as 'das anläßlich der Reichswerbung für "nordisches Gold" entstandene Funkspiel'.[65] It is unfortunate that the loss of the text precludes analysis of a play evidently submitted in response to a propaganda slogan. In the 1984 edition, however, the following is suggested, 'Das Verzeichnis der Stimmen (das Mädchen; der Mann; die Mücke; der Eisriese – S.P.) deutet auf ein Traumspiel in der Art von "Ein Fahrstuhl ist nicht mehr zu halten" und "Ballade im Eisfenster"'. (ii,413) This is plausible enough comment, consistent with an established pattern, as Huchel sought to steer a course through acceptable treatment of a subject without adopting the strident tones of overt and aggressive Nazi propaganda.

As with 'Der Bernsteinwald', the context of the production of 'Gott im Ährenlicht' offers a basis for some comment despite our only vague knowledge of the content. Once again Huchel employed the favoured form of the cantata, this time for a piece which, one can read in the 1984 edition, 'wurde unmittelbar vor der Übertragung der "Morgenfeier" aus der Potsdamer Garnisonskirche anläßlich des Erntedankfestes gesendet'. (ii,415) Lennartz offers the following characterisation, 'Immer wieder tritt die starke lyrische Begabung aus Liedern zutage, die in die Handlung verwoben sind, z.B. in der farbig bewegten, klangvollen Kantate über die Erntezeit und den Herbst "Gott im Ährenlicht" (1936), die den Duft und die Stimmung einer großen Ernte einfängt'.[66] However, we see here much more blatantly than in other examples examined hitherto how Huchel's lyrical gift was deployed on a very special occasion in the Nazi calendar, celebrated in an equally special place in Nazi image-building. The Nazis' efforts to extract maximum propaganda effect from harvest thanksgiving have been well documented. If little else can be established regarding Huchel's involvement in this piece of Nazi cultish practice, it can be said that by late 1936 he could not say no to an invitation to participate.

The contradictions at this time between the private and the public spheres emerge in a story told by both Huchel himself and his wife after the war, though with somewhat different emphases. According to Dora Huchel, the Huchels were not fortunate in their choice of neighbours at Jägerstraße 5. The house owners and co-residents were Nazi supporters and the Huchels' unconventional lifestyle did not meet with their approval. All their worst suspicions were confirmed in an incident in early 1936, when the Huchels were visited by Horst Lange. Lange, who – not unusually – had been drinking, flew into a rage and began to curse Hitler at the top of his voice. The neighbours could not fail to hear Lange's drunken invective and reported it to the Michendorf police. As the head of the offending household, Huchel was at once summoned to the police station. According to his wife's testimony, he simply did not follow this instruction, so she went along in his place. The affair dragged on for a few months, but finally things were smoothed over. Huchel's own early post-war account, which also places the incident in 1936, makes no mention of Lange and suggests that he himself was questioned by the person in charge of the Michendorf NSDAP.[67] The owners of the house felt justified in taking their own action against the Huchels and served them with notice to quit. As a temporary measure, in the summer of 1936 they moved into accommodation near Huchel's parents in Alt-Langerwisch, Am Wolkenberg 27. It was there that Huchel was consulted by Lange as he struggled to complete his novel *Schwarze Weide* for Goverts and Claassen. Lange wrote to Claassen of Huchel that summer that he 'mir stets ein gerechter Kritiker gewesen ist'.[68] With Huchel's advice and that of Elisabeth Langgässer, Lange was able to bring *Schwarze Weide* to a conclusion. When it appeared the following year, Lange thanked Huchel and his wife with a dedication that follows the motto which acts as the book's final statement, 'Alles, was da kreucht, wird mit der Geissel zur Weide getrieben. Für Piese und Dora, in der Hoffnung, dass sie mein Sorgenkind gut aufnehmen werden. Berlin Sept 1937 H.'.[69]

By then, the Huchels had moved into permanent accommodation of quite generous proportions back on the Willichslust development in Michendorf. For eighty marks a month – apparently not always paid [70] – they rented a house at Waldstraße 32, which had a large garden backing on to woodland. The Huchels would stay there until after the war, developing friendships with a number of their neighbours. Huchel's parents would presently join them on Waldstraße. This chapter in Huchel's life, like a number of others, has figured only sketchily in post-war accounts through references in Oda Schaefer's memoirs and Christoph Meckel's account of his father's life. Taking their cue from Huchel's post-war statements, a number of accounts stress Huchel's rural isolation in these years, yet this is a quite misleading picture of Huchel's life in the mid- to late 1930s. Waldstraße 32 became something of a meeting place for the Huchels and their Berlin friends, for whom Michendorf represented a pleasant break from life in the nearby capital. During the war years, as the bombing of Berlin intensified, the house would provide a refuge for friends such as Lange and Schaefer, Hans and Edith Nowak, Günther and Bobba Birkenfeld, and Eich and his first wife Else. At the same time, Berlin was just a short rail journey from Michendorf, so Huchel could pursue his literary projects in the capital without difficulty.

A Tightening of the Screw

In late 1936, the re-organisation was set in train which would shift the emphasis in programming policy for the period leading up to the war. Radio production was more directly instrumentalised for propaganda purposes. It was now increasingly difficult for Huchel to maintain the distance that informs his better work from 1935-6. While in the later 1930s he continued to produce light entertainment, he was exposed to greater pressure to produce other work more overtly supportive of the regime's policies. He responded to this pressure with an even more pronounced ambiguity and on one occasion with what has been construed as dissent, before the outbreak of war made for fresh demands. Indeed, Huchel's plays from the late 1930s and 1940 highlight graphically the very inconsistencies and contradictions in the development of an essentially non-Nazi writer operating in a highly repressive and volatile historical context, in which the stultifying atmosphere of the peace in time gave way to the peculiar pressures of war.

Under the new programming policy fresh primacy was given to overt political propaganda. Wessels notes the encouragement of 'gemeinschaftsbildende Sendungen'[71] during this phase of strengthened Nazi control of the radio, which saw the dismissal of figures such as Werner Pleister and Harald Braun. As Germany embarked on its expansionist plans, listeners were encouraged to identify with the 'Volksgemeinschaft' rather than with particular German regions. Two of Huchel's plays, both realistic adventure stories and as such a fresh departure for him, reflect this new orientation, though in each case Huchel's treatment did not quite deliver what policy makers might have hoped for. Both plays are set on the high seas and show the influence of Traven's novel *Das Totenschiff*. 'Brigg Santa Fé. Eine Weihnachtsballade' was broadcast from Leipzig on 23 December 1937, 'Die Freundschaft von Port Said. Ein Spiel zwischen Heimat und Übersee' by the Berlin short wave station on 7 April 1938. A recording of the latter was recently found at the Czech radio archive near Prague and re-broadcast by Südwestfunk on 16 January 1994.

Like the earlier Leipzig broadcast of 'Der letzte Knecht', 'Brigg Santa Fé' was directed by Hans Zeise-Gött. Huchel's correspondence with his wife reveals that the main contact at Leipzig was Veit Roßkopf, earlier mentioned by Eich in his letter to Kuhnert. In December 1937, Huchel wrote to his wife of his planned meeting with Roßkopf together with Kuhnert and Eich, with whom he was enjoying a Franconian holiday based at Kuhnert's house in Hohenfeld, something they would repeat with Martin Raschke the following September.[72] Both Eich and Kuhnert added their signature to the letter, in which Huchel reported that he was captivated by the Franconian experience and was greatly enjoying his male company. He suggested to his wife that when their daughter was older they should take a second honeymoon along the Main; so much of the landscape was reminiscent of the Wachau area near Vienna, which they had visited in 1926, shortly after they had met. Huchel estimated that they would not be back in Michendorf until just before Christmas. They had driven Eich's car so hard every day that it had broken down and had been towed into a garage. Repairs would be completed on 19 December at the earliest. Their return journey would take in Rothenburg, Dinkelsbühl, Bamberg, Jena and Leipzig, where they would meet Roßkopf. From Leipzig they would travel straight back to Michendorf, in time for him to see to all the Christmas preparations. Huchel also discussed with his wife in the letter the arrangements for the dismissal, apparently for some breach of trust, of their girl in service, Helene Itau.[73] It is likely that their discussions with Roßkopf virtually coincided with the broadcast of 'Brigg Santa Fé' on 23 December. By now, Huchel could not always find non-Nazi figures to work alongside. Despite his reservations, he was drawn into a network in which Roßkopf as a manager and Eich and Kuhnert as authors were involved with work more in line with propaganda needs. Huchel's correspondence with his wife reveals that it was a period of further collaboration with Eich and Kuhnert, which, it seems, involved co-authorship of texts.[74] Huchel's daughter recalls,

> Es wurde auch zusammen gearbeitet, Günter Eich und mein Vater hatten wohl gemeinsame Projekte z.B., aber auch mit den anderen wurde manchmal gearbeitet, wobei ich mich natürlich, da ich ja Kind war, an den Inhalt dieser Arbeit nicht erinnern kann. Jedoch, daß es oft Hörspiele waren oder daß man gemeinsam die Bücher, Manuskripte und auch die Gedichte gegenseitig durchging oder vortrug. Man zog sich ins Arbeitszimmer zurück oder lag draußen ... Ich und meine zahlreichen Spielkameraden, Freunde, Freundinnen wurden dann oft von Haus und Hof verwiesen. 'Wir brauchen jetzt Ruhe,' sagte mein Vater dann, 'tobt mal woanders' hieß es auch, 'Ruhe, wir arbeiten!' schrie man uns auch zu vom Dachstubenfenster oder aus einer Ecke im Garten. Manchmal kamen auch Leute vom Funk, Lektoren, Sendeleiter. Im Zusammenhang mit Hörspielen erinnere ich mich an Namen z.B. jemanden, der Linnekogel hieß und auch Heller.[75]

'Brigg Santa Fé' may be one of the joint projects. It draws upon the 1920s' tradition of the musical with lines such as the following,

> Lieber Baas, wer hält das Steuer,
> Wenn der Wind zur Hölle rennt!?
> Sieh, am Cap lischt aus das Feuer
> und die große Kälte brennt!
> Bring die Brigg aus Eis und Schnee,
> Kapitän der 'Santa Fé'!
> Steure in die offene See![76]

The ship is trapped in the ice off Canada in the weeks immediately before Christmas 1857. Rations are severely depleted. The captain decides that the three German passengers, a man, his pregnant wife and his mother, should be given more than the crew. Two sailors mutiny, making off with the rations over the ice. They trick the

German man to go with them. However, on Christmas Day his wife gives birth. A summary, most likely written by Huchel himself, continues the story,

> Und mit der Geburt des Kindes geschieht auch die Wiedergeburt der Schiffsmannschaft. Alle ahnen dumpf, daß neues Leben mit dem Kind geboren wurde, und die wunderbare Gewißheit, daß das Kind der 'Santa Fé' den Tod auf der Brigg besiegt hat, läßt die Leute ihre Todesfurcht überwinden und schweißt sie zu einer gläubigen Schicksalsgemeinschaft zusammen. (ii,417-8)

The ice begins to break and the ship is gradually freed to continue its passage. Tragedy is averted through the miraculous effect of the German child's birth. The reference in the summary to 'einer gläubigen Schicksalsgemeinschaft' suggests a treatment quite in line with the new propagandist requirement. Interestingly enough, however, the text itself does not quite measure up, since Huchel refrains from making the obvious ideological points that the story invites and the summary seems to promise.

A similar point can be made about 'Die Freundschaft von Port Said', which was repeated three times by May 1939 after a prominent initial production by the Berlin short wave station to celebrate the station's fifth anniversary. In staggered fashion, it was broadcast to all parts of the globe. This explains why, exceptionally, a recording was made. Gerhard Heller, who was employed there between 1936 and 1939, recalled that he had commissioned the play as a collaborative piece by Huchel and Eich.[77] The play echoes 'Brigg Santa Fé' in that it is a story of Germans abroad suffering in adversity on board a ship. The play's summary states that the play 'berichtet von dem Schicksalsweg eines jungen Deutschen', (ii,419) Thomas, emigrating to Australia. Now a farmer there, Thomas tells his wife the tale of his passage. The inexperienced German of good family gets into bad company in the bars of Port Said, where he is robbed and misses his boat. He is rescued by the older German stoker, Paul, who smuggles him on board his Dutch ship, where he is discovered. The two Germans stick together in the face of some of the foreign crew's hostility. Forced to work as a trimmer, 'besteht der junge Deutsche die erste große Prüfung seines Lebens, als er sich unter den farbigen Trimmern behaupten kann'. (ii,419) The black trimmer Johnson is particularly menacing but Thomas shows no fear. The selfless Paul helps his young compatriot, and his exemplary behaviour rubs off on Thomas, who 'erlebt die wunderbare Kameradschaft des Heizers und erfährt eine innere Wandlung'. (ii,419) In a raging storm Paul sacrifices his own life to rescue Thomas. Safely in Australia, Thomas sees a vision of his friend, who stands 'wie auf einem Heiligenbildchen über der "dürren Weide" im "Schein des Kesselfeuers" ... und zur Besinnung mahnt'.[78] The plays closes with Thomas' words to his wife, 'Ich sah ihn im Schein der Kesselfeuer arbeiten. Und ich beschloss, seiner würdig zu sein'.[79] The ending thus fits in with the theme of individual self-sacrifice in the interest of the wider community. Through its affirmation of traditional 'German' virtues such as loyalty, honesty and hard work the play could be construed as a contribution to the raising of German consciousness orchestrated by the Nazis in the build-up to war. It is, finally, difficult to see in this play evidence of an 'antinationalistische Haltung', whatever Huchel might have believed privately.[80] However, what was seemingly given with one hand was withheld with the other: the play did not deliver a clear ideological perspective, since the focus throughout in the text is on the growth of a friendship, not on the growing awareness of Germanness, which the summary somewhat misleadingly foregrounds.

A telling index of Huchel's internal conflict in that same year, 1938, is the composition of two poems to which he later appended that dating when they were published after the war, 'Cap d'Antibes' (i,96) and 'Zwölf Nächte'. (i,94) The former is part of his memorial to Hans A. Joachim, who, as Huchel's letters to his wife show, was never far from his thoughts. It presents an interplay of Huchel's memories of the South of France in the late 1920s – the country in which Joachim was living in exile in 1938 – and the reality of Germany in 1938, the year of *Reichskristallnacht*. The poem opens with a reference to November, the month of *Kristallnacht*, presenting a scene of a hostile nature, which is also in the process of decaying. The central stanza echoes the message of 'Strophen aus einem Herbst', inverting, too, the cosmic vision of 'Havelnacht' and 'Die Sternenreuse', 'Des Himmels Zisterne,/ aus der ich trank/ siderische Wasser,/ ist dunkel und leer'. The final stanza can be read as a premonition of Joachim's later murder by the Nazis, 'Die Tränen der Toten/ schmeckt salzig der Mund./ Wohin ziehn die Boten? Nichts tun sie kund'. Huchel and his friend had indeed now become irrevocably separated as the wholly negative and radical dynamic of National Socialism began fully to reveal itself. 'Zwölf Nächte' thematises the pain and bloody destruction of the age, 'Du findest nur den Schmerz der Zeit,/ die Erde feucht von Blut./ Und unterm Schutt, zum Biß bereit,/ der Schlangen nackte Brut'. The poem's final stanzas mark both a re-affirmation and an extension of the message of 1933 in 'Späteste Söhne , ...' Thus, action is recommended against the 'nackte Brut', 'Zertritt ihr Haupt und scheu den Biß./ Horch in den Wind, bleib stumm'. This is followed by the assurance, 'Doch nicht erstickt der Nacht Gewalt/ der Seele stilles Licht./ Weht auch der Hauch der Asche kalt,/ Die Finsternis zerbricht'.

Yet for all the rejection of what Nazism stood for, action against the regime individually or as a member of a resistance group was never a course that Huchel opted for. The same went for a number of people in his circle such as Lange, Nowak and Birkenfeld, while for others such as Kuhnert, Raschke, Meckel and Eich there was less in the way of outright rejection. Indeed, at times there was open support for National Socialism from this latter group. In this way, the circle that Huchel moved in magnified the ambiguity of his own position.

If we seek to do justice to the range of his work in the years immediately before the outbreak of war, then it is necessary to consider that the new policy emphasis for radio on more overt propaganda did not wholly exclude other types of play and that in 1937-8 Huchel produced two comedies, 'Taten und Abenteuer des Löwentöters Tartarin von Tarascon. Ein Lustspiel mit vielen Liedern frei nach Daudet' and 'Zille Martha. Eine Komödie'. In the former, broadcast on 18 September 1937, Huchel continued his collaboration with Zeise-Gött at Leipzig. Huchel's comedy enjoyed such success that by May 1939 it had been broadcast four more times. In this depiction of the lovable, self-deluding Tartarin, Huchel was able to deploy the ironic humour, which his friends so valued in him but which has no place in his poetry. The summary is an accurate reflection of the play's content,

> Das Lustspiel ist eine freie und volkstümliche Bearbeitung ... Wie Tartarin in der Menagerie Mataine eine 'furchtbar-schreckliche' Begegnung mit einem Löwen hat und von seiner Vaterstadt beim Wort genommen wird, in Afrika Löwenfelle zu erbeuten, welch wunderliche Jagd- und Liebesabenteuer der tatendurstige Tarasconese im bunt besiedelten Algerien bestehen muß, um einen zahmen und blinden Löwen erlegen zu können, und wie der ausgeplünderte und um alle Träume betrogene Held nach Tarascon zurückkehrt, um schließlich doch als Löwentöter gefeiert zu werden, das ist der Inhalt der Handlung.
> (ii,417)

Huchel's other comedy 'Zille Martha', broadcast on 21 June 1938 in the series 'Berliner Volksstücke', also enjoyed great popularity. In 1939, it was judged by the listeners of the Reichssender Berlin one of the plays which 'im vergangenen Jahr am besten gefallen haben'.[81] Its appeal derived no doubt in part from the local colour in the portrayal of life on the Zille Martha, a Havel barge. Its popularity may well also be linked to the involvement as producer of Helmut Hansen, who both produced and played the part of the 'Landbote' in Eich and Raschke's hugely successful series 'Die Monatsbilder des Königswusterhäuser Landboten'. As we have seen, Hansen was one of the prominent Nazis at the Masurenallee with whom Eich embarked upon collaboration in 1933. Huchel himself could no longer avoid collaboration with such figures. Not that, as far as can be ascertained, 'Zille Martha' was informed by overt Nazi propaganda despite a notice which described the play as the 'Geschichte zweier Flußschiffer, die dasselbe Mädchen lieben, darüber in erbitterten Streit geraten, aber in höchster Not zu opferbereiter Kameradschaft zurückfinden'.[82] While this notice reproduces the familiar Nazi propaganda slogan as was then required, the summary points in the direction of a popular, light-hearted tale of love and adventure,

> Der junge Havelschiffer Paul und sein Bootsmann Franz sind zwei Schürzenjäger, wie sie im Buche stehen. Jedes Tanzvergnügen in den Dörfern am Wege, den die 'Zille Martha' nimmt, endet mit einer wüsten Rauferei. Jedesmal dreht es sich bei der Keilerei um ein

Mädchen. Die beiden Schiffer haben auf der Fahrt Zeit, über die Dorfschöne nachzuden-
ken. aber seltsamerweise sind die Gedanken der beiden jungen Schiffer in Katzow, einem
kleinen Dorf, fest vor Anker gegangen. Beide haben dort das Mädchen gefunden, das sie
einmal heiraten wollen. Und nichts ist natürlicher, als daß sie eines Abends, als ihre 'Zille'
an Katzow vorbeigeschleppt werden soll, sich einfach vom Schleppzug abhängen. Sie
erleben aber in Katzow eine tolle Überraschung. (ii,418)

For Lennartz, 'Das lustige Berliner Alltagshörspiel "Zille Martha" (38), in dem zwei
Havelschiffer das gleiche Mädchen lieben, ist weiterer Beweis für die ausgesproche-
ne Funkbegabung Huchels'.[83] The loss of the manuscript is all the more regrettable
since there has been some controversy in recent years over possible links between
Huchel's play and Helmut Käutner's film 'Unter den Brücken'. The film was
completed in the autumn of 1944 and shares with 'Zille Martha' a plot in which two
'Havelschiffer' fall in love with the same girl. Hans Dieter Schäfer writes, 'Oda
Schaefer erinnerte sich, daß Helmut Käutner von "Zille Martha" angeregt wurde;
Huchel soll 1944 am Drehbuch mitgearbeitet haben'.[84] The 1984 edition contains
the following note, 'Die verschiedentlich geäußerte Vermutung, das Hörspiel habe
als Vorlage zu Helmut Käutners Film vor Kriegsende, "Unter den Brücken",
gedient, ist von P.H. selbst, wie Frau Monica Huchel mitteilt, zurückgewiesen
worden'. (ii,418) Other information suggests that the matter should not be deemed
closed. Huchel's wartime letters to his wife reveal that he was involved in film
scriptwriting from just after the time of his conscription in August 1941 until
October 1944.[85] In 1981, Dora Huchel recalled that during the later war years 'ging
eine große Summe auf die Michendorfer Bank für einen Film, wahrscheinlich "Unter
den Brücken"'. If there is no doubt that Käutner collaborated with Walter Ulbrich
in producing a script which drew on Leo de Laforgue's *Unter den Brücken von
Paris*, then the independent testimonies of Oda Schaefer and Dora Huchel, as well
as the evidence of thematic affinities, strongly suggest that 'Zille Martha' was drawn
upon for Käutner's film. In time additional archive information may emerge so that
firmer conclusions can be drawn.

Open Dissent?

Shortly after the first broadcast of 'Zille Martha', Dora and Susanne Huchel visited
the Lassels in Kronstadt. They flew from Berlin to Budapest on 18 July, just three
days before Susanne's birthday. Huchel remained in Michendorf, where he pressed
on with quite a gruelling writing schedule for the radio. Only a matter of hours after
their departure on 18 July he sent them a postcard, which was followed at the end
of the month by a letter in response to one from his wife.[86] He described the
pressures he was under with his work: Leipzig were pressing for 'Margarethe
Minde', and he had now agreed to submit it by mid-August, even though he still had

forty pages to write after he had worked through papers in the Staatsbibiliothek. He also had a pressing piece of work to do for the short wave station. He mentioned Eich, who was still at his house on the Baltic coast, and Kuhnert, from whom he had received 150 marks. The money had gone towards paying some bills. He went on to inform his wife that in order to take his mind off such problems he had bought a huge black leather sofa for fifteen marks. Finally he had been further consoled by the news that Leipzig were repeating 'Die Freundschaft von Port Said' on 15 August. Eich returned from the Baltic and on 10 August he visited Hermann Kasack with Huchel.[87] Not long after his wife and daughter's return from Kronstadt, Huchel, too, would take a break, travelling in early September with his friends Eich and Raschke to visit Kuhnert in Hohenfeld.[88]

Despite the above evidence of financial difficulties, it would be wrong to conclude that in the mid- to later 1930s the Huchels were especially poor. Huchel's income from his radio work was on a par with the average income in the mid-1930s of someone working in an administrative grade in law or education. Then there was the financial support from Kronstadt. The Huchels' income was thus broadly in line with their neighbours and certainly sufficient to keep a girl in service, whose dismissal was clearly not for financial reasons. What is more, despite the fact that Huchel always opposed the Nazis' policies, gradually as the 1930s progressed, he accepted working arrangements with figures such as Roßkopf, which made for a reasonably comfortable life but brought with them a degree of dependence which would become seriously compromising following the outbreak of war.

As an established radio author, in the late 1930s Huchel drew an increasing proportion of his income from repeats of his plays. For all the stress he felt under in mid-1938, he was not under such great pressure to produce fresh material on a regular basis. In fact only one play, 'Margarethe Minde', was first broadcast before the outbreak of war. This play supplies further evidence of Huchel's equivocal position as a dissenting collaborator. It was broadcast from Leipzig on 22 June 1939 and directed by Hans-Peter Schmiedel, Roßkopf's colleague in the arts department. The extant text, published in the 1984 edition, together with the other information referred to above by Huchel in correspondence with his wife, reveals that Huchel took considerable trouble over this play, which was broadcast almost a year after he discussed it with his wife.

The editor of the 1984 edition points out Huchel's relative independence from Theodor Fontane in his use of sources, (ii,419-20) which is corroborated by Huchel's reference to the use of original material in the Staatsbibliothek. The play is thus more than just an adaptation in the manner of other pieces. Vieregg draws attention to the magical and prophetic quality of the opening scene, whose power is underscored by Huchel's use – exceptionally – of blank verse. In his afterword to the edition, Vieregg singles out 'Margarethe Minde' in order to make quite specific claims for Huchel as a 'literary opponent' of National Socialism, 'Der Text kann als Beitrag jener literarischen Opposition gedeutet werden, die ihre Kritik als

Parabel und Gleichnis formulierte'. (ii,405-6) He adds that Huchel's critique of the Nazi regime 'muß gut verstanden worden sein. Entsprechend vorsichtig verhielten sich die Rundfunkanstalten; im Gegensatz zu anderen mehrfach gesendeten Hörspielen wurde "Margarethe Minde" nicht wiederholt'. (ii,406) In fact, the outbreak of war shortly after the play's broadcast was followed by the suspension of radio play production. Considerable emphasis was placed on war propaganda when it was resumed. In those circumstances, prospects of a repeat were somewhat diminished.

To make this point is not, however, to deny that 'Margarethe Minde' contains formulations that can be interpreted as critical of the regime. Vieregg cites two key speeches by sympathetic characters, Morten and Helmreich. They occur near the beginning and the end of the play and thus establish a framework for interpretation. Morten's speech in the opening scene evokes a doom-laden atmosphere of evil, which can also be found in some of Huchel's poems from the late 1930s such as 'Zwölf Nächte', which were published only after the war,

> Die dumpfe Erde brütet Unheil nur,
>
> Seit der Saturn dem Mars sich nähert –
>
> Ja, was für Zeiten! Mensch und Tiere zittern,
>
> Bricht über sie die Nacht herein! (ii,44-5)

When near the end Helmreich assumes the judge's role, he exclaims,

> Ungern, ihr Bürger, walt' ich dieses Amts!
>
> Wer möchte hier noch Richter sein? – Die Stadt,
>
> Sie war voll Rechts, nun ist sie eine Mördergrube! –
>
> Zornhaus der Hölle, öffne dich!! Verschling
>
> Doch diese Brut, die über Tangermünde kam!
>
> Im Blutdunst des Verbrechens lebt hier alles! (ii,97)

Vieregg draws attention to Huchel's allusions in this passage to Isiah's apocalyptic prophesies and especially to chapter one verse 21, 'Wie geht das zu, daß die fromme Stadt zur Hure geworden ist? Sie war voll Rechts, Gerechtigkeit wohnte darin, nun aber – Mörder'. The first half of the speech can certainly be construed as conveying 'die Ängste und Anklage des Jahres 1939 zwar in zeitlicher Verfremdung, doch im höchsten Maße anspielungsreich', (ii,406) and their position invites such an interpretation of the play as a whole. Yet the second half of the speech contains terms that were deployed by the Nazis and their supporters in their attacks on the Weimar Republic. Many listeners would have made this link.

Wessels, who makes this point, suggests that listeners would in any case have understood the piece as a historical play.[89] Even though one might accept that Huchel's intention was to express dissent with the Nazi regime, the passage invites other interpretations and as such illustrates a fundamental difficulty for the would-be dissenting writer operating within the framework of the official literature under the dictatorship.

A further point can be made. While there can be no denying Huchel's personal rejection of all that Nazism stood for, 'Margarethe Minde' and 'Die Herbstkantate' provide the only evidence among available radio manuscripts of a dissenting stance. Indeed, there is much evidence, if not of explicit support, then of conformism to elements of programming policy. It is therefore misleading to stylise Huchel on the basis of 'Margarethe Minde' as an authentic representative of the 'literary opposition'. Like many of his friends and contemporaries Huchel was pulled first one way then another, experiencing the inner conflict characteristic of the dissenting collaborator. The range and unevenness of his radio work testifies to a precarious balancing act as the political circumstances elicited ever more contradictory responses.

Like other writers in the *Kolonne* Circle, Huchel was filled with dismay at the course his career had taken. Horst Lange surely spoke for Huchel and others, when on 27 February 1939 he wrote wistfully to Ernst Kreuder that friends 'mit denen man vor 7, 8 Jahren eine kleine Front jugendlicher Begabungen gebildet hat' had in the meantime 'einträgliche und weniger anstrengende Beschäftigungen'.[90] Lange himself was seeking still to build upon the critical acclaim that had greeted publication of *Schwarze Weide*, but he, too, was being drawn into the network of radio and, increasingly, filmscript writing, on which many of his friends and acquaintances were squandering their talents. Lange was one of a number whose careers would never recover. Not so Eich and Huchel.

Wartime Propaganda

In 1981, Dora Huchel recalled that in the summer of 1939 the Huchels and their daughter once again enjoyed the Lassel family's hospitality in what would prove to be Huchel's final visit to Kronstadt. Dora Huchel later wrote,

> Überlegung, ob Kronstadt in ferner Zukunft noch möglich sein würde, führte zu schnellem Reiseentschluß. Wieder hatten wir einen herrlichen Sommer, zum Teil im Erholungsheim Freck mit dem wunderschönen Park zwischen Kronstadt und Hermannstadt. Huchel konnte nun an vielen zusätzlichen Kg. zehren. Wir kamen im Spätherbst alle drei sehr erfrischt gerade zur Apfelernte in unserem Michendorfer Garten an. Vorher aber, noch in Kronstadt, Nachricht vom Tod der Großmutter mütterlicherseits. Huchels einzige Reaktion: 'Nun bin ich ein reicher Junge'. Als wir im September 1939 in Michendorf

ankamen, Huchels große Wut, er hatte nichts geerbt. Seine Mutter und ihr Bruder lagen
im Streit um die Hypothekenzinsen vom Langerwischer Grundstück – für ihn fiel nichts
ab.

The truth regarding the Zimmermann estate finally emerged after Emilie
Zimmermann's death. Like Marie Huchel, who had cared for her mother for the best
part of two decades, Huchel, the only surviving grandchild, expected appreciable
and lasting financial benefit. Yet Marie's brother inherited the lot, and Huchel's
hopes were dashed that, like his wife, he would be able to draw a sinecure. The
story goes that in her anger Marie Huchel attacked her brother and brawled with him
on the roadside in Alt-Langerwisch. And it was he who came off worse.

When the Huchels returned to Germany in September 1939 it was to a
country at war following the German attack on Poland, and Britain and France's
declaration of war on Germany. The anti-militarist Huchel had absolutely no desire
to be conscripted into the German armed forces. For nearly two years his talent as
an established radio author and subsequently as a film author was valued sufficiently
to ensure that conscription could be put off. Yet the immediate situation in
September 1939 was difficult. All radio play production was suspended and Huchel
was deprived of his main source of income. As a freelancer, who according to an
internal memorandum of the Reichsschrifttumskammer dated 24 July 1940 had 'in
erster Linie für den Funk gearbeitet',[91] Huchel had from the mid-1930s onwards
become increasingly dependent on his radio work to support his family. The
difficulties which now stemmed from Huchel's financial dependence on the radio
as his major source of income can be charted through Reichsschrifttumskammer
correspondence. It reveals the rapid deterioration of his financial situation following
the suspension of broadcasting in September 1939 and again in the second half of
1940, when any semblance of a coherent radio play schedule was abandoned. The
correspondence demonstrates that far from being identified as a 'literary opponent',
Huchel as an established author was in the early war years deemed worthy of
financial support. On 7 October 1939 Huchel was sent the following letter from the
Deutsche Schillerstiftung in der Reichsschrifttumskammer, Weimar,

> Auf Anregung von dritter Seite lasse ich Ihnen heute durch Postscheck aus unserer
> *Notstandskasse* eine einmalige Beihilfe von
> *RM 150. – (einhundertfünfzig)*
> zur Erleichterung Ihrer wirtschaftlichen Lage zugehen.
> Gleichzeitig bitte ich Sie, den beiliegenden Fragebogen ausgefüllt und unterzeichnet
> zurückzureichen und wesentliche Proben Ihres dichterischen Schaffens aus nueerer (sic)
> Zeit beizufügen.

Huchel's room for manoeuvre had been further reduced. When radio play production was resumed it was on the basis of war propaganda, particularly anti-British work, though even now some space was left for light entertainment and more ambitious literary productions. In October 1939, the journal *Nationalsozialistische Rundfunkkorrespondenz* stated, 'Die Ausrichtung dieser Hörspiele wird natürlich von den Ereignissen der Zeit bestimmt sein, aber auch die lustigen Unterhaltungsspiele werden nicht zu kurz kommen'.[92] Anti-British propaganda took up a large slice of radio play time in the coming months. Pressure to produce politically relevant work culminated in a short conference at the Masurenallee on 22-3 January 1940, where writers were addressed by party officials and Goebbels. There is no record of Huchel's having being present. It must be said that writers were not actually coerced into producing such work. Wessels has pointed out that Paul Alverdes and Georg Britting both declined.[93] On the other hand, a large number of writers who were by no means hard-core Nazis such as Huchel's friends Eich and Kuhnert were ready to deploy their talents in the campaign against the British. Under some pressure financially as well as ideologically and guided by the wish to avoid conscription, Huchel, too, participated in the anti-British campaign with his next play 'Die Greuel von Denshawai', an adaptation of George Bernard Shaw's 'Denshawai Horror'. It was first broadcast from Danzig on 23 January 1940 and repeated from Breslau on 5 April that same year.[94]

When after the war Huchel put distance between himself and his radio work from the 1930s, it was surely primarily in order to cover up the embarrassing fact of involvement in Nazi war propaganda. Knowledge about this episode would have put a halt to his rapid rise in the East Berlin cultural hierarchy and could, in later conflicts, have been used to blackmail him. Huchel took this secret with him to the grave. No mention of 'Die Greuel von Denshawai' is made in the 1984 edition nor has an extant manuscript been identified. In 1989, however, Glenn Cuomo drew attention to details of a broadcast and the Peter Huchel Collection contains a copy, extensively annotated in Huchel's hand, of Siegfried Trebitsch's translation of Shaw's text, on the basis of which I undertook a reconstruction of the play.[95] Huchel's annotations underscore the anti-British tenor of Shaw's report of British colonial brutality and injustice in Egypt. The addition of the decent common soldier Bob Williams, who is outraged at the behaviour of his superiors, fits in with the Nazi propaganda aim to identify the British ruling classes as the real enemy. In his annotations, for example, Huchel takes over from Shaw the views attributed to Lord Cromer and Shaw's sarcastic comment on them,

'Ich habe,' fügt er hinzu, 'nahezu dreißig Jahre meines Lebens mit dem ernstlichen Bestreben hingebracht, die sittliche und materielle Lage des ägyptischen Volkes zu heben. Ich bin von einer Anzahl sehr tüchtiger Beamten dabei unterstützt worden, die alle, ich darf wohl sagen, von dem gleichen Geiste beseelt waren, wie ich selbst'. Ägypten mag

wohl schaudern, wenn es die Worte liest. Wenn die ersten dreißig Jahre durch dies
Begebnis in Denshawai gekrönt worden sind, wie wird Ägypten am Ende weiterer dreißig
Jahre sittlichen Aufschwungs aussehen, 'beseelt von dem gleichen Geist'?

In encouraging such a critique of the British ruling classes, the Nazis and their
propagandists exploited negative, popular images of Britain which had enjoyed
some currency in the German population since before the First World War and
which had been nurtured, too, among German intellectuals by Shaw's work, which
remained popular in Germany in the 1930s. The Peter Huchel Collection contains
as many as eleven Shaw translations. Nor should one forget that in these years
Shaw's unfavourable comparison of the British parliamentary system with the
European fascist dictatorships was eagerly seized upon in Germany.

According to his own testimony, in conversation with Kundera, Huchel
produced a second 'anti-colonial' piece, an adaptation taken from Kipling's stories
Soldiers Three.[96] The text had, he informed Kundera, been lost. Like Huchel's Shaw
adaptation, stories in *Soldiers Three* contrast the common soldier favourably with
the officer caste of British colonial rule. Again, this play is not mentioned in the
1984 edition and no further information has as yet come to light. As is the way with
these things, however, details will no doubt be unearthed in time.

It emerged recently, for example, that Huchel's adaptation of Goethe's
Hermann und Dorothea was broadcast from Leipzig on 17 March 1940 and that it
includes a prologue by Huchel, which contains the following lines,

> Wo die Geschütze so nah
> Wie im eigenen Herzen dröhnen,
> Dort an der Grenze zogen sie fort,
> schweigend unter den schweigenden Wolken;
> Viel an der Zahl,
> Und manche bekümmerten Herzens.
> ...
> Dort an der Grenze im Westen,
> Wo immer ein Schicksal wohnt,
> Lebten vor Zeiten sie auch,
> Hermann und Dorothea.
> Deiner gedenken wir heut,
> Du herrliches Paar,
> Das sich im Feuer des Krieges
> Suchte und fand. Seid ihr nicht

Näher dem Herzen der Lebenden heute? –

...

Schicksal, es treibt uns hinauf

Und stürzt uns hinab!

Aber was klagend begann,

Nicht immer endets in Tränen;

Denn Leiden gehn unter

Im Herzen des ewigen Volks.

Dies sagt Euch das Spiel

Von Hermann und Dorothea.[97]

The immediate and old enemy on the Western Front was France, now in union with Britain. Goethe's text is used to make a link with the present conflict in a manner which assures listeners that the outcome will be favourable despite suffering, which is deemed both necessary and justified. Indeed, the suffering of the individual is subsumed within the collective 'Herzen des ewigen Volks'. Whatever Huchel's personal beliefs – and we cannot forget here both his love of France and the early pain of his elder brother's death on the Western Front in the First World War which was decisive in his adoption of an anti-militarist stance – he delivered the propaganda message, guiding listeners in their understanding of an adaptation which stays close to Goethe's original. The final lines, spoken by Hermann, read, 'Und gedächte jeder wie ich, so stünde die Macht auf/ gegen die Macht, und wir erfreuten uns alle des Friedens'. Hermann declares his readiness to fight the enemy in order to secure peace, a peace won, according to the logic of Huchel's adaptation, on Germany's terms against the powers ranged against it in the West.

In this piece, as in his other radio work from this time, Huchel adopts quite unequivocally the patriotic German attitude that was required by the regime. Yet, one must ask, too, if during the early war years Huchel came personally to identify with the officially fostered patriotism? A snapshot of Huchel's private view of developments in the war is provided in Horst Lange's diary entry for 4 June 1940 following the attack on France, 'Die Zerstörung wächst. Paris ist bombadiert. "La belle et douce France" – sagte neulich Huchel ganz traurig und verzweifelt, als wir vom Krieg sprachen. Brände, Trümmer und Schädelstätten. Die Gewalt, die Barbarei, die sinkenden Welten'.[98] This passage serves to point up the conflict that Huchel now found himself in. He had much greater affection for French culture, which he knew so well from the 1920s, than for the rather remote British class society, with which the French were allied. His anti-militarist attitude is well documented in his letters to his wife. His rejection of Nazi ideology is beyond dispute. Yet, more can be said regarding his view of Britain and its Empire. Why should Huchel, at the turn of the 1960s, have told Kundera of his 'anti-colonial' piece, the adaptation from Kipling's *Soldiers Three*? Clearly, in the early post-war period in the Eastern Bloc, the perception was maintained of Britain as an aggressive capitalist and imperialist power. The perception of Britain as a power hostile to Germany's interests had a history rooted in the Wilhelmine period. Huchel's conservative upbringing would certainly have instilled that into him. Nor, following his conversion to the Left in the 1920s, would any re-appraisal of that image have been necessary. Indeed, precisely in the work of a figure such as Shaw it would have been re-affirmed. Following the outbreak of war, as we have seen, the Nazis played on such popular images of the British. We should not forget that at the time the USA was a long way from joining in the war and that the Soviet Union had signed its non-aggression pact with Germany. There is nothing in Huchel's hand from the time which suggests that he would have regarded a Germany defeated by Britain and its Empire as a liberation from Nazism. Why should Germany expect anything better from the British than the treatment meted out to the inhabitants of its colonies? It is necessary to maintain a sense of the historical moment here and an awareness of the extent to which, from a German perspective, Britain in late 1939 and early 1940 constituted the threat of an escalation to the instability of continental Europe. A measure of this is the fact that so many writers who were not hard-core Nazis joined in the anti-British propaganda campaign on the radio. As we have seen, they include not only Huchel but also his friends Eich and Kuhnert.

After the repeat of 'Die Greuel von Denshawai' in April, on 30 May 1940 the Berlin short wave station broadcast Huchel's 'Peter Paul Rubens. Sein Werk und sein Leben. Szenen und Dialoge'. The 1984 edition states, 'Die Sendung wurde, im Rahmen des täglichen Nachmittagprogramms *Ditjes en Datjes voor Insulinde*, in niederländischer Sprache nach Niederländisch-Indien (Indonesien) ausgestrahlt'. (ii,420) Any puzzlement over the translation of Huchel's work into Dutch for a German broadcast to Indonesia is resolved if one recalls that German troops overran Holland and Belgium in an attack lasting four days, from 10 to 14 May 1940. This created a fresh demand for material from radio authors and Huchel promptly produced his slight text. As is appropriate in a situation in which the Germans were seeking to win over the population of newly conquered territories, Huchel's text is by no means agitatory. Just as Germany was placing itself at the forefront of the new Europe, so too could the 300th anniversary of Rubens' death be celebrated in terms of the status he achieved as a pan-European artist born in Germany. Mention of Rubens' penchant for the monumental would not, of course, go amiss.

As far as has been ascertained hitherto, 'Peter Paul Rubens' was Huchel's final radio play text before the genre disappeared from the air waves in June 1940. His dependence on the medium meant that he stayed with it until the end of the radio play and continued to do occasional radio work later. By July 1940 Huchel was once again in financial difficulties. He approached the Reichsschrifttumskammer for help. Following his personal appeal, a letter was sent from there on 24 July 1940 to the Deutsche Schillerstiftung. It contains the following,

Hier hat soeben Peter Huchel vorgesproche (sic). Wie Sie wissen, hat Huchel in erster Linie für den Funk gearbeitet. In den Jahren 1935 und 1936 hat er z.B. darauf je rund RM 3000, -- Einnahmen gehabt, die namentlich aus Hörspielen, Hörfolgen und Lesestunden usw. herrühren. Alverdes hat für *Das Innere Reich* mehrere Beiträge erworben. Am Verlagsalmanach des Langen-Müller Verlages hat Huchel mitgearbeitet bezw. ihn zusammengestellt. Bei Wilhelm Heyne in Dresden liegen die *Lieder der Stille* und bei Klotz in Gotha *Das Lied der Arbeit*. Durch die Unmöglichkeit der Sender, Wortsendungen literarischer Art zu übernehmen, ist Huchel wie leider so viele andere im Augenblick restlos aufgeworfen. An Miets- und Kohlenschulden haben sich über RM 280, -- angehäuft. Wir müssen hier schnell helfen. Ich schlage vor, dass Sie aus der Notstandskasse noch in diesem Monat RM 150, -- bewilligen und den gleichen Betrag Anfang August wiederholen und nach Möglichkeit Anfang September noch einmal RM 150, -- zahlen.

Copies of letters subsequently sent to Huchel confirm that the three payments were made to an author who was clearly viewed as possessing sufficiently sound credentials. It appears that no further payments were made beyond September 1940, although it was only in August 1941 that Huchel was called up into the Luftwaffe.

Little is known for certain about Huchel's literary activities during these months. He arranged for the re-publication in 1941 of 'Holunder', the Viennese love poem which had a particular sentimental value for the Huchels. Beyond that, it is plausible to assume that in this period he began to produce filmscripts for film companies based in Berlin and Potsdam-Babelsberg, where Ufa was based. It is suggested in the 1984 edition that Huchel's film work may date from 1938. Yet in the questionnaire that he filled in for the Reichsschrifttumskammer in May 1939 Huchel left the film section blank – and he was normally conscientious when filling in these forms. Wessels writes that the switch from radio to film work was undertaken by many after mid-1940,

In gleichem Maße wie die Dramaturgen, sahen sich auch die freien Mitarbeiter, die Autoren, gezwungen, sich endgültig neu zu orientieren. Insbesondere bedauerte das RSHA (Reichssicherheitshauptamt – S.P.), daß die durch ihre antienglischen Hörspiele im Gedächtnis gebliebenen Autoren Kuhnert, Eich und Prugel zum Film überwechselten.[99]

In November 1940 Eich took part in a film scriptwriting course conducted by Frank Maraun for Ufa.[100] The name Maraun crops up in Monica Huchel's mémoirs, though in a somewhat confusing way. She recalls her husband saying of Maraun that he had

> bei Goebbels im Reichsrundfunk gearbeitet und hin und wieder Hörspiele von Huchel,
> Hans Nowak und einigen anderen angenommen hatte. Die Unverfänglichen wurden auch
> gesendet, andere – wie das über Lincoln , der in seiner Loge erschossen worden war, was
> bezüglich Hitler zur Nachahmung hätte anregen können – bezahlte Maraun und legte sie
> in seine Schublade, wo sie blieben, bis alles vorüber war, während Huchel und seine
> Freunde von dem Geld lebten.[101]

Yet Maraun, as we have seen, was employed in film. He boasted to Gottfried Benn that through his work he 'besäße das ganz besondere Wohlwollen u. das immer für ihn offene Ohr des Propagandaministers'.[102] Huchel's professional contact with Maraun in the Third Reich must therefore have been not in radio but in film. In conversation with Kundera, Huchel stated that three or four of his scenarios were deposited with Ufa at Babelsberg.[103] None of them had been turned into films. Huchel in fact to some extent echoes Wolfgang Koeppen's testimony regarding his scriptwriting in claiming that he was commissioned to do work by film companies in full knowledge that nothing would come of them.[104] This was the fate of the vast majority of scripts produced for the greedy and well financed medium. Yet in the 1984 edition, one can read that Huchel added the following in conversation with Kundera, 'Die Projekte seien aber nicht realisiert worden, da er – P.H. als früherer Mitarbeiter so "jüdischer" Presseerzeugnisse wie *Die Vossische Zeitung* und *Die literarische Welt* der Reichsfilmkammer nicht genehm gewesen sei. Dieser Erklärung ist glauben zu schenken'. (ii,421) Huchel's wartime letters to his wife, however, indicate collaboration with film companies over a period of some four years during the war. In the letters there is no hint whatsoever that Huchel personally or the work he was producing were anything but acceptable. Huchel's statement to Kundera was a variation on his early post-war claim that his two film scripts had been banned by the Propaganda Ministry.[105] Both statements fit in the familiar pattern of self-justification in the immediate post-war period and beyond. Perhaps more credibly, Huchel informed Kundera that Heinrich George had been interested in his scenarios.[106] He speculated that George might have been their instigator. George's interest did not lead to anything, Huchel added, less credibly, 'vielleicht wegen dem Namen des Autors'. (ii,421) The scenarios were linked to the themes of the poetry. In one of them 'Der Bauer durchbricht den Damm, damit die Felder sich verbessern'.

The 1984 edition contains two 'Filmnovellen', 'Der Nobiskrug' and 'Das Fräulein von Soor'. Both of them provided quite acceptable material for the film medium as it operated under wartime conditions. The latter treats a patriotic theme from Prussian history, the struggle against Napoleon's army of occupation. As such it was quite in keeping with mainstream Nazi propaganda, which linked Prussia's struggle in the Wars of Liberation with the Reich's in mid-twentieth century Europe. Without resorting to the crude chauvinism of hard-line Nazi propagandists, Huchel underscores German nationalist sentiment through his story of love and the self-sacrifice in the Prussian cause, which his eponymous heroine accepts. The rural setting in the Brandenburg village of Lunow adds local colour in terms of landscape and character depiction. The doughty inhabitants of the Brandenburg Marches are contrasted favourably with the soldiers from the Palatinate who wear French uniforms. Their leader, Féral, and his adjutant, Privas, show clear character weaknesses in stereotypical 'French' fashion: Féral is distracted from his duties by women, Privas by drink. Aided by the villagers, Prussian soldiers in hiding in Lunow escape from under the noses of the French troops. Yet it is Fräulein Charlotte von Soor's heroism in donning a Prussian uniform and acting as a decoy that is crucial as the Prussian soldiers cross the Oder 'um zu den verbündeten Russen zu stoßen'. (ii,182) Mention of the allied Russian forces is repeated on that same page. This detail is not only historically credible; it would, of course, only have been possible to play upon a Prussian alliance with Russia for a short period in the Third Reich, the duration of the German-Soviet pact from 22 August 1939 until 22 June 1941. This detail enables us to locate the composition of 'Das Fräulein von Soor' in that period, probably in its latter half.

In the case of the second 'Filmnovelle' in the 1984 edition 'waren die Pläne weit gediehen; für "Der Nobiskrug" liegt ein gemeinsam mit Otto Linnekogel verfaßtes Drehbuch mit dem Titel "Sturmnacht" vor'. (ii,421) As we have seen, Susanne Huchel recalled her father's collaboration with Linnekogel. Linnekogel, a writer and artist, had been writing scripts since 1937 and in 1939-40 directed two films, one of them being called 'Herz ohne Heimat'. 'Der Nobiskrug' contains elements familiar from Huchel's poetry from the early to mid-1930s. The setting is rural Brandenburg, and the characters, 'Fischer', 'Kuhbeschwörer' and 'Knecht', have all been encountered before in poems, the imagery of which is also often reproduced. A summary of the plot at the beginning of the novella conveys the following, 'Wie Sebald sein Verbrechen sühnt und durch eine befreiende Tat seiner Verpflichtung der Allgemeinheit gegenüber nachkommt – das ist die Fabel des Stoffs'. (ii,129) As such, without employing the aggressive tones of Nazi propaganda, the story underlines an ethical stance officially fostered: the primacy of the individual's responsibility towards the community.

The story was both acceptable and unremarkable; sufficiently so, perhaps, to ensure the continuation of a freelance engagement with film companies, which would guarantee an income and act as a justification for avoiding conscription. This Huchel managed to do until August 1941 when, following the German attack on the Soviet Union, he too was called upon to defend his country.

The Soldier

Huchel's years as a soldier provide no exception in the pattern of myth-making and creation of legends that has characterised the depiction of his life hitherto. A number of publications have drawn attention to his acquaintance with the Soviet Union and its culture gained as a soldier. It is not difficult to appreciate the value of such supposed links in the immediate post-war years in East Berlin. Apparently relying on Huchel's own testimony, Kantorowicz reported that Huchel 'nahm an Vormärschen und Rückmärschen im Osten teil', while Bernhard Gajek writes of 'fünf Jahre des Soldatenseins in Rußland'.[107] This was apparently followed by 'imprisonment in the Soviet Union',[108] where 'Als Kriegsgefangerer hat er die Sowjetunion kennengelernt'[109] before returning to Germany to participate in the anti-fascist reconstruction. This was, of course, the path followed by many German soldiers who as PoWs became involved in the anti-fascist work of the Nationalkomitee Freies Deutschland set up in 1943 in Soviet PoW camps. Huchel's own involvement in this conspiratorial organisation is at least hinted at, in some cases perhaps involuntarily, in the above quotations.

Huchel did not serve on the Eastern Front nor was he a PoW in the Soviet Union. His correspondence with his wife reveals that he saw service only within the borders of Germany and for the most part within easy reach of Berlin so that he might pursue his projects in radio and film. In many publications, it has been stated that Huchel was conscripted in 1940 and by Lommer, using the familiar hyperbole, that he was 'zur "Wehrmacht" gepreßt – als Quittung für seine unbeugsame, den Machthabern verdächtige Haltung'.[110] The 1984 edition comes closer to the truth with the brief statement that from 1941 to 1945 Huchel was a 'Soldat in einer Flak-Einheit bei Berlin'. (i,460)

Huchel was thirty-eight when on 15 August 1941 he joined a Luftwaffe signals regiment, the 11 (Flugmeldedienst Reserve) Luftgau Nachrichtenregiment 3. Basic training took place at Hottengrund near Kladow. References to Hottengrund in letters from later that year indicate that, above all as a result of the treatment meted out by brutal NCOs, basic training was a nightmarish experience for someone to whom the harshness of military discipline was futile and demeaning. It is possible that Huchel was referring to Hottengrund when in 1971 he said, '1940 (sic) habe ich vor gesammelter Truppe meinen Feldwebel niedergeschlagen, der uns triezte. Georg von der Vring hat mich gerettet'. (ii,371) It is impossible to establish whether Huchel's protests at the NCOs' behaviour went so far. It can be said that there is no reference to such an incident in his letters nor any sense that he had been given a black mark by his superiors.

After Hottengrund, 'Funker' Huchel was deployed at various locations in North Germany, monitoring British aircraft movements. His first posting was to Joachimsthal in the Uckermark. In a note to his wife from the beginning of October he supplied the address of his lodgings with master baker Welck's family at Horst-

Wessel-Straße 64. Joachimsthal was, however, only the briefest of interludes, since a few days later he was transferred to a unit stationed on the estate of Behrenhoff near Greifswald. From there in just three weeks he wrote as many as ten cards and letters. These letters, like those following from other later postings, contain regular requests and subsequent thanks for cigarettes, food and clothing. The correspondence from Behrenhoff describes the simple pleasure of life on the remote estate with his ten comrades. The letters of 9 and 14 October contain quite extensive depictions of the estate and of the delicious food prepared for them in the kitchen. In the letter of 16 October he describes the relaxed atmosphere fostered by a head of section who was a First World War veteran: there was just half an hour's drilling per week, everyone knew his job and went about it without any fuss. He evidently enjoyed the company of soldiers who in peacetime had been simple working men in Pomerania and the Uckermark, though later in the month he wrote wistfully of a visit to Greifswald, where the sight of a bookshop window had prompted thoughts of a world far away from the daily conversations centring on the pleasures of food and sleep. He found his duties quite strenuous: they were organised around a rota of twenty-four hours on watch and twenty-four hours rest. When on watch the cycle he followed was one hour spent up the watch tower, one hour manning the telephone and one hour on standby. Exposure through the night to the harsh autumn weather was clearly wearing, yet in a letter such as that of 9 October he registered a sense of satisfaction at his developing skills as a plane spotter. And for all his antipathy to war and military discipline, he was conscientious in his work. Nor was his 'good' attitude lost on his superiors: on 31 October he announced that he had been selected for the more demanding duties at flight command in Neubrandenburg. Yet he was a reluctant hero, as his decidedly unenthusiastic response to this posting demonstrates. For all that, the extent of the esteem in which he was held by his superiors would emerge in the later war years when discussion turned to the quite realistic option of officer training.

The posting to Neubrandenburg was most untimely, since he had been exploring a transfer to flight command at Grunewald, which was both nearer home and as close as he could possibly be to his literary contacts in Berlin. Huchel's friend Günther Birkenfeld was already stationed there, in a position where he could exert influence in Huchel's favour. Through Birkenfeld, Willi Schäferdiek at the short wave station and Jürgen Eggebrecht at the 'Stabstelle Papier', Huchel would in the coming months pursue the transfer, which in the event only came about at the beginning of 1943. Huchel also lost no time in winning Schäferdiek's support for his application to take leave in order to do radio work. A request for three weeks was initially refused but two weeks were finally granted from 8 January 1942. Unfortunately no details of the content of this or later work are available. In the letter of 23 October he discussed with his wife the publication of his poem 'Späte Zeit' (i,94) in *Die Dame*.[111] Huchel had been extremely angry to discover that the editors had substituted 'Im nassen Sand', a phrase from the poem, for his own title.

It would appear that 'Späte Zeit' had been too defeatist for them in spite of the poem's reference, surely drawing on Huchel's recent experiences as a plane spotter, to the 'fremder Hund' in the German skies. The poem had been submitted in a competition organised by *Die Dame* for war poetry. The poem displays a subtle blend of imagery drawn from nature, mythology and warfare ('Über allen Jägern jagt/ hoch im Wind ein fremder Hund') within a composition informed by a sombre mood of impending death ('Herbst schoß seine Schüsse ab/ leise Schüsse übers Grab'). This elegiac treatment of war, though published with a title that no longer drew attention to this mood, is far from the German heroism officially fostered. By the same token, however, the context of publication places it far away from the 1933 date of composition which Huchel gave it after the war, with its implication of an anti-fascist statement.[112]

The transfer to Neubrandenburg took place at the beginning of November. He would stay there until well into 1942. Thirteen letters and cards from Neubrandenburg have survived. The earliest is from 1/2 November – written during the transfer – and the latest from early February. The correspondence documents his continuing pre-occupation with the proposed transfer to Grunewald, as well as with his radio and film work. Arrangements at Neubrandenburg regarding both accommodation and work were quite different and much less agreeable than at Behrenhoff. He had quarters in the small, bare attic of a house and had to cater for himself using bread and milk coupons. The loneliness and drabness of his situation made him think back to his friendship with Hans A. Joachim in the mid-1920s and to what he called his Expressionist phase. Although his nighttime duties at flight command were inside rather than exposed to the rough autumn weather, there was the prospect of greater responsibility, of courses and of more frequent drilling. In early November, he lamented the pointlessness of what he was doing and wondered just how long it would go on. Yet he busied his mind with compositions and literary plans. In mid-November he discussed with his wife a project with Ufa, on the basis of which he hoped to secure a short spell of leave. In the event it was not granted and in later November he found his literary talents being harnessed by the officer at Neubrandenburg responsible for the organisation of Christmas festivities. Huchel was required to follow the officer's instructions in producing a thoroughly Christian play. In mid-December he quoted from one of the speeches of the traditional character Ruprecht, explaining to his wife how the words were to be spoken by a sergeant, who was totally lacking in any rhetorical skills. Following performances on 20 and 21 December Huchel reported to his wife just how ludicrous a business it had all been. Yet the play scarcely afforded a distraction from his duties. In letters from the end of December and the end of January he reported upon his monitoring of enemy aircraft. The British had been flying not only to Hamburg, Bremen, Hanover and Berlin, but as far as Warsaw and Prague before turning for home. He and his wife discussed prospects for an end to the war, for which both longed and which both, unsurprisingly at the time, evidently expected to be a German victory.

While Dora Huchel, it seems, thought a swift end to the war possible, her husband urged caution, suggesting, with uncanny accuracy, that it might take as long as four years. In January, he wrote that those in his regiment who had been born in 1908 and 1909 were being transferred to the infantry for deployment on the Eastern Front. He expected that his time would come. All the same, he was able to look forward to leave over Easter and to the prospect that his transfer to Grunewald would finally come through.

After early February 1942 the sequence of letters is interrupted until 19 August 1942, the date of a card sent from the posting to Gollin, a tiny village in the Uckermark near Templin. In all he sent eight cards and letters to his family from Gollin between 19 August and 30 November 1942. After flight command at Neubrandenburg, he was back with a small unit taking his turn up the watch tower. He lodged first with the Schumachers, a quite young family who had a small-holding, and towards the end of the posting with the more elderly Brenneckens. There had evidently been some tensions with the Schumachers due to what appears to have been Frau Schumacher's attraction to the lodger. Though Huchel protested to his wife that Frau Schumacher was not his type, it was not his way to give an admirer an unequivocal sign. On 21 August he wrote to his wife that when off duty he was helping the Schumachers with the harvest. This was a way of increasing his food allocation. For all the image of the poet rooted in peasant life cultivated by Huchel, it would appear that this was his only direct experience of farm work. Hardly surprisingly, it was so tiring that he had to postpone any work on his own compositions. Yet he was rewarded with three weeks leave in early September in order to recover from his exertions.

After he had returned to Gollin, in a letter of 28 October 1942 he pondered upon his options in order to avoid the worst of what might be coming in the war. His letter reveals the ability to safeguard his own immediate interests through foresight and some strategic planning. He was confident that the transfer for which he had been waiting so long would probably go ahead, but he and his wife had been considering other options. His father would be delighted at the thought that he might apply for an officer training course, yet he was pessimistic about his chances of success even though he evidently expected that he would be accepted for training.[113] He was aware, too, that girls were being trained to do signals work previously done by men, who would be redeployed in the spring of 1943 in the flak or the dreaded infantry. The sense of terror he felt was caused not only by the prospect of the Eastern Front and the horrors of the Russian winter; the memory of his brother's death as an infantryman was surely a further factor. For such reasons, he was still considering an application to join a propaganda company. Many of his fellow writers had followed that path.

It must be said at this juncture that throughout his life Huchel was much more strongly motivated by careful consideration of his immediate interests than has been appreciated hitherto by critics who have accepted at face value the image of the uncompromising poet and countryman suffering in rural isolation. His decision to remain in Germany in 1933, which was followed by his reluctant and partial incorporation in the official literature, in time brought with it a narrowing of options in which there were no longer any 'good' choices to be made. What has been called his 'Seßhaftigkeit', his inability to set himself free from the course upon which he was embarked, made in the final analysis for a critical lack of intellectual mobility and flexibility.[114] These qualities were very much needed, though as always at a premium, in the highly unstable world of twentieth-century Germany. Many writers were, like Huchel, caught in situations in which they adapted as best they could. Retrospectively, they would distance themselves from their part in events in a manner frequently nauseating to behold but which emerged from the logic of their situation, which they deemed compelling, as they sought still to pursue their careers.

On 30 November 1942 he reported his success in persuading his superiors that he should be transferred nearer to Berlin so that he could do the film work that had been asked of him. His transfer to Ferch, only a short distance from Michendorf, came through almost immediately, to date from 3 December. This meant, too, that he could live at home. Soon afterwards the transfer to flight command at Grunewald was finally completed. He lived at Hubertusallee 50, just a short walk from the Masurenallee. From Hubertusallee, he wrote a card on 28 January 1943 explaining that a planned weekend at home would have to be postponed because of his duties. He was, in fact, able to stay at home frequently during his long posting at Grunewald. A consequence is the absence of correspondence from that period. Over Whitsuntide 1943, Dora and Susanne Huchel made what would be their last visit to Kronstadt. Only one item from Huchel's correspondence with his wife and daughter during that stay has survived: a card to Susanne dated 12 June and written in Michendorf. As Susanne Huchel recalled, this period also saw Huchel's affair with a local woman, Frau Maß, whose husband had been sent to the Eastern Front and would die at Stalingrad. As ever, Dora Huchel did nothing about the affair and her expectation was fulfilled that Huchel would soon tire of Frau Maß.

A further testimony relating to Huchel's Grunewald posting is the brief portrait written shortly after the war by Günther Birkenfeld. Birkenfeld, as we have seen, had been instrumental in Huchel's transfer to Grunewald. Birkenfeld writes,

> Zwischen den vielen Alarmen, Schlaflosigkeit und allgemeiner Überreiztheit, saß er da im engen Wachkabuff unseres Bunkers, tagelang, nächtelang, und starrte vor sich hin über einer dünnen Oktavkladde, in die er mitunter eine Zeile schrieb, zumeist aber das Leere hinwegdichtete, von fiebernder Nervosität oder auch schon von wütiger Erbitterung angefüllt, von der Wut des Vaganten hinter Kerkermauern.[115]

Amidst all the early post-war hyperbole, one should not forget that Huchel had engineered for himself a position which was much more favourable than that of many of his compatriots. His literary talents and connections had demonstrably contributed to the attainment of that position.

The extant correspondence recommences only in September 1944. A number of letters from the period until then were destroyed by Soviet soldiers when they occupied Michendorf in April 1945. On 20 September 1944, Huchel sent his wife a postcard of Schiller's birthplace at Marbach am Neckar. The card was written at the Ossweil barracks (formerly the Karlsschule, where Schiller was educated) in Ludwigsburg. It was the first of nine cards and letters sent from Ludwigsburg between September and the end of October, after which Huchel returned to the Berlin area. Huchel's correspondence from Ludwigsburg indicates that he had been accepted for the officer training programme which he had been considering in October 1942. Huchel also sent his wife a copy of Goethe's *Maximen und Reflexionen*, published by Alfred Kröner in Stuttgart in 1943, with the dedication 'Für Dora in einsamen Nächten! Peter'.[116] He dated the dedication 19 September 1944. During the later stages of the war, Huchel also put together a hand-written collection of his poems, which he dedicated to his wife. He took it with him in 1947 when he removed his possessions from Waldstraße 32 in Michendorf. No mention of the collection is made in the 1984 edition.

By September 1944, the tide had turned decisively against Germany on both the Eastern and the new Western Front, while in Germany itself some of the conservative élite around Stauffenberg and his co-conspirators had come out against Hitler. Huchel's letters to his wife reflect something of the new mood engendered by these developments and record, too, something of the mounting evidence of impending defeat. In his postcard from Marbach, Huchel cited Schiller's words 'In tyrannis' and on 24 October he adopted a tone of scarcely veiled sarcasm in relation to the supposed powers of the German secret weapons such as the V2 rockets deployed since September against British targets. He had received eye-witness reports of the German army's sudden collapse in the face of the German assault in Romania, and he sought to re-assure his wife that her family would survive. In fact, Dora's mother Josefine Lassel was run over by a Soviet tank as it swept through Kronstadt. From Ludwigsburg, he had watched the enemy air attacks on Stuttgart, which had been reduced to rubble. He had failed in his attempts to contact Georg von der Vring, who had probably left the city. Such scenes of destruction would feed into the war poetry which Huchel published in the early post-war years. He asked his wife to send him the Bergengruens' address at Achenkirch in Austria, presumably as a possible refuge. This demonstrates a continuing link with Susanne's godmother and her husband, who had been excluded from the Reichsschrifttumskammer due to his oppositional stance. Meanwhile, in Ludwigsburg Huchel was sitting a series of examinations, some of which related to technical and scientific matters, while others addressed questions of leadership and organisation. He predicted failure at every stage. It seems that this happened only with the final examination, following which he was permitted a short period of leave before returned in the rank of 'Obergefreiter', in British terms senior aircraftsman, to his comrades in the Berlin area.

In the meantime the Huchels' house had become a refuge for Berlin friends seeking to escape the relentless bombing that had reduced much of the city to rubble. Susanne Huchel recalls,

> Das Haus war verhältnismäßig groß, aber dadurch, daß es verhältnismäßig viele Leute waren, wurde es immer enger, zum Schluß sehr eng, weil es immer mehr wurde. Etliche Freunde flohen oftmals aus dem zerbombten Berlin zu uns, zumal der Angriff auf Potsdam beinahe vor unserer Tür stattfand ... Ich mußte oft auf einem schmalen Sofa schlafen oder zu normaleren Leuten, wie man sagte, fliehen ... Am Abend wurde immer herumgedreht am Radio und versucht auch, aus dem Ausland Informationen zu bekommen ... Mit mir als Wache.[117]

Despite Marie Huchel's wish that her granddaughter should join the Nazi girls' organisation, her parents discouraged her. The result was that she was singled out by her schoolteacher, a distant relative by the name of Wedekind, who suggested that her parents should show a better example. Susanne Huchel recalls what she had to put up with at home during the war years, focusing on Eich and his first wife, whom she knew as Evelyn, a morphine addict,

> Sie war also – peinlich genug für Günter Eich – eine sogenannte Cabaret-Sängerin und sang scheußliche billige Stücke, z.B. also so etwas wie Schiri Biribi in großen Abend-Toiletten bei uns und bei meiner Großmutter, die aber davon sehr beeindruckt war. Durch den Zustand von Evelyn entstanden große Irritationen, zumal mein Vater noch jemanden aus den Soldat-Baracken anschleppte, eine Dame, die Aida St. Paul hieß und sich mit Wohltätigkeitspaketen in diesen Baracken beschäftigte und von unseren Freunden 'die Sardinenbüchse' genannt wurde. Diese beiden Damen stritten ununterbrochen und wurden dann von dem Hausarzt und meinem Vater aus dem Haus hinausgeworfen, auf jeden Fall dringend gebeten, das Haus zu verlassen. Das war also kaum mehr zum Aushalten.

Amid all the chaos that accompanied the German collapse Huchel, even at this late stage of the war, still had irons in the fire. Through his wife, he was maintaining contact with people from the Berlin film world, among them a Dr. Born. His wife reported in 1981 that late in the war Huchel was paid a large amount for a film project. The money was deposited in the Michendorf bank and survived the war but lost much of its value. It is quite possible that the sum involved related to the use of

Huchel's radio play manuscript 'Zille Martha' in Käutner's film 'Unter den Brücken', if not necessarily to Huchel's actual involvement in writing the filmscript.

As the allies closed in on Berlin, Huchel was finally deployed to an aircraft monitoring unit at Dahnsdorf near Belzig, to the south-west of Michendorf. It was from there that on 19 April 1945 he sent his wife his final wartime letter, only days before Michendorf and his own position were captured by Soviet troops. On 19 April, Huchel was expecting that it would be the Americans who would sweep through from the Magdeburg Front. His unit was only lightly armed and could put up little resistance. He hoped that the Americans would simply bypass their insignificant position. He planned to blow up his signals equipment and the tower, and then make his way as best he could. In a most poignant message, he sought to comfort his wife that all would be well and that they would be back together soon. He noted down for her Sebastian Haffner's address in Cambridge and asked her to make a copy of his poem 'Sommerabend'. She should ensure that it was kept in trustworthy hands. 'Sommerabend', as I have argued above, can be understood as an epitaph for the two Huchel boys, should he now join his elder brother in death on the battlefield. Dora and Susanne Huchel recalled that this was something his mother fully expected would happen.

The letter of 19 April 1945 demonstrates that Huchel continued to do his duty until almost the very end. The Belzig area was overrun by Soviet troops sweeping round the south of Berlin between 20 and 24 April, when according to the 1984 edition he 'setzt ... sich von einer zersprengten Truppe ab'. (i,460) Huchel's own account shows his movement in a northwesterly direction from Belzig in order to escape the Soviets advancing from one direction and the Americans from the other.[118] There is clearly no truth in the story that circulated in the post-war years, spread by Kantorowicz and others, to the effect that Huchel deserted to the Soviets, however much this improbable act might have commended itself after the war in East Berlin. The myth of imprisonment in the Soviet Union noted already above is embellished by Kantorowicz as follows,

> Er wartete nur auf den Moment, wo er überlaufen konnte. Dummköpfe werden das Mangel an Vaterlandsliebe nennen, es war aber nur seine mangelnde Liebe für den Nazismus: es war in Wahrheit eine heroische Tat, sich von den Verderbern Deutschlands abzusetzen. Er hat mit ihr seine Haltung während dieser ganzen Jahre gekrönt.[119]

Huchel's genuine hatred of Nazism is all but lost in the hyperbole, which here, as so often, retrospectively lends his behaviour an ideological slant which fits in with the political culture of East Berlin. In this case, however, the hyperbole masks an act of defiance by Huchel, which demonstrates courage born out of an instinct for survival at the very last.

After his unit's position was blown up, they were not immediately captured. The officer in charge marched his men off in a northwesterly direction into the area to the west of Berlin where German forces remained quite strong, stalling the American advance on the Elbe Front. The officer evidently intended that the unit should continue the hopeless fight to the bitter end. Yet, according to one of Huchel's comrades, Kurt Zackor, Huchel filled his rifle with sand rather than continue the senseless struggle. This act shows the courage of someone who knows the game is up and can see no point in further death, not least his own. According to Monica Huchel, in the general confusion of the final days of the war, Zackor rescued him from being shot.[120] At the last, Huchel did, indeed, lay down his arms, and then made off from the fighting. Like so many of his countrymen he was left relying on a spirit of self-preservation, which, coupled with the luck that seldom deserted him, would stand him in good stead as the profound uncertainties of the final days of the war were rapidly transformed into the beginning of a new life in a key position with the occupying Soviet forces.

Part 2
The Search for a Society

6
Working for the Soviets: from Bourgeois Sympathiser to Anti-Fascist

'O daß ich atme noch und lebe'

As Huchel made off from his decimated unit in late April 1945, survival could be his only concern. He continued to move in a northwesterly direction within the pocket of land to the west of Berlin still occupied by German troops. Not least in order to avoid capture by them, he got rid of his uniform, perhaps hoping that he might melt back into civilian life. In or out of uniform, the risks were great. His actions during these days bear out the point which he made in the 1970s in the West that it was pure chance that he fell into Soviet hands. By the same token, his movements contradict the earlier message of desertion to the Soviets. No German soldiers willingly placed themselves in the care of the Red Army during the final days of the war!

According to his public statements, it was only after months of imprisonment at the Rüdersdorf PoW camp that he was released in the autumn of 1945 to work at the Soviet-licensed Radio Berlin. Following Huchel's death, Monica Huchel – as we shall see below – maintained this position until it was queried, and in her mémoirs she acknowledged that the period of imprisonment prior to employment at Radio Berlin was merely a matter of days. That is not to say that Rüdersdorf was not also a significant port of call in Huchel's activities in the spring and summer of 1945. As we shall see, Huchel's work during that period involved both Radio Berlin and Rüdersdorf.

In other respects, in her mémoirs Monica Huchel remains faithful to her husband's account of events and reproduces something of the raconteur's manner, as her description of the last days of his war shows,

In der Nacht setzte Huchel sich ab, versteckte sich in einer Scheune und zerriß sein Soldbuch. Er fand eine alte Hose und nahm sich die Jacke von einer Vogelscheuche, nicht ahnend, daß er als Zivilist viel gefährdeter war als in Uniform. Es gab damals keine Zivilisten mehr. Das wußte jeder. Zwei Tage blieb er ohne Essen und Trinken in der Scheune, bis sie beschossen wurde und er die Schreie von Frauen hörte, die vergewaltigt wurden. Dann schwamm er durch ein Gewässer, das vermutlich ein Havelarm war. Als er an der Straße stand, wurde er eingereiht in einen endlosen Zug Gefangener und geriet in die Rüdersdorfer Kalkbergwerke, wo es verdorbenene Blutwurst gab und Huchel Tannenspitzen aß. Nach den ersten chaotischen Tagen kamen russische Kulturoffiziere und befragten die einzelnen Gefangenen. Huchel erzählte, was er bislang getan hatte, und kurz darauf kam ein Lastwagen, der ihn und einige andere Gefangene im Berliner Rundfunk an der Masurenallee absetzte.[1]

Some details of the account figure in the cycle 'Der Rückzug', (i,100) which was published in *Gedichte*. The cycle, whose title, no doubt, fuelled certain assumptions about Huchel's involvement on the Eastern Front, contains some of his most powerful war poetry. As such, 'Der Rückzug' foreshadows 'Das Gesetz' and other poems published in the early 1950s as well as verse collected in 1963 in *Chausseen Chausseen*. Like the poems of the early 1950s, it contains some flights of rhetoric that were pared back for re-publication in *Die Sternenreuse* in 1967. The cycle opens with the famous lines, 'Ich sah des Krieges Ruhm./ Als wärs des Todes Säbelkorb,/ durchklirrt von Schnee, am Straßenrand/ lag eines Pferdes Geripp'e'. (i,100) Employing a graphic realism, Huchel testifies to the horror with which the final bloody stages of the war filled him, 'Zwischen den beiden/ Sicheln des Mondes wurde ich alt/ wie der blutgetränkte Fluß voll treibender Leichen,/ wie der aschig trauernde Wald'. (i,100) The 'große Schlichtheit' of nature poetry composed within the formal parameters of the *Volkslied* was swept away in the shock of the final collapse. The elegiac tone was left to run on and on: long and short lines alternate without any set pattern, and they are no longer bound by rhyme in the unfolding scene of destruction, which is echoed in the harsh dissonance of many of the cycle's consonant sounds. The cycle sees Huchel adopting the more expressive language that characterises the deliberately public, that is to say rhetorical manner of his early post-war verse. As already in 'Späte Zeit', he extends his range to take in the vocabulary of modern mechanised warfare, in which machines are deployed to cause death and destruction to humans and nature, and where the burnt-out shells of tanks are abandoned amid the debris and decaying flesh. The cycle, moreover, illustrates how Huchel contrasts 'zarte Gegenbilder' with an unloved reality, originally his suburban childhood but now warfare. This finds expression in the contrast between the destruction of war and finely drawn creatures, 'Weißbrustige Schwalbe,/ dein Schnabel ritzt/ das grau sich kräuselnde Wasser/ an Schilf und Toten vorbei/ im gleitenden Flug'. (i,100) The survival of the swallow points to the regenerative capacity of nature, thematised in the final stanza of the cycle, 'Und es wächst im Nebel das Korn,/ noch überwölbt von Finsternis,/ hinter dem Hang vergorener Herbste,/ Wasser und Schlamm, leuchtet die Sichel/ im Widderhorn'. (i,107) At the end the crescent comes together with Huchel's personal sign, the 'Widderhorn', which signifies both his birth sign and his gift of song. In the face of appalling destruction, the poet asserts through his song the primacy of elemental nature as possessing properties beyond the capacity of man to destroy the planet.

The reassurance of these final lines, which some of a more radical temper might feel to be rather too comforting and which Huchel would certainly no longer feel able to share by the early 1960s, comes only after the evocation of extreme danger conveyed in the main body of the cycle. There the story is told of refuge in the barn, which is followed by 'Die Schattenchaussee'. (i,102) It begins, 'Sie spürten mich auf. Der Wind war ihr Hund./ sie schritten die Schattenchausseen./ Ich lag zwischen Weiden auf moorigem Grund/ im Nebel verschilfter Seen'. In addition to those he imagines pursuing him, he sees 'Den Trupp von Toten, im Tod noch versprengt', of whom he says, 'Sie hatten dem großen Sterben gedient/ und Sterben war ihr Gewinn'. Nor does he exclude himself from this harsh lesson that dead comrades had got their dues, 'Da sah ich mich im grauen Zug,/ der langsam im Nebel zerrann'. This acknowledgement of the survivor's guilt is followed by the recognition of his pure good fortune in surviving to witness the end of Nazism, 'O daß ich atme noch und lebe,/ den Spuk erkennend, der nicht gilt!' However much he had rejected everything Nazism had stood for, he had become caught up in its barbaric conduct of the war. Yet he had survived Nazism and it was legitimate for him to point out that he had never been taken in by it, though, like millions of others, he could not have begun to imagine the excesses that would flow from it. In the final section the cycle evokes the swim across the Havel, 'O Nacht der Trauer, Nacht April,/ die ich im Feuerdunst durchschwamm'. (i,106) In Monica Huchel's mémoirs, this episode is followed by Huchel's immediate capture and brief imprisonment at Rüdersdorf. Yet there is much more to be said.

By the time he was captured by the Soviets near Rathenow, Huchel had travelled quite a distance. After sweeping round the north of Berlin, the Soviet 47th Army, which included Konrad Wolf, son of Friedrich and brother of Markus, as an interpreter, was held up near Rathenow on 27th April after taking Gatow airfield and clearing the West Bank of the Havel. It would appear that Huchel was captured by the 47th Army. As we have seen, in public statements made in the West in the 1970s Huchel obscured the course of events after he fell into Soviet hands and emerged that autumn in their employment at Radio Berlin. The station occupied the same building on the Masurenallee where he had worked on a freelance basis before 1945. It is not sufficient here to point to his accustomed reticence. Collaboration with the Soviets was a sensitive issue, especially in the West. Huchel had little interest in engaging in discussion of the complexities of Soviet aims and actions, as well as the motives of those who collaborated with them. Nor has critical literature fostered such an awareness. One West German critic, for example, could only countenance Huchel's involvement with the Soviets on a strictly cultural basis, which the critic took explicitly to exclude any political dimension.[2] For the Soviets, of course, culture could not be construed as anything other than part and parcel of general policy formulation and implementation. Huchel himself was only too aware of this. Despite the relative paucity of archival information about the period immediately after 8 May 1945, various bits of knowledge can be pieced together, which show in some detail how Huchel negotiated the transition to the post-war era and how he came to rise so quickly in the hierarchy at Radio Berlin under the Soviets.

During his years in the GDR there was no public discussion of his early post-war radio career beyond the acknowledgement that he had participated in the reconstruction of that key feature of Berlin cultural life. As we have seen, in the 1970s in the West Huchel remained reticent about this period, expanding little on the notion of the play of chance at its outset. The 1984 edition contains the laconic statement that after he was captured he was placed 'in ein Lager in den Rüdersdor-fer Kalkwerken östlich von Berlin, wo er kulturelle Veranstaltungen organisiert. Ende 1945 wird er beauftragt, im Berliner Haus des Rundfunks (Masurenallee, sowjetische Enklave) eine Hörspielabteilung einzurichten'. (ii,460) Monica Huchel amplified upon this as follows in a letter reproduced in the edition (though she would modify crucial details in her mémoirs),

> Mein Mann befand sich – nach Kriegsende – in einem Kriegsgefangenenlager in Rüdersdorf bei Berlin (Rüdersdorfer Kalkwerke) in sowjetischer Gefangenschaft. Dort war es so gräßlich, daß man entweder nur der Verzweiflung anheimfallen oder irgendwie betriebsam sein konnte. Er entschloß sich für das letztere und betätigte sich kulturell, unterstützt von sowjetischen Kulturoffizieren, die solche Lager besuchten und dort Gespräche führten. Dabei erfuhren die Sowjets auch, daß H. Hörspiele geschrieben hatte. Nach längerer Lagerzeit wurde er dann, eines Tages, zusammen mit einigen Technikern, Musikern u.a. auf einem Lastwagen, ohne zu wissen wohin es ging, zum Berliner Haus des Rundfunks in der Masurenallee gebracht. Das Rundfunkhaus und noch zwei Privathäuser waren sowjetische Enklave. Er wurde beauftragt, im Funk eine Hörspielabteilung einzurichten. Das war im Spätherbst 1945. Er hat oft zu mir gesagt, wie sehr es ihn verblüfft habe, mit welcher Sicherheit diese ersten sowjetischen Offiziere darauf vertraut hatten, er würde schon alles Hörspieltechnische *so* machen, wie sie es sich vorstellten. (ii,407)

Other information demonstrates that the 'official' version of events contained in the edition is fundamentally flawed. As we have seen, in her mémoirs Monica Huchel drastically reduces the duration of his captivity from a longish period to a matter of days. By the late autumn of 1945, Soviet officers had reasons beyond Huchel's radio experience and cultural activities in Rüdersdorf for placing their trust in him. Huchel, as his widow acknowledges in her mémoirs, was taken to work at the Soviet-controlled radio station at a much earlier date following his identification as someone with appropriate experience. Records show that he was registered as living at Berlin 19, Bayernallee 44 as early as 8 May 1945, though Huchel's choice of that date for his registration was more symbolic than strictly accurate in empirical terms.[3] Bayernallee 44 was commandeered by the Soviets for their officers and approved

German intellectuals, most of them KPD figures as they returned from Moscow. The Soviets captured the radio building on 2 May and on 13 May broadcasting resumed. In charge was Hans Mahle, a member of the Ulbricht group that returned to Berlin from Moscow on 30 April. In a conversation with me at his home in Berlin on 11 September 1996, Mahle explained that he was the first to occupy a flat at Bayernallee 44, on 13 May 1945. He subsequently permitted key personnel to use the other flats in the house. They included Huchel and Markus Wolf, who rose to become the Cold War's most famous spymaster.

Together with Mahle, five other KPD figures were responsible for the first programmes, Artur Mannbar, Matthäus Klein, Otto Fischer, Erwin Wilke and Fritz Erpenbeck. Mahle confirmed that Huchel was employed at Radio Berlin as early as May 1945. He said, 'Huchel war unter den ersten Leuten, die wir dann genommen haben' in the days following the resumption of broadcasting. Huchel was brought to the radio station personally by the Soviet commandant from Rüdersdorf. There he had impressed the Soviets with his ability to cheer up his comrades through his organisation of theatre and other cultural events. The experience of radio drama and the Christmas play in 1941 had stood him in good stead. Throughout all the chaos of the previous weeks, he had kept with him a hand-written collection of his poems. He had shown them to the Soviet commandant, claiming that he had been involved in German literary life but that his poems had been banned by the Nazis. With characteristic charm and acumen, Huchel rapidly won over the Soviets during his few days of captivity. It was they who legitimised him when they took him to Radio Berlin and offered him to Mahle as a suitable employee in the cultural sphere.

He was interviewed by Mahle and Matthäus Klein, a pastor and member of the anti-fascist Free Germany movement, whom Mahle employed as head of personnel. Huchel told Mahle and Klein the story of the Nazis' banning of his verse. He showed them the hand-written collection, of which Mahle remarked to me that he could not judge the extent of their putative anti-fascist message. Huchel had, however, been recommended by the Soviets and was accordingly set to work.

Mahle recalled that, probably still in May, Huchel came to see him and said, 'Herr Mahle, wie ist denn das? Da wohnt meine Familie, da wohnt meine Mutter'. Huchel's parents lived at Waldstraße 31, just over the way from his wife and daughter, who lived at number 32. Mahle granted Huchel his wish and made available a battered old Opel and a Soviet driver, by whom he himself had been taken to the radio station from Karlshorst shortly before. Yet if Huchel travelled to Michendorf, one thing is clear: he did not go to Waldstraße to see his family. He would resume contact with them only in late August. Had he got other unfinished business to attend to? We shall probably never find out what he did on that day. It can, though, be said that Michendorf is a small place, and his presence in a car driven by a Soviet soldier would have been noticed and remarked upon to his family. It can also be said that Huchel quite deliberately declined the opportunity that he had engineered to re-assure himself and his family that all was well. His behaviour is an index of his estrangement at that time above all from his wife, which she was unwilling to accept then or, indeed, later. It must be said that she would scarcely have welcomed the news of his collaboration with the Soviets. Nor would he later confide to his wife that he had worked at Radio Berlin before September 1945. He spun her the yarn that he had secretly become involved in the Free Germany movement in the latter stages of the war. That supposed activity had guaranteed him his post-war position. There was a certain logic to the claim, in that Klein and others with whom he worked at Radio Berlin in the anti-fascist re-construction were members of that organisation. Significantly, Huchel would never make the claim on any other occasion, not least in official questionnaires, in which membership of Free Germany would have acted as important legitimation. His deployment of the story to his wife could be used a cover for his 'secret' movements as well as to safeguard him from the – in her eyes, serious – charge of collaboration as a 'Russen-Knecht'.

Although he never acknowledged it in public, Huchel was, then, involved in the German capital's post-fascist cultural life almost from the beginning. By 22 May, the station was already broadcasting as many as nineteen hours a day. Among those KPD figures returning from Moscow who worked at Radio Berlin was Markus Wolf. On 4 June 1945, he wrote to his parents Friedrich and Else, who were still in Moscow, 'Wir sind hier 6 Mann Deutsche und ein Major mit 600 Mann der "Alten" zusammen. (Das alles natürlich unter uns.) Das Ausmisten ist leider nur zu einem kleinen Teil möglich, da viele, ja die meisten gebraucht werden'.[4]

Wolf's letter indicates the scale of the personnel problems faced by the Soviets and their KPD collaborators in their efforts to set up a viable anti-fascist radio service. This had been identified in Moscow as something to which the highest priority had to be given, together with the establishment of a newspaper, the *Deutsche Volkszeitung*, which later became *Neues Deutschland*. It was necessary to set to work straight away as many people as possible with the appropriate skills. More considered selection would have to come later. Already on the inside track, Huchel could, as necessary, point not only to his experience as a freelance radio author but also to a degree of technical knowledge through his training in signals. Later, he could use his position in Berlin literary life before 1933 with *Die literarische Welt* and in the artists' colony as further legitimation. He could present himself quite plausibly as a 'bourgeois intellectual' with Leftist sympathies. That was, moreover, precisely the sort of figure that the Soviets were seeking to recruit in order to implement their policy for Germany. Even though the years from 1933 had not been marked by the anti-fascist activity of those now released from concentration camps or of friends such as Kantorowicz and Bloch, who would presently return from exile and whom he would use as referees in the immediate post-war years, before 1933 he had moved in 'progressive' circles, in which Marxism had certainly been a subject of discussion. Huchel's ability to demonstrate appropriate knowledge and connections would certainly have a bearing on his movements in the summer of 1945 and beyond.

Having been recruited by the Soviets in May 1945 to work at Radio Berlin, Huchel cannot from that point on be regarded as a prisoner-of-war. Though this position was not without its dangers, Huchel was shrewd enough to exploit it in such a way that he came to play an influential part at Radio Berlin in the development of what was the greatest concentration of creative talent in Berlin during the immediate post-war years. Mahle was favourably impressed by Huchel's good work and after some four weeks named him 'Leiter des künstlerischen Wortes'. From this position, from June onwards Huchel was in a position to exert a strong influence on programming for the arts.

Through broadcasts of Theodor Plievier's 'Stalingrad' on 15 July 1945, Horst Lommer's 'Das tausendjährige Reich' on 6 September 1945 and of Friedrich Wolf's 'Professor Mamlock' on 8 November 1945, the anti-fascist orientation of radio drama was established. It was accompanied by productions of German classics, beginning with Lessing's 'Nathan der Weise' on 2 August 1945 and Goethe's 'Iphigenie' on 30 August 1945. They were followed by further pieces from the canon, German and international, reflecting a strategy designed to recover humanist values undermined by Nazism. The strategy also reflected a scepticism towards experimental modernism which Huchel broadly shared with Soviet cultural officers. Their training had, of course, encouraged them to recognise such work as an outgrowth of a western capitalist system. Huchel had his reservations about capitalism as well, but his reservations about experimental modernism were more an expression of his temperament and of the fact that he had entered Berlin literary life in 1930 at a key stylistic watershed. As experimental modernism became the vogue in the West during the deepening Cold War, there was correspondingly less and less room for modernist work *tout court* in the schedules of Radio Berlin.

It is clear that when in the early summer months of 1945 a somewhat more searching selection procedure was instigated, Huchel was in a very strong position. Quite apart from his background, Huchel had proved himself to be an intelligent and conscientious worker, who possessed rare literary talents, which were not lost on the well-educated Soviet cultural officers responsible for selection. They themselves had been carefully selected for their knowledge of German culture and were skilfully deployed in what was essentially a charm offensive, the aim of which was the renewal of Berlin cultural life in conjunction with appropriate German partners.

Why did the Soviets elect to launch this charm offensive to win over a people responsible for the devastation of their country? Since 1989, research has brought out ever more clearly that in the immediate post-war years the aim of Soviet policy was not to adopt a revolutionary strategy but instead to secure Soviet interests through negotiation with the Western Allies.[5] Stalin recognised that the Soviet Union's security concerns and its legitimate claims for reparations could most realistically be pursued through an agreement which would maintain a united Germany within a system which he – like the KPD in 1945 – described as a parliamentary democracy. Western politicians were, understandably, sceptical about

Stalin's conception of parliamentary democracy. Not all leading Moscow politicians shared the ageing Stalin's analysis, though none, of course, dared openly to challenge him. The same went for elements in the Soviet Military Administration in Germany (SMAD) as well as in the KPD, primarily – and crucially – Walter Ulbricht. Stalin, of course, relied precisely on these people to implement his German policy. Differences of opinion would presently be translated into the fundamental contradiction between the pursuit of the all-German approach and the emerging reality of the separate German socialist state, which, as a policy priority, Stalin never actually wanted. This contradiction was reproduced at all levels of the Soviet Zone (SBZ)/GDR, including cultural policy. This, in turn, would lead to the wholly paradoxical situation, in which – put at its bluntest – the non-Stalinists such as Huchel and Arnold Zweig were the most notable supporters of Stalin's policy for Germany, while Stalinists such as Alexander Abusch supported Ulbricht's Stalinisation of the GDR in the face of Stalin's German policy. The key cultural politician of the first post-war decade, Johannes R.Becher, was caught hopelessly between both camps.

The KPD's proclamation on 11 June 1945 of the 'Aufrichtung eines antifaschistischen, demokratischen Regimes, einer parlamentarisch-demokratischen Republik'[5] is not to be dismissed as mere rhetoric. It was rather the expression of Stalin's policy. The agreements reached at the Potsdam Conference were hailed at the time by the Soviets as a triumph for their diplomacy. It is only against this background that one can begin to appreciate the import of Anton Ackermann's call in February 1946 for a 'besonderen deutschen Weg zum Sozialismus', which was explicitly not to be that of Sovietisation. Stalin held the view that once the fatal divisions of the German working class parties had been overcome, a united working-class party would be in a position to secure a majority in elections throughout Germany and to proceed with a programme of socialism by parliamentary means, as the Labour Party, for example, was doing in Britain. Indeed, even beyond Stalin's death in 1953 and up until 1955, priority in Soviet policy was given to unification rather than the separate development of a socialist state. Under Walter Ulbricht's leadership, as the Cold War deepened, elements of the SED continually sought to assert their separatist agenda for the construction of socialism, and this led to great tensions between East Berlin and Moscow throughout the early post-war period, which fed through into cultural policy and its practical application, which, within the discourse of Marxism-Leninism, lurched between an all-German and a specifically GDR path.

Successful implementation of Soviet policy depended crucially on the recruitment of bourgeois sympathisers such as Huchel, who might act as a magnet to attract the many German intellectuals whose sympathies similarly lay with socialism. In these circumstances, there was an, on the face of it, unlikely readiness on the part of Soviet officers to acknowledge that many of those intellectuals who had stayed in Germany had entered into certain compromises without by any means becoming Nazis themselves. It was vital to win them over and mobilize them. Huchel was one of those figures who was welcomed as someone who had never supported Nazism and who, drawing on his own reserves of idealism as well as a pragmatic appreciation of the situation, was most willing to engage in political and cultural reconstruction out of the sincerely-held belief that a better Germany must now be built. Huchel had not participated in the socialist struggle against Nazism, and many of those who had would regard him as an opportunist and resent his cultivation by the Soviets. Yet he had learnt what at the time beyond any doubt he took to be the lesson that the recurrence of fascism could only be prevented by democratic socialism. This view came to inform his activity in the early post-war period, including his attitude towards the 'restoration' of capitalism in the western zones/ Federal Republic. For Huchel personally, his collaboration with the Soviets marked a great opportunity to cast off the frustrations and uncomfortable compromises of the Nazi years. He could now think of deploying his literary talents and personal skills in order to make a real contribution to society. This contrasted with the past, when he had adopted a rather passive role, viewing himself, in his role of poet, as someone on the margins of social processes. It was not lost on him that despite the attempt to maintain an independent position, he had looked on helplessly as, willy-nilly, he had been drawn into the net of radio propaganda and his integrity as a writer had been compromised. In the immediate post-war years Huchel would throw himself into his work, first with Radio Berlin, then with *Sinn und Form*, determined to make good what had happened in the past on a personal as well as a broader social and political level. This determination was born out of a sense of personal failure, which would act as a spur in the challenges to come.

He had reason to be grateful to the Soviets for the opportunities they gave him after they captured him in late April 1945. It is certain that he would never have received such favourable treatment had it been down to the KPD alone. In the 1970s, Huchel remarked in conversation with Rudolph, 'Die Zusammenarbeit mit den sowjetischen Offizieren war nicht immer einfach, aber alles in allem doch recht kollegial'. It has been pointed out by a number of commentators that Huchel came to enjoy Soviet support at the highest level. Werner Wilk, for instance, who knew Huchel in this period at Radio Berlin, refers to his support from 'einen sehr einflußreichen russischen Offizier'.[6] Mahle, for his part, always felt that Huchel had 'einen Stein im Brett bei den Russen'. It has not proved possible to identify the officer referred to by Wilk with absolute certainty, but it must have been one of the control officers deployed directly at the radio station or at SMAD headquarters at Karlshorst. Among those in the latter category were Major Sergey Tulpanov, head of the SMAD's information section, Major Alexander Dimshitz, a literary historian who headed the SMAD's cultural section, Major Mulin, who was in charge of radio, and Major Patent. A key figure at Radio Berlin was Major Seva Rosanov, whose German was excellent following schooling in Berlin as the son of Soviet diplomats. He was a writer as well as a literary translator, chiefly from German into Russian.

Support of the order suggested by Wilk can only have come from that level in the hierarchy. Certainly, Huchel and Monica Huchel both mentioned Patent, but he would have had dealings with Rosanov and Mulin. It was the latter whom Mahle identified as the key figure concerning the management of personnel at Radio Berlin.

Huchel was one of the few people among the 600 initially employed at the radio station who were selected for special training, through which they were groomed for key posts in administrative as well as artistic spheres. The expectation was that they would be capable of working in both areas. Huchel never referred to this training in public. As we have seen, in the 1984 edition Monica Huchel merely followed him in claiming that in the months in Rüdersdorf he had opted to become involved in cultural work rather than give in to the general mood of despair. Yet, as is so often the case in the Huchel story, the reality was somewhat different.

Rüdersdorf

Rüdersdorf was used not only as a PoW camp, it was also the site of the SMAD's anti-fascist school, which was run by Major Wilhelm Ludwigovitch Martens of the Soviet Army's Intelligence Corps. A small number of Germans were prepared there for key positions in the emerging new structures. It was to Rüdersdorf that those Germans at Radio Berlin who had been selected for training were sent. Huchel was one of them. As we have seen, Huchel never divulged this information in public. In a questionnaire completed on 18 May 1948, however,[7] Huchel stated that, in addition to his selection for the SMAD school in August-September 1945, in Rüdersdorf he was put in charge of the 'Antifa-Aktiv', through which he implemented Soviet political and cultural re-education policies for his former comrades-in-arms. This position of responsibility amounts to much more than Huchel's personal decision to take a lead in putting on cultural events for his compatriots. Indeed, it testifies clearly to the degree of trust that Huchel had built up with the Soviets, who placed him in this post. His account of 1948 is consistent with the fact that he went to Rüdersdorf as a figure recruited by the Soviets with a political and cultural brief. There is nothing sinister about that. While there, he had as his assistant the nineteen-year-old Herbert Stöhr. Stöhr recalls that Huchel enjoyed a degree of freedom that one would not normally associate with a PoW. He was allowed to travel between Rüdersdorf and Berlin with musicians whom he had recruited to give concerts.[8] This memory is in keeping with Monica Huchel's account of the journey by lorry with musicians from Rüdersdorf to the Masurenallee, where Huchel had his other base.

Apart from the short initial period of captivity, Huchel was in Rüdersdorf only for his crash course at the SMAD school in August and early September 1945. In late August, he took the step of contacting his family for the first time since the letter that he had sent from Dahnsdorf on 19 April. On 26 August and 2 September, he sent notes home from 'R'.[9] In them, he informed his wife and daughter that he was enjoying more than adequate food and tobacco rations and was spending his time studying. Details of this preferential treatment contrast sharply with Monica Huchel's depiction of Huchel eating rotten black pudding and pine cones in Rüdersdorf, though such a diet clearly cannot be ruled out during the first few days of captivity. His studies certainly included material about the Soviet Union, its history, political system and culture, though Soviet policy for Germany implied a broader curriculum. It is quite possible that Huchel's copy of a German-language edition of Mayakovsky's *Ausgewählte Gedichte*, which was published in Moscow in 1941, comes from that time.[10] Signed by Huchel, the text includes an introduction with a number of margin marks placed against key passages, in which socialist views on poetry and the poet's relationship to the social whole are discussed. Huchel was certainly also introduced in Rüdersdorf to administrative and management issues, which would figure in the duties that he later assumed. To some extent, his schooling nearly a year earlier in Ludwigsburg would have come in handy. Already on 26 August, the 'PoW' knew that he would be able to return home in mid- or late September, and he confirmed this arrangement on 2 September. It goes without saying that this information would not have been available to the average, run-of-the-mill prisoner. Both notes reveal that he was in good spirits in the quite acceptable circumstances of his 'confinement'. He knew that he would soon be on his way back to Radio Berlin where he would occupy a post that would give him further opportunities to deploy his talents within the programme of antifascist reconstruction.

The Return to Radio Berlin and to Civilian Life

Huchel was released on 15 September and had five days leave before, on 20 September, he resumed his duties at the radio station. Dora Huchel recalled his return home to Michendorf as follows,

> Ich sah ihn schon am Gartenzaun – wie in solchen Situationen – gingen Traum und Realität ineinander. Kindern ist so etwas nach der ersten Freude eher selbstverständlich. Von Sorgen und Ängsten umeinander befreit, für Susanne und mich endlich auch ein Schutz gegen die damals tagtäglich Frauen aufrührenden Russen.

Huchel depicted his return to the village in 'Heimkehr' (i,109), appropriately the final poem in *Gedichte*. The poem begins with the scene of destruction that awaited him, 'In der schwindenden Sichel des Mondes/ kehrte ich heim und sah das Dorf,/ verödete Häuser und Ratten'. The crescent moon of 'Der Rückzug' is picked up in order to suggest the cycle of death and re-birth which continues on a cosmic plane despite the orgy of destruction that has taken place on earth. For all that no one gathered in the harvest, the poem finishes with a visionary scene of regeneration. At its centre is the mythical female figure familiar from 'Die Magd' onwards, 'kam eine Frau aus wendischem Wald'. She is the key representative of a rural culture that endures despite the inroads of Prusso-Christianity, capitalism and Nazism. The poem ends with the invocation of the Great Mother in a manner that can only have appealed to Soviet readers,

> Da war es die Mutter der Frühe,
>
> unter dem alten Himmel
>
> die Mutter der Völker.
>
> Sie ging durch Nebel und Wind.
>
> Pflügend den steinigen Acker,
>
> trieb sie das schwarzgefleckte
>
> sichelhörnige Rind.

The poem's grandiose ending affirms the basis of life beneath the maternal principle, re-establishing, too, the linkage between the earth and the cosmic order in the imagery of the 'sichelhörnige Rind'.

According to Dora Huchel's account, as early as September 1945 Huchel's collaboration with the Soviets was the source of a conflict between them, which would grow in the coming months. Dora Huchel writes,

> Huchels Mitteilung von der hochbezahlten Stellung im sowjetisch lizensierten Berliner Rundfunk nahm ich äußerst skeptisch auf ... Ich versuchte, ihn sogar dazu zu bewegen, auf geschickte Weise den einträglichen Posten am Rundfunk zu verlassen, zumal wenn er berichtete, daß schon wieder 'nur noch ein Hut am Nagel hing', da sein Besitzer 'abgeholt' worden sei. Die Russen-Pajoks 'für die oberen Zehntausend' verführten mich nicht dazu, diese Laufbahn zu begrüßen. Huchel war zwar keinesfalls unglücklich in dieser Stellung, doch glaubte ich, daß er in anderer Stellung eine kompromißlosere Arbeit finden würde. Vielleicht trug diese meine Einstellung zu der Trennung bei, die bei einer grundsätzlichen Auseinandersetzung ihren schmerzlichen Anfang nahm.

As Dora Huchel saw it, after four years in which they had spent much time apart during the war and its aftermath, difficulties in adjusting were exacerbated by the conflict over the direction of Huchel's post-war career. Yet for Huchel himself, through a mix of good fortune, shrewdness and basic agreement on the approach to cultural and political reconstruction, fuelled by a rekindled idealism, he had worked himself into a position with the Soviets that he could scarcely have expected, at a time when any employment whatsoever was at a premium and there was no longer anything forthcoming from Kronstadt. In the meantime, the other Allies had arrived in Berlin and four sectors had been established. Dora Huchel believed that other opportunities might now arise. The Huchels' friend, Günther Birkenfeld, for instance, quickly became established with the Americans, and Huchel came to enjoy contacts in that quarter. Yet over a number of months Huchel had become accepted by the Soviets in a manner that promised further opportunities in the development of radio that he found appealing. He surely felt that he had grounds to be less sceptical than his wife about Soviet motives. At the time, the prospects they were holding out were not so very different from those offered by the other Allies. The agreements recently reached at the Potsdam Conference gave grounds for hope that, despite French misgivings, Soviet policy could be implemented for a new, united Germany.

When Huchel returned to the Masurenallee and to the top-floor flat at Bayernallee 44, it was to a Soviet enclave in Charlottenburg in the British Sector. The enclave was the product of bartering between the British and the Soviets, who had surrendered Gatow airstrip in exchange for the continuing occupation of the radio station and the area around the Masurenallee. It would prove to be a controversial outpost, from which East Berlin would attempt to influence opinion in the West of the city, not only through radio but through the *Sinn und Form* venture which had its first editorial seat at Bayernallee 44 from 1948-50. The Soviets finally agreed to surrender the radio station in the early 1950s and it became the home of Sender Freies Berlin. In the autumn of 1945, Huchel's duties were not restricted to the artistic sphere nor, indeed, to radio play productions. His crash course in Rüdersdorf had prepared him for an administrative role and on 20 September 1945 he assumed the post of personal assistant to the 'Sendeleiter'. That post was occupied by Jenö Vida, who had been imprisoned in Dachau from 1938 to 1945 because he had illegally broadcast anti-fascist material. Huchel never publicly acknowledged his post as administrative assistant to Vida, though it obviously had a bearing on his rise over the next two years at Radio Berlin, when his time was divided between administrative/managerial and artistic work, with the emphasis more often on the former.

Material rewards were now forthcoming, as for the first time in his life Huchel now officially assumed a post as a full-time employee. His salary was 600 marks per month but this would soon rise steeply and, apart from a minor blip at the turn of the 1950s, he would be firmly in the bracket of the high earning cultural elite in the SBZ/GDR for the next decade and a half. The demands made on him would, of course, grow proportionately. As was usual for intellectuals in the SBZ/GDR, Huchel presently assumed other duties which went along with his role in cultural life.

Yet, only a matter of days after his resumption of duties at Radio Berlin, Huchel had quite different problems to contend with. At 8.30 in the evening of 30 September 1945 Fritz Huchel died aged 78 at home at Waldstraße 31 in Michendorf.[11] Fritz Huchel's son would die at exactly the same age in 1981. The funeral in Michendorf reflected the severe deprivations of the immediate post-war years. Susanne Huchel recalls the event as resembling a scene from the Middle Ages. A horse and cart were hired and her father took his place alongside the coachman, while the other mourners walked along behind. There is no longer any trace of Fritz Huchel's grave in the Michendorf cemetery. Huchel chose to remember his father through 'Letzte Fahrt', which was among his first post-war publications in 1946 in the anthology *Das Gedicht in unserer Zeit*.

In the autumn of 1945 there was no time for Huchel to recover from the physical and emotional trials of the past year. On 3 November, Elisabeth Langgässer brought Oda Schaefer up to date with developments in their old Berlin circle, writing that she and her husband Wilhelm Hoffmann had seen Huchel at the radio station, 'Huchel sieht sehr blass u. elend aus u. ist erst kürzlich aus russ. Gefangenschaft zurückgekommen – ein treuer und herzlicher Freund für Euch beide und uns!'[12] There were, it seems, clear limits to the degree of intimacy Huchel was prepared to enter into with his old friends. In fact, Huchel's friendship with Schaefer and Horst Lange would henceforth be restricted to the occasional letter following their decision to settle in Bavaria, though in the late 1940s Huchel made a great effort to publish Lange in *Sinn und Form*.

His other area of duties, the artistic sphere, was described by him both as dramaturg and as literary lector. This area of duties was broadly conceived, including musical as well as literary and dramatic productions. Huchel enjoyed close contact with the young female cultural officer, Lieutenant Sakva, who was deployed in the literary section, where, among other things, she was responsible for radio drama. Max Seydewitz, a Social Democrat, who was put in charge of Radio Berlin in 1946, writes of her, 'Diese junge Genossin ... kannte von deutscher Kunst und Literatur, auch der aus der jüngsten Vergangenheit, viel mehr als die meisten Mitarbeiter der Abteilung'.[13] She would have found an informed conversation partner in Huchel. A good working relationship with Sakva can be assumed; it would surely have been a pre-requisite for Huchel's advance.

Susanne Huchel recalled her father's involvement in broadcasts by Russian choirs. The classics, too, were a staple feature of programming. His major task, however, was to set up a studio for radio drama. He did this with evident success, dealing with the technical and administrative side, as well as attracting talented authors. Among old friends from radio work in the Nazi years who were now also employed in radio drama were Oskar von Arnim, Pelz von Felinau and Geno Ohlschläger. Langässer and Wilhelm Hoffmann did occasional work. Hedda Zinner, wife of Fritz Erpenbeck, was one of the people who were engaged in the same sphere following her return from Moscow exile in June 1945.

Huchel was involved in a number of series that were broadcast on a regular basis. 'Autorenstunde' presented readings by contemporary writers, including Langgässer, August Scholtis, Hedda Zinner and Hermann Kasack. 'Das Meister-werk der Literatur' was devoted to readings from the classics of world literature, among them Petrarch, Tolstoy's *Anna Karenina* and Elizabeth Barret-Browning. Other programmes were 'Erzieher zur Menschlichkeit', 'Theater-, Film- und Funkspiegel' and 'Das Gedicht'. In a letter of 20 February 1946, Langgässer wrote to Schaefer and Lange of her recent work at the radio station,

> Ich ... laufe ... zum Funkhaus, zum 'Horizont' ... ergattere Aufträge, schreibe Spiele für den Jugendfunk ... über 'Pawlow', ein Leben für die Naturwissenschaften, über die 'Curie', die Huch und Gott weiß wen alles und habe jetzt am 27. Februar eine 'Autoren-stunde' in der Reihe erlauchter Geister wie Becher, Fallada usw., wobei mich Paul Wiegler einführt.[14]

In the same letter, she describes her very strong friendship with Huchel, his critical acumen and the enormous attraction towards him that she felt,

> Auch zwischen Piese und mir seid Ihr beiden der Gegenstand häufiger Erörterungen – so ungefähr wie zwei unzuverlässige, geliebte Enkelkinder, um die sich die Großeltern Sorgen machen! Lacht nicht – wir, die wir, jeder an seiner Stelle, den berliner Markt der Eitelkeiten und den grotesk-traurigen Jahrmarkt im besonderen der gepeinigten Menschheit durchschauen (mein Gott, wie sie nach Anerkennung lechzen, wie unverwan-delt sie aus allen Feuern und Leidensproben hervorgegangen sind!) – wir, Huchel und ich, stehen hier am Rande des Literaturbetriebes – – zwei melancholische Pinguine, die ab und zu ihre Flügel spreizen und leise mit dem Schnabel klappern. Neulich war er abends bei uns zu heißem Tee mit Rum-'Aroma' und nachweihnachtlichen Plätzchen, ich las ihm den Anfang, das 'Proszenium', meines neuen Romans vor und war begeistert von seinem unglaublichen Einfühlungsvermögen, seinem klugen, absolut sicheren Urteil und seinen so garnicht intellektuellen, sondern durchaus substanziellen Erkenntnissen. Beim Anschauen H.[uchel]'s geht es mir ähnlich, Odalein, wie bei Dir – ich könnte ihn stundenlang betrachten ohne eine Spur von Sexualität. Leider wird er von dem Funkbetrieb fast aufgefressen, und ich finde es jammervoll um seine künstlerische Substanz, die entweder darunter leiden oder sich wie ein Igel zusammenkugeln und verkleinern muß.

The passage includes reference to a number of the qualities for which Huchel was valued by literary friends and colleagues. In writing of Huchel's extraordinary capacity for empathy in his critical understanding of her new novel, *Das unauslöschliche Siegel*, Langgässer echoes Lange, who in the mid-1930s so much appreciated Huchel's views on his *Schwarze Weide*. The comments of both demonstrate that, despite the fact that Huchel's own talent did not extend to prose, he was a gifted critic of it, as he was of other genres, though again, he never actually wrote reviews or works of criticism. He deployed his critical acumen on a professional basis in the selection of material for broadcast and would go on to do so to such great effect with *Sinn und Form*. Indeed, over the coming decade and a half the editor's selection of material by others would represent Huchel's major contribution to German literary life. It was in his capacity as an editor with a unique all-German brief rather than as a poet in his own right that Huchel would come to occupy such as key mediating function in the German literary world of the Cold War years. In a sense then, Langgässer's fears for Huchel's creativity were borne out. The poet generally had to take a back seat while Huchel became a constant, though enigmatic presence in a literary market place fascinated, like Langgässer and Schaefer, by the extraordinary charisma which he exuded from the unique position that *Sinn und Form* occupied.

His work in radio was a valuable editorial training ground. The weekly broadcast 'Das Gedicht' was later described as including,

> das Werk der Verstorbenen wie der Lebenden ... Verse unseres Vaterlandes wie der Welt ... Goethes 'Sah ein Knab' ein Röslein stehn', Heines 'Leise zieht durch mein Gemüt', Dehmels 'Liegt eine Stadt im Tal' ... Bald spricht zu uns der dichterische Nachwuchs, bald haben die Dichter jenseits unserer Grenzen das Wort. Franzosen, Italiener, Russen, Amerikaner sorgsam gewählt und von Künstlern vorgetragen.[15]

This account illustrates how both in terms of international flavour and the appreciation of the German lyric tradition Huchel's approach was informed by a breadth in line with policy aims. His organisational skills and taste in the choice of personnel and material ensured the growth of his reputation.

A KPD figure such as Zinner appreciated Huchel's skills and political good faith, yet had her ideological reservations, as her brief portrait of Huchel in her mémoirs shows. It is reminiscent of portraits by other KPD/SED figures such as Kantorowicz and Karola Bloch, in that it draws attention to what Zinner, like Bloch, perceived as Huchel's political limitations, though it must be said that these putative deficiencies need to be weighed against the particular sectarian view of politics and public life cultivated in KPD/SED circles. Zinner writes,

> Die Hörspielabteilung des Berliner Rundfunks wurde damals von Peter Huchel geleitet, einem feinfühligen, sehr verschlossenen Naturlyriker, der merkwürdigerweise für das Genre Hörspiel viel übrig hatte und etwas davon verstand. Huchel war Antifaschist, einer, der sauber durch die Nazizeit gekommen war, aber ich hatte immer den Eindruck, alles

bei ihm sei nur gefühlsmäßig verankert. Im Grunde war er ein unpolitischer Mensch, der Ursachen und Wirkungen politischer Erscheinungen oft nicht in Einklang zu bringen vermochte.[16]

It was, of course, inconceivable that anyone in Huchel's position could have been anything other than an anti-fascist. It is unclear if Zinner was aware under what circumstances Huchel had learnt his trade, and she could certainly not have known of the extent of his compromises in plying it. Her account illustrates how Huchel was accepted by a returning KPD figure as someone legitimised by the Soviets. Huchel's difficulties at the radio station would begin later, when the SED's influence in practice came to outweigh that of the SMAD officers. Huchel was not political in the manner of a KPD/SED member like Zinner or, for that matter, Karola Bloch, since he had never internalised party dogma which was reproduced as the occasion demanded as articles of faith. It was not least for this reason that Huchel always stood out from many of his peers in the SBZ/GDR. This is the way the Soviets wanted it, but, by the same token, many KPD/SED figures came to resent the prominence and privileges that Huchel gradually gained. Figures well disposed to him such as Zinner and Karola Bloch labelled him 'unpolitical', yet Huchel was playing the political game according to different rules. For all the differences that she recognised, Zinner was appreciative of the help Huchel gave her in her work,

> In dem von Peter Huchel gegründeten Hörspielstudio ... fand ich Anregung und Hilfe. Und wenn Huchel mir zu dem Hörspiel 'Kolchis' ... sagte, wenn es einen Nationalpreis für Hörspiele gäbe, würde er ihn mir für die 'Kolchis' zuerkennen, war das für mich die beste Bestätigung, daß ich gelernt hatte.[17]

Zinner's characterisation of the radio play department under Huchel shows how productive collaboration there was,

> Unter Huchels Leitung fanden in der Masurenallee regelmäßig Zusammenkünfte von Hörspielautoren und Regisseuren statt, bei denen Kritik an bereits gesendeten Arbeiten geübt, aber auch Themen für neue überlegt und besprochen wurden. Was ich besonders schön fand, war, daß man nicht nur Themen für die eigene Arbeit zur Diskussion stellte, sondern es häufig vorkam, daß jemand eine Idee, eine besonders hörspielgeeignete Geschichte erzählte, mit der Bemerkung: 'Für mich ist das nichts, aber vielleicht interessiert sich jemand von den Kollegen dafür'. Die Diskussionen, die bei diesen Gelegenheiten oft recht leidenschaftlich geführt wurden, haben mir nicht nur sehr bei der Gestaltung meiner praktischen Hörspielarbeit geholfen, manche meiner theoretischen

Artikel, etwa 'Das Hörspiel als Kunstform', 'Was wird aus dem Hörspiel?' und andere
wurden durch solche Diskussionen angeregt. Unter den Teilnehmern dieser Zusammen-
künfte befanden sich so bekannte Rundfunkleute wie Alfred Braun, Hannes Küpper, Pelz
von Fehlinau.[18]

Huchel's talent in stimulating discussion derived in all probability much less from
any overt attempt to lead a discussion than from his quiet discretion, even personal
reticence and the fact that he was a very good listener and sympathetic critic, who
had a gift for promoting constructive dialogue. After he had set out the framework
for participants he would allow discussion to develop freely, only occasionally
joining in to summarise or to clarify issues and to bring proceedings to a conclusion.
That is certainly the impression left by one of the few documents which show
Huchel working in such a capacity, the record of an 'Arbeitstagung des künstlerischen Wortes' held at Radio Berlin on 25 and 26 November 1947, which we shall
examine presently.

Promotion

Official recognition was not long coming at Radio Berlin. On 16 May 1946 Huchel
was promoted to head dramaturg. His salary was 1,000 marks, which had risen to
1,200 by August when further promotion followed. It was not only his employers
who were appreciative of his work. At a time when the Huchels' marriage was
about to collapse irretrievably, on 21 May 1946 their Potsdam friend Rudolf Elter,
whose untimely death came the following year, wrote to Dora Huchel offering his
family's congratulations on her husband's success,

> Der glänzende und verdiente Erfolg Ihres Mannes hat die gesamte Sippe mit herzlicher
> Freude erfüllt, u. wir möchten zuerst Piese, dann aber auch Ihnen als der Leidensgenossin
> während so vieler schwerer Jahre unsere aufrichtigen Glückwünsche aussprechen. Zwar
> verhehle ich meine Besorgnis nicht, daß Piese einer derart 'exponierten' Stellung bald
> überdrüssig werden kann, doch ist im Augenblick nur Anlaß zu heiterer Genugtuung.
> Meine Mutter sagte kürzlich bewundernd: 'Piese ganz gross', nachdem sie eine schöne
> Mozart-Sendung gehört hatte. Wir hoffen, dass recht viele Zuhörer so denken.[19]

A further bone of contention between Huchel and his wife was her negative
response to his news that he had been offered a ministerial post in Potsdam,
presumably in the cultural sphere. In 1981, she recalled, 'Die Übersiedlung samt
Transport von Sack und Pack könne jederzeit starten, meinte er, während ich mich
ganz und gar dagegen sträubte: Es war mir klar, wie schäbige Kompromisse so ein

Posten bedeuten würde'. In the event, Huchel did not take this post, but any basis for understanding between husband and wife was fast disappearing. She was clearly concerned that her husband, who was not a party member, could easily be used as an acceptable front and be manipulated or discarded as was expedient. Events in those years and later demonstrate that her fears were not entirely misplaced. Yet she did not fully appreciate her husband's relationship with the occupying power and the hopes that he invested in Soviet policy for Germany.

He would confide to a number of people in the GDR, among them Ulrich Dietzel, that, following the merger of the KPD and SPD as the Socialist Unity Party in April 1946, he had intended to join the SED. He had, however, discussed his intention with Soviet officers who advised him against this step. They explained that he was more valuable to them as a non-aligned figure working to preserve cultural unity. Huchel accepted their advice, which – as things turned out – would in subsequent years with *Sinn und Form* save him from subjection to party discipline but at the same time leave *Sinn und Form* rather exposed and outside the SED's lines of communication. Huchel's acceptance of Soviet advice, however, demonstrates that he was fully aware of the role he was being asked to play and consented fully to playing it. In his subsequent work, be it with Radio Berlin, with *Sinn und Form* or in other activities, Huchel rightly regarded himself as operating on a plane of cultural diplomacy elevated well above any political line that Ulbricht might be following. He brought to bear a sophistication and idealism that was wholly foreign to Ulbricht and his followers, and in time he would make the policy of German cultural unity his own, when the SED had abandoned it. Initially resented by certain SED figures at Radio Berlin, Huchel was presently actively opposed there, as the SMAD withdrew for the SED to take command. Yet, Soviet cultural officers and a German cultural politician of the standing of Johannes R. Becher continued to see in Huchel a guarantor of the all-German policy on which they were set.

Throughout 1946 Huchel's star was still very much rising in radio. In the first major re-organisation that took place at the station in August 1946, Hans Mahle was promoted from Director General of the station to a post overseeing all radio operations in all the Soviet Zone. He was replaced at Radio Berlin by Max Seydewitz, whose background in the SPD had taken him into exile in Sweden. In the re-organisation, Huchel was given the posts of Director of Programming and Director of Radio Berlin itself and of the 'Deutschlandsender'. This was a very steep rise indeed and it was matched by substantial financial reward. As we have seen, he had begun in September 1945 with 600 marks a month but less than a year later his salary was 1550 marks with a bonus of 600 marks.[20] A chauffeur-driven limousine, a most improbable trapping for Huchel, went with his new responsibilities in one of the top managerial positions.[21]

Huchel's rise coincided with Wilhelm Girnus' appointment as Seydewitz's deputy. After years spent in prison and a concentration camp under the Nazis for illegal KPD activity, from December 1945 Girnus had been responsible for radio in the body set up by the Soviets for German self-management, the 'Deutsche Selbstverwaltung für Volksbildung'. A figure with a highly irascible manner combined with a dogmatic certainty in politics, both exacerbated by the brutal treatment meted out to him by the Nazis, Girnus was a powerful enemy within the SED hierarchy, who had great reservations about Huchel which presently he would not conceal.

Despite his rise, then, Huchel had good reason to be wary. Among the old friends who had been seeking to re-establish contact with him was Eich. Huchel was evidently not responding to Eich's advances. In September 1946, Eich asked their mutual acquaintance, Hermann Kasack, 'Haben Sie Huchel gesehen? Warum ist er so völlig verstummt? Man kann es mit Arbeitsüberlastung und Schreibfaulheit kaum erklären'.[22] It is quite plausible to conclude that at this stage Huchel did not wish to compromise his sensitive, new position through contact with someone who, as he himself knew, had gone much further in his compromises with the Nazis in his radio work.

Monica Melis

As he reshaped his life in an atmosphere of increasing estrangement from his wife, Huchel was receptive to fresh emotional experiences. The radio station was a place which afforded many opportunities for the casual liaisons that Huchel enjoyed. This was something that Dora Huchel had learnt to live with in the 1930s, but things had changed greatly since then. The new world that her husband moved in was foreign to her and one she did not particularly wish to get to know. In the period of their growing estrangement, Huchel had more than one affair and their marriage had essentially collapsed by June 1946.

In an interview in the mid-1980s, Monica Huchel recalled, with great precision, that her first meeting with Huchel had taken place on 6 October 1946.[23] In her mémoirs, however, she writes that the meeting took place shortly after May 1946.[24] In 1953, following the Huchels' divorce, Monica Melis would become his second wife. She was born in 1914 in Essen, where, according to her own account, she spent a difficult childhood and adolescence following her father's death in the First World War. She was an attractive woman in her early thirties when she got to know Huchel. Shortly after May 1945 she began to carve out a career for herself as a journalist with the *Deutsche Volkszeitung*, later re-named *Neues Deutschland*. In those chaotic days, the normal rules of engagement were suspended. It does, though, seem quite improbable that it was only a chance meeting in a cinema with Enno Kind that brought her immediate employment on a newspaper of such strategic importance and that, without any background in journalism, she was offered a basic salary of 600 marks per month with an additional fee per line.[25] Though a medical assistant by training before the war, she discovered a talent for reviewing plays, films and radio broadcasts. She later took in sessions at the courts and social issues. In that way, she managed to feed and clothe herself, her two young children, Catharina and Roger, and the woman who looked after them. Roger Melis is today one of Berlin's best known portrait photographers of writers and artists, while Catharina worked on a Potsdam newspaper before her early death in 1981. Monica Melis' first marriage to the sculptor Fritz Melis collapsed during the war, and she instigated divorce proceedings on 23 July 1945. She survived the war by using native cunning and the determination born out of the adversity she had known in her early years. She, too, then was ripe for fresh emotional involvement.

In her mémoirs she recalls how the Berlin authorities arranged a bus tour of Mecklenburg and Pomerania for journalists in Berlin associated with the performing arts, so that they could see what was being played in the provinces,

> Es waren Journalisten aus allen vier Sektoren geladen. Morgens um zehn Uhr traf man sich am Bahnhof Zoo. Ich stellte fest, daß ich die einzige Frau war. Als es hieß: Jetzt fahren wir los, kam ein Taxi, aus dem ein Mann in Hut und Gamaschen stieg und in den schon fast die Türen schließenden Bus sprang. Er wurde von Herbert Ihering heftig begrüßt. Wir waren zehn Tage unterwegs, abends hingen wir in Hotelbars herum, und allmählich wurde mir offenbar, daß dieser Mann in den Gamaschen Peter Huchel hieß. Seit dieser Reise haben wir uns nicht mehr getrennt.[26]

The Peter Huchel that Monica Melis got to know was the influential media man, a member of the management team at Radio Berlin. She could surely not begin to guess just how recent his elevation to that status had been, nor for that matter how swift his sidelining would be. Only later did she discover that he was a poet. At the start of their relationship and in fact later, neither of them was inclined to dwell on their lives before 1945. Like so many people emerging from the traumas of the war years, they wished to look forward and to build a new life. Certainly, Huchel's new partner was more closely attuned to his aspirations in those years than his first wife. While Dora Huchel regarded with suspicion his active involvement in cultural life, Monica Melis was, like him, using her energies to discover new skills in fresh spheres. While she did not possess Huchel's creative talents, she was happy to enter into his world on the terms he set. Later, Monica Melis would sacrifice her independence to join him on the *Sinn und Form* venture. She later wrote, quite candidly, 'In all den Jahren mit Huchel lebte ich in ständiger Verfügbarkeit'.[27] She acknowledged, too, that she accepted her husband's judgment on political matters rather than forming her own opinions. Yet, throughout all the years of their relationship Monica Huchel would be the staunchest of supports, possessing a determination and instinct for survival that Huchel's first wife had never been required to develop. These qualities would be tested to the extreme during the early years of their relationship. Not only was Dora Huchel unwilling to give up her claims on Huchel; despite the increasing estrangement between him and his wife, Huchel, too, could not bring himself to make the decisive break. Monica Huchel writes, 'Diese Ehe belastete ihn sehr, aber es war eben auch Huchel, der es nicht fertiggebracht hatte, sich einer Frau gegenüber eindeutig zu verhalten, mit der er nicht leben wollte. Ich war längst geschieden, alles war geregelt, während die Ehe Huchels auf eine Weise an uns hing, daß daran eine neue Liebe hätte zerbrechen können'.[28] We see here in Huchel's indecision, his inability to make a big decision affecting his life, what great inhibitions he had about surrendering what he already had and knew, and how loath he was to move on to something new and unfamiliar. The story illustrates Huchel's characteristic 'Seßhaftigkeit', which Erich Arendt found quite unattractive in his friend.[29]

During the early stages of the relationship with Monica Melis, Huchel was having another affair at Radio Berlin. As the years went by, Monica, like Dora, would learn to turn a blind eye to his infidelities, adopting the same basic attitude that he would always come back. Huchel and Monica Melis soon moved in together, using his flat on the Bayernallee and hers at Dahlmannstraße 4b. During the day they pursued their professional duties, while in the evening they met at such venues for artists and intellectuals as Die Möwe and the Klubhaus der Kulturschaffenden, which was part of the Kulturbund at Jägerstraße 2-3. It was only consistent with Huchel's position that he should become a member of that organisation, which had been established in the summer of 1945 under Johannes R.Becher's presidency as an umbrella organisation for the arts. The visitors' book of the Klubhaus contains the names Huchel and Melis among the visitors on 16 November 1946.[30] Also present were Becher, Alexander Abusch, Ruth Hoffmann and Paul Wiegler.[31] The attraction of the Klubhaus extended beyond the plentiful supplies of food and drink for the intellectual elite. The Klubhaus was central to the aim promoted by Becher of bringing together artists and intellectuals from a variety of backgrounds to create a strong anti-fascist front. For Huchel, who, as Monica Huchel writes, knew hundreds of people, the Klubhaus was an ideal place to do business for the radio as well as, in time, to re-launch his own literary career, which he had temporarily put on ice.

The Kulturbund

The Kulturbund was founded in Berlin on 8 August 1945. Among those present on that day were Becher, Ihering, Wiegler, Ackermann, Ernst Lemmer, Mahle, Klaus Gysi, Lommer, Günther Weisenborn and Wolfgang Harich. Despite Becher's wish that Bernhard Kellermann should be elected its first President, those present argued that Becher should take the post himself. At the first meeting of the Presidium on 24 August 1945 Wiegler, head lector at the Aufbau Verlag, which was established as the publishing arm of the Kulturbund, reported on plans to produce a journal. The plans bear a marked similarity to the thinking that later went into *Sinn und Form*. Wiegler explained,

> Zu dem Verlagsprogramm gehören dann Zeitschriftenwerk, oder vielmehr Zeitschriftenunternehmungen, und ich darf diesen Plural gebrauchen, da nunmehr der kulturpolitischen Monatsschrift *Aufbau* eine literarische Monatsschrift folgen soll, die für den Oktober vorbereitet wird und die gewidmet sein soll der Literatur in engerem Sinn, der Kritik, der Philosophie, und die ja in gleichem Maße zu berücksichtigen hat Bildende Kunst und Musik, um dieses Programm, das man von hier erwartet, ganz zu erfüllen.[32]

The Kulturbund rapidly established links with other new institutions in Berlin cultural life. On 1 October 1945, Radio Berlin began its daily broadcast 'Stimme des Kulturbundes'. Cläre Jung, who headed the department 'Kulturpolitik und Volksbildung', was responsible for this programme, in which Becher took an active interest. The influence of the Kulturbund grew and, in the spirit of institutional collaboration, it was only natural that Huchel should accept an invitation from the Kulturbund's literature commission to give a talk at its Klubhaus in early December 1946. Shortly afterwards, in early 1947 Huchel would accept an invitation to join the literature commission. As far as can be ascertained, the paper which he read in early December 1946, 'Probleme des Hörspiels', marked his first significant public appearance outside the radio station after the war.[33] According to the Kulturbund's own memorandum of the event, it was very well attended, with some 120 guests.[34] Huchel was introduced by Günther Weisenborn. The memo writer's evaluation, produced according to the SMAD's guidelines, was that it had been 'very interesting'. Reports appeared in *Vorwärts* (4.12.46), *Tägliche Rundschau* (8.12.46) and *Der Morgen* (22.12.46).

Beyond providing some insight into Huchel's approach to radio drama, the talk, like the slightly later 'Rede zum "Tag des freien Buches"', (ii,261-5) which was delivered on 10 May 1947 at the Humboldt University, documents something of his contribution to anti-fascist reconstruction. The speeches, which can profitably be read in conjunction with each other, are of interest in two further respects. Firstly, the manner in which Huchel treats the question of culture in the Third Reich reveals the discomfort of someone who had participated in that now stigmatised world. Furthermore, the fluctuating, often contradictory terms of reference that he chose testify to the difficulty experienced by a writer with an essentially 'bourgeois' background in a cultural context in which, for all the all-German strategy, partisan socialist positions were being promoted strongly, since the SED ultimately knew no other way.

The 'Rede über das Hörspiel' can be divided into two main sections, a potted history of the radio play and recommendations for present practice. Huchel refers back to the Weimar Republic in order to establish a respectable radio play tradition, singling out the experimental contributions of the Marxists Friedrich Wolf and Bertolt Brecht and quoting from *Die Weltbühne* to distinguish the 'besondere[n] sprachliche[n] Form' (ii,256) of the radio play from the visual medium of the theatre. Huchel, who had acquired all his practical experience of radio play work in the Third Reich, restricts his comments on that period to the following,

> Dann kam das Jahr 1933. Und wie auf allen Kunstgebieten, so erntete auch auf dem Gebiet des Hörspiels ein rein künstlerisches Formstreben keinen Dank und keine Anerkennung mehr. Die alles vergiftende politische Tendenzlüge bemächtigte sich auch des Funks und des Hörspiels, so daß der wertvollere Teil der Hörerschaft, der nach menschlicher und künstlerischer Erhebung verlangte, sehr bald das Interesse am Hören verlor. (ii,256)

Huchel's reticence regarding his own work and that of others is, of course, more than understandable given the opprobrium attaching to art produced in the Third Reich. The uncomfortable nature of his own position as an expert unable and unwilling to refer publicly to his own source of experience is evident. This meant, too, that Huchel, understandably enough, went along with a wholly simplified view of radio and indeed the arts in general in the Third Reich. Had he sought to present a more nuanced picture he might easily have drawn attention to himself and to aspects of his radio work in the Third Reich that, in the climate of the immediate post-war years, were best forgotten. In addition, the language of Huchel's analysis at this stage (e.g. 'ein rein künstlerisches Formstreben', 'politische Tendenzlüge' and 'nach menschlicher und künstlerischer Erhebung') reveals a rather traditionalist, even 'formalist', 'bourgeois' aesthetic understanding clearly at odds with Marxist categories.

Moving on to recommendations for present practice, Huchel made statements which were generally of a rather obvious kind, to which no exception could be taken. He recommended simplicity and accessibility,

> Wahrscheinlich dürften aber diejenigen Hörspiele vorzuziehen sein, die sich ganz aufs dramatische Wort einstellen, die keiner Exposition bedürfen, die auf jedes Beiwerk verzichten und die von der Geräuschkulisse entweder gar keinen oder den allersparsamsten Gebrauch machen. (ii,258)

Similar thinking informs his advice on the choice of subject matter,

> In einer unvergleichlich bewegten Zeit wie der unsrigen dürfte es dem Hörspielautor nicht
> schwerfallen, einen packenden, allgemein interessierenden Stoff zu finden. Das Leben in
> einer verwüsteten Stadt, die elternlosen Kinder, die Heimkehrer ... Aber auch die ganze
> Vergangenheit der Menschheit und die ganze Zukunft der Menschheit bietet ihren Stoff
> dem Hörspieldichter an. (ii,260)

Huchel's recommendations here are conventional formulations for standard realist practice and omit any reference to a socialist orientation. Huchel was, of course, doing precisely what the Soviet officers wanted him to. Yet it should not be forgotten that as a writer who had stayed in Germany, Huchel had not been party to the debates on the nature of realism conducted in exile by many socialist writers who returned to the Soviet Zone. His espousal here and elsewhere of an aesthetic that had not developed significantly beyond the 'bourgeois' position that he had adopted in the early 1930s made his position increasingly dubious for a number of his German communist peers.

Huchel's talk at the Klubhaus provoked lively discussion. As *Vorwärts* reported, demands that Radio Berlin should now really promote the radio drama were met with the announcement, reported in the *Tägliche Rundschau*, that the station was inviting submissions in a radio play competition and was offering 1,000 marks as first prize. The *Tägliche Rundschau* noted that the discussion

> drehte sich naturgemäß um hörspieltechnische Formprobleme, an denen sich die
> anwesenden Autoren sehr interessiert zeigten. Aber auch der Wunsch nach aktuellen
> Hörspielstoffen, wie es beispielsweise die Bodenreform, die Neusiedler, die Heimkehrer
> usw. sind, wurde angesprochen. Mit Recht wies Generalintendant Hans Mahle auf die
> erzieherische Bedeutung des Hörspiels hin.

Zinner was among the authors present. *Der Morgen* reported her as calling for 'ein eigenes Ensemble von Sprechstimmen, die auch für Sprechchöre eingesetzt werden können'. And it was Zinner who won the first prize in the competition for her work 'Erde', which was broadcast in 1947. Huchel was a member of the jury which selected her play from 1130 entries. Fellow jurors were Wolfgang Langhoff, Walter Franck, Boris Blacher, Girnus and Ihering. In their different ways, all but Franck would in coming years have roles to play in Huchel's life in the GDR.

Kantorowicz's Return

Shortly after his successful evening at the Klubhaus, Huchel was spending an evening there in January 1947 when one of his oldest friends, Alfred Kantorowicz, came through the door. The Kulturbund was the first port of call for many returning emigrés. They were guaranteed a friendly reception and a good feed. Kantorowicz recalled,

> Der Klub war fast leer, aber von einem entfernten Tisch erhob sich ein Mann mittlerer Jahre und kam auf mich zu mit der Frage, ob ich es denn wirklich sei. Es war mein Jugendfreund, der märkische Lyriker Peter Huchel, den ich zuletzt im Jahre 1933 gesehen hatte.[35]

There was much to catch up on. The intervening years had seen the KPD activist Kantorowicz working for Willi Münzenberg in Paris, fighting in the Spanish Civil War and escaping from Vichy France to the United States. There he had been employed by CBS radio before being accused by the Hearst press of spying for the communists. Kantorowicz had one item of news which confirmed Huchel's worst fears about their old friend Joachim. Kantorowicz told Huchel that Joachim had fallen into Gestapo hands and nothing had been heard from him since.

Huchel invited Kantorowicz back to what the latter described as Huchel's 'zerbomte(r) Behausung', where he spent the night 'neben dem kleinen eisernen Ofen, den wir beständig mit Holzresten und Abfällen füttern mußten, damit er im Umkreis von etwa einem Meter ein wenig Wärme spende'.[36] Huchel, in fact, took Kantorowicz not to his own flat at Bayernallee but to Monica Melis' on Dahlmannstraße, where Huchel was officially registered from 19 May that year.[37]

The following morning, Huchel summoned a chauffeur-driven limousine from Radio Berlin to take Kantorowicz to his appointment with Johannes R. Becher in the district reserved for top functionaries on the edge of Pankow. Kantorowicz's later depiction of his meeting with Becher in his *Deutsches Tagebuch* conveys all the loathing and, it must be said, envy which Kantorowicz felt towards Becher. Differences would come out into the open only later. For the time being, Becher and SMAD officers were content to acknowledge that in Kantorowicz they had a figure with great energy and drive, who had a host of contacts, not least with Heinrich Mann, whom Becher and others wanted to see back in Berlin as a symbol of anti-fascist unity. Very quickly, Kantorowicz was granted a licence to set up a publishing house in Pankow. He gave it the name Ost und West, quite in keeping with the Soviets' all-German strategy, and chose *Ost und West*, too, as the title for the influential, though short-lived journal that he set up as its flagship.

In the two or so years of its existence between 1947 and 1949, Huchel was a contributor to *Ost und West*, as, with Kantorowicz's help, he went about re-establishing himself as a poet. Indeed, Kantorowicz did much to promote Huchel's anti-fascist credentials in those years. As we shall see, their relationship soured in the early to mid-1950s, when, with Becher's support, Huchel joined the artistic élite in the East Berlin Academy of Arts, while at the very same time Becher personally ensured that Kantorowicz was excluded.

Re-emergence

Having established himself in an influential and lucrative position at Radio Berlin, in April 1947 Huchel took four weeks' leave in order, at last, to pursue his own literary work. However, his letter of 19 May 1947 to Max Schroeder at the Aufbau Verlag indicates that even then he could not divest himself of all the responsibilities that he had acquired. Indeed, it is a measure of the influence that Huchel had gained beyond his immediate sphere that he wrote to Schroeder, an old friend from the artists' colony,

> Könntest Du nicht Kanto[rowicz] veranlassen, daß er uns einmal mit Ende zu sich lädt, damit wir dort im privaten Kreis über das schlecht geleitete Feuilleton des *Neuen Deutschland* sprechen könnten? Es ist in letzter Zeit wieder so viel Unsinn fabriziert worden, daß unbedingt etwas passieren muß.[38]

Huchel's relationship with Monica Melis meant that he was well-informed about *Neues Deutschland*. He was evidently one of the people who could be expected to have a view that counted in such matters. In addition to his position with Radio Berlin, he was now a member of the Kulturbund's literature commission along with Schroeder, Weisenborn, Ihering, Friedrich Wolf, Herbert Roch, Gerhard Pöhl and Ruth Hoffmann.[39] It was evidently part of the brief of the commission to keep an eye on such matters. That said, it is unclear if any action ensued, or whether the proposed meeting ever took place.

It emerges in Huchel's letter to Schroeder that he had been asked in his capacity as a poet in the commission to evaluate verse that had been submitted by new writers, who were hoping that they would be published by Aufbau. Huchel conveyed to Schroeder his opinion that none of the material he had been given to read was suitable. It was because of such negative judgements that the commission rapidly gained the reputation as an élitist forum that was not sufficiently concerned with fostering the range of new talent that was emerging. Clear proof of tensions would emerge in Huchel's later evaluations.

Given Huchel's position in cultural life, it was only appropriate that Aufbau should publish Huchel's verse. Later that year, on 19 September 1947, he signed a contract for the collection that appeared late the following year as *Gedichte*. There was much work to be done to lick it into shape. He had left behind in Michendorf many of his belongings, including his personal archive and his library. The archive was needed in the preparation of a manuscript. He returned to the family home with Monica Melis and took away as much material as he could lay his hands on in a hasty search through the house. What was left – and this was very substantial – in time found its way via West Berlin and Mora, Sweden, to the John Rylands University Library in Manchester. The material now in Manchester and the papers consulted for the 1984 edition as well as others deposited at the Deutsches Literaturarchiv Marbach and in Huchel's house in Staufen reveal as hollow the public statements made in June 1947 by Kantorowicz and Lommer that Huchel's personal archive had been destroyed during the war.

It was Kantorowicz and Lommer who supplied the first post-war critical assessments of Huchel's life and work. In them, they set the tone for Huchel's early post-war reception. As we have already seen, in doing so, they introduced confusing and downright misleading statements, which continue to bedevil Huchel research fifty years on. It must be said that their statements were wholly in keeping with an established discourse which sought to ensure the distance of the subject treated from the culture of the Third Reich and to project an anti-fascist continuity. In this way, Huchel could be legitimised for the post- and anti-fascist context. One must add that in the prevailing climate it would have been downright dangerous to attempt a properly balanced public appreciation of a non-Nazi artist's position in the Third Reich. Distinctions were lost sight of and, as happens in times of crisis, myth-making replaced dispassionate analysis. It just so happened that, with a little help from his friends, Huchel was singularly well-equipped to negotiate such a situation.

The point of the story of the archive's destruction was, of course, that Huchel was free to present himself afresh, stripped of any unwelcome constraints deriving from his pre-1945 life and work. It then became a quite straightforward matter to present Huchel simply as an anti-fascist, as we see in the following passage that Lommer wrote,

> Huchel dichtete weiter. Aber nicht für die Reichskulturkammer. Er dichtete für uns, seine Freunde, und für die Stunde der Befreiung, an die er trotz aller Erfolge der gehaßten Machthaber unerschütterlich glaubte. Es ist ein tragisches Verhängnis, daß fast alle Werke aus dieser Zeit verbrannten. Weniges blieb übrig, weniges konnte ich selbst sicherstellen.[40]

It is a measure of Huchel's readiness to identify with Lommer's exculpatory panegyric that the account of his life that Huchel submitted on 18 May 1948 as part of his formal application for the *Sinn und Form* editorship included reference to Lommer's article as a source of reliable information about him.[41] Huchel suggested further that from 1935 until the end of the war he and Lommer had been the closest of companions in Michendorf. In the late 1940s, Lommer's appeared to be a good address. A founder member of the Kulturbund, he made a name for himself with the broadcast by Radio Berlin in 1945 of his satire, *Das tausendjährige Reich*. It was published by Aufbau in 1947 and became a popular success. Yet for all Lommer's initial attempts to ingratiate himself in East Berlin through his strident anti-American statements in *Die Weltbühne* and the *Tägliche Rundschau*, he was not held in particularly high esteem.[42] By 1951 he had fled to West Berlin, where he recanted in a document released to the press. This event was reported in *Die neue Zeit* on 29 March 1951 under the title 'Ein Gott wurde angebetet, der keiner war. Ein Dokument als exemplarisches Beispiel der geistigen Barbarei'. In the article the gravest of doubts were expressed about Lommer's integrity. It was apparently lost on that commentator, as it would be on later ones, that Lommer's own anti-fascist credentials were further blemished by his involvement as an actor in the notorious anti-semitic film 'Jud Süß'.[43] Unsurprisingly, the opportunist Lommer's recantation was followed by Huchel's removal of any reference to him and the 1947 article in an updated version of the CV that he produced in 1951.[44]

Huchel was more gifted, more astute and better connected than Lommer. On 10 May 1947, Huchel was invited to join Kantorowicz on the platform at the Humboldt University for the 'Tag des freien Buches', an event organised to commemorate the fourteenth anniversary of the Nazis' burning of books. Huchel's speech represented a contribution to the reconciliation of 'inner' and 'outer' emigration. Huchel pleaded for a renewal of the German humanist tradition after its decimation by the National Socialists. The speech begins with a self-critical intention,

> wenn eine grundsätzliche Neubesinnung auf die wirklichen Werte der Dichtung und der Kunst sich geltend machen soll, dann müssen wir, so glaube ich wenigstens, es vor unserem Gewissen verantworten, wie weit wir Schriftsteller dazu beigetragen haben, daß es heute in Deutschland notwendig ist, einen Tag des freien Buches zu begehen. (ii,261)

Huchel re-affirms his own credentials, already assured by his choice as speaker as well as through his position with the Soviets, by reference to his close acquaintance with Kantorowicz, Ernst Bloch and Friedrich Burschell at the beginning of the 1930s in Berlin. His own position on the Left in the Weimar Republic is thus guaranteed. His diagnosis of the failure of intellectuals to combat successfully the rise of National Socialism follows the familiar path of reference to the split in the parties of the Left and criticism of those 'ängstlich oder hochmütig der Zeit ausweichende[n] Schriftsteller[n], die sich hinter der reinen Kunst verschanzten'. (ii,261) Huchel's own distance from such a stance is seemingly guaranteed by reference earlier to his relations with Bloch, Kantorowicz and Burschell. Yet, as we have seen, Huchel's own position in the 1930s was by no means as clear-cut. There were clearly limits to the public self-criticism that Huchel was prepared to indulge in. To have done so would, it must be said, have been damaging. Thus, he chose to dwell only briefly on his career between 1933 and 1945, restricting himself to the following,

> Meine Damen und Herren, ich gehöre zu den Schriftstellern, die zwölf Jahre Hitlerdiktatur miterlebten. Zweimal war ich in dieser Zeit allerdings mehrere Monate lang im Ausland und hatte das Glück, von dort aus Verbindungen zu einigen emigrierten Freunden aufnehmen zu können. Und da ich bis zum Jahre 38 Besuch aus England bekam, war ich nicht ganz isoliert. (ii,262)

Given his position in the Berlin cultural hierarchy, it is at the very least arguable that Huchel did not actually need to produce such an interpretation of his life in order to ensure continued credibility. And yet, even if we must question Huchel's stylisation of his past, we must consider the pressures of the time and add that there is no reason to doubt that he was sincere in his support for anti-fascist reconstruction. By May 1947, he had come some way to viewing art as necessarily containing a political dimension. Thus, while praising the moral stance of those few writers who stayed in Germany and who 'sich geistig nicht gleichschalten ließen', (ii,263) he nonetheless criticised their writing (and implicitly much of his own from that time) because of its adherence to the tradition of inwardness,

> unsere besten Dichter – und ich meine jetzt die wieder, die ideologisch keineswegs mit den Nazis paktierten – auch dann noch ins Gebirge der dichterischen Schau stiegen und auf den höchsten Eisfirnen, losgelöst von jeder Realität in methaphysischer (sic) Einsamkeit mit dem Unendlichen Zwiesprache hielten, als am Fuße des Gebirges schon längst Städte und Dörfer in Flammen aufgingen und Menschen erschlagen wurden. Es war eine Flucht vor der Verantwortung. (ii,264)

In its moral intensity, Huchel's argument corresponds closely – though different imagery is used to express the idea – to that produced by Huchel's friend Langgässer later that year at the First Writers' Conference. While for Langgässer Christianity provided the writer with the means to overcome the ethical abdication that had occurred under Nazism, Huchel's answer was decidedly different,

> Und selbst dort, wo sie in die Zeit vorstießen, kämpften sie, einsam und dunkel, gegen das Schicksal an, statt gegen politische und gesellschaftliche Mächte zu kämpfen ... ein Jahrzehnt faschistischer Diktatur und völliger Isoliertheit hat genügt, die deutsche Literatur zu ersticken. (ii,264)

It would appear that Huchel included himself in this criticism. As we shall see presently, a number of early post-war compositions indicate the desire to overcome what he and many others had come to see as the fatal division of art and politics. It is consistent with his position in the Soviet Zone that he should conclude his speech with two final points: firstly, with a warning against the possible resurgence of fascism 'unter anderer Maske', (ii,264) the allusion to the perceived role of the Western Allies being reinforced by reference to the 'Drohung eines neuen imperialistischen Krieges' (ii,264); secondly, with words of praise for prominent representatives 'des freien deutschen Geistes, wie Thomas Mann, Heinrich Mann, Albert Einstein ... Johannes R. Becher, Anna Seghers, Ludwig Renn'. (ii,265) Yet the fact that he had not joined them surely compounded a sense of discomfort, alluded to only in general terms, deriving from the thought that throughout the Third Reich he had accommodated himself to the restrictions placed on writers.

Huchel could, however, rely on the support of friends like Kantorowicz. He was included in the book *verboten und verbrannt*, which was compiled by Kantorowicz together with Richard Drews and published in 1947. In it, one can read of Huchel, 'Während der Hitlerzeit hat er geschwiegen'.[45] On 4 June 1947, Kantorowicz organised an evening at the Klubhaus dedicated to Huchel's poetry, which was read not by Huchel himself but by the actors Siegfried Niemann and Paul Klinger. The latter had worked on Huchel's 'Herbstkantate' in 1935. On 5 June, *Neues Deutschland* reported that Kantorowicz introduced Huchel, 'Vor allem ist es Dr. Alfred Kantorowicz, der an einem Autorenabend ("Forum der Dichtung") mit den äußeren Umständen bekannt machte'.[46] The audience were told of 'die Nacht der Nazityrannei, die Huchel zwar überstand, aber schweigend, allen Verlockungen trotzend. Und nun spricht er nach 14 Jahren zum ersten Male wieder zur Öffentlichkeit'. The report in *Der Morgen* on 6 June 1947 echoed Kantorowicz's and Lommer's fiction, 'ein großer Teil dessen, was er im Krieg schrieb, ist bei einem Bombenangriff verlorengegangen'.[47] The visitors' book at the Klubhaus for the evening of 4 June includes the following names, indicating that they probably attended the Huchel event: Alexander Abusch, Heinz Willmann, Friedrich Wolf, the Birkenfelds, Langgässer, Wolfgang Weyrauch, Ruth Hoffmann, Lommer, Erich Weinert and Becher.[48] Huchel's own party, entered in his hand, includes, himself, Klinger, Niemann, Monica Melis and Götz Kozuschek. On 14 June 1947, the Kulturbund sent its report on the evening to the SMAD.[49] It stated that the evening had been devoted to the work 'des fortschrittlichen jungen Dichters'. Lest we forget, this member of the 'young generation' was forty-four years of age! The report continued, 'der Saal war voll besetzt' and 'der Abend kann als gelungen bezeichnet werden'. As the list of guests shows, Becher was among those present. He evidently took a liking to his fellow poet and would presently enlist him for the great literary enterprise he had been planning on and off with Paul Wiegler.[50]

Kantorowicz included Huchel's poetry in the first number of *Ost und West*, which appeared in July 1947. Kantorowicz outlined his programme in an editorial, in which he wrote that the 'Beiträge zu kulturellen und politischen Fragen der Zeit' were designed to build bridges between East and West, an undertaking in keeping with Soviet policy but one which many SED figures viewed with suspicion. In this respect *Ost und West* anticipated *Sinn und Form*, as it did, indeed, in its international breadth. In the first number, Huchel's name can be found alongside those of Heinrich Mann, Georges Bernanos, Theodore Dreiser, Ilya Ehrenburg, Carson McCullers, Alexander Blok and Brecht. Huchel's verse was prefaced by a portrait by Günther Birkenfeld, who, as we saw earlier, drew on his memories of their time together at Grunewald during the war. 1947 saw them still collaborating in Berlin cultural life, before the Cold War division put them in opposing camps. Birkenfeld's portrait stresses Huchel's striking visual impact, something remarked upon by Italiaander and Haas, as well as Langgässer. Birkenfeld conveys, too, the image of Huchel as the Bohemian adventurer,

> Halblange Saffianstiefel und ein besticktes bulgarisches oder ukrainisches Hemd würden ihm gut stehen. Ebenso gut kann man ihn sich in einem kleinen Literatencafé auf dem Montmartre vorstellen – auf dem er sich übrigens leibhaftig herumgetrieben hat, ebenso wie in verlassenen Weinbauerhäusern, in denen es spukte, tief in der Provence, in Städten und Dörfern des Balkans. Und wenn er barfuß in Hemd und Hose über die märkischen Felder bei Potsdam schweift, von denen er stammt, mit leicht gesenktem Kopf einen sandigen, von hohen Birken gesäumten Fuhrweg entlanggeht, nein, eher schon entlang-döst, so kommt aus der Vergangenheit ein Wendenbursche herauf.[51]

Birkenfeld further characterises his friend as a 'Lyriker komplexer Natur', the sort who 'zäh und mühevoll, unter Entsagungen und Leiden sich durcharbeiten, immer auf der Flucht und Suche, immer auf der Wanderschaft'. He links these characteristics with Huchel's constant dissatisfaction with his own compositions and his unwillingness to release his work even for friends to read, let alone for publication. Huchel, now in his mid-forties, had still not published his first collection. The six poems that he released for publication in *Ost und West* included very special verse for him personally. The poems were 'Sommerabend', 'Die Sternenreuse', 'Cap d'Antibes', 'Zwölf Nächte', 'Die Schattenchaussee' and 'September'. Only the final composition does not fit readily in the pattern. It was fitting that the October number should include 'Oktoberlicht'. As we have seen, this poem had special significance for Huchel's friendship with Kantorowicz, since it was composed during the summer they spent together at Kladow in 1931.[52]

Setback

By the autumn of 1947, Huchel's influence at Radio Berlin had reached its peak. The deepening splits at the onset of the Cold War forced the pace of changes in political structures which were taking place as the Soviets gradually relinquished control to the SED in key areas, among them radio. In September 1947, Huchel was 'promoted' sideways to 'Künstlerischer Direktor' and was thus divested of his responsibilities as director of programming, a marked erosion of his powers. In mid-February 1948, a new department, 'Künstlerische Direktion', was finally formally established to accommodate him, though it had existed in practice since his new appointment.[53] An account of his career at the radio station provided by the personnel department in 1952 indicates that this new area of responsibility included the 'Abteilung Künstlerisches Wort' and 'Ferner wurde er mit der Leitung des "Künstlerischen Beirats" beauftragt und zur Beratung der Intendanz in allen künstlerischen und kulturellen Fragen herangezogen'.[54] As we shall see, the 'Abteilung Künstlerisches Wort' offered some new challenges, but the 'Beirat' was, as the word implies, only an advisory body.

In a short, unpublished statement entitled '1948', which was evidently a draft for the autobiography for which he was contracted by Suhrkamp in the 1970s, Huchel recalled with a certain pique that Girnus replaced him as director of programming despite the fact that Girnus, as Huchel saw it, had only limited experience in radio.[55] It was, of course, Huchel's rival Girnus who would take over as editor of *Sinn und Form* in 1964 following Bodo Uhse's brief interregnum. In her mémoirs, Monica Huchel went so far as to claim that Girnus himself was responsible for Huchel's demotion.[56] In any case, as she acknowledges, the result was that Party members occupied all key positions while Huchel's influence dwindled and 'Der Rundfunk wurde ihm zuwider'. Huchel's agreement with the Soviets that he should remain outside the SED seemingly counted for nothing anymore.

In '1948', Huchel wrote that he was now sidelined and his duties restricted to radio play seminars and to courses for authors, for which he was at least praised in *Sonntag* in February 1948. One of the few surviving documents relating to his activities at Radio Berlin shows that on 25 and 26 November 1947 he presided over a short conference organised by the 'Abteilung Künstlerisches Wort', which covered the range of cultural broadcasts for radio professionals from other stations in the Soviet Zone such as Leipzig.[57] In his closing address, Huchel quoted Georg Lukács in order to stress the responsibility that German writers had in overcoming Nazism and promoting fresh values, 'Die Zukunftsverantwortung der deutschen Literatur ist groß, es geht um die Erweckung der Seele des deutschen Volkes zu neuem Leben'. His differences with Girnus, however, emerged in his pointed comment that perhaps not all those present would agree with every aspect of Girnus' paper. In his final summary, however, Huchel was at pains to acknowledge the common ground that they shared in their belief that the writer had a social function.

Among other speakers were Hedda Zinner, her husband the influential Fritz Erpenbeck, Alfred Braun and Hannes Küpper. Lommer's political piece 'Raffke 1947' was held up as a good example of how to combine humour with a serious point. Throughout, Huchel insisted on the crucial importance of quality in programme-making, however difficult it might be to find authors who could deliver.[58] He acknowledged that a weakness of the first day's programme had been its excessive abstraction but believed that those present would be able to take away with them fresh ideas for their practice at their own stations. He concluded by thanking Soviet officers for their part in organising the conference and singled out especially Lieutenant Sakva.

It was around this time, too, that Huchel favourably impressed Becher. Monica Huchel recalls,

> Ende 1947 oder Anfang 1948 fand im großen Sendesaal in der Masurenallee eine Lesung
> von Johannes R. Becher statt. Die einleitenden Worte sollte Friedrich Wolf sprechen, der
> aber nicht kam. Der Saal war voll, alles wartete, und es wurde beschlossen, daß Huchel
> einspringen müsse. Diese Rede muß Huchel besonders gelungen sein, denn er vermutete
> später, daß Becher ihm deshalb sein Projekt *Sinn und Form* antrug.[59]

The poet Becher no doubt appreciated the understanding of his work shown by a fellow poet. Not long after, in 1948, Huchel would conduct a radio interview with Becher about the meeting of the International PEN Club that Becher had attended in Copenhagen from 1 to 5 June 1948. The interview was published that year in *Aufbau*. In Becher, Huchel found someone with great power within the cultural sphere, who believed in him both as a poet and for his personal skills. When Huchel's position at Radio Berlin became untenable, a fresh opportunity would open up for him with *Sinn und Form*, which was equally prestigious and certainly more to his taste. While still at Radio Berlin, Huchel made just one isolated attempt to build upon his own work as a radio author through a new production of his Faust adaptation of the mid-1930s.[60]

He had continued his activities outside Radio Berlin in such organisations as the Kulturbund's literature commission. A document in the Kulturbund's archive refers to a meeting between the commission and young authors on 13 February 1948.[61] The event was run by Birkenfeld. In the second of two sessions, Huchel spoke about the poetry that he had been asked to assess. His comments were even less encouraging than those in his letter of May 1947 to Max Schroeder. In his view, the poetry was far inferior to the prose discussed at the first session. There was no point in having any of it read to the assembled audience. The memo notes, 'Er brachte weiterhin zum Ausdruck, daß die eingesandte Lyrik ein an Frieda Schanz erinnerndes Niveau aufwies und daß außerdem nicht einmal Stilarten in Anlehnung an bekannte Dichter zu verzeichnen waren'. Some of the young poets evidently protested at these harsh words. The document indicates that Huchel asked that his judgement should not be regarded as unalterable. He suggested that a second event should be organised, at which some of the work could be read and discussed. This was agreed to by those present. Evidently, the sort of work which young poets were being encouraged to produce in the Soviet Zone was anathema to him. Those present had, however, included a certain Horst-Harry Bienek from Köthen, who in the report on the event was deemed the most promising of the young writers. After his return home from Berlin, on 24 March 1948 the young Bienek wrote to Frau Kelbe at the Kulturbund and asked her to forward some of his poems to Huchel. She replied on 13 April, informing Bienek that she had passed the material on to Huchel.[62] There is no further record of correspondence in the Kulturbund's archive. It is, however, germane to note that in 1951 Huchel published Bienek's poem 'Mit einem Wort' in the special fourth number of *Sinn und Form* for that year, which in a print-run of 40,000 accompanied the 'Weltfestspiele der Jugend und Studenten für den Frieden' in Berlin from 5 to 19 August 1951.

As on 10 May 1947, on 10 May 1948 Huchel was involved in the commemoration of the burning of the books. This time, the venue was the Klubhaus of the Kulturbund. A report appeared under the title 'Fünfzehn Jahre später' in the West Berlin *Tagesspiegel* on 13 May 1948. The report cited the anti-western statements of Kantorowicz and Johannes Stroux, and glossed Huchel's contribution as follows,

> Unter anderer Maske erscheine heute ein neuer 'Faschismus', meinte Peter Huchel getreu den Tendenzen von Radio Berlin; in seinem Warnruf an die deutschen Autoren, sich vor einer Flucht aus der Verantwortung zu hüten, tauchte das gefährliche Wort von der 'jungen nationalen Dichtung' auf.

Huchel at this stage placed himself firmly in the East Berlin camp, in opposition to what he evidently viewed as the resurgent fascism of the West. He was prepared, too, the report indicates, to play on German nationalist sentiment as he combatted those in the West, as he saw it, opposed to unity. The report went on to contrast Huchel's 'einseitige Phraseologie' with the more balanced contribution by Hans Mayer from Frankfurt am Main. Mayer had been working for the Americans at the Frankfurt radio station but was actually in the process of negotiating a move to a professorship in Leipzig. This was Huchel's first meeting with Mayer, who in coming years would be one of Huchel's most brilliant essayists with *Sinn und Form* and would later recall, 'Das begann – daran kann ich mich genau erinnern – auf der Treppe des Ost-Berliner Kulturbundhauses in der Jägerstraße'.[63]

It was consistent with his position in the cultural elite that, as a non-aligned figure, he should become a delegate for Charlottenburg at the Deutscher Volks-kongreß.[64] From 1946 to 1949, that body was used by the SED and the SMAD as an organisation to promote German unity and peace. Huchel was, of course, a 'plant' in the British Sector. Becher's correspondence with Radio Berlin the following year demonstrates that the decision initially to place the editorial seat for *Sinn und Form* at Bayernallee 44 was motivated by the same consideration to have all-German representation in the western sectors.[65] At this stage, Huchel was evidently sufficiently convinced by Soviet policy to play the game according to the terms set out by the Soviets and Becher.

From Radio Berlin to *Sinn und Form*: Becher's role

For a few months in 1948 Huchel continued his duties in radio. He oiled the wheels of cooperation with such key organisations such as the Aufbau Verlag. From the library of 'Künstlerische Direktion', which existed in practice though not yet formally constituted, he sent the Aufbau Verlag his New Year greetings on 30 December 1947 with the words, 'Sie haben stets Ihre Neuerscheinungen zur Verfügung gestellt, und wir konnten mit Ihrer Hilfe ein gutes literarisches und aktuelles Sendeprogramm durchführen'.[66] He also took steps to recruit the staff that he needed for his department. In her unpublished mémoirs, Cläre Jung recalls that in early 1948 she accepted his invitation to move across from another department to join him in the 'Künstlerische Direktion'.[67] She recounts their telephone conversation, in which Huchel explained that among their tasks they would have 'musikalische und dramaturgische Studios zu entwickeln, öffentliche Diskussionen zu veranstalten über künstlerische und politische Probleme und Verbindungen aufzunehmen'. Huchel, according to Jung, led a team of eight in all, which included Else von Holländer-Lossow (reader, dramaturg and translator), Professor Max Butting (music studio), Dr Karl Block (drama studio), Edith Härting-Liebknecht (administration) and two secretaries, Erna Heidemann and Marta-Lore Krüger-Weth. Cläre Jung agreed to front public discussions and do the ground work for them. The discussions were quite big occasions,

> Für die öffentlichen Diskussionen wurde der Sendesaal zur Verfügung gestellt, ein Raum, der etwa 300 Personen faßte. Aber es gab Abende, an denen die Plätze kaum ausreichten. Diese Diskussionen hatten bald eine solche Popularität erreicht, daß sich schon ein gewisses Stammpublikum herausbildete, daß sich aus allen Teilen Berlins zusammensetzte.

The discussions were recorded and some later broadcast. Some details of the programme for these occasions have survived.[68] Huchel had overall responsibility and one can see his hand in the choice of speakers invited for the first discussion on the evening of 15 March, 'Was hat die deutsche Jugend zu erwarten?' Huchel's friends Kantorowicz and Birkenfeld participated together with Professor Heinrich Franck, a Dr Sellenheim and Edith Baumann. The discussion on another evening was Wie sehen Heimkehrer das heutige Deutschland?'. Speakers were Maximilian Scheer, Hedda Zinner, Heinz Schmidt, Eduard Claudius and Victor Stern. Other topics chosen in the series, which ran until 16 August, include 'Die Stadt: eine gute Wohnung?'; 'Braucht Deutschland seine Techniker, Ingenieure und Chemiker?'; 'Können wir uns selber helfen?'; 'Polnische Wirtschaft?'; and 'Was will der Zweijahresplan?'

The political events of the summer of 1948 put a stop to the series. Indeed, two of the titles above, 'Können wir uns selber helfen?' and 'Was will der Zweijahresplan?', point to the adoption of topics in line with the requirements of the SED and SMAD in the rapidly polarising situation. The split escalated with the introduction of separate currencies in East and West, which was followed by the Soviet blockade of West Berlin. These events caused enormous problems for the Soviet-run Radio Berlin, situated as it was in Charlottenburg in the British Sector. Indeed, the British had been jamming broadcasts since 1946. The Berlin crisis brought to a halt the type of programming of which Huchel was an exponent, which was designed to bring together East and West. More partisan attitudes were struck and greater ideological discipline enforced. Cläre Jung writes that in the plan for 1949 there was no longer any place for the 'Künstlerische Direktion'. Huchel's reference of 1952 from Radio Berlin explains, 'Infolge Auflösung der Abteilung wurde der mit Herrn Huchel bestehende Vertrag mit Wirkung vom 31.3.1949 gekündigt'.[69]

An article of 29 October 1948 in the West Berlin *Tagesspiegel* reported Huchel's impending departure from the radio station as resulting from a purge,

Seit Beginn dieser Woche wird laut DENA Angestellten von Radio Berlin, die nicht 'linientreu' sind oder die in dem Verdacht stehen, es nicht zu sein, nahegelegt, 'aus Gesundheitsrücksichten' ihre Kündigung einzureichen. Der Sprecher Alfred Braun hat bereits sein Arbeitsverhältnis gelöst. Der künstlerische Direktor Peter Huchel übt seine Tätigkeit ebenfalls nicht mehr aus. Mehrere Angestellte vom 'Künstlerischen Wort' sowie Mitarbeiter des 'Jugendfunks' reichten ihre Kündigung ein. Die 'Säuberung' wird von dem Personalchef Trojan (SED) geleitet.[70]

Whatever pressures Huchel might have been exposed to, as far as his own situation was concerned the report scarcely began to capture the reality of his situation. Huchel ceased working at Radio Berlin in September 1948 in order to devote himself full-time to the job of editing *Sinn und Form* from the beginning of the following month. He had, though, been involved in planning the journal from an earlier date. As he acknowledged in an account of his career produced on 29 June 1951, he continued to draw his salary of 1550 marks from the radio station until the end of March 1949. From 1 April 1949, he drew the more modest starting salary of 800 marks with 700 marks bonus for *Sinn und Form*.[71] This favourable interim arrangement did not later prevent him from complaining bitterly to Rütten und Loening, publisher of *Sinn und Form*, about the fact that he had had to work without a salary for the first six months![72]

He had been pencilled in for the *Sinn und Form* post by the spring of 1948 and provided career details on 18 May 1948.[73] On 24 April 1948, Johannes R. Becher wrote to Thomas Mann, requesting the latter's permission to use the title of Mann's journal *Maß und Wert* for a proposed new publication. Becher wrote,

> Nachdem wir absichtlich einige Jahre haben verstreichen lassen, um einen Überblick zu gewinnen über die in Deutschland vorhandenen literarischen Kräfte, wollen wir nun daran gehen, eine repräsentative literarische Zeitschrift zu gründen. Als Herausgeber sind vorgesehen Herr Paul Wiegler und ich, und Peter Huchel hat sich bereit erklärt, die Redaktion zu übernehmen.[74]

In the event, Mann did not agree to release his title and Becher settled on *Sinn und Form*. In the piece entitled '1948' as well as in interviews with Rudolph and Hansjakob Stehle, Huchel stated that he had been extremely reluctant to become involved in the project. In '1948', he wrote that after his experiences with Radio Berlin he had few illusions what would be in store for a non-aligned figure like himself. He added that though he hardly knew Becher he found it impossible not to go along with his wish that they should meet in Becher's office at the Kulturbund to discuss the project. In conversation with Stehle, he put it as follows, 'Ich hatte eigentlich gar keine Lust, aber Becher ließ nicht von mir ab'. (ii,374) Huchel, according to this account, found it impossible to resist the powerful Becher and submitted to his wishes. There is clearly something in that, but surely Huchel would not have entered into an agreement of this sort with Becher if he had not found the project attractive. As we shall see, Huchel was, indeed, deeply attracted by it, for all his misgivings about the mercurial Becher, which would be amply borne out. Huchel's problem when later talking about this matter in the West, however, was his understandable reluctance to acknowledge just how much he became Becher's creature in the late 1940s and early 1950s.

In conversation with Rudolph, he did acknowledge that he was an object of Becher's strategic thinking, 'Wie er ausgerechnet auf mich kam, kann ich nur dadurch erklären, daß er einen parteipolitisch nicht fixierten Mann brauchte'. He pointed out to Stehle that Soviet officers were motivated by the same consideration, 'Die sowjetischen Kulturoffiziere legten Wert darauf, einen leitenden Mann zu haben, der nicht in der Partei war'. (ii,374) In other words, *Sinn und Form* was a vehicle for the all-German policy which emanated from Moscow and gained expression in that wing of the SED occupied by Ackermann, who had proclaimed the 'besonderen deutschen Weg zum Sozialismus', a path which, ultimately vainly, Becher sought to follow, not to mention others such as Brecht and Arnold Zweig, as well as Huchel himself.

Yet there was also already an institutional basis in place for Huchel's collaboration with Becher: the Kulturbund. This link was surely also surely a factor in Becher's choice of Huchel to edit the journal. Like so many other early post-war enterprises in Berlin, *Sinn und Form* emerged from the Kulturbund. Preliminary discussions took place well before the crisis of the summer of 1948, after which the cultural and political atmosphere between the East and the West was poisoned for the foreseeable future. As we have seen, the idea of a high-quality literary journal to complement *Aufbau* was proposed by Wiegler at the Kulturbund as early as August 1945. Becher and Wiegler pursued the idea on and off in the interim, as Becher's letters show.[75] No doubt with one eye on Becher's abysmal reputation in the West and the other on the fact that Becher clearly used Huchel and dropped him when it became expedient to do so, Huchel later sought to play down his influence on the journal. He said to Stehle, 'Ich leitete die Zeitschrift ohne Rücksicht auf persönliche Verbindungen, auch wenn Johannes R. Becher, der damals Präsident des Kulturbundes war, gerne eine Becher-Zeitschrift aus ihr gemacht hätte'. (ii,374) Yet, at the same time Huchel conceded to Stehle that until 1953 Becher's patronage was integral to the journal's survival. It was only consistent with this constellation of personalities and its institutional basis that Huchel should have invited Wiegler and Becher to attend a first editorial meeting on 25 May 1948 at the Kulturbund.[76] They were joined by the publisher Ulrich Riemerschmidt and the printer, Eduard Stichnote, both of whom Huchel knew from Potsdam.

Though he does not make the point explicitly, the reference to Becher's position as President of the Kulturbund is of greater relevance still, since, until *Sinn und Form* was taken over by the German Academy of Arts in the autumn of 1950, Huchel actually reported on *Sinn und Form* matters to the Kulturbund's literature commission. After *Sinn und Form* was taken over by the East Berlin Academy, Huchel reported to its literature section, of which Becher was the Secretary as well as being Vice-President of the Academy to Zweig's President. Until 1953 the journal would in fact be much more of a 'Becher-Zeitschrift' than Huchel later cared to remember. Critics, too, have been disinclined to acknowledge that it owed its early success in no small measure to that influence: in the early days, it was Becher who had the links with all the major figures who were won for the journal. Commentators before 1989 in the West and since 1989 in Germany as a whole have tended to go along with Huchel's depiction: accounts such as Wittstock's, Zimmermann's and Hilton's stylise him from the outset as the isolated and beleaguered figure that later he became in his struggles with SED cultural politicians of the stamp of Alexander Abusch, Alfred Kurella and Kurt Hager.[77] Such accounts nourished the myth of Huchel's opposition from the start to GDR totalitarianism, just as he had, of course, been an opponent of Nazi totalitarianism. The dearth of hard and fast information about the GDR in the West (and in the GDR itself!) positively encouraged the growth of such myth-making, which Huchel did little to discourage. In fact, as we shall see, Huchel, who had collaborated closely with the Soviets, would in the early years of the *Sinn und Form* project come to represent the acceptable face in the West of Becher's ambitions in literary and cultural politics. At that time, there was certainly enough common ground between them politically for Huchel to accept such a role, whatever his personal misgivings. He was certainly well equipped to perform the high-level cultural diplomacy that his new post required.

To illustrate this point, one needs only to point to the role that Huchel played with some success in the Schutzverband Deutscher Autoren (SDA). On 13 April 1948, Huchel was proposed as a new member of the executive of the SDA, which included Birkenfeld, Lommer, Kantorowicz, Becher and Friedrich Wolf.[78] Lommer agreed to contact Huchel in order to establish if his work at the radio station would permit him to attend meetings on a regular basis. It evidently would: Huchel was elected to the executive and the membership commission on 29 April 1948. Soon afterwards, on 20 July 1948, following the currency reform, the first signs of a serious split in the organisation occurred. Birkenfeld proposed that the SDA should withdraw its affiliation with the Freier Deutscher Gewerkschaftsbund. On this occasion, at a meeting of 30 July 1948, Weisenborn's compromise was accepted, though by 13 November 1948 Weisenborn had resigned from the organisation. Huchel and Kantorowicz had asked him to re-consider and he was thinking the matter over. In the meantime, Huchel, with votes from Roland Schacht, Birkenfeld, Kantorowicz and Wolf, beat Wiegler and Ilse Langner in the election for a new chairman. At the meeting of the executive on 21 December 1948, Becher's call for a boycott of *Der Tagesspiegel* was discussed, even though, as Schacht pointed out, he was not present to represent his case. Huchel, however, intervened on Becher's behalf, 'Wie Herr Huchel mitteilt, ist Herr Becher dafür, daß dieser Punkt auch ohne ihn besprochen wird'. In the event, Schacht's proposal was accepted that the matter shuld be put to the membership. At the same meeting, Huchel also undertook to represent Hedda Zinner, who, it was agreed, had been defamed in the introduction broadcast by Nordwestdeutscher Rundfunk to her adaptation of Anna Seghers' *Das siebte Kreuz*. Evidently taking very seriously the social dimension of his role, he reported on the economic plight of Herbert Roch and secured support for him. It was in keeping with the role that he assumed with the SDA and *Sinn und Form* that in the early 1950s he should, as we shall see, become a proponent of the 'Gesamtdeutsche Arbeit' undertaken by the GDR Writers' Union in Berlin and in the Federal Republic.

Despite his experience with Radio Berlin, for Huchel there were actually any number of good reasons why, in the spring of 1948, he should accept Becher's offer.

It meant that he would continue working at a high level in cultural life with good remuneration, on an enterprise which fitted perfectly his skills and temperament. Radio had been the main focus of his literary activities for a decade and a half, yet the recent demotion meant that it was not difficult for him to leave. The new post meant, however, that for the foreseeable future opportunities would remain limited for him to work on his own compositions. He took the opportunity presented by the transition from Radio Berlin to *Sinn und Form* to do the remaining work on the collection for which he was contracted with Aufbau.

Gedichte

In his letter to Max Schroeder of May 1947, Huchel referred to his 'Arbeit am eigenen Manuskript', and in September of that year he signed a contract with the Aufbau Verlag. The path to publication was, however, not smooth. His relations with the Aufbau Verlag worsened after publication of *Gedichte*, the course of events illustrating how fraught Huchel's relations with his publishers could become. It is certainly true that Aufbau, like most other publishers, was not a model of efficiency, tact and even-handedness in its dealings with authors. Central to the problems in the relationship, however, was Huchel's extreme indecision, which had been a major factor in the non-appearance of *Der Knabenteich* and would recur later. Another was his insistence on special treatment before and after publication, which resulted in the issuing of frequent demands and ultimatums. One point of conflict is dealt with in Erich Wendt's letter to Huchel of 24 November 1947, which indicates that Huchel was unhappy with the contractual point that two thirds of the print-run should be in paper covers rather than bound between hard covers. Huchel's view prevailed that the whole print-run should be between hard covers. We shall return to other difficulties presently.

Friends such as Birkenfeld, Kantorowicz and Werner Wilk testify just how reluctant Huchel was to release even an individual poem for publication and how he continually changed his compositions, for which no definitive version could be established. Monica Huchel recalls how she and Huchel travelled to the Baltic coast for three weeks in the summer of 1948 in order to assemble the collection.[79] As he had done with his first wife, Huchel drew Monica into the process of composition, selection and organisation. Generally he could count on their approbation but she recalls that she withheld it for 'Sommerabend'. Monica rightly objected to the kitsch in lines such as 'Knaben, schön ist das Leben, wenn es noch stark ist und gut'. He refused to accept her judgment and after quite a serious difference of opinion he included the poem anyway. It would appear that he did not divulge to her the reason for his particular attachment to this poem, which, as we have seen, emerges in his last wartime letter to his first wife on 19 April 1945. Monica Huchel's account continues,

Ich merkte, wie Huchel es hinauszögerte, dem Verlag das Manuskript zu geben. Er baute
es wieder und wieder um. Auch später mußte ich ihm die Gedichte irgendwann aus der
Hand reißen, sonst wären sie nie erschienen. Immer wollte er sie noch zurückhalten. Bis
zur allerletzten Minute, bevor ich sie in den Briefkasten werfen konnte, zweifelte und
veränderte er daran ... Bei der Qual, die die Zusammensetzung eines Gedichtbandes für
ihn bedeutete, ist es nicht verwunderlich, daß Huchel so wenig Bücher publiziert hat und
daß die Abstände dazwischen sehr groß waren.[80]

We have seen how already in his letter to Raschke of September 1931 Huchel
referred to his uncertainty in the evaluation of his own work, which contrasts with
the sense of gratitude towards him felt by friends such as Lange and Langgässer.
They benefited from what they regarded as his informed and judicious assessment
of their work, which they went on to publish to critical acclaim. Yet Huchel was
gripped by an indecision about his own work which inhibited the development of his
own profile as a poet.

The Aufbau Verlag's archive contains a copy of the fourth draft of the proofs
of *Gedichte*, which includes alterations in Huchel's hand for the Potsdam printer
Eduard Stichnote. The proofs reveal very late corrections to eight poems, 'Kindheit
in Alt-Langerwisch', 'Krähenwinter', 'Alte Feuerstelle', 'Der Hafen', 'Wintersee',
'Zunehmender Mond', 'Der Rückzug' and 'Griechischer Morgen'. In the case of
'Wintersee' they amounted to the inversion of the poem's two stanzas, a change that
was, however, subsequently revoked. In addition to alterations to the body of
poems, Huchel appended the year 1933 to 'Späte Zeit'. This explains the
discrepancy between the 1933 dating on page 77 of *Gedichte* and the 1935 dating
given in the 'Anmerkungen' on page 100. Yet, as we have seen, the claim that the
poem was first published in 1935, as the note states, is in itself misleading. The
dating illustrates the point made to me by Dora Huchel in 1981 that Huchel was on
occasion quite cavalier in such matters.

A letter from Huchel to the Aufbau Verlag dated 22 September 1948 indicates
that prior to publication further tensions had developed. Huchel, at this stage still
using the Radio Berlin address, complained bitterly that the radio station had been
sent the 'Korrekturen meines Gedichtbandes' - presumably for review purposes -
even though the 'Fahnen noch nicht von mir imprimiert waren und ... das Buch um
viele Stücke verändert und erweitert worden ist'.[81] Claiming that a contract had not
yet been signed, Huchel threatened to withdraw the volume 'wenn noch einmal so
fabrikmäßig und dilettantisch von Ihrer Seite aus verfahren wird'. The book
appeared in late 1948 in a print-run of 9,500, of which 1,200 copies were reserved
for the Stahlberg Verlag in Karlsruhe. Huchel's friend Gerhard Heller had a stake
in Stahlberg, which obtained a licence to distribute the collection in the West. In this
way, publication in the West was assured for Huchel's first book. All his subsequent

books were published only in the West, and as a result not one of his collections was actually published in the GDR.

A note on page 100 of *Gedichte* points out that all the poems collected were composed between 1925 and 1947. Only 17 of the 73 texts in the index of *Der Knabenteich* were acceptable to Huchel now. Although a number of texts had first been published in the Third Reich, this information was for the most part withheld. Details of first publication were provided for some poems: 'Die Magd 1931, Der Knabenteich 1932, Kinder im Herbst 1932, Löwenzahn 1932, Alte Feuerstelle 1932, Der Zauberer im Frühling 1932, Oktoberlicht 1932, Herkunft 1933, Der Herbst 1933, Havelnacht 1933, Späte Zeit 1935'. In addition, Huchel wrote, 'Corenc, Löwenzahn, Totenregen, Cimetière, Das Himmelsfenster, Die Sternenreuse, Der Herbst wurden 1927 und 1928 in Paris und Südfrankreich geschrieben'.

As he would with his later volumes, Huchel took the greatest of care over the arrangement of his verse, dividing it into three sections entitled 'Herkunft', 'Die Sternenreuse' and 'Zwölf Nächte'. In this way, the collection charts a poetic biography, which corresponds to the myth of the self articulated in the poems composed from the mid-1920s onwards. Individual poems have been examined in the present study's exploration of the poetic biography. My comments will correspondingly focus on the architecture of the collection and its reception.

'Herkunft' begins with the poem of the same title and includes the verse celebrating the childhood world of Alt-Langerwisch. This section conveys the impression that the rural childhood had been, as Huchel later put it, 'der eigentliche Urgrund des Schaffens'. The cosmic metaphor of 'Die Sternenreuse', which expresses the poet's visionary sensibility, is used to characterise the sequence of poems which begins with those composed in Paris and the South of France from 1927 to 1929. The section closes with poems taken from the cycle 'Strophen aus einem Herbst', which was originally published in 1935 in *Das innere Reich*. The cosmic vision and Romantic yearning are thus finally confronted by their opposite, a vision blighted and a poetic personality in the grip of despair and melancholy. The final section, 'Zwölf Nächte', which can be readily understood as a metaphor for the Nazi years, continues the story with verse placed more explicitly within that spatial and temporal setting. In this way, the contrasting visions of the previous sections are taken up within a much more direct confrontation with history. The poetic truth of the collection culminating in 'Zwölf Nächte' is certainly in keeping with the broad sweep of Huchel's development as understood in the present study.

'Zwölf Nächte' includes the cycle 'Deutschland', which contains verse composed by Huchel during the Third Reich in a tone which, as Dora Huchel recalled, was only for private consumption. The oppositional views expressed there remained unpublished during the Nazi years. The section opens with 'Späte Zeit'. Its 1933 dating invited the anti-Nazi reading that was later reproduced by critics. The section closes with poems composed at the end of the war such as 'Der Rückzug' and 'Heimkehr', which convey the idea of regeneration after the death and destruction of war. It was consistent with Huchel's position in the cultural hierarchy of the Soviet Zone that among the final poems there should be 'Griechischer Morgen', dated 1947, which expressed support for Greek communist partisans in their vain struggle. It also contains Huchel's response to Brecht's statement in 'An die Nachgeborenen', 'Was sind das für Zeiten, wo/ Ein Gespräch über Bäume fast ein Verbrechen ist/ Weil es ein Schweigen über so viele Untaten einschließt!'. Following Brecht, Huchel's poem contains the following question in its first stanza, 'tauiger Ölbaum, Wasser des Bachs,/ darf ich euch preisen,/ eh nicht der Mensch den Menschen erlöst?' Yet the poem concludes with the execution of a partisan, whose 'Auge preist/ unsterbliches Land,/ das Freiheit heißt,/ atmende Erde, Feuer der Frühe'. Huchel's insistence on the significance of the continuing Utopian otherness of nature points up a fundamental difference between the two poets, who for all that and other differences would become allies in the face of SED dogmatism. The collection also contains other poems unpublished before 1945 which thematise social injustice, 'Der polnische Schnitter', 'Dezember' (though an earlier version without the explicit social comment was published in the mid-1930s) and 'Die Hirtenstrophe'. Surprisingly, Huchel did not find a place in his collection for his 'Lenz', which in the event would be first published only in 1957. 'Die Hirtenstrophe' (i,67)[82] ends with the couplet 'Die Erde aufgeteilt gerecht,/ wir hättens gern gesehn'. While pre-1945 publications articulate Huchel's sympathy for those excluded from the rural community, the call for the equitable distribution of land cannot be found in any pre-1945 publication, however important the issue became for Huchel in the early post-war period, when the first stage of the land reform in the Soviet Zone took place, which Huchel strongly supported. Similarly, the Polish reaper's cry 'kehre ich heim ins östliche Land,/ in die Röte des Morgens' cannot be heard in any pre-war publication. Critics influenced by the position of 'Der polnische Schnitter' among the poems in 'Herkunft' have argued that this poem must belong among Huchel's compositions from the 1920s.[83] Yet there is no evidence to support this contention. The poem does not, for example, figure in the index of poems for *Der Knabenteich*. As a result, claims regarding the socially revolutionary aspect of Huchel's early verse lack substance. There can be no doubting his early sympathy for the poor and the sincerity and artistic accomplishment of the verse calling for social justice through revolution in the immediate post-war period. However, a greater degree of caution is needed than has hitherto been displayed in locating the development of these concerns in the early Huchel and the Huchel of the middle years. It must be said that he rather blurred distinctions in the interest of promoting the image of an active anti-fascism in the early post-war years.

Only too aware of the dangers to which nature poetry such as his own was exposed through zealous, ideologically motivated critics in the Soviet Zone, Huchel went to considerable lengths in exercising control over the distribution of review copies. That was one of the reasons for his extreme annoyance with the Aufbau

Verlag after the proofs were sent to Radio Berlin without his authorisation. That same letter of 22 September 1948 contains the following,

Mit Herrn Wendt wie auch mit Herrn Schroeder habe ich folgende Vereinbarung getroffen: Alle Besprechungsexemplare werden von mir selbst an die in Frage kommenden Blätter und Rezensenten verschickt, und ohne mein Wissen soll weder an Presse noch Rundfunk ein Besprechungsstück gegeben werden.

Huchel, highly sensitive to criticism, displayed the extreme caution that we have already witnessed in his dissemination of his work. Among the named reviewers were Huchel's friends Horst Lange (*Die Welt*, 21 August 1949), Herbert Roch (*Ost und West*, 3 (1949), No. 5, 91-2), Ernst Reissig, (*Aufbau*, 5 (1949), No. 11, 1013-8) and Herbert Ihering (*Sonntag*, 29 May 1949). Roch's eulogy is surely one of the most vacuous reviews ever written about a serious poet. As we have seen, Roch owed Huchel a favour after the latter had interceded on his behalf at the SDA in order to secure Roch some financial support. Reissig, who had lived it up with Huchel and Dora Lassel on the Côte d'Azur twenty years earlier, produced a much more informed and considered piece, pointing to Huchel's affinities with Loerke and Lehmann, Droste-Hülshoff, Storm and Liliencron, whilst rightly insisting on Huchel's original achievement. Similarly, Lange described Huchel as 'einer der wenigen ursprünglichen und echten Lyriker' in the German-speaking world, who had conveyed his experiences in the 'sensiblste Form, die die Literatur bereithält'. Alluding to the events at the Huchels' house in early 1936 when they were denounced following Lange's drunken invective against Hitler, he went so far as to suggest that Huchel should be made an honorary citizen of Michendorf: 'weiß ich doch genau, wie er, "die unsichere und verdächtige Existenz", unter dem Mißtrauen seiner Mitbürger jahrelang gelitten hat'. Yet Huchel's wartime correspondence with its mention of neighbours such as the Abels demonstrates that the Huchels were by no means without friends in Michendorf on the Willichslust estate, even though there were others only too willing to denounce the Bohemian *Kolonne* group that gathered at the Huchels' house.

Huchel also managed to place his collection in safe hands with the anonymous reviewer for the *Tägliche Rundschau*, the SMAD's organ. On 6 May 1949 the collection was described as 'eine der reifsten Lyrikgaben dieses Jahres'. Huchel himself was described as 'ein guter Deutscher', who in his verse had 'Abrechnung gehalten mit dem zerstörenden Raubzug des Faschismus'. After 1945 there had entered into his verse 'ein neuer lebenszugewandter Klang ... einer Freudigkeit des Beginnens, wenn auch zwischen brandschwarzen Mauerresten'. In this way, the 'progressive' quality of his verse could be identified. This conclusion was shared by the reviewer in *Berliner Zeitung* on 9 July 1949. However, this view was not shared by all. Werner Wilk writes,

Schon 1948 ... äußerte Peter Nell, der nachmalige Hauptabteilungsleiter im Becherschen Kulturministerium, daß er mit den Sachen nichts anfangen könne, ja daß er sie im Hinblick auf die Entwicklung in der sowjetischen Zone für gefährlich halte. Er drückte damit etwas mehr als die Verwirrung aus, die diese Publikation in Parteikreisen hervorrief, er formulierte, was viele Funktionäre dachten.[84]

Wilk's statement captures the great distance that always existed between Huchel and many SED cultural officials, who resented the promotion of this 'bourgeois' figure by the Soviets and now by Becher following his choice of Huchel to edit *Sinn und Form*. If Huchel managed to limit the damage in reviews of his work, then that was at the expense of wider discussion. This inhibited sales in a climate that, in the West as well as the East, was no longer as receptive to poetry as had been the case immediately after 1945. As a result, as Hans-Jürgen Heise later wrote, 'ging man, im Osten wie im Westen, relativ uninteressiert über Huchel hinweg'.[85] Nor did the Aufbau Verlag subsequently do much to promote the work of a writer, whom at this stage they did not place in the first rank. This led to a further deterioration in relations. The conflict with the Aufbau Verlag would come to a head in the mid-1950s.

Revolutionary Romanticism:
a founding myth for a new Germany

There was much truth in the comment made by the reviewer in *Tägliche Rundschau* that Huchel's compositions after 1945 contained 'ein(en) neue(n) lebenszugewand-te(n) Klang ... einer Freudigkeit des Beginnens'. Before embarking on the story of Huchel's editorship of *Sinn und Form*, it is appropriate to examine the early post-war Huchel sound in the new verse that he published in the GDR until the mid-1950s. Like so much else in the Huchel story, this period of his poetic development has been lost from sight, obscured by later developments in his poetry following the deterioration in his relations with SED cultural politicians. The point has been made that in the unfinished cycle 'Das Gesetz' (i,283) Huchel expressed his support for the programme of land reform, yet 'Das Gesetz' has been viewed as an isolated episode. The Huchel of the 1950s has generally been sought and found in the collection *Chausseen Chausseen* of 1963. Yet that collection is not a suitable guide to the Huchel of at least the first half of the 1950s. One need only point to the fact that the political dimension originally present in 'In der Heimat', (i,408) which appeared in 1951 dedicated to Johannes R. Becher, no longer figures in 'Die Pappeln'. (i,145) Similarly, the title poem of the collection reads very differently in the context of its first publication within 'Das Gesetz'. An examination of the poetry from the early 1950s proceeding from 'Das Gesetz' demonstrates that it was not an isolated composition but quite typical of Huchel's new work at the time.

In the early 1950s, Huchel made a number of statements about his poetic intentions in a series of notes accompanying his composition of 'Das Gesetz', (ii,293) some of which Eduard Zak included in his monograph of 1953. Maintaining that his poetry was rooted in the language of the rural working people, Huchel exclaimed,

Es ist das Volk mit seiner Sprache: Stake, Stoppelsturz, Hungerharke, Klaubholz, Kachelloch, Gröps, drämmern. Die Dichtung hat sich, wenn sie in Gefahr geriet, blaß und gekünstelt zu werden, immer wieder aus der Sprache des Volkes erneuert. Wenn sich der Dichter mit der Sprache der Arbeit, der Arbeitsvorgänge, das heißt mit der Sprache des Volkes beschäftigt, wenn er diese nicht poetisch verbrämt, wohl aber zu seiner eigenen Sprache werden läßt, so wird er im Gedicht ganz neue Wege gehen können.[86]

Huchel, indeed, sought to forge a fresh poetic idiom, which would unite his emotional attachment to, and knowledge of the rural world with his enthusiasm for the land reform. The rhetorical qualities identified in 'Der Rückzug' are taken up in an affirmative vision, which testifies to an early post-war idealism that was, however, progressively eroded and had disappeared for good by the early 1960s.

Huchel began work on 'Das Gesetz' in the summer of 1949. (ii,435) An extract from the cycle was published in 1950 in *Sinn und Form*.[87] Other extracts from the cycle followed in *Sinn und Form*: in 1951 'Chronik des Dorfes Wendisch-Luch' (i,293) appeared; in 1952 'Chronik: Bericht des Pfarrers vom Untergang seiner Gemeinde' (i,142); and in 1955 'Chausseen Chausseen. Chronik Dezember 1942'. (i,144) In addition to 'In der Heimat', 'Dezembergang', which was published in *Neues Deutschland* on Christmas Day 1953, (i,295) belongs to this distinctive group of new poems published in the early years of the GDR. As a chronicle of contemporary events, they represent a clear development on the third section of *Gedichte*, in that they take the story forward from wartime and homecoming to include the reconstruction of life in the countryside. The poems move, then, between the destruction of war and the re-building of peacetime, which has transformed the rural world. The key to that transformation is the programme of land reform initiated by the SMAD in September 1945. Large landowners were expropriated, and farmworkers and refugees from the East were given their land. In *Gedichte*, Huchel had published poems lamenting the injustice of the farmworkers' lot. The poems of the early 1950s turn the lament into a celebration of what at the time looked to Huchel to be the successful implementation of Soviet policy.

These poems show just how closely Huchel came to identify with Soviet policy aims for Germany. He evidently shared the Soviet view that the programme would prove popular throughout Germany. The British, it should be recalled, had forbidden the implementation of such a programme in their zone against the wishes of the people. In the poetry of the early 1950s, Huchel, moreover, granted to the Soviets and, by extension, the SED the cultural legitimation that he had sought to withhold from the Nazis. In keeping with his view of the social role of the poet that he had developed since 1945, Huchel now constructed an idiom which was designed to have a much more popular appeal, trading in the esoteric for the accessible and, with that, a degree of subtlety for rhetorical effect. Hence, for a while, the more marginal stance of the sceptic was abandoned for a voice more confidently affirmative of social developments, as a strain of idealism came to the fore which matched a mood of fresh optimism.

In his enthusiastic espousal of the land reform, Huchel was one of the few poets who responded successfully to the many calls by the cultural politicians of the SED and the SMAD for the depiction of the revolutionary changes that had taken place in the countryside. Huchel forged an idiom that was now more realistic than magic, which answered Dimshitz's call for a Revolutionary Romanticism.[88] As a nature poet of some distinction, Huchel was well-nigh unique in the SBZ/GDR. Johannes Bobrowski, for example, had not yet come on the scene. Others such as Lehmann, Krolow or Eich were in the West, while Loerke was dead. Following Marx's scathing comments about the idiocy of the countryside, poets of the left had generally shunned the countryside as hopelessly backward. The Nazis' appropriation of German blood and soil had simply served to confirm established attitudes. However, Soviet policy identified the German peasantry as an important section of the population to be won over through its land reform. Huchel was almost alone in being able to draw upon his immersion in the tradition of nature poetry, which he brought to bear on the new situation.

'Das Gesetz' opens with the majestic topos of an elemental nature grander and more powerful than the deeds or, indeed, misdeeds of humans, 'Aber noch dreht sich,/ Sterne und Steine schleudernd/ das alte Schöpfrad der Nacht'. In this way, the cycle provides continuity with the message of the final section of *Gedichte*. Despite the destruction of war, elemental nature remains intact and order can therefore be created out of chaos. This message is reflected in a similarly re-assuring depiction of the German people, 'O des Volkes vergessenes Leben!/ Hielt es nicht immer bereit/ die Schlüssel zum Tor der Tiefe?' Some fifty years on, this rather sanguine view of the people would surely not go unchallenged, nor, one might argue, should it have in 1950. 'Das Gesetz' and the other compositions from the time, in fact, consistently represent the orthodox position that Nazism was the responsibility of the property-owning classes, not the people, the receptacle of a sound national consciousness. Stalin himself had after all said that the Hitlers came and went but the German people would remain. The idea of the essential soundness of the people was thus legitimised in the GDR, and the term itself was used despite the disrepute it had fallen into through the Nazis. It plays a prominent role in Huchel's cycle and the notes he made accompanying its composition.

While West Germany's founding myth was that of individual freedom secured in the teeth of totalitarianism, the GDR's beginning was stylised as the common people's successful struggle against pernicious capitalism. Indeed, Huchel's cycle contrasts the wisdom of the people with the limitations of individual endeavour, which is dismissed with the following words, 'und hadernd geht/ das Vergangene um/ auf modernden Füßen'. For a while the intimate link between the people and the 'Brunnen' in the depths of the earth was broken, 'Doch das durstige Schicksal/ fand euch verschüttet'. The sections that follow make clear that it is the immediate past of Nazism and war that is meant by the euphemistic 'durstige Schicksal'. What is more, the sections on wartime destruction, not only in 'Das Gesetz' but also in other poems such as 'Chronik: Bericht des Pfarrers vom Untergang seiner Gemeinde', focus the reader's attention on the hardships experienced by the German people at the end of the war as they took to the 'Kreuzwege der Flucht', as refugees from the East fleeing in the face of what we can readily take as the Red Army's advance on the Eastern Front. In this way, that very important group of the refugees is integrated in the founding myth. Yet by the same token, this focus on German suffering in the war does little to foster a critical attitude towards the reasons why that suffering came about in the first place. Huchel's priority lay elsewhere, in promoting awareness about the revolutionary changes that had taken place thanks to the land reform. Not least for that reason, in 'Chronik: Bericht des Pfarrers vom Untergang seiner Gemeinde' he depicted the very helplessness of the church in the face of suffering and destruction caused by war.

'Das Gesetz' moves on to treat the wretched conditions of life in the country after wartime destruction. Huchel invokes the familiar figures of the toiling old woman and the child. The 'Greisin' is depicted as a more complex figure than the mythical 'Mutter der Frühe' in 'Heimkehr'. The poet asks, 'was wohl wußte ...die Greisin vom wahren Tag?' She continues to possess magic powers over her local world ('Auf den Knien/ die Truhe der Nacht,/ in der sie Wiesen und Flüsse/ der Heimat schleppte'). She continues, too, to spin 'das weiße Garn', yet the thread has escaped her and 'wehte zerrissen über die Felder'. The old values of the 'Heimat' embodied by her are called into question. The depiction of the old woman in 'Chronik des Dorfes Wendisch-Luch' is similar, in that her consciousness, too, remains unreconstructed.

In 'Das Gesetz', the 'Greisin' is contrasted with the child, who emerges as the symbol for regeneration. The child's unsullied innocence stands out against all the darkness, death and suffering, 'Aber das Kind war nahe dem Tag'. Regeneration can, however, only proceed following liberation from the 'Mörder', who flee from the advancing army, 'doch unter der hallenden Öde/ des Landes zog näher das Heer,/ ... / Es brachen die morschen Bretter der Lüge'. The promulgation of the land reform is celebrated in the lines,

O Gesetz,

mit dem Pflug in den Acker geschrieben,

mit dem Beil in die Bäume gekerbt!

Gesetz, das das Siegel der Herren zerbrochen,

zerrissen ihr Testament!

The dark ages are over. It is a time of new beginning, in which the people can take full possession of their world, 'Zwischen Acker und Stern,/ o Volk, die ganze Tiefe ist dein!' Huchel adopts a quite uncharacteristic voice, as he exhorts the 'Volk' to rise to the new challenge,

So legt den neuen Grund!

Volk der Chausseen,

zertrümmerter Trecks!

Reißt um den Grenzstein des Guts!

The exhortation continues as the poet names the elements of work that have to be completed before the year ends. The balance between nature and rural life is established on a fresh and just basis due to the new terms of the ownership of the land. The poem concludes on the confident note that the work has been done and that the 'Volk' has been redeemed through hard work, 'Dezemberrissiger Acker,/ auftauende Erde im März,/ Mühsal und Gnade trägt der Mensch'. One is, of course, reminded that the same message of the value of hard work was conveyed in West Germany during the 1950s and that this enabled the population to sidestep potentially uncomfortable questions about Nazism, while those in power generally benefited from discipline at the work place.

Other poems from this group are written in the manner of a socialist pastoral. A case in point is 'Dezembergang', which celebrates a successful year, 'Das Jahr, es gab uns Brot, nicht Steine./ Es gab dem Volk das ganze Korn'. Similarly, we can read in 'In der Heimat' lines such as

Schön ist die Heimat,

wenn über der grünen Messingscheibe

des Teichs der Kranich schreit

und das Gold sich häuft

im blauen Oktobergewölbe;

wenn Korn und Milch in der Kammer schlafen,

die rußige Schmiede des Alls
beginnt ihr Feuer zu schüren.

Today's reader is struck by the narrowness of the poet's chosen perspective that was shaped by the requirements of the politics of reconstruction, which he embraced enthusiastically. Huchel avoids any critical discussion of the German people's role in Nazism, let alone the Holocaust. The blame lies with the property-owning classes that have been dispossessed. There is no sense that German culture has suffered a profound and irreversible fracture, since nature and the German people, aided by the Red Army, act as sources of regeneration in Huchel's mythologising of recent history. It must be said, finally, that in the early 1950s all this went with the grain with the poet himself, who had little interest in looking back at the Nazi period but like the rest of his generation was looking forward to build a better Germany.

Sinn und Form: within the Contradictions of Cultural Policy

From the Foundation to the Adoption by the Academy

Becher's letter to Thomas Mann of 24 April 1948, in which he unsuccessfully requested the release of Mann's title and invited Mann to contribute to the new venture, indicates the direction of Becher's thinking for the new project. It would be the making of Huchel's reputation as he moved onto centre stage in post-war literary life. From now on, *Sinn und Form* was the focus of Huchel's day-to-day life. He would come to identify with the venture in a way that few people would fully appreciate. Its mission to promote German cultural unity would strike a chord deep within him, motivated as he was by the desire to overcome the insufficiencies that had so marked his life to date. The appreciation of Huchel's life from 1948 onwards is intimately bound up with the journal. What follows, though, is not a history of the journal itself. The next four chapters, dealing with Huchel's life as the editor of *Sinn und Form*, chart his, on the face of it, quite unlikely success story, given that he pursued his editorial work within the milieu of that heavily bureaucratic and politicised, albeit highly subsidised, world of the arts engendered by the SED's brand of socialism.

The need had long been perceived by Soviet cultural officers and by Becher for a journal which would project the quality of German intellectual life in terms of the continuity of 'progressive' traditions. As we have seen, as early as August 1945 Paul Wiegler had announced at a meeting of the Kulturbund the intention to produce a monthly literary journal of national and international standing. Becher's correspondence with Wiegler and Sergey Tulpanov shows that he continued intermittently to give some thought to the project until it took on a concrete form in 1948. It was agreed that the journal should serve the literary-pedagogic purpose of re-introducing humanist values lost under Nazism and act as a rallying point for those who believed in the indivisibility of German cultural life. In this way, its aims were a further expression of Soviet policy for Germany, which maintained an all-German orientation in the face of what were presented as western attempts to divide the country, though division was scarcely at odds with Ulbricht's own stance.

It was envisaged that the project would have at its core the array of figures with an international reputation who returned to Germany from exile to participate in the construction of what they hoped would become a socialist Germany. In a manner similar to Brecht's Berliner Ensemble and Felsenstein's Komische Oper, *Sinn und Form* was conceived as a magnet, a prestige project designed to impress and influence opinion outside the Soviet Zone. Huchel would later quote from the wording of his contract when he pointed out that he was entrusted by Becher with the task 'dieser Zeitschrift "eine hohe wissenschaftliche und literarische Qualität zu sichern und sie als führendes Organ auf dem Gebiet der Literaturkritik zu ge-

stalten'''. (ii,326) Werner Wilk, who was involved at the planning stage as a senior
member of the publisher's editorial staff, later recalled the terms of editorial policy

> Es sollte die große, repräsentative deutsche Zeitschrift sein, die mit Gedicht, Novelle,
> Romanausschnitt und Essay die Strömungen der deutschen und internationalen Literatur
> aufzuspüren und zu dokumentieren hatte. Sie sollte keine Polemik, keine Manifestation
> (außer der künstlerischen Werte) und keine Kritiken enthalten ... Sie sollte 'gesamt-
> deutsch' – wie man später sagte – sein, sich aus tagespolitischen Forderungen und
> Erörterungen heraushalten und Beiträge von Schriftstellern aus allen deutschen
> Besatzungszonen bringen, soweit sie den künstlerischen Anforderungen entsprachen und
> keine dubiose Vergangenheit hatten.[1]

As Wilk states, Huchel never intended to realise the contractually agreed aim to
include reviews. In this way, he sought to steer clear of becoming pinned down to
a specific line in cultural politics within the controversies of the moment such as the
Formalism Debate of the early 1950s. The 'representative' approach reflects
continuing confidence in East Berlin that, despite the many setbacks, the avoidance
of an explicitly revolutionary policy would help to create broadly-based support
amongst the cultural élite for a socialist Germany. The choice of personnel, as well
as of the title and the design of the journal, was also a product of this 'representative' thinking, the ambiguities in which would presently emerge in the polarisation
of German intellectual life in the 1950s. Becher's name was balanced through the
presence of Wiegler as co-founder, though Wiegler died soon after. Widely
respected as the author of a distinguished history of German literature and through
his long association with the Ullstein Verlag, Wiegler enjoyed, in Hans Mayer's
words, 'einen angesehenen bürgerlichen Literaturnamen'.[2] Not altogether unlike
Wiegler, Huchel had an essentially 'bürgerlichen Literaturnamen', well-known in
Berlin circles from the 1930s. An early reviewer of *Sinn und Form*, Alfred
Andersch, characterised Huchel with telling acuity as 'eigentlich kein Marxist,
sondern ein "bürgerlicher" Lyriker hohen Ranges, dem wohl am ehesten Absichten
zuzutrauen sind, wie sie innerhalb des Nazi-Staates die sogenannte "innere
Emigration" beherrscht haben'.[3] Subsequent events show that Andersch probably
understood Huchel's motivation better than Becher. In his choice of Huchel, Becher
had the support of cultural officers, who, as we have seen, were looking for that
rather scarce commodity of a reliable non-SED figure and regarded Huchel as such.

Planning for the new venture proceeded through the summer of 1948.
Becher's choice of the title *Sinn und Form* echoed the classicistic balance of
Mann's title. With studied irony, Huchel would later remark that he personally
found Becher's choice too 'formalistisch'. (ii,374) The design, essentially unaltered
today after nearly half a century, emerged from lengthy discussions which included

Huchel and the Potsdam figures, publisher Ulrich Riemerschmidt of Rütten und Loening and the Potsdamer Verlagsgesellschaft, printer Eduard Stichnote, and Suhrkamp editor Hermann Kasack. All three would presently move to the West.

Huchel was busy recruiting collaborators below the level of the major names, whose contributions Becher secured. Huchel, for instance, wrote to Henri Bergmiller on 14 June 1948,[4] outlining the new project and inviting him to contribute as a translator from the French,

> Es handelt sich um eine Literaturzeitschrift, die ausländische Dichtung, also wertvolles Schrifttum vermitteln soll. Alles, was zur leichteren Literatur oder zum Feuilleton gehört, kommt nicht in Frage. Besonders interessiert uns die Literatur aus der französischen Widerstandsbewegung.

Shortly afterwards, on 28 June 1948, Heinz-Winfried Sabais wrote to Becher, reporting his conversation with Huchel about the project and offering his editorial services,

> Peter Huchel erläuterte mir letzthin noch sehr ausführlich den Plan der künftigen Zeitschrift *Sinn und Form*. Wir haben uns dabei aneinander ein wenig in Ekstase geredet. Ich glaube, daß diese Zeitschrift eine große und strenge Aufgabe erfüllen wird und denke dabei nicht an die Art, aber an die Funktion der *Blätter für die Kunst* Stefan Georges, freilich ohne deren Seelenlosigkeit und reaktionäre Tendenz. Wenn ich es richtig verstehe, hieß diese Funktion, die Dichtung über die Gartenlaube und über die Orphile hinwegzu-retten, Courts-Mahler und Rilke (zu einigen Strecken) zu überwinden, Tradition und Fortschritt zu vereinen.[5]

Following the first editorial meeting in May at the Kulturbund, Becher arranged for a further meeting at the beginning of August 1948 at the house which had been placed at his disposal by the Kulturbund in the fashionable Baltic resort of Ahrenshoop. This arrangement was typical of the unbureaucratic Becher. It would appear to be this meeting to which Monica Huchel is referring when she writes of her trip to Ahrenshoop with Huchel in the summer of 1948.[6] She is mistaken in stating that it was only at this meeting that Becher offered Huchel the post of editor-in-chief.

The stay at Ahrenshoop was, however, significant in another respect: Monica became pregnant. She recalls Huchel's response to the news, 'Wieso ein Kind?'[7] Starting another family was far from Huchel's mind in those years. His partner already had two young children. The role of the devoted father did not come naturally to him, getting in the way of his literary plans and ambitions. However, when their son Stephan was born on 2 May 1949 in the hospital on Eschenallee in Charlottenburg, Huchel, in Monica Huchel's words, 'wurde ganz und gar Vater'.[8]

The editorial meeting at Ahrenshoop was attended by Becher, Huchel and Riemerschmidt. The content of the opening issues was agreed upon. Following his return to Potsdam, on 10 August 1948 Riemerschmidt wrote to Huchel, who had stayed on at Ahrenshoop with Monica to work on *Gedichte*. He reported on progress with the first number and planning for later ones, adding of Ahrenshoop, 'hoffentlich hat sich inzwischen alles besser angelassen, als es nach dem ersten Eindruck zu sein schien'.[9] Publicity material was produced, advertising the forthcoming launch in January 1949. The material reveals that the ideas behind the founding of *Sinn und Form* – and it should not be forgotten to what extent they were Becher's – were far removed from the normative aesthetic of Socialist Realism, which would come to represent the official literary and cultural dogma in the GDR,

> Mit SINN UND FORM wird eine Literaturzeitschrift vorgelegt, deren Herausgabe nur gerechtfertigt ist, wenn sie – fern von jedem Ästhetizismus – dem Geist der Sprache und der Dichtung dient. Denn nur unter dieser Voraussetzung kann sie eine der wesentlichen und repräsentativen periodisch erscheinenden literarischen Veröffentlichungen in Deutschland werden. Die Auswahl der Beiträge erfolgt in erster Linie nach den Gesichtspunkten, die für eine derartige Umschau stets gegolten haben sollten: all den Stimmen Gehör zu verschaffen, die im Sinne menschlichen und gesellschaftlichen Fortschritts, des Humanismus und der geistigen Vertiefung mit künstlerischen Mitteln das Wort formen oder mit kritischen die literarischen Erscheinungen der deutschen und ausländischen Geisteswelt aus gründlichem Wissen bewerten.[10]

The published statement studiously avoided the references to socialism in an earlier draft.[11] Riemerschmidt had in fact taken a huge gamble in securing such a journal on behalf of the Potsdamer Verlagsgesellschaft and Rütten und Loening. Rütten und Loening, with its proud tradition of producing bibliophile editions, was, it is true, an appropriate choice as publisher for *Sinn und Form*. Yet, as the publicity material makes amply clear, the journal had been pitched at the quality end of the market, and any realistic assessment of sales would have to conclude that that market was quite limited. If the association meant that further prestige would in time accrue for the publisher, who would hope to attract top authors, then after the currency reform there was the certainty that *Sinn und Form* would always require heavy subsidies. The cavalier Riemerschmidt was, it seems, more interested in securing an agreement with the influential Becher than with working out the detail of costs.

The result was that the financial basis for the undertaking was not properly worked out. A contract dated 15 October 1948 was agreed between the publisher and Becher in his capacity as President of the Kulturbund.[12] The journal would have

160 pages and appear every two months with a print-run of 10,000. The price was 4 marks per number. In fact, the initial print-run was only 2,500 and during Huchel's years never rose above 6,000. A substantial proportion was earmarked for the West, and its distribution in the GDR was always quite deliberately limited. Becher was guaranteed as much as 1,500 marks per number and was recognised as the owner of the intellectual property in the title. *Sinn und Form was* Becher's journal, as Huchel knew well enough. Much else was left unresolved. This created great practical difficulties for the editorial staff, as well as unremitting tensions with the publisher. Matters would come to a head in early 1951 following the adoption of *Sinn und Form* by the Academy, when Rütten und Loening threatened to pull out because they could no longer bear costs that were much higher than Riemerschmidt's initial estimates. By that stage, Riemerschmidt himself had departed for the West, leaving behind much chaos and confusion.

In truth, it is little short of a miracle that the journal survived the mess of its foundation. It was carried by Huchel's efforts, supported by Becher's authority and the knowledge that it would presently have a more secure home in the Academy. Enormous complications ensued from the fact that the editorial seat was initially Bayernallee 44. Huchel worked from his flat together with his editor Hilde Westphal, who moved with him from Radio Berlin, and secretary Charlotte Narr. Narr was supplied by the publisher. They were joined by Monica Huchel in August 1949. As we know, Bayernallee 44 was in the Soviet enclave near Radio Berlin in Charlottenburg in the British Sector. The choice of Bayernallee did not simply follow from the fact that Huchel already lived there. Becher explained the strategic significance of this choice to the head of Radio Berlin in a letter of 2 November 1949.[13] He described *Sinn und Form* as 'kulturpolitisch von grösster Wichtigkeit' and explained, 'Aus wohlüberlegten Gründen befindet sich die Redaktion in Westberlin'. Quite simply, *Sinn und Form* was aimed at West Berlin, West Germany and the western world. The journal was hence a quite deliberate East Berlin 'plant' in the West, much in the same way as Huchel had been as a delegate of the Volkskongreß for Charlottenburg. The significance of *Sinn und Form*'s anomalous position would not be lost on western critics.

For all the problems, the first issue was ready before Christmas 1948. Becher thanked Riemerschmidt and Stichnote for their efforts on 17 December 1948.[14] He sent Wilhelm Pieck and Otto Grotewohl two copies each of the first issue on 21 December 1948.[15] On the same day, copies went out from Becher, along with a letter inviting contributions, to Alfred Döblin, Lion Feuchtwanger, Heinrich Mann and Thomas Mann.[16] In January 1949, Huchel went on the radio to publicise the journal in conversation with Hermann Kasack. Kasack's story 'Der Webstuhl' appeared in the first issue. He also contributed an essay, introducing unpublished poems from Oskar Loerke's papers, for which he was responsible. It was Kasack, too, who supplied Huchel with unpublished poems by Gertrud Kolmar for the next issue. [17] Yet soon after, Kasack would flee to the West, following Soviet attempts to recruit him as a spy on account of his work in the Potsdam Kulturbund.[18]

In his radio conversation with Kasack, Huchel echoed and amplified upon the points already made in publicity material. He sought to deflect any criticism that might come from the East as well as the West, stating, 'Wir werden uns nicht uniformieren. Wir werden aber auch keine literarischen Moden unterstützen, die aus den Überresten einer bürgerlichen Ästhetik kommen. Für blosses Virtuosentum, für einen extremen Subjektivismus haben wir keinen Raum'.[19] One of the first and most prized responses to the first issue came on 4 February 1949, when Thomas Mann replied to Becher,

> Die Zeitschrift wirkt außerordentlich vornehm und wird, dieser Eröffnungsausgabe nach zu schließen, wohl rasch den ersten Platz unter den deutschen literarischen Revuen einnehmen. Es ist kein unbedeutender Beitrag darin, und diejenigen, die ich nicht nur überflogen, sondern ernstlich gelesen habe, waren mir eine wirkliche Bereicherung. Dies gilt für die erschütternden Gedichte von Loerke, wie für den Ramuzschen Dostojewski-Aufsatz, das schöne, gedankenvolle und feierliche Stück aus Reisingers Salamis-Roman und auch für den klugen Essay von Niekisch.
>
> Möge das ganze produktive Deutschland Ihnen, Ihrem Mitherausgeber und der Redaktion behilflich sein, die Zeitschrift auf dieser Höhe zu halten. 'Ad multos annos' wie der Gebildete sagt. Und die besten persönlichen Wünsche.[20]

The qualities of the new venture were not lost on those in the West with similar ambitions. Comparing *Sinn und Form* with the *Neue Rundschau*, Andersch noted that 'die klassisch-edle Typographie (Eduard Stichnote) erreicht, ähnlich wie Anna Simons seinerzeit in der *Corona*, im Bodoni-Satz von *Sinn und Form* einen Höhepunkt des statischen Klassizismus'.[21] The design of the first number drew admiring comments from Hans Paeschke, editor of the Baden-Baden journal *Merkur*. He wrote to Kasack, whom he knew to have been involved in the planning, 'Das Papier ist freilich sowjeto-plutokratisch und der Druck einfach herrlich, das kann Stichnote keiner nachmachen'.[22] He went on to confess his surprise 'daß *Sinn und Form* überhaupt in soviel Repräsentationsexemplaren in den Westen kommt und noch dazu mit so repräsentativen Herausgebern'. As many as 250 copies were distributed free of charge,[23] a figure that doubled after *Sinn und Form* became the Academy's journal. Seduced by the design and attracted by the personnel involved, Paeschke saved face with scathing comments about the content and the intentions behind *Sinn und Form*,

Was übrigens den Inhalt betrifft, so ist es ein höchst lauer Aufguss von zum Teil längst Erschienenem und ein recht schwacher Versuch, sowjetische Ideologie poetisch zu bemänteln. Zwei, drei Hefte weiter und man wird beim Stalinismus angelangt sein. Mir greifts halt ans Herz, Loerke und auch Sie in dieser Umgebung zu sehen.

A month later, Paeschke describes *Sinn und Form* as a 'kulturpolitischen Versuch im Sinn des trojanischen Pferdes, vom Kommunismus in unsere Mauer geschickt'.[24] The image was also deployed in a review by the West Berlin writer Wolfdietrich Schnurre, who pointed out, 'Der Lizenzerteiler wird schamhaft verschwiegen; dafür ist im Impressum zu lesen, daß sich die Redaktion in Berlin-Charlottenburg, Bayernallee 44 befindet. Für Uneingeweihte: das ist zwar der britische Sektor, aber 44 ist von den Russen für Radio Berlin beschlagnahmt, mit dem ja auch Huchel verheiratet ist'.[25] Schnurre's review indicates the extent to which, even before the founding of the two German states, attitudes towards products of the Soviet Zone had hardened among those active in the cultural sphere in the West. Clearly, a certain scepticism was not wholly misplaced towards an undertaking that quite deliberately employed camouflage tactics in its choice of an editorial seat and remained silent about the fact that it was licensed by the Soviets. For Schnurre, these things said it all. Andersch's review two years later is similarly coloured by a profound mistrust towards what by then he identified as the Stalinist GDR.

As for the content of the first issue, in his essay on Loerke, Kasack went so far as to present him as an authentic representative of a literary resistance to Nazism in Germany, a poet whose work embraced aesthetic sophistication and political probity. It helped to set the tone in an approach which, as Uwe Schoor has shown in his analysis of the content of the journal's first year, sought to bring together anti- and non-fascist writing in the exploration of the related themes of 'Knechtschaft und Auflehnung'.[26] Loerke's poetry was followed in the next issue by Gertrud Kolmar's, the Jewish poet who was murdered by the Nazis in a concentration camp. Literature from France (Romain Rolland and resistance poetry) and the Soviet Union (Pushkin and Mayakovsky) figured. Among prominent German authors included in the first few issues are Theodor Adorno and Max Horkheimer, Ernst Bloch, Hermann Broch, Gerhart Hauptmann, Georg Kaiser, Werner Krauss, Ernst Niekisch and Anna Seghers. Other international figures include Louis Aragon, Federico García Lorca, Georg Lukács and Mao Tse Tung. Their work amounted to what Schoor calls, 'Der Versuch, ein literarisches Bildungsangebot in Form lernbarer Widersprüche zu strukturieren',[27] in which editorial guidance for the reader was kept to an absolute minimum.

The early coup that did much to establish the journal's reputation was the publication in the summer of 1949 of the first special number dedicated to Bertolt Brecht's work. Brecht returned to Berlin in October 1948 and took up residence at the Hotel Adlon. It was there and at the Klubhaus that Huchel discussed with Brecht the content of the special number. They renewed an acquaintance which, though never previously close, went back to the 1920s and which would grow through the years of collaboration on *Sinn und Form* and in the Academy before Brecht's untimely death in 1956. Theirs was an unlikely alliance, given their obvious differences, yet it becomes readily comprehensible in the climate of cultural politics engendered by the SED in the early 1950s. Brecht immediately grasped the significance of the new venture. He wrote to Bertold Viertel on 14 December 1948, 'Außerdem möchte Peter Huchel für seine neue Zeitschrift *Sinn und Form*, die sehr repäsentativ wird, Ihren Brecht-Aufsatz'.[28] In the event Viertel's piece was not included in a publication that made literary history. The volume contained essays by Hans Mayer, Ihering and Niekisch as well as major pieces by Brecht, which had been written in exile. They were his *Kleines Organon für das Theater*, *Der kaukasische Kreidekreis*, *Die Geschäfte des Herrn Julius Caesar* and a small selection of poems. The volume was rounded off by Gerhard Nellhaus' Brecht bibliography. Brecht wrote to Huchel on 1 July 1949,

> ich habe Ihnen für das ausgezeichnete Sonderheft zu danken, es ist eigentlich die erste Produktion, die mich mit den Deutschen zusammenbringt, meine eigenen Bemühungen abgerechnet ... Aber ich habe auch die ersten drei Hefte jetzt gelesen, und ich bewundere diese geistreiche und planmäßige Kontribution zum Aufbau und Umbau. Ihre Ansicht, daß dieser *im großen* gemacht werden muß, nach einem *breiten* Plan und durch eine allgemeine Entfaltung der Produktivität im Materiellen und Formalen, tritt überall hin deutlich und erfrischend zutage.[29]

He praised Huchel for publishing Lorca, Majakovsky and Bloch, and singled out Stephan Hermlin, 'dessen Gedichte mir sehr gefielen'. As Brecht's biographer, Werner Mittenzwei, has written, *Sinn und Form* became Brecht's 'wichtigste literarische Plattform, von der aus er die Öffentlichkeit in sorgfältiger Auswahl mit neuen oder bereits im Exil entstandenen Arbeiten bekannt machte. Seit 1950 erschienen in fast jedem zweiten Heft Beiträge von ihm'.[30] Not only that, Brecht could rely on Huchel to place *Sinn und Form* at his disposal in order to take a stand against what Schoor, following Mittenzwei, calls 'Mißstände und Fehlentwicklungen auf künstlerischem Gebiet'.[31] The Formalism Debate and the crisis of 1953 are cases in point. Huchel ensured that the journal's close association with Brecht was carried on after his death. Following the second Brecht special number in 1957, Huchel chose to introduce several issues with unpublished material from the Brecht Archive.

    It is an index of the enormous ideological tensions in East Berlin cultural life that, for all Becher's standing, as early as the spring and early summer of 1949 the first attacks were launched on *Sinn und Form* in reviews which appeared in the

Berliner Zeitung on 27 April and in the *Tägliche Rundschau* on 14 June. In the former, Susanne Kerkhoff took issue with the publication of Kolmar's poetry, writing of 'kranker Symbolismus, die besessene Erotik ihrer Verse'. This was deeply upsetting for Huchel. More than two decades later, he would allude in an interview to the attack on a figure whose fate he deplored and whose work he deemed eminently suitable for remembrance. The reviewer in the *Tägliche Rundschau* commented,

> Wir erkannten und anerkannten im ersten Heft den Willen der Herausgeber, die Literaturprobleme der Gegenwart real und durch konkrete humanistische Beispiele wie Romain Rolland, Wladimir Majakowski und Gerhart Hauptmann, erhärtet im fortschritt-lichen Geist zu deuten ... Die beiden letzten Hefte enthalten zwar gewichtige Beiträge, von guten Federn geschrieben, aber das Ganze ist (mit Ausnahme des Brecht-Sonderheftes) in eine dünne Höhenluft gesteigert, die die Gefahr in sich birgt, daß man vor lauter Ferne und Gehobenheit die Nähe nicht mehr sieht.

Well before the Formalism Debate proper took place in 1951-2, the reviewer warned of 'formalistische(r) Tendenzen' and went on to offer the following advice, 'Will man nicht zu sehr ins Experimentieren geraten, wird man das Maß am Menschen nehmen müssen, und zwar am Menschen unserer Tage, der durchaus nicht mehr die ästhetischen Feuerwerke der zwanziger Jahre sucht und schätzt'. For the reviewer, present-day Germans needed to be addressed not in the modernist idiom of the Weimar Republic but with a clarity and sobriety deriving from the humanist tradition of German classicism. In that way, *Sinn und Form* might overcome the 'allzu große Distanz' that it had put between the population and itself in the opening numbers. It was on such terms that the Formalism Debate was conducted shortly afterwards, as if 20th century modernism in general and Expressionism in particular could be simply dismissed as a pernicious deviation. The fact of the matter was that for the major talents such as Brecht there could simply be no way back, despite all his efforts to accommodate himself politically. Huchel's own work might scarcely fit in with avant-gardist movements but his taste was decidedly catholic. He was, moreover, always on the side of artists when faced by dogmatic cultural politicians. In 1949, the threat from the dogmatists did not yet look so grave. Huchel could for the time being draw comfort from the knowledge that such reviewers simply did not understand the nature of the enterprise he was involved in. That lack of comprehension was not so very serious since he enjoyed the backing of the SMAD as well as Becher, who understood the value of his high-level cultural diplomacy between East and West.

Narrow-minded reviewers in East Berlin were not Huchel's only problem. Cold War cultural politics and economics did not easily mix after the introduction of separate currencies in East and West Berlin. On 25 April 1949 Huchel reported to the Kulturbund's literature commission that he would not be able to publish Lange's new novella due to financial constraints.[32] That was regrettable, since this extraordinarily gifted writer was in a desperate situation. Similarly, the occasion of Becher's letter to the head of Radio Berlin on 2 November 1949 was Huchel's complaint that he had not been permitted to use his ration coupons at the radio station's shop. Huchel was paid in East German marks and used for editorial purposes a large amount of the 200 West German marks he was allowed to change. For this reason, Becher asked that Huchel be allowed to use the shop. On a less mundane level, shortly afterwards, on 26 January 1950, Huchel turned to Becher once more, requesting that he be permitted to exchange at least 1,000 marks per month.[33] He advanced four points in support of his request: the need to pay good fees for original material by foreign authors; the need to do the same for reputable West German authors (he cited Günter Eich); authors such as Hans Reisinger, Kasack and Lange had been dropped from recent numbers because fees could not be paid; and, finally, the editorial office could only function because Huchel's own salary was being used to pay the rent, electricity and other recurrent costs.

Mention of Eich and Lange in the publicity material for the journal shows how, after the currency reform but before the division of Germany, Huchel sought, ultimately without success, to integrate within the *Sinn und Form* project his close friends from the 1930s, whom he rightly regarded as amongst the most gifted writers who had stayed in Germany. Even though subsequently other West German writers such as Hans Henny Jahnn would contribute regularly, Eich featured only twice (including translations from the Chinese) and Lange not at all. The examples of Eich and Lange also illustrate the wisdom of Huchel's choice as an editor whom western writers felt they could trust. Their non-publication, however, demonstrates the great practical difficulties in capitalising on that trust. More than anyone else in the East Berlin cultural orbit, Huchel had the brief to cultivate western writers and intellectuals. His background in Goldberg's and Willy Haas' circles, then in the *Kolonne* Circle, was the basis of the trust that he enjoyed. In Huchel's view, it could only be preserved by a fundamental openness to various literary orientations deemed generally progressive and by the avoidance of the rhetoric of the class struggle and partisan, pro-GDR sloganising. While for many in the GDR, who for a while went along with this, such a stance was merely a matter of expediency, for Huchel the class struggle had no place in his East-West cultural diplomacy. To that extent, Huchel always remained the bourgeois intellectual recruited by Becher. Huchel's reference in his conversation with Kasack to the 'remnants of a bourgeois aesthetic' was untypical. His opponents in East Berlin, of course, felt justified in asking where that left socialist principles? When, in time, he was forced to choose between the practice of socialism in the GDR and the goal of German cultural unity, Huchel could only opt for the latter.

He never tired of telling Becher and anyone else who would listen that, despite all the difficulties, his journal had got off to the best possible start. In his letter to Becher of 26 January 1950, for instance, Huchel proclaimed the 'Tatsache, daß sich die Zeitschrift *Sinn und Form* in kurzer Zeit, wie es aus sämtlichen Kritiken der in- und ausländlischen Presse zu ersehen ist, eklatant durchgesetzt hat und selbst von der westlichen Kritik zu den besten Literaturblättern Europas gezählt wird'. We see how at the very beginning Huchel, a skilled self-publicist, went about creating what became the legend of *Sinn und Form*. Huchel could also refer to messages of support like the one he received from Nelly Sachs on 30 March 1950, 'Ein Quell ist der Inhalt wieder, daraus ich Erquickung trank. Ich danke Ihnen, daß ich dabei sein darf, bei den Dichtern, aus denen die ewige Flamme glüht'. She wished him well, too, with his own 'tiefe(n) Dichtung'.[34] Yet, of course, Huchel's mission made his an anomalous and exposed position in East Berlin cultural life, and this in turn made for a dangerous degree of dependence on the mercurial Becher, who, as is well-known, was a man of divided loyalties. For all his passionate espousal of the cause of his fellow poets, Becher the SED cultural politician with his place on the Central Committee ultimately accepted party discipline with all its ramifications.

At the turn of the 1950s, there was still a feeling among non-SED writers that, as Arnold Zweig put it to Lion Feuchtwanger, 'Jedenfalls wird sich auch der Moskauer talk über Formalism und dergl. hier schnell verflüchtigen, wir alle ignorieren ihn achselzuckend'.[35] Zweig could not possibly have guessed what lay ahead in the coming years, during which his work was subjected to the most humiliating treatment by officious bureaucrats and cultural politicians, nor that by 1959 he would be pleading with politicians on the occasion of Feuchtwanger's death, 'Wir waren eine Mannschaft 1948, als ich hier zurückkam, und wir sind jetzt so wenige geblieben, daß Sie uns gestatten müssen, unsere Kräfte jetzt nur noch auf unsere eigene Arbeit zu konzentrieren'.[36] Zweig's sad commentary contrasts with the enthusiasm of his early post-war correspondence. On 20 October 1949, he reported to Feuchtwanger on the offices that he had assumed and his sense of involvement in historic decisions. He praised Soviet cultural policy and he reported that there 'entwickelt sich die Zurückdrängung der Aggression auch nach Westen hin. Der Bonner Puppenstaat höhlt sich von innen aus'.[37] In a slightly earlier letter of 9 July 1949, Zweig praised *Sinn und Form* and not long afterwards he would begin to develop a closer interest in the journal as plans were laid to bring it under the wing of the German Academy of Arts, once that foundation had been established on 24 March 1950 as a successor institution to the Prussian Academy of Arts.

Heinrich Mann had agreed to become the Academy's first President but died before returning to Germany from the USA. Zweig, another 'bourgeois humanist', was nominated in his place. The Academy was conceived along the lines of Soviet policy as an institution which would represent the arts throughout Germany. Given the Academy's own all-German approach, it was appropriate that *Sinn und Form* should become its house journal. Already on 1 November 1949, Gustav Seitz had informed Mann, 'Die neue Akademie übernimmt, wie Sie sicherlich wissen, die sehr schöne Literaturzeitschrift *Sinn und Form*'.[38] The fact that *Sinn und Form* could become established and could survive for so long in the turbulent climate of the early 1950s with its original character intact was in some large measure due to the support not only of Brecht but also of Zweig in his capacity as President of the Academy from 1950 to the end of 1952. Initially, Becher's role, too, was wholly supportive but that would change amidst the vagaries of policy.

Becher and Arnold Zweig Take *Sinn und Form* under the Academy's Wing

Together with Becher, Zweig was instrumental in effecting the change in the journal's status. At the Academy's first Plenary Session on 3 April 1950, it was announced that the Academy would now proceed, in line with a memorandum of 2 April 1950, with the 'Ausgestaltung und Unterstützung der Zeitschrift *Sinn und Form*'.[38] Given its predominantly literary character, *Sinn und Form* would be the organ of the Academy's Literature Section. The change of status simultaneously enhanced the standing of the journal and its editor and made the position much more complex, since *Sinn und Form* was now located squarely within the fraught relations between the Academy and the SED. From 1950, Huchel's hopes for the journal as well as his personal ambitions would be channelled through the prestigious Academy. As we have seen, *Sinn und Form* and the Academy were both expressions of Soviet policy for Germany, and shared aims could be identified. Yet Soviet policy conflicted directly with the SED's aim to consolidate its power base within the territory of the GDR. The SED would find the Academy and its journal wanting when it demanded a more partisan stance in cultural politics. As the leading SED cultural politician, Becher had staked much on the all-German path, to which he was, in any case, emotionally deeply attached. At the beginning of the 1950s, he saw the Academy and *Sinn und Form* as the vehicles for the realisation of his all-German vision.

Sinn und Form was on the agenda at the first meeting of the Literature Section on 24 May 1950, which was attended by its founding members Becher, Brecht, Kellermann, Seghers and Zweig.[39] Rudolph Engel, the Director of the Academy, reported upon his negotiations with the publishing house and with the editorial staff. The essential issue was 'ob die Akademie durch finanzielle Unterstützung maßgeblich Einfluß auf die Gestaltung der Zeitschrift nehmen soll'. All questions relating to *Sinn und Form* were to be discussed with Huchel and Riemerschmidt on 8 June. There is no extant record of that meeting, nor is there any indication in the records of later meetings that Zweig and Becher, the two key figures, had succeeded in resolving matters.

The journal was formally adopted by the Section when it met on 13 July 1950, with Huchel and Riemerschmidt in attendance.[40] Zweig met with Becher after the meeting on 13 July to discuss the journal[41] and visited Becher for a 'Konferenz über unsere Zeitschrift *Sinn und Form*' in mid-September. Yet theirs was an uneasy relationship and matters remained in the air. Zweig also met with the Huchels on 19 September. Despite continuing uncertainties, at a Plenary Session on 6 November 1950 it was announced that the journal had been adopted. There was a clear determination to improve on the journal's first year, 'Die Sektion nahm sich vor, sie in alter Form aber mit neuen Inhalten erscheinen zu lassen, um sie zu einer wirklichen literarischen Zeitschrift auszubauen'.[42] In the fifth number of 1950, Zweig signalled his intentions by announcing that in future *Sinn und Form* would act as the Academy's 'Sprachrohr und geistiges Visier'.[43] He explained,

> Wir haben niemals die Aufgabe der Literatur darin gesehen, die Leistungen von Vers und Prosa gewalttätig oder ziervoll in die Höhe zu schrauben, solange nicht im Grundbau der Gesellschaft eine gerechtere Ordnung und ein menschenfreundlicherer Drang waltete als in den Jahrzehnten seit dem Ende des Naturalismus. Unsere Absicht ist es, in dieser Zeitschrift *Sinn und Form* wie bisher, nur noch geordneter um ein Ziel, das Notwendige zu gestalten, kristallinisch, blumenhaft oder im Lied, wie sich's uns aufdrängt und vorschreibt.

Zweig rightly insisted on the need for a greater focus in the journal's content. That had not always been present in earlier issues. Zweig's elegant prose also testifies to the fundamental belief which he shared with Huchel in the *Sinn und Form* project that the aesthetic and the social dimensions of art were indivisible. Not only that, Zweig went on to characterise the arts as 'Fühlfäden ... , welche die Gesellschaft ins noch Ungeformte vortastet und vortreibt'. This perception lay at the root of his great and idealistic commitment to the work of the Academy. Yet that very commitment would be constantly undermined by dogmatic cultural politicians.

The Removal to Wilhelmshorst

In the same number as Zweig's announcement, one could read that the editorial seat had moved from Bayernallee to Wilhelmshorst near Potsdam. There was no longer the need for any pretence now the journal was with the Academy, and in any case the Soviets were returning Bayernallee 44 to its owner. Suitable accommodation was not easy to come by in Berlin, where the Academy itself was situated, and it could in any case be argued that it was equally important to be close to the publishing house, which still had its seat in Potsdam. Having established himself in the new cultural hierarchy in East Berlin, Huchel elected to move back to the cluster of villages south of Potsdam, which he knew from his childhood and where he had lived from the mid-1930s to the mid-1940s with his first family. In the meantime,

Dora and Susanne Huchel had given up the house in Michendorf and moved to the Wilmersdorf area of West Berlin.

Wilhelmshorst is the most elegant of that cluster of villages to the south of Potsdam. Like Michendorf, Wilhelmshorst enjoyed good rail links with Potsdam and Berlin, so that, like Willichslust, it was a place favoured by commuters and other professionals. Despite physical proximity to the traditional Brandenburg village of Langerwisch, Wilhelmshorst was far removed from any peasant farming community. Wilhelmshorst was a new development of villas and detached houses set in parkland and surrounded by woods.

In addressing the question of why Huchel chose to move out to Wilhelmshorst, Werner Wilk dismisses the idea that it was part of any careful calculation and writes, 'Diese Episode gehört zum Privatesten der Biographie und entbehrt keineswegs grotesker Züge'.[44] On the basis of what has been established in the early stages of the present study, one can only assume that Wilk was aware of the psychological tangle of Huchel's background and of the reality beneath Huchel's self-stylisation. It would certainly appear to be true that, just as he had been in 1934 when he returned from the lengthy stay in Kronstadt, Huchel was attracted by the emotional attachment and sense of security which he felt towards that 'Gegend, die mir am vertrautesten ist, die Gegend um Potsdam'. (ii,248) Monica Huchel recalls, 'Eines Tages zeigte mir Huchel die Gegend, wo er aufgewachsen war, Langerwisch bei Wilhelmshorst. Ich dachte, hier möchte ich leben. Wir mieteten zunächst ein Haus am Kirchweg in Wilhelmshorst, dann zogen wir in ein Haus am Eulenkamp, durch dessen Terrasse eine Kiefer wuchs'.[45]

The elegant Wilhelmshorst might have been a million miles from Langerwisch. Although they went to live at Kirchweg 2, both kept an official registration in Berlin.[46] After Dahlmannstraße, Huchel had once more registered at Bayernallee on 16 October 1949. He transferred his registration on 1 July 1950 to Berlin-Oberschönweide, Zeppelinstraße 117. He was in fact using Erich Arendt's address. On 7 March 1952 he 'moved' to Libauerstraße 8 in Berlin, before on 17 April 1953 he gave Eulenkamp 6 as his address. This was just after Huchel's second marriage, following the conclusion of his long, drawn-out divorce in March 1953, which Dora Huchel had resisted to the bitter end. Huchel's pretence over his address surely related to the divorce issue. Similarly, on 4 February 1953, Huchel, in his role as Monica Melis' boss, requested the extension of her pass so that she could travel to work at Eulenkamp 6 from her address at Fredericiastraße 4a in Berlin-Charlottenburg.[47]

The house they rented was big enough to house them and their three children as well as leaving some space for editorial work. They were joined there each day by Charlotte Narr, affectionately nicknamed 'die Närrin', and by Hilda Westphal. The family business could thus be conducted in the comfort of the couple's own home, an arrangement which suited Huchel admirably. His working habits could not easily be accommodated within normal office hours: he liked to sleep in during the morning and work late into the night, when he would conduct lengthy telephone conversations with his authors.

He had managed to tailor his professional situation almost totally according to his own wishes. At the same time as the link with the Academy was being established, Huchel moved the journal well away from its new parent institution. This would not escape his opponents in the Academy. A number of members resented the distance between the Academy and the journal's seat, a distance viewed not just in physical, but also aesthetic and ideological terms. As Wilk suggests, it would be overstating things to regard the removal to Wilhelmshorst as part of a grand plan by Huchel. Nonetheless, in time the distance between Wilhelmshorst and Berlin was used by him to maintain *Sinn und Form* much as he wanted it. As the 1950s progressed, the journal and Huchel's name became inextricably linked.

Relations with the Literature Section

Whenever over the years Huchel was criticised because *Sinn und Form* did not reflect sufficiently closely the work of Academy members, his stock reply was that the fault did not lie with him but with those Academy members who had shown little interest in the development of the journal. There was certainly some truth in this defence, and the extent to which it was true increased as the years went by and the stand-off between Huchel and the Academy became more pronounced. This was not the case at the beginning. The Section had concluded that the Academy's financial stake should be matched by a commensurate influence in editorial matters. In the early stages, much thought and effort was invested in promoting the venture by the Section. Yet, despite Zweig's talk of fresh content and a greater focus, there was a lack of clarity about how best to proceed. It emerged very quickly that the meetings of the Section were not the most effective forum for discussion of the journal's needs, not least because Huchel, not yet an Academy member, was himself not present. Nor was Huchel enamoured of the regular meetings of the Section's editorial board. As we shall now see, a sequence of meetings in late 1950 and early 1951 charts the difficulties that were encountered and the solutions that were found on Huchel's initiative. Yet shortly afterwards, those solutions would themselves be called into question.

On 12 December 1950, in the editor's absence, the Section embarked on the formulation of policy for the journal.[48] It was resolved that a column called 'Notizen', 'Anmerkungen' or 'Marginalien' should be introduced so that the Academy could comment on matters of immediate importance. Brecht proposed the inclusion of previously published material 'zur Belebung und Aktualisierung des Inhalts, besonders im Hinblick auf westdeutsche Erfordernisse'. Huchel was not happy with either idea. He channelled his response to the first through Annemarie Auer, the administrative assistant to the Section. She informed Zweig in a letter of

27 December 1950 that Huchel would prefer any Academy communications to be included as loose-leaf supplements,

> Da die Zeitschrift nur alle zwei Monate erscheint, überdies jedes Heft eine Herstellungszeit von 4-6 Wochen braucht, würden fest eingedruckte Mitteilungen veralten. Der Sonderdruck hingegen bietet immer die Möglichkeit, aktuell wichtige Dinge einzurücken und rechtzeitig zu bringen.[49]

Huchel requested the Section's support for his proposal, which he presented in terms of practical considerations as well as with an eye on the notion that *Sinn und Form* should be seen to be dealing with enduring values rather than with ephemera. Similarly, Brecht's proposal ran counter to the rather elevated position that Huchel and, indeed, Becher wished the journal to assume. Huchel quietly ignored Brecht's proposal but Brecht would return to it, or variations upon it, in coming years.

Huchel took part in a monthly editorial meeting on 20 December, which was also attended by Becher, Ihering and Paul Rilla.[50] The aim was the 'Inhaltliche Erweiterung und Belebung der Zeitschrift'. Becher wanted to see discussion or, preferably, publication of the West German authors Usinger, Rinser, Leonhard Frank, Penzoldt, Edschmidt and Weisenborn. In this way, the journal could demonstrate 'die Einheit des deutschen Kulturlebens'. Though nothing came of Becher's proposal of specific names, there was no dispute over the general policy aim. Financial issues were once again aired. It was acknowledged that the proposed expansion and especially the inclusion of West German writers meant higher fees. Huchel was encouraged to discuss the matter with Erich Wendt of the Aufbau Verlag and with Franz Henschel of the publishing house of the same name, before coming back to the Section with proposals for a new budget. Becher's suggestion, presumably as an interim measure, was that West German authors should be paid in East German marks but that the fees should be tripled. In keeping with the working relationship between Huchel and Becher, Huchel received from Becher material for the next number as well as instructions on other editorial matters.[51]

Becher's correspondence with *Sinn und Form* from the early 1950s shows that he regularly submitted his own work and that of others. Huchel later asserted that he struck a bargain with Becher that neither should publish more than the other and that he himself used this agreement in order to keep Becher's contributions to a minimum by publishing his own only sparingly. Yet a comparison of work published by the two of them shows that, leaving aside the two special numbers for Becher, Becher published double the amount that Huchel did and that he figured in what he evidently regarded as his own journal every year from 1949 until his death in 1958. On 7 June 1950, for instance, nine poems and Paul Rilla's essay 'Der Weg Johannes R. Bechers' were dispatched from Becher's office.[52] There was no question of not complying with Becher's request to publish the material: it duly appeared in the fourth number that year. In the same way, the material that Becher supplied for the special number devoted to him which appeared in 1951 was all incorporated. Similarly, it was Becher who discovered Günter Kunert for *Sinn und Form*, as Becher's letter of 7 February 1950 demonstrates.[53]

Others members of the Section were busy seeking out material for the journal. The link with the Academy and its prominent literary figures meant that there was no shortage of suitable work, even if it did not all result in publication. In a letter to Feuchtwanger of 16 December 1950, Zweig told his friend, 'Die Zweimonatschrift *Sinn und Form* haben wir als Organ der Akademie übernommen und werden bald an Sie mit der Frage herantreten, ob wir nicht ein geschlossenes "Goya"-Kapitel von Ihnen zum Vorabdruck erhalten können'.[54] That idea came to nothing but Zweig's and Brecht's friendship with Feuchtwanger provided the link by which his work came to appear in *Sinn und Form* regularly throughout the 1950s. Similarly, on 16 September 1950 Brecht sent Huchel his 'Erziehung der Hirse', which appeared in issue five of that year.[55] At the meeting of the Section on 30 January 1951, Anna Seghers pleaded for an end to the polemic over the issue of realism and for the publication of 'wesentliche Texte'.[56] She handed over to Annemarie Auer four pieces, which she felt were suitable for *Sinn und Form*. This time, however, none of the pieces found their way into the journal.

Given the central position that Huchel and *Sinn und Form* were coming to acquire in the life of the Academy, it was only a matter of time before Huchel was elected to that body. As early as 30 January 1951, at a meeting of the Section, he was nominated by Brecht, who referred to Huchel as 'der ausgezeichnete Lyriker'.[57] On its own, the editorship of the Academy's journal could not, at least in those days, be advanced as sufficient proof of artistic excellence. Together with other nominées, Huchel had to wait for nearly two more years, as the Academy was kept waiting by an SED leadership dissatisfied with its development.[58]

The next editorial meeting for *Sinn und Form* under the aegis of the Section was chaired by Zweig on 1 February 1951.[59] The group was, in fact, required to discuss all publishing projects that the Section was involved in, something that Huchel was clearly uncomfortable with. Ihering, Auer and Engel attended on 1 February, while the Huchels represented the editorial staff. He gained approval for the first issue of 1951 and for his plan for the rest of the year. Significantly, the following year it was Becher who would present the plan in the form of instructions. In February 1951, Huchel explained that he wished to establish a group of regular contributors for various areas, which 'ständig aktiv an der Gestaltung der Zeitschrift mitwirkt und eine Erweiterung und Vertiefung ihres Inhaltes herbeiführen hilft'. He suggested Werner Krauss and Paul Rilla as essayists, Rilla and Ihering to cover film and theatre, and Zweig, Becher and Brecht for literature. All were or would become regular contributors and did much to give *Sinn und Form* its distinctive character. In addition, he suggested the introduction of a 'kulturpolitische Chronik' to be written by Kantorowicz and a young author, possibly Paul Wiens. As Auer's note to Engel of 8 February 1951 makes clear, Huchel's idea of drawing Kantorowicz into the work of *Sinn und Form* and with that into the Section was scuppered by Becher.[60] Huchel, not inclined to challenge Becher on this matter, let it drop. His old friend, who had done what he could to promote him after his return from exile, felt that he had been poorly treated. Kantorowicz's resentment would grow. He would later write that Huchel 'dem Druck von Becher sich beugend, mich preisgab'.[61]

At the meeting of the Section on 28 February,[62] Huchel was proposed for the Goethe Prize of the city of Berlin 'der Heimatgebundenheit seiner Verse wegen'. He had powerful backers in the Section. Becher, its Secretary, provided the supporting statement. That document of 15 March 1951 contains the following,

> Peter Huchel hat in seinen Gedichten, erschienen 1948 im Aufbau-Verlag, insbesondere seiner märkischen Heimat, der großen Tradition Fontanes folgend, ein unvergängliches Denkmal gesetzt. Huchels Gedichte sind Heimatdichtung im besten Sinne des Wortes. Huchels Dichtung hält sich nicht nur frei von jeder Art von 'Verpreußung', sondern er verbindet seine Liebe zur märkischen Landschaft mit einer echten Humanität und einem tiefen Demokratismus, die ihn befähigen, einen neuen Ton in der deutschen Heimatdichtung zu finden.[63]

The text conveys quite clearly what the German patriot Becher saw in Huchel's poetry. He regarded Huchel's verse as a vehicle for cultural integration due to its strong sense of tradition and regional ties, combined with a 'progressive' political stance. It seems that in Becher's eyes Huchel could do no wrong. Huchel's response to the nomination was that he would only accept such a prize if it were first class. Huchel was evidently prepared to follow Brecht's rejection of the 'grading' system of prizes. In the event, there was no need to maintain the threat: it was later established that the prize could be awarded only every second year and that the next time would be 1952.

Discussion on 28 February included editorial matters. In the light of his dissatisfaction with meetings of the editorial group to date, Huchel made an alternative proposal – essentially an extension of his proposal from the start of the month – which was accepted,

> Abgesehen von der bestehenden Gepflogenheit, Tenor und Inhalt der Zeitschrift jeweils mit dem Präsidenten und dem Vizepräsidenten abzustimmen, bat Herr Huchel um eine Kommission für *Sinn und Form*, die aus den Herren Ihering, Rilla, Brecht, Krauss, Herzfelde besteht. Die Redaktion *Sinn und Form* kann diese Arbeitskommission nach ihrem Ermessen zusammenrufen.

The commission was in all but name an advisory board. Huchel could henceforth dispense with cumbersome consultations with people not always closely involved with his work. As President and Vice-President, Zweig and Becher would remain his most important points of contact. He could now exercise much more personal control over the journal than had been the case since its adoption by the Academy. Huchel thus notched up a notable early success in securing a degree of freedom of action. It would soon be seriously threatened. It must be said, though, that the great tensions and conflicts of the coming years could not be avoided come what may, since they derived from much broader contradictions, of which *Sinn und Form* was just one expression. The first tasks for the new commission were a special number for Becher's sixtieth birthday and another for the Weltjugendfestspiele that coming August in Berlin. The latter in particular would prove to be a singularly trying experience.

Starnberg

Following an initiative by Becher, Huchel became involved in further cultural diplomacy with the West. At that same meeting of the Section on 28 February it was agreed that Huchel, Becher, Uhse, Hermlin and Rilla would travel to Starnberg at Easter for a meeting with a group of Munich writers. As things turned out, Becher did not travel with the East Berlin group, rightly suspecting that his presence would have made it even more difficult to reach understandings. Starnberg was the first attempt to set up a forum for the exchange of views between East and West German writers outside the fragmenting German PEN framework. Becher's election to the PEN executive had prompted Plievier, Birkenfeld and Rudolf Pechel to declare that they would stay away as long as Becher remained in that position. At the German PEN meeting in Wiesbaden on 4-7 December 1950, which had been attended by only Becher and Hermlin from the East, a proposal had been made to exclude GDR writers from the organisation. Though later dropped, the proposal sent a clear enough signal to Becher, who, in pursuit of the aim of cultural and political unity, made plans to remedy the situation.

In an attempt to keep the East-West dialogue open, on 10 January 1951 the Section, led by Becher, issued an 'Aufruf der Schriftsteller an die westdeutschen Intellektuellen', urging a meeting to discuss peace and re-unification. Huchel joined them in that appeal, expressing his solidarity with Becher, Brecht, Seghers and Zweig.[64] Borrowing imagery from his 1947 speech to commemorate the burning of books, he appealed to fellow writers that they should learn from experience and reject the 'almost idyllic nihilism' i.e. of the West and identify instead with the 'people'.

Munich writers connected with the publisher Willi Weismann responded on 9 February 1951, proposing Munich as a venue for a meeting of writers from East and West. It was upon Becher's initiative that Weismann acted as the host, inviting more than fifty writers from the Munich area, including Hans Werner Richter, Ernst Penzoldt, Walter Kolbenhoff, Johannes Tralow, Georg Schwarz and Irma Loos. The meeting took place on 26-7 March.

Huchel did not play any significant role in the main discussion, the record of which shows just how delicate relations were between figures essentially well disposed to each other but on opposite sides in the Cold War. For Huchel, Starnberg also, of course, provided an opportunity to establish links for *Sinn und Form*. One lasting benefit was his meeting there with Hans Henny Jahnn, President of the Hamburg Academy of Arts. In Jahnn, Huchel found a friend and regular contributor to *Sinn und Form*, who as an opponent of the Adenauer government was prepared, whenever possible, to support GDR writers' initiatives in the cause of German unity.

Following an introduction by Tralow and a response by Uhse, conciliatory speeches were delivered by Penzoldt and Hermlin.[65] Thesing suggested that a basis for an exchange of opinions be established outside the political realm. This was opposed by Hans Werner Richter, who found support among those present by arguing that political questions must be addressed in order to ascertain the extent to which collaboration might be possible. Tralow took up the idea of developing an all-German journal as an expression of unity among writers despite the political division. While Willi Bredel agreed with Richter that the political dimension could not be excluded, he suggested that it might be considered in the framework of discussions seeking to secure unity among writers through work on the proposed journal. Agreement was reached on three main points: they should all make efforts to help maintain peace; they should cultivate the exchange of literature between East and West; and they should found the all-German journal. They agreed to come together again at regular intervals in the future. A resolution was issued condemning the publication of neo-fascist literature in Germany. A group was chosen to pursue the goal of establishing the journal. It included Walter von Molo, Penzoldt, Tralow, Kolbenhoff, Weismann, Becher, Zweig, Brecht, Hermlin, Uhse, Huchel and Jahnn. For a while, plans for the journal were pursued in East Berlin within the Writers' Union. In its 'Plan für die Arbeit in Westdeutschland und Westberlin' of June 1951, a proposal was made for an appeal to be issued by Brecht, Becher and Seghers to Hermann Hesse, Feuchtwanger, Thomas Mann, Penzoldt, Döblin, Jahnn and Rudolf Alexander Schröder, encouraging them to collaborate in publishing the all-German venture.[66] 30,000 West German marks would be needed.

On his return from Starnberg, Huchel followed up the meeting in the manner required by Becher. On 30 May 1951, he issued a circular to all PEN Club members in which he proposed a special meeting in Berlin, 'Um eine Krise im PEN-Club zu vermeiden' and 'die Vorgänge im PEN-Zentrum kameradschaftlich zu klären'.[67] In his reply of 9 June, Jahnn welcomed Huchel's initiative and expressed his support for the executive elected in Wiesbaden, to which Becher, of course, belonged. Jahnn, however, warned Huchel of the ideological pressures to which West German writers were now being subjected by the Bonn government. They would not be without effect on the future history of the German PEN. Nor, indeed, did Huchel's proposal for a meeting in Berlin gain the necessary support of fifteen members.

Steps were later taken in the Writers' Union to build upon what had been achieved at Starnberg. A letter was sent from the Writers' Union to the Cultural Department of the Central Committee on 17 December 1952, proposing that GDR writers, including Huchel, should send letters to West German colleagues. In that way, relations might be improved at a time of diminishing contact.[68] As an example of the sort of message that might be sent, the letter referred to Huchel's 'Mahnung an die Schriftsteller',[69] an appeal to West German writers to keep alive the idea of cultural unity despite the political division. Huchel had called upon all German intellectuals to oppose the ratification of the General Treaty signed by West Germany and the Western Allies in 1952. Yet such calls came to nothing in an atmosphere in which, as was increasingly acknowledged in the Academy, West German writers rather tired of the constant appeals addressed to them from East Berlin.

Crossing Swords with Publishers

Life was becoming busier than ever, bringing tensions, with which Huchel was temperamentally and physically not always best suited to cope. The discreet, diplomatic manner could give way to outbursts of rage when his life was made unduly difficult. Becher's letter of 15 January 1951 to Walter Gerull, Riemerschmidt's replacement as head of Rütten und Loening, sees Becher attempting to smooth over a row between Huchel and Gerull. The letter also testifies to Becher's great esteem for Huchel and his concern for his well-being,

> Ich bitte Dich sehr, uns den Huchel nicht zu verstimmen, der ein ausgezeichneter Mitarbeiter ist und nach jeder Richtung hin von uns geschätzt wird und auf den wir auch angewiesen sind, nämlich was die Herausgabe der Zeitschrift der Akademie betrifft. Also nochmals, ich bitte Dich sehr um Entgegenkommen. Dabei ist es nicht gut einen Brief zu schreiben, in dem solche Worte wie 'überschnappende Stimme' vorkommen usw. ... Huchel ist außerdem ziemlich herzkrank.[70]

The major bone of contention between the journal and its publisher remained finance. Gerull was adamant that now this prestigious but loss-making organ was a joint venture with the Academy a more equitable distribution of costs should be established. Gerull demonstrated his determination not to be, as he saw it, fobbed off by vague promises from Becher and the Academy by stating that Rütten und Loening would cease to publish *Sinn und Form* from 1 April 1951 unless fresh arrangements were put in place. The publisher could in any case no longer pay

Westphal's salary. Huchel and his editorial staff found themselves in the middle of this row, though Huchel, encouraged by Becher and aware of where his real interests lay, intervened with letters to Engel on 22 March and Zweig on 31 March in order to provide the Academy with ammunition in its negotiations with Rütten und Loening.[71]

His letter to Engel was written before the Munich trip. Huchel described the publisher's decisions as endangering the very existence of the journal, nor did he conceal his outrage at Gerull for what he regarded as the high-handed manner in which he was treating Huchel and his staff. He painted a desolate picture of Rütten und Loening and of its feeble efforts to support *Sinn und Form* even though the journal had done much to enhance the publisher's reputation. The letter which followed to Zweig was written after negotiations between Engel and Gerull had failed. Huchel reminded Zweig that the Section had agreed to secure the financial future of the journal yet nothing had been done. He had in the meantime produced detailed budgetary calculations, as Becher had encouraged him to. He sent Zweig a breakdown of the present editorial budget (nearly 3,000 marks per month) and added a second column setting out the budget that was really needed. (4,500 marks per month) This latter included Westphal's salary, which would be found from monies freed off by Becher's decision to waive his fee per number. Huchel estimated that, taking everything into account, the journal required a subsidy of no less than 7,200 marks per issue.

Zweig invited Huchel and his wife to discuss the matter at the Academy on 2 April. There Zweig was informed that the background to present difficulties lay in the fact that 'RuL seine Osthälfte im Stich gelassen hat'.[72] This interpretation of events was a convenient shorthand for a whole series of omissions. The only solution lay in more financial input from the state to cover the required subsidy. Following a redistribution of the costs shared by the publisher and the Academy, the latter came up with a subsidy as high as 10,000 marks per issue, which was scaled down to 8,500 marks following rationalisation at the publisher's end.[73] This was a measure of the importance that the Academy leadership attached to *Sinn und Form*. If it was a huge vote of confidence in the journal, it also implied an interest that would manifest itself through more active involvement in editorial policy. For the time being, Huchel was able to return to editorial business, satisfied that at last *Sinn und Form* had been placed on a sound financial footing. He was offered a fresh contract with Rütten und Loening on 24 September 1951, which brought together the two elements of his pay, so that the salary of 800 marks and the bonus of 700 marks would be consolidated in a monthly sum of 1,500.[74] In the event, Huchel signed a coveted individual contract of 2,000 marks per month the following year with the Academy. It was the type of contract that was reserved for especially valued members of the intelligentsia.

In the early 1950s, Huchel was also negotiating with the Aufbau Verlag over his own work. Despite the difficult relations between author and publisher over

Gedichte, in the early 1950s it made sense for both parties to continue their collaboration. The Aufbau Verlag was established as the GDR's leading publisher of *belles lettres* and Huchel was a member of the East Berlin cultural élite. Following the publication of the extract from 'Das Gesetz' in *Sinn und Form*, Huchel and the publisher sought an agreement for the publication of the whole cycle. Huchel evidently also promised Günter Caspar further extracts for the publisher's house journal. Caspar wrote to Huchel on 16 January 1951, 'Natürlich sind wir bitterböse auf Sie ... ganz sicher hatten Sie uns zum 5. 1. 51 Teile aus dem "Gesetz" zugesagt'.[75] On 1 August 1951, however, Max Schroeder wrote a memo to his new boss, Walter Janka, in which he proposed terms for the whole cycle and supplied a supporting statement. Schroeder explained, 'Das Buch kann natürlich im Moment kein großes Geschäft werden, aber es wird repräsentativen Charakter für den Verlag haben'.[76] The subject of the land reform was something that, in Schroeder's view, should figure in the publisher's list. Schroeder was also, no doubt, aware that Huchel had been nominated for the GDR's 'Deutscher Nationalpreis' for Art and Literature, Third Class. He would know, too, that with Becher's support, approval of Huchel's name was a formality.

Janka incorporated Schroeder's proposal of an advance of 1,000 marks in the contract, which he sent to Huchel on 9 August 1951.[77] He sent a reminder to Huchel on 20 September. Yet Huchel did not react. When he wrote to Janka about another matter on 22 March 1952, he made no reference to 'Das Gesetz'. Another reminder was sent on 2 July 1952. Huchel's interest had clearly cooled, but he returned the contract on 25 July 1952. In an accompanying letter, he insisted that, like his previous book, 'Das Gesetz' should be bound in hard covers, not produced with a paper cover. This would be merely in keeping with the SDA's policy. He informed the publisher that he wanted provision in the contract for a small print-run to be distributed by Willi Weismann under licence. He added, rather tartly, 'Ich glaube kaum, daß Sie aus kulturpolitischen Gründen dagegen Einspruch erheben werden'.[78] The SED member Janka replied in kind on 31 July 1952, 'Werter Genosse Huchel! Wir danken für die um zwölf Monate verspätete Rücksendung des Verlagsvertrages'.[79] It is hard to believe when reading this exchange that a decade later Janka and Huchel would begin a close friendship after they had both been put through the mill by the SED. Janka explained that Weismann should liaise directly with the Aufbau Verlag. It would not be necessary to amend the author's contract, as Huchel had assumed. He informed Huchel that the advance had been paid into his account. The deadline for the submission of the manuscript was now 1 November 1952 rather than 1 November 1951, which had originally been mooted.

Yet the deadline in 1952 would also pass without the work's completion. It would appear, nonetheless, that in the very early 1950s Huchel still intended to complete 'Das Gesetz'. As we have seen, he published an extract in *Sinn und Form* as late as 1955. Yet in mid-1952, the SED embarked on the collectivisation of the land on the Soviet model, taking away from the small farmers what had been given to them in 1945. The reform of 1945 had provided the cornerstone around which 'Das Gesetz' was written as an expression of Huchel's enthusiasm. It is not difficult to see in its non-completion Huchel's disillusion with the change in policy in mid-1952. His subject matter had in effect been rendered redundant by events. In a letter to Schroeder of 4 October 1952, Huchel went out of his way to underline his commitment to another project, writing, 'Ich arbeite an der Ballade der Malaya, erweitere sie vorsichtig, um nicht die Urfassung zu zerstören – alles im Hinblick auf unsere Absprache. Nenne nur den letzten Termin für die Ablieferung'.[80] In the event, only extracts from this story of the struggle of Chinese partisan fighters would appear in 1956 in *Neue Deutsche Literatur*. And, despite the more cheerful tone adopted towards his old friend Schroeder, Huchel's relations with the Aufbau Verlag and with Janka did not improve. Matters would come to a head in 1955.

Becher's Sixtieth Birthday

The immediate concern for Huchel in early 1951 was the special issue of *Sinn und Form* for Becher's sixtieth birthday on 22 May 1951. On 5 March Becher had written to Huchel, informing him that he was satisfied with the manuscript for the special number, which was to be entitled 'Sterne unendliches Glühen. Die Sowjetunion in meinem Gedicht 1919-1951'.[81] Mistrustful of Rütten und Loening's capacity to deliver for this crucial project, Huchel sent Becher a memo of an agreement that he had reached on 6 May with Alfred Protte, Rütten und Loening's production manager and one of the few members of their staff in whom he had confidence.[82] Huchel was adamant that arrangements for the prompt distribution of the volume, for which Rütten und Loening was responsible, should be set down in black and white. Lest there be any suggestion that Huchel himself might be responsible for any delays, the final sentence of the document signed by Huchel and Protte reads, 'Herr Protte verpflichtet sich, für die Einhaltung der obengenannten Termine persönlich einzutreten'.

The volume was ready on time for an occasion that was organised with great pomp and ceremony by the Kulturbund for its President.[83] The Huchels were among the guests, who included the politicians Walter Ulbricht, Wilhelm Pieck and Friedrich Ebert, cultural politicians such as Paul Wandel, Alexander Abusch and Wilhelm Girnus as well as intellectuals such as Ernst Bloch. The event is presented in particularly scathing terms by Kantorowicz,[84] who claims that preparations took the best part of a year. In addition to a Festschrift published by Aufbau 'mit Beiträgen derer, die ihn nicht aus der Nähe kennen wie Thomas Mann oder Hermann Hesse', Kantorowicz noted, 'Zugleich das Sonderheft der von ihm selbst herausgegebenen Zeitschrift *Sinn und Form*'. The State Opera House on Unter den Linden was used for the occasion. It opened with Bach's Brandenburg Concerto, followed by a speech by Wandel and music by Haydn. After the interval, Hans Sandig conducted the youth choir of the Mitteldeutscher Rundfunk with Ernst Busch as soloist. Helene Weigel offered a recitation. Celebrations continued the following day in the Haus der Regierung, where Ulbricht delivered a speech. Guests moved on to the Academy, where Becher was awarded an honorary doctorate by the Humboldt University. And so it went on with the speeches and honours. As we can see, the personality cult was not restricted to Ulbricht. The implacably hostile Kantorowicz penned the following lines to commemorate the occasion, drawing sarcastically on Becher's autobiography *Abschied*,

Böse warst du schon ganz jung

Abschied nahmst du da,

Abschied von Erinnerung

Durch Narkotika.

Warst ein Revolutionär,

Als du Abschied nahmst,

Doch ein hoher Funktionär,

Als Du wiederkamst.

...

Heut bist Du so feierlich

Wie ein heil'ger Gral.

Nenne nicht mehr *Becher* Dich,

Heiß Dich jetzt *Pokal*.

The special number of *Sinn und Form* was one of the finest of the trophies. It contained over 300 pages of poems tracing the revolutionary development of Becher's verse. 10,000 copies were printed and yet, despite Becher's all-German aspirations review copies were distributed only in the GDR.[85] Such was Becher's reputation in the West by now that distribution there would only have given cause for comments even more scathing than Kantorowicz's.

While Kantorowicz was very much marginalised due to Becher's personal animosity, Huchel was, as Kantorowicz saw it, part of the Becher orbit. He did what was expected of him, and in the second issue of *Sinn und Form* he published his poem 'In der Heimat', which he dedicated to Becher. The title, of course, echoed Becher's characterisation of Huchel's verse. The poem was later collected in 1963 in *Chausseen Chausseen* in much pared-back form under the title 'Die Pappeln'. As we have seen, in its original form it very much fits in with the pastoral tones of socialist reconstruction in the countryside after the devastation of fascism and the war found in 'Das Gesetz' and other poems from the early to the mid-1950s. 'In der Heimat' contains the lines,

Schön ist die Heimat,

wenn über der grünen Messingscheibe

des Teichs der Kranich schreit

und das Gold sich häuft

im blauen Oktobergewölbe:

wenn Korn und Milch in der Kammer schlafen,

die rußige Schmiede des Alls

beginnt ihr Feuer zu schüren.

The sense of affinity felt by the poet towards those tilling the soil is expressed in the final two lines of the poem, 'Er pflügt auch mein Herz/ und senkt sein Saatgut in mein Wort'. By 1963 this feeling that poet and labourer were involved in a common cause had been lost. The final lines in 'Die Pappeln' are sinister, in keeping with Huchel's later mood, 'Und Asche fällt/ Auf den Schatten der Fledermäuse'.

While Huchel's socialist pastoral of the early 1950s appealed to Becher, it was less well received in other quarters. Huchel declined an offer to contribute to the *Tägliche Rundschau* on Becher's birthday.[86] The paper had been due to publish an extract from 'Das Gesetz' after it had appeared in *Sinn und Form*. Huchel heard that it was withdrawn at the last minute because a gentleman with an aristocratic name, who had never heard of Huchel, had 'helped the cycle on its way' into the waste paper basket on the grounds that it was a formalist work. Huchel wrote that as long as people of that ilk continued to 'haunt' the editorial offices at the *Tägliche Rundschau* he would decline to expose himself to the sort of treatment that he had never experienced before in the thirty years of his literary career.

The Weltfestspiele Farce

In 1951, Huchel proceeded with the production of the second special number, for the 'Weltfestspiele der Jugend und Studenten für den Frieden', which were held in Berlin from 5 to 19 August 1951. As we have seen, preparation of this issue was a test for the new arrangements secured by Huchel. It was doubly important to make a success of the issue, since *Sinn und Form* was being used as an organ representing the state, which was host to guests from many parts of the world. It was agreed that a special subsidy of 35,000 marks should be granted for a one-off print-run of 40,000 copies. Yet the financial constraints were still such that the special number had to take the place of the fourth issue for 1951.

The Section proceeded with planning while Huchel was in hospital in March. He was informed that all members had been asked to contribute.[87] On 16 March, he was reminded that Zweig's 'Das Spiel vom Herrn und vom Jockel' was intended for publication in that number. Yet, as Huchel's letter to Engel of 16 June makes clear, he was having difficulty in putting the number together. Contributions from abroad were still arriving at what was a very late date. He complained that he had not received a single original contribution from Academy members. It was with some relief that Engel wrote to Huchel on 17 July, thanking him for getting the number ready on time.[88] He wanted to check that Huchel had proceeded as agreed, 'Haben Sie mit Herrn Becher die Zusammenstellung und den Inhalt des Heftes abgestimmt?' He queried the absence of representative figures such as Becher and Zweig in this of all numbers. He inquired finally, 'Haben sie den Beitrag Bredels über Pawlenko erhalten? Ich halte es für außerordentlich wichtig, ihn in die nächste Nummer aufzunehmen, und bitte um Ihre Nachricht'. It was a fresh departure for Engel to be directing Huchel's work in his way. Bredel had actually written the essay about the recently deceased Soviet author at Engel's request. Engel's intervention in editorial matters was an index of growing tensions: in many people's eyes, *Sinn und Form* was an expensive item that should be brought under proper ideological control. We shall return to this point and the significance of the Bredel piece presently. Huchel's reply to Engel of 19 July shows him at pains to justify his position by pointing out that it was no fault of his if contributions had not materialised as expected.[89] He explained that he had had to inform Zweig that for editorial reasons he had not been able to include his piece. Zweig was at a PEN Club meeting in Lausanne and it had hence not been possible to discuss the matter with him. He had written to him separately. Huchel regretted that the Academy President could not be included, especially as all other members had failed to deliver. Huchel went on, 'Auch Herrn Becher hatte ich in Anwesenheit seiner Frau – und zwar in der Akademie während der Becher-Ausstellung – dringendst meine Bitte vorgetragen, für dieses Heft eine Arbeit zur Verfügung zu stellen. Leider vergeblich'. He reminded Engel that he was his witness and that Engel could testify to how often he had requested contributions during meetings. He had nothing to add on the matter.

Huchel wrote separately to Zweig on 19 July,[90] setting out the reasons why it had not proved possible to include his piece. Above all, it contained passages dealing with warfare which could easily have been misconstrued. Huchel had not wanted to make any changes to the manuscript without Zweig's permission. Unfortunately, the production schedule meant that he could not wait for Zweig's return from Lausanne. Following his return, on 25 July Zweig met with Huchel and his editorial staff to discuss the content of the number, something Huchel had evidently not been able to do with Becher. Zweig noted in his diary, 'Eine sehr erfolgreiche und interessante Arbeitssitzung ... Wir brachten ...*Sinn und Form* in beste Ordnung'.[91] Huchel's worst fears had thus not been confirmed after all. It had proved possible to include contributions by a number of prominent authors from abroad. Among them were Viteslav Nezval, Mao Tse Tung, Lukács and Pablo Neruda. The number opened with Stalin's 'Über den Frieden'. German contributors included Bloch, Renn, Brecht, Herzfelde, Mayer, Hermlin, Bienek and Huchel himself with his 'Chronik des Dorfes Wendisch-Luch'. His correspondence with his secretary from July (ii, 335) shows that it was only with the greatest of difficulty that he managed to complete in time a work that, as we have seen, he described as 'Aus der Chronik "Das Gesetz"'. As he wrote to Charlotte Narr, he attached the greatest importance to ensuring that he himself was represented in the number. The poem that he had chosen demonstrated his commitment to the revolutionary changes since 1945. On 11 August, Huchel informed Engel of final arrangements for the distribution of the number.[92] Yet through no fault of his own, the arrangements proved a disaster. In a report dated 28 September compiled in the Section, Walter Seifert, a member of the Freie Deutsche Jugend, (FDJ) was identified as the figure responsible for not collecting 32,000 copies from the publisher.[93] Nonetheless, the publisher had then delivered them to the FDJ's warehouse, where they had remained. Due to the FDJ, the enormous investment in *Sinn und Form* had been for nothing. The FDJ evidently had no interest whatsoever in what *Sinn und Form* had to contribute to the festival.

Falling out with Willi Bredel and Friedrich Wolf: under Pressure from the SED

Huchel could not be held responsible for the fiasco, but his correspondence with Engel reveals that he no longer enjoyed the Academy Director's confidence and that he was at pains to justify his position. By the early summer of 1951, Engel would have been aware of a document completed in June 1951 by Hans Schlösser of the Central Committee's Cultural Department, which was highly critical of the Academy.[94] Becher was censured for his failure to give an ideological lead. Schlösser noted that Becher had spoken against the 'Bildung eines Parteiaktivs', since this would be an undemocratic act. Schlösser called for Becher to be replaced as Secretary of the Literature Section. The document also noted that *Sinn und Form* 'objektivistische, unkritische und ästhetisierende Züge aufweist'. In the context of the Formalism Debate that was now dominating cultural life, this was a damning judgment. As a prominent SED cultural politician, Becher could rescue his position by accepting party discipline. Huchel's position would be much more difficult to retrieve if the SED chose to act on Schlösser's report.

The manner adopted by Engel towards Huchel over the Bredel essay becomes more readily comprehensible when set against this background. Bredel was a valued SED figure and a writer of partisan work. Engel was clearly seeking to test Huchel's response at a time when Huchel was also falling out with another prominent SED figure, Friedrich Wolf. On 10 July, Wolf complained to Becher about Huchel's treatment of him over his essay 'Talent und Aussage'.[95] He wrote,

Hätte ich vor wenigen Tagen nicht in Gegenwart von Arnold Zweig zufällig bei Huchel

anfragen lassen, so wüßte ich heute noch nicht, daß der bereits gesetzte Aufsatz 'zurückgestellt' wurde. Ist die Redaktion unserer Zeitschr. der Akademie berechtigt, so mit einer Arbeit eines Akademiemitgliedes zu verfahren? ... Daß der 'Chefredakteur' von *Sinn und Form* mir mit einem 2 Zeilenwisch meine Arbeit (Fahnen) zurückschicken läßt, ist schon keine Frage der Kinderstube mehr, sondern eine Verletzung des primitivsten Anstandes unter Schriftstellern. Ich bitte Dich, Herrn Huchel hierüber zu belehren.

He added that he had sent Zweig a copy of the letter with a view to the matter being discussed at the next meeting of the Section. In Wolf, Huchel made a powerful enemy, who would not be assuaged by Becher.[96] Becher explained in his reply to Wolf that he would have wished to deal with the matter informally between comrades but that this was no longer possible because Wolf had copied the letter to Zweig, who now had to rule on the matter as President.[97] Becher continued, 'Huchel werde ich Deinem Wunsche gemäß darauf aufmerksam machen, daß er seinen Ton zu ändern hat'. At this stage, however, Becher went on to protect Huchel. In the first draft of his letter, he explained,

Sonst trifft ihn keine Schuld, denn angesichts der internationalen PEN-Club-Tagung in Lausanne wird er für unsere Zeitschrift, die ja hauptsächlich für Westdeutschland bestimmt ist, die Anordnung getroffen haben, vorerst keine Beiträge kulturpolitischer Art zu bringen, sondern den Abschluß der Lausanner Tagung abzuwarten.

In the version that was sent, however, Becher changed 'wird er ... die Anordnung getroffen haben' to the impersonal 'wurde ... die Anordnung getroffen', thus absolving Huchel of any responsibility for what had in fact been his decision, which in all probability was linked with Lausanne. Wolf, however, had little time for such a conciliatory stance towards the West. His partisan stance was shared by many others, including Bredel. Huchel closed his letter to Engel of 19 July with the following, 'Falls es Ihnen recht ist, werde ich Sie am Dienstag nächster Woche um 11 Uhr aufsuchen; dann können wir auch über den Aufsatz Bredels sprechen'. On 1 August, Bredel enquired of Engel what the position was with the essay. A memo was written in the Section on 20 August recording Huchel's message that he had spoken with Bredel about the essay.[98] Huchel's position was opposed to Engel's. He argued that *Sinn und Form* was 'keine aktuelle Zeitschrift' and that the author's death was too long ago for an appreciation to be published. It would be better at some point in the future to publish 'eine gründliche Untersuchung der Werke Pawlenkos'. Huchel reported that Bredel shared his opinion and that he would try to find another journal for his essay. Huchel had informed Engel as to how things stood. He underscored his position in a letter to Becher on 11 August 1951, confident that he could count on his support. Huchel wrote, 'Wie müssen tiefer loten, um im besten Sinne aktuell zu sein'.[99]

Yet Huchel had snubbed another powerful SED figure who would neither forgive nor forget. In a letter to Engel a year later, on 23 August 1952,[100] Huchel acknowledged that Bredel continued to take exception to his decision, 'bis auf den heutigen Tag. Ich bedaure Bredels unversöhnliche Einstellung sehr – denn diese ist wohl auch der Grund, weshalb Bredel in SINN UND FORM nicht über Zweig schreiben möchte'. Events would soon show that Huchel could expect as little sympathy for his position from Engel as he could from Bredel or, for that matter, Wolf.

More Cultural Diplomacy with the West

As yet, voices raised against Huchel's editorial practice, however powerful, did not add up to serious opposition to his continuing rise. Supported by Becher and with the approval of Zweig and Brecht, on 7 October 1951 Huchel was rewarded for his efforts, but especially for his poetry, with the GDR's 'Deutscher Nationalpreis' for Art and Literature. He was praised for his 'wertvollen Gedichte, die die neue deutsche Lyrik wesentlich bereichern'. Even though the prize was Third Class Huchel accepted despite his earlier threat. Kantorowicz viewed the award as follows, 'Im dritten Rang sah man Eduard Claudius als Protegé des Apparats und Peter Huchel als Protegé Bechers (doch freut's mich für ihn, daß er dabei ist, er wird wohl die 25000 Mark in einem Häuschen auf dem Lande anlegen)'.[101] He would have a further year to wait before election to the Academy, but he was in any case now invited to attend all meetings of the Literature Section.[102]

The day following the award, Huchel left for Hamburg. He was accompanied by Werner Baum of the Writers' Union. Baum had provided a glowing report in his 'Anlage zur Charakteristik über Peter Huchel' of 31 July 1951, writing,

> In der schwierigen Situation, die sich in der Arbeit der Berliner Schriftsteller infolge der verräterischen Handlungsweise des Dr. Schendell (of the S.D.A. – S.P.) ergeben hatte, hat sich Peter Huchel als ein unermüdlicher Agitator für die Einheit der Schriftsteller in Berlin gezeigt und bewährt. Zweimal hat er in größeren öffentlichen Versammlungen zu den Westberliner Schriftstellern mit Erfolg gesprochen und war trotz seiner schweren Krankheit unermüdlich tätig, um den Schutzverband Deutscher Autoren in Berlin vor dem Verfall zu bewahren. Hauptsächlich dank seiner Initiative und seiner verständnisvollen kulturpolitischen Anleitung ist es gelungen, eine solche Grundlage für die gemeinsame Arbeit aller Berliner Schriftsteller zu schaffen, wie wir sie in der entsprechenden Weise kaum in einer anderen Organisation finden können.[103]

There should be no underestimating the size of Huchel's task. The credibility of his position in the West owed next to nothing to SED policy. Huchel was in Hamburg with Baum from 18 to 21 October.[104] On the first day, they discussed guidelines for fees for radio work with West German authors. On the following days, they met with Jahnn, Harry Reuß-Löwenstein, (President of the Verband Deutscher Autoren - GesamtVerband), Hermann Quistorf (Reuß-Löwenstein's deputy), Friedrich H. Prehm, Hans Erich Nossack, Weisenborn 'und mit einer Reihe uns ohnehin nahestehender Schriftsteller'. Of them, Peter Martin Lampel and Herbert Lestiboudois would be coming to Berlin at the beginning of November. Baum and Huchel attended a book exhibition in Hamburg. Baum was scathing in his report, 'Die ganze Buchwoche offenbarte mit erschreckender Deutlichkeit die katastrophale Lage der westdeutschen Literatur und Schriftsteller'.

From Hamburg, Huchel travelled with Weisenborn to the general meeting of the German PEN Club, which took place in Düsseldorf from 23 to 25 October. The few West German writers who attended felt that they were steamrollered into decisions by their colleagues from the East, whose delegation included Becher, Hermlin, Huchel, Mayer, Renn, Ehm Welk and Zweig. The group from the East was able to secure majorities in elections. Following pressure from the Bonn Interior Ministry, a number of West German writers signed a statement regretting the absence of other West German writers. They announced their intention to found a West German PEN Club, in which they were joined by other colleagues. They included Huchel's friends from the 1930s, Lange, Schaefer, Bergengruen and Birkenfeld. The political split of the Cold War was now felt keenly by writers, many of whose friendships could from now on survive only from a distance, if at all. The efforts of Huchel and others from East Berlin to maintain the unity of the German PEN Club had come to nothing in the face of pressure from Bonn and the suspicion felt by West German writers towards the Stalinist East. The powers-that-be in East Berlin were, however, not inclined to accept this situation. As Huchel reported to Jahnn on 4 January 1952, 'Gleich nach der PEN-Tagung faßte man dann meine Frankfurter Reise mit der Rückfahrt über Hamburg ins Auge'.[105] Papers had, however, not been granted by the authorities in Düsseldorf. Given the intervention of the Bonn Interior Ministry in the PEN affair, one can see why.

Jahnn's letters to Huchel testify to the difficulties that Jahnn's neutralist stance caused for him. In a letter of 26 or 27 October 1951, Jahnn wrote, concerning his prospective election as a corresponding member of the East Berlin Academy, 'Mich jetzt in die Akademie zu wählen, wäre geradezu vernichtend für mich'.[106] He suggested that the only way really to help him would be for the Academy to nominate him for the Nobel Prize. He clearly had a point. In a later letter, of 27 March 1952, Jahnn wrote, 'Für alle Schriftsteller und Schaffende schlechthin, die den Kurs der Bonner Regierung nicht bejahen, wird das Dasein in ökonomischer Beziehung hier im Westen immer schwieriger'.[107] Jahnn sought to respond to calls for solidarity among intellectuals against Bonn, which were published in *Sinn und Form* by the East Berlin Academy and its members. Yet he did not always feel able to do so.

A case in point was Brecht's open letter of 26 September 1951, which ended with the famous lines, 'Das große Karthago führte drei Kriege. Es war noch mächtig nach dem ersten, noch bewohnbar nach dem zweiten. Es war nicht mehr auffindbar nach dem dritten'. Brecht's letter also contained a call, clearly directed against the West, for freedom of publication and performance of all works with the exception of 'Schriften und Kunstwerke, welche den Krieg verherrlichen oder als unvermeidbar hinstellen, und für solche, welche den Völkerhaß fördern'. Jahnn, faced with repeated difficulties from the GDR authorities in having his books published there, – he evidently did not know of Brecht's own difficulties – responded to Huchel on 1 April 1952,

> Natürlich weiß ich von mir selbst, daß ich ein Individualist bin; aber den Krieg habe ich
> seit jeher abgelehnt, und daß mein Ziel die Verständigung ist, folgt als Selbstverständlich-
> keit daraus. Aber die Welt der Gegensätze ist nun einmal mit groben Waffen ausgerüstet.
> Das Gefühl, daß ich mitten zwischen den Fronten stehe, wird in mir immer deutlicher, so
> daß mein Unbehagen wächst.[108]

Brecht's open letter was treated with scorn in many circles in the West, and Huchel included an attack on those who had maligned Brecht in a speech delivered on 1 February 1952 before the 'Groß-Berliner Komitee der Kulturschaffenden', an East Berlin front organisation through which he pursued the cultural diplomacy for which he had been praised by Baum. The speech was published later that year in *Aufbau*. Huchel interpreted the attacks as evidence of 'eine maßlose, hinterhältige Hetze gegen den Frieden'. (ii,279) He argued the case, as he would throughout the 1950s, for the preservation of cultural unity in Berlin despite the city's political division. Polemicising with untypical ferocity, Huchel drew a parallel between the actions of the Nazis in 1933 and those of the western allies, especially the USA, 'Wir schreiben das Jahr 1952, und die ersten Vorboten der Barbarei sind schon lange wieder in die Mauern unserer Stadt eingezogen! Noch können wir sie zurückschlagen!' (ii,270) Undoubtedly, these words and others of a similar tone in the speech contributed to the image of Huchel as an orthodox cultural functionary, an image that enjoyed some currency in the West during the 1950s. Yet, although Huchel ascribed divisions in the cultural sphere exclusively to the 'tödliche Umarmung der amerikanischen Kulturpolitik', (ii,283) the speech also contained a plea for an end to the 'Sektiererwesen in der Literaturkritik' (ii,282) in East Berlin caused by those eager to uncover wherever they looked evidence of Western Formalism. Thus, while Huchel's comments against the West placed him firmly in the GDR camp, he identified himself with those members of the Academy, including Brecht, Zweig and Hanns Eisler, who put up strong, if not always ultimately effective resistance to attempts to undermine their position with charges of Formalism. In East Berlin things would get worse before, for a time at least, they got better.

Escalating Pressure for Change: Formalism, Brecht and Barlach

Following his return from Düsseldorf, Huchel delivered an up-beat report on West German responses to *Sinn und Form* to a meeting of the Section on 6 November.[109] Yet the SED's dissatisfaction with the Academy's work had filtered through to all levels of the institution. Brecht responded to Huchel by proposing an initiative designed to take advantage of the journal's distribution in West Germany and its possible impact there. He suggested that GDR writers such as Bredel, Marchwitza, Wolf, Renn, Michael Tschesno and Kuba should be approached to write reportage about the economic and cultural development of the GDR, principally in the countryside. Huchel, it was said, 'der selbst einige interessante und lohnende Objekte im Land Brandenburg kennt, wird zunächst versuchen, Michael Tschesno für eine solche Arbeit zu gewinnen'. Nothing came of Brecht's initiative, yet it cannot have been by chance that he proposed this fresh orientation and authors such as Wolf and Bredel only shortly after Huchel's differences with them and the evaluation of the journal in the SED hierarchy as 'objektivistisch'. Brecht's attempt to bring Huchel and *Sinn und Form* together with more partisan authors came to nothing, principally as a result of Huchel's own fundamental lack of enthusiasm for such writing, which, with its explicit commitment to the class struggle, he could only see as undermining *Sinn und Form*'s all-German mission. Brecht, of course, was disposed to adopt a partisan attitude and to show much more nimble footwork than Huchel, who was not prepared to follow Brecht's urgings. Had he done so, a particular problem might yet have been averted that would presently assume much greater proportions.

If this was an area in which he was unwilling to make any compromises, concerned that he would open the gates to much dross, that is not to say that he was not on occasion prepared to make concessions in other areas. One example of self-imposed censorship undertaken in concert with one of his authors can be found in Bloch's letter to him of 15 November 1951.[110] Bloch wrote, explaining his decision to omit from a piece for Huchel the section 'Ineinander nächtlicher und täglicher Traumspiele, seine Auflösung', 'Die Verkürzung entstand, indem ich – bei dem gegenwärtigen niedrigen Niveau – Probleme des Surrealismus, die hierher gehören ... weggelassen habe. Sonst hätte *Sinn und Form* Unannehmlichkeiten'. Similarly, in response to Wolf's wish to initiate a discussion in the Academy of Huchel's treatment of him and his essay, Huchel sought to defuse that situation by undertaking in future to pass on to the editorial commission all manuscripts by members of the Section submitted for publication in *Sinn und Form*.

Yet Huchel increasingly found himself between a rock and a hard place, as he came under attack for something that he had published by another member of the Section. He was summoned to Becher's office following his publication of Brecht's defence of Barlach. An excerpt from Ernst Barlach's papers, part of the drama *Der Graf von Ratzeburg*, had been published in *Sinn und Form* in 1950, followed in

1951 by two pages of *Aufzeichnungen aus einem Taschenbuche von 1906*. When at the turn of 1951-2 the Academy's Barlach exhibition became the focus of the Formalism campaign, in its first number of 1952 *Sinn und Form* published Brecht's defence of Barlach, which *Neues Deutschland* had refused to print. It was in *Neues Deutschland* that Girnus had launched his savage attack on Barlach. Huchel later recalled, 'Damals galt in der DDR die Parole: Wer für Barlach ist, unterstützt den amerikanischen Imperialismus. Also wurde ich zu Becher zitiert, der mich beschimpfte'. (ii,374) Huchel would take up the the matter again the following year in his open letter to the communist writer from Hamburg, Herbert Lestiboudois. The letter was written shortly after the tumultuous events surrounding 17 June 1953, when Brecht seized the moment to save Huchel and *Sinn und Form*. Huchel's sense of gratitude towards Brecht and renewed confidence in tackling the dogmatists both emerge clearly in the following statement,

> Was allein die Barlach-Affäre angerichtet hat, als man es wagte, in so herabsetzendem Sinne über diesen großen deutschen Bildhauer zu schreiben, ist leider noch nicht in seinem ganzen Umfang erkannt. Es war ein Glück, daß es damals nicht bei dem Pyrrhussieg des flachsten kritischen Journalismus blieb und daß die Stimme der wirklichen Autorität, die Stimme Bertolt Brechts, auch für Westdeutschland hörbar wurde. (ii,291)

The atmosphere following the 17 June 1953 contrasted markedly with early 1952, which, in turn, contrasted with early 1951, when, as we have seen, Huchel had made the running with his plans for the coming year. On 15 January 1952, Annemarie Auer, the administrator for the Literature Section, wrote to Huchel at Eulenkamp 6, informing him of the passage concerning *Sinn und Form* which had been formulated by Becher for the coming year's work in the Section,

> Die Zeitschrift *Sinn und Form* soll im Laufe des kommenden Jahres weiter in Richtung einer repräsentativen gesamtdeutschen Literaturzeitschrift ausgebaut werden; besonders wird sich die Redaktion der Zeitschrift dem Ausbau eines literaturwissenschaftlichen und literaturkritischen Teils zu widmen haben.[111]

The mention of academic articles and reviews was particularly loaded at that juncture, given the ideological fervour promoted by the SED. The journal's future was the subject of discussion at the level of a Plenary Session on 26 February.[112] Engel began by representing the party's view that the Academy had not been performing the role with which it had been entrusted, namely to take a clear public stance on questions related to the arts. Friedrich Wolf proposed the foundation of a new 'kunsttheoretische Zeitschrift' to deal with such matters. Becher countered,

Unsere Zeitschrift *Sinn und Form* reicht aus, um auch diese Fragen regelmäßig in 8 bis 12 Seiten zu behandeln. Daraus ergibt sich, daß die Zeitschrift nicht mehr alle zwei Monate erscheinen kann, sondern sie muß jeden Monat herausgegeben werden. Auch Fragen der bildenden Kunst gehören ja herein.

Becher's statement was far from being a defence of the status quo. Such far-reaching proposals implied a great shift in the journal's identity and a re-structuring of editorial work, not to mention the likely need for even greater subsidies. Following discussion, it was agreed that

Die Zeitschrift *Sinn und Form* wird ergänzt durch kunstkritische Stellungnahmen der Akademiemitglieder. (Hier steht die Frage qualifizierter Mitarbeiter. Herr Huchel kann das nicht allein verantwortlich übernehmen. Herr Rilla wird vorgeschlagen, fällt aber wegen Krankheit vorläufig aus. Weitere Vorschläge wurden gemacht: Heinz Lüdecke und Alfred Kurella.)

Consideration of Kurella and Lüdecke is, of course, quite in step with the course that the SED wished the Academy to adopt. At the time, Kurella was still in Moscow. Huchel would meet him there in May 1953 and encourage him to return to East Berlin, apparently quite unaware of the reputation of a man of whom it was said that he had betrayed his own brother in the Great Terror. In the event, Kurella returned to East Berlin in 1954. From then on, he made his presence felt in GDR cultural life, using the power that accrued from his close links with the Moscow security services. In time, *Sinn und Form* would become the object of his attentions.

Despite the resolution of the Plenary Session, it remained unclear quite how the changes proposed for the journal would be brought about. Should they be implemented, it was certain that Huchel's editorial control would be reduced through the introduction of editorial staff of at least equal standing to himself. The names discussed indicate that any figure chosen would in all likelihood be well versed in Marxist aesthetics from an SED point-of-view. It was the first time that the issue of a second editor was raised, but it would not be the last. Engel's closing words at the Plenary Session, announcing that the Presidium had resolved to formulate 'eine grundsätzliche Erklärung über die kulturpolitische Aufgabe der Akademie', showed that the pressure for the adoption by the Academy of positions in keeping with SED policy would not relent.

In keeping with the hierarchical structure of the Academy, the 'Ausbau der Zeitschrift *Sinn und Form*' was taken up at a meeting of the Section on 5 March 1952, at which Huchel was, as usual, present by invitation.[113] In the absence of Brecht and Zweig, he had only one ally, Ihering, at the poorly attended meeting. Meanwhile Becher, Wolf and Engel ensured that the position already represented at the Plenary Session would be developed upon, not least because Becher was at last responding to SED pressure. The various points and resolutions of the previous months were rehearsed, with a view to their implementation. Preparations were to be made for *Sinn und Form* to appear monthly. The intention, spelt out in the minutes, was that 'die Zeitschrift sich aktualisiert und Buchkritiken, sowie Probleme der Sprachpflege, Berichte aus dem wirtschaftlchen und kulturellen Leben der DDR und spezielle Arbeitsmitteilungen der Akademie bieten soll'. Reference was also made to the extension of *Sinn und Form*'s range, agreed at the Plenary Session to include theoretical and aesthetic questions, and with that the necessary additional editorial staff. The introduction of a new editor was considered but in the light of unspecified difficulties, perhaps financial, Huchel proposed an alternative: that the Section might establish a working relationship with specific authors. It was agreed that Georg Piltz, Melchior Vischer, Dr. Behrsing and Wieland Herzfelde should be invited to discuss their possible input in the presence of members of the Section. There is no record of such discussions ever having taken place. Here as elsewhere Huchel, who had little to gain from such changes, simply acquiesced in the institutional lethargy which so marked various attempts by the Academy over the years to turn *Sinn und Form* into a journal more to the liking of the management and the SED hierarchy.

On 5 March, the prospects of major changes and a diminution of Huchel's influence were real enough. Wolf added his own recommendation, upon which, as the minute of the meeting indicates, Huchel was expected to act, 'Auf Anregung von Herrn Friedr. Wolf fährt Herr Huchel demnächst nach Leipzig, um mit einigen Absolventen des Studiengangs des Instituts für Publizistik Verbindung aufzunehmen, die evtl. zur ständigen Mitarbeit zu gewinnen'. The underlying enmity and mistrust are not difficult to detect in Wolf's encouragement to Huchel to look to young authors schooled in the GDR. It can be safely assumed that he did not act upon Wolf's advice. He did, though, write to Becher two days later, on 7 March 1952.[114] His letter indicates just how bad the feeling had been at the meeting and that the minutes do not fully convey the depth of criticism directed primarily by Wolf, it seems, at the journal's editorial staff. For the first but not the last time Becher had not stood by Huchel as the latter would have expected, given that his role extended well beyond *Sinn und Form* as Becher's acceptable face in cultural diplomacy with the West.

Huchel wrote ostensibly in order to elicit Becher's opinion about two passages in texts submitted for publication. However, he prefaced this request with the following statement,

Sie werden verstehen, daß ich nach der letzten Sitzung in der Akademie Sie darum angehen muß, denn ich muß es ablehnen, weiterhin allein die Verantwortung auf mich zu nehmen – so gern und mit allem Verantwortungsbewußtsein ich es auch bisher getan habe. Doch das Protokoll – ein Dokument der Umfälschung fast aller Vorgänge; und das nicht zum ersten Mal! – hat mir sehr zu denken gegeben.

Huchel's letter records a clear change in both tone and substance in response to what he rightly perceived as Becher's betrayal. The arguments concerning the journal's identity and mission, for which he had previously been able to rely on Becher's support, now counted for nothing. Now at latest, Huchel had clear evidence of whom he was dealing with in his working relationship with Becher, whose passionate belief in poetry and the poet's calling to rescue civilisation rapidly fell by the wayside in his subjection to what the SED required of him. And so it was increasingly in the early 1950s.

Huchel went on in his letter to ask Becher's opinion about a passage in Zweig's 'Blick auf Gogol 1952' and Konrad Farner's 'Aus dem Reisetagebuch eines Schweizers'. Regarding the latter, Huchel referred to some passages in which Farner recorded his open discussion with Soviet friends about art. He feared that some comments could be 'vielleicht für sehr dumme Leute verfänglich'. Huchel explained, however, that he had only come to see them in such a light 'nach der letzten Aussprache in der Akademie, aus der ich entnahm, daß jeder Beitrag in SINN UND FORM evtl. mit der offiziellen Meinung der Deutschen Akademie der Künste verwechselt werden könnte'. He informed Becher that in his piece Zweig had insisted on the retention of the phrase, 'Da sie, *wie Generationen später unser großer Dichter und Plastiker Ernst Barlach*, vom überwundenen Klassizismus her ...' Huchel added, 'Herr Zweig hat auch bei dieser Gelegenheit nicht ohne Vorwurf über die Ablehnung der Veröffentlichung seiner Barlachrede und anderer Manuskripte mit mir gesprochen – und zwar mit der Äußerung, er werde sich ein solches redaktionelles Eingreifen nicht mehr gefallen lassen, seine Manuskripte hätten so zu erscheinen, wie er sie schreibe'. Huchel could scarcely afford to fall out with an ally such as Zweig. Yet Huchel had already received a dressing-down from Becher over Barlach and could not afford to provoke his wrath again.

Huchel went on to draw attention to the fact that Zweig had given him a further manuscript for *Sinn und Form*, 'Abschied von Hamsun'. Huchel told Becher that in his view it should not appear in the journal. Nor did it in fact. Huchel's letter, though, shows just how exposed his position had become, as his previous supporters began to desert him in the turbulent period that led up to the 17 June 1953. The offending sentence in 'Blick auf Gogol 1952' was printed, yet Huchel's fears were certainly not misplaced. Shortly after, on 26 March 1952, Huchel confided to Jahnn,

Dazu kommt, daß ich seit der Übernahme der Zeitschrift durch die Deutsche Akademie der Künste nicht mehr die volle Aktionsfreiheit besitze, die ich vorher hatte. Besonders in letzter Zeit habe ich – das sei Ihnen vertraulich mitgeteilt – manches einstecken müssen, und es ist nicht immer leicht, die Zeitschrift auf der gewohnten Höhe zu halten. Ich blicke oft mit Schmerz auf die ersten beiden Jahrgänge zurück. Ich hoffe aber, daß eine endgültige Aussprache mit Becher manches klären wird.[115]

The way forward was full of traps. It was by now too much to hope that he would receive from Becher the guarantees that he sought for future collaboration. He was surely by now aware that his work in cultural diplomacy between the two German states could in time count for nothing.

Election to the Elite in the Midst of the Ideological Struggle

Despite his deteriorating relations with Becher, throughout 1952, in the months immediately preceding his election to the Academy, Huchel performed actively in the role that he had been allocated in cultural politics. He wrote to Engel on 15 March 1952,[116] proposing a joint publishing project with other German academies. His idea was to re-issue works of art that had been destroyed in the two world wars. Engel encouraged him to pursue the idea, but it was not in the event developed. Otherwise, he offered minor concessions on matters of editorial policy in the attempt to accommodate some of the points that had been made, without fundamentally weakening his position.

His letter to Roland Schacht of 9 May 1952 sees him going about SDA business, which, as he was well aware, was under the control of the Writers' Union.[117] On 19 June, the Writers' Union put on an event to draw attention to the plight of André Stil, a member of the French Communist Party's Central Committee and editor of *L'humanité*, who had been arrested on 25 May 1952 in Paris. He had called for demonstrations against General Matthew Bunker Ridgway, who was about to take up his post as Supreme Commander of NATO at Fontainbleu.[118] Huchel responded by writing 'Gerechtigkeit, sofortige Freiheit für André Stil', which was published in the August number of *Aufbau*. Despite an earlier spat with the *Tägliche Rundschau* over *Das Gesetz*, on 26 July he responded to a request for material by the editor Theuerkauf. He offered 'In der Heimat', which was published on 8 August 1952.[119] This time there was no dedication to Becher.

On 11 June 1952, Huchel offered his editorial services for a project floated in the Academy, the publication of an almanac.[120] Ironically, it was with the offer to edit an almanac for the Academy that Bredel would seek to buy Huchel off in 1962. Wishing in 1952 not to appear obstructive in the development of *Sinn und Form* Huchel announced that 'nunmehr ein Glossenteil mit Marginalien eingerichtet wurde'. [121] He announced, too, the plan to include film reviews. This can be seen as a belated response to Wolf's observation in his letter to Becher of 10 July 1951 that hitherto *Sinn und Form* had totally ignored this important medium. The new, final section, entitled Umschau und Kritik' and introduced in the fourth number of 1952, was not separately marked on the contents page. It began with R. Hinton Thomas' essay 'Friedrich Wolfs Entwicklung als Dramatiker'. Yet the positioning there, tucked in at the back, was surely a calculated snub: Huchel could not resist taking his revenge on Wolf, upon whom this was surely not lost. The same number saw some treatment of film in Johannes Altmann's report on the Cannes Film Festival. Until 1955, when Herbert Ihering began a regular column for that section, 'Bemerkungen zu Theater und Film', it was generally used for announcements by the Academy and for short essays on literary matters, which were, however, by no means always devoted to matters of contemporary interest as had been envisaged. They were often, instead, pieces that Huchel did not want to include in the main body of the journal.

He followed up these announcements with identically worded letters to Becher and Brecht on 14 June 1952,[122] along with which he enclosed a copy of a recent letter from the Swiss communist Konrad Farner, a contributor to *Sinn und Form*, who sang the journal's praises. These words from a western intellectual were welcome proof that *Sinn und Form* was fulfilling its mission. Farner remarked, with words that could scarcely have been improved upon if Huchel had prompted him, 'Meine Freunde und ich finden, daß *Sinn und Form* wohl das Organ der DAK sein soll, aber nicht in der Hauptsache das Organ gewichtiger Mitglieder der Akademie'. Huchel described Farner's letter to Becher and Brecht as 'vielleicht für die weiteren Besprechungen über *Sinn und Form* nicht ohne Bedeutung'. At this stage, he still had everything to fight for and was well aware where it was important to exercise his influence.

It was at the meeting of 11 June, too, that the matter of Huchel's election to the Academy, mooted as early as 28 February 1951, was taken up again, along with the nominations of Renn and Kantorowicz. The delay had been due to SED dissatisfaction with the Academy's work to date. That is to say, the Academy under the politically non-aligned Zweig's leadership had failed to give a clear lead since it had not adopted a sufficiently partisan attitude in matters of cultural politics. Engel, as we have seen, was in the process of making sure that things would change, and the SED was now prepared to allow some movement on the issue of further elections of Academy members. SED pressure would become overwhelming in the wake of the Second Party Conference of the SED in July 1952, when it was announced that the construction of the foundations of socialism would proceed apace with the West German state's integration within the structures of the West. At latest now, the basis upon which the Academy was founded – an all-German institution with representative membership – was declared anachronistic and the imposition of Party discipline in key posts was demanded. This could not but affect Huchel, the fragility of whose position as the editor of *Sinn und Form* was rapidly exposed, just as, paradoxically enough, he was elevated to membership of the Academy.

It is a measure of the tensions and counter-currents of the turbulent early 1950s, as well as of the wholly contradictory role played by Becher, that while in the summer of 1952 Becher and Engel were planning the changes that would follow from the Party conference, including Zweig's replacement by Becher, Becher in his capacity as Secretary of the Section was also preparing the text which presented the case for Huchel's election to the Academy. On 22 August 1952, Engel wrote to Becher about the future of the Academy and its journal, urging him 'nochmals mit aller Energie an die Dinge heranzugehen, um diesem schönen Instrument, das in unsere Hände gegeben ist, "Sinn und Form" zu geben'.[123] Becher's text supporting Huchel, dated 9 September 1952, highlights three aspects of Huchel's achievement: as a poet; with Radio Berlin; and with *Sinn und Form*.[124] The text begins, 'Das Wirken Peter Huchels ist seit jeher durch die fortschrittlichen Kräfte im deutschen Volke bestimmt'. The characterisation of the poetry drew to some extent on the text produced the previous year prior to the award of the National Prize. His work with Radio Berlin was described as 'Pionierarbeit beim Aufbau des demokratischen Rundfunks', while the final section reads, 'Durch die Begründung der Zeitschrift *Sinn und Form* (gemeinsam mit J. R. Becher und Paul Wiegler), durch ihre redaktionelle Betreuung und Weiterführung als Zeitschrift der Akademie hat sich Peter Huchel um die Deutsche Akademie der Künste verdient gemacht'. Though not at that time sufficient on its own, editorship of the Academy's journal was clearly a crucial factor in the election, just as it would be with later editors, who could thus provide the essential link between Academy members and editorial staff.

Huchel's election to the Academy was approved at a Plenary Session on 26 September 1952.[125] Renn was also elected, but not Kantorowicz, who later wrote that he and Huchel had spoken for the last time in 1952. On 28 March 1953, Kantorowicz made an entry in his diary, which signals his profound disillusion with Huchel. This was, ironically enough, at the very time when it was Huchel's turn to feel the heat. In later years, Huchel's relationships with other close friends, Bloch and Hermlin, not to mention his 'discovery' Johannes Bobrowski, would come under similar strain as the pressures to which GDR intellectuals were exposed gave rise to misunderstandings, as well as fears of exclusion and betrayal, real or imagined. Kantorowicz's diary entry reads, 'Zu den menschlichen Enttäuschungen, die man nachgerade mit einem Achselzucken zur Kenntnis nimmt und abtut, gehört auch das Verhalten meines einstigen Jugendfreundes Peter Huchel. Seine Fügsamkeit geht über das Notwendige hinaus'.[126] Kantorowicz continued the entry by recounting a dream about the Nazi period, in which Huchel encouraged Kantorowicz to follow him into Goering's ministry since 'er diese Beziehung für sich vorteilhaft eingefädelt hatte. So war nun einmal die Lage. Man mußte sich darein schicken'.[127] Kantorowicz discussed the dream with Max Schroeder, who found the simple explanation that Goering was Becher. The dream also hints at Kantorowicz's doubts about the stories that Huchel had told him about his life in the Nazi years, which Kantorowicz had repeated during the re-launch of Huchel's literary career in 1947. Kantorowicz's treatment by the editorial staff of *Sinn und Form* in late 1953 and 1954 over his 'Zola' essay, in which he explored the relations between the Mann brothers during the First World War, would confirm all his worst suspicions about his former friend. The fact that by then Kantorowicz had only a very partial view of Huchel's position is itself an index of their estrangement.

In late 1952, Kantorowicz remained marginalised in the Academy in his role as head of the Heinrich Mann Archive, and his bitterness increased. Despite Zweig's protests, at a meeting of the Presidium on 11 September, Kantorowicz's name was replaced by that of Alexander Abusch as a nominée of the Literature Section.[128] At the Plenary Session on 26 September Becher stated that Abusch 'Wurde von uns in einer Sitzung als Kandidat vorgeschlagen!'[129] Zweig countered, 'In einer Sitzung der Sektion Dichtkunst, in der die Kandidatur von Abusch beschlossen wurde, war ich nicht dabei'. Abusch's name had, indeed, not been discussed at a meeting. However, Engel immediately supported Becher, and Abusch's name was pushed through together with Hans Rodenberg's despite the protests from members of the Performing Arts Section. Both were needed by the SED, as preparations were finalised for the struggle for ideological control in the Academy that was about to be launched.

Huchel's letter of acceptance to Engel dated 30 September contained conventional formulations expressing his pleasure at having been singled out for such an honour, especially on account of his close working relationship with the Literature Section.[130] In his reply of 1 November, Engel informed Huchel that his name had been placed before the Minister President of the GDR for approval.[131] Huchel was invited to attend the Academy as a member for the first time on 10 November. The occasion was the celebration of Arnold Zweig's birthday. The invitation was all the more fitting since Huchel had just completed a third special number of *Sinn und Form* for Zweig to mark the occasion. At the celebrations Huchel was also handed the certificate confirming his election, which brought with it an annual sinecure of 10,000 marks. The intellectual élite was, indeed, treated generously in material terms by the state. Huchel received the sinecure until he left the GDR in 1971.

Yet two days after the celebrations, Huchel was writing to Werner Baum at the Writers' Union, complaining about the behaviour of a member of that organisation's executive,

In Anbetracht dessen, daß der von mir sehr verehrte Kollege Hans Marchwitza vorgestern vor der Arnold-Zweig-Geburtstagsfeier in Gegenwart Hans Mayers und zweier Thüringer Schriftsteller stundenlang meine Arbeit als 'Unsinn und Uniform' – wie er sich geistreich ausdrückte – beschimpft hat, halte ich es für besser, daß mein Zustand in bezug auf die Verbandsfragen vorläufig noch ein latenter bleibt. So ist es mir auch weiterhin möglich, alle Dinge mit Humor aufzunehmen. Von einem Vorsitzenden meines Verbandes aber müßte ich eine Unterscheidung zwischen Kritik und Anpöbelei verlangen. Und warum wollen wir einander das Leben so schwer machen?[132]

Marchwitza was just one more enemy among the proletarian writers like Bredel, who deeply resented the prominence enjoyed by the 'bourgeois' Huchel and his journal. Their view was simply that Huchel was not with them in their political struggle conducted with the weapon of literature. As Stephan Hermlin later acknowledged, Huchel was, indeed, not open to the sort of writing that these figures produced, dismissing it all and pledging that the likes of Bredel and Marchwitza would never appear in *Sinn und Form* as long as he was editor. Such intransigence was dangerous at the best of times in the workers' and peasants' state. In time it would prove fateful, and as we shall see, it is quite extraordinary that Huchel survived as long as he did.

In the same letter to Baum, Huchel added that he was still on the executive of the SDA. He informed Baum, too, that his mother had had a stroke and was in hospital. She would recover and live until 1961, but at the time Huchel handed Eduard Zak the poem 'Erinnerung', which was included as a facsimile in Zak's study *Der Dichter Peter Huchel*, the first monograph on Huchel, which appeared the following year. It would be a fateful year for the new state, and Huchel was caught up in the turmoil as the currents and counter-currents in the politics of the GDR and the Soviet Union almost brought Huchel and *Sinn und Form* crashing down in the months leading up to 17 June 1953. In this atmosphere, an innocent note to Huchel from Auer on 9 October would have the most ominous consequences. She wrote,

> Wir bitten Sie, den Aufsatz Ernst Fischers über die Faustdichtung Hanns Eislers durchzusehen und der Sektion Ihre Stellungnahme in kurzer Notiz mitzuteilen. Für eine baldige Entsprechung unseres Wunsches wären wir dankbar, weil die alsbaldige Veröffentlichung des Essays entweder als Einzelpublikation oder angeschlossen an den Text selbst in Aussicht genommen worden ist.[133]

There is no record of a reply from Huchel. Auer's note followed an agreement at the Presidium on 8 October that Eisler's text should be published before the essay.[134] At the end of the month, on 30 October, this was changed to the plan that Fischer's essay should appear as an independent Academy publication.[135] In the event, Huchel published both texts in the final number of 1952. He was eager to add to *Sinn und Form*'s international reputation through the re-working of the Faust legend by Eisler, underpinned by Fischer's interpretation. Yet the publications provoked outrage among SED cultural politicians. They were angered by Fischer's discussion of the 'misery' of German history at a time when they were seeking to generate an image of the GDR as the embodiment of a 'progressive' strand in German historical development. Not only that, the German classics represented an inviolable humanist heritage that should not be tampered with. According to the SED view, this heritage was a potent weapon to be deployed against the frivolous and pernicious Formalism then prevalent in the West, with which the German people surely could not identify.

It goes without saying that the SED view was based on a massive over-estimation of the power of art to influence political attitudes, something that derives from a similar over-estimation of the power of ideology. For figures such as Wolf and Bredel, Huchel's publication of Eisler/Fischer was simply confirmation of what they already knew about the editor's unreliability and lack of judgment. For those with ambitions in GDR cultural politics, such publications were useful pretexts to justify the course of action now being planned.

1953: the Struggle for Control. Brecht's Confrontation with Abusch

As a politically non-aligned figure, Huchel was excluded from the flow of information and instructions to which an SED figure like Marchwitza was party. The latter probably had good reason to feel that he could be so outspoken about *Sinn und Form* on 10 November. Two days later, F.C.Weiskopf reported to Willi Bredel upon Becher's visit to him in Prague,

> Dabei erwähnte er die Notwendigkeit, die Redaktion der von der Akademie herausgegebenen Zeitschrift neuzubesetzen, weil gewisse Änderungen im Charakter der Zeitschrift vorgenommen werden sollen. Und in diesem Zusammenhang warf er die Frage auf, ob das nicht eine Sache für mich wäre.[136]

Weiskopf was very keen to return to Berlin and to take the job despite his and Bredel's reservations, expressed in scornful terms in other letters, about what *Sinn und Form* stood for.[137] Despite the recognition the Academy's all-German standing would be impaired, the SED leadership had pushed Becher to take over as Academy President from Zweig, and he was now adopting the energetic approach encouraged by Engel earlier that year. He made his acceptance of the Presidency conditional upon the election of a suitable successor as Secretary of the Literature Section. The person elected would do much of the work for the unbureaucratic Becher in the Section and the Presidium. The Presidium was the key committee, the membership of which comprised the secretaries of the four Sections as well as the President and Director. The immediate aim, achieved by the SED, was for all the positions in the Presidium to be occupied by SED figures. Friedrich Wolf turned down the job of Secretary to the Literature Section, so Becher turned to his ally at the Kulturbund, Alexander Abusch. Abusch, versed in conspirative work during exile, had been stripped of his post as Secretary of the Politburo in 1950 on suspicion of involvement with Noel Field. He was subjected to a thorough investigation by the SED, during which, on 30 May 1951, he was recruited by the Stasi as IM Ernst.[138] It can therefore be safely assumed that from May 1951 onwards Abusch was collaborating with the Stasi. By insisting on Abusch's election as Secretary, in the face of bitter opposition from Zweig, Becher helped Abusch back on his feet within institutional life. Yet Becher would live to rue the day, as in the months before his death in 1958 Becher, by then the Minister of Culture, was deceived by Abusch, his deputy, who stepped into the dying man's shoes.

Even the Cultural Department of the Central Committee had reservations about Abusch. Gustav Just wrote to Hans Lauter on 9 December 1952, 'Die Wahl des Genossen Abusch als Sekretär der Sektion hat manches für sich und manches gegen sich. Abusch wird sicher eine bestimmte Arbeit leisten, ob er aber versteht, alle Mitglieder der Sektion heranzuziehen, ist fraglich'.[139] In his mémoirs Abusch wrote of his period in office in the Academy, 'Es war zumindest keine schlechte Periode in der Entwicklung der Sektion'.[140] Yet archive materials demonstrate that Zweig's and Just's reservations were amply justified. Documents shed light, too, on the atmosphere of intimidation and repression that prevailed in the early 1950s, in which a figure like Abusch could wreak such havoc. In his eagerness to fulfil the task set him and his boss, Becher, by the SED, he recognised no limits and inflicted great damage on individuals as well as the fabric of the new institution. One of his victims was Huchel, another Eisler. In each case Brecht did his utmost to hold the line on behalf of artists and writers. It was pure chance that, whereas Brecht was finally able to help Huchel, he had not been able to save his friend Eisler from the worst. Such was the play of events in this turbulent period, culminating in the 17 June 1953, that in the disarray following that date, Brecht was able to help Huchel back from close to oblivion, while the attack on Eisler had, from Abusch's point-of-view, been successfully completed by 10 June, a time when Brecht's authority reached its lowest ebb.

Huchel cannot have been aware of the storm that was about to break around him when he attended his first Academy meeting, a Plenary Session, on 10 January 1953. Zweig, who was much more in the picture following the pressure brought to bear on him to make way for Becher, noted sardonically in his diary later that day, 'Um 2 (!) Akademie Sitzung. Als ich 1/4 3 komme, alles schon im Gang unter Bechers Vorsitz. Es wird eine Kartei-Betriebs-Akademie, aber wir müssen vorläufig den Krieg abwehren'.[141] Zweig had already had a hint of what was in store for *Sinn und Form* at the meeting of the Presidium on 9 December 1952, which he had chaired for the last time.[142] There he had described the journal as a 'beachtliche Leistung' of the Academy and surely expected Becher's agreement. Becher was after all the journal's co-founder and was known for his support of it. Yet on 9 December, Becher replied, 'Über letztere ist Herr Vizepräsident Becher anderer Ansicht, da sie s. M. nach immer mehr und mehr an literarischem Wert verliere ... Aber das sei nicht das Ausschlaggebende, vielmehr fehle der Akademie eine Leitung ... die ideologische Führung'. Becher stated quite bluntly that the journal's failure, like that of the Academy itself, was to be attributed to the absence of ideological leadership in the SED's sense. As Becher had already explained to Weiskopf, this was reason why changes had to be made. Evidence of literary failings could always be advanced to justify this action.

On 10 January, however, this assessment had not gone beyond the Presidium. At the Plenary Session, Huchel was very active.[143] He supported Becher's proposal that the forthcoming 95th birthday of Heinrich Zille should be marked by a publication in his honour. Yet his enthusiasm for the high fees for authors paid by the Sachsen-Verlag was not shared by Otto Nagel, who had worked with Zille and who pointed out that Zille's 'Sorge war immer: Kann Bruder Arbeiter das auch kaufen, – ich verzichte lieber auf einen Teil meines Honorars, aber das Buch muß billig sein. Diese Riesenhonorare sind also sehr schön für den, der diese Arbeit macht, aber nicht für den, der es nachher kaufen soll'. It was agreed that an inexpensive volume should be prepared. When discussion turned to the Academy's further response to the Federal Republic's signing of the General Treaty with the Western Allies, Huchel proposed that a declaration be sent to West German academies as well as others abroad with the request for their support in opposing the Treaty. He argued that any declaration should be couched in, as he put it, dignified terms, far removed from the language of politics. With Becher's encouragement, Huchel continued to demonstrate his grasp of cultural diplomacy by suggesting a delay until February in sending out the statement. When Becher moved on to the issue of West Berlin radio propaganda against the GDR, Huchel drew upon his experience in that medium to argue that Rias' 'Insulaner' could only be countered by East Berlin's production of a better cabaret. Though he did not spell out how this might be achieved, he did suggest that Radio Berlin should invite Berlin workers to the studio and record their responses to the abuse of proletarians perpetrated in the Rias series. Huchel pointed out that the very actors who had worked for Radio Berlin were now doing this work for Rias. He concluded, 'Ich bin wirklich ein humaner Mensch, aber hier kann man nur noch mit dem Revolver handeln, so widerlich sind jetzt diese Sendungen, die Herr Neumann macht'.

Only a matter of days later, on 15 January, the attack on *Sinn und Form* was launched in the Presidium. The minutes contain the following record,

Die Frage *Sinn und Form* steht schon sehr lange zur Debatte. Hier muß unbedingt eine Änderung herbeigeführt werden. Den letzten Anstoß gab der Fischer-Artikel über die Faust-Oper von Prof. Hanns Eisler. Herr Langhoff betrachtet den Artikel als eine unseren Bemühungen entgegengesetzte Arbeit. Als Hauptglied käme als Zentralfigur der Renegat d.h. die deutsche Misere der Intelligenz zum Ausdruck. Die Chefredaktion hätte vorhin überprüfen müssen, ob sie den Druck übernehmen kann. Herr Vizepräsident Dr Becher hat sich über die Umbesetzung der Chefredaktion schon lange Gedanken gemacht und schlägt vor, sobald Weiskopf nach Berlin kommt, ihm die Redaktion verantwortlich zu übertragen. Es steht somit die Frage der Umgestaltung der Zeitschrift *Sinn und Form* und ihre Erweiterung.[144]

It was in this way that Eisler's text and, above all, Fischer's essay were used as a pretext for getting rid of Huchel. The ideological correction of Eisler and Fischer was another job for Abusch, which was carried out in parallel to the campaign against *Sinn und Form*, in a series of Wednesday meetings (the 'Mittwoch-Gesellschaften') in the Academy in May and early June. He co-ordinated both campaigns through the Presidium and the Literature Section, and delivered the introductory speech attacking Eisler and Fischer at the first Wednesday meeting on 13 May. He presented lists of participants to the Presidium and thereby ensured a majority of speakers, led by Wilhelm Girnus, aginst the avant-gardist Eisler and his main supporter, Brecht. They were remorselessly pressurized and pushed further and further into a corner. The effect on Eisler, an SED member, was devastating. He left Berlin for Vienna and later that year wrote to the Central Committee, 'Nach der Faustus-Attacke merkte ich, daß mir jeder Impuls, Musik zu schreiben, abhanden gekommen war. So kam ich in einen Zustand tiefster Depression, wie ich sie kaum jemals erfahren habe'.[145]

Now that all key positions in the Academy were occupied by reliable SED figures, one would expect that the internal 'discussions' over *Sinn und Form* would be concluded in a satisfactory manner for the SED. Yet, despite careful planning and initial success in the execution of the campaign, quite improbably, the desired result eluded the party. The analysis of events reveals to what extent in early 1953, in the realm of culture as elsewhere, the SED overestimated its capacity to implement policies which demanded, simultaneously, rapid restructuring on socialist lines coupled with drastic savings targets.

The lavishly subsidised journal was subjected to rigorous financial scrutiny at the start of 1953. The editor's salary was a prime target. Engel wrote to Huchel on 13 January, informing him of the intention, 'Ihren Einzelvertrag im gegenseitigen Einvernehmen so zu ändern, daß Sie in Zukunft statt DM 2.000 -- monatlich den Betrag von DM 1.200 monatlich erhalten'.[146] The reduction was justified by reference to the monthly sinecure of just over 800 marks that Huchel now received as an Academy member and to the fact that his post as editor to some extent overlapped with his role as an Academy member. Taken together, in fact, Huchel's sinecure and salary made him the top earner among Academy employees, including Engel himself. As Engel's letter suggested, any change could only be undertaken with Huchel's agreement. He simply did not respond to Engel. His very inactivity illustrates the strength of Huchel's material position as a member of the GDR's privileged intelligentsia. Kantorowicz knew very well what he was talking about, when he later wrote of Huchel's situation,

Seinen westdeutschen Freunden, die ihm vorwarfen, daß er den Zwangsstaat nicht verlasse, ihm durch seine bloße Anwesenheit als Aushängeschild nütze, hätte er die Frage stellen können, wer einem Dichter, der im Jahr kaum mehr als zehn bis fünfzehn spröde Gedichte schrieb, der so gar nicht zum Tagesschreiber taugte und weder fähig noch willens war, sich dem antikommunistischen Racket zu verdingen, auf dieser Seite der Demarkationslinie mit Frau und Kindern ein sorgenfreies Leben ermöglichen würde.[147]

Yet the further point was, of course, that much was expected in return for the material privileges. In February, the Literature Section scrutinised the print-run and the number of free copies for the West. In April, the Finance Ministry informed the Academy that all subsidies for journals were being removed with immediate effect.

Meanwhile, on 21 January the journal was attacked in the Literature Section because of the Eisler/Fischer publications.[148] Friedrich Wolf led the attack, arguing that in many respects Eisler's work flew in the face of historical facts and failed to address some of the most important issues. On 20 March, Abusch's proposal was accepted that the first of the Wednesday meetings should be introduced by a number of pieces in *Sinn und Form*. Huchel was instructed to request contributions from Abusch himself, Langhoff, (another member of the Presidium) Wolf and Hans Mayer. In this way, a clear majority against Eisler/Fischer was guaranteed, and *Sinn und Form* would have the opportunity to engage in a little self-criticism. There is no evidence to suggest that Huchel acted upon Abusch's proposal.

Wolf continued the attack on the journal and its editor in a letter to Abusch dated 25 March, which he read out the following day at a Plenary Session.[149] He drew attention to the latest issue, the content of which in the form of Oskar Maria Graf's poems revealed 'einen schweren Mangel der Schriftleitung'. Wolf adjudged Graf's poem 'Und doch' to contain 'eine kosmopolitische Diktion in Reinkultur'. In 'Hymne an das Volk' he found 'Blu-Bo-Zeilen ... eine schändliche und feindliche Ideologie'. He described 'Die Empörung' as 'förmlich das "seelische" Fazit dieser dekadenten Seelenjodler'. He reserved his particular sense of outrage for the lines 'Einst hieß ich Kain, nun bin ich Neger aus dem Süden/ Und Jude oder Christ, der in dem anderen keinen Menschen sieht'. Wolf commented, 'Soviel mir erinnerlich ist, erschlug Kain seinen Bruder Abel. Also würde – falls die Sprache überhaupt noch einen Sinn hat – nach Grafs Diktion nicht Klukluxklan der Mörder der Neger sein, sondern der Neger = Kain den armen unschuldigen Klukluxklan erschlagen'. He asked, 'Ist es möglich, daß der Chefredakteur der Zeitschrift über all diesen uns feindlichen Sinn hinwegliest?' Wolf's view was that the journal was not operating at the level expected of it. He deemed the editorial staff 'politisch und künstlerisch für unfähig, die Zeitschrift *Sinn und Form* verantwortlich weiter zu redigieren'. He aligned himself with the Presidium in demanding that the whole matter should be dealt with. His letter concluded with his expression of profound mistrust of the editorial staff. At the Plenary Session, he warned that if the Academy did nothing, it, too, would be to blame, 'Die Ideologie der Zeitschrift *Sinn und Form* muß sauber und klar gehalten sein. Die Zeitschrift zeigt einen ganzen Komplex vieler Mängel auf'. He proposed three things to address the problem: firstly, the Literature Section, which was responsible for the journal, should convene a discussion to be attended by Wolf himself, Abusch, Brecht and Willi Bredel; secondly, the Academy needed to formulate its view on the Eisler/Fischer publication; and thirdly, the Academy should formulate its criticism of Graf's poetry.

Time was running short at the meeting, and Becher's proposal from the chair was adopted that Abusch should write an essay treating the fundamental issues, excluding the Graf poems, which should be treated separately. Thus, Abusch, and Abusch alone this time, was asked once again to write a piece for *Sinn und Form* on the Eisler/Fischer publication. It later emerged that the intention was to publish his essay 'im Namen der Redaktion'.[150]

Huchel himself can only have felt the deepest anger and humiliation at this attack sanctioned by Becher. Evidently, he was scarcely able to mount any defence, and such was the atmosphere that no one stood up to support him. That same day, Arnold Zweig noted in his diary, 'Plenarsitzung, wo Huchel von Wolf angegriffen wurde und sich schlecht verteidigte'.[151] The minutes of the meeting contain the following, 'Herr Huchel erklärt zu den Vorwürfen, nachdem er 4 Jahre verantwortlich die Redaktion der Zeitschrift *Sinn und Form* geleitet hat, daß er die Konzequenzen daraus ziehen müsse'.

This was the green light for Abusch. Although the Literature Section was supposed to continue the discussion about the journal's future in the group of four (Wolf, Brecht, Bredel and Abusch, with Abusch as the convenor), nothing happened until the end of June. Instead, in April and May, Huchel's removal was pushed through in the Presidium. He himself was sent to Moscow in May with a delegation from the Writers' Union. It must be said that his own later comment, 'Ich war ahnungslos abgereist', (ii,375) does not tally with the course of events. The Presidium used the government's savings plans as a means to strengthen Huchel in his apparent resolve to resign. Engel wrote to Huchel on 7 April, 'Wir sind nicht imstande, für die weitere Herausgabe von *Sinn und Form* irgend welche Mittel zur Verfügung zu stellen, bevor nicht eine grundsätzliche neue Regelung über die zuständigen Behörden erfolgt ist'.[152] This was the position represented in the Presidium on 8 April, when Weiskopf and Günter Caspar were discussed as possible successors.[153] It is quite grotesque that the meeting went on to agree to the belated celebration of Huchel's fiftieth birthday at the Academy. Equally grotesque was the instruction that a special issue of *Sinn und Form* should be prepared for Friedrich Wolf. Predictably enough, the issue never got off the ground. Becher sent Huchel the usual telegram with birthday greetings from the Academy and a collection of Dürer prints.[154] Huchel thanked Becher in a letter of 13 April, remarking that the Dürer volume was particularly welcome since he had lost all his books during the war, including all his Dürer.[155] Maybe Becher's present encouraged him to try and re-gain Becher's support. On 17 April he sent Becher a very positive review of *Sinn und Form* published in *De groene Amsterdamer* on 11 March.[156]

Meanwhile, Auer had prepared a document on *Sinn und Form* for discussion at the Presidium.[157] It contained a list of proposals and resolutions about the journal, with reference to the extent to which they had or had not been adopted. A further document for the Presidium was a second letter from Friedrich Wolf dated 12 April.[158] Wolf suggested that, given the government's need to make savings, the journal should become the almanac that had earlier been mooted. Huchel's opponents were, though, biding their time, waiting for him to go to Moscow before they continued their campaign against him. Shortly before his departure, the Stasi collected their first item of information about him, a reference from the Writers' Union written by its Secretary, Kuba. Kuba's evaluation was thoroughly positive, 'Er ist nicht nur ein hervorragender Lyriker, der die Probleme des Aufbaues unserer Landwirtschaft wirklich beherrscht, sondern setzt sich auch mit besonderem Nachdruck und mit Erfolg im Kampf um die Herstellung der Einheit Deutschlands ein'.[159] At the Presidium, it was agreed on 29 April,

> Die von Herrn Prof. Wolf vorgeschlagene Kommission, bestehend aus Herrn Abusch, Brecht, Bredel und Wolf, wird für die nächste Zeit von Herrn Abusch zusammengerufen, während die Diskussion mit Herrn Huchel als verantwortlichem Redakteur bis zu seiner Rückkehr aus der SU zurückgestellt werden muß.[160]

In this way, a clear distinction was made between the work of the commission, to which Huchel did not belong, and a discussion with him, which would take place after his return. On 9 May, however, Auer wrote to Brecht on Abusch's instructions concerning the commission's work,

> Er (Abusch – S.P.) hält es jedoch für zweckmäßig, die nächste Sektionssitzung, auf der über *Sinn und Form* diskutiert werden soll, erst Ende des Monats nach Rückkehr von Herrn Peter Huchel und den anderen Sektionsmitgliedern aus der Sowjetunion durchzuführen und hofft auf Ihr Einverständnis.[161]

Through putting Brecht off, Abusch saw to it that during Huchel's absence the Presidium was the only forum in which *Sinn und Form* was discussed. On 13 May, the day of the first Wednesday meeting, the crucial meeting of the Presidium took place at which the systematic attack on *Sinn und Form* was launched.[162] Six resolutions were passed which meant the end for the editor and for the journal in the form in which it had hitherto appeared. Engel and Abusch were given the responsibility for the implementation of the resolutions. The editorial staff were stripped of responsibility for the content: all material for publication had to be presented to the Presidium for counter-signing. Huchel was sacked from the earliest possible date permitted by his contract, 30 November 1953. (Contracts did apparently mean something at that time in the GDR!) Four issues were scheduled to appear before then. They were to appear as double issues. In this way, costs could be reduced and the editorial staff could be controlled more easily. The first double issue was to appear at the end of June and contain the text by Becher and the music by Ernst Hermann Meyer, which had been written to celebrate Ulbricht's sixtieth birthday. This occasion would set the tone for the whole issue. It also had to include Anna Seghers' words spoken in memory of the poet Erich Weinert, who had recently died. A substantial essay on Weinert would appear later. The instructions relating to Weinert are surely to be understood against the background of the recent publication in *Sinn und Form* of the Weinert article by the then Polish Marxist Marceli Ranicki, better known nowadays as Germany's most celebrated literary critic and media performer, Marcel Reich-Ranicki. Becher was angered by Ranicki's unflattering comparison of his Expressionist poetry with Weinert's early verse in passages such as the following,

> Man darf daran erinnern, daß fast sämtliche Gedichte Bechers, die aus jener Zeit stammen, heute schon in Vergessenheit geraten sind. Doch auch damals, als sie entstanden, waren sie, obwohl sie den Hoffnungen der deutschen Arbeiterklasse Ausdruck verliehen – für den Durchschnittsleser nicht verständlich.[163]

It is not difficult to see Huchel's publication of Ranicki's Weinert article as an act of revenge against Becher. The same number contained statements by members of the Literature Section on Stalin's death, on 5 March 1953. Huchel's brief statement, in keeping with the general tone, reads,

> Stalin hat seine Gedanken verwirklicht und damit den Anbruch einer neuen Epoche: der Mensch, frei von Hunger und Ausbeutung, wird endlich sichtbar. Das ist sein Vermächtnis, das bis in die fernsten Tage Zeugnis ablegen wird für die Größe seines Gewissens, für die Größe seines Genies.[164]

The fifth resolution passed on 13 May was that negotiations should begin with the Finance Ministry in order to secure the subsidies required to prosecute the publication plans. Needless to say, the subsidies were readily forthcoming. The final resolution was that *Sinn und Form* should become a journal not just of the Literature Section but of the whole Academy. Abusch was primarily responsible for the implementation of this resolution and for collaboration with the editorial staff. He thus effectively had the journal under his control. On 15 May, the resolutions were communicated to the editorial staff and the publisher.[165] On the same day, Engel sent Huchel his dismissal letter.[166] In it, Engel requested that Huchel should attend a meeting of the Presidium immediately after his return from Moscow. The following day, Engel sent Wandel a report on progress to date.[167]

For all the resolutions and the forthcoming essay by Abusch, one ingredient was still missing before the campaign could be deemed a real success: a public display of self-criticism by the editor. While Huchel was still in the Soviet Union, his wife, the senior member of the editorial staff, was summoned to the Academy. She writes,

> Becher ... reichte mir einen Text, unter den Peter Huchels Name gesetzt war. Es war eine Selbstbezichtigung, in der sich Huchel schwerer künstlerischer und ideologischer Verfehlungen schuldig bekannte. Ich sagte: 'Nach dem zweiten Satz weiß doch jeder, daß Peter Huchel so etwas nie geschrieben haben würde'. Da sprang Becher auf und schrie: 'Ich habe es dir ja gleich gesagt, das macht die nicht!' Erst jetzt sah ich in dem großen dunklen Büro Alexander Abusch sitzen, und es wurde mir in diesem Augenblick klar, daß Abusch der Verfasser dieses Textes war.[168]

Unfortunately, it has not proved possible to trace this text, which on 2 July Huchel would describe as the 'unmöglichen Vorspann' to Abusch's essay.[169]

Shortly afterwards, a second opportunity for Huchel to engage in self-criticism presented itself. The Hamburg writer Herbert Lestiboudois, whom Huchel had met in Hamburg in 1951 and who enjoyed close contacts with the Writers' Union as well as with Abusch, whose guest he had been in November 1951, sent an open letter to Huchel via the editorial office of the Writers' Union's new journal, *Neue Deutsche Literatur*. Bredel had been instrumental in setting up the journal, which he regarded quite explicitly as a counterweight to *Sinn und Form*.[170] In his open letter, Lestiboudois took issue with Huchel's 'Mahnung an die Schriftsteller', his follow-up piece to the Starnberg meeting, in which he sought to consolidate what had been achieved there. Lestiboudois replied that

> Der Weg der Deutschen Demokratischen Republik insofern richtiger und erfolgreicher auch [war], als dort eben durch Menschen mit einem starken politischen Bewußtsein politische *Tatsachen* geschaffen wurden, die auch den geistigen Menschen, den Schriftsteller zu *seinem Glück zwangen*, ein politisches Bewußtsein in sich zu entwickeln.[171]

Günther Cwojdrak, an editor at *Neue Deutsche Literatur*, encouraged Huchel to produce an appropriate answer in a letter of 22 May, writing, 'Ich denke, daß im

Prinzip an den Ausführungen Lestiboudois vieles richtig ist, bei einer gewissen sektierenden Neigung allerdings, zu der man vermutlich ein paar Worte sagen müßte'.[172] In the event, Huchel sent off his reply only on 6 August, by which time his situation had radically improved and he was strong enough to adopt a position broadly in line with his speech the previous year to the 'Groß-Berliner Komitee der Kulturschaffenden'.[173]

In the meantime, the double issue was being prepared as instructed in Huchel's absence. He returned on 2 June from a trip which had taken him as far north as Leningrad and Rasliv, as far south as Stalingrad and Tbilisi.[174] On 8 June, a letter was sent by Monica Huchel to Becher's office, reminding him that the manuscript for the Ulbricht cantata would have to be in the editors' hands by 13 June, otherwise the journal could not appear on 30 June, as agreed.[175] As instructed in the dismissal letter, Huchel attended a meeting of the Presidium on 10 June.[176] There he was obliged to give his assent to his dismissal and signal his willingness to produce the remaining issues on the terms laid down. Understandably, he did not later mention this dimension of his treatment, preferring with hindsight to stress his ability to determine the situation, 'Als ich aus Moskau zurückkam, war ich entschlossen, die Chefredaktion unter solchen Umständen niederzulegen'. (ii,375) On another occasion, he spoke of his intention at that time 'mich anderen Aufgaben – auf Grund bestimmter Angebote aus dem Ausland – zu[zu]wenden'. (ii,326) What these offers were, he did not specify. One is bound to add, nor could he have, if pressed. He was, in fact, only in a position to determine his own fate from the beginning of July.

Certainly, on 10 June he had no choice in the matter. At that same meeting, Becher's view was accepted that now was the time to convene the group from the Literature Section. It should formulate proposals for the restructuring of the journal for presentation to the Presidium. Huchel had never been seen as part of that group and would therefore have no part to play in its discussions.[177]

Later that month, on 26 June, Abusch reported that the group had been due to meet on 18 June but – in Abusch's words – 'da hatten wir andere Sorgen'.[178] The uprising of 17 June and the profound shock it triggered in the East Berlin political establishment undoubtedly worked decisively in Huchel's favour. Curiously, he himself never made the link in public statements. Instead, he always drew attention to the role played by Brecht, who, according to Huchel, 'intervened' while he was still in Moscow. On another occasion, he explained, 'Brecht, der von diesen Manipulationen hörte, erhob Einspruch und erwirkte, daß es nicht zu einer Umbesetzung der Redaktion kam. Nach meiner Rückkehr aus Moskau sagte ich zu Brecht, ich wolle die Chefredaktion dennoch niederlegen'. (ii,326) Yet there is no evidence whatsoever that the dismissal was rescinded before 17 June. The sequence of events was quite different from what Huchel later suggested.

Until that point in time, Abusch was conspicuously successful. At the final Wednesday Meeting of 10 June, Brecht and Eisler generally remained on the defensive, though there were already signs that they could exploit the New Course agreed between East Berlin and Moscow. Abusch was undoubtedly aware that ideological control in the Academy could only be secured if Brecht, its most gifted personality, could be persuaded of its necessity. Brecht, the non-SED Marxist, was already under extreme pressure from the SED because of his allegedly 'formalist' approach to the theatre, most recently with regard to his interpretation of *Urfaust* and at the Academy's Stanislavsky Conference, which had been staged as an anti-Brecht event. The objections to his *Urfaust* were similar to those voiced over Eisler/Fischer. In mid-1953 in the Academy, the ideological conflict came to a head. In the fierce arguments of that summer, Abusch was the most vociferous and insistent proponent of the dogmatists' position, while Brecht was the most tenacious defender of artists' interests. At first, it looked as if Abusch would prevail, but Brecht managed to turn the huge shock triggered by the 17 June to his own advantage and that of his fellow artists and intellectuals. That, at least, was the immediate outcome within the confines of the Academy, whilst outside Brecht pledged his support to Ulbricht. The bigger drama was being played out in Moscow. It led to Beria'a arrest, which would save Ulbricht's skin and this, in turn, would in time play into the hands of Abusch and other dogmatists.

Academy members met in emergency session on 17 and 18 June.[179] On 17 June, Abusch and Engel proposed presenting a statement as a declaration of loyalty to the government and as a contribution to the re-establishment of order. However, Brecht's counter-proposal was accepted that such a statement could only be made once the government itself had spoken. In the circumstances, individual members might voice their support through work on the radio and similar activity. Furthermore, Academy members should apply themselves to the question of the 'Neugestaltung des Kulturlebens' in keeping with the New Course. Brecht was immediately alive to opportunities that the crisis presented to roll back some of the repressive apparatus that had been applied against the GDR cultural élite, though he was, on the other hand, at pains to stress his loyalty to the SED in the context of the German-German division. On 18 June, Brecht was elected to a group which met on 20 June to discuss the question 'Was muß in der Kulturpolitik geändert oder positiv entwickelt werden?' Other members of the group were Becher, Eisler, Felsenstein, Langhoff, Nagel, Fritz Cremer and Ernst Hermann Meyer, who was included despite Brecht's opposition. Huchel himself was not present at these meetings. Brecht was instrumental in the formulation of the eight 'Vorschläge der Deutschen Akademie der Künste', which went forward to the government and were later published in *Sinn und Form*. Among other things, the proposals aimed at the abolition of the State Commission for the Arts, in effect a censor's office, where Girnus and Helmut Holtzhauer ruled the roost. The Commission was duly disbanded.

The proposals were presented to a Plenary Session of the Academy on 26 June.[180] Again, Huchel stayed away. He would appear in the Academy for a further Plenary Session on 30 June, at which the Academy's proposals for the government

were again discussed. During the discussion of the proposals on 26 June, Wolf
broached the subject of *Sinn und Form*, evidently believing that it was now simply
a matter of proceeding with the restructuring of the journal. He rehearsed his idea
of turning it into an almanac, having once again drawn attention to the supposed
failings of the editorial staff. This time, however, he encountered much stiffer
opposition. Hanns Eisler spoke against him, saying,

> Ich glaube, *Sinn und Form* war trotz all der Schwächen, die sie hatte, eine ganz
> hervorrgende Publikation der Akademie. Ich weiß von meinen Freunden in Westdeutsch-
> land und auch in Österreich, daß es die einzige Zeitschrift aus der DDR ist, die –
> allerdings in sehr begrenzten Kreisen – drüben ankommt. Ich glaube allerdings auch, daß
> die Arbeit von *Sinn und Form* verbessert werden muß, und zwar daß sie etwas aktualisiert
> werden muß. Das könnte am besten dadurch geschehen, daß man den sehr tüchtigen
> Huchel nicht überfährt, sondern ihn läßt und ihm durch ein Redaktionskollegium auf die
> Beine hilft.

For Eisler, then, *Sinn und Form* was one of those aspects of GDR cultural life that
should be developed in a positive manner. Ihering supported Eisler, whereupon
Becher intervened from the Chair. Turning demonstratively to Brecht, with whom
he had now presumably discussed the matter, he said, 'Wir haben eine Kommission
gewählt, die sich ernsthaft mit *Sinn und Form* beschäftigen soll. Stimmt das,
Brecht?' Brecht replied, 'Nein, die Kommission ist leider nicht zustande gekommen'. Brecht ignored Abusch's protests and took issue with Wolf. He contrasted the
things criticised by Wolf with three years' worth of publications and the, in the
circumstances, huge success of the journal in the West. The emphasis on the West
in statements by both Eisler and Brecht was, of course, quite deliberate, signalling
as it did their commitment to the all-German policy that the SED had been prepared
to jettison from mid-1952 onwards. Brecht returned to Abusch, whose name he had
underlined twice in a memo beneath 'Huchel' and 'Academy'.[181] He took up where
Eisler had left off, saying,

> Ich bin selbstverständlich auch absolut dafür, daß man diese Zeitschrift unter allen
> Umständen verbessert. Ich bin auch dafür, daß man Huchel dabei Hilfe angedeihen läßt.
> Darüber, wie man das macht, kann man sprechen, aber jedenfalls nicht eine solche Hilfe,
> wie sie ihm im letzten Heft durch Abusch geworden ist. Dagegen bin ich absolut. Da ist
> folgendes passiert: Wir hatten hier eine sehr anständige Diskussion über den *Faustus*,
> wobei sich zwei diametral entgegengesetzte Meinungen zeigten. Es wurde eigentlich sehr
> fair diskutiert. Daraufhin sollte das nächste Heft, das Abusch zu leiten, zu überwachen
> hatte, wie wir, glaube ich, bestimmt hatten, ausschließlich einen Artikel gerade von

Abusch enthalten, aber – so wurde mir mitgeteilt, vielleicht können Sie mich korrigieren – noch nicht einmal z.B. die Gegenthesen. Das fing also ganz hübsch an mit einer sehr eigentümlichen Art und Weise, hier Einfluß zu gewinnen.

Brecht added that the group, with its original or new membership, was the appropriate forum for a discussion about *Sinn und Form*. Becher, no longer constrained by the party discipline of the previous months, changed sides. He said,

Ich möchte prinzipiell etwas sagen. Wir dürfen jetzt nicht in die Richtung hineinkommen, daß der arme Huchel keine Fehler machen darf, während die anderen es dürfen, – wobei ich sofort Selbstkritik übe: wir haben Huchel mit Beiträgen, Anregungen usw. scheußlich im Stich gelassen.

This was decisive for the future course of the argument. Abusch, though, did not give up easily. He countered, 'Lieber Brecht, es tut mir sehr leid, daß Sie erstens ein sehr schlechtes Gedächtnis haben und sich zweitens von irgendjemand irgend etwas zutragen lassen, was der Wahrheit diametral entgegengesetzt ist'. But Abusch's own memory was not so reliable, even though he referred back to the minutes of meetings such as that of the Literature Section on 20 March. He said, 'Auf meinen Vorschlag wurde beschlossen, daß Brecht, Ihering, Langhoff, Rilla, Abusch und noch ein Sechster – so daß also verschiedene Meinungen zu Worte kommen – aufgefordert werden sollen, zu dem *Faustus* Stellung zu nehmen'. There had been no mention of Brecht, Rilla and Ihering at that meeting, only of the quite different grouping of Abusch, Langhoff, Wolf and Hans Mayer. Abusch now said the following about Becher's later request that he alone should write an essay dealing with fundamental issues,

Als die Rede von den Beiträgen war, die keiner der Aufgeforderten gechrieben hatte, [machte Becher] den Vorschlag, ich sollte einen Artikel im Namen der Redaktion schreiben... Das wurde zwischen Tür und Angel in der Weise gemacht, daß man mich überhaupt nicht fragte, ob ich einen solchen Artikel schreiben wollte. Ich habe danach erklärt, ich arbeitete bereits an einem Artikel und sei bereit, diesen Artikel zu schreiben, aber nicht im Namen der Redaktion – denn ich bin weder die Redaktion von *Sinn und Form* noch die Redaktion von *Aufbau* oder von irgendetwas anderem – und ich sei bereit, diesen Artikel in *Sinn und Form* zu veröffentlichen.

He returned to the question of the other contributions to the *Faustus* discussion. Huchel had informed him on 24 June that Brecht wished to publish his counter-arguments alongside Abusch's essay. Abusch had answered, 'Das ist nichts anderes, als wir damals vorgeschlagen haben'. In his memoirs, Abusch places this episode in the context of the Wednesday meetings. As ever, he does little to play down his key, mediating role in events, though the forced simplicity of his style betrays him,

> Am Ende des Abends fragte mich Brecht: 'Wie geht es nun weiter?' Ich sagte ihm: 'Wir drucken in *Sinn und Form* Ihre Thesen im Anschluß an meinen Aufsatz. Dann haben die Leser der Zeitschrift beides. Sind Sie einverstanden damit?' Brecht und Becher und auch Peter Huchel waren damit einverstanden. So geschah es dann in Heft 3/4 des Jahrganges 1953 von *Sinn und Form*.[182]

At the Plenary Session Abusch went on to hold the absent Huchel responsible for the fact that the third number of the journal had not appeared on time, that is to say for the first Wednesday meeting. Abusch blamed its non-appearance on Huchel's absence in the Soviet Union, even though it was the result of the Presidium's resolution to combine issues three and four. He then went on the attack himself, arguing that the vibrant relationship that should exist between the journal and its parent institution was missing. He found it outrageous that the editorial office was 'irgendwo in einem Dorf weit hinter Potsdam'. He proposed discussion of two points, which in any case many Academy members, including Brecht, wanted to have talked about: the fact that the journal was felt by some not to represent the GDR sufficiently and that it did not reflect adequately the work done in the Academy. Abusch was at his most abysmal, though, in his statement,

> Ich wollte keine Diskussion in Abwesenheit von Huchel führen. Deshalb ist die Kommission, die Wolf vorschlug, nicht zustandegekommen. Wolf schlug eine Kommission vor, und ich sagte, eine Diskussion über *Sinn und Form* kann nur stattfinden in Gegenwart von Huchel, wenn Huchel die volle Möglichkeit hat, sich zu den Dingen zu äußern, daß wir die Probleme und auch die positiven Vorschläge für eine eventuelle Neugestaltung von *Sinn und Form* wirklich diskutieren können.

In reality, of course, Abusch had prosecuted Huchel's removal through the Presidium, so that later he would have a free hand to pursue the restructuring of the journal in the grouping chosen by the Literature Section. As we have seen, there would have been no place for Huchel in these discussions. Now, however, Abusch immediately agreed with Wolf's call to include Huchel in any discussions about the journal's future. He was duly elected to the freshly constituted grouping. The balance of its membership indicates the wish to find an approach supportive of the present editor, whilst keeping alive the idea of extending the remit of the journal to include the whole spectrum of the Academy's activities. Max Schwimmer, Paul Dessau and Ihering joined the group, and Arnold Zweig agreed to chair its first meeting, which took place on 2 July. Eisler also attended.

Abusch and Wolf were now in a clear minority against Brecht and his allies, principally Eisler, Dessau, Ihering and Huchel. Brecht was now fully in the picture about Abusch's scheming. Huchel was surely referring to this meeting when, later, he said, 'Während einer peinlichen Sitzung kam es zu einem schweren Zusammenstoß zwischen Brecht und Abusch. Nie zuvor hatte ich Brecht so aufgeregt gesehen – die handgreiflichen Einzelheiten möchte ich auch heute nicht schildern'. (ii,375) Zweig noted in his diary that day, 'Ab ½3 Sitzungen (sic) des Ausschusses für *Sinn und Form*. Heftige Auftritte von Huchel, Brecht gegen Abusch. Meine Leitung erfolgreich: bis Ende des Jahres bleibt alles'.[183]

Two versions of the minutes of this meeting exist: a quite full record of statements by individuals, and what is manifestly a later version, which summarises their views in a decidedly sober tone.[184] Yet even the later version bears the following hand-written note, 'Vom St. Sekretär genehmigt. Auf Wunsch v. Hrn. Abusch nicht verschickt'. Given the content, this wish is quite understandable.

The first version makes clear that at the start of the meeting Huchel attacked the measures taken by the Presidium against *Sinn und Form*, but that, especially, he attacked Abusch personally. He found the restrictions placed on the editorial staff outrageous, as he did the preamble to Abusch's essay, which had been written in the name of the editorial staff but which 'inzwischen rückgängig gemacht worden ist'. He attacked Abusch for instructing that his essay should be placed in the journal at the same point as Eisler's own piece. Monica Huchel had evidently wanted to put it at the back! In the event, it appeared in a quite prominent position, followed by Brecht's counter-arguments.

Zweig sought to pursue two basic questions. How could *Sinn und Form* be restructured? And how could Huchel be kept on to work on the journal? Despite Abusch's opposition, Zweig argued successfully that until the end of the year *Sinn und Form* should continue to appear as usual. There was no more talk about Huchel's dismissal. Brecht stressed that 'die alten rechtlichen Verhältnisse wieder gelten, daß die *Redaktion* wieder voll für die Zeitschrift verantwortlich ist'. But Huchel seemed in no way convinced that he should continue. He stressed that 'er es leichter habe, wenn er nicht mehr der Chefredakteur sei'.

Brecht then mounted a savage attack on the Presidium. He found it outrageous that the editor's responsibility should have been taken away from him during his absence. He doubted whether the Presidium in its actions had reflected the wishes of the Academy's membership. Therefore,

wird Brecht dem Plenum vorschlagen, daß außer dem Präsidenten sämtliche Ständigen Sekretäre nochmals zur Wahl gestellt werden. Er wird auch begründen, warum er eine

Neuwahl der Sekretäre für erforderlich hält. Die Zusammensetzung des Präsidiums entspricht nicht den Erfordernissen der gegenwärtigen Situation. Wir brauchen hier jemand, der das Vertrauen der gesamten Sektion besitzt. Auch die Wahl des Vizepräsidenten muß nachgeholt werden!

He could not have put it more clearly. He galvanised others, including Huchel, who could now scarcely walk away after Brecht's massive show of support. Huchel later reported, 'Brecht bestimmte mich, weiterhin Chefredakteur zu bleiben. Er sagte: Sie müssen Ihren Laden verteidigen, genauso wie ich meinen Laden verteidige. Das Berliner Ensemble und *Sinn und Form* sind die beste Visitenkarte der DDR'. (ii,327) As we have seen, in March he had not been able to defend himself, nor, indeed, had Brecht supported him. Huchel now made good his earlier capitulation by demanding a discussion about the 'verlesene kritische Stellungnahme Friedrich Wolfs gegen *Sinn und Form* und gegen Huchel persönlich'. In Abusch's view, Wolf had attempted, with the best possible intentions, to resolve conflicts that had arisen around *Sinn und Form*. Huchel then took up Wolf's proposal of an editorial collective. Brecht, however, argued against, adding his own criticism of *Sinn und Form* with the following words, 'Wir brauchen Beiträge, die die großen historischen Errungenschaften der DDR beschreiben, so daß die Leute in Westdeutschland und in der DDR sie wirklich als sachlich aufnehmen und verstehen können. Die Fakten sind überwältigend'.

In saying this, Brecht was demonstrating the strict limits to any critique of SED rule that he was prepared to countenance in the light of the 17 June. He was alluding, too, to the proposals that he had made a year earlier – which Huchel had not acted upon – for publications in the journal of reportage dealing with cultural and economic developments in the GDR. Brecht added pointedly, 'Wenn Huchel dazu ein Kollektiv braucht, dann soll er selbst eins wählen und über diese Vorschläge mit der Akademie sprechen'. However improbably, Wolf now supported Brecht, and Huchel adopted a more conciliatory tone. He referred to Wolf's help in mediating what he described as an important recent publication by Smirin. He excused himself for speaking so long and for his 'allzu heftig geäußerten Vorwurf' directed against Abusch. Wolf repeated his suggestion that an almanac should replace *Sinn und Form*, but no one was really interested in this idea anymore. Suddenly, Abusch was transformed into a visionary and partisan of the all-German path, recently re-affirmed in the New Course. Abusch enthused, 'Für *Sinn und Form* kann es, auf Grund der internationalen Entspannungen und der Aussicht auf die Einigung Deutschlands, ungeahnte Möglichkeiten geben'. Huchel declared his willingness to remain as editor until the end of the year and he was asked to prepare the next two issues. The meeting ended in blissful harmony. It was agreed that the group would re-convene in September, after the summer break.

The Academy leadership accommodated itself to the new situation. On 11 July Engel wrote to the publisher, 'Für die Fertigstellung des neuen Heftes bitten wir, davon Kenntnis zu nehmen, daß Herr Huchel für die Redaktion voll inhaltlich verantwortlich ist. Unsere Anweisung im Schreiben vom 15. Mai 1953 wird damit aufgehoben'.[185] There was no mention of Ulbricht's birthday in the double issue now that Abusch's hand had been removed, nor was there room for the cantata composed by Becher to Meyer's music.[186] Huchel included Hans Mayer's essay on Richard Wagner, which Abusch had thrown out. The latter would not forget this and the treatment of Ulbricht. Huchel also included Brecht's reply to Abusch's essay as well as the Academy's eight proposals to the government. Issues five and six appeared individually.

For all the conciliatory tone finally adopted at the meeting presided over by Zweig, Huchel saw no reason yet to forgive and forget Engel's role, especially since Engel had not yet revoked the dismissal notice in writing. On 21 July Huchel was approached by the Academy with the request that he should formulate the statements supporting the award of the National Prize to four non-GDR writers, Thomas Mann, Lion Feuchtwanger, Leonhard Frank and Reinhold Schneider.[187] Huchel declined to undertake such work as long as the views about his literary judgment recently expressed by Engel, Abusch, Becher and Wolf continued to enjoy currency. None the less, on 31 July, Huchel felt sufficiently safe again to make allusions to the intrigues against him in a letter to Günter Caspar, who had asked him for a poem for an anniversary issue of *Aufbau*. Huchel told him that he had long had in mind a poem about Lenin in Rasliv. He probably had no idea that Caspar was one of the figures who had been lined up to replace him.[188]

After the summer break, the Literature Section's group met again on 29 September to consider the journal's future.[189] The group was well enough disposed towards Huchel but was aware of the need to move the discussion on. The issues from early 1952 remained on the agenda. These included the need for a 'thematische Erweiterung, Bereicherung und Belebung'. The journal should publish contributions dealing with fundamental issues in aesthetics relating to all the arts. It should also publish the Academy's debates about aesthetic and artistic matters as well as about cultural politics. There was a need to include work by young GDR intellectuals and to find space for discussion of the GDR's cultural achievements, such as the opening up of secondary and higher education to all. Following Brecht's lead, the task was identified 'eines offensiven Kampfes gegen die in Westdeutschland zu beobachtende kulturfeindliche Entwicklung, gegen die Militarisierung und Entmenschlichung des Geisteslebens'. A properly constituted advisory board was founded, including two representatives from the Literature Section and one each from the other Sections. Room 106 in the main Academy building would be reserved for regular consultations with the editorial staff.

The very next day, 30 September, Huchel wrote to Engel by registered letter. He argued, 'Nach dem Ergebnis der letzten Kommissionssitzung ist wohl anzunehmen, daß Sie nunmehr auch die Kündigung vom 15. Mai 1953 schriftlich zurücknehmen werden'.[190] Engel passed the letter on to Becher and Abusch, asking for their advice. On 14 October, it was agreed at the Presidium that 'Nachdem sein Einzelvertrag mit dem 30.11.1953 abläuft, wird ihm von diesem Zeitpunkt ab ein Vertrag als Chefredakteur in Höhe von 1,200 - monatlich angeboten. Aussprache darüber in der nächsten Präsidiumssitzung am 21. 10. 1953 in Anwesenheit von Herrn Huchel'.[191] The offer from the start of the year was back on the table. Yet the Presidium was now not sufficiently strong to push this through. Huchel declared his opposition to the proposal at the meeting. What was more, 'Auch eine sofortige Zustimmung für eine Vergütung von DM 1,500 -- konnte Herr Huchel nicht geben, sondern bat sich Bedenkzeit aus'. Engel put the offer in writing on 29 October.[192] Huchel, though, held out until the beginning of 1954, when Becher agreed to 1,750 marks for Huchel and a rise of 250 marks for his wife! Engel and Huchel signed the new contract on 4 January 1954.[193]

Becher's mind was by now, in any case, on other matters. One of the outcomes of the debates after 17 June was the founding of the Ministry of Culture. Becher was named Minister, and once more he took Abusch with him to set things up. They both gave up their duties at the Academy in late 1953. Such was the disarray in the SED's cultural politics that no plans were laid for the succession in the Academy. Far from being the instrument to implement SED policy, the Presidium was now scarcely capable of functioning at all. The pressure to which Huchel had been exposed now virtually disappeared, and he was left more or less to his own devices. In keeping with his own interests and strengths, he felt that *Sinn und Form* had to remain primarily a literary journal. Any extension of the journal's remit would have required the appointment of a second editor alongside Huchel. This, in turn, would have meant a diminution of Huchel's control over a venture which, as we have seen, he ran almost as a family business far away from the Academy in Wilhelmshorst. It can be safely assumed that Huchel himself did nothing to promote the extension of the journal's brief or, for that matter, to give it the more agitatory profile that Brecht periodically called for. Huchel would certainly have viewed this as offending against *Sinn und Form*'s all-German mission. In later years, he would not be forgiven for this, following the abandonment of the all-German policy.

For those who knew his poetry well, he gave a clear signal of withdrawal from the affirmative position that can be traced through his verse published in *Sinn und Form* and elsewhere in the early 1950s. The fifth issue of 1953 contained at its mid-point his poem 'Eine Herbstnacht', which signalled a reversion to the voice of the early 1930s, in search of the self through the rural childhood. It opens with the lines,

Wo bist du, damals sinkender Tag?

Septemberhügel, auf dem ich lag

Im jähen blätterstürzenden Wind,

Doch ganz von der Ruhe der Bäume umschlungen.

Huchel found his way back in this poem, as in others published in the mid-1950s such as 'Damals', 'Widmung: Für Hans Henny Jahnn' and 'Caputher Heuweg', to a contemplative, visionary, poetic attitude, in which he shows himself to have more in common with Mörike than with any of his GDR peers. During the mid-1950s, three poetic strands co-existed uncomfortably in Huchel's publications. Only with the publication of *Chausseen Chausseen* in 1963 did Huchel begin to move towards the resolution of his artistic dilemmas in the 1950s. Yet, as we shall see, there were limits to what he could achieve by that stage.

After the traumatic break with Becher, it was Brecht who in the years until his untimely death in August 1956 would be *Sinn und Form*'s most influential protector. During these years, he also occupied a prominent role in the Academy as Vice-President. After Brecht had stood up in the Academy for the artists and intellectuals against SED dogmatists of Abusch's stamp, whilst simultaneously professing his support for the SED leadership, the Academy and its journal enjoyed a period relatively free of SED interference in the period until the autumn of 1956, though it was not so much a 'thaw' as a policy vacuum that shaped the atmosphere until 1956. Following the Hungarian Uprising, the dogmatists would again have their day. Yet as we shall see, the particular circumstances that obtained in the Academy, most notably the absence from 1957 until 1961 of a Director to act as a conduit for SED policy and the presence from 1956 until 1962 of a President, Otto Nagel, who had little interest in such matters, meant that, most improbably in the 'totalitarian' state, the day of reckoning was deferred for a whole decade after the débacle of 1953.

Cultural Diplomacy without the Dogmatists:
The Creation of the *Sinn und Form* Legend

Courting Thomas Mann: the Definitive Break with Kantorowicz

As things settled down after the high drama of 1953, Huchel returned to the business of editing his journal. He remained mindful of his role as a cultural diplomat, mediating between East and West. As ever, his efforts were channelled principally through *Sinn und Form*. He remained loyal and conscientious despite the gulf that had opened up between him and prominent figures in the Academy. The Academy, as we have seen, was no longer capable of functioning as an instrument of SED cultural policy, which had in any case suffered a severe setback. Huchel was able to go about his business now with little interference from the Academy and the SED. It was in the years from 1954 to 1956 that the journal came to bear his unmistakable stamp. In the mid-1950s, he made himself and *Sinn und Form* into an all-German institution virtually independent of the Academy at a time when, ironically enough and much to Ulbricht's relief, the all-German policy was abandoned by the Soviet Union and hence by the SED. The abandonment of that policy meant that the days of the *Sinn und Form* project as it had been originally conceived were necessarily numbered. For the political class, there remained only rhetorical posturings over the German Question, which had in practice been 'solved' for the foreseeable future by division.

By mid-1953, Huchel was well aware of the redoubling of efforts, spearheaded by Becher, to secure Thomas Mann's blessing for the GDR. Huchel was, we recall, the Academy member who had been approached to write the supporting statement for the award to Mann of the GDR National Prize. Mann had remained conspicuously neutral on the German Question from his home in Switzerland. Plans were being laid at the Aufbau Verlag for a collected edition of Mann's works, to be edited by Hans Mayer, which would be ready for Mann's 80th birthday on 6 June 1955. That was achieved as planned, but, despite the fact that Mann travelled to Weimar in 1955 to deliver the same speech on Schiller's 150th birthday that he had just delivered in Stuttgart, Mann denied the GDR the propaganda coup which it craved when he declined the award of the National Prize.

In the autumn of 1953, Huchel played his part in the courting of Mann. On 20 September 1953, he requested Mann's permission to reproduce a lecture on Tolstoy that Mann had delivered to students at Princeton in 1939. Huchel engaged in quite shameless flattery, assuring Mann that during his recent trip to the Soviet Union 'Ihr Name den ersten Platz einnimmt, wenn von der zeitgenössischen deutschen Literatur gesprochen wird'. He informed Mann that it was not only Moscow intellectuals who enthused about him, adding that 'Ihr Name auch in den breitesten Schichten des sowjetischen Volkes lebendig ist'. He cited the example of 'ein etwa fünfzigjähriger

Maschinist' on a boat on the river Don, who exclaimed, 'Thomas Mann sehr großer Schriftsteller!'[1] In a letter of 4 October, Mann granted permission for the text of the Princeton lecture to be re-printed, and this duly happened in the fifth issue of 1953, which was dedicated to the celebration of Tolstoy's 125th birthday.[2]

Clearly, Huchel was not going to do anything which would damage the GDR's relations with the younger Mann brother. However, on 13 November Kantorowicz, head of the Heinrich Mann Archive, submitted his study, 'Der Zola-Essay als Brennpunkt der weltanschaulichen Beziehungen zwischen Heinrich und Thomas Mann'. For a figure on the Left like Kantorowicz, Heinrich Mann's political stance at the outbreak of the First World War could only be much more sympathetic than Thomas' nationalist attitudes, from which he had, of course, long since distanced himself. From Huchel's point-of-view, it would clearly be unhelpful for *Sinn und Form*, the GDR's most prestigious literary journal that was regularly dispatched to Mann, to be seen to be reminding the world of things that both Thomas Mann and the GDR had no interest in resurrecting. In a letter to Kantorowicz of 27 November 1953, Huchel explained that he feared that Mann's feelings might be hurt by the publication of the material.[3] He suggested that together they should try to find a more acceptable form for the study. It emerges from the letter, however, that by this stage Kantorowicz deeply mistrusted Huchel's motives. In his later account of the episode, Kantorowicz treats the matter as further evidence of Huchel's willingness to do Becher's bidding in the full knowledge of Becher's animosity towards Kantorowicz. Yet, the available evidence in this case indicates that, to some large extent, Kantorowicz misunderstood Huchel's motives, determined as they were by the need not to upset Thomas Mann. By now, the ominous figure of Becher clouded Kantorowicz's judgments of other issues.

Kantorowicz, thus, later construed Huchel's unwillingness to publish the essay in its original form as related to his reluctance to be seen to support the marginalised Kantorowicz's increasingly unguarded criticism of the SED regime. Huchel may well, indeed, have been reluctant to join Kantorowicz in his personal crusade. Kantorowicz later wrote, plausibly enough, that in his Zola essay he had attempted 'den Widerstand gegen die Zwangsherrschaft, deren Mitträger Johannes R.Becher geworden war, unüberhörbar beziehungsweise unübersehbar zu machen'.[4] He went on to explain that he had sent Huchel the manuscript because 'Gerade ihn wünschte ich zu verständigen, daß für mich die Zeit der "äußersten Prüfungen" gekommen sei. Er hat mich seitdem gemieden'.[5] For Kantorowicz, Huchel failed the test that he had set him. Yet, by this point Huchel might well have felt unsure exactly what Kantorowicz expected of him. For his part, Huchel must surely have been exasperated at Kantorowicz's failure to grasp the need not to alienate Mann.

In a strictly formal letter of 2 March 1954, Kantorowicz was informed that the journal's newly constituted advisory board had considered his study at its meeting on 28 January.[6] Renn, Brecht and Ihering all rejected publication without alterations. The 11 March was proposed as a date for a meeting which Ihering would attend. Huchel reported to Engel on 1 April 1954 that Kantorowicz refused to discuss the matter further and insisted on payment for the work in its present form.[7] Engel had agreed to take the essay off Huchel's hands, and Huchel was keen to ensure that that meant payment, too. He went on to point out – and here personal animosity came into play – that the essay comprised 1,150 lines, of which 715 lines were quotation and only 435 Kantorowicz's own text. Huchel reminded Engel that Kantorowicz was paid for his work in the Heinrich Mann Archive and invited him to consider whether Kantorowicz should receive full payment for the quotations! Huchel's pettiness here is quite unpleasant and surely not excused by the stridency of his former friend in their recent dealings.

Stasi Interest

Early 1954 saw Huchel seeking to maintain a sense of common purpose and identity among Berlin writers. Indeed, Walter Ulbricht had only recently called for the creation of an all-German body of artists and intellectuals to promote unity before the Conference of the Four Powers over the future of Germany in Geneva. The Stasi commented upon the willingness of western figures to engage in such activity in its report of an event organised by Huchel's body, the SDA, which he attended at the student meeting house in Charlottenburg on 22 January 1954.[8] The occasion was a reading by Günther Weisenborn from his unpublished novel *Der dritte Blick.*[9] As well as an observer from the Stasi, representatives were present from the western 'K5'. Huchel spoke in order to allay fears among those from the West that their readiness to participate in a 'gesamtdeutsches Kulturgespräch' might be used by the East to make certain demands on them. Huchel is reported as saying that since 1945 he 'stets enge Verbindung mit westdeutschen Geistesschaffenden unterhalte und ihm das von keiner Seite verboten oder verübelt worden sei, sondern im Gegenteil sogar gefördert wurde'. That was certainly true! The report notes Huchel's later, overtly political contribution as follows,

> Herr Huchel machte am Schluß der Veranstaltung die Anwesenden mit einem angeblichen Vorschlag der DDR bekannt, wonach eine Delegation aus Westdeutschland durch die Gefängnisse der DDR gehen soll, um die 'unschuldig Verurteilten' festzustellen und umgekehrt, eine Delegation der DDR durch die westdeutschen Gefängnisse gehen soll, um die dort unschuldig Verurteilten festzustellen und auch diejenigen, die schon wieder zum Kriege hetzen und frei herumlaufen dürfen.

Shortly afterwards, the Stasi compiled a short report on Huchel, characterising him as someone who worked for the SDA as well as *Sinn und Form*. It went on,

Huchel ist Lyriker und beteiligt sich aktiv an Veranstaltungen, die der Schutzverband in Westberlin im Ramen (sic) des gesamtdeutschen Gesprächs veranstaltet. Zu derartigen Veanstaltungen spricht er in unserem Sinn und im Auftrag des Schutzverbandes zu gesamtdeutschen Problemen ... Politisch wird er als indifferent eingeschätzt, der aber mit den Zielen der DDR einverstanden ist und mit der Partei sympatisiert. (sic) Seine Haltung ist oft schwankend.[10]

According to the Stasi's evaluation, Huchel was not at this stage perceived as a subversive. Indeed, if one makes allowance for the particular Stasi/SED perspective, the evaluation captures something of the very real ambiguities of his political position in the GDR.

Hubertusweg

Their financial and professional situation once again secure, the Huchels went through with the purchase of Hubertusweg 43-45 in Wilhelmshorst in the spring of 1954. They used the proceeds from the award of the National Prize, the 25,000 marks just covering the cost. It is an elegant and roomy, detached property on three floors, set in its own grounds among the fir trees of Wilhelmshorst. In its generous proportions and attractive setting in Wilhelmshorst, the property was a worthy successor to the Zimmermanns' farmhouse in Alt-Langerwisch. Huchel himself evidently saw it in such terms, as a visitor, Walter Jens, would later recall, 'Unvergeßlich der Augenblick, da Huchel uns in seinem Haus vom Grund und Boden sprach, den er, da er ihm kraft unverzichtbarer Erb-Vollmacht gebühre, mit Hilfe eines Preises zurückgekauft habe'.[11] After a decade and half, he made good what he regarded as the deception perpetrated by his uncle. He had not, in fact, bought back the same property. Nonetheless, he evidently regarded the purchase of Hubertusweg 43-45 as a symbolic act, which made good the injustice of 1939, over which his mother and uncle had brawled on the roadside.

The Huchels would stay at Hubertusweg 43-45 for the seventeen years they remained in the GDR. In the early 1990s, a stone plaque was placed in the garden in Huchel's memory. Huchel had his study on the top floor, well away from the rest of the house. The editorial office was located on the ground floor. They had a live-in domestic, Fräulein Gerda Riepert. The following year, they would be granted the use of two rooms for editorial work in the nearby Hubertusweg 35-39 by the Wilhelmshorst council.[12] The decision followed a period of some tension between the council housing commission and Huchel, when his initial request had not been granted. On 7 September 1955 he actually resorted to threats, 'Jede negative Entscheidung in meiner Angelegenheit kann ich nicht anders als gegen mich persönlich gerichtet auffassen'.[13] In the two rooms, Charlotte Narr assembled the journal's archive. In the mid-1960s, after Huchel had ceased to edit *Sinn und Form*, the rooms would become the subject of a bitter and quite absurd dispute between Huchel and the local council.

Spats with Publishers

1954 saw further evidence of Huchel's strained relations with his publisher. Janka wrote to Huchel on 11 January 1954, drawing his attention to Stahlberg's inclusion in its publicity material of a collection of Huchel's verse.[14] Janka, evidently unaware of the licence arrangement with Stahlberg in 1948, wanted to know if the poems in question were different from those for which he was under contract with the Aufbau Verlag. Huchel replied on 14 January that he had not had any contact with Stahlberg for years but supposed that the publisher had been prompted to re-advertise the collection following a reference to it in an anthology, *Ergriffenes Dasein*.[15] He added that his verse had been included in the anthology without his knowledge. He went on to give full vent to his bitterness at what he saw as the Aufbau Verlag's discriminatory treatment of his work and person, complaining that the publisher 'selbst nach der Verleihung des Nationalpreises an mich so gut wie gar nichts für die Verbreitung meines Buches getan hat, obwohl zahlreiche positive Besprechungen vorliegen, und dieses Buch in keiner Buchhandlung zu finden ist'. He suggested that he was valued more highly by West German publishers. Janka countered on 25 January in what had become the familiar ritual between publisher and author, 'Wir wollten Ihnen keineswegs irgend einen Vorwurf machen, sondern es lag uns lediglich daran, nachzuprüfen, ob Ihre Rechte irgendwie verletzt worden wären'.[16] Not long afterwards, in July that year, Huchel began negotiations with Fritz Hünich of the Insel Verlag in Leipzig, with a view to the publication of a volume of some fifty poems. The collection was announced in the Insel programme for 1955 but nothing came of it.[17]

In the summer, Huchel became involved in another of his ritualistic disputes with the *Tägliche Rundschau*, this time over his poem 'Lenin in Rasliw'. (i,298) The first mention of the poem comes in Huchel's letter of 31 July 1953 to Günter Casper of the Aufbau Verlag.[18] Caspar had approached Huchel with an invitation to contribute to an anthology. Huchel replied that he had long been meaning to write a poem about Lenin's exile in Rasliv and his life in the 'Laubhütte', which he had visited that May. A year later, Huchel wrote to Theuerkauf of the *Tägliche Rundschau*, offering 'Lenin in Rasliw' for publication in July, an appropriate month since Lenin had been in Rasliv in July and August.[19] He added that *Aufbau* wanted to publish the poem come what may. Theuerkauf responded on 20 July as follows,

Wir können uns nicht entschließen, das uns angebotene Gedicht zu übernehmen. Sie haben die größte Aufmerksamkeit der Schilderung der Landschaft gewidmet, und das Wesen Lenins kommt nur schwach heraus. Eine Unrichtigkeit sehen wir in den ersten beiden

Zeilen der zweiten Strophe. Es kam nicht täglich ein Bote aus Petrograd, und die Bemerkung ' ... kostbar ist ihm die Einsamkeit' paßt doch nicht zu Lenin. Auch der Vergleich mit Tolstoi scheint uns nicht glücklich.[20]

Once again, it is apparent to what extent Huchel's artistic and intellectual horizons differed from those of many of his peers in East Berlin, however much he clearly wished at this stage to demonstrate his support for Eastern Bloc policies through his portrait of Lenin. Huchel passed his poem and Theuerkauf's letter on to Brecht and to Max Schroeder at the Aufbau Verlag, who shared Huchel's outrage in his reply to Huchel on 26 July 1954, 'Der Brief des Kollegen Theuerkauf ist ein Affront'.[21] He assured Huchel that the poem would appear in *Aufbau*, which it duly did in September that year. A cursory reading of the poem confirms what one already knows: artistically and temperamentally, Huchel was simply not capable of producing portraits of iron-willed revolutionary leaders of the type Theuerkauf evidently expected.[22]

A Growing Influence

As the 1950s progressed, Huchel's own work continued to take a back seat as, through the Academy and *Sinn und Form*, he played an increasingly prominent, mediating role in cultural matters. He used his position in the Academy to propose Bloch for the National Prize[23] and promoted the case for Mayer's membership of the Academy.[24] He succeeded with Bloch but not with Mayer. *Sinn und Form* was, for the time being, not a subject of discussion in the Academy's committees. Zweig, however, still saw it as his task to follow up the resolutions of the committee he had chaired in 1953. He wrote to Louis Fürnberg in May 1954 and outlined continuing problems. He sought to win Fürnberg for the idea of editing *Sinn und Form* together with Huchel,

Wir brauchen Dich, lieber Louis, in Berlin, und zwar in der Akademie der Künste und mit Huchel als Hauptherausgeber von *Sinn und Form*. Von Weimar aus ist das nicht zu machen, unsere Zweimonatsschrift krankt schon daran, daß Huchel in Wilhelmshorst sitzt und ebenda seine Redaktion und er nur zweimal wöchentlich in Berlin ist ... Die *Neue Deutsche Literatur* hat aber durch Weiskopf einen solchen Aufschwung genommen, daß sich *Sinn und Form* nur halten kann und seinen Standard sogar verbessern, wenn es seine redaktionellen Kräfte verdoppelt.[25]

Fürnberg declined and nothing came of Zweig's initiative, though the feeling remained strong in East Berlin, by no means simply among cultural politicians who wanted to make the journal an instrument of their policies, that *Sinn und Form* could only realise its full potential if it was strengthened at a senior editorial level.

Huchel was, none the less, able in the mid-1950s to take advantage of the somewhat more relaxed relations between the two German states to travel further afield in the West and to build upon his journal's growing international reputation. Through the expenditure of much energy in travel and in the cultivation of contacts, the journal and its editor achieved the long-desired breakthrough in West Germany. He undertook these trips with the express support of the East Berlin authorities in line with the all-German strategy. Indeed, they were organised in consultation with the Academy and the commission for all-German work in the Writers' Union, of which Huchel was a member.[26] While in January 1953 he had reported to Jahnn that Hamburg had 'mein Einreisegesuch für Westdeutschland abgelehnt',[27] in a letter to Ludvík Kundera of 23 February 1955 he wrote that during the previous few months he had spent more time in the West than at his desk.[28] Venues in 1954 included Düsseldorf, the International PEN Congress in Amsterdam from 19-26 June and the meeting of the Hölderlin Society in May in Bad Homburg. By the mid-1950s, Huchel was conducting a correspondence with a range of western writers. Apart from Thomas Mann, they included Hans Bender, Hans Magnus Enzensberger, Konrad Farner, Ernst Fischer, Peter Hacks, Peter Hamm, Rudolf Hartung, Helmut Heißenbüttel, Walter Höllerer, Italiaander, Jahnn, Walter Jens, Kasack, Alfred Kelletat, Wolfgang Koeppen, Ernst Kreuder, Heinz Ludwig Schneider, Weisenborn and Weyrauch. In this way, Huchel also began to build up a lobby of western opinion that would provide strong support when things began to get tough in the later 1950s. Among GDR correspondents were Bloch, Eisler, Mayer, Hermlin, Werner Krauss and Rolf Schneider.

In September 1954, he was joined by Mayer in a high-level mission to visit the aged Alfred Döblin at his home in the Black Forest. On the way, they called in at Freiburg to visit Huchel's old friend from the *Kolonne* Circle in the 1930s, Eberhard Meckel, whose achievements would presently be eclipsed by those of his son, Christoph. Contact with the *Kolonne* writers was at best sporadic in the 1950s. Huchel's relations with Döblin had never been as close, though his link with him went back further. In late 1929, we will recall, he and Joachim had paid Döblin a visit one evening. Döblin had just published *Berlin Alexanderplatz*, his great experimental novel, with the success of which he is invariably associated. For Becher and others in East Berlin, he was one of those major international figures in the West, whom they wished to win over. Like Jahnn, Döblin was disaffected at his treatment in West Germany, where he had been shunned by publishers and had made his main home in Paris again. It should not be forgotten that his treatment in West Germany was not unconnected to the fact that he had returned to Germany at the end of the war wearing a French officer's uniform and had been instrumentally involved in the organisation of cultural life in the French zone. He had joined together with Becher to ensure that the works of their fellow Expressionist,

Gottfried Benn, were banned on account of Benn's support for the Nazis in the early stages of the regime. It is a measure of the climate in the intellectual life of the Federal Republic during its early years that Benn had re-emerged as the acknowledged master while Döblin was isolated and spurned.

Naturally enough, Döblin welcomed the attentions of his visitors from East Berlin. Following their visit, Huchel wrote to Döblin's wife Erna on 16 September 1954, seeking to arrange a publication in *Sinn und Form* of Döblin's 'Der Tierfreund oder das zweite Paradies', which he had been given to read.[29] Although that publication did not materialise, the Döblins also sent Huchel the manuscript of the *Hamlet* novel, with the authorisation for an excerpt to be printed in the fifth issue of 1954. In his next letter to Döblin dated 27 September 1954, Huchel lavished praise on the novel, writing that he had selected the whole of the King Lear section as the lengthy opening piece that would set the tone for the double number 5/6, which was due to appear in mid-November.[30] Huchel pointed to the company of Jahnn, Farner, Brecht, Bloch and Ihering in that issue. These names demonstrate Huchel's success in attracting established, 'weighty' names from the whole of the German-speaking world. He might have included Thomas Mann, Johannes R.Becher, Hans Mayer, Ludwig Renn and Leonhard Frank, too, not to mention Eberhard Meckel, whose poems Huchel printed by way of thanks for his efforts in preparing for the visit to Döblin.

Huchel himself was evidently pleased with his own efforts, writing to the publisher on 11 October 1954, 'bei aller kritischen Einstellung meiner Arbeit gegenüber kann ich wohl diesmal sagen, daß wir in sechs Jahren ein solches gewichtiges Heft (SuF 5+6/54) noch nicht herausgebracht haben'.[31] Wolfgang Koeppen, one of those West German writers to whom the journal was sent on a regular basis, wrote to Huchel on 28 December 1954 congratulating him on the issue,[32] as did Ernst Bloch. Bloch wrote on 11 January 1955, 'So eine Komposition ist noch kaum dagewesen; und das in unserer Langeweile, im fast ringsum widrigen Jargon. Ich drücke Dir die Hand'.[33] *Wege zueinander*, published in Cologne, chimed in with 'ein wunderbarer Zusammenklang deutscher Kultureinheit mit den geistigen Kräften der Welt',[34] while the *Deutsche Volkszeitung* of Düsseldorf proclaimed, in line with East Berlin policy,

> Man kann dieses Kompendium, das Peter Huchel als Beitrag zur zeitgnössischen Literatur Deutschlands, für die es keine Zonengrenzen gibt, der Öffentlichkeit vorlegt, nicht aus der Hand geben, ohne ernsthaft darüber nachzudenken, welche Möglichkeiten dem Geistesleben unserer Nation geboten sein könnten, wenn man dem Beispiel Huchels folgen würde. Denn hier, in *Sinn und Form*, ist die Einheit der deutschen Literatur eine Tatsache, schwarz auf weiß.[35]

It was not only those organs controlled by East Berlin that acknowledged *Sinn und Form*'s unique contribution to German literary and cultural life during the Cold War. A number of West German intellectuals deeply suspicious of the GDR were prepared to make an exception for *Sinn und Form*, which, increasingly, they came to identify with Huchel rather than with the parent institution, let alone the state, which, of course, provided the funds. On 22 February 1955, Jahnn, whom Huchel and Brecht had proposed for membership of the Academy on 17 June 1954, but without success, described that same double issue as 'besonders gehaltvoll' and reported further that *Sinn und Form*

> hier im Westen gelesen wird, und ich darf hinzufügen, daß ich über die Zeitschrift übereinstimmnd gute Urteile höre. Eine Anzahl meiner Kollegen bezeichnen sie als die einzige würdige deutsche Literaturzeitschrift überhaupt. Mein Freund Hans Erich Nossack war jedenfalls von der letzten Nummer so angetan, daß er sich entschloß, Ihnen gelegentlich Arbeiten von sich zur Verfügung zu stellen.[36]

Nossack sent Huchel the manuscript of his play *Die Hauptprobe*, the first two acts of which were published in 1955. In this way, following his great success in late 1954, Huchel increasingly attracted some of the most interesting names of his generation in West German literature to the journal which by now had come to bear his stamp.

Günter Eich and the Gruppe 47

It could not be expected that the renewal of the friendship with Eberhard Meckel might lead to the re-establishment of the close friendships of the 1930s with the *Kolonne* Circle. Raschke had died in the war, Langgässer following her return to West Germany, and the others had gone their separate ways in the West. There, only Eich had fulfilled his early promise, not least through his association with the Gruppe 47, whose prize he won at its first meeting. Eich's standing certainly matched Huchel's own. The rest of the Circle remained marginal in post-war German literature, even the gifted Lange. As we have seen, in the later 1940s Huchel attempted to publish both Eich and Lange, and Lange reviewed *Gedichte* in *Die Welt*. In further recognition of Meckel's efforts with Döblin, Huchel mediated the publication by the Aufbau Verlag of a selection of Meckel's poems. Yet that was really the only productive exchange between Huchel and his old friends during these years. Meckel's son, Christoph, summarises relations between his father and the *Kolonne* poets in the 1950s as follows, 'Er besuchte noch Horst Lange und Günter Eich, er selber wurde von Goes und Huchel besucht, man schickte einander die neuen Publikationen, aber das alles blieb ohne Folgen für ihn. Die Freundschaften der dreißiger Jahre wurden von keiner Seite wiederaufgenommen'.[37]

That said, the Döblin episode demonstrates that while there was no real development of earlier friendships, there was still a sense that as members of an informal network they could rely on each other, however sporadic their contact. That certainly goes for Huchel's relations with Lange and Schaefer. With the latter, Huchel maintained an infrequent correspondence in the mid-1950s, Huchel generally expressing his sense of shame at his failure to respond to Schaefer's more frequent letters.[38] She had been keeping him informed about royalties from the Stahlberg Verlag, which he had authorised her to look after on his behalf. In fact, by 26 May 1958 they would amount to a princely 207.72 marks, which he had not collected. Schaefer teased him by suggesting that she might send them to Dora!

There had always been much tension in Huchel's relations with Eich. It re-emerged during a rare meeting in the post-war period. It was a measure of Huchel's growing standing in West Germany that he was invited to attend the meeting of the Gruppe 47 held at Burg Rothenfels in October 1954. Hans Werner Richter's invitation paved the way for Huchel to win young West German writers for collaboration on *Sinn und Form*, as well as to re-establish contact with old acquaintances like Eich. Whatever hopes might have been invested in Burg Rothenfels by Huchel and his host, his first and only meeting with the Gruppe 47 turned out to be a most unfortunate experience. His participation was reported as follows in the West German press,

> Eine Attraktion der Tagung war der Besuch des ostzonalen Schriftstellers Peter Huchel, der die Zeitschrift *Sinn und Form* in Ost-Berlin herausgibt – einer der ernstzunehmenden Literaten aus dem Osten. Das literarische Ost-West-Gespräch blieb jedoch leider in den Anfängen stecken, da selbst ein Mann wie Peter Huchel in starrer östlicher Meinungsuniformität verharrt. Das war für die Teilnehmer der Tagung eine betrübliche Einsicht.[39]

The conflict was not forgotten, as Hans Mayer points out in his autobiography, where he is a little more explicit about it,

> Fast kam es zu Tätlichkeiten zwischen so alten und erprobten Freunden wie Peter Huchel und Günter Eich. Das war eine Schauermär. Später haben mir beide davon berichtet, unter Lachen. Ausgangspunkt des Krachs muß ein politischer Disput gewesen sein. Wobei es nicht nüchtern zuging. Trotzdem: Huchel hat nie wieder eine Einladung angenommen, oder erhalten. Mir riet er ab, als mich Richter ... einlud.[40]

One is bound to ask what Eich and Huchel said and did not say independently of each other to Mayer, who had spent the Nazi years in exile? The obvious reading of the dispute, confirmed by other sources, is that a West German friend was challenging Huchel to explain why he stayed in the 'Soviet Zone'.[41] Indeed, the press report indicates that this was an important dimension of the conflict and that Huchel demonstrated his loyalty to the GDR. Yet, as we know, the tensions between Eich and Huchel ran much deeper, since their first political row in 1935. In the meantime, in the GDR Huchel had been stylised as an anti-fascist, yet Eich would have had some difficulty in identifying Huchel with that image and can be expected to have said so. He had, though, little to gain by explaining this to Mayer, since, by the same token, in the Federal Republic Eich had been stylised as an Inner Emigrant, yet Huchel knew different and could have responded in kind. In truth, both were representative figures for what the East and the West had respectively done in creating ideologically convenient myths to deal with the problem of Nazism. Mayer, of course, knew well enough about the creation of these myths in general terms, yet he certainly knew little about his friends' activities in the Nazi years. Had he done so, he would have known, too, that since their row in 1935, their friendship had often been uneasy. The title of the poem 'Nicht geführte Gespräche', which Eich later dedicated to Huchel, indicates that after the war their friendship became more latent than real. On 17 October 1954, immediately after the row, Eich wrote a postcard from Würzburg to his friend Rainer Brambach. He explained, 'Hier sollte Peter Huchel unterschreiben, aber er fuhr im Zorn davon'.[42]

Quite apart from the damage that the meeting did to relations between Eich and Huchel, the débacle of Burg Rothenfels effectively closed off relations between *Sinn und Form* and the Gruppe 47. Despite broad agreement over the question of German cultural unity, the desirability of re-unification and opposition to the Adenauer 'restoration', it would appear that for influential members of the Gruppe 47, Huchel, under pressure, had shown himself to be too closely aligned with a communist system to which they were fundamentally opposed. Of those younger writers linked with the Gruppe 47 from the mid-1950s, only Helmut Heißenbüttel (1956) and Hans Magnus Enzensberger (1957) had work published in Huchel's journal during that period. Wolfgang Bächler had been associated with both ventures from an earlier stage, and the older Wolfgang Weyrauch contributed in 1955, although he, like Enzensberger and Heißenbüttel, had not been at Burg Rothenfels.

It was, then, doubly important that Huchel should continue to cultivate a figure of Döblin's standing. He resumed correspondence with Döblin on 15 November 1954, when he reported that both Rütten und Loening and the Aufbau Verlag were extremely interested in publishing the *Hamlet* novel.[43] He explained that because Rütten und Loening published *Sinn und Form*, their editor Wolfgang Richter had had the first bite of the cherry and was pushing for *Hamlet* to be typeset at once, something deeply regretted by Aufbau. Huchel was confident that the novel would be published by the one or the other in 1955. In fact, Rütten und Loening published the book in 1956. Huchel offered to travel to Paris with a representative from the publisher's if Döblin wished. He wrote that he had also been busy promoting the idea of a new edition of *Berlin Alexanderplatz*. The publishing house Das neue Leben would probably offer the best deal; Rütten und Loening and Aufbau would do it come what may. Huchel finally enquired of Döblin if it would be possible to consider publication of a selection of Döblin's oeuvre in the GDR. Showing his accustomed tact and acumen in dealing with major writers, he wrote that he recognised that the feasibility of such a venture depended on any agreement Döblin might have with West German publishers. In this way, Huchel succeeded in bringing Döblin's name back to the attention of publishers and can be said to have had a hand in the Döblin renaissance which the author himself did not live to see.[44]

Confronting the Aufbau Verlag

In early 1955, matters came to a head with the Aufbau Verlag over Huchel's own work. The licence arrangement with Stahlberg made for a dimension of confusion in the granting of permissions for West German anthologies which exacerbated the already strained relations between authors and publisher. On 31 January 1955, Huchel demanded that, once and for all, his relationship with the Aufbau Verlag should be placed on a proper footing.[45] He asked for exact figures of the print-run for his collection and for sales. He advanced his familiar complaint that he had not been promoted like other authors, despite the positive reception in the West and the opportunity to capitalise on this 'gesamtdeutschen Aspekt'. He also pointed out that he might have expected Aufbau to produce a new edition after the award of the National Prize, even though the matter had never actually been the subject of discussion between him and the publisher.

Janka did not reply until 26 April 1955, when he informed Huchel that three years earlier more than half the print-run of *Gedichte* had been destroyed in a fire.[46] Much stock not irreparably damaged in the fire had been distributed to pensioners and the poor. He went on to point out that sales had not in actual fact been affected: 1,822 copies had been sold by Aufbau during the seven years since publication and 341 copies remained unsold.

Huchel was, quite justifiably, outraged. He gave full vent to his anger in a letter sent by recorded delivery on 2 May 1955,[47] in which, at points, he uses language that echoes the charges issued by the father in Kafka's *Das Urteil*, 'wie leicht wäre es gewesen, mich so mit schönen Lügen einzudecken, daß ich von den Fakten nichts bemerkt hätte'. He pointed out that beyond the quite extraordinary circumstance that he had not been informed of the fire, his assent was surely needed for the distribution without charge of 1,362 copies of his book, for which he might have expected royalties. The books had, in any case, he wrote, been distributed to groups 'die sich wohl mehr für Schuhwerk und andere Dinge des täglichen Bedarfs interessieren. Weshalb hat der Verlag meine Gedichte nicht an Studenten und an Volksbüchereien verteilen lassen?' He added that librarians were constantly complaining to him that they simply did not have the money to purchase his poems.

Huchel concluded his letter with the words, 'Wozu sollen wir noch lange hin und her reden? Streichen Sie mich also aus Ihrem Verlagsverzeichnis'.

This was, however, not the last word on the matter, and it is certainly misleading to conclude from Huchel's letter that his subsequent actions represented a 'rejection of any idea of a reprint' of *Gedichte*.[48] It is important not to mistake the quite justified anger displayed by Huchel as determining the position he subsequently assumed. We have seen the roots of his always uneasy relations with the Aufbau Verlag. It would certainly be wrong to read into Janka's attitude towards Huchel evidence that the former was doing the SED's bidding in marginalising a figure who in 1952 was falling into disgrace.[49] Had that been the case, Janka would now have been happy simply to drop Huchel. As subsequent events would show, Janka was not the type to engage in Stalinist manipulations.

Instead, Janka attempted to patch up relations with Huchel. On 23 May he wrote, 'Wir sollten, wie schon wiederholt von mir angeregt und eigentlich auch in Weimar vereinbart, uns bald einmal zusammensetzen und alles weitere besprechen'.[50] He suggested a meeting at Französische Straße with Huchel's friend Max Schroeder and Günter Caspar. This proposal evidently bore fruit. Janka sent Huchel contracts for the cycle 'Ballade (sic) aus Malaya' and a new edition of *Gedichte*, which Huchel duly signed on 23 June.[51] Huchel wrote to Caspar on 21 September 1955, sending 'Spruch für Wilhelm Pieck' and four 'Jugendgedichte'.[52] The latter were subsequently published in *Aufbau*, the former some years later in an anthology dedicated to Pieck.[53] On 27 June, Huchel informed his friend and Czech translator, Ludvík Kundera, '"Malaya" erscheint zum Jahresende im Aufbau-Verlag'. (ii,337) On 1 July 1955, Janka arranged payment to Huchel of 2,211 marks, the equivalent of the author's 15% royalties for the 4,761 copies damaged in the fire.[54] Although in the 1950s Huchel signed contracts with Aufbau for 'Das Gesetz' as well as the two projects mentioned above, none of them was ever completed. In the late 1950s, Huchel clearly intended to produce a new edition of *Gedichte* with the Aufbau Verlag.[55] Despite an agreement with Rütten und Loening, his next volume *Chausseen Chausseen* was published only in the Federal Republic, by S. Fischer in 1963. Thus, not a single volume of Huchel's poems appeared in the GDR during the existence of that state.

Pre-eminence

In the mid-1950s, Huchel's position in the GDR cultural hierarchy was at its strongest. He enjoyed Brecht's support in the Academy and beyond at a time when the SED leadership was not showing its teeth as it had done in the *Kulturkampf* of the early 1950s. On 20 February 1955 Huchel went on the radio to introduce his journal in the slot reserved for the Academy, 'Stunde der Akademie'.[56] Indeed, the GDR's Minister President, Otto Grotewohl, was unreserved in his praise of *Sinn und Form* in a keynote speech which he delivered in Dresden in June 1955,

In unserer Republik sind in so kurzer Zeit so entscheidende literarische Zeitschriften wie
Sinn und Form oder das Organ des Schriftstellerverbandes *Neue Deutsche Literatur*
entstanden, deren Bedeutung auch maßgebliche Kreise der Bundesrepublik nicht leugnen
können und die sie als führende Organe zeitgenössischen literarischen Lebens anerkennen
müssen.[57]

In 1955 Huchel was awarded the GDR's Fontane Prize, a fitting distinction for a
poet who treated rural Brandenburg in his verse. There is also evidence of greater
interest in Huchel's poetry outside Germany. Brecht recommended Huchel, together
with Kuba and Hermlin, in a letter of 21 April 1955 to his Italian translator Gilda
Musa, who was looking for new work to translate.[58] Huchel would later answer her
questions about his poems.[59] Her translations of Huchel's poetry appeared in the
anthology *Poesia Tedesca del Dopoquerra*, which was published in 1958 in Milan.
He himself on 19 March 1958 would recommend to her Hermlin and Johannes
Bobrowski, describing the latter as the most gifted of the young GDR poets.[60]

It was Huchel who 'discovered' Bobrowski in 1955. In a sense, they were
made for each other, even though they would never actually form a close friendship.
While almost all young GDR poets were Brechtians, Bobrowski's roots, like
Huchel's, were very firmly in the German lyric tradition of the 18th and 19th
centuries. Bobrowski's earliest compositions from the 1930s place him in the same
'bürgerlich' tradition to which Huchel belonged in those years. On 1 June 1955,
Bobrowski sent *Sinn und Form* a selection of fifteen poems, requesting a critical
assessment.[61] Huchel immediately spotted Bobrowski's rare talent and responded
by telegram on 13 June, requesting him to come and meet him in the Academy at 2
pm on 16 June.[62] Bobrowski idolised Huchel, using the old-fashioned address
'Meister' to indicate his veneration.[63] Huchel must have been torn between
amusement and embarrassment. In any case, the distance that Bobrowski placed
between himself and the 'Meister' served to some large extent to determine the
nature of their relationship. It was extremely difficult in these circumstances for
Huchel to develop a genuine friendship. It was, though, clear to Huchel that he
should publish Bobrowski, and he resolved to do so at once, selecting five poems
for the fourth issue of his journal in 1955. Huchel thus launched Bobrowski's career,
for which the latter always remained deeply grateful. In his letter of thanks for the
forthcoming publication, dated 5 August 1955, Bobrowski adopted the role of the
ungainly apprentice that rather irritatingly characterises his correspondence with
Huchel, whose equal as a poet he certainly was, 'Nun ist das Dankeschön also
heraus, nachdem ich schon ein paarmal einen Brief an Sie begonnen hatte. Die
gerieten aber jugendlicher, als es für mich irgend zulässig sein kann. Ich tu mich
überhaupt schwierig auf dem Papier'.[64] Huchel would publish two further batches

of Bobrowki's poems in the late 1950s before Bobrowski achieved his breakthrough in the early 1960s.

A New Idiom: 'Für Ernst Bloch'

That same summer in which he discovered Bobrowski, the poet Huchel himself entered new territory with his publication of his poem 'Für Ernst Bloch. Zu seinem 70. Geburtstag' in the third issue of *Sinn und Form*. Huchel's poem was followed in the journal by Hans Heinz Holz's essay on Bloch's *Prinzip Hoffnung*. These contributions were 'framed' by two pieces by Brecht, an extract from *Galilei* and 'Der Friede ist das A und O'. All these pieces were in the second half of the number. The main thematic focus of the issue, comprising the first half, was Thomas Mann's 80th birthday. It opened with an extract from Thomas Mann's 'Versuch über Schiller', the speech delivered by Mann in Stuttgart and Weimar on the 150th anniversary of Schiller's death. Congratulations to Mann were published from, among others, Becher and Jahnn. They were followed by essays by Hugo Siebenschein and Hans Mayer. The issue also included the announcement that Mann had been elected an honorary member of the Academy on his 80th birthday.

Huchel's poem for Bloch, written in June 1955, (i,404) was thus included amongst exalted company in a particularly 'representative' number. The affirmative tone of the early 1950s has gone. Gone, too, is the tone of the poems of childhood reproduced in 'Herbstnacht', as well as in other compositions first published in the mid-1950s such as 'Caputher Heuweg' and 'Damals'. The new composition, later collected in *Chausseen Chausseen* as 'Widmung. Für Ernst Bloch', represents a first, decisive step by Huchel in the articulation of the more difficult, modernist idiom resistant to ideology à la Adorno that characterises much of *Chausseen Chausseen*. Huchel draws upon imagery from poems of the late 1930s and early 1940s such as 'Späte Zeit' in order, for the first time in the GDR, to convey his sense of a world inhabited by dark forced preying upon the vulnerable,

> Am Hohlweg wechselt schneller das Wild.
>
> Und wie ein Hall aus fernen Jahren
>
> Dröhnt über Wälder weit ein Schuß.
>
> Es schweifen wieder die Unsichtbaren.

It is perhaps tempting simply to read this poem off against a specifically GDR reality, in which Huchel had his dealings with dark forces, as did Bloch. There is certainly that dimension to the poem, and to that extent Huchel himself can be seen here to be articulating the sort of sentiment that Kantorowicz suggested he was unwilling to publish. The poem is informed by the pessimism of someone all too accustomed to the arbitrariness of German authoritarianism. Ironically, it was safer in the mid-1950s to publish such sentiments than it was earlier or, for that matter, later. Yet, as Uwe Schoor suggests, it makes sense to read this and other poems later collected in *Chausseen Chausseen* in the Cold War context, in which Huchel was operating in the 1950s. His several warnings in the late 1940s and 1950s about the policies of the West were not intended as mere rhetoric, even though by the late 1970s he had obviously changed his opinion. The poem contrasts the rapacious activity of the hunter with the thinker, whose path brings him close to the 'golden smoke' reminiscent of Hölderlin. The thinker is granted privileged insight into the deeper workings of the world, 'Er ahnt, was noch die Nacht verschweigt'. In a letter to Gilda Musa, Huchel explained the direction of his thinking by reference to the imagery of the 'Feuerbild' in the poem's opening lines and 'Des Winters Sternbild' in the closing line.[65] He wrote that in a time of great turmoil it was necessary to protect and preserve eternal values. This was the sense of 'Du mußt es bewahren'. The message was not so much different from that in poems from the late 1930s, but the imagery is much less direct and less conventional, making demands on the reader far beyond anything Huchel had published earlier. It is at the very least interesting in this context that early the following year Huchel received a request from Brecht's friend Käthe Rülicke for the loan of a collection of poems by T.S. Eliot, about which they had spoken at the Academy.[66]

'Für Ernst Bloch' was a beginning on a path towards western modernism, yet it would be a mistake to view all of Huchel's poetry from 1955 onwards in such terms. In fact, this idiom co-existed rather uneasily with the poetry of childhood and with the residue of the affirmative verse composed since the late 1940s, of which 'Bericht aus Malaya' represented the latest example. It would appear early the following year in *Neue Deutsche Literatur*.

Pressing Home the Advantage

In mid-1955, Huchel felt that he had good grounds for complaining to Becher about what he evidently regarded as discriminatory treatment. He wrote on 27 June, pointing out that unlike other editors-in-chief he had not been permitted to travel to the PEN conference in Vienna.[67] He had thus missed an opportunity to strengthen existing links and to create new ones. He assured Becher that he would not have come back empty-handed. That summer Huchel missed out, too, on a holiday to the Baltic coast.[68] Thomas Mann's death meant hasty arrangements for suitable publications in Mann's memory. Georg Lukács supplied 'Der letzte große Vertreter des kritischen Realismus', written on 13 August 1955, the day after Mann's death. Lukács' essay was followed in the journal by a brief selection of Mann's correspondence with Huchel, Rilla, Seghers, Hermlin and Gustav Seitz, as well as Lukács.

The two numbers in which Mann figured so prominently in 1955 illustrate the way in which the Academy's representative, all-German journal was used for celebration and commemoration. As the 1950s progressed, it also maintained its initial orientation as a forum for figures whose horizons were not principally those of the post-war division and of the literary groupings it had spawned. As we have seen, Bobrowski, Huchel's major 'find' in the mid-1950s, was then already in his mid-thirties and belonged to the same pre-war 'bürgerlich' tradition as Huchel himself. Erich Arendt, whose own work and whose translations were published, was, like Huchel, Becher, Brecht and Zweig, of the older generation. It is true that Huchel gave early opportunities to Fühmann, Kunert, Kipphardt, Bienek and Hacks, but there was an emphasis on established names, whose work might be viewed as transcending the post-war division. This was not lost on those Academy members who wished to see greater representation of young GDR intellectuals. Until the mid-1950s, Huchel's approach was underpinned by the Marxist re-interpretation of the European tradition undertaken in major essays by Lukács, Mayer, Bloch, Fischer, Rilla, Farner and Werner Krauss. As one might expect, the major focus was on the Enlightenment, Weimar classicism and nineteenth-century realism, although Mayer, Fischer, Farner and Bloch also treated writers and themes associated with twentieth-century modernism.

It is a measure of the strength of Huchel's position in the mid-1950s, reflected in Grotewohl's speech, that on 27 September 1955 he wrote by registered mail to Engel with the demand that, from 1 October, his salary should be returned to the old level of 2,000 marks a month.[69] The letter had been preceded by informal agreement that this should happen. Only through the reversion to his former salary, Huchel said, could unfinished business be completed, which it was Engel's responsibility to deal with. He went on,

> Sollten Sie aus irgendwelchen Gründen meiner Bitte nicht nachkommen können, so darf ich wohl von Ihnen einen schriftlichen Bescheid darüber erwarten, weshalb ich seit zwei Jahren einen finanziellen Verlust hinnehmen muß, obwohl meine Arbeit an *Sinn und Form* vom Ministerpräsidenten wie vom Minister für Kultur anerkannt worden ist.

Huchel went on to demand a rise for 'meinen Redakteur', by which he meant his wife, Monica. He pointed out that his editor had been employed on *Neues Deutschland* from 1945, where, he claimed, she had earned double her present salary of 810 marks. He requested a positive response by 8 October at the latest, 'denn ich möchte ungern meine Angelegenheit an höherer Stelle vortragen. Sie können aber versichert sein, daß ich eine weitere Verzögerung nachgerade als eine solche Mißachtung meiner Person ansehen würde, daß ich dagegen mit allen Mitteln protestieren müßte'. It is the letter of a person confident of his position and determined to drive home his advantage against someone whose part in his earlier humiliation Huchel had not forgotten. Engel had no defence to mount and replied on 29 September 1955,

Es hätte des massiven Briefes nicht bedurft, um, wie wir schon mündlich verabredet hatten, ab 1. Oktober 1955 Ihren Einzelvertrag auf die Summe von 2.000 -- aufzurunden. Gerade der Erfolg der Zeitschrift in der letzten Zeit läßt die Wiederherstellung des ursprünglichen Vertrages als eine Selbstverständlichkeit erscheinen.[70]

He could, however, hold out no prospect of a rise for Huchel's editor. The way had been cleared for the journal to be ordered direct from West Germany as well as in the GDR by post, and this justified a rise in the journal's print-run to 6,000. Huchel's individual contract was revised in line with his demand with effect from 1 October. Huchel continued to press home his advantage. Pointing to his success in the West, he wrote to Engel on 23 October, 'Deshalb behagt mir manchmal der Ton nicht, in dem man mich zu belehren versucht'.[71] In this way, he sought further to diminish any vestiges of control exercised by Engel and the Academy.

A Voice of Authority

The autumn of 1955 saw an attempt by the Munich writer, Kurt Ziesel, who had given strong support to the Nazis in his writing, to enlist Huchel in a campaign against Hermann Kasack. Kasack, we will recall, had collaborated with Huchel in 1948-9 before he had fled to the West. Kasack subsequently became the President of the Deutsche Akademie für Sprache und Dichtkunst in Darmstadt. He enraged the East Berlin Academy with his article 'Sinn und Möglichkeit einer Deutschen Akademie', which he published in the *Frankfurter Allgemeine Zeitung* on 29 May 1954. His article was his contribution to the propaganda war that surrounded the founding of the West Berlin Academy of Arts as a rival to the East Berlin Academy. He wrote that the 'sowjetische Akademie in Ost-Berlin jedem Mitglied jährlich 12. 000 -- Mark vergütet, ihm freilich damit die freie Meinung abkauft'. Huchel, together with Brecht and Hermlin, was named by Kasack. The East Berlin Academy, represented by the GDR's star lawyer Dr Friedrich Karl Kaul, pursued redress for this slander in the courts in Stuttgart, but to no avail.

When Ziesel wrote to Huchel on 17 October 1955, he obviously had hopes of enlisting Huchel against Kasack.[72] Ziesel named Dr Oskar Jancke from Stuttgart, whom Huchel knew from the PEN-Club, as a figure who had suggested that Huchel might be in possession of material that could incriminate Kasack, whom Ziesel clearly intended to expose. In his brief reply to Ziesel on 25 October 1955, Huchel declined to supply any such material, of which Jancke had, in his view, spoken in a misleading manner without Huchel's agreement.[73] Quite what, if anything Huchel had in his possession remains a mystery. We should, though, recall the hysterical anti-communism of the Federal Republic in its first decade, when Kasack's earlier collaboration with the Soviets and their allies (such as Huchel) might easily have been held against him. Whatever Kasack had said about Huchel and the other

Academy members, Huchel was above denunciation of that sort and did not rise to Ziesel's bait. He clearly had no wish to see a further deterioration in relations with Kasack, whose role in Darmstadt was of continuing relevance for his own work, quite apart from the fact that the last thing Huchel needed in his cultural diplomacy was headline association with the likes of Ziesel!

A mark of Huchel's own confidence and that of GDR writers more generally vis-à-vis the dogmatists in East Berlin in the mid-1950s is the short speech that he delivered at the Kulturbund's Klubhaus on 12 January 1956 during the discussion of lyric poetry at the GDR Writers' Congress.[74] In his unpublished speech he declared that production literature was passé, as was, too, a type of criticism which was ideologically correct but ignorant of literary practice. Dogmatic critics had, Huchel continued, failed to foster a new literature dealing with the new reality of life in the rural world, which had, of course, been Huchel's own subject matter in the early 1950s. He called upon young writers not to engage in imitation but to have the courage to go their own way, with due respect for melody, rhyme, imagery and meaning, as opposed to rather mindless experimentation, although he was by no means opposed in principle to experimentation.

Huchel's speech is a good example of the type of statements that were being made by eminent figures like his friend Hans Mayer, as they sought to exploit the ideological uncertainty in the SED. SED cultural politicians and figures such as Engel simply did not have the authority at this time to mount any challenge to Huchel. At the same time, that did not mean that a figure such as Brecht had abandoned his own aims for *Sinn und Form*, which, as we have seen, differed from Huchel's own in respect of Brecht's commitment to partisan politics. These Huchel viewed as incompatible with his all-German mission. This difference emerges in a memo of Brecht's proposals for the agenda of a meeting of the Academy's Presidium scheduled for February 1956.[75] In Brecht's view, 'Die Redaktion *Sinn und Form* soll verbreitert und aktiviert werden, um so schnell als möglich aus *Sinn und Form* ein Organ des Kampfes für die Ziele der DDR zu machen'. The proposal was to be made once again that Louis Fürnberg be summoned from his post in Weimar to Berlin in order to join the editorial staff. A second point from Brecht was, 'Aufträge sollen erteilt werden, um Aufsätze und literarische Werke zu schaffen mit kämpferischem Inhalt zur Veröffentlichung über die Akademie und in *Sinn und Form*'. As far as can be ascertained, nothing came of these proposals. They indicate clearly once more to what extent Huchel's relationship with Brecht was predicated on their shared antipathy towards SED dogmatists, and much less on shared convictions.

Yet, Huchel's standing in the mid-1950s is underscored in a report written by Harald Hauser for the Writers' Union of a meeting of the 'Sektion Literatur und Verlagswesen des Deutschen Kulturtages' in Bremen on 24/25 March 1956.[76] This all-German occasion organised by the Writers' Union was attended on the GDR side by Huchel, Arendt, Georg Maurer and Kurella. The occasion was, however, a far cry from the Starnberg meeting and the hopes of the early 1950s. No West German writer of any repute could be persuaded to go along. Hauser wrote,

> Eine solche Persönlichkeit wie Peter Huchel überragt die westdeutschen Diskussionsteilnehmer um ein Bedeutendes. Es kommt so zu keiner echten Auseinandersetzung. Es mangelt den westdeutschen Teilnehmern an Bedeutung. Sie sind in Westdeutschland selbst meiner Meinung nach ziemlich bedeutungslos. Es käme darauf an, westdeutsche Intellektuelle, die gegenwärtig noch nicht mit uns sprechen, durch eine kühne Themenstellung für ein echtes Streitgespräch zu gewinnen.

It was in truth impossible to breathe any new life into such activities, though it was not in Huchel's interest to say so. Generally, any opportunity to travel to the West was good for *Sinn und Form* and for his own reputation as a poet. He travelled with Ihering to Hamburg from 25-28 April 1956 on Academy business to hold talks with Jahnn in his capacity as President of the Hamburg Academy and to attend the premiere of Jahnn's *Thomas Chatterton*. He held discussions there, too, with Weyrauch, Weisenborn and Hans Georg Brenner, who worked for the Claassen Verlag. Following his return to Wilhelmshorst, Huchel congratulated Jahnn on the performance of his play. He explained why he had not rung him immediately before embarking on the train journey back to Berlin,

> Meine Abfahrt aus Hamburg war eine sehr nervöse; das Reisebüro hatte mir am Vortag nur Zuschlagkarten, nicht die Fahrtkarte selbst, ausgehändigt, so daß mich der Beamte an der Sperre nicht in den Zug ließ. In letzter Minute mußte ich noch einige Sachen verkaufen, um eine Fahrkarte 3. Klasse zu erstehen. Dabei verlor ich meine Brille.[77]

Such were the perils of 'inter-zonal' travel in the Germany of the 1950s. On 12 June, he corresponded with Walter Höllerer concerning the publication of 'Letzte Fahrt' in Höllerer's *Transit*.[78] He explained that on 28 March he had written to a Dr Unseld, pointing out that his poem must have the date 1932 attached. Höllerer, Huchel felt, would surely understand why. As we have seen, 'Letzte Fahrt' was first published in the mid-1930s, and West German editors such as Hans Bender were well-known for boycotting writers who had published during the Third Reich. Huchel's response, here as on other occasions, was to date the poem outside that stigmatised era.

In the early summer Huchel flew to Moscow, where he met Constantin Fedin. In East Berlin, he left behind much intellectual ferment around the Aufbau Verlag, where Wolfgang Harich was leading reformist discussions. Huchel himself was not part of that grouping, though Harich was one of his authors. In July 1956, Huchel was a member of the GDR delegation that travelled to the meeting of the International PEN Club in London. The same month, he travelled to Munich with Hermlin and Mayer in order to cultivate sympathetic West German writers. On 20 July, for example, Huchel wrote to Koeppen, saying that they would like to meet up with him during their visit.[79] 1956 saw further trips to Verona and Poland. In Poland, in August, Huchel and his wife got to know Roman Karst, editor of *Twórczość*, and Marcel Reich-Ranicki, whose essay on Erich Weinert Huchel had published in 1953. Monica Huchel writes that in the Carpathian Mountains they received Helene Weigel's telegram informing them of Brecht's death on 14 August 1956.[80] Reich-Ranicki recalls giving Huchel the news on the morning of 15 August, when he picked him up from the Bristol Hotel. Huchel apparently replied to Reich-Ranicki, 'Um Gottes willen – was wird aus *Sinn und Form* werden?'[81] Huchel sent a telegram to Helene Weigel, offering his condolences.[82]

Later that year, on 5 November, following the Hungarian Uprising, Huchel wrote to Oda Schaefer, lamenting Brecht's death as that of a friend who had been a strong supporter of *Sinn und Form*.[83] He might have added that such support was now going to be much needed. Later, in conversation, Huchel was less inclined to see his relationship with Brecht as a friendship. He told Hans Dieter Schmidt, 'Ein Freund war ich ihm wohl nicht. Das hätte nämlich bedeutet, daß er mich in seine Dienste genommen hätte. Immer hat er alle, die um ihn waren, für seine Zwecke eingespannt'.[84] This is certainly an accurate characterisation of Brecht, and Huchel did manage to keep some distance in Wilhelmshorst, yet there was a debt which Brecht owed to Huchel for the first Brecht special number and an even bigger one that Huchel owed to Brecht from 1953. Without Brecht, Huchel's work could only become more difficult. Work on the second Brecht special number the following year would demonstrate that.

The same day that he wrote to Schaefer, Huchel sent a letter to Rolf Italiaander, Willy Haas' former secretary, who was now General Secretary of the Hamburg Academy. Haas, too, now lived in Hamburg, where he worked on *Die Welt*. Huchel's reflective mood led him to take stock of Haas' decisive influence on him at the turn of the 1930s in words already quoted earlier in this study, 'Alles, was mit Willy Haas zusammenhängt, ist mehr für mich als eine Erinnerung an wichtige Jahre, in denen man versuchte, zu sich selber zu gelangen. Nichts ist mit dieser Zeit zu vergleichen. Ich verdanke Haas viel, ohne seinen Zuspruch wäre wohl manches falsch gegangen'.[85] The early 1930s stood out as all the more attractive against the rapidly deteriorating situation of late 1956. He offered Italiaander a poem composed in the early 1930s, 'Havelnacht', for the anthology *Berliner Cocktail* that Italiaander was editing with Haas. He also offered 'Caputher Heuweg', explaining that he had never written poems directly about Berlin, only the area around Berlin. Nothing would happen to alter that attachment to the Havel and the villages south of Potsdam, where he lived.

Repression and Re-alignment

As we have seen, though Huchel was not directly involved in the discussions at the Aufbau Verlag, he had spoken up in January 1956 and had published his poem 'Für Ernst Bloch'. It was clear where his sympathies lay, and he had regularly published a number of those authors who had been directly involved and who were now in the firing line. Lukács had previously been a guarantor for critical orthodoxy in *Sinn und Form*, but he was now disgraced. Following his involvement in the deposed Hungarian government, he was imprisoned and his writings subsequently criticised for their emphasis on the bourgeois tradition to the exclusion of proletarian-revolutionary achievements. Hans Mayer, too, was attacked on this count, as well as for his defence of the avant-garde against the charge of decadence. In June 1956, Mayer had also publicly challenged the authority of the SED on cultural matters after having been debarred from speaking at the Writers' Congress that January. There was a plan to arrest Ernst Bloch but Ulbricht was mindful of the outcry that would have caused so soon after the award of the National Prize. Instead, Bloch was accused of fomenting seditious activities and compelled to retire from his professorship. Despite Ulbricht's written assurance to Bloch that he would not be prevented from publishing, the public denunciation of Bloch was so severe that, in the short term at least, publication was impossible.

The most brutal treatment was reserved for Wolfgang Harich, Walter Janka, Heinz Zöger and Gustav Just. All had been involved in reformist discussions at the Aufbau Verlag, about which Becher was kept informed. Indeed, at this time Becher wrote texts highly critical of the development of socialism, which he subsequently withdrew from publication and which appeared in *Sinn und Form* in 1988.[86] Harich had made no secret of his wish to see Ulbricht replaced and had ridiculed him to his face. Extraordinarily, Janka, following talks with Becher and Seghers, had been about to travel to Hungary to rescue Lukács. All four figures were arrested, put on trial and given long prison sentences. Leading intellectuals such as Seghers and Becher were conspicuous by their silence. The affair marked the end of Becher's influence as Minister of Culture. It saw the beginning of the rise of the dogmatists, Abusch and Kurella. Together with Kurt Hager and with the support of Otto Gotsche, Ulbricht's secretary, they would dominate GDR cultural politics in the late 1950s and 1960s.

Almost at a stroke, Huchel lost arguably his most talented authors. He could still risk publishing Mayer, but Bloch and Lukács were beyond the pale.[87] Looking back on the events of the autumn in a letter to Feuchtwanger of 3 December 1956, Zweig lamented, 'Immer wieder sagt einer aus unserem Kreise: "Das müßte man dem Brecht sagen! Der würde sich einen Fall des Wolfgang Harich nicht haben gefallen lassen"'.[88] It is true that there was no longer anyone of Brecht's stature in the intellectual community. Yet it must also be said that conditions for successful resistance to the neo-Stalinist restoration with its dogmatic repression were singularly unfavourable. The story of 17 June 1953 shows that Brecht had the courage and wit to act decisively when the political tide turned, but as long as it had been running against him, he, too, had been helpless. Nor would he openly challenge the SED leadership. Now, the tide was running strongly in the dogmatists' favour.

With Brecht's death, the waning of Becher's authority, the marginalisation of Zweig and the routing of the 'revisionists', orthodox cultural politicians were able to consolidate powerful positions in the SED hierarchy, which they held until Ulbricht was replaced by Honecker in 1971. From 1957, they looked for ways to exert greater influence in the Academy, where hitherto, principally through the influence of Brecht, the balance of power amongst members had generally lain with the non-orthodox. Yet their capacity to impose themselves upon the Academy and its journal was initially constrained by the absence of a Director to carry out their orders, following Engel's departure in 1957, and by the presence as President of Otto Nagel, who had little interest in such matters.

The rise of the dogmatists was, however, consistent with the flow of events in the struggle between the two German states. By the mid-1950s, the Federal Republic and the GDR had become integrated within their respective power blocs, each in practice pursuing a path of separate development. Indeed, 1955 had seen the Soviet Union's effective abandonment of Stalin's German policy. While there was still some propaganda value in the ideas of re-unification and cultural unity, their relevance for practical politics was drastically diminished. In the GDR, renewed efforts were made to focus attention on the task of the construction of a socialist society. A campaign was initiated in 1957 against what were viewed as residual bourgeois elements in the cultural sphere, and contacts with the West were actively discouraged. The Writers' Union's all-German work was all but abandoned. The campaign set the tone for the rest of the decade and beyond, the construction of the Berlin Wall in August 1961 representing its logical conclusion. For the exponents of this strategy, an undertaking such as *Sinn und Form* was at best a distraction, at worst a pernicious influence.

The War of Attrition

Remembering Brecht

The period from late 1956 onwards represented, in Hans Mayer's words, 'sechs Jahre der Agonie' for Huchel and his journal.[1] Despite the heavily bureaucratised cultural life of East Berlin, since 1953 he had become used to doing more or less as he wished. He had come to enjoy a remarkable degree of independence, upon which he had capitalised in establishing *Sinn und Form* as a virtually free-standing institution for the promotion of German cultural unity, with which his name became synonymous. In this way, idealism and institutional status came together in a manner which represented the fulfilment of two key competing strands of Huchel's personality: his deep desire to overcome the wretched inadequacies of the present and his search for stability. This was a potent combination, all the more so since the repression of early 1953 and of 1956 meant that the practice of state socialism had come to hold few attractions for him. It explains, too, why Huchel came to identify so closely with his journal, and why he was prepared to go to such lengths to defend his achievement in the years to come. After the autumn of 1956, he was called upon to do precisely that in an Academy in which the working atmosphere changed dramatically. Above all, he was determined not to slide into compromises in the manner that he had in the Third Reich. The fact that he was not an SED member worked to his advantage in that respect at least, since he was not bound into the system by party discipline. In the 1970s, Huchel recalled that, as the going got tougher, Walter Felsenstein and Herbert Ihering were among the prominent figures whom he could count on. Neither of them was a party member. Yet, by 1960 there were strict limits to their influence, as Abusch and Kurella began to get the measure of the Academy.

Huchel's major task in early 1957 was the second Brecht special number. He wrote to Jahnn on 24 August 1956, inviting him to contribute.[2] Huchel's letter shows that his original intention had been to publish the special number in the autumn of 1956. He gave Jahnn a deadline of 20 September, but this rapidly proved unrealistic. The project's cultural-political importance in the rapidly changing climate certainly did not escape Huchel, who was determined to put everything he could into it. According to the Academy's account of progress, written by Theo Piana, head of the 'Arbeitsgruppe Archive und Publikationen', Huchel informed him of his plans on 18 September 1956.[3] By the time he wrote to Jahnn again on 5 November, the deadline had been put back to the start of November.(sic) Huchel urged Jahnn to submit his piece by the middle of the month. This was particularly important since,

Einige 'westliche' Beiträge versuchen, den Dichter Brecht vom politischen Menschen Brecht scharf zu trennen. Man vergleicht seine Parteiloyalität mit Vergils Bewunderung

für die Alleinherrschaft des Augustus und Shakespeares für die Tudor-Monarchie. Und
meint, daß jetzt nach Brechts Tode der Blick endlich frei geworden sei für den 'reinen
Dichter'. Diese Art der Analyse entspricht aber weder der Wahrheit, noch ist sie im Sinne
Brechts.[4]

In time, the SED would have its own designs on Brecht, the 'socialist classic'.
While Huchel worked on the Brecht project, Jahnn had his designs on Huchel. In
November 1956, he asked him for a c.v. and on 22 February the following year he
wrote to congratulate him on his election as a corresponding member of the
Hamburg Academy. This represented a significant mark of acceptance in the Federal
Republic for the GDR poet and editor. The following day, 23 February, Huchel
wrote to Otto Nagel, informing him of this distinction, which he had accepted.[5] In
his letter of acceptance to Jahnn on 24 February 1957, Huchel commented,

> Diese Berufung ist mir insofern eine besondere Freude, als ich mich einem großen Kreis
> der Mitglieder wie Alfred Döblin, Willy Haas, Hans Erich Nossack, Günter Weisenborn,
> Peter Martin Lampel, Rolf Italiaander und nicht zuletzt Ihnen, verehrter Hans Henny
> Jahnn, seit Jahren freundschaftlich verbunden weiß.[6]

Meanwhile, he conceived the Brecht project in the grandest terms and, increasingly
aware of the scale of the coming publication, approached the Academy for support.
If he imagined that all the stops would be pulled out for Brecht at this juncture, he
was wrong. According to Piana, Huchel requested an additional three and a half
tonnes of paper on 30 November, which Piana and his colleagues managed to come
up with in December. On 20 December, Huchel wrote to Engel, requesting a special
subsidy of 10,000 marks, of which 5,000 should be in western currency. Engel
passed this on to Piana. Piana convened a meeting with Rütten und Loening on 2
January, but the publisher was not in a position to come up with the western
currency. On 6 February, the Academy received Huchel's final estimate of costs.
The additional subsidy required was 12,000 marks, of which 5,335 should be in
various western currencies. Attempts were made to secure the foreign currency,
despite the difficulty in doing so, which was communicated to Huchel on 12
February. On 20 February, it emerged that three and a half tonnes were not
sufficient: the same amount again was required. Attempts were made to identify a
source. Piana wrote a memo to the Literature Section on 28 February 1957, in which
he outlined the difficulties in meeting Huchel's demands.[7] They required raising the
subsidy for a special number from 17,000 to 37,000 marks and the amount of paper
by seven tonnes, only three and a half of which had been secured. There was little
chance of securing the 20,000 marks needed, not least because 5,000 of the 20,000
had to be in western currency. In any case, *Sinn und Form* received an annual

subsidy of 51,000 marks. Piana proposed that the project should be executed as a book. It should be produced not in paper covers 'sondern mit einem repräsentativen Einband'. It could be sold for between 10 and 14 marks. In that way, no subsidy would be necessary. Huchel had, however, evidently already planned to use the resources earmarked for issues one and two in 1957 for the special number. Also, Rütten und Loening would have to shelve plans for another book to make way for it. Piana wrote to Huchel on 4 March 1957.[8] He suggested using the first three numbers for 1957 as a way out of the dilemma. Huchel agreed to this. On 20 March, a further discussion took place with Rütten und Loening. In his 'Stellungnahme' Piana complained that the memo of the meeting, produced by the publisher, sought to place all responsibility for the procurement of the paper and the currency on the Academy's shoulders. This was unprecedented in the relationship between Academy and publisher. Not only that, Huchel now had the temerity to complain to the Academy in a letter of 16 April 1957, 'Ich bin nicht nur erstaunt darüber, wie gleichgültig verfahren wird, ich bin im höchsten Maße verärgert'.[9]

Huchel had, in fact, already written on 4 April but received no reply. On 16 April, he was adamant that at the meeting in early January representatives of the Academy and the publisher had agreed that the necessary foreign currency would be procured to pay the fee for the most important contribution, the Brecht bibliography, upon which Walter Nubel had been working for a decade. Huchel had informed Nubel that payment would be made in dollars, yet it turned out that no source for the funding had been identified.

In his 'Stellungnahme', Piana conceded that he and his colleagues had, like Huchel, assumed – wrongly as it had turned out – that Brecht's name would suffice to overcome all problems. That it was not was surely an index of the shift in cultural politics that had already taken place. Piana pointed out that they would be able to secure the paper but not the foreign currency. He concluded by stating that his group was no longer able to bear the responsibility for the matter alone.

The currency issue was taken over by the Literature Section in conjunction with the Presidium and, following the tensions of the previous months, the matter was resolved in line with Huchel's needs. Nubel's bibliography was included in a publication that stretched to over 600 pages and, like the first Brecht special number, was deemed a landmark in Brecht research, not merely a vehicle for remembering the GDR's greatest writer. The outcome clearly vindicated Huchel's insistence on approaching the matter on a grand scale.

However, much damage had been done in personal relations. Piana was outraged at what he saw as Huchel's high-handed manner and prefaced his 'Stellungnahme' with the following,

Die Redaktion der Zeitschrift *Sinn und Form* arbeitete m. W. bisher völlig selbständig als Einrichtung der Akademie. Erst seit den Beratungen um den Haushaltsplan 1957 wurde die Redaktion auf Vorschlag von Herrn Direktor Engel der Sektion Dichtkunst und Sprachpflege angeschlossen. Dies erfolgte im Herbst vorigen Jahres.

Piana knew full well that the times were now past when such a degree of independence as Huchel had enjoyed with his highly subsidised journal would be tolerated indefinitely. This independence would be seriously called into question in late 1957, both inside the Academy and in the first public attack on the journal launched by Kurt Hager, before, belatedly, the ideological attack proper began at the turn of the 1960s.

Taking up Old Themes, Re-visiting Old Haunts

In a letter to Lutz Weltmann on 31 May 1957, Huchel reflected, 'Es ist ein überaus diffiziles, ja undankbares Amt, eine Zeitschrift im Jahrzehnt des kalten Krieges redigieren zu müssen'.[10] That was the challenge that he had accepted and to which he had risen, but after the exertions over the past couple of years he sought now to devote more time to his own compositions and plans. On 7 May 1957, he sent Max Schwimmer, a member of his dormant advisory board, photos from which Schwimmer could produce a drawing. He thanked Schwimmer for his efforts on 24 May 1957.[11] That same month, he wrote to Peter Hamm[2] and Günther Deicke[3] repeating allegations that had first surfaced in the first monograph on Huchel written by Eduard Zak in 1953. Huchel asked Deicke not to include Karl Krolow's poems in an anthology that he was preparing. Like Zak, he charged Krolow with plagiarism of Huchel's work. Zak had written that while after 1933 Huchel

> schwieg und es vorzog, vergessen zu werden, erschienen die lyrischen Werke einer Reihe von Dichtern, die, wenn nicht ihre künstlerische Existenz, so doch ihre vielbeachtete 'Eigenart' von Peter Huchel bezogen hatten ... Ganze dichterische Bilder sind wortgetreu, neue Wortbildungen (Zusammensetzungen) buchstabengetreu aus Huchels Gedichten, die man in alten Jahrgängen der Zeitschriften begraben wähnte, von dieser schnellfertigen 'Schule' übernommen worden, so daß sich der Dichter, um Mißdeutungen vorzubeugen, gezwungen sah, in seinem 1948 erschienenen Gedichtband das Ersterscheinungsjahr vieler Stücke anzumerken. Auf die Aufnahme gewisser Gedichte mußte er, da sich die Anleihen bis in die jüngste Zeit fortsetzten, sogar überhaupt verzichten. (Zu diesen gehört das ... Gedicht 'Die Kammer', aus dem eine so charakteristische Verszeile wie 'Der Herbstdochtschein ins Fenster kam' von dem Lyriker Karl Krolow bedenkenlos adoptiert worden ist, denn bei diesem heißt es: 'Es wird der Herbstdochtschein im Fenster wohnen', ganz zu schweigen von anderen typischen Vokabeln wie 'Einsam Kammer', 'Blattlaternen' und so weiter.)[14]

Huchel's references in his letters to Hamm and Deicke in 1957 were to exactly the same lines and phrases. It is inconceivable that he was not behind Zak's initial attack. Some poets would have reacted with less outrage to Krolow's borrowings. Huchel was not one of them, and his reply points to the insecurity to which the poet was prey about his reputation. He wrote to Deicke of his intention, nevertheless, to proceed with the publication of more of the early poems that had appeared in *Die literarische Welt*.

Soon after, though, he was on his travels with his wife, this time an extended trip through the Soviet Union. As he wrote to Kundera on 27 June 1957, this time the trip, from which they had just returned following a thirty-hour flight, had taken them as far as Armenia, Baku and the Ararat.[15] They had visited Yasnaya Polyana, where they had got to know Bulgakov, Tolstoy's last secretary, who gave them a copy of his recently completed book on the last year of Tolstoy's life. In his next letter to Kundera on 6 August 1957, Huchel reported on their forthcoming month's holiday on the Black Sea coast, which he had planned around an invitation from that country's Writers' Union.[16] He would be flying with his wife and their son to Sosopol in Bulgaria. During the holiday, Huchel returned to Balçik, the port that he had been to in 1930 on his honeymoon. In 1963, *Chausseen Chausseen* would include 'Schlucht bei Baltschik', a poem in which Huchel married the pared-back, modernist idiom of 'Für Ernst Bloch' with the visionary, magical qualities of his verse from the later 1920s in the evocation of a world presided over by female powers. He also visited Momtschil, which Monica Huchel recalled as a 'winzige Zigeuneransiedlung unweit von Baltschik, mit winzigen, weiß gekalkten Häuschen, ein paar Zigeunerfamilien und ein paar Pferden'. (i,400) It was precisely the sort of marginal peasant community that Huchel had visited on the Magura with his first wife on their honeymoon and which so stimulated his imagination. On this occasion, he took home with him the memories which in time yielded 'Momtschil', (i,126) a vision of that rural community which is imbued with a sense of wonder and magic. In this verse, there is no longer any trace of any beneficial effect on the rural world that derives specifically from socialism. He published 'Momtschil' in *Sinn und Form* in 1959 before it was collected in *Chausseen Chausseen*.

Meeting the New Western Poets: in the Midst of the Gathering Storm

On his return to Germany, Huchel concluded arrangements for the employment of a new editor, Fritz Erpel, a Potsdam germanist. The appointment was approved by the Academy's Presidium on 27 September 1957.[17] The minutes of that meeting record that Huchel had not discussed the appointment with the Literature Section and had presented its Secretary, Bodo Uhse, with a *fait accompli*. Here as elsewhere, Huchel excluded Academy members from a decision in which they clearly had an interest. This cannot have helped relations. The minute also reads, 'Die Schreibart und der Stil von Herrn Huchel an die Akademie – das ist nicht das erste Mal – bedürfen einer Korrektur'. Uhse was delegated to talk to Huchel about the matter. It would not end there.

Also in September, Huchel, together with Mayer, received an invitation to attend a weekend meeting, from 11 to 13 October, which was organised by the last West German outpost of the Kulturbund in Wuppertal. The meeting was dedicated to the topic 'Literaturkritik – kritisch betrachtet'. As Mayer recalls, the organiser Hans-Jürgen Leep was keen to have the editor of *Sinn und Form* present rather than Huchel the poet. Yet the occasion would be equally important for Huchel the poet, as the list of western writers invited indicates. They included Ingeborg Bachmann, Paul Celan, Hans Magnus Enzensberger, Walter Jens and Heinrich Böll. The event was a revelation for both Mayer and Huchel. The relationships established and ideas exchanged would have a profound effect on the development of both. They encountered writers who were having what would prove to be a lasting impact in shaping a western German literature. They found in them much that was both new and to their liking, including things which their existing contacts such as the older Jahnn and Döblin could not offer. Mayer recalls,

> Am schönsten war der geheime Abschluß, den einige Teilnehmer der Runde für nötig hielten, nachdem die Tagung bereits geschlossen war. Wir haben lange an jenem Sonntagabend des 13. Oktober 1957 beim Wein miteinander geredet. Poeten und Interpreten einer offiziell geteilten, doch nicht teilbaren Literatur: Huchel und die Bachmann, Celan und Jens, Enzensberger und ich. Heinrich Böll, den wir dabeihaben wollten, mußte zurück nach Köln.[18]

Mayer would ensure that relations were developed through invitations to read in Leipzig, Huchel through invitations to Wilhelmshorst, where Bachmann, Enzensberger and Jens all visited him.[19] Jens and Mayer would be instrumental in the promotion of Huchel's poetry in the years to come. They were joined by Reich-Ranicki, who moved to West Germany, leaving behind his Polish secret service career and his Marxism. Thus, Huchel would have on his side the three most influential critics of their generation in the West Germany of the 1960s and beyond. They would not let him down in the struggles to come.

However rosy the prospects for collaboration looked on Huchel's and Mayer's return journey to Berlin, a storm cloud was gathering in East Berlin cultural politics. Having effectively replaced Becher as Minister of Culture when Becher, seriously ill, was wholly discredited in Ulbricht's eyes, Abusch went about organising the ideological offensive that was launched at the SED Central Committee's Cultural Conference in Berlin on 23-4 October. Abusch himself led the attack on Bloch, Mayer and 'bourgeois decadence', the dragon that had once more to be slain in order to ensure socialist progress. It fell to Kurt Hager, Secretary of the Central Committee with responsibility for culture, to lead the attack on *Sinn und Form*. Hager began his speech by referring to the pernicious Petöfi Circle in Hungary, including Lukács. He linked that grouping with the Harich-Janka group in Berlin and with Bloch. He then turned to attack Huchel's journal. The attack was conducted in the following terms,

> Deshalb kämpfen wir gegen den Neutralismus, die unpolitische Haltung, die Selbstisolie-
> rung, die beschauliche Betrachtungsweise. So wünscht man sich als Leser der Zeitschrift
> *Sinn und Form*, die von der Akademie der Künste und angesehenen Schriftstellern
> herausgegeben wird, daß sie einmal aus ihrer feinen Zurückhaltung und Beschaulichkeit,
> die etwas von der Art englischer Lords an sich hat, ihrer noblen Betrachtungsweise und
> philosophischen Skurrilität heraustreten möchte und einmal parteilich zu den so nahen und
> so wichtigen, so großen und erhabenen Problemen des Schönen in unserem sozialistischen
> Aufbau, des Heldenhaften im Kampf gegen den deutschen Imperialismus und Militarismus,
> des Sinns unserer Diskussionen über den sozialistischen Realismus, Stellung nehmen
> möchte.[20]

Hager readily acknowledged the literary quality of Huchel's journal, yet he criticised the absence of a genuine relationship between *Sinn und Form* and the Academy. This point would be raised repeatedly in the coming years. Indeed, Hager's statement set the tone for the coming conflict. A meeting between Huchel, Hager and Kurella was arranged for 4 November, also the date of the next meeting of the Literature Section, at which Hager's speech was to be discussed. Huchel prepared himself for the meeting with Hager and Kurella, which the latter probably did not attend, by setting out a number of points on two sides of a sheet of paper which has survived among his papers.[21] It is unclear to what extent he deployed the arguments that he set down in note form. He later recounted the episode to Hans Mayer. In Mayer's account, Huchel took up Hager's reference to English lords, offering the following reply, 'Sehen Sie, Herr Hager, in einem Manuskript hätte ich Ihnen das Adjektiv "englisch" sogleich gestrichen'.[22]

Huchel's notes demonstrate that his intention was to enter into a constructive dialogue, if that was at all possible, while holding on firmly to key principles. He welcomed the prospect of a more productive relationship with the Academy but pointed out that the journal had been conceived as a purely literary organ, not as a journal of cultural politics. Its publication every two months meant that it 'den aktuellen Ereignissen nachhinken muß. Ihre Aufgabe ist, eine tiefere Aktualität sichtbar zu machen'. He referred in his notes to the journal's international standing and to the enthusiastic reviews. He mentioned Brecht's praise as well as Grote-wohl's. He sought to counter the charge that in his journal literature had not been used as a weapon. He referred to work by Rilla, Smirin, Neruda, Stil, Laxness,

Brecht's 'Erziehung der Hirse', Greek resistance poetry, Eluard's essay 'Die Gelegenheitsdichtung', Arnold Kettle, Ralph Fox and Attila József. He intended to remind Hager of the Weltfestspiel débacle and to challenge his assertion that *Sinn und Form* had adopted a neutral position. He noted the difficult conditions under which he had to operate, complaining of lack of support from the Academy, lack of finance and absence of recognition for the work he had done. There was a reference, too, to the sacking in 1953. The notes conclude, 'Uniformierung? Wie schwer es ist, eine Zeitschrift von literarischem Rang aufzubauen – wie leicht es ist, eine Zeitschrift zu zerstören'.

At the meeting of the Literature Section later the same day, Huchel referred to his 'kollegial geführte Unterredung' with Hager.[23] Somehow, the meeting managed to agree that Hager's words at the conference had not constituted an attack on the journal! Bredel, however, demanded that an advisory board should be put in place and that its role should extend beyond advice to include making editorial decisions. Once again, the curtailment of Huchel's editorial independence was firmly on the agenda. Huchel responded by citing Brecht's successful opposition to the same proposal on 2 July 1953. The matter was to be discussed further at the Presidium on 10 December 1957.[24] Hager, Kurella, Zweig, Hermlin and Huchel were invited to the meeting. Both Hager and Kurella cried off, so the discussion was put off until the following February. Again, it proved impossible to assemble the group on that occasion. The matter was left in the Academy administration's hands, with the instruction to find a date that same month. The meeting, however, never happened: the Director, Engel, had departed, and, quite extraordinarily, this key post remained vacant until it was filled by Karl Hossinger in 1961. For the time being, Huchel was saved by the incompetence of an Academy bureaucracy which he had long come to expect, though by now he actually relied upon for his survival.

The affair served only to increase Huchel's growing alienation from the Academy. Huchel had attended the meetings of the Literature Section on a regular basis, but from late 1957 his attendance became quite infrequent. As so often, he signalled his distress at his situation through the publication in *Sinn und Form* of a poem which captured his mood. In late 1953, that poem had been 'Eine Herbstnacht' and in 1955 'Für Ernst Bloch'. In the final issue of 1957 he finally published 'Lenz', a poem which – we will recall – he had written all of thirty years earlier in Paris but which had stayed in his drawer. His letter to his secretary of 11 December 1957 (ii,338-9) sees him making the usual last-minute adjustments to the manuscript. In an undated letter to Günter Caspar, he made the acceptance of 'Lenz' the condition for inclusion of his other poems in the anthology *Deutsches Gedichtbuch*, which was edited for the Aufbau Verlag by Uwe Berger and Günther Deicke.[25] He described 'Lenz' to Caspar as 'dieses für eine gewisse Entwicklungsphase typische Gedicht', while he wrote to Kundera on 31 January 1958, 'In der rechten Stimmung grub ich in diesen Wochen die Jugendverse "Lenz" aus'. (ii,340) He described the poem further to his translator as a litany. As we have seen, the poem combines criticism of the abuse of authority and privilege with a sense of the tragedy of undeserved human suffering. It was, however, the poem's message contained in the final refrain that was surely more pertinent as an expression of Huchel's mood,

> Lenz, dich friert an dieser Welt!
>
> Und du weißt es und dir graut.
>
> Gott hat dich zu arm bekleidet
>
> mit der staubgeborenen Haut.
>
> Und der Mensch am Menschen leidet.

The hope of 'Griechischer Morgen' had been abandoned, idealism had found no outlet in the practice of socialism, which spawned idealism's polar opposite, despair. Increasingly, all that remained was the prospect of suffering. In this way, ideas that had first been treated in the late 1920s acquired renewed significance for the poet in the late 1950s. The theme of suffering would assume a highly personal tone in the poetry of the 1960s and 1970s, as Huchel came to face the prospect of his own mortality.

Predictably, Hager's public attack on Huchel was followed up by the Stasi. In a report of the Hauptabteilung V/6/I in Berlin dated 3 December 1957, Lieutenant Seiß collated available information about Huchel, which was drawn from the surveillance of Ernst Bloch, undertaken under the code name 'Wild', following Bloch's address, Wilhelm-Wild-Straße 8 in Leipzig.[26] An imprisoned woman recalled a meeting of participants of the Writers' Congress in March (sic) 1956 at the Newa Hotel. She recalled that on that evening Harich had been in conversation with Bloch, Lukács, Leonhard Frank, Janka, Huchel and Becher. The informant 'Hubert' had drawn attention to the fact that Harich and Bloch had published in *Sinn und Form*. Mayer's conversation with Bloch of 27 February 1957 was drawn upon. It was reported as follows,

> Neulich hätte er (Mayer – S.P.) in Frankfurt mit 'Teddy' (Theodor W. Adorno – S.P.)
> gesprochen. Dieser sei nicht mehr Amerikaner ... Er sagte dann wörtlich: Die sehen doch,
> daß Ernst und ich und **** und Peter HUCHEL und andere dem System hier von Grund
> auf feindlich sind.

Huchel's visit to Wuppertal with Mayer was known about. It was noted that there they had come into contact with members of the Gruppe 47. Huchel's visit to England was referred to. Mayer was further reported as saying on 19 October 1957 in Leipzig, 'Nach seiner Meinung würde es keinen richtigen Meinungsstreit mehr geben. So würde man jetzt auch von einem Prof. Mayer-Kreis sprechen. Zu diesem

Kreis würde man rechnen: HUCHEL, HERMLIN, Dieter KUHNERT und Peter HERZ'. Beyond the earlier information about Huchel's work in West Berlin on behalf of the SDA, that was the extent of the Stasi's knowledge about Huchel in late 1957. Seiß discussed Huchel with his colleague Ruck on 10 December 1957. Ruck undertook to investigate Huchel further in the Academy. From late 1957 until mid-1959, that file seemingly remained dormant. The Stasi compiled a report of Huchel's meeting with the Blochs at the Johannishof Hotel in November 1957, and Huchel was suspected of belonging to the 'Bloch Circle'.[27] Meanwhile, Huchel and Bloch continued to hold out the hope that Bloch could once again be published in *Sinn und Form*. Bloch wrote to Huchel on 6 August 1958, for example, 'Ganz nebenbei: sobald irgendwann die Kategorie Möglichkeit wieder ins Haus stehen sollte, bleibt das Manuskript über einen unbekannten Wagner (ich meine Musik, nicht Person) für *Sinn und Form* bereit'.[28]

Yet, despite Ulbricht's written assurance, Bloch's 'Kategorie Möglichkeit' would never become a real possibility. It was remarkable enough that, for the time being, Huchel retained his post. It was surely only because of the particular situation of the Academy that *Sinn und Form* escaped the radical changes which affected other leading GDR papers and journals. Between 1956 and 1958 the editorial staff of *Sonntag* were dismissed, Willi Bredel was sacked as editor of *Neue Deutsche Literatur*, and *Aufbau*, whose editor was Bodo Uhse, was discontinued. Under the Presidency of Otto Nagel, there was no agenda for such changes in the Academy. The reckoning would be all the more bloody when it came.

Gedichte: the New Edition for the Aufbau Verlag

Huchel had clearly been feeling the pressure of the last few month when, on 7 May 1958, he wrote to Jahnn excusing his silence by writing, 'die Zeitschrift hat gerade im letzten Halbjahr in jeder Beziehung große Anforderungen an mich gestellt, so daß ich selbst für eine kurze Reise die notwendige Ruhe einfach nicht fand'.[29] He had, in fact, been intending to take three months' leave from his editorial duties following Fritz Erpel's appointment. He had wanted to work on the new edition of *Gedichte* for the Aufbau Verlag, but this had proved impossible. On 31 January 1958 he responded to Kundera's inquiry concerning the composition of the new edition as follows,

> Zu Ihrem und meinem Kummer sei es gesagt, daß ich beim besten Willen nicht vorausse-
> hen kann, wie die zweite und vermehrte Auflage aussehen wird. Ich wollte am 1. Januar
> für ein Vierteljahr in Urlaub gehen, mich frei machen von aller Redaktionsarbeit – da kam
> wieder einmal einiges dazwischen. Das allein ist der Grund, weshalb ich mich nicht
> aufraffen konnte, an Sie zu schreiben, obwohl ich oft an sie dachte. Doch was sollte ich
> Ihnen, lieber Freund, schon mitteilen? (ii,340)

Kundera was keen that his translation of Huchel's *Gedichte* should be in step with the new edition. In his letter of 31 January, which, incidentally, shows just how much help Huchel gave his translator, we can see that Huchel preferred to give Kundera latitude to include what he wanted rather than to tie himself to a definite arrangement for the new edition he was planning. He was considering the inclusion of some unpublished or uncollected material from the 1920s and early 1930s, but, when pressed by Kundera, responded on 12 March 1958 that it would, on balance, be better not to change the arrangement of the original *Gedichte* for the Czech edition. He added, 'je mehr ich mich mit meinen Jugendversen beschäftige, desto stärker wird mir bewußt, daß ich mit der Publikation dieser Arbeiten noch einige Jahre warten sollte'. (ii,344) He explained, 'Diese Auswahl hängt schließlich weder von mir noch vom Verlag ab, es spielt die Zeit eine Rolle, in der diese Verse, meist vor dreißig Jahren, geschrieben wurden, wie auch die Zeit, in der wir leben'. In the late 1950s and early 1960s, the necessary symbiosis could not be achieved. Indeed, when the revised edition was finally published in the West by Piper in 1967 as *Die Sternenreuse*, only 'Lenz' of those early poems he had been considering was included. Despite Huchel's intentions in late 1957 and early 1958, the climate of the times militated against him doing the work necessary in order to fulfil his agreement with the Aufbau Verlag.

Continuing to Steer an All-German Course

Following Hager's attack, there was no discernible change in editorial policy. As we know, Huchel believed that the introduction of more Socialist Realism and the adoption of a decidedly partisan stance were incompatible with the journal's established identity as a high-quality, all-German organ. His refusal to incorporate such work did nothing to defuse the situation: his editorial stance was open to interpretation – and was indeed so interpreted – as a snub not only to partisan Socialist Realists but to the state itself. For Huchel's opponents, his stance demonstrated that his loyalties lay not with the GDR and socialist art but with the 'bourgeois aestheticism' of the West. He had, indeed, in many ways remained the 'bürgerlicher Lyriker' identified by Andersch at the beginning of the 1950s. The ambiguities inherent in the original conception of *Sinn und Form* were now forced into the open by the stark ideological alternative represented by the two German states. Huchel had achieved a representative status for himself and his journal whilst remaining true to its original conception, within which he had invested his personal aspirations. Yet for his opponents in the GDR, in the fundamentally changed climate of cultural politics in the late 1950s, this now amounted to a hijacking of the journal in the interests of an anachronistic all-German vision.

If GDR cultural politicians believed that he would yield to pressure, they underestimated the extent to which Huchel, stubborn and resourceful if not suited to the rigours of a protracted struggle, identified personally with the achievements of *Sinn und Form*. They also underestimated the extent to which the journal and its editor had become synonymous with German literature of the highest quality among influential circles in the West. Such was the journal's standing in that quarter that Huchel could now count on support in times of need, especially from figures such as Jens and Reich-Ranicki. Much of that support was quite genuinely an attempt to help a friend and colleague. Yet, certain West German pundits were also eager to seize a stick with which to beat the GDR in the propaganda war. In some cases, it is well-nigh impossible to separate the one from the other. Thus, in the late 1950s Huchel continued to cultivate western contacts, and he, in turn, was increasingly cultivated in West Germany. Certainly, at this stage he still saw his future in the GDR, though less out of a sense of loyalty to the state than of attachment to his journal and to his home in Wilhelmshorst. He undoubtedly hoped that pressure from influential western circles what would help him to withstand what would be only a temporary climate of hostility towards *Sinn und Form*. He had, after all, survived in 1953. This time, however, things were different, as the building of the Berlin Wall in August 1961 would conclusively demonstrate.

Despite the attack of late 1957, he continued to make valuable contributions to the Literature Section's meetings whenever he attended. He made one such proposal, described as an 'ausgezeichneten Vorschlag', on 3 March 1958, when he suggested that a series of public readings at the Academy should be launched.[30] The readings should draw on unpublished works by famous authors deposited in the Academy's archives. The provisional list included the names Heinrich Mann and Friedrich Wolf. Similarly, in April 1958 Huchel willingly complied with the request to deliver the speech on the occasion of his friend Stephan Hermlin's award of the F.C.Weiskopf Prize. Huchel's speech was published on 27 April in *Sonntag*, the title 'Drum gebt mir eine neue Sprache' citing Hermlin's verse. Huchel praised Hermlin for the clarity of his poetry and the integrity of his anti-fascism.[31] He argued for the modernity of Hermlin's language, whilst mocking the pretensions of western modernism,

> Hier gibt es kein Transit mit falschen Pässen, keinen Aprèsgardismus, der sich avantgardistisch gebärdet, keine bloße Virtuosität der Montage, keine Sprache, die eine unabhängige Existenz führen möchte, die sich nur noch an einen kleinen Kreis pervertierten Geschmacks wendet und sich allenfalls als sterile Schönheit dem Untergang anbietet.
>
> (ii,297)

We can see here how, in public in the GDR if not in the pages of *Sinn und Form*, let alone on trips to the West, Huchel – seeking still to ingratiate himself in East Berlin – would on occasion deploy the rhetoric of partisan cultural politics against the West. Who were these poets? Those who were published by Walter Höllerer in *Transit*? Who were their audience? Those who listened to Huchel at his readings in the West? Hermlin was, of course, excluded from all the charges that Huchel laid at the feet of the fraudulent 'Aprèsgardismus'. He concluded that his friend's formally rigorous, pellucid verse was a fine example of his maxim, 'Quellwasser, auf den Boden geschüttet, hat nur geringen Glanz – in ein Glas gegossen, ist es voll Licht'. (ii,298)

Poetry: Re-discovering the Mediterranean

Shortly afterwards, on 7 May 1958, Huchel reported to Jahnn that he had received a visit from Fritz Hünich of the Insel Verlag in Leipzig.[32] Huchel had recommended Jahnn to Hünich. Huchel had, of course, negotiated with Hünich in 1954, and Insel had advertised a forthcoming collection in their programme for 1955. He would continue to discuss the matter with Hünich, and Insel sent Huchel a contract on 2 December 1960. Despite reminders in 1961, the contract was never signed and Huchel finally entered into an agreement with the West German publisher, S. Fischer.

In the late 1950s, there was increasing interest in Huchel's poetry in West Germany. He informed Jahnn in that same letter that he would be reading at the Volkshochschule in Düsseldorf in June, and in Munich and Tübingen in September. He had been invited to Tübingen by Jens, while the Munich invitation had been issued by the Tukan Circle, organisers of the fourth International German Writers' Congress on 7 September 1958.[33] Jahnn himself visited Huchel in Wilhelmshorst at the end of August.

Foreign travel was, however, much more limited. As a member of the nomenclature, though, he had more opportunities than most, amongst them a trip to Venice with Hermlin in August 1958, where he was made a member of the city's Society of Culture. The Huchels converted the trip into an Italian summer holiday. They would return to Italy the following year. As we have seen, in 1957 he had returned to the Black Sea after thirty years and had been inspired to compose 'Schlucht bei Baltschik' and 'Momtschil'. He had visited Verona earlier in the 1950s, but his Italian holidays now represented a return to a Mediterranean culture and landscape which had first fired his poetic imagination when he visited Corsica with Dora in 1928 and wrote 'Die Insel Aloe'. The fruits of the fresh encounter with the Mediterranean would become fully apparent in the first section of *Chausseen Chausseen*. Among the places they visited in 1958 was Forio on Ischia. (i,399) Forio was the setting for his poem 'Chiesa del Soccorso', (i,121) which is, indeed, the name of the local church. The poem signals Huchel's renewed pre-occupation with a religious interpretation of life, as he distanced himself from secular socialism. The poem explores the fate of souls within the Saviour's sphere of influence, 'Odem der salzigen Brandung/ Erquicke die Seelen'. Religion, however, meant not so much a return to the Lutheran Protestantism of his upbringing but to the mysticism to which Huchel had been so receptive in the 1920s and early 1930s. Together with images of the Mediterranean, which acted as a counterpoint to the bleakness and barrenness of the North German world, mysticism would come increasingly to the fore in Huchel's later verse, pre-occupied as he was by the problem of death, which the mystics addressed.

Becher's Death

Huchel's return to Wilhelmshorst was followed that autumn by Becher's death on 11 October 1958. Like Hans Mayer, Huchel was aware that for all Becher's weaknesses and deceit, he had a sense of literary quality which was lost on the likes of Abusch. Huchel wrote to the Academy proposing the special number required to follow Becher's death.[34] Yet, in the name of the Central Committee, Ulbricht himself issued instructions, 'eine durchdachte Konzeption', for the special number.[35] Marianne Lange was earmarked to participate in its preparation. There was no difficulty over finance this time. Huchel's problems came from a different quarter and were merely magnified by the Becher project. On 11 December, he confided to Jahnn, 'mit welcher Fracht ich gerade noch mein schwaches Segelschiff über Wasser halten kann'.[36] He informed Jahnn that he had been prevented by the flu from attending Becher's burial, at which Jahnn had spoken as President of the Hamburg Academy. He requested a contribution from Jahnn for the special issue, revealing that it was for him 'eine recht diffizile Arbeit, die neben der Zusammen-stellung der laufenden Nummern meine Kraft in stärkstem Maße überfordert'.[37] He felt under intense pressure. He later recalled an exchange in the Academy when he had been required to report on the journal's first ten years,

> Da stellte dann Alexander Abusch eine Frage, deren Antwort er selber schon kannte: Haben Sie den Geburtstag von Walter Ulbricht nicht wenigstens einmal gewürdigt? Ich verneinte, und dann nahm Herr Professor Kurella die Hefte in seine gepflegten Finger, hob sie hoch, ließ sie herunterfallen und rief: In den ganzen zehn Jahren wurde die Existenz der DDR nicht erwähnt (was übrigens nicht stimmte). (ii,376)

The affair surrounding Ulbricht's aborted birthday issue in 1953 had not been forgotten. Work on the Becher number dragged on through 1959. Becher's widow Lilly insisted on playing an active part in it. Huchel finally confided to Jahnn on 12 September 1959, 'die letzten Monate, die ich mich mit der Zusammenstellung der ebenso umfangreichen wie zähen Sonderpublikation J[ohannes] R. B[echer] zu beschäftigen hatte, waren für mich in jeder Beziehung derart strapaziös, daß ich gesundheitlich wie nervlich völlig erledigt bin'.[38] The strain was now beginning to tell on a man who, by now in his late fifties, had coped with the peculiar pressures of the East Berlin cultural bureaucracy for a decade now. Those pressures would by no means diminish in the years to come.

Renewed Interest from the SED and the Stasi

In the meantime, both the SED and the Stasi had re-activated their interest in Huchel. Lieutenant Adamzik in Potsdam noted on 15 February 1959 the informant 'Michael's' information that Huchel never attended meetings of the Writers' Union, that he 'fest im Sattel sitzt ... und soll ein ganz bürgerlicher Mensch sein'.[39] The re-mobilisation of the SED hierarchy began on 2 April 1959. Like all other institutions, the Academy was full of people embarked on a career and out to impress. At that time, one of them was Ulrich Dietzel, a very able academic, originally employed by Kantorowicz in the Heinrich Mann Archive. In 1957, Kantorowicz had fled to the West. Later, Dietzel did outstanding work in building up the Academy's archives and after 1989 performed the duties of Academy Director with skill, though his was an impossible job. In April 1959 he sought out Kurella at his office in order to draw to his attention difficulties in the Literature Section.[40] There was clearly no point in trying to achieve anything through the Academy's own virtually non-existent management structure. The memo of his request for an interview with Kurella, written by Kurella's deputy Erhard Scherner, includes reference to the 'Willkür einzelner Akademiemitglieder' as the determining factor in the work of the Literature Section. That was the case despite the fact that four of the fifteen members of the Section were also members of the SED Central Committee. The four were Abusch, Bredel, Gotsche and Kurella. The memo continues,

> Auf die Zeitschrift *Sinn und Form* nähme die Akademie bisher so gut wie keinen Einfluß. Sicher ärgere sich Peter Huchel über jeden Angriff gegen die Zeitschrift, beklage sich aber gleichfalls, daß er wenig Hinweise und Hilfe erhalte. Bestimmt habe er Interesse, sich einmal über die Perspektive der Zeitschrift auszusprechen. Genosse Dietzel erinnerte daran, daß der Auftrag der Kulturkonferenz bisher nicht ausgeführt worden sei, daß die Genossen Abusch, Hager, und Kurella zusammen mit der Akademie über *Sinn und Form* beratschlagen und Veränderungen einleiten.

Dietzel thus picked up the point made by Piana that Huchel enjoyed virtual independence from the Academy. More importantly, though, he referred to the unfinished business of the 'Kulturkonferenz' eighteen months earlier. Now that the matter was fed back into the bureaucracy, it was to be expected that it would be acted upon again.

The Stasi, meanwhile, had been observing Reverend Karl Kleinschmidt of Schwerin cathedral, father of Sebastian Kleinschmidt, the present editor of *Sinn und Form*. On 27 May 1959, a report was filed, which referred to Huchel's link with Kleinschmidt.[41] This had prompted the Stasi to begin investigating Huchel, about whom at the time the Stasi possessed 'kein operatives Material'. The Stasi received the following assessment from a 'reliable unofficial source',

> In seiner Grundhaltung ist Huchel ein anständiger und positiver Mensch, jedoch mit vielen bürgerlichen Eigenschaften und Auffassungen behaftet. Der GI hat den Eindruck, daß H. seit längerer Zeit in einem ungünstigen Fahrwasser segelt. Nach Meinung des GI ist Huchel nicht der treibende Teil, sondern wird beeinflusst von einem Personenkreis der Akademie der Künste. Zu diesen Personen zählen UHSE, HERMLIN, FÜHMANN und BREDEL, die teilweise in sogenannten Nebenfragen opponieren. Sehr deutlich drückte sich das auf der Bitterfelder Konferenz aus, wo z.B. UHSE äußerte: 'wenn dort so eine Atmosphäre herrscht wie auf der Kulturkonferenz in Berlin, verlasse ich die Tagung'. Uhse hat die Tagung nicht verlassen, obwohl er sehr unruhig war als Genosse Walter Ulbricht in seinem Diskussionsbeitrag u.a. sagte, daß es an der Zeit wäre, in der Akademie der Künste aufzuräumen.
>
> Der GI ist der Meinung, daß es sich bei den genannten Personen im einzelnen um gute brauchbare Genossen handelt. Als Gruppierung erwiesen sie sich unfruchtbar, aber nicht gefährlich.[42]

It is difficult to imagine Huchel belonging to the same 'group' as Bredel. The Stasi undertook to gather further intelligence about the 'group'. Meanwhile, details of Huchel's career supplied by the poet himself to his employer on 10 February 1956 were copied by the Stasi and deposited in their file on Huchel. The unofficial informant's evaluation of Huchel's character was accurate up to a point, yet by this stage in his career he was much less susceptible to influence by other Academy members than was assumed. It certainly made no sense whatsoever to lump Huchel in with Uhse, let alone Bredel, though he had much more in common with Fühmann and Hermlin. In truth, though, Huchel's affinities and sympathies by now lay more with friends in Hamburg, not to mention Bachmann and Celan, than with East Berlin literary circles, with which his material existence was bound up.

The relationship with the Hamburg Academy was further cemented when Jahnn wrote to Huchel on 28 May 1959.[43] Jahnn announced that his Academy had agreed to award Huchel its major distinction, its bronze 'Plakette'. Thomas Mann had been a previous recipient in 1955. Jahnn explained that the award was in recognition of his achievements as a poet and as an editor. He saw this as a way of marking *Sinn und Form*'s first decade. The award would be made in Hamburg and a number of East Berlin Academy members would be invited. Jahnn saw the occasion as an opportunity to re-affirm relations between artists in East and West. The date of the ceremony would be fixed later.

The award was, indeed, a rare distinction for a GDR writer in the West in the late 1950s. Huchel sent his formal letter of acceptance on 4 June 1959. He wrote,

> Ich bin mir bewußt, daß – im Vergleich zu dem, was man hätte leisten können, ginge nicht infolge der unseligen Spaltung Deutschlands auch ein Riß durch die deutsche Kultur, – das Ergebnis meiner Bemühungen oft hinter meinen Wünschen zurückbleiben mußte. Aber ich darf die Ehrung der Hamburger Akademie wohl in der Gewißheit annehmen: meine Arbeit ist nicht umsonst gewesen.[44]

The award was the first of a long list of honours that Huchel would receive in West Germany during the two remaining decades of his life. This contrasted starkly with the stony silence that would presently descend over him in the GDR.

That same month of May 1959, no doubt prompted by the announcement of the Hamburg Academy's award, the first of many articles supportive of Huchel appeared in the West German press. It was published on 23 May in the Hamburg daily *Die Welt* and written by Marcel Reich-Ranicki, under the title 'Peter Huchel: Ein Mann ließ sich nicht irre machen'. Reich-Ranicki wrote that, unlike Seghers and Zweig, Huchel had not been deflected from his purpose by the cultural functionaries. He added that it was self-evident that the development of the 'Soviet Zone' could only disillusion a man like Huchel. Reich-Ranicki demonstrated his expert knowledge of Eastern Bloc cultural affairs in his description of *Sinn und Form*'s position and function. He added, 'Zwar ist der Spielraum, den man dieser für das literarische Leben der Sowjetzone durchaus nicht typischen Zeitschrift gönnt, im vergangenen Jahr wieder wesentlich enger geworden, doch haben sich die Gerüchte, Huchel sei abgesetzt worden, erfreulicherweise als falsch erwiesen'. The rumour mill would continue to turn in the coming years until the reality finally matched the prophesies. Reich-Ranicki's article did not escape the Stasi. In a report of 13 July 1959, one can read of Huchel and his work,

> In einigen westdeutschen Zeitungen u. a. in der *Welt* [wurden] Gedichte abgedruckt, die mit positiven Kritiken beurteilt wurden. Ferner erhielt Huchel vor einiger Zeit in Westdeutschland einen 'Kunstpreis'. In den Artikeln zu seinen Gedichten wurde er sehr gelobt, im Gegensatz zu anderen fortschrittlichen Schriftstellern wie Kuba, Marschwitza u.a. Es kann der Eindruck entstehen, daß versucht wird, den Huchel mit dem Ziel der Abwerbung ideologisch zu beeinflussen.[45]

As so often, Stasi officers' appreciation was hardly sophisticated. It must be said that the efforts of Hager, Abusch and Kurella could only make the West appear more attractive, whatever reservations Huchel might have about Adenauer and his government, as well as the Western Alliance.

The Stasi now collected information about an invitation that Huchel had received from a West Berlin literary grouping, the 'Gruppe Vier + ', whose Secretary was Johannes Teufel, on 6 July 1959.[46] The report, written by Captain Zörner in Potsdam, notes, 'Über Peter Huchel, der selbst Lyriker ist, können hier kaum Ermittlungen geführt werden, da er im Schriftsteller-Verband nie zu sehen ist'. He was obviously right to steer clear of the Writers' Union, which was a nest of informants.

The Academy's Boycott of the Hamburg Award

Jahnn wrote on 9 September, informing Huchel that the ceremony in Hamburg would be on 3 October.[47] The same day he wrote to Otto Nagel, inviting him to attend and to bring with him members of the Literature and Theatre Sections. Hans Scharoun, President of the West Berlin Academy, would also be present.[48] Huchel replied to Jahnn on 12 September 1959.[49] He explained to Jahnn that he had booked his holiday in Italy for October, since he had assumed that the award ceremony would take place in September. It might make sense to delay the ceremony until November. November would also be better for the East Berlin Academy, because the Academy was wrapped up in its preparations for its tenth anniversary.[50] He also had to draw to Jahnn's attention the fact that the East Berlin Academy had not officially recognised the award, since the Academy had not been officially notified. He was, though, sure that Jahnn's recent letter to Nagel would have put things right.

In the event, the ceremony was arranged for 7 November. Huchel went to Italy in September for a three-week holiday. When he left, he was not well.[51] This time, the Italian holiday took in Monterosso, a small village on the coast just west of La Spezia. Again, the place name would be taken over as the title of a poem in the first section of *Chausseen Chausseen*. And again, the poem treated the question of salvation.

Following his return, the necessary arrangements were put in place for the Hamburg trip. Nagel informed Jahnn by telegram on 30 October 1959 that neither he nor other members of the Presidium would be travelling with Huchel.[52] It was, appropriately enough, Willy Haas who had been chosen to deliver the laudation in Hamburg. Yet Uhse, Secretary of the Literature Section in East Berlin, wrote to Huchel on 26 October 1959, explaining that the Academy could not support the event since Haas had made no secret of his views on the GDR.[53]

Huchel travelled to Hamburg without fellow academicians. Haas praised Huchel the editor and the poet. Of the editor, he said that he had far outdone his own efforts as Huchel's mentor on *Die literarische Welt* and that he had 'die von uns beiden so tief bedauerte politische Zweiteilung Deutschlands ohne viel Umstände zu einer geistigen Einheit zusammengeschweißt'.[54] Huchel's poetry was for Haas

zunächst ein Produkt der Erde, des Pflanzenreichs, der Natur, der Landschaft ... ein Werk
der chthonischen Alchimie, der Naturmystik, wenn man will, und - ich sage das nicht
ohne geheime Bosheit - eine Dichtung von 'Blut und Boden', die einzige echte, die wir
in der deutschen Literatur unserer Zeit mit Recht so nennen dürfen - neben der Lyrik des
älteren Wilhelm Lehmann.[55]

Haas knew his old friend's poetry better than most, and for him the comparison with
Lehmann was unproblematic. He went on to state that, as far as he was aware,
Huchel had published nothing whatsoever in the Third Reich. He had remained
resolutely silent, as befitted a poet of his rank. This is just yet another example of
the ritual distancing from the culture of the Third Reich that was undertaken after
the war. As usual, the distancing was accompanied by the affirmation of the poet's
moral rectitude. Finally, for Haas, it was absurd that after the war in the West
Huchel's poetry had remained 'so gut wie unbekannt'.[56]

In reply, Huchel acknowledged the role that Haas had played in the early
stages of his career. He referred specifically to Haas' library and to his discovery
there of St. Augustine. Engaging in his own self-stylisation, he contrasted Haas'
library with his grandfather's curious collection of material, which had provided, so
he said, his first reading matter. He continued by offering, for the first time, a
negative interpretation of St Augustine's 'Großer Hof des Gedächtnisses, daselbst
Himmel, Erde und Meer gegenwärtig sind'. He commented that it 'kann nicht nur
verfinstert werden - er kann ausgelöscht werden'. (ii,300) The veneer of optimism
during the reconstruction phase of the early 1950s had now peeled off, the poet
being left to confront the stark reality of man's destructive potential, as demonstrated by the war begun by Nazi Germany and constantly present in the nuclear
threat. This pessimism would henceforth be a hallmark of Huchel's poetry.

Jahnn's Death

As President of the Hamburg Academy, Jahnn presented the 'Plakette' to Huchel.
Huchel later told the story that only a matter of days after, Jahnn, blind drunk, rang
Huchel from Potsdam railway station.[57] Huchel went to see him and Jahnn explained
that he had attended a congress in Weimar and had spent the night drinking with
Ulbricht and others. Jahnn had accused them of being criminals. Only too aware of
his recent heart attack, they none the less plied him with cognac until he was out of
his mind. Jahnn boarded the train for Hamburg once more, on which he had another
heart attack before he died a few days later, on 29 November. Together with Bredel,
Huchel represented the East Berlin Academy at Jahnn's funeral, which degenerated
into a farce, 'als die Tochter des Toten die Schleifen an dem von Ulbrichts
Kondolenzgesandtem überbrachten Kranz zerschnitt'.[58] On 18 December, Huchel

returned to Hamburg to speak of his memories of Jahnn at the Hamburg Academy. Jahnn's death was a great blow. Huchel was robbed of a friend and of a figure upon whom he had been able to rely throughout the 1950s as his single most important contact in the Federal Republic. One by one, the great names of the first half of the 20th century whom he had published in *Sinn und Form* had passed away: Mann, Brecht, Döblin, Becher and now Jahnn.[59]

Cementing Relations with the Young Western Poets

On that same 18 December that Huchel was speaking in Hamburg, his friend Stephan Hermlin was attempting to boost Huchel's standing in East Berlin. At a meeting of the Literature Section, Hermlin proposed Huchel for the new Johannes R. Becher prize.[60] By contrast, a Stasi informant 'Feuerherd', the writer Bernhard Seeger, reported on 21 January 1960 that Huchel was the only GDR writer who was a member of a West German academy, that his poems were published regularly in the West and hardly ever in the East. His verdict was that Huchel was a 'sehr billiger und gewandter Poet', who did not deserve the nomination for the Becher Prize, which had also been made by comrade Erdmann of the Kulturbund.[61]

    The previous autumn Hans Mayer had consulted Huchel after Hans Werner Richter had issued Mayer, the GDR's star critic, with his first invitation to attend a meeting of the Gruppe 47. Mindful of his experience in 1954, Huchel advised him not to attend, but the opportunity was too good for Mayer to miss. In October 1959, Mayer travelled to the meeting at Schloß Elmau. Johannes Müller, whose group Huchel had joined briefly with Joachim in late 1925, was no longer there, but Mayer was sceptical about the choice of a place that had Nazi associations. He was, however, won over by the Gruppe 47, captivated above all by the new poetry of Enzensberger and Günter Grass, and by Bachmann's unpublished prose. The impression that he had gained at Wuppertal in 1957 was amply confirmed. Mayer was determined to introduce this new work to the GDR. He managed to arrange a symposium in his favourite lecture room 40 at the University of Leipzig on 30-31 March 1960. The event was one of Mayer's most cherished memories of his time in Leipzig.[62] One session was devoted to poetry. Mayer invited his friends Hermlin and Huchel from the GDR, Enzensberger and Bachmann from the West. The session was led by Walter Jens. Another session was led by Inge Jens. It dealt with Thomas Mann's correspondence with Ernst Bertram, which she had edited. The poets read from their work on 30 March and talked until late into the night after a reception at the Hotel International. Ernst and Karola Bloch were invited, Werner Krauss and Georg Maurer, too. Jens delivered a paper the following day, in which he interpreted a poem by each of the guests, one by Maurer and Marie Luise Kaschnitz's 'Gennazino'. Jens' paper was followed by discussion, in which Mayer's students, not so much his poets, took the lead. Mayer recalled with justified pride, 'Viele

Zuhörer, das weiß ich, haben sich damals eine kostbare Erinnerung mitgenommen'.[63]

Falling out with Bloch

For Huchel, the occasion was marred by tensions that had built up between him and Bloch. Following Bloch's marginalisation, their contact had become less frequent, and Bloch suspected Huchel of dropping him at a time when Bloch entertained fresh hopes of publishing again in the GDR. Huchel had last been in Leipzig on 25 March 1958, when he met up with Bloch. At the start of 1960, Huchel had enquired about Bloch in a telephone conversation with Mayer, during which Mayer conveyed to Huchel Bloch's opinion about him, which was in no way flattering. During the three days in Leipzig in late March 1960, Huchel had respected what he took to be Bloch's wish that they should keep their distance from one another. Following his return home, on 2 April Huchel phoned Bloch to try and set the record straight. To no avail. The following day – it was Huchel's birthday – Bloch fired off an angry letter to him. The letter was not published in the edition of Bloch's letters, which contains his correspondence with Huchel. Nor was Huchel's reply of 7 April, in which he responded to Bloch's reproaches.[64] The first reproach, which Huchel had attempted to clear up by phone, was that he had rejected for publication Mayer's essay on Schiller dedicated to Bloch. Huchel enclosed a photocopy of Mayer's letter to him of 11 November 1959, which stated that Mayer had reserved that work for the West German *Jahrbuch der Deutschen Schiller-Gesellschaft*. Bloch's second reproach concerned Huchel's poem 'Für Ernst Bloch'. Huchel assured Bloch that he had always chosen the poem for readings in recent years, be they in Berlin, Prague or Düsseldorf. He had selected it for Leipzig, too, but at the dinner on 29 March Mayer had suddenly suggested that it be read there. Bloch had passed comment on its omission from Huchel's reading the following day, apparently suggesting that Huchel had quietly forgotten his friend now that he had become marginalised in GDR cultural life. Huchel pointed to the fact that the poem had recently been included in four anthologies, one in Italy, one in France, one in West Germany and, finally, in the GDR PEN almanac published by the Verlag der Nation. In conclusion, Huchel explained that the phone call and his present letter were intended merely to record a number of facts, nothing else. Their relationship should remain as Bloch wanted it. Huchel included a memo of Frau Narr's, supporting his version of events in October/November 1959.

After the break with Kantorowicz, the falling-out with Bloch is the second example of a long-standing friendship put under the severest strain in the unhealthy atmosphere of mutual suspicion engendered by the SED's marginalisation of figures who went against their views in cultural politics. Both Bloch and Kantorowicz felt that they had been shabbily treated by their old friend, whom they suspected of compromising too much in order to protect his own position. Yet, from an SED point-of-view, Huchel had conspicuously failed to do enough to satisfy the party's cultural politicians, even though he had not gone so far as to provoke their wrath by actually publishing Bloch again. Indeed, presently relentless pressure would be brought to bear on Huchel. In the circumstances of Huchel's own marginalisation, Bobrowski and Hermlin, two fellow poets with whom he felt a special affinity, would be found wanting by Huchel. The failings of Bobrowski and Hermlin have been highlighted in publications since 1989.[65] It is salutary to consider these failings in the same context as the tensions in Huchel's friendships with Kantorowicz and Bloch. This suggests the need for careful appreciation of the complex issues and emotions at stake in an environment of extreme pressure. One should not fall into the trap of playing off the integrity of one figure against the apparent lack in others. At different times, the moment of truth came for Kantorowicz, Bloch, Huchel and Hermlin, if less obviously Bobrowski. Whatever weaknesses earlier or later, Kantorowicz, Bloch, Huchel and Hermlin all showed courage in standing up to pressures.

Indeed, while the break with Kantorowicz was irrevocable, Huchel and Bloch managed to patch things up. It is unclear from archival sources available to me who made the next move, after Huchel, in his letter of 7 April, had left the door open for Bloch. In the early summer, Huchel did two things, no doubt determined to demonstrate his loyalty to his friend, who had entered into discussions with the SED concerning possible public expressions of loyalty to the GDR and the SED, which might result in permission to publish in *Sinn und Form*.[66] No doubt aware of this situation, Huchel wrote to Abusch, inquiring whether he might now proceed to publish Bloch. He also had chapters 45-47 of Bloch's *Prinzip Hoffnung* set by his printer. However, he received no reply from Abusch, who knew that Bloch had declined to provide exactly the type of statement that the SED required. On 19 December 1960, Huchel shelved plans for the publication.[67] It can be assumed that all the important discussions of this matter between Huchel and Bloch were conducted by phone. Their published correspondence during this period is restricted to brief, though friendly exchanges. On 8 June 1960, Bloch sent Huchel his recommendation of a young poet from his home region, the Palatinate, Susanne Margarete Stirn-Faschon.[68] Huchel responded on 8 July with his greetings on the occasion of Bloch's 75th birthday.[69] A year later, when the Berlin Wall was built, Bloch was on holiday with his family in Bavaria. The Blochs elected not to return to the GDR.

Kurella Begins the Attack

In early 1960, the East Berlin rumour mill began to turn once more with stories of *Sinn und Form*'s imminent demise. Following Dietzel's intervention with Kurella, the latter was, indeed, preparing the ground to move against Huchel. The context was the SED Cultural Conference, which had passed a resolution that the work of the Academy should be fully investigated. Those in the West who enjoyed good contacts with East Berlin, not least with Huchel himself, picked up the rumours and passed them on. Thus, in May 1960, two supportive articles appeared in West Germany. The Stasi duly copied for their records Reich-Ranicki's 'Das Fähnlein eines Aufrichtigen' and Peter Jokostra's 'In der Schußlinie der Doktrinäre'.[70] Reich-Ranicki raised many hackles in East Berlin with his description of *Sinn und Form* as 'gewissermaßen eine liberalerer (sic) Enklave im geistigen Leben der Zone'. The phrase would reverberate through the many meetings and statements of the coming years. Jokostra, meanwhile, characterised Huchel as 'der einzige verantwortungsbewußte Sachwalter deutschen Sprachgutes in der Zone'.

Nor did it escape the Stasi's attention that since April 1960 Hermlin had been Secretary of the Academy's Literature Section. Huchel had supported Hermlin's appointment in a letter to Dietzel on 12 May 1960 and had nominated him for the Johannes R. Becher Prize.[71] It was noted by the Stasi officer that there had been what was called a lack of progress in the development of *Sinn und Form*.[72] It fell to Hermlin to convene a meeting at which, following earlier failures to do so, *Sinn und Form* would be the subject of discussion. Huchel informed Dietzel that he was hoping to attend the meetings despite the fact that he had been in some pain, suffering, he wrote, from an abscess that had required surgical treatment.

The conflict of interest for Hermlin was clear: on the one hand he was an SED member, on the other Huchel was his friend, with whom he shared many artistic views that could not be accommodated in the dogmatists' terms of reference. Yet as a party member he had received his instruction that the debate over the future of Huchel's journal should now be conducted in the Academy's committees. There was no question but that he would comply with that instruction. In time, it would prove impossible for Hermlin to reconcile his conflicting interests. He chaired a meeting of the Literature Section on 2 June 1960, at which it was agreed that a special meeting of the Section should take place. In addition to Huchel, the President and all the Secretaries of the Sections were invited to attend.[73] The meeting took place on 23 June 1960. The minutes of that meeting of 23 June and of those that followed in the Academy were published in *Sinn und Form* in 1992.[74]

Hermlin was in the chair. Some fundamental issues required clarification, not least whether the Literature Section or the Presidium was ultimately responsible for the journal. Hermlin's own view, which was not Huchel's, was that the Presidium should be responsible, since *Sinn und Form* was the journal of the whole Academy. Like so many issues now on the table, this matter had been batted back and forth in the early 1950s. The Academy's policy aim had always been the extension of the journal's brief, while Huchel had always seen it as a literary journal. That was his great strength, and in that way, of course, he could best maintain his editorial independence. Yet Hermlin wished to explore how far the journal could come truly to represent the range of the Academy's interests through the publication of material from all Sections. The range of expertise on the advisory board had been intended to facilitate this. At this early point in the discussion, however, one board member, Ludwig Renn, resigned because the board had, to his knowledge, never actually met. Support for Huchel came from Walter Felsenstein, yet Kurella intervened. Predictably enough, he, like Hermlin, emphasised the journal's role as an organ for the whole Academy.

In reply, Huchel claimed that when the advisory board was founded in 1953, it was on the understanding that it would only meet to discuss contributions dealing with non-literary matters. He did not deny that it had long been dormant.[75] Like his critics, he had recourse to arguments that had been rehearsed ad nauseam in the early 1950s. He insisted that the journal had been and should in the future be primarily a literary journal. As always, he was able to refer to its very positive critical reception. He drew attention to the difficult conditions under which he and his staff had to work. At this stage, he felt it was still appropriate to refer to the extraordinary level of trust invested by the government in him and his staff, which they were at pains to justify.

For Kurella, it was time to stop beating about the bush. The journal existed at several removes from the Academy. It was pitched at a level that was far away from any recognisable reality. Only a small circle of people contributed, yet surely the journal's task was to draw attention to the Academy's activities. Huchel replied that in Rilla and Brecht he had lost two excellent essayists. Academy members simply did not produce sufficient material to fill the journal's pages. Anna Seghers then spoke, attempting to mediate. The journal's links with West German figures were very useful. Academy members had done little to support *Sinn und Form*. She felt, however, that Huchel could do more to initiate discussions and establish new contacts, especially now that key figures such as Becher were no longer there. She saw no reason why other Sections should not contribute and, like Brecht before her, she wanted to see more of GDR life reflected in *Sinn und Form*'s pages in a manner comprehensible abroad. Joining the discussion, Arnold Zweig pleaded for the maintenance of the journal's literary quality. Recollecting the statements that had accompanied its foundation, he regarded *Sinn und Form* as an undertaking that had repaired some of the damage done to German culture by Nazism. Yet that was no longer deemed sufficient by Kurella.

Otto Nagel renewed the pressure on Huchel, referring to the resolution that *Sinn und Form* should reflect the whole spectrum of the Academy's activities. Huchel challenged him to name anyone in his Section who would write for the journal on a regular basis. He asked if Nagel's Section could formulate a plan which would guarantee *Sinn und Form* regular contributions. He then raised the issue of editorial responsibility, recollecting that he had been left to carry the can over the publication of Brecht's Barlach essay.

Kurella had little time for such matters. He demanded a plan for the journal which would place it firmly within the context of the Academy's activities and within the GDR's cultural policies. He then moved the terms of the debate on much further, questioning the role and function of the Academy and maintaining that the journal must inform readers about GDR cultural life. He suggested treatment of the forthcoming Arbeiterfestspiele. Huchel expressed his interest in receiving such a piece from Kurella. It did not materialise.

Apparently hoping that concessions might once more suffice, Huchel declared his willingness to resume the practice of arranging a regular time when authors could meet with him at the Academy. He also agreed with Felsenstein's suggestion that each Section should nominate a member for the advisory board. Yet, fearing there was a hidden agenda, he went on to suggest, 'es könne sich herausstellen, daß bereits der Beschluß gefaßt sei, die Zeitschrift solle aufhören zu bestehen. Dann bitte er, das ihm gleich zu sagen, und es gäbe auch keine "Flurgespräche" mehr über *Sinn und Form*'. Both Kurella and Nagel flatly rejected Huchel's suggestion, querying who might have wished to put such rumours into circulation. For Nagel, it was self-evident that it could scarcely be said of Hermlin that he of all people could have arranged the discussion with a view to torpedoing *Sinn und Form*. There, for the moment, the matter rested.

Huchel's Defence

Following the June meeting, Huchel compiled a very detailed 'Bericht über *Sinn und Form*', in which he catalogued the journal's achievements in response to the criticisms made on 23 June. It was completed on 12 July 1960. It was a very clear signal to Huchel's opponents that he was not going to give up without a struggle. In a letter to Kundera of 17 August 1960, Huchel suggested that he had been taken unawares by recent events, which he compared to being engulfed by a sudden landslide.[76] He followed the comparison through, writing that he was finding his way back to the daylight. His nerves were in a bad way. He was in need of a holiday, but the planned trip to Sicily had been cancelled. Instead, he was about to leave for the Baltic coast for two weeks with his wife and son. In a letter of 10 November that year to August Closs, Huchel conveyed his state of mind during that holiday, when he completed the poem 'In der Bretagne'. Its opening stanza reads,

> Wohin, ihr Wolken, ihr Vogelschwärme?
> Kalt weht die Chaussee ins Jahr,
> Wo einst der Acker warm von der Wärme
> Des brütenden Rebhuhns war. (i,133)

He wrote to Closs that isolated images had remained dormant since he had passed through the north of Brittany in the autumn of 1927. He continued, 'Jetzt erst, in diesem September an der Ostsee, kam es zur Niederschrift des kleinen Gedichts. vielleicht nur deshalb, weil ich mich an der verregneten kalten Ostsee nicht wohl fühlte und manchmal an die Nordküste der Bretagne und an ein warmes Herdfeuer denken mußte'. (ii,346-7)

The events of the autumn served only to darken his mood. Before the next meeting of the Literature Section on 22 September, Erhard Scherner, Kurella's assistant, wrote as follows to Siegfried Wagner of the Cultural Department of the Central Committee, 'Huchels Bericht ist kaum mehr als eine Rechtfertigung des Bisherigen. Von der auf der letzten Beratung geforderten neuen Konzeption der Zeitschrift enthält er kaum einen Hauch'. Scherner went on to bad-mouth Huchel,

> Ich darf noch aufmerksam machen, daß uns die Genossen des DSV während des Sommerkurses mit westdeutschen Schriftstellern mitteilten, daß der Besuch einiger westdeutscher Schriftsteller in der Wohnung von Peter Huchel (Erich Arendt war ebenfalls anwesend) deprimierend auf die jungen Westdeutschen gewirkt habe.

As we have seen, the Writers' Union was full of spies. Huchel knew this well enough and was less and less inclined to keep up the appearance of loyalty.

Meanwhile, Hermlin was keen to ensure that the discussion should continue in the Literature Section with the full participation of all interested parties. He evidently viewed open debate as the way to deal with his own conflict of interests. He wrote to Kurella and Abusch on 22 September, urging them to attend all meetings of the Section, not just on isolated occasions. Huchel's report was circulated with the agenda for the meeting and acted as a basis for discussion on 22 September and on 27 October.

On 22 September, Huchel began by conceding that 'noch einiges fehlt, was das Bild der literarischen Zeitschrift quantitativ bereichern würde'. He went on, however, to enumerate twelve points of fundamental importance regarding the journal's 'Konzeption'. He took issue with Kurella's criticism, confronting it squarely with a clearer definition of the journal's character. He insisted that there should be no simplification of complex issues. He outlined five areas which should continue to be cultivated: the literary essay; progressive world literature; the cultural heritage of world literature and its elucidation in terms of historical materialism; critical engagement with contemporary artistic tendencies and movements; and literary documents. Huchel appended a host of significant achievements in each area, mentioning Academy membership wherever relevant. He continued by stressing the importance of collaboration with West German academies, mentioning contacts with Hamburg, Mainz and West Berlin, all of which he had cultivated successfully. There can be absolutely no doubt that he had achieved what he had originally been engaged to achieve. In that way, *Sinn und Form*, if not the Academy itself, had come to enjoy such high standing in the West. Yet times had changed.

The discussion on 22 September became simply a re-run of the June meeting. Kurella attacked the journal's achievements, while Huchel mounted his defence. But any defence that he cared to mount would never be deemed enough now. Before the argument was resumed on 27 October, Huchel and *Sinn und Form* became the subject of a rancorous exchange of letters between Hermlin and members of the Hamburg Academy. Speculation had continued to mount as to whether Huchel could survive the hostile climate in GDR cultural life and there were even rumours that he had been arrested. On a visit to Hamburg, Uhse was informed of this rumour by Günter Weisenborn, who had heard it from Italiaander, who was the General Secretary of the Hamburg Academy.[77] In a letter to Italiaander of 27 September 1960, Hermlin suggested, quite improbably, that Huchel might take action against Italiaander for spreading the rumour. He challenged Italiaander to explain why he was spreading such untruths and what steps he was intending to take in order to correct the impression he had given, which might affect relations between the academies. Martin Beheim-Schwarzbach, Chairman of the Hamburg Academy's Literature Section, replied to Hermlin on 16 October 1960. He dismissed Hermlin out of hand, arguing that it had all been idle, insignificant chatter. The tone adopted by Hermlin would do nothing to help relations between the academies. The basis for the rumour was apparently the fact that Huchel had not replied to letters for some time. In Hermlin's view, to base a rumour on such flimsy evidence amounted to crass irresponsibility. In his reply on 25 October 1960, Hermlin accordingly represented the view that intellectuals should attempt to counteract the political division of the Cold War by giving a good example. Rumours of the sort spread about Huchel only contributed to the Cold War mentality. It is difficult to imagine that the Hamburg Academy heeded Hermlin.

On 27 October, Huchel was supported in the Academy by his old friend Ihering. Ihering was also a member of the West Berlin Academy and reported that the feeling there was that there was no point in producing a journal as long as *Sinn und Form* remained so good. He also spoke on Felsenstein's behalf, conveying his opinion that *Sinn und Form* was an excellent journal and should continue as it was. Huchel then raised the stakes. Remarking that the editorial staff appeared not to enjoy the Academy's confidence, 'er selber stelle, wenn es sein muß, sein Amt zur Verfügung'. Kurella took this as his cue to argue that the inclusion of material from all the Academy's sections would 'natürlich eine radikale Änderung bedeuten und ein Verschwinden von *Sinn und Form* in der bisherigen Form'. Hermlin sought a compromise position: *Sinn und Form* should remain a literary journal but contributions from the other arts had a place there as long as they were presented in an acceptable literary form. Huchel responded positively to Hermlin's suggestion. He went on to point out that other material might find its way into a special section of the almanac that the Academy had long been planning to produce. Yet he added that if it was felt that an organ should be produced representing the work of the four sections, he was prepared to work on it, 'nur solle man dann *Sinn und Form* eingehen lassen'. Kurella seized his chance to put to the Section the fundamental question about the journal's future character, but he did not receive the support he had expected. The membership came out in favour of maintaining *Sinn und Form* as a literary journal.

The lengthy discussion moved on. Uhse argued that the journal needed to have proper representation in Berlin. There should be closer contacts with young writers. Kurella stated quite bluntly that the journal was simply out of step with the contemporary reality of the GDR. He explained that the principles that had previously underpinned the journal's activities were no longer valid,

> Es gibt bei uns immer noch einen Begriff der gesamtdeutschen Arbeit, der abgestorben ist. Wir haben ein humanistisches Bildungsideal verteidigt, das uns bedroht erschien sowohl bei uns wie im Westen. Wir fanden uns auf einer Mittellinie, die die Grundlage für eine Wiedervereinigung sein konnte. Politisch liegen die Dinge heute ganz anders und stellen uns vor ganz neue Aufgaben.

There was much truth in these words, which met with general approval, yet they cannot have been welcome to Huchel, whose career with *Sinn und Form* and in the GDR in general was intimately connected with the all-German mission which he was not prepared to abandon without a fight. Kurella observed that the points he had made were of relevance for the Academy as a whole and would have to be discussed in that context. In this way, Kurella signalled the SED's intention to bring the Academy into line with SED policy, which would take precedence over further debate about *Sinn und Form*.

Anger and Disillusion; under Surveillance

The abysmal state of relations between Huchel and the GDR cultural bureaucracy emerges in a memo of 7 January 1961 produced by an employee of the Writers' Union, Baumert. It was written for internal consumption but was later commandeered by the Stasi.[78] Baumert noted that he had phoned Huchel to inform him of arrangements for a reception for Putrament, a meeting by the Schwielowsee at the Writers' Union's Friedrich-Wolf-Heim in Petzow and the formulation of the invitations to the All-German Writers' Congress for Peace and Disarmament due to take place at Weimar on 28-9 January 1961. Huchel had accepted an invitation to open the congress, and his name was on the Academy's call to support the congress that was issued on 21 November 1960.[79] Huchel, however, told Baumert over the phone 'in sehr scharfer Form und erregter Weise ..., daß er keine Absicht habe, weiterhin mit dem DSV zusammenzuarbeiten'. A whole catalogue of complaints had evidently been preying on Huchel's mind. He began by saying that he had worked for the GDR for years but had received little recognition. He complained that resolutions he had composed at the Writers' Union's behest had not been printed; he was not considered for foreign travel on Writers' Union business and for delegations, such as the one to Palermo; the Secretary of the Writers' Union, Alfred Schulz, had attacked and slandered *Sinn und Form* abroad; he was permitted to promote certain writers in his journal, for example the Swedish writer Lunkvist, yet when Lunkvist visited the GDR Huchel was not informed. When he nonetheless saw such writers, they were always accompanied by a Writers' Union employee. He added that employees of the Writers' Union drove cars, while he had to entertain young West German writers out of his own pocket. It was time for younger colleagues to take over, 'er wolle nichts mehr tun'. Baumert noted that Huchel became calmer after he had aired his grievances. It is self-evident that Huchel had grave reservations about adopting the representative role which he had accepted for the forthcoming congress in Weimar. Fearful of what Huchel might now do, Baumert proposed in his memo that he should visit Huchel during his trip to Petzow, 'um mit ihm ein Gespräch über die Arbeit nach Westdeutschland zu führen'. He also hoped to set up a meeting, 'an dem das Sekretariat und einige Mitglieder des Vorstandes (evtl. Anna Seghers) teilnehmen könnten'.

A meeting with Seghers took place later that month but Huchel felt she had failed to understand his complaints. The meeting must have preceded his trip to Weimar with Arendt and Bobrowski. As arranged, Huchel delivered the opening address. Rolf Haufs recorded his memory of the occasion in his poem 'Bildnis Peter Huchel', which captures the spell of silence which Huchel cast,

> In Weimar sah ich Sie wieder
>
> Als Präsident einer kulturellen Veranstaltung
>
> Wieder haben Sie nur geschwiegen
>
> Wie macht er das, dachte ich
>
> Als Präsident. Kein Zeichen
>
> Keine Bewegung wem denn das Wort erteilt war [80]

It must be said that the occasion scarcely merited the title all-German anymore. A Stasi report on Huchel's behaviour at the congress shows him as far from silent, indeed unguardedly outspoken in his attacks on the Writers' Union, cultural politicians and other aspects of GDR life, including the role of Soviet armed forces. The Stasi report was from 'Marion', an employee of the Writers' Union.[81] Initially with humour, Huchel had exclaimed to her, 'Ich bewundere Sie, daß Sie es unter den Verrückten aushalten!' However, 'Marion' reported that Huchel 'in einer inoffiziellen Sitzung in Weimar mächtig gegen die Funktionäre losgezogen sei, warum und wieso ist dem GI nicht bekannt'. Seghers, as President of the Writers' Union, had attempted to mediate. Klaus Völker later wrote that after the congress Huchel and Seghers apologised to writers because cultural politicians of Abusch's stamp had placed 'hauptsächlich betagte westdeutsche Friedenskämpfer auf die Rednerliste'.[82] Huchel was outraged because two West German authors had been arrested for a short period of time by the Soviets because they had photographed a Soviet building. 'Marion' reported that Huchel 'soll über diese Handlungsweise der sowjetischen Genossen sehr empört gewesen sein und wollte eine Protestresolution loslassen'.

Huchel's increasing outspokenness is reflected in a further report in Stasi files of a conversation with him at the Weimar Congress on 29 January 1961. It was conducted by a Writers' Union employee, possibly 'Marion'.[83] Arendt, Bobrowski and a young West Berliner were also present. When Huchel heard where the informant worked, he announced that he intended to resign from that organisation. He gave as his reason Schulz's defamatory statements about *Sinn und Form* in Bulgaria. He complained that his income from his poetry in the GDR was 30 marks a month. 10 marks of that went in his contribution to the Writers' Union. He received no royalties for his poetry broadcast on the radio because the Writers' Union had reached an agreement with the state radio stations that was not in authors' interest. He and his friend Arendt had for a long time wanted to travel abroad, but they had been repeatedly passed over. Things had been different in earlier years, but the Writers' Union employee who had included them in her plans had been moved elsewhere because she was not in the party. He was also not informed when poets came to the GDR from abroad. They came to see him anyway and some of them told him that the Writers' Union was not interested in their visiting him. When they came, they were always accompanied. Huchel wanted to know why, since he wanted to talk to the writer, not with the Writers' Union employee. He was reported as saying, 'Max Zimmering hätte richtig gehandelt, als er so einen Begleiter mal rausschmiss'. He added that he himself was too polite to do that! Huchel rehearsed various complaints that he had already brought to Seghers' notice, but there were others, among them,

> daß sich Claudius den Fontane-Preis selbst verliehen hätte und er ihn erst im darauffolgen-
> den Jahr bekam, wo er dann auch bestimmte Forderungen stellte. Während einer
> Bulgarienreise klappte es mit seinen Devisen nicht. Dem zuständigen Kulturreferent der
> Botschaft war sein Name nicht bekannt und er mußte seine Uhr eintauschen.

These complaints related to events as far back as 1954-5 and 1957. They show that Huchel had reached the point where he was prepared to dredge up any old, petty complaints to hurl at the representatives of a cultural bureaucracy that he saw as having such a baleful effect on GDR cultural life.

It was only logical that, on 14 April 1961, the Stasi should bring together all that was known to them about Huchel. The report amounted to just over three pages.[84] It reveals to what extent the Stasi was a surveillance organisation, its employees generally not equipped to undertake more sophisticated work. Thus, the information compiled about Huchel's career in its broad outline was simply taken over from the c.v. that he himself had filled in for his employer. Had they conducted careful research into his radio career in the Third Reich, they could have found material, with which they could blackmail him. That was, of course, common practice, though incriminating material was generally drawn from surveillance, not from more demanding research.

The report goes over much familiar ground, but the tone is much more sharply critical than in the early 1950s. Huchel is characterised as politically indifferent; furthermore, 'in seiner Haltung ist er oft Schwankungen unterlegen'. His political stance is described as follows,

> Nach einem Ermittlungsbericht vom Dezember 1957 wird H. im Wohngebiet so eingeschätzt, daß er nur nach außen hin eine fortschrittliche Einstellung zeigt. Er erzählte dem ABV (Abschnittsbevollmächtigter der Volkspolizei – S.P.) im Wohngebiet, daß er von der SED den Auftrag erhielt, nicht in die SED einzutreten mit der Begründung, daß er angeblich seine umfangreichen Verbindungen nach dem Westen so besser ausnutzen könnte. Weiter äußerte er dem ABV gegenüber, daß er sehr viel in Mannheim und Baden zu tun habe. Dort hätte er sehr viele Bekannte.
>
> Unter dem Siegel der Verschwiegenheit berichtete er dem ABV, daß er in Mannheim von den Amerikanern eingeladen wurde. Der ABV sollte darüber nicht sprechen.

Well aware of the ABV's role as a conduit for information to the state security service, Huchel could not resist teasing him with the story of his invitation from the Americans. There was clearly some truth in his assertion that he had many friends in Baden. Among them was Gerhard Heller, for example. Of prime interest, however, is his statement that he had not joined the SED because that would have been counterproductive, given his role in fostering links with western figures. It is certainly the case that an element in the agreement between Huchel, Becher and representatives of the SMAD was Huchel's status as a non-SED figure, who would be acceptable to western intellectuals as he presented the GDR's case. As we have seen, he told others that in the immediate post-war years he had wanted to join the SED but had been advised against doing so. However incredible all this might seem, given the evolution of relations between Huchel and SED cultural politicians in the 1950s and 1960s, the story is consistent with his early post-war development.

Since Hager's attack in late 1957, Huchel's attendance at meetings of the Academy had become less frequent. A rare contribution to an issue unrelated to *Sinn und Form* was during a discussion of poetry in the spring of 1961.[85] Huchel found the discussion 'recht erfreulich' because it had attracted the interest of people 'aus den verschiedensten Kreisen'. The memo of the meeting continues, 'Seine Meinung sei immer noch, schreibende Arbeiter, schreibende Bauern nicht mit Gewalt zu einer miesen und platten Ausdrucksweise zu dringen. Man sollte sie ermuntern, ihre eigene Sprache, die eine Volkssprache ist, zu beherrschen'. These sentiments were familiar enough from his speech in honour of Hermlin in 1958, as was his view that 'die sogenannte Avantgarde in der Lyrik oft nur eine Aprèsgarde sei. Und es sei schwierig zu erkennen, ob es nicht oft nur "Oberlehrerdichtung" sei'. Huchel's words reflect, too, his deep disapproval of exhortations such as 'Greif' zur Feder, Kumpel' that emerged from the Bitterfeld Conference in 1959. Huchel would later remark that the Bitterfeld Conference signalled to him the beginning of the end of his editorship of *Sinn und Form*.

Despite the pressure to which he had been subjected, during 1961 Huchel's editorial line remained essentially unaltered. There were contributions from Krauss, Mayer, Zweig, Fischer and Fühmann, as well as Celan's translations of Esenin. Fischer argued for a re-evaluation of Kleist, Mayer wrote about Hofmannsthal and Richard Strauss, Jahnn, Bobrowski and Georg Kaiser all figured, while an opening was provided for the younger Reiner Kunze, Christoph Meckel and Klaus Wagenbach, who worked as a reader for S. Fischer. Kunert published his first poems in *Sinn und Form* since the early 1950s. Given this company, the inclusion in the second issue of a short prose piece by Willi Bredel and of an essay to mark Bredel's sixtieth birthday by Alfred Klein, head of the Academy's research project on proletarian-revolutionary literature, remained very much the exception. There had been no change of heart in the face of Kurella's strictures.

Recognition in the West

As the tensions grew in the East, Huchel's stock in the West was rising. He accepted invitations to read from his poetry in Düsseldorf in April 1961 and in Tübingen in June. A review of the Düsseldorf reading, 'Ein deutscher Lyriker', appeared in the *Rheinische Post* on 25 April 1961. Huchel had been invited to share the platform with Marie Luise Kaschnitz in the series 'Das neue Werk'. Her poetry, like Huchel's, had appeared in *Die Dame* in the 1930s. Like Huchel, she had fundamentally 'modernised' her style after 1945, though he had done so only from the mid-1950s after his excursion into thesocialist pastoral. The meeting between the two of them - it would have been the first - did not in the event come off due to Kaschnitz's commitments in Italy. The reviewer presumed his readership's unfamiliarity with Huchel, writing, 'Wer ist Peter Huchel? Mögen sich besonders diejenigen gefragt haben, die nicht erschienen waren. Diese Frage stellen, heißt - über den gegebenen Anlaß hinaus - ein trauriges Gegenwartskapitel aufschlagen'. The reviewer regretted the fatal estrangement between East and West Germany on the cultural plane. Walter Jens' new book, *Deutsche Literatur der Gegenwart*, was cited as an authoritative source of information about 'einen großen deutschen Poeten'. Such words of unreserved praise instigated Huchel's belated recognition in West Germany, in which Jens played a crucial role, especially through his *Deutsche Literatur der Gegenwart*. Jens' own efforts in cultural mediation between the two Germanies were reflected in his words, 'Wehe uns ..., wenn Hans Mayer und Peter Huchel, hier als Stalinisten, dort als revisionistische Liberale beschimpft, nicht mehr zeigen dürfen, daß es eine Mitte gibt'.[86] Together with Bachmann, Eich and Celan, Huchel was described by Jens as 'die größte Potenz auf lyrischem Felde'. In this way, Huchel was re-united with Eich within the grouping of the foremost contemporary German poets. This can only have been music to the ears of someone who had published only one collection of poems, and that as long ago as 1948.

At the Düsseldorf reading, Huchel was introduced by Dr Rathke of the city's Kunstverein. Huchel drew on work from all phases of his development for a reading whose delivery was described as follows, 'Er tat das mit jener, selbstvortragenden Lyrikern eigenen leisen Monotonie, die das Wort als Klang begreift und deshalb zusätzliche Färbung für überdrüssig erachtet'. This was a particularly apt characterisation of Huchel's delivery. He won over his audience with a reading described in the following terms,

> Ob er als junger Wanderer das Leiden des Menschen am Menschen in seinem durch Büchner inspirierten 'Lenz' zu streng gereimtem Aufschrei formte, ob er die besonders aus der Jugend so vertraute Natur, die ihm Metapher des ewigen Lebenszyklus ist, in ebenso prägnanten wie eigenwilligen Bildern tages- und jahreszeitlich abwandelte ('Frühe', 'Sommerabend', 'Eine Herbstnacht', 'Dezember'), ob er das Grauen des Krieges an der radikalen Zerstörung unserer herkömmlichen Bibelvorstellung indirekt sichtbar machte ('Chausseen Chausseen', 'Chronik'), ob er in noch unveröffentlichten Italiengedichten die unter brennender Sonne so eng verschwisterten Gegensätze in das chiffrehafte Symbol freier Rhythmen bannte, sie alle werden getragen von dem starken Atem reiner Poesie.

By now, Huchel was making very selective use in the West of the verse of the early 1950s. The poems of wartime destruction remained part of the repertoire, but not those which overtly supported a reconstruction on socialist lines which had gone horribly wrong. 'Das Gesetz' now rang hollow. Poems such as 'Chausseen Chausseen' and 'Bericht des Pfarrers vom Untergang seiner Gemeinde' were stripped out of the cycle and presented as free-standing compositions.

Another journey to the West followed when Bobrowski accompanied Huchel to the meeting of the Hölderlin Society in Tübingen on 26-28 May. Prior to the trip, Bobrowski visited Huchel on 17 May. Bobrowski's letters to Huchel from this period show that he had lost none of his awkwardness towards Huchel, who seldom answered Bobrowski's letters personally. Bobrowski visited again on 11 June. Two days later, he wrote to Christoph Meckel, 'Huchel hat großartige neue Gedichte. Er zeigte sie mit einer bubenhaften Schüchternheit vor'.[87] The material for *Chausseen Chausseen* was starting to take shape.

Huchel read from some of the new work, though principally from earlier poetry, when he swiftly returned to Tübingen in mid-June for a reading at which he was introduced by Walter Jens. The reading was reported in the *Stuttgarter Zeitung* on 14 June 1961. The review opened with the observation that 'obwohl er schon seit nahezu vier Jahrzehnten dichtet, ist er als lyrischer Dichter erst in jüngster Zeit bekannter geworden'. The reviewer took his guidance from Jens in placing Huchel in the same bracket as Celan, Eich, Kaschnitz and Bachmann. The message was getting through. The reviewer identified three key elements in Huchel's verse: the social dimension illustrated by 'Lenz'; the hymnic celebration of nature as in 'Eine Herbstnacht' ('das sind Klänge tiefempfundener, erdhafter Naturmystik'); and, finally, the experience of war. The new elements such as the Mediterranean verse that would emerge fully in *Chausseen Chausseen* were either not foregrounded by Huchel or not picked out by the reviewer. He read a number of older compositions, among them 'Havelnacht' and 'Letzte Fahrt', and some recent ones such as 'In der Heimat', (now much changed) 'Damals' and 'Sibylle des Sommers'.[88] It was published that year, together with 'Chiesa del Soccorso', 'In der Bretagne' and 'Südliche Insel' (which was dedicated to Jens) in S. Fischer's house journal *Neue Rundschau*. Huchel in fact stopped off in Frankfurt am Main during his Tübingen trip to hold talks with Gottfried Bermann Fischer. The publication of the poems was the first fruit of a relationship which was formalised in a general contract for Huchel's works. In the event, *Chausseen Chausseen*, which appeared in late 1963, would be the only substantial product of that relationship.

Bobrowski's reputation was now also rapidly growing. It was boosted by the publication of *Sarmatische Zeit* in the West in 1961. He visited Wilhelmshorst again on 21 July 1961. Bobrowski was keen to follow up Huchel's offer to help arrange a reading for him in Düsseldorf. Huchel, for his part, was being courted by a number of West German publishers keen to produce a collection of his verse. The previous year, on 17 August 1960, he had reported to Kundera the interest shown by Fritz Hünich of Insel in Leipzig, as well as by Suhrkamp and Piper in the West.[89] On 14 July 1961, he wrote to Kundera of his readings in Düsseldorf and Tübingen and of the fact that in the past months a number of West German publishers – he named Suhrkamp, S. Fischer, Luchterhand and Piper – had literally been rushing into his house and offering him the most lucrative contracts.[90] Even that had not been enough to cheer him up, although he certainly was pleased at the prospect of being able to say goodbye to the Aufbau Verlag. As we have seen, S. Fischer, whose tradition was synonymous with the best in 20th century German literature, won the race, apparently with the agreement that Huchel's next collection would be published in the GDR by Rütten und Loening.[91] 1961 also saw the last publication of formulaic, affirmative verse, with the poems 'Spruch. Für Wilhelm Pieck' (i,312) and another

'Spruch' (i,312) in celebration of the tenth anniversary of the Academy's foundation.

He said his goodbyes to the Aufbau Verlag in no uncertain terms in a letter to Günter Caspar dated 22 August 1961, writing that

> ich das Vertragsverhältnis mit dem Aufbau-Verlag bereits seit Jahren als erloschen ansehe. Das ist auch der Grund, weshalb ich in den letzten Jahren davon Abstand genommen habe, Beschwerde bei Ihrer Verlagsleitung hinsichtlich der Behandlung meiner Person als Autor wie der Nichtförderung meiner Lyrik einzulegen. [92]

Huchel had, we should recall, made an effort to complete a new edition of *Gedichte* as recently as 1958. Without it and the other uncompleted projects for which contracts had been signed, there was little that the Aufbau Verlag could do to promote his work. He informed Caspar that he had arranged for the advance which he had received from the publisher to be returned. That should have been the end of Huchel's relationship with the Aufbau Verlag, but by one of those twists of fate Rütten und Loening was presently taken under the wing of the Aufbau-Verlag and the issue of Rütten und Loening's publication of Huchel's next volume in the GDR would be dealt with by the head of the Aufbau Verlag, Klaus Gysi, in the highly charged atmosphere following Huchel's departure from *Sinn und Form*.

The Private and the Public: Family Worries and the Building of the Berlin Wall

Quite apart from his own projects and difficulties, Huchel was now greatly pre-occupied by family problems. Marie Huchel, now in her mid-eighties, had survived for a decade since her stroke in the early 1950s. She had continued to live in Michendorf until she moved into an old people's home in Teltow. She was now very frail. In addition, the health and development of Huchel's son, Stephan, gave grounds for serious concern. He was an extremely withdrawn, delicate child, who was diagnosed by Dr Herwig Hesse as suffering from a sclerosis of the thoracic spine and from a heart defect with exertion-induced cyanosis.[93] Stephan Huchel would in fact die, aged just forty-one, in 1990. The Huchels had planned another Italian holiday for August 1961. Stephan fell ill with bronchitis, the holiday was delayed and on 13 August work began on the building of the Berlin Wall. What Huchel had believed never could happen, was now happening: the border was sealed.[94]

Monica Huchel recalls in her memoirs that as President of the Writers' Union, Anna Seghers sent round a circular urging members to explain to writers abroad why this measure had been necessary. Seghers' circular, in fact, followed the open letter to members of the Writers' Union issued by Günter Grass and Wolfdietrich

Schnurre, challenging them to either condemn or support the GDR's action. The
letter was directed especially at members of the Writers' Union's executive, on
which Huchel still actually served. Stephan Hermlin and a number of others
supported the GDR in their replies.[95] Huchel did not. Monica Huchel writes, 'Als
Otto Gotsche, ein kleiner, unangenehmer Mann, diesen Brief vorbeibrachte, riß
Huchel die Haustür auf und warf ihn hinaus, während er hinter ihm her schrie:
"Sagen Sie Frau Seghers, sie soll sich einen anderen suchen"'.[96] Huchel was, after
all, prepared to follow Max Zimmering's example. The well-connected Gotsche –
he was Ulbricht's secretary – would never forgive him for this.

Some time after, Huchel wrote 'Bericht', (i,352) a 'Witz-, Spott- und
Wutgedicht auf die Mauer', (i,457) as Monica Huchel recalled. The poem is of
interest not least because, for all Huchel's conflicts with the GDR authorities, it
retains a perspective on this event which continues to see two sides in the Cold War.
Key lines are reminiscent of Brecht's parabolic approach, which is, on occasion, to
be found elsewhere in Huchel's post-war poetry,

> Die Verwalter der Welt,
>
> Männer in mächtigen Hosen,
>
> Männer in engen Hosen,
>
> Prüfen die Festigkeit
>
> des raschen Bauwerks.

Monica Huchel explained that the 'Männer in mächtigen Hosen' were meant to be
the Soviets, the 'Männer in engen Hosen' the western allies. It follows from the
logic of this juxtaposition that the lie referred to later in the poem cannot have been
produced on just one side. For Huchel, with the building of the Wall, virtually all
hopes of a constructive dialogue between East and West disappeared for the
foreseeable future. The Cold Warriors had won and the efforts of those like himself
who had maintained a dialogue against the odds had come to nothing. It was a
severe blow to him personally and to all those who opposed the division of
Germany. It was only with the accession to power of Willy Brandt that a dialogue
based on the principle of peaceful co-existence would be launched.

The above comments on Huchel's response to the building of the Wall are
consistent with Monica Huchel's statement that, had they been permitted to travel
to Italy for their holiday, they would have returned despite the building of the Wall.
Their situation was different from the Blochs'. Their life was in Wilhelmshorst with
the journal.[97] As we know, they enjoyed a very comfortable material existence there.
It is evident from Monica Huchel's statement that they could not at that stage
countenance what would happen in 1962, let alone the restrictions that would be
imposed from 1963. It was simply not possible to think through all the ramifications
of the building of the Wall.

Though Italy was ruled out, they followed Erich and Katja Arendt to the Black Sea coast at the end of August. They sent a postcard to Bobrowski from Nessebar in Bulgaria in September. Huchel wrote the following words, 'Auf dem Weg nach Sizilien traf ich in der Karawanserei Nessebar Arendts, die nach Paris reisten. Auch im alten Thrakien reifen die Feigen und schreien die Esel'.[98] 'Thrakien' (i,116) became the title of one of his new visionary poems, meditating upon problems of time, death and language, which was published in *Chausseen Chausseen*.

They had left Monica Huchel's child from her first marriage, Roger Melis, who was now twenty-one, to look after the house in Wilhelmshorst. During their absence, two of his friends fled to the West. He stayed behind but felt deeply distressed, as they saw when they returned. Huchel's response was to introduce his step-son to West Germans of his own generation. Instead of travelling to the meeting at Petzow organised by the Writers' Union, Huchel invited three young West Germans, Klaus Völker, Peter Hamm and Christoph Meckel, to visit him in Wilhelmshorst. Klaus Völker recalls of the visit on 9 October that Huchel wanted to show Roger that the West was not a bed of roses.[99]

The visit was a success and the worries subsided. It was, however, followed by Marie Huchel's death in Teltow on 17 October 1961. Like Fritz, she belonged to a world that Huchel had long ago put behind him. Yet, for all her ways, somewhere Marie still represented that Brandenburg peasant culture to which her son was deeply attached. This common emotional identity provided the focus for Huchel's mourning for his mother, whose death he had anticipated as long ago as the early 1950s with his poem 'Erinnerung'.

Huchel's mood remained dark. Shortly afterwards, on 6 November 1961, Baumert of the Writers' Union reported upon a conversation with Huchel that, he claimed, had been very depressing for him, especially as hitherto he had seen Huchel as an important literary force for 'our republic'. Huchel had simply exploded during his conversation with Baumert, who did not know how to judge Huchel's outburst. Baumert concluded his memo, which found its way to the Stasi, 'Jedenfalls scheint mir sein heutiger Zustand als Besorgnis erregend'.[100]

It has not proved possible to identify with absolute certainty a specific source of Huchel's anger. There was certainly no shortage of grounds for profound dissatisfaction. His dark mood at the time is conveyed in his composition at the end of November (i,409) of 'An taube Ohren der Geschlechter', Huchel's famous warning of nuclear holocaust, which contains the lines,

Der Weg ist leer, der Baum verbrannt.
Die Öde saugt den Atem aus.

Die Stimme wird zu Sand

Und wirbelt hoch und stützt den Himmel

Mit einer Säule, die zerstäubt.

It is certainly germane to consideration of Huchel's anger that in early November 1961 the Soviet Union broke the nuclear test ban, exploding thirty atomic bombs in the atmosphere.

It is unlikely that in November 1961 he was aware of plans for cuts to the budget for *Sinn und Form*. In December 1961 the Academy entered into negotiations with the Finance Ministry and Rütten und Loening with a view to reducing the subsidy for *Sinn und Form*.[101] It was agreed that the number of free copies would be reduced by 250, that is to say, halved; the contribution to production and distribution costs would by reduced by 1,500 marks per issue; the Academy would be responsible for all monies relating to the editorial team; and the annual subsidy would be reduced from 51,000 marks to 37,500 marks a year. These were just the opening shots in the next stage of the campaign against Huchel's *Sinn und Form*, which would be conducted throughout 1962 and on into 1963. After the humiliation of 1953 and the botched affair of 1957, Abusch, Kurella and Hager were now much more firmly in control of the cultural bureaucracy and strong enough to bring both the Academy and *Sinn und Form* into line. This time there would be no mistakes.

The Crunch

Abusch directs operations

On 12 January 1962, Abusch informed Karl Hossinger, the Academy Director, that a fundamental discussion was planned for *Sinn und Form*.[1] As Deputy to the Chair of the GDR Council of Ministers with special responsibility for culture, Abusch, had reached the height of his powers. He was determined to act decisively against the Academy in general and *Sinn und Form* in particular. Both were to be transformed into unambiguously socialist organs in support of the GDR.

Shortly afterwards, on 8 February 1962, he wrote to Nagel, requesting an analysis of the journal's content over the past three years. Like Kurella, he talked about the need for the journal to reflect the work of the Academy and life in the GDR. He also sought clarification about the role of what he called a 'Redaktionskomitee', whether measures agreed upon for *Sinn und Form* had been implemented, and if not, why not. The Presidium complied with Abusch's instruction at its next meeting on 12 February,[2] and on 21 February the Literature Section, in Huchel's absence, passed on the instruction to proceed with the analysis to its academic assistants, Eberhard Meißner, Ulrich Dietzel and Gert Hillesheim.

It was Abusch's view that the necessary changes could only be achieved through the replacement of the Academy's leadership. On 22 February, he sent Kurella his account of a meeting that he had conducted with Nagel on 8 February. Abusch reported that he had explained to Nagel the ideological reasons why a new President had to be elected. He had assured Nagel, just as Zweig had been assured in 1952, that he would leave with honour in order to pursue his own artistic projects. Abusch concluded that Nagel 'überzeugte sich, ... daß dieser Weg der richtige ist'.

On 9 February, Hossinger and Nagel wrote to Huchel, requesting that he should prepare a special issue devoted to the history of socialist literature following a recent conference on the subject.[3] There is no record of any reply from Huchel, though the lecture that they recommended by Alfred Klein on proletarian-revolutionary literature was published in the second issue of the journal. They wrote to Huchel again on 2 March, informing him that the analysis of the journal's content was proceeding on the terms outlined by Abusch.[4] Later that month, Hossinger reported to Huchel that new financial arrangements had been agreed by the Academy and the publisher.[5]

An extraordinary meeting was planned between the Academy and the Council of Ministers on 30 March. This was preceded by the presentation of a paper by the Academy on 19 March, which detailed the path that it had to take in order to be transformed into a socialist institution. *Sinn und Form* was referred to explicitly. Both leadership and content would have to be changed to reflect the Academy's new ideological tasks. Therefore, 'Dem parteilosen Chefredakteur Huchel ist ein ideologisch zuverlässiger Genosse Schriftsteller mit gleichen Rechten an die Seite zu stellen'. The old issue of a second editor was revived on an explicitly ideological basis. The journal was to be brought into line, whilst it continued to benefit from Huchel's good name abroad. These two goals could not, however, be reconciled, since Huchel's assent was required for a plan that spelt the end of an editorial approach that was predicated on the avoidance of the very partisanship set out in the Academy's paper.

The Academy's paper was approved at the meeting on 30 March. Willi Bredel, who had been earmarked to replace Nagel, spoke against *Sinn und Form*, arguing that it was a 'Wanderer zwischen zwei Welten' and that this situation must change. Huchel was sent a copy of the Academy's circular which announced the proposed changes to the leadership and content of *Sinn und Form*. Monica Huchel recollects that she and other members of the editorial staff at first kept the circular from him.[6] He had long since begun to withdraw and was preoccupied with the collection of poems that he was preparing for S. Fischer. She prepared him for the news by asking him, as the occasion permitted, if he could imagine life without the journal, and when she was convinced that he really wanted to give up she let him have sight of the circular.

Not surprisingly, his health had begun to suffer under the relentless pressure. We have charted a number of his complaints over the years. He was, in fact, in the habit of supplying his correspondents with quite precise details of his medical condition. His wife, we recall, enjoyed a training as a medical assistant before the war, while it had always been Fritz Huchel's hope that his son would become a doctor. He certainly ensured that he was conversant with the terms of diagnoses. On 10 April 1962, he wrote to Kundera that he had been in bad health over the previous weeks, when he had also been extremely depressed. He was just starting another course of injections for a crippling arthritis in his right shoulder.[7] His wife, who had earlier suffered from severe weight loss ('Abmagerung'), was now having her thyroid gland examined at the Charité hospital in Berlin. Stephan was, of course, a constant worry. Their live-in domestic help had now left them, too.

Tending the Poet's Image

Huchel left it to Fritz Erpel to deal with his correspondence to Livia Wittmann, who – so Huchel informed Kundera – inspired him to write 'Hinter den weißen Netzen des Mittags'. (i,122) Wittmann, a Hungarian germanist, was proposing to write about Huchel, and Erpel supplied her with material and advice on Huchel's behalf. He recommended Jens' *Deutsche Literatur der Gegenwart*, which, as we have seen, placed Huchel in company in which he was very happy to be seen. Erpel distanced Huchel's poetry from the label 'Heimatdichtung' that Zak had attached to it in the early 1950s, a term used by Becher, too, and echoed, we recall, in compositions such as 'In der Heimat'. Huchel had, in the meantime, given up his early post-war ambitions to contribute to a new national literature through a socialist re-definition of 'Heimat'. Erpel drew attention instead to 'Lenz' as indicative of Huchel's true concerns. 'Lenz', as we know, assumed an emblematic status in Huchel's work from the late 1950s, which it had certainly not previously possessed. Erpel argued that Huchel's nature poems had been published in the 1920s before Wilhelm Lehmann's, so he did not belong to the Lehmann 'school' of nature poetry identified in the West. In fact, Lehmann's nature poetry was first published in journals such as *Die literarische Welt* and *Vossische Zeitung* in 1929, Huchel's the following year in the same outlets. Not that that made him a member of a Lehmann 'school'. Erpel proposed the term 'realist' as appropriate for Huchel, 'dessen Arbeiten von provinzialistischen Einflüssen so weit entfernt sind wie von allen bloß formal artistischen'. (ii,348) The categories employed by Erpel are quite transparent, designed as they were to steer Huchel away from certain concepts that had acquired unfavourable connotations. In the face of a narrow West German conception of nature poetry, Huchel would, understandably, continue to argue for the distance between his beginnings and those of Lehmann and his 'followers', including the *Kolonne* poets. Clearly there were differences, as there always are. Yet the similarities cannot simply be ignored. In the early 1960s, as the reception of his poetry in West Germany was only properly beginning, Huchel was concerned to cultivate an image in the West that placed him in the company of the new voices of the younger generation represented by Bachmann, Celan and Enzensberger, not as a 'member' of the Lehmann 'school', which really was a figment of the West German critical imagination and really something of a cliché. Certainly, since 1945 Huchel's path had been quite different from Lehmann's and that of the *Kolonne* Circle. Huchel's poetry continued to evolve into the 1960s, while the elderly Lehmann's was no longer susceptible to development. Comparison with Eich was surely a different matter.

Bredel Replaces Nagel

In the Academy, Huchel was really a helpless by-stander as matters were taking their course along the lines laid down by Abusch. Decisions regarding the future of the journal were taken by the Academy's management in conjunction with Abusch and Kurella, then presented to the membership for rubber-stamping. The newly-elected President, Bredel, spoke of the tasks for the Academy and its journal at a Plenary Session on 30 May 1962. Among other things, he said, 'Unser sozialistischer Staat hat ... nicht die Absicht, unter Aufbringung großer Geldmittel eine Zeitschrift zu finanzieren, die bürgerlichen Ästheten und sogenannten literarischen Feinschmeckern vom Schlage Willy Haas Freude macht und Erbauung gibt'.[8]

The gloves were off. Later that day, Bredel, in the first entry in the diary of his Presidency, cast doubt on the authenticity of Huchel's apologies for absence due to illness.[9] Bredel's long-standing enmity towards Huchel emerges in the following,

'Bei Huchel ist meines Erachtens ausgesprochene Verachtung, zumindest Mißachtung anderer die Triebkraft und – grundsätzliche Opposition ideologisch und kulturell gegen unsere Kulturpolitik'. These were Bredel's sincerely held views about his partner in forthcoming negotiations. On the following day, 1 June, one of the new President's first tasks was to instruct Huchel to publish the speeches from the meeting of 30 May. In the event, Huchel managed to reach an agreement with Bredel to publish only Hermlin's brief statement at that meeting in the third issue. He appended a note to the effect that the other contributions, including Bredel's, were available in the Academy's brochure *Die nationale Aufgabe der Deutschen Akademie der Künste zu Berlin*. The brochure was distributed with that third issue.

In his letter of 1 June, Bredel continued by inviting Huchel to discuss with him matters relating to *Sinn und Form*. Huchel agreed to a meeting, on the condition that he was provided with transport to the Academy since his doctor had forbidden him any physical exertion.[10] The meeting was arranged for Thursday 14 June at 3 pm. In addition to Huchel and Bredel, Hossinger and Hermlin were present. Huchel later described the sequence of meetings instigated in June as follows,

> Ab Juli 1962 suchten mich der damalige Präsident der Deutschen Akademie der Künste, Willi Bredel, und deren Direktor, Dr Hossinger, mehrfach auf, um mein Einverständnis für eine bloß nominelle Mitwirkung an *Sinn und Form* – die eigentliche Chefredaktion sollte Bodo Uhse übernehmen – zu erreichen. Einen solchen Kompromiß lehnte ich ab. Da sich Uhse jedoch eine längere Einarbeitungsfrist ausbedungen hatte, bat mich der Präsident, den Jahrgang 1962 noch zu Ende zu führen. Unter der Bedingung, daß man mich dann nach Ablauf des Jahres nach Italien gehen lasse, sagte ich sofort zu. (ii,327)

Understandably enough, certain issues are simplified and the chronology of events somewhat distorted, as Huchel presents himself as the victim of hostile forces, which, of course, he was. His omission of Hermlin indicates that he did not wish to discuss the actions of a friend, which, in his view, culminated in betrayal. Elsewhere, in the 1970s, Huchel added, somewhat less plausibly, 'Man sagte mir: Sie brauchen ja nur ein paar Stunden zu kommen, wenn die Nummer schon fertig ist, und Sie bekommen das gleiche Geld. Ich kannte diesen stalinistischen Trick und lehnte diese Art von Bestechung ab'. (ii,377)

On 15 June, Hossinger wrote a record of the previous day's meeting. At the very start of the meeting Huchel declared his intention to resign, referring to his ill health. This was in keeping with the outcome of his conversations with his wife. However, instead of seizing upon this, Bredel, supported by Hermlin, sought to explain why change was necessary. Hermlin was proposed as a co-editor, but he would not entertain this. Huchel rejected Uhse and Scherner as co-editor. The issues were similar to the early 1950s, when Huchel had sat out the threat to his editorial independence, which then receded. Yet circumstances had changed fundamentally. Discussion turned to the editorial team and to the question whether all the staff were fully occupied. The Academy's representatives evidently wished to put an end to *Sinn und Form* as the family concern it had been. The option of deploying Monica Huchel elsewhere was discussed, possibly on the proposed new Academy almanac. The editorial seat was another issue. In 1953, Abusch had complained that it was in some village beyond Potsdam. The building of the Berlin Wall had further impaired communications between Wilhelmshorst and the Academy. A two-hour car journey was required to travel the relatively short distance. Come what may, some of the editorial work would in the future have to be undertaken at the Academy on a permanent basis. The analysis of *Sinn und Form* would be discussed at the Literature Section. It was agreed that a further meeting of the same group would take place at Wilhelmshorst after the Literature Section had met. Bredel noted in his diary on the evening of 14 June, 'Aussprache mit P.Huchel über *Sinn und Form*. Moralischer und kulturpolitischer Sieg. Er will am 25. (Sektionssitzung) kommen und sich der Kritik stellen. Hoffe, wir kommen mit ihm zusammen zur Neugestaltung der Zeitschrift'.[11] Yet, as we know from his earlier assessment of Huchel and his intentions, Bredel would not be too concerned if the re-structuring was accomplished without Huchel.

The Academy Leadership Moves Matters on

The analysis of the journal's content in 1960 and 1961 had in the meantime been completed. Meißner sent Kurella a copy on 7 June, informing him that Hermlin wanted Kurella to join a small group from the Literature Section, which would make recommendations on the basis of the analysis. Hermlin himself would be in the group, together with Wieland Herzfelde and Franz Fühmann. Hermlin thus ensured that this group would, on balance, be, in Hans Mayer's words, 'aus Leuten zusammengesetzt, die ihrem Akademiekollegen helfen wollten'.[12] Yet the analysis confirmed what Abusch, Kurella and Hager wanted to hear about the paucity of GDR literature, especially by young authors, of essays about GDR culture and, latterly, of Marxist criticism, especially by young essayists. There is no doubt that Huchel had left himself exposed by his reluctance to promote such work. Brecht had warned against doing this long ago.

The group, excluding Kurella, met on 19 June and all had criticisms to make of editorial practice, focusing particularly on a perceived lack of interest in cultivating potential contributors from the GDR.[13] *Sinn und Form* was on the agenda at the meeting of the Literature Section on 25 June.[14] Uhse noted in his diary the following day, 'Gestern nachmittag Sitzung in der Akademie. Die Seghers, Renn, Hermlin, Abusch und viele andere ... nachher zu *Sinn und Form* der Beschluß, daß ich entweder mit oder ohne Huchel die Zeitschrift weiterführen soll'.[15] This time, the status quo was no longer an option. Uhse entered into negotiations with the

Academy in July, yet they proved difficult, and when Bredel and Hossinger travelled to Wilhelmshorst to talk to the Huchels on 27 July, they were by no means certain that Uhse would take the job. Hermlin was also invited on 27 July but turned up only at 4.30 pm., when negotiations were over. He had chosen the easy way out of his conflicting loyalties. Hossinger's record of the meeting sets out Huchel's position, which was essentially unchanged.[16] Huchel was not prepared to countenance any change to the editorial arrangements, nor to edit *Sinn und Form* as a journal of the whole Academy under the new conditions that had been agreed on 25 June. He suggested that in future the journal might be given another name, presumably to distinguish it clearly from the journal that he had edited.[17]

According to Hossinger's summary of the discussion, it was agreed that Huchel would leave his post at the end of the year. He would edit the remaining issues. Because, as Hossinger saw it, the Academy had accepted Huchel's resignation 'erübrigt sich durch diese Vereinbarung die formale Kündigung des Einzelvertrages'. There will be occasion to return to Hossinger's note, since it would have a great bearing on the later legal dispute over Huchel's pension rights. Huchel had not been dismissed from his post. Bredel proposed, subject to agreement by the Presidium, that Huchel and his wife should assume responsibility for editing the Academy's proposed almanac. They would be employed on a freelance basis. At this stage, they had apparently declared that they were willing to do this. That would soon change. As had happened in 1953, Huchel's editorial independence was removed, 'Für die Konzeption der restlichen Hefte dieses Jahres wird Dr h.c. Bredel als Präsident von Peter Huchel die rechtzeitige Vorlage der Konzeption und des Inhaltes erhalten'. Yet Huchel would find a way to circumvent this control. He wished to take his leave of his readership personally in the final issue of the year, but Bredel insisted that a statement from the Academy President would be more appropriate.

By 8 August, Bredel and Uhse had reached agreement that the latter would take over from Huchel on 1 January 1963, but would begin preparing the ground already on 1 October.[18] On 8 August, Hossinger wrote to Huchel, seeking to confirm the major points agreed at their meeting on 27 July. Then, on 30 August, Hans Bentzien, the Minister of Culture, wrote to Bredel, evidently to ensure that his resolve would not waver. He complained that the content of issues two and three of *Sinn und Form* directly contradicted GDR cultural policy and the mission of the Academy. He requested that Bredel should put measures in place which would ensure that *Sinn und Form* could no longer pursue its pernicious work. No doubt Bredel believed that the arrangements he had already put in place would be sufficient. They would not be.

Huchel Fights Back

By now, the comments that Bredel had made about the journal on 30 May had been published. When Hossinger next met Huchel in early September to discuss the transfer of papers, Huchel expressed his outrage at what Bredel had said. Ernst Fischer, Hans Mayer and Werner Krauss had all encouraged him to defend himself against Bredel's charges. He had had time to think through some of the implications of what had been happening. Hossinger noted that as a result of his resignation and the ending of his personal contract Huchel was very worried about his future. Huchel went on the offensive, describing the Academy's actions against him as a 'Fußtritt' and as a great injustice, after he had edited the journal for so many years. Hossinger, referring to the earlier discussion which had included Bredel, assured Huchel that they would take steps to ensure that, despite the premature ending of Huchel's contract, his right to a pension would remain as agreed in the revision to his contract of 6 December 1960. This was a real concern for Huchel who was by now 59 and aware that he had no chance of securing elsewhere a post of such intellectual distinction and with such material reward. The agreement reached in 1960 guaranteed him 60% of his final salary, that is to say 1,200 marks per month. That calculation took no account of his sinecure from the Academy. Huchel had every right to expect that the Academy would keep its word over his pension. As it turned out, the subsequent wrangling over the pension was one of the pettiest and spiteful elements of Huchel's treatment by high-ranking SED politicians.

Hossinger sought to assure Huchel that the fee of between 8,000 and 10,000 marks per annum for editing the almanac would provide an income. Again, this would be supplemented by the sinecure. Yet the situation was rapidly deteriorating and, given statements such as Bredel's and Bentzien's, there was surely already by this stage little prospect that this project could be realised with the Huchels. Huchel now expressed his reservations about the proposal, arguing that the fee was not sufficient. According to Hossinger's record, Huchel also suggested that the monograph about Huchel, upon which Ludvík Kundera was working for the Academy, should be put on ice. In the event, the book was never completed. Unusually, Hossinger noted impressions as well as facts in his memo, writing, 'Ich habe persönlich den Eindruck, daß er sich in den vergangenen Wochen ohne Ergebnis bemüht hat, eine anderweitige Beschäftigung zu finden'. It is not wholly inconceivable that Huchel, encouraged by the support he had received from the West, had for a while toyed with the idea of transplanting *Sinn und Form* to the Federal Republic. That would fit in with Huchel's suggestion that the Academy should re-name its own journal. If Huchel did entertain the idea of a transplant, he must rapidly have abandoned it as wholly unrealistic. The great interest shown in the West in *Sinn und Form* derived not least from its wholly anomalous position in the GDR. As a result of that, the journal and its editor came to be surrounded by a mystique, which Huchel was particularly adept at cultivating. Yet once in the West, it would be stripped of that mystique and it would prove difficult to distinguish it from other journals such as *Merkur* and *Neue Rundschau*. Quite apart from that, for any publisher or Academy in the West, a venture on the scale of *Sinn und Form* would have been a thoroughly daunting prospect, maintained as it was by large state subsidies.

When Hossinger turned to the agreement that the coming issues should be produced in conjunction with the Presidium, Huchel declared that the fourth issue was already with the printer, while five and six would appear as a double issue. The appearance in the fourth issue of Ernst Fischer's lengthy essay on Kafka can have done nothing to defuse the situation. Having failed to exercise control over number four, Hossinger was determined that nothing should slip on the double issue. He noted that the plan for the number would be ready in two weeks. Monica Huchel agreed to present it to Bredel, but Huchel protested in advance against any change to his plan. The transfer of material to Uhse was an equally fraught matter. Huchel did not conceal his hostility towards Uhse, whilst agreeing to pass on all unpublished material. In practice, this did not happen. Huchel insisted on retaining the correspondence with authors that he had conducted personally. This he did, taking some of it with him to the West in 1971 but leaving a substantial amount at his house in Wilhelmshorst, where Erich Arendt lived after Huchel's departure. After Arendt's death, the material was discovered and catalogued by Barbara Heinze of the Academy's Archives as the Teilbestand *Sinn und Form*.

Bredel Counters Western Support

In mid-September, reports began to appear in the West German press that the journal was about to fold. Reich-Ranicki wrote what amounted to an obituary in *Die Zeit* on 14 September. On 17 September Bredel noted in his diary, 'Huchel macht Schwierigkeiten, wahrscheinlich aufgestachelt'.[19] In similar vein to Reich-Ranicki, on 17 September Joachim Günther, editor of the West Berlin journal *Neue Deutsche Hefte*, wrote his 'Epilog auf *Sinn und Form*' in the *Frankfurter Allgemeine Zeitung*, even though, as he acknowledged, he had no hard and fast evidence to support the rumoured death. Günther had evidently not sought to contact Huchel personally. *Der Spiegel*, however, had. In a piece published on 19 September, 'DDR-Zeitschrift: Zwischen zwei Welten', Huchel was quoted as follows, 'Ich bin nur bis zum Ende des Jahres für *Sinn und Form* verantwortlich. Was dann geschieht, weiß ich nicht. Das sind die Fakten; eine Auslegung kann ich nicht geben'. Huchel's very reticence did nothing to quell speculation, but then why should he seek to do so? It was for the Academy to act upon the matter. Hermlin, as Secretary of the Literature Section, wrote on the Academy's behalf to Dr Leonhard of *Die Zeit* on 17 September, just as, two years earlier he had written to the Hamburg Academy.[20] He requested the correction of the hasty and inaccurate assertions made by Reich-Ranicki. As usual, little notice was taken. Abusch wrote to Bredel, urging him to produce a statement to clear the air.[21] Bredel formulated a press release, which was in the event held back and then published at the beginning of the double issue that appeared at the end of the year. He countered the rumour of the journal's imminent demise, explaining that its intellectual trajectory would change. In line with the resolution passed at the Plenary Session on 30 May, the journal would reflect the work of all the Academy's sections, the development of a socialist national culture and artistic life in the GDR. It would be a forum for the discussion of issues in cultural politics and introduce German readers to cultural treasures from around the world. The statement concluded, 'Der bisherige Chefredakteur Peter Huchel scheidet auf eigenen Wunsch mit Jahresende aus'. Bredel's statement originally also referred to the fact that Huchel would be editing the almanac, but this was omitted at Huchel's request.

Bredel reported on the matter to the Presidium on 19 September. Huchel had come to regard the Academy's measures as 'ein ungerechtfertigtes Vorgehen gegen seine eigene Person'. Bredel stated, 'Inzwischen ist in Westdeutschland ein Krieg über *Sinn und Form* entbrannt'. For Bredel, Huchel had changed his attitude between June and September, following the press reports and probable advice from friends. He cited Huchel's statement to *Der Spiegel* as evidence of that. Bredel proposed that Huchel should be invited to the Academy in order to clarify questions still open, to explore his future role and thereby to provide re-assurances. Bredel here was functioning in the usual GDR managerial manner, assuming that individuals had to be found a place within the system. In assessing the degree of Bredel's sincerity here, we should recall that Huchel's friend, Hans Mayer, later wrote of Bredel's role in this affair that he 'vieles zu verhindern suchte'.[22] By no means does Bredel come out of the affair as well as Mayer suggests. We have seen how Bredel's crass statement in May antagonised Huchel. However, as the situation deteriorated, the efforts that he made to prevent the worst were nullified by the intransigence of his superiors, whose thirst for revenge was great, and, to some extent, by Huchel himself, who, quite understandably, of course, turned his back on the Academy, both as a member and an employee. Already, the affair was close to spiralling out of Bredel's control.

Huchel's Bitterness and Regrets; Bredel's Efforts to Keep the Lid on the Affair

Huchel met with Hossinger again in late September. Hossinger still had hopes of ensuring a smooth transition of editorial arrangements.[23] Yet Huchel insisted on talking about the grave injustice that had been perpetrated towards him. Hossinger maintained the official line that Huchel had resigned. Huchel replied that the employment of Uhse alongside him was unacceptable and that he had been forced to resign. That is the line that is taken in the 1984 Huchel edition, where one can read, 'Huchel wird gezwungen, die Leitung von *Sinn und Form* im November an Bodo Uhse abzugeben'. (i,461) It is unclear where the reference to November comes from. Huchel denied that he was behind the West German rumour mill. He had been rung up by *Der Spiegel*, which had distorted the statement he made to their journalist.

Naturally enough, Huchel maintained contact with influential western figures during this period. Among them were Hans Bender, Klaus Wagenbach and Fritz J.Raddatz. His letter to Raddatz of 18 October contains a particularly colourful description of his situation,

> Ich bin von meinem alten Jeep gesprungen. Aber mir paßte nicht der Anstrich, mit dem
> der Wagen versehen werden sollte. Und noch weniger der mir offerierte Beifahrer; den
> kenne ich allzu gut. Wenn er sich einmal, durch Zufall, für die Firma verfährt, dann steigen
> ihm sofort die Tränen in die Augen. Und was mich anlangt, so hat er oft genug versucht,
> mir Nägel auf die Fahrbahn zu streuen. Und überhaupt: in dieser Kumpanei ist keine steile
> Kurve zu nehmen. Vierzehn Jahre, eine lange Zeit. Erst jetzt merke ich, wie sehr ich an
> diesem verbeulten Vehikel hänge.[24]

Through the imagery of him driving the old jeep, Huchel manages to convey something of the great affection and the excitement that he felt as editor of *Sinn und Form*. All that would be lost through the involvement of an SED member like Uhse.

Hossinger was told by Huchel in late September that the plan for the final number was not yet quite ready. Hossinger duly recorded this in his memo but took no action. He could have used the instruments of the state in order to check on progress at the publisher's or at the printer's. This was not done. Had he taken such action, he would have discovered that Huchel was sending material to the printer for the final issue from 7 October until 2 November.[25] The material included poems by Huchel such as 'Soldatenfriedhof', 'Der Garten des Theophrast' and 'Traum im Tellereisen', all of which he composed that October. Each of these poems captures an aspect of his sombre mood that autumn. 'Soldatenfriedhof' is an ironic comment on a grotesque society where militarism and regimentation go hand in hand. 'Der Garten des Theophrast', which he dedicated to his son, laments the breaking of the East-West dialogue that he had so carefully nurtured in the manner of Theophrastus. Finally, 'Traum im Tellereisen' treats the violent entrapment of the poetic vision of a better world that Huchel had vainly sought to foster. Huchel was concocting a powerful brew for that final double issue.

It was only on 27 October that Hossinger confirmed to Huchel receipt of the plan for the final number. Bredel approved the plan but would later angrily claim that Huchel then changed it without his knowledge. A copy of the plan that Huchel submitted to the Academy has not yet surfaced, which would permit a systematic comparison. What can be ascertained is that there were two late additions to the table of contents, Aragon's 'Rede in Prag' and Walther Huder's piece about

Barlach, 'Besuch in Güstrow'.[26] Huchel's publication of the former certainly angered Uhse, who had earmarked it as the keynote piece for his first issue![27] Yet, on their own the two additions would surely not have been sufficient to provoke Bredel's anger.

The note of the meeting with Huchel concluded with Hossinger's reminder to himself that he should cancel the rental arrangement for the editorial rooms next to Huchel's house that had been acquired in 1955. This Hossinger duly did, and the Wilhelmshorst housing commission subsequently determined to re-allocate them. We shall return to that story presently.

In early October, Uhse began work. One of his first tasks was to recruit an advisory board. Among others, Hermlin agreed to serve with Uhse, though Felsenstein did not.[28] The evidence of Hermlin's agreement contradicts his statement made in 1988, 'ihren Redaktionsbeirat verließ ich vor genau fünfundzwanzig Jahren, aus Solidarität mit dem damals abgesetzten Chefredakteur Peter Huchel'.[29] He made a similar statement in the early 1990s, 'Ich ... trat aus dem Kollegium aus, als Huchel seine Tätigkeit als Redakteur beenden mußte'.[30] In late 1962 Hermlin did not perform an act of solidarity with Huchel. It would, indeed, have been very difficult to countenance such an act in the climate that prevailed. Very soon, however, Hermlin, too, was subjected to intense pressure by Abusch and Kurella, and forced to resign as Secretary of the Literature Section. This experience would come to dominate his memory of a period, in which he, like Huchel, became a victim of the dogmatists.

In early October, Huchel took up Hossinger's suggestion that he should meet with Bredel.[31] Bredel now offered Huchel an early retirement deal, which he had discussed with Gotsche. Despite his treatment at Huchel's hands in August 1961, Gotsche recommended a generous settlement of an affair which was beginning to be a great embarrassment. Huchel later suspected that he had Gotsche to thank for all the years of isolation that were to follow. He said of the later 1960s, 'Sämtliche Briefe, die ich schrieb, gingen durch die Hände Gotsches, des persönlichen Sekretärs von Ulbricht. Ich glaube, daß ich ihm diese bitteren Jahre zu verdanken habe'. (ii,381) Things were somewhat different. The plan agreed by Bredel and Gotsche, and presented to Huchel by Bredel, was shortly afterwards vetoed by Abusch and the party group in the Academy.[32] Abusch was at this stage, it seems, motivated more by revenge against an old adversary than by the need to minimise the political fall-out from the affair.

Following the claims made about pension, Bredel had made another promise that he could not keep. Even though he had secured support at the highest level in the hierarchy, his authority was undermined by Abusch and others. The Academy's officers were in an impossible position as they attempted to continue negotiations with Huchel, who already had little faith in what they told him. It was left to Hossinger to pick up the pieces in an affair that was rapidly unravelling.

Not before time, in mid-October, Hossinger took expert advice on Huchel's pension.[33] Three options were explored. One possible solution was based on health grounds, another was an honorary pension and the third related to the terms of his personal contract, even though that had ceased to have effect through Huchel's resignation. None of these three options could, however, become operable until Huchel's 65th birthday in 1968. Casting around for a solution, Hossinger now devised a package for Huchel's 'Beschäftigung und finanzielle Sicherstellung', as he put it, until 1968. He presented his plan to Bredel on 23 October.[34] He began by proposing that Huchel and his wife should continue to be employed by the Academy. He then listed five points. As an Academy member, Huchel received 10,000 marks annually. He should be offered a fee of 12,000 per annum to edit the almanac. Monica Huchel could earn between 3,000 and 5,000 marks from translation work done for the Academy. A collection of Huchel's poems should be published by the Aufbau Verlag! *Sinn und Form* should publish his poems, too!! Finally, Hossinger suggested that agreement might be reached that the pension which Huchel was due from April 1968 could be frozen until then. In the meantime, he might be granted an honorary pension. He was later informed by an insurance expert that this proposal was a legal impossibility.[35] An exception could be made only with the express approval of the Presidium of the Council of Ministers. The hapless Hossinger really was grasping at straws as he searched for a way out of his and Bredel's embarrassment. The consequences for Huchel were potentially very serious, as he himself was aware. There was no prospect anymore of Huchel's agreeing to work on the almanac. He had absolutely no desire to be published by Aufbau or in a *Sinn und Form* edited by Uhse. The only thing that Huchel was actually guaranteed was his sinecure, and that only as long as he was an Academy member. Bredel crossed out that point in Hossinger's calculations, commenting, 'Punkt 1 zählt nicht. Das erhält auch jeder andere Faulenzer. Mit den übrigen Punkten bin ich einverstanden. Bin auch für eine Unterhaltung mit Huchel'.

The Huchels travelled to Berlin on 9 November for their meeting with Bredel and Hossinger. Bredel explained to Huchel that the early retirement plan had been rejected by the majority of Academy members. Another way had to be found to help him. Huchel declined to edit the almanac. He said that he wanted to concentrate on his writing and look after his health. He laid claim to his pension on the terms presented previously by Bredel and asked to be permitted to travel to Italy. Both Huchel (ii,327) and his wife later place the request to travel to Italy earlier in the year.[36] There is no record to support the Huchels' later assertion that they made the granting of the trip to Italy a condition for editing the remaining issues in 1962. They also both later suggested that already earlier in the year they wanted to leave the GDR for good. Again, there is no evidence to support that version of events. The intention to leave for good crystallised as the situation deteriorated in the late autumn and beyond. Huchel had a long-standing invitation from Gottfried Bermann Fischer to visit him at his house in Camaiore in Italy. Bermann Fischer renewed the invitation, first issued in the summer of 1961, in a letter of 13 November 1962.[37] It can be assumed that the letter was produced at Huchel's prompting, since it could act as a convenient pretext for him and his family in their efforts to leave. He certainly used it as such, though to no avail. In a letter to Livia Wittmann on 29 November 1962, (ii,349) Huchel referred to Bermann Fischer's invitation, though by then he doubted whether he would be able to take it up. Nor, he feared, would he be able to take up her invitation to visit her in Budapest, Kundera's to go to Brno and another invitation to Warsaw.

Hossinger was still trying to sort out the transfer of material, which the Huchels continued to insist was not ready. Huchel, meanwhile, wrote to Hans Bender on 11 December explaining that he would now not be able to supply the piece on *Sinn und Form* that he had promised for Bender's *Akzente*. Such a piece could be construed as resentment, an impression that he wanted to avoid 'nachdem die Polemik um *Sinn und Form* über Monate hin und mit aller Härte geführt worden ist'.[38] The letter suggests that Huchel did not anticipate the storm that would break over the final issue.

He telephoned Hossinger on 20 December, seeking confirmation that he would receive his pension of 1,200 marks from his 65th birthday.[39] He informed Hossinger that his lawyer had advised him to maintain that the Academy had not yet shown that he had done his job unsatisfactorily, that if the contract had been terminated during their negotiations in mid-August, he was entitled to 1½ months salary in 1963 and if no agreement was reached on his pension, he reserved the right to go to court. Huchel and Hossinger reached agreement on 28 December as the date for the transfer of material. Hossinger wrote to Huchel on 21 December, assuring him that he would receive his pension on his 65th birthday or earlier if he was no longer fit for work.[40] Yet Hossinger had no guarantee that such approval would be given! In fact, on 22 December Hossinger drafted a proposal, for approval by the Council of Ministers, for a special case to be made for Huchel's pension.[41] The draft was sent to Abusch's office that same day. Huchel's long-term financial security was now in Abusch's hands. As we know, he owed Huchel no favours.

Huchel and Hossinger next spoke when Hossinger came to collect the editorial material on 28 December. His memo of the next day shows that the atmosphere had, predictably enough, not been good.[42] The by now familiar grievances were rehearsed, and Huchel gave Hossinger Bermann Fischer's invitation. It was agreed that Huchel should apply through the Academy for permission to travel to Italy. In another memo of 29 December, Hossinger reported that Frau Narr had referred him to 10-12 files which contained correspondence with authors since 1960.[43] Earlier correspondence had been destroyed, he was told, apart from the letters removed by Huchel as his personal correspondence. Huchel would later refer to the destruction of some 4,000 letters in a fire in his garden. (ii,381) Hossinger would return to pick up material a few days later. Yet in practice, no proper hand-over of material took place and Uhse was left in a quite hopeless position in the first few months of 1963, before his death that summer. In Hossinger's account of events, he was at pains to stress that the content of the double issue was not known to him at that point in time since it was sent from the printer's to the Academy only on 27 December.[44]

Three days into the New Year, Huchel wrote to Bredel, requesting the Academy's support for his application to travel to Italy with his family for two months or so, probably in the summer of 1963. They would be the guests of Bermann Fischer.[45] Huchel informed Bredel that the S. Fischer Verlag and the Hamburg Academy had agreed to act on his behalf in order to obtain the necessary papers in West Berlin. He went on to explain that since they did not yet know the exact dates, they would like a general exit visa. He suggested that his request differed in no way from that of other Academy members. Hossinger passed the matter on to Abusch's office on 7 January 1963.[46] There, for the time being, the matter rested.

A Final *Tour de Force*

Meanwhile, the double issue had appeared. A review by Reich-Ranicki, 'Ein anderer Sinn, eine andere Form. Der Dichter und Redakteur Peter Huchel ist in Ungnade gefallen', appeared in *Die Zeit* on 4 January 1963. In the absence of any expression of thanks from Bredel to Huchel in his statement at the beginning of that number, Reich-Ranicki wrote, 'Wir jedoch wollen ihm, der in der DDR eine Zeitschrift redigiert hat, die für uns alle wichtig war, in aller Öffentlichkeit danken. Er sollte wissen, daß er nicht allein ist'. Reich-Ranicki continued with words about Huchel's poetry that were heeded in many quarters in the following years, as Huchel's standing as a poet was buoyed on the wave of sympathy felt towards the erstwhile editor, 'Jene aber, die in der Bundesrepublik Literaturpreise verleihen, seien auf die Gedichte Peter Huchels hingewiesen ... Dies, meinen wir, ist große deutsche Lyrik unserer Zeit'. Reich-Ranicki thus added his influential voice to Jens' assessment of Huchel's poetry. Together with Hans Mayer, who moved to the West in 1963, these critics were crucial not only in Huchel's belated recognition as a poet in the West, but also in keeping alive throughout the 1960s the issue of his treatment by the GDR authorities. Indeed, his last act with *Sinn und Form* had so antagonised influential figures in East Berlin that it would be nearly a decade before he could enjoy that recognition in the West.

Under Bredel's nose, Huchel had arranged for an extremely demonstrative departure. It contained Ernst Fischer's 'Entfremdung, Dekadenz, Realismus' and Sartre's 'Die Abrüstung der Kultur', his plea at the Moscow World Peace Congress for an end to dogmatism in USSR cultural politics. Essays by Mayer and Krauss featured, Huchel's own poems and those of Eich and Celan. There was a story by Ilse Aichinger. The issue opened with Brecht's 'Rede über die Widerstandskraft der Vernunft', which was written in 1936. It begins,

Angesichts der überaus strengen Maßnahmen, die in den faschistischen Staaten gegenwärtig gegen die Vernunft ergriffen werden, dieser ebenso methodischen wie gewalttätigen Maßnahmen, ist es erlaubt, zu fragen, ob die menschliche Vernunft diesem gewaltigen Ansturm überhaupt wird widerstehen können.

The use of Brecht to supply the scarcely veiled comparison between Nazism and the GDR was regarded as the ultimate insult by the SED. Abusch called a meeting for 9 January at his office. It was attended by Kurella, Bentzien and all members of the Academy's Presidium with the exception of Hermlin. Hermlin had come under heavy fire after the poetry evening that he had organised at the Academy on 11 December 1962, when he had introduced young poets, among them Wolf Biermann, Volker Braun, Bernd Jentzsch, and Sarah and Rainer Kirsch. Hermlin had long been mistrusted because of his unregenerate 'bourgeois' tastes. The decision to remove him from his post as Secretary to the Literature Section was taken at the meeting on 9 January and the attempt was subsequently made to force him to admit his failings. He, however, acted quickly. He sent his resignation letter to Bredel on 13 January 1963, withdrawing from both the post of Secretary and from the advisory board of *Sinn und Form*.[47] From this point on, Hermlin, like Huchel, was in the wilderness. He refused to supply the self-criticism that had been demanded of him.

Abusch claimed that Huchel's final issue of *Sinn und Form* had demonstrated his intolerance towards other artistic attitudes, since it was so one-sidedly against the GDR's cultural politics. However, he criticised the Academy leadership for permitting this to happen. Bredel replied that it was only in the final months that the situation had crystallised. That was true enough, and he had played his part in the outcome that had been achieved. He claimed that the plan which Huchel had given him for the final number had simply not contained a number of pieces that actually appeared. Bredel could scarcely contain his anger, exclaiming, 'Ich halte Huchel kulturpolitisch für einen dummen und plumpen Gegner'. The agitated Bredel declined to enter into further negotiations with Huchel, no doubt unwilling to repeat the debacle of the pension. The whole business had in truth over-taxed Bredel, whose own health deteriorated. He died following a heart attack in October 1964.

A public attack on Huchel, as well as on the Academy and its President, followed at the sixth SED Party Conference on 15-21 January. Paul Verner criticised the SED group in the Academy for tolerating its 'stille Enklave des Liberalismus' for so long. He asked how the Academy could possibly have raised Huchel's salary and gone on now to propose his early retirement? At this point, Walter Ulbricht interjected, 'Der hat einen Sondervertrag!' Bredel sought to defend the Academy's actions, arguing that despite all their efforts, Huchel had been determined to show 'wes Geistes Kind er ist und was er unter loyaler Mitarbeit versteht'. He took through the story of Huchel's deception and announced that Huchel intended to go to court. He was uncertain what the outcome would be.

Hager, who had spent the years of exile in Britain, replied with his familiar, sarcastic comparison of the Academy with the House of Lords,

> Aber bisher ging es in der Akademie der Künste ... offenbar zu wie im englischen
> Oberhaus, wo ein Lord dem anderen nicht wehtut und der Präsident keine Macht hat.
> (Heiterkeit und Beifall) Die erhabene, geradezu majestätische Isoliertheit im Elfenbeinturm
> hinderten aber weder Peter Huchel noch andere Mitglieder der Akademie, den Angriff
> gegen die Politik der Partei und gegen den sozialistischen Realismus zu führen.

The speeches were reported in detail in the GDR media and the West German press. On 24 January, for example, *Die Welt* wrote of a 'Strafgericht über die Poeten'. As we have seen, Huchel was not in good health. He had clearly not anticipated attacks of such vehemence. He had seriously miscalculated if he believed that he could get away with what he had done. He later said, 'Meine Annahme, der Fall *Sinn und Form* sei nach Herausgabe des letzten Heftes abgeschlossen, erwies sich als trügerisch. Das Kesseltreiben sollte erst beginnen'. (ii,328)

He had not, though, lost the sympathy of fellow writers in the Academy such as Zweig, who himself had suffered at the hands of cultural politicians and bureaucrats. Zweig wrote to Huchel on 25 January. He began by referring to differences between them from the early 1950s. Nor had he forgotten that Huchel had rejected three of his pieces on Freud. However, Zweig went on to express his solidarity with Huchel after the attacks launched against him. He praised *Sinn und Form* as the best literary journal in the German language, writing, 'Immer wird *Sinn und Form* verbunden bleiben mit dem Namen Peter Huchel, seinen Gedichten, seiner Persönlichkeit als Herausgeber, seiner und Frau Monicas Sorge für das vortreffliche Deutsch'. Huchel replied on 4 February, thanking him for his kind words. He outlined the grave situation in which he found himself,

> Es wäre töricht, die Wirkung einer solchen Kampagne zu unterschätzen, sie bietet
> manchen Leuten eine vorzügliche Handhabe, meine wirtschaftliche Existenz vollkommen
> zu zerstören. Allen Ernstes, was mit uns werden soll, liegt noch ganz im Ungewissen. Die
> Frage, wie wir uns überhaupt in den nächsten Jahren durchschlagen sollen, stand niemals
> drohender vor uns.

He said that Rütten und Loening had deferred publication of his collection until the affair had subsided. Klaus Wagenbach, S. Fischer's reader, had not been permitted to visit him. He spelt out what this all meant for him, 'Unausgesprochenes Reiseverbot, unausgesprochenes Rundfunkverbot, unausgesprochenes Publikationsverbot, schließlich vollständige Isolierung'. After occupying a position for well over a decade which had given him a unique standing in the German literary world, Huchel had simply been swept off the grand stage. More than likely, he would be consigned in his final years to a life of obscurity, with little influence in literary affairs.

Into the bargain, the Huchels had lost two salaries worth together nearly 3,000 marks per month. They had plunged from being a high-earning family to having a regular income that amounted only to 10,000 marks per year from the Academy and 210 marks per month that Monica Huchel received as an invalid allowance on account of her thyroid gland trouble.[48] It must be said that it was hardly possible in the GDR to spend the amount that they had earned over the years. A substantial sum of 45,000 had accumulated in a savings account, and Monica Huchel earned money through translation work. Nonetheless, they had a house to maintain and their sickly fourteen-year old son to support for the foreseeable future. His school-fellows in Potsdam took their cue from the GDR media, teasing the defenceless Stephan as a traitor's son.

The Break with Bobrowski

Huchel's professional prospects were indeed bleak. Hitherto, only a fragmentary picture of his years of isolation until 1971 has been available. Yet much archive information is now available, and much of it has latterly been brought into the public sphere, so that a more informed picture can be constructed.[49] Despite Zweig's support in his letter, Huchel later claimed that figures of his generation such as Zweig broke with him overnight. Huchel in fact withdrew a dedication to Zweig from the poem published in *Chausseen Chausseen* as 'In memoriam Paul Eluard'. (i,154) Huchel's friendship with Hermlin, too, had come under great strain, yet the first relationship to break down was with his protégé Bobrowski.

Bobrowski had latterly sprung to prominence in the Federal Republic. Publication of his two collections, *Sarmatische Zeit* and *Schattenland Ströme*. was followed in October 1962 by the award of the prize of the Gruppe 47 at its meeting in West Berlin. Bobrowski maintained the deferential tone towards Huchel in his dedication in *Sarmatische Zeit*, which reads, 'Herrn Peter Huchel, meinem Meister, in Verehrung und Dankbarkeit. Johannes Bobrowski'.[50] Huchel remained for Bobrowski the embodiment of the poet and man of letters. Yet even at that stage, Huchel later maintained, he had developed his reservations about Bobrowski.[51] He disliked Bobrowski's contempt for the anti-fascist movement and the anti-fascist schools in the Soviet Union, which Bobrowski had attended. For a long time, Bobrowski kept his membership of the CDU secret. Huchel also objected to the cynicism, 'womit Bobrowski in den letzten Jahren politische Erklärungen und Aufrufe unterschrieb und in Westdeutschland sich darüber lustig machte'.

Huchel's own situation was deteriorating in inverse proportion to Bobrowski's success, and Huchel evidently felt that Bobrowski owed him at least a sign of his solidarity in his hour of need. Bobrowski neglected to give such a sign. Indeed, Huchel's wife later recalled that Bobrowski simply ignored her at a reading in the Academy.[52] The reading in question was the poetry evening organised by Hermlin on 11 December 1962.[53] Huchel refers to that evening in his censorious letter to Bobrowski on 14 February 1963. Reinhard Tgahrt is apparently referring to the same episode, when he writes of Bobrowski's omission 'Für Peter Huchel nicht im rechten Moment und deutlich genug eingetreten zu sein (obwohl es zuletzt an einer erwarteten kleinen Geste lag, die ihm im Dezember 1962 freilich aus vielen Gründen schwerfiel)'.[54] It was clearly not just Bobrowski's relationship to Huchel himself that was a problem.

The matter came to a head when Christoph Meckel visited Bobrowski at his home in Friedrichshagen. It was around the end of January or beginning of February. Meckel asked to ring Huchel, who told him in no uncertain terms of his deep disappointment, indeed his anger at Bobrowski's silence. Bobrowski wrote to Huchel on 7 February full of contrition.[55] He acknowledged his 'Unvermögen, in derartigen Situationen überhaupt zu reagieren'. He sought to counter Huchel's reproach that he had been more concerned with his own career advancement than with expressing his support for the disgraced Huchel. Huchel responded to 'Herr Bobrowski' on 14 February.[56] He pointed out that during visits from friends, who 'auf Sie und unsere vermeintliche Freundschaft kamen', he had been 'in die peinliche Situation gebracht [worden], der Wahrheit entsprechend zu argumentie-ren'. Huchel referred to Bobrowski's absence in recent months, his behaviour during Meckel's call and 'nach der Akademie-Lesung, wo es Sie weder Zeit noch Mühe gekostet hätte, en passant ein menschliches Wort zu finden'. Bobrowski replied on 20 February, insisting that it had never been his intention to distance himself from Huchel. He begged Huchel's forgiveness.[57] Huchel did not answer.

Making an Example of Huchel

Offers of help were forthcoming from the West and from within the GDR, but they were blocked. On 28 February, for example, the Hamburg Academy invited Huchel to celebrate his sixtieth birthday with them.[58] There would be a reading from his work on the occasion. They wished to mark it with the publication of some of his poems. They also wished to publish a critical appreciation of his work in their almanac. The letter was passed on to Hossinger. Hans Mayer, too, sought to arrange for a birthday invitation to Leipzig University, but, as he told the Huchels, the SED intervened to block his initiative.[59]

Mayer was asked to write a piece for *Die Zeit* in order to mark the occasion.[60] In the event, Dieter E. Zimmer's name appeared as the author of the article 'In der Mitte der Dinge die Trauer', which appeared on 5 April. Meanwhile, Monica Huchel wrote to Hossinger on 18 March informing him that Huchel was in hospital.[61] On his behalf, she asked Hossinger for a decision as to whether her husband could travel to Hamburg. Hossinger consulted with Abusch's office on 21 March.[62] It was already 8 April when Hossinger replied to Monica Huchel that there could be no question of permission to travel being granted at that point in time.[63]

The SED hierarchy was determined to put on a show of its authority over Huchel and *Sinn und Form*. At a meeting of the politburo on 19 March 1963, *Sinn und Form* and Huchel were attacked for nurturing the ideology of a reconciliation between socialism and capitalism. It was argued that the German Question was a class question and that socialism was the way forward for the whole of Germany. Gerd Bucerius of *Die Zeit* was identified as a kindred spirit in this ideology of reconciliation. The Academy was criticised, too, for leaving untouched for so long this 'Insel der Seligen', as the journal was described in the crude sloganising of the Cold War in East Berlin. A further public demonstration of the SED's determination to stamp on Huchel came when Hager again attacked *Sinn und Form* in familiar Cold War language in his speech delivered before writers and artists on 25 March.

A Sombre Sixtieth Birthday

Huchel, meanwhile, celebrated his sixtieth birthday at home in Wilhelmshorst with his family and a small circle of friends. Among them were Huchel's doctor Herwig Hesse and his wife. Hans Mayer recalls travelling from Leipzig; Erich Arendt and Stephan Hermlin came from Berlin.[64] Like Huchel, Hermlin had been attacked by Hager. Hesse recalls conversation centring on the control exercised by the state over literature.[65] Hermlin and Mayer fell out, and Mayer left early. The mood was subdued, there was little further difference of opinion, until Hermlin, as he was leaving, astounded his friends by reminding them, 'Aber ich bin doch ein Kommunist!'[66]

Mayer recalls that 'Irgendeine Berliner Instanz hatte ein Blumentöpfchen geschickt'. The flowers were presented by Hanna Kaemmel on behalf of the Writers' Union. She gave him a card from the Union as well as hand-written greetings from Paul Wiens on behalf of the Berlin executive committee, to which Huchel still belonged. She wrote a report about the visit, which was forwarded to the Cultural Department of the Central Committee, and from there to Hager.[67] Huchel had received her in a downstairs room at 4 pm., away from his guests, who were upstairs. He was sarcastic about what Kaemmel called the 'Blumenschale', saying how pleased he was that the Writers' Union had had the courage to congratulate him with such a fine present. She noted her impression of the effect of recent events on him, which was that he regarded what had happened as a 'schicksalhaftes Unglück ... Er zeigte weder Verstimmung, noch Empörung, sondern tiefe Traurigkeit'. He was concerned about his financial position, afraid that after Hager's last speech he would be excluded from the Academy and would lose his sinecure. He said that his state of health made it difficult for him to travel to Berlin for meetings of the Writers' Union's executive. He felt it would be best if he resigned now rather than running the risk of being excluded on the pretext of poor attendance. Kaemmel agreed to take the matter up in Berlin. Her view was that what had happened should not affect Huchel's other literary projects and plans with GDR publishers.

Huchel's assessment of his situation was decidedly sombre, when he wrote to Günter Eich on 10 April,

> Eine mächtige Maschine hat mich aufs tote Gleis rangiert, die blockierte Strecke ist abzusehen, hier also wirst du verrosten. Ein Leben ohne Aussicht auf irgendeine Veränderung ist uninteressant. Und was einem manchmal durch Haut und Knochen geht, es ist nicht notwendig, Ihnen das mitzuteilen. Sie haben ähnliche Situationen in Ihren 'Träumen' erschreckend genau registriert.[68]

The West Berlin Fontane Prize: Kurella's Threats and Mistrust of Hermlin

Almost immediately, there was a further escalation in the affair when the West Berlin Academy announced its decision to award Huchel its Fontane Prize. The jury, consisting of Dieter Hildebrandt, Kurt Ihlenfeld and Rudolf Hartung, heeded Reich-Ranicki's words. The decision was interpreted in East Berlin as a highly provocative act. For Huchel, however, it was not only a heartening signal of western support, the prize money of 10,000 marks was also welcome. Now the SED hierarchy went utterly over the top in a response that testifies not only to the arrogance of those firmly in power in their own state but also to their profound anxiety regarding the threat posed by the larger western neighbour and its 'outpost', West Berlin.

Academy members and other figures were encouraged to try and dissuade him from accepting the prize. The award was due to take place on Sunday, 21 April. Stephan Hermlin recalled in a letter of 19 August 1993 that Siegfried Wagner had called him with the request that he should travel to Wilhelmshorst in order 'auf ihn einzuwirken, er möge den Preis nicht annehmen. Ich wies dieses Ansinnen zurück'.[69] He later claimed that his intention had been not to dissuade Huchel from accepting the prize. On the contrary, he wished to demonstrate his support.[70] Monica Huchel recalls that Hermlin, Bredel and Erich Wendt rang the Saturday before the prize was due to be awarded.[71] Hermlin tried to reach Huchel four times in all. Monica Huchel was encouraged by Wendt in her assumption that Hermlin's message would be the same as Wendt's and Bredel's, although Wendt had not actually spoken to Hermlin. On each occasion, Monica Huchel answered that her husband was not at home. He had, indeed, gone to ground at the Hesses in nearby Caputh.[72] Heinrich Böll accepted the prize in Huchel's absence, who wrote to express his thanks on 22 April.[73] Hartung delivered an appreciation of Huchel's achievements as a poet, studiously avoiding any mention of his editorial work and recent conflicts. Yet, of course, Huchel was praised in the western press for his tenacious opposition to the East Berlin dogmatists. This was like a red rag to a bull. On 23 April Kurella, Hermlin's replacement as Secretary of the Literature Section, paid Huchel a visit. Hesse recollects how Huchel imitated the stutterer Kurella as he acted out the scene,

Eines Tages stand Alfred Kurella persönlich in seinem Haus, man begegnete sich zur beiderseitigen Überraschung in der Küche. Huchel machte mir vor, indem er Kurellas Sprechweise imitierte, wie man sich gegenseitig anschrie. Huchel wies Kurella ab: 'Ich gehöre nicht zu Ihrer Kirche und akzeptiere nicht die Beschlüsse Ihres heiligen Konzils!'.[74]

Similarly, Huchel recalled that Kurella, 'ließ gewaltige Drohungen vom Stapel, um mich zur Ablehnung des Preises zu bewegen: Er habe schon manchen aus falschem Stolz in den Tod gehen sehen, rief er'. (ii,378) Half an hour later, Kurella's limousine returned and the chauffeur delivered a letter, which, Huchel could only assume, Kurella had written in preparation before the visit. In Kurella's view, the Fontane Prize was not an award of the West Berlin Academy as such but rather of the West Berlin Senate. On that basis, Kurella proposed that Huchel should decline the award. He went on to assure Huchel that by such an act he would regain many friends that he had lost, who, like Kurella and Huchel, were opposed to the politics of Brandt's Senate. But Huchel, of course, was not opposed to Brandt! Then followed Kurella's threat, 'Umgekehrt wird es uns schwer sein, wenn Sie sich nicht in dieser Weise von dem Brandt-Senat distanzieren, mit Ihnen über alle die vielen Einzelfragen zu reden, die Sie in unserem Gespräch in Form von Widerspruch, Klagen, Gekränktsein vorgebracht haben'. (ii,379)

Kurella asked Huchel to think things over and to contact Hossinger the following morning to convey to him his final decision on the matter. Huchel did not react. Kurella reported to a Plenary Session on 30 May that Huchel had said to him, 'Ja, ich weiß, was ich angenommen habe. Ich habe nicht die Absicht, die Annahme dieses Preises zu verweigern. Ich weiß, daß man beschlossen hat, mich zu vernichten. Ich werde hier zugrundegehen'.

The affair escalated further in East Berlin. Huchel later maintained that, following Kurella's visit, he received 'keine Post, keine Zeitschriften mehr'. (ii,379) This was not literally true, which is not to deny that Huchel was subjected to quite unacceptable treatment by the Stasi. His post certainly was controlled and items were confiscated, but it was not quite the blanket isolation that he later suggested. Huchel conveyed his mood of bitter resignation in the poem 'April 63', (i,217) which was later collected in *Gezählte Tage*,

Ich bette mich ein

in die eisige Mulde meiner Jahre.

Ich spalte Holz,

das zähe splittrige Holz der Einsamkeit.

Yet his mood was not one of unmitigated despair. The poet follows the play of five young jays in the trees and ends with his contemplation of the 'leimigen Hüllen der Knospen' as they gleam. It would, though, become ever more difficult to muster such images of renewal through his familiar counterpointing technique, given the sense of futility that surrounded him.

Stasi headquarters in East Berlin alerted the Potsdam office on 29 April that systematic surveillance of Huchel was now necessary.[75] On the same day, one of the Stasi's star informants, 'Martin', better known as Hermann Kant, reported upon a conversation with his friend Stephan Hermlin, during which Hermlin allegedly said that he

> hält die Auszeichnung *Peter HUCHELS* von der Westberliner Akademie der Künste mit
> dem 'Fontane-Preis' als (sic) eine Provokation. HERMLIN vertritt den Standpunkt, daß
> Peter HUCHEL die Annahme der Auszeichnung ablehnen muß, sollte er dieses nicht tun,
> *dann muß man Peter HUCHEL aus der Akademie ausschließen.*[76]

Following publication of this document in the early 1990s, Hermlin strenuously denied that he had ever recommended that Huchel or anyone else should be excluded from the Academy.[77] As we have seen, he later claimed that he had wished to encourage Huchel to accept the prize. Yet, at that time an SED member like Hermlin could not but have been against Huchel's acceptance of the Fontane Prize. He would, moreover, surely have seen it as his duty as a friend to advise Huchel against accepting. In that way, he could hope to reconcile his conflict of interests. Regarding Kant's report, as someone who had himself recently been castigated and sent into the wilderness, it is highly unlikely that Hermlin would have drawn the conclusion that Huchel should be excluded from the Academy. That was on the agenda of those like Bredel and Abusch, who had engineered Hermlin's own disgrace. Nothing in Hermlin's behaviour in 1963 indicates that he was seeking to curry favour in that way. Is it possible that Hermlin's friend Kant was feeding such a view into the security apparatus to demonstrate that, despite everything that had been said and done, Hermlin was absolutely loyal?

Hermlin never wavered in the view that Huchel was for him a friend. He was evidently less enamoured of Monica Huchel. She certainly encouraged her husband in the view that Hermlin was behaving in a duplicitous manner. She based this on her assumption that Hermlin's message to her husband would have been the same as Wendt's and Bredel's. For his part, Hermlin has never forgiven her for the role that, in his eyes, she played in destroying his friendship with Huchel. Hermlin was asked to speak at a ceremony when, in the early 1990s, a plaque in Huchel's honour was placed in the garden of Hubertusweg 43-45. Hermlin agreed to do so only on the condition that Monica Huchel did not attend.[78]

Systematic Stasi Surveillance: Hager Attacks Again

In early May, the Stasi began to draw up plans for Huchel's systematic surveillance, seeking to identify suitable informants in Wilhelmshorst.[79] From 20 May, his telephone conversations were tapped.[80] On 27 May, Bredel received a letter from Paul Février, inviting Huchel to the Biennales Internationales de Poésie in Brussels on 5-9 September 1963.[81] The reply that Février was sent by Bredel on 23 July had been dictated by Kurella. Predictably, it was laced with Cold War rhetoric. Huchel would not be going to Brussels. He was once again attacked by Hager in a speech at the conference of the Writers' Union. The text of the speech was published in *Neues Deutschland* on 28 May 1963 under the title 'Wir freuen uns über jedes gelungene Werk'. Hager reported on Huchel's attitude during attempts to bring him round to the SED's way of thinking. Huchel had demonstrated his distance from the GDR and its ideology by referring repeatedly to 'euer Staat' and 'euer Marxismus'. Hager argued that Huchel was surely old enough to appreciate what sort of politicians were to be found in West Berlin. In what was the crudest public statement deployed against Huchel, Hager went on, 'Und wenn er das nicht gemerkt hat, wenn er so naiv sein sollte, dann sind wir bereit, ihm einen Pionier aus einer Pionierorganisation zu schicken, der ihn darüber aufklärt'. For Hager, Huchel's acceptance of the Fontane Prize was the final straw. Hager was by no means alone in this view. Many people with a stake in the GDR who had previously been not unfavourably disposed to him, now abandoned him. Until his departure to the West in 1971, he was ostracised by such people. Such was the sense of anger and bitterness in the SED hierarchy that 'selbst liberalere Geister unter den DDR-Funktionären bei Nennung seines Namens fanatisch sich verhärten'.[82] Huchel was resolved to have no further truck with GDR literary life. He withdrew into his private sphere, where he was joined by others like Walter Janka and Wolf Biermann, who were ostracised by the SED.

The Academy's Condemnation

The Huchel affair was the subject of a lengthy debate at a Plenary Session of the Academy on 30 May. Bredel opened proceedings, explaining how the development of *Sinn und Form* had been diametrically opposed to that of the GDR during the 1950s and early 1960s. This was correct, even if that fact does not necessarily reflect well on the GDR, nor, for that matter, on the Federal Republic and the other actors in the Cold War. Bredel commented that during his negotiations with Huchel, the latter had acted 'als wäre die Zeitschrift inzwischen sein privatkapitalistisches Unternehmen geworden, und die Akademie hätte ihm da gar nichts dreinzureden'. He returned to Huchel's disloyalty over the final issue. Bredel confessed that he had been so upset by the affair that at the Party Conference he had been not able to contain himself and had behaved in a manner unbecoming for an Academy President. We see here how the affair simply demanded too much of Bredel, whom Abusch had pushed into the front line. Hossinger, too, claimed that the negotiations had been a great strain on his health. Bredel concluded by saying that the Academy must adopt a clear position on the matter of Huchel's acceptance of the Fontane Prize.

Kurella then spoke, pointing out that Huchel had willingly allowed himself to be depicted as a martyr in the western campaign against the East. He was applauded when he said of Huchel that 'wir diese Haltung verurteilen müssen'. It was finally agreed that Ihering should be delegated to go to Wilhelmshorst in order to invite Huchel to come to the Academy and discuss the situation. The Plenary Session passed a resolution nem. con., condemning Huchel's acceptance of the Fontane Prize. Depending on the outcome of Ihering's deliberations with Huchel, it would be released to the press. Further steps might follow in the Academy. A meeting between Huchel and Ihering was arranged for mid-June but Charlotte Narr phoned Hossinger to request a delay due to Huchel's bad state of health.[83] There the matter rested for the time being.

Stasi Suspicions of 'Republikflucht'

In early June, the Stasi believed that Huchel and his family were preparing to be smuggled out of the GDR. On 8 June, an unnamed Stasi informant with links to a West Berlin student group that specialised in smuggling out GDR citizens reported that a person fitting Huchel's description was to be whisked out via Czechoslovakia, using Austrian passports.[84] On 10 June, it was confirmed that Huchel was, indeed, the person in question.[85] It was expected that Huchel would take his family with him. The Stasi alerted border controls and sought to establish whether Huchel had applied to leave the GDR to visit a neighbouring socialist country. They established that he had not. Other Stasi papers contain references to links, via Roger Melis, with Klaus Völker and Günter Bruno Fuchs, who are identified as members of the West Berlin group.[86] According to the Stasi, the escape was abandoned when one of the chain of helpers pulled out at the last minute. Was this all a figment of the Stasi's imagination? Certainly, none of those named in the alleged abortive flight has told such a story. Suspicions were revived in December when the Stasi intercepted a letter from Monica Huchel to a friend in Frankfurt, in which she wrote, actually, she later explained, with reference to difficulties between their dog Sascha and their new tom-cat,'deshalb müssen Schleusen gebaut werden und eine gedachte KOEXIS-

TENZ kann nur sehr sukzessiv eingerichtet werden'.[87] The Stasi suspected that the Huchels were about to try to break through the border.

Poetry Plans: Bobrowski Mediates with Rütten und Loening

Meanwhile, in a letter of 4 June, which certainly reached Huchel, Bobrowski made a first attempt to mend relations.[88] Bobrowski had attended the Writers' Union conference that had been addressed by Hager. Bobrowski strove to demonstrate that he had learned from recent experience. He wrote that the conference had shown him that it was futile simply to wait for an improvement in the political climate. He revealed that he had been behind an inquiry made by Rose Nyland concerning the fate of Huchel's collection of poems due to be published by Rütten und Loening. Bentzien had said that the collection had not been rejected. The letter ended with Bobrowski's plea that Huchel might now acknowledge him. Huchel did not respond.

Huchel was not now particularly interested in Bobrowski's information about Rütten und Loening and Bentzien. He had turned his back on much of GDR life, just as the GDR, as he saw it, had discarded him. This information does, however, indicate that some people in the SED hierarchy, whether for tactical reasons or out of a concern for Huchel's welfare, wished still to re-integrate him in GDR literary life. He himself spoke on the telephone about the collection on 20 June to a representative of S. Fischer.[89] He was at the time clearly still entertaining thoughts of a collection for Rütten und Loening but it would be a quite different collection from the one that S. Fischer was producing. He was aware that after all that had happened, it was unlikely that such a collection would finally appear. On 5 August 1963, Huchel was actually sent a letter from Rütten und Loening, in which the publisher expressed continuing interest in a collection of Huchel's verse.[90] There is no record of any reply from Huchel.

In mid-June, Huchel's telephone conversations with representatives of S. Fischer in Frankfurt regarding *Chausseen Chausseen* continued to be tapped. On 18 June, Huchel conveyed his feelings of isolation; he had received no visitors for months and had received little post.[91] Shortly, after, the Stasi compiled a list of Huchel's post that had been confiscated and destroyed. In June and July, there were twelve items, principally western journals.[92] On 3 July, Charlotte Narr wrote to Kundera on Huchel's behalf. Kundera was already translating the new collection into Czech. Narr warned him, 'Als ich in den Urlaub fuhr, war mein Meister noch immer mit dem *Um*schreiben der Manuskripte für S.Fischer beschäftigt – es hat sich *sehr* viel, auch in den älteren Arbeiten, verändert, so daß ich nur dringend Geduld anraten kann, damit nicht Fassungen ercheinen, die er nicht gutheißt'. (i,396) There can be no doubt that recent events had triggered major revisions. It is not always easy to identify exactly what changes were made at this late stage, since few manuscripts are extant and the proofs no longer exist. (i,395) As we shall see in greater detail presently, there is a clearly discernible tendency not only to great condensation of expression but also to the rigorous exclusion of an affirmative socialist dimension in the older works referred to by Narr.

Exclusion from the Academy? Western Initiatives

At Hossinger's prompting, Ihering phoned Huchel on 3 July.[93] Huchel said that his state of health had improved and that he would be prepared to receive a visit from Ihering. He went on to say, however, that in the light of what had been done to him, his only wish now was to leave the GDR. He had been subjected to character assassination. Ihering, who, like Felsenstein, lived in West Berlin, made it clear that he supported Huchel in his acceptance of the Fontane Prize.

Hossinger reported the conversation to Bredel, whose view was that there was now no point in trying to enter into a dialogue with Huchel. That was true enough. Bredel proposed informing Hager as Head of the SED's Ideological Commission. Hager should also receive a copy of the Plenary Session's resolution condemning Huchel. Bredel wanted to see the resolution published. In the light of the gulf between Huchel and the Academy, it was appropriate that he should now leave the GDR. Bredel intended to seek the support of Kurella, Secretary of the SED group in the Academy, for his approach to Hager, which would be undertaken in concert with Abusch. On 16 July, Hossinger produced a memo of a meeting between Bredel and Kurella, which resulted in a plan of action, to be forwarded to Abusch and Siegfried Wagner, and from them, on to Hager. There was one crucial addition to the points made by Bredel. It can be assumed that it was Kurella who now proposed, on behalf of the Literature Section, though, as far as can be ascertained, without prior consultation with its members, that Huchel should be excluded from the Academy. Huchel would, meanwhile, be encouraged to approach the appropriate organs of the state to pursue the matter of his departure from the GDR. There is no record that Huchel was thus encouraged at that stage. There was a further exchange of letters that month between Bredel and Kurella, in which the former sought, quite abjectly, once again to justify his position and actions in the Huchel affair.[94] There the matter rested for the summer.

On 17 July, Huchel received welcome news from the West that the Hamburg Academy had elected him an honorary member.[95] On 5 August, he talked with Klaus Wagenbach of S. Fischer.[96] He told Wagenbach that, following his own promptings, Hans Werner Richter had issued him with an invitation to attend the next meeting of the Gruppe 47. Richter said that he had intended to do so in any case. 1954 has simply been unfortunate. Wagenbach encouraged Huchel to submit an application in order to travel to the meeting, but Huchel was understandably despondent about his chances of success. He said that, come what may, he was going to submit an official application to leave the GDR for good. There was no point in staying. He could by now look forward to the appearance of *Chausseen Chausseen* in the West. On 23 August he received a telegram from S. Fischer, informing him that his corrections had arrived.[97] He was very happy with the changes that he had made and with the overall organisation of the collection. He had included late poems such as 'Polybios'. (i,149) He would have liked to include more but had run out of time.

The *Sinn und Form* Archive

Huchel would later report in the West that petty officialdom now took its cue from the likes of Hager, instigating persecution on a local level in Wilhelmshorst. Huchel later recalled,

> Nachdem ich dann am 28. Mai 1963 auf der Delegiertenkonferenz des Schriftstellerverbandes öffentlich gemaßregelt worden war, fühlte sich auch der Gemeinderat meines Wohnorts Wilhelmshorst ermuntert, zu persönlichen Schickanen zu übergehen. Bei Nacht und Nebel erschien ein kleiner Funktionär mit drei Polizisten und einem Lastwagen und räumte aus einem Zimmer, das wir dazu gemietet hatten, mein ganzes persönliches Archiv aus. Briefe von Thomas Mann, von Brecht, von Bloch, von Döblin, die ganzen Jahrgänge von *Sinn und Form*, die Wörterbücher. Ich stand dabei und schimpfte, aber der Funktionär hatte seine Sprüche auswendig gelernt: Er zitierte Kurt Hager, der mich den 'englischen Lord von Wilhelmshorst' genannt hatte, berief sich auf den sechsten Parteitag, auf dem ich als Arbeiterverräter beschimpft worden war. (ii,379-80)

The story has been reproduced by critics in essentially the same form, the removal of the archive having apparently taken Huchel totally by surprise.[98] Thus, one can read of the archive in the 1984 edition,

> Manches ging später in der DDR verloren, vor allem Briefe, als im Frühjahr 1963, veranlaßt durch die örtliche Behörde Wilhelmshorst, eine Zwangsexmittierung des *Sinn und Form*-Archivs stattfand. Als Monate später, durch Gerichtsbeschluß, Huchel das Material wieder zugänglich gemacht wurde, war das meiste – durch die Verlagerung in einen durch Nässe unbenutzbar gewordenen Gemüsekeller – bis zur Unkenntlichkeit in Auflösung begriffen. Huchels Sekretärin gelang es, ein paar noch nicht völlig zerstörte Manuskripte zu retten. (ii,403)

As it stands, this story is a classic representation of Huchel's victimisation in the GDR. Yet, in virtually every detail, it is in great need of correction – which is not to say that Huchel was not victimised. It was surely a petty matter, but there was pettiness on both sides. We recall Hossinger's frustration at the fact that the Huchels refused to cooperate in the hand-over of the *Sinn und Form* archive to the Academy. We recall, too, that Hossinger cancelled the Academy's rental arrangement for *Sinn und Form*'s editorial offices at Hubertusweg 35-39 with effect from the end of 1962. After that date, the local Wilhelmshorst council began to explore what use the rooms could be put to for the accommodation of local people. Huchel certainly no longer had any exclusive right to them. The threatening manner that he had employed when seeking to secure use of them in 1955 would not have been forgotten. It might well have been felt that his own house was now sufficiently spacious for his needs. Finally, far from following on directly after the conference in the spring of 1963, Huchel's dispute with the Wilhelmshorst council was a long, drawn-out affair.

Something of its complexity emerges in a report written for the Stasi by an informant, an insurance man, who signed himself Ulrich.[99] For him, it was self-evident that Huchel no longer had any claim on the rooms. He recalled that throughout all the wranglings, Huchel was, however, able to deflect attention away from the issue by discrediting the deputy mayoress, since it had emerged that she had compromised herself politically in the Nazi period. It had also become known that one of her colleagues, who worked in the local SED offices, had wrongly been categorised as someone persecuted by the Nazis. Though the SED cleared the mayoress, the local rumour mill continued to turn and Huchel was able to exploit this to his benefit, especially as the local SED was split over the issue of the mayoress and therefore unable to function effectively. The affair dragged on for many months and Huchel cunningly managed to put off the day of reckoning. It emerges from 'Ulrich's' report, for instance, that Huchel had some success through inviting Herr Juhl, a council employee, into his home and plying him with drink.[100]

Extant correspondence shows that, after months of negotiation, the matter was discussed at the meeting of the Wilhelmshorst housing commission on 20 August 1963. The meeting ruled that the rooms should be re-allocated. Huchel immediately protested at this decision in a registered letter that he fired off the following day.[101] Among other things, he complained that Frau Pramor, who occupied the rest of the house and wanted the rooms to be allocated to a member of her family, had had recourse to unfair methods, such as switching off the electricity at the mains! She had also produced false assertions about which members of her family lived in her house. For his part, Huchel wanted the rooms for his step-son, whom he had encouraged to move into Hubertusweg 35-39! It emerges clearly that Huchel had been asked to remove his archive but had declined, referring to the lack of space in his house and its unsuitability due to the style of its construction. He went on the attack, claiming that as a member of the intelligentsia he had long been discriminated against in the local community. He had not, he said, moved from West Berlin into the GDR all those years ago just to be exposed to such treatment. And so he went on, finally threatening court action if the local council proceeded with its threat forcibly to remove his archive. Following this threat, the situation remained deadlocked until late 1964. In a telephone conversation with Wagenbach on 20

September 1963, Huchel acknowledged that it was simply in his character to respond in this way. He knew that he should not and that he should pull back, but he could not stop when he could see that it was all 'reine Schickanen'.[102] It truly was a petty matter, which would later be endowed with a symbolic meaning quite at odds with the reality of events.

The Final Break with Hermlin

In what was a further erosion of the grouping to which Huchel had belonged in the GDR, on 1 September 1963 Hans Mayer gave a press conference in Hamburg to announce that he would not be returning to Leipzig from a trip to the Federal Republic. Shortly after, on 12 September, Huchel conducted a telephone conversation of some length with another member of that grouping, Hermlin. The conversation was tapped by the Stasi.[103] It was Hermlin's last attempt to resurrect a friendship that was already essentially finished. Hermlin said that he would like to visit Huchel. Initially, Huchel responded positively. They would have an opportunity to talk. Hermlin said that he would arrange things as Huchel wished, 'Er wüßte nur nicht, was Herr Hu. gegen ihm (sic) hat'. Huchel replied that he 'es Herrn He. damals sehr übel genommen hat, daß er sich an dieser Sache beteiligte', by which he meant the affair surrounding the Fontane Prize. By Hermlin's involvement, he meant the telephone calls. Hermlin, alluding to Monica Huchel's role in the affair, complained that Huchel had refused to speak to him. Huchel said that he had simply not been there. Hermlin stressed that he had wanted to mediate as a friend. Alluding to his own marginalisation, he pointed out that he, too, had had his worries in the last few months. As a friend, he had wished to share Huchel's worries but that was clearly not wanted, and Huchel had cold-shouldered him. Huchel disputed that. He went on, though, to state that Hermlin's call had been part of a sequence that had ended with Kurella's sinister death threats. He cited his wife's report that Erich Wendt had confirmed that Hermlin had been calling about the same thing as himself. Was Hermlin saying that she had lied? Hermlin explained that he had not talked to Wendt for months, the last time was certainly long before April. At this point, Huchel offered his apologies to Hermlin. Hermlin then went on to claim that many people had tried to prevail upon him to talk to Huchel about the matter but he had refused to do so. Presumably, by this he meant that he had refused to do so on the terms they wanted. Again, Huchel apologised to Hermlin and said that he would have to tackle Wendt because he had lied. This was, of course, not necessarily the case. Hermlin went on to explain that, of course, he had wanted to talk to Huchel about this matter. If the radio was full of it, then naturally he wanted to speak to him about it. Huchel's response again hardened. Why should they talk about it, 'solle er nun noch einmal den dummen Hund spielen'? Huchel sought to make Hermlin concede that he had rung about the same matter as the others. Hermlin's response was that he 'zum Teufel noch einmal, das Recht habe, sich Sorgen zu machen'.

These were Hermlin's last words. Huchel's final riposte was that 'er nicht wüßte, was es hier heißt, sich Sorgen machen. Herr He. solle sich lieber Sorgen machen, wenn sie ihn hier gefangen halten'. These words signalled the definitive end of their friendship. Both felt misunderstood and shabbily treated by the other. They would never speak again. Huchel never mentioned the matter in public. In the obituary that Hermlin wrote in *Die Zeit* after Huchel's death in 1981, he wrote, 'Aber gerade er, der mich geehrt hatte, tat mir später Unrecht, und gerade zu einer Zeit, da ich seiner Hilfe besonders bedurfte'.[104]

Ulbricht's Ruling

Wagenbach kept Huchel informed of progress on the production of *Chausseen Chausseen*, which would appear on schedule for the Frankfurt Book Fair that autumn. On 3 September, Huchel had requested the relevant papers from the Writers' Union to apply for permission to travel to the meeting of the Gruppe 47 at Saalgau between 24 and 28 October. After consulting the Central Committee, the Writers' Union sent Huchel a negative response on 25 September.[105] Only Bobrowski and Max Walter Schulz were permitted to travel. Bobrowski sent 'Herr Huchel' a brief note before he went to Saalgau.[106] As usual, Huchel did not respond.

Again, there was slippage in the SED bureaucracy's dealing with the Huchel affair. Wagenbach attempted to intercede with Hager on Huchel's behalf.[107] After some delay, the Academy pushed on with its plan for Huchel, which had been formulated by Bredel and Kurella, and agreed with Abusch and Wagner. On 18 November, Hossinger complied with Abusch's request for basic details about Huchel and his family, which would be ready for use if the plan was accepted.[108] Later, on 9 December, he sent Abusch's office further details.[109] On 23 November, Hager received the letter, written by Abusch and signed by Abusch and Wagner, which set out their proposals.[110] They explained that all those Academy members who were simultaneously members of the SED Central Committee had discussed the matter with Wagner. They wrote that Huchel was playing the invalid and the martyr, and was doing so with monies from the Academy. To exclude him from the Academy would mean removing his only real source of income, the payment of which was not, however, sustainable in the longer term for political and moral reasons. They expected no change in his attitude, and, to break the deadlock, they proposed that Huchel be granted a 'Sondererlaubnis', with which he could leave the GDR. Acutely aware of the propaganda dimensions of the affair in the Federal Republic, they calculated that such an approach would benefit the GDR, provided that the timing was right and appropriate arrangements made. Before any reply was forthcoming, Huchel received and accepted an invitation to deliver the annual series of lectures on poetry at the University of Frankfurt am Main during the summer semester 1965. Huchel's excellent contacts with the West thus helped to keep up some pressure on the SED leadership. On 12 December, Bredel fired off a letter to

Hager, complaining that despite all his efforts to deal with the situation, no firm decisions had been reached in the hierarchy. This was damaging to the Academy's proper functioning. It was therefore time to put an end to the affair.

The reply that was finally forthcoming in December cannot have pleased Bredel and others in the Academy. A hand-written note in the former SED Central Archive demonstrates that the matter was finally ruled upon by Ulbricht himself.[111] Bredel et al. had wanted to be rid of Huchel and to send him on his way, after first demonstratively excluding him from the Academy. Ulbricht was not inclined to let Huchel off so lightly. Huchel himself later speculated that Ulbricht's secretary, Gotsche, had a decisive say in the matter. (ii,381) That may well be, but there is as yet no direct proof. Ulbricht made five points which effectively put paid to any progress in the Huchel affair for the foreseeable future. Ulbricht's first point was that Huchel should remain an Academy member, his second that he should continue to receive his regular payment. Attempts should be made to 'normalise' the situation. It followed that Huchel should not be granted a 'Sondererlaubnis' but should remain a citizen of the GDR. The normalisation process should include, if possible, the publication of a volume of Huchel's verse by the Aufbau Verlag. Wagner, Abusch, Kurella and Bredel were to be informed of this decision. Ulbricht's role, it scarcely needs saying, was crucial in the future course of the Huchel affair. It did now, indeed, look as if Huchel, as he feared, would end his days in obscurity in the GDR.

The Years of Isolation

Chausseen Chausseen: Controversy *in absentia*

Like *Gedichte* and the later *Gezählte Tage*, *Chausseen Chausseen* appeared just after Huchel had crossed a major threshold in his life. Indeed, the publication history of all three collections suggests that Huchel needed to live through and beyond the critical point in a phase in his life before he could commit himself to the release of a work in a form that he found acceptable. As a summation of experience to that date, each collection marked the culmination of a set of thematic concerns. While *Gedichte* had represented hope rekindled after fascism, *Chausseen Chausseen* articulated the painful recognition of the illusory nature of that hope, amply confirmed by the events of 1962-3. Poems in the collection contain clear statements of his anger and despair following the *Sinn und Form* affair. Yet the collection goes beyond that to articulate his deep pessimism at the state of the world in the grip of the Cold War, whose actors, major and minor, threaten to compound in terminal fashion the destruction and horror of Nazism. His themes did not yet focus specifically on the restrictions on his own life imposed by the SED and its agents in the manner adopted in *Gezählte Tage*. In *Chausseen Chausseen*, Huchel adopted the grand poetic style, which was certainly a departure from *Gedichte*. He frequently slipped into the masks of figures from classical literature or employed allusions to biblical and other sources in order to project a seemingly timeless voice which prophesied destruction. In this way, *Chausseen Chausseen* established the tone for the quite substantial output of verse that Huchel published in the 1960s and 1970s.

It was in keeping with the classical underpinning to his warning of senseless destruction that Huchel should choose to introduce *Chausseen Chausseen* with the quotation from St Augustine that he had first used in 1932 and on which he had commented in 1959 in Hamburg, 'Der "große Hof des Gedächtnisses, daselbst Himmel, Erde und Meer gegenwärtig sind", kann nicht nur verfinstert werden – er kann ausgelöscht werden'. (ii,300) The ominous potential for destruction hangs over the whole collection, darkening the course of the poetic biography charted by *Chausseen Chausseen*, like *Gedichte* before it. Once again, Huchel devoted much attention to the 'architecture' of his collection. Each of the five sections has its particular focus, and the arrangement of the sections invites the reader to explore thematic relations between the sections, much in the same way as Huchel's compositional technique for his journal.

The first section evokes principally the Mediterranean world and the classical heritage of Italy and Greece; the second includes French and Balkan settings; the third section is made up primarily of poems treating rural Brandenburg and childhood; war poems are concentrated in section four; and section five is devoted to Huchel's challenge to an age of which he had come to despair. The central section acts as a fulcrum, around which other experience can be arranged. It is no accident that the three poems of childhood, 'Damals', 'Caputher Heuweg' and 'Eine Herbstnacht' – all written in Huchel's idiom of 1930 – occupy the central position in that section and hence in the whole collection. In this way, Huchel re-affirmed the poetic identity that he had developed in the early 1930s. This lent Huchel's poetry a dimension that many in the West regarded as curiously anachronistic in the early 1960s, whilst other, conservative critics singled out this work for their particular praise. In the hymnic 'Eine Herbstnacht', (i,138) reminiscent of Mörike, the poet puts the question, 'Wo bist du, damals sinkender Tag?', and his magical identity with his 'Heimat' is re-affirmed in the lines that follow,

> Septemberhügel, auf dem ich lag
> Im jähen blätterstürzenden Wind,
> Doch ganz von der Ruhe der Bäume umschlungen –
> Kraniche waren noch Huldigungen
> Der Herbstnacht an das spähende Kind.

These poems of childhood are flanked by, on the one hand, poems which he dedicated to his friends Bloch, Jahnn and Kundera, on the other hand, by verse in which he articulates a bold, visionary energy to be found in some of his late Brandenburg verse. In 'Auffliegende Schwäne', (i,139) for example, the early-morning darkness of the lake is suddenly breached,

> Ein jähes Weiß,
> Mit Füßen und Flügeln das Wasser peitschend,
> Facht an den Wind. Sie fliegen auf,
> Die winterbösen Majestäten.
> Es pfeift metallen.
> Duck dich ins Röhricht.
> Schneidende Degen
> Sind ihre Federn.

The first two sections include poems treating the experiences of landscapes and peoples that, already in the 1920s and early 1930s, acted as a creative counterpoint to Brandenburg. However, Huchel quite pointedly chose to open the collection with a recent Brandenburg poem, 'Das Zeichen'. (i,113) The poem's title signals Huchel's resumption of his poetic dialogue with his old friend, Eich. The dark negativity of 'Das Zeichen' records quite explicitly his disillusion with rural life in the GDR drained of its magic potential following the collectivization of agriculture, which was pushed through in 1960. This disillusion is amply illustrated in lines such as 'Ich ging durch das Dorf/ und sah das Gewohnte' and 'Nichts war zu deuten./ Es stand im Herdbuch'.

Existential concerns, articulated through the mediums of classical literature and biblical motifs, predominate in the encounter with the Mediterranean, principally in the Italian poems referred to earlier, which were inspired by the places that Huchel visited on holiday in the late 1950s. Poems such as 'Schlucht bei Baltschik' and 'In der Bretagne', meanwhile, betoken Huchel's attraction to a mysticism rooted in folklore. 'In der Bretagne' (i,133) ends

> O Marguerite,
>
> Streich mit der Hand
>
> Die Asche von des Herdes Glut.
>
> Es leuchtet auf das alte Blut
>
> Im Feuer der Legenden.

Huchel explained the significance of the name Marguerite in a letter of 10 November 1960 to August Closs, 'Die Kunkelspinnerin Marguerite Philippe war, wie Sie sicherlich wissen werden, die bretonische "Viehmännin"; sie ließ sich vom Volk die alten Märchen und Legenden erzählen, wenn sie durch Morbihan wallfahrte und aus den Brunnen heilkräftiges Wasser für die Kranken schöpfte'. (ii,346) Rural Brittany was one of those rather remote areas away from the urban world, in which the poet, perhaps recalling Goldberg, identified residual traces of an authentic ethnic culture. Many of Huchel's concerns, both long-standing and more immediate, come together in the complex imagery of 'Le Pouldu'. (i,131) Huchel evokes his intense identification with the dilemmas faced by his fellow artist, Gauguin, as the painter sought to tear himself away from rural Brittany, his attachment to which parallels Huchel's attachment to Brandenburg,

> ... Geh fort, Gauguin.
>
> Laß alles zurück,
>
> Die Einfalt des Landes,
>
> Das Holzschuhgeklapper auf blankem Granit,
>
> Das Kreuz aus Stein,
>
> Von Stimmen umwittert.
>
> Und auf der Lippe des Sommers
>
> Das kühle Feuer der Distel.

The difficulty of leaving derives from a deep immersion in valued cultural traditions. In effect, the collection works through the thematic juxtaposition of those valued traditions with their wanton destruction, which is foregrounded in section four. The shocking description of death in the war poems of that section is best illustrated by 'Chausseen'. (i,141) Culled from 'Das Gesetz', the poem's modified ending reads,

> Tote,
>
> Über die Gleise geschleudert,
>
> Den erstickten Schrei
>
> Wie einen Stein am Gaumen.
>
> Ein schwarzes
>
> Summendes Tuch aus Fliegen
>
> Schloß ihre Wunden.

The grotesque finality of the imagery contrasts starkly with the very sense of culture that permeates the earlier sections. Section five drives home the point that the lessons of history have not been learnt. 'An taube Ohren der Geschlechter' sees Huchel adopt the mask of the Greek historian Polybius, who accompanied Scipio to Carthage, the destruction of which he later recorded. Huchel was, of course, responding to Brecht's famous statement about the three-fold destruction of Carthage that Huchel had published in 1951 in *Sinn und Form*. Events in the intervening years had served to plunge him into a deep despondency, from which he would never really emerge. In the final poem in the collection, 'Psalm', (i,157) he adopts the voice of the prophet, warning of impending nuclear disaster, identifying those responsible in their bunkers, and spelling out the consequences for mankind. The poem ends,

> Und nicht erforscht wird werden
>
> Ein Geschlecht,
>
> Eifrig bemüht,
>
> Sich zu vernichten.

'Psalm' is one of Huchel's most powerful and compelling statements. The most poignantly elegiac expression of Huchel's state of mind in the early 1960s comes in poems that he first published in his final issue of *Sinn und Form*. They are 'Winterpsalm', which he dedicated to Hans Mayer, 'Traum im Tellereisen' and 'Der Garten des Theophrast', which he wrote for his son Stephan. In their lament over the wilful destruction of a living culture, the two latter poems bring together the thematic threads of earlier sections. 'Traum im Tellereisen', for example, begins,

'Gefangen bist du, Traum./ Dein Knöchel brennt,/ Zerschlagen im Tellereisen', while 'Der Garten des Theophrast' ends with the lines, 'Sie gaben Befehl, die Wurzel zu roden./ Es sinkt dein Licht, schutzloses Laub'. (i,155)

Through the arrangement of his verse, Huchel conveys to the reader his message that humans have repeatedly and truly perversely squandered the great potential to create a rich culture in the environment within which they have been placed. He had come to see the events of his own lifetime as a continuation of an eternal cycle of suffering, which forces for good could not break. Adumbrated already in 1927 in 'Lenz', to the end of his life this would essentially remain the bitter lesson that Huchel drew from experience. When he came to the West, it was this experience alone that he allowed to count, especially when faced by the neo-Marxist ideas of the New Left.

When *Chausseen Chausseen* appeared in the late autumn of 1963, public discussion took place exclusively in the West. Given the recent favourable reception there of Bobrowski's work, Huchel surely had hopes of a significant breakthrough. With the support of figures such as Jens, this was virtually guaranteed. Yet, as we shall now see, opinion became so divided that the absent Huchel was plunged into fresh controversy that he can scarcely have anticipated.

The 'official' GDR reception was restricted to an article by Dieter Schlenstedt which was actually published in the West Berlin magazine *Alternative*.[1] Schlenstedt sought to play down the significance of the poet's deep pessimism. In letters, Bobrowski was lavish in his praise. He wrote to Kundera on 13 November 1963, 'Ich bin wie erstarrt vor Bewunderung. Das ist etwas anderes als ein Gedichtband: eine Rehabilitierung der lyrischen Gattung überhaupt'.[2] He found the following words in correspondence with Huchel, 'Mit Bewunderung und Ehrfurcht – es ist nicht anders zu sagen – lese ich Ihr Buch und, bei aller Bitterkeit, doch auch mit großer Freude: daß Ihnen die Kraft geblieben und neue dazu gekommen ist'.[3]

There was much truth in Bobrowski's few, well-chosen words: the major changes that Narr had reported to Kundera testify to the recent surge in energy, deriving not least from the repudiation of old positions. The reception accorded to the collection in some quarters of the West German press tended rather to reproduce the hyperbole of Bobrowski's letter to Kundera, fuelled as the western reception was by media coverage of the *Sinn und Form* affair. The marketing people at S. Fischer were clearly determined to reap maximum benefit from the publicity and the great wave of sympathy in the West that had accompanied Huchel's struggle with the SED cultural politicians. Marcel Reich-Ranicki's words of the previous year found their way on to the dust-cover, 'Dies, meinen wir, ist große deutsche Lyrik unserer Zeit'. They supplied the cue for further hyperbole – and for a backlash from more fastidious or sceptical souls, among them some fellow poets mistrustful of sudden fame. Far away in Wilhelmshorst, Huchel found himself again in the midst of controversy, played out this time in the West German media centres of Hamburg and Frankfurt.

In the influential *Frankfurter Allgemeine Zeitung*, the conservative Hans Egon Holthusen queried the hyperbole, 'Weiß man in deutschen Verleger- (und Kritiker-) kreisen zwischen Horaz und Huchel oder meinetwegen zwischen Mörike und Huchel nicht mehr zu unterscheiden? Zum Kuckuck mit solchen Schaumschlägereien!'[4] In his review in *Die Zeit*, Jens, since the late 1950s Huchel's most vigorous advocate, not only offered a perceptive reading of the collection, he also used the occasion to draw attention to the plight of someone most deserving of respect.[5] The review began,

> Sehr weit von uns entfernt, in Wilhelmshorst bei Potsdam, lebt zusammen mit seinem Sohn ein einsamer Mann – ein großer Schriftsteller ... Die Zeichen sind düster, und es wäre falsch, so zu tun, als ergäben die vor uns liegenden achtundvierzig Gedichte einen Band wie jeden anderen auch.

Returning to the same point near the end of the review, Jens finally spoke of Huchel as 'ein Mann, vor dessen Kunst wir uns verneigen', who had shown, 'daß es auch in unserer Zeit noch möglich ist, das Schwierige einfach zu sagen; er hat bewiesen, daß die Dunkelheit dort endet, wo Genialität und moralische Kraft, Kalkül und Zeugnis sich vereinen'. Jens took as his point of reference the ending of 'Verona', (i,117)

> Dieser Stein,
> Im Wasser der Etsch,
> Lebt groß in seiner Stille.
> Und in der Mitte der Dinge
> Die Trauer.

He commented, 'Die Trauer soll, groß, für sich selbst stehen – sie allein gibt den Gedichten das Pathos und den hohen lyrischen Ernst, den Klang der Elegie und jenen Ton der Schwermut, der sich vor allem dort einstellt, wo die Kriegsrealität, 'frostiger Lehm', 'Asche und Schlamm', auf zarte Gegenbilder stößt'. We have seen that this stylistic feature informs earlier compositions such as 'Der Rückzug' and that Jens rightly identifies it as integral to Huchel's poetry, poised as it is between idyll and elegy. The sum of Huchel's experience was such that the latter was increasingly foregrounded, a tendency which in later collections would lead to a slackening in the poetry's stylistic tensions.

Jens identified as a major stylistic development in *Chausseen Chausseen* a movement towards 'Verknappung und abstrakte Raffung' in free verse which generally dispensed with the rhymes that had still characterised *Gedichte*. Jens referred to earlier versions of poems first published in *Sinn und Form* such as 'Hinter den weißen Netzen des Mittags' in order to demonstrate how, in *Chausseen Chausseen*, inordinately direct expressions were avoided and individual words deployed as ciphers for complex states of affairs. At times, this impaired the narrative quality of the verse but lent the imagery a sharper and more pronounced focus, fascinating yet resistant to interpretation. As Jens had argued in *Deutsche Literatur der Gegenwart*, Huchel's idiom could be said to belong to the same modernist wave as Bachmann's and Celan's, not to mention Kaschnitz, Sachs and Eich, poets of Huchel's generation who had transformed their style after 1945. The more circuitous route via the socialist pastoral that Huchel had taken in the late 1940s and early 1950s was now forgotten, as Jens celebrated Huchel's mastery of the range of poetic forms in which scarcely a word was out of place.

In exploring the stylistic reduction in Huchel's verse, Jens examined poems first published from the mid-1950s to the early 1960s, that is to say, following the decisive shift signalled by the poem dedicated to Bloch. In this way, Jens – like all other western reviewers – avoids the somewhat delicate issue of the ideological dimension of changes made to earlier compositions produced in the affirmative mode such as 'Das Gesetz' and 'In der Heimat', not to mention 'Bericht aus Malaya'. Hardly surprisingly, *Chausseen Chausseen* no longer included any explicit support for the idea of a socialist Germany. It is true that another reviewer, Peter Härtling, wrote that Huchel had written a poem about Lenin, but neither Härtling nor anyone else saw fit to pursue the matter.[6] It was as if the 'aberration' of the late 1940s and early 1950s had never happened and that *Chausseen Chausseen*, as it was presented in 1963, was representative of his output since *Gedichte*. Härtling was seemingly unaware of the fact that 'In der Heimat', a poem whose changes he discusses at some length, had originally been dedicated to Johannes R. Becher. Nor did he register the fact that the original version was a celebration of the regeneration of rural life effected by the land reform carried out in the Soviet Zone, as witnessed by the 'I' of the poem, who had emerged from the chaos and destruction of the war. For Härtling, 'In der Heimat' was simply 'ungleich weitschweifiger, deskriptiver ... Allein die Titeländerung bezeugt Huchels Wunsch, durch Indirektes direkt zu sein. Das odenhafte "In der Heimat" weicht dem signifikanten, Vorstellungen und Emotionen wie in einem schlanken Stamm zusammenpressenden "Die Pappeln"'. Actually, much of the original's politically affirmative, pastoral imagery was excised, as were the final lines linking the 'I' and the ploughman, 'Er pflügt auch mein Herz/ und senkt sein Saatgut in mein Wort'. Indeed, the 'I' is removed from the poem altogether, and with that the lines which convey the sense of a shared community. The final lines are replaced by imagery which evokes an atmosphere of threat and insecurity, 'Und Asche fällt/ Auf den Schatten der Fledermäuse'.

The omission from discussion of Huchel's excision of the affirmative dimension of his early post-war verse illustrates West German critics' uncertainty – and in many cases quite understandable ignorance – in dealing with Huchel's poetry. He was a well-nigh unique phenomenon in the indigenous development of the genre since 1930. The difficulty for some critics, if not for Jens and Härtling, centred on the evaluation of a collection by a poet whose earliest publications they knew but whose sudden fame was accompanied by his appropriation of modernist techniques, towards which, for much of his career, he had shown a marked scepticism, notwithstanding 'Für Ernst Bloch'.

Among those who mistrusted the hyperbole was Wilhelm Lehmann. Lehmann received a letter from the young poet and critic, Hans Dieter Schäfer, which was full of praise for Huchel's work. This irritated the elderly Lehmann. He alluded to Schäfer's letter in correspondence with Hans Bender on 8 December 1963. He wrote,

> Wenig bin ich erbaut von den Gedichten Huchels, die mir ein junger Enthusiast als 'sehr gut' zustellte. Wenn Rezensenten doch begreifen wollten, daß sie mit Superlativen ihrem Sujet nur schaden. P.H. würde sich außerdem kaum darüber freuen, daß man das Lob seiner Dichtung mit dem Lob seiner ehrlichen menschlich-politischen Haltung erwähnt.[7]

Huchel was surely glad of any support he could get. Lehmann went on to make points that he expanded upon shortly afterwards in his review 'Maß des Lobes',[8] 'Abgesehen davon, daß Huchel dem Leser, mir jedenfalls, unvorstellbare Vorstellungen über eine allgemeine Lyrizität hinaus zumutet, ... finde ich keine Authentik aus erster Hand'. In Lehmann's view, the collection betrayed Huchel's subjection of his imagination to a 'drängenden Willen', which resulted in forced and unconvincing imagery. We have seen Huchel's use of the genitive metaphor 'Lippe des Sommers' in 'Le Pouldu'. Lehmann criticised 'Landschaft hinter Warschau' as follows,

> Der Einbruch des Lichts ist ein großes Thema. Was wird damit gewonnen, daß es mit einem Wasservogel verglichen wird, der die Zehen spreizt? Ist er selbst Licht, wieso glänzt dann als etwas Besonderes seine Schwimmhaut aus dünnem Nebel? Das Partikuläre in hohen Ehren, aber sich den Himmel flacher als einen Hundegaumen vorzustellen, will nicht gelingen.

Lehmann was joined in his criticism of Huchel's imagery by Holthusen, who deplored the proliferation of the technique of the genitive metaphor. Certainly, one is bound to agree with Lehmann and Holthusen that the joints showed in what was not a uniformly successful transformation of Huchel's style, even if many of their comments served to confirm their own highly traditionalist attitudes. Holthusen was attracted precisely by those poems in Huchel's collection composed in his idiom of 1930. He wrote,

> Huchel ist am stärksten immer dann, wenn er sich auf seinen Instinkt für die im besten Sinne einfache, beinahe treuherzige Motivbildung verläßt, und wenn er auch bei der Formung des Verses der zeitgemäßen Tendenz zum Manirierten und Outrierten widersteht. Wo das im Grunde erzkonservative Muster seines Weltverstehens sich mit poetischem Glück erfüllt, wo das innig Erlebte nicht mit bloß dekorativ glitzernden Metaphern behängt wird, sondern 'im Bilde' wiederaufersteht, dort ist er unangreifbar.

Again, Holthusen's view contained certain elements of truth, not least his identification of the deep strain of cultural conservatism within Huchel which co-existed uneasily with his more progressive social attitudes, Yet Holthusen would restrict the poet's appeal to the half dozen or so traditionally constructed poems in the collection such as 'Damals', 'Caputher Heuweg', 'Eine Herbstnacht' and 'Sibylle des Sommers'.

If a conservative like Holthusen could find something to his taste, then *Chausseen Chausseen* left rather at a loss those many young West Germans fundamentally opposed to anything that smacked of the internal German cultural climate of the 1930s and 1940s, with its, at best, subdued modernism. One such figure, Wolf Wondratschek, found himself agreeing with much of Lehmann's and Holthusen's criticisms.[9] Klaus V. Reinke went much further, writing of Huchel's 'Nicht-Entwicklung' and adding the savage comment that 'Huchel bei den Tendenzen von 1940 stehengeblieben ist'.[10] What for Jens and Härtling was Huchel's remarkable reinvigoration of traditional imagery was for Reinke a passé use of 'Asche-und-Wind-Bilder'. Huchel's use of the genitive metaphor was 'hoffnungslos von gestern', as was his use of internal rhyme. Reinke's utterly condescending conclusion was that Huchel's poetry was 'ein bißchen verstaubt und rührend'.

A more generous approach was adopted by other critics such as Kurt Hohoff and Rino Sanders.[11] Even though he was taking a point too far in arguing that Huchel's verse had little in common with the post-war West German development of modernism, Hohoff, like Sanders, brought to bear a fundamental sympathy for the stylistic development in Huchel's verse from *Gedichte* to *Chausseen Chausseen*. Unsurprisingly, Sanders' essay, together with Jens', was later included in *Über Peter Huchel*. Yet, as we have seen, the reception was a much more complex affair than either that volume or even the later *Materialien* volume dedicated to Huchel suggested. In the final analysis, it was less the dissident's sudden fame than the apparent stylistic shifts that provoked contradictory responses, stoking a controversy that erupted again in 1972 following the publication of *Gezählte Tage*.

The Attempts at 'Normalisation': Huchel's Inner Emigration

After the attacks of 1963, the name Peter Huchel was rarely mentioned in public in the GDR. After he had left for the West in 1971, he described this period as 'acht Jahre totale Isolation'. (ii,313) For the West German media, Huchel represented a new phenomenon in German-German relations: he was the first intellectual seriously to fall foul of the SED after the building of the Berlin Wall; and the first, therefore, who could be detained in the country as long as it suited the authorities. In that respect, his position was, of course, no different from that of any other GDR citizen below pensionable age after the building of the Wall, and in the West his fate was taken to symbolise that of a whole population held against its wishes on the other side of the German-German border. But the attention span of the West German media was limited, as East Berlin politicians had anticipated, and the furore over Huchel presently died down, the media bandwaggon moving on to other newsworthy items. It would return to Huchel periodically over the coming years, whenever his loyal supporters in the West succeeded in putting his name forward for an award, wrote articles on his birthday or created publicity with a protest against the East Berlin authorities' attitude towards him. He himself demonstrated great resourcefulness in orchestrating western publicity from the isolation of his home in Wilhelmshorst. Yet in 1963, Ulbricht had Huchel exactly where he wanted him. Huchel could be used as an example to deter others from embarking on a similar course.

One of Ulbricht's measures designed to bring about a 'normalisation' of Huchel's situation was the publication of a collection of his verse by the Aufbau Verlag. On 7 January 1964, Klaus Gysi, head of Aufbau and Rütten und Loening, as well as being a Stasi informant, followed up Rütten und Loening's letter to Huchel of the previous August, repeating the publisher's interest in the volume that had long been mooted.[12] Huchel did not reply. The GDR government's interest in this matter was underscored when a letter was sent to Gysi from the Ministry of Culture on 21 January 1964, which read, 'Eine Streichung des Titels Huchel, *Gedichte*, sehen wir als verfrüht an. Wir bitten Sie, noch das Ergebnis Ihrer Bemühungen abzuwarten'.[13] Until November 1966, the publisher repeatedly attempted, though without success, to re-establish contact with Huchel.[14] Thereafter, the Aufbau Verlag's correspondence with Huchel was restricted to birthday greetings in 1967, 1968 and 1969.

As with so many other matters relating to Huchel's years in the GDR, these things became public knowledge only after 1989. Although Huchel had no way of knowing specifically about the instructions that Ulbricht had issued, he was well aware that the SED was interested in re-establishing a facade of normality. After he came to the West, he made a number of statements in which he alluded to this. On one occasion he said, 'Ich hätte höchstens noch erreichen können, daß er ein paar Gedichte, so à la Naturgedichte, vom Aufbau Verlag gedruckt worden wären. Und wenn man mich dann gedruckt hätte, dann hätte man doch wiederum damit zeigen wollen, wie frei der Betreffende lebt – und das hat mich nicht interessiert'. (ii,384) He refused any collaboration with official representatives of the GDR, recalling later, 'Immer wieder kamen hohe Herren, im Ministerrang sogar, zu mir, und wenn ich mich beklagte, gingen sie darüber hinweg und versuchten, gemütlich zu plaudern. Diese Art stalinistischer Gemeinheit empörte mich'. (ii,382) On one occasion, he was invited to compare his situation to the one described by Stefan Heym in his *Der König-David-Bericht*, in which an intellectual was simply silenced by the state. Huchel replied, 'Das war genau meine Situation. Denn man hat doch alles versucht, mich in so eine Vereinsamung hineinzudrängen'. (ii,383) However, he went on to make the following important qualification, 'Man hat aber in den ersten Jahren auch immer wieder versucht, mit mir Kontakt aufzunehmen. Das gelang nicht, weil die Leute mit Forderungen kamen, die ich einfach nicht erfüllen konnte'. (ii,381) In a similar vein, on another occasion he stated that cultural politicians and others did not give up the hope that 'ich vielleicht doch wieder irgendwo für sie arbeiten würde'. (ii,381) On another occasion still, referring initially to the Academy's proposal of two editors for *Sinn und Form*, he commented, 'Ich kannte diesen stalinistischen Trick und lehnte diese Art von Bestechung ab. Es gab auch in den folgenden Jahren, als ich schon isoliert zu Hause saß, immer wieder solche Vorschläge. Ich wußte, wenn ich den kleinen Finger reichen würde, nähme man gleich die ganze Hand'. (ii,377)

As Huchel acknowledged on these various occasions, the SED strategy was by no means a blanket ban. Yet this was the assumption in many quarters in the West, especially in the media, in which there was the usual Cold War simplification of a rather more complex state of affairs.[15] Hans Mayer was much more circumspect than many others, when in 1968 he concluded an essay about his friend with the statement, 'In dem Staat, zu dessen Bürgern er zählt, hat man seit mehr als sechs Jahren keine Zeile von ihm gedruckt. Seine Gedichte erscheinen dort nicht. Was man ihm angetan hat, kann nicht verziehen werden'.[16] Elsewhere one could read, 'da nichts von ihm veröffentlicht werden durfte, stand er praktisch unter Schreibverbot'.[17] In the first western monograph on Huchel, Axel Vieregg was quite categorical. He wrote of 1962 as the year of Huchel's 'Publikationsverbot' in the GDR,[18] which would last until 1971. Vieregg investigated the political dimension of Huchel's GDR poetry on the basis that he was in a situation in which 'es ihm verwehrt ist, sich seines Mediums, der Sprache des Gedichtes, offen zu bedienen'[19] and in which he had not been permitted to publish 'den damals letzten Band seiner Gedichte, *Chausseen Chausseen*, in der DDR'.[20] Vieregg noted that between 1963 and May 1971 fourteen poems by Huchel appeared in West German journals, the implication being that publication would not have been permitted in the GDR. Huchel's situation in the GDR, withdrawn and reduced to silence in the countryside, was, moreover, compared by Vieregg and others with the apparently parallel situation that Huchel had experienced during the Third Reich. Yet that congruence was not given.

Huchel's resolute resistance to SED blandishments demonstrates something slightly different, his determination to make amends for earlier compromises by displaying an unbending attitude. This time, Huchel was resolved to withdraw completely from any involvement in the literary culture over which the SED had gained a stranglehold. He never again set foot in the Academy and rarely attended literary gatherings. He had, it is true, always spent most of his time working at home. Yet his resolution to remain within the domestic sphere of his house in Wilhelmshorst represents an act of withholding intellectual assent that can be best described as inner emigration. He was not put under house arrest, as was often asserted in the western media, though his house was subjected to Stasi surveillance. Within his own four walls, he cultivated his own values and beliefs, no longer having the slightest regard for official views. He was outspoken about the SED to an extent that visitors recall as downright dangerous. He described his highly political, domestic situation in a series of poems which in their very directness stand out from much of his difficult late verse. One such poem is 'Exil', (i,178) which was written during the early stages of Huchel's isolation and picks up from 'Le Pouldu' the dilemma of staying or leaving.[21] The poem begins by evoking the poet's isolated withdrawal within the domestic sphere, 'Am Abend nahen die Freunde,/ die Schatten der Hügel/ ... und führen Gespräche mit meinem Schweigen'. The title suggests both his present state of internal exile and the possibility of leaving for what the poet understands would be exile from his country. The poem rehearses these two options, 'Geh mit dem Wind,/ sagen die Schatten' and 'Sei getreu, sagt der Stein'. The dilemma is very real: the prospect of staying did not fill Huchel with unmitigated despair, despite the bleakness of his situation. As we know, he was deeply attached to that rural world south of Potsdam. Indeed, the poem ends on a note which echoes the vision of nature's regeneration at the end of 'April 63',

> Die dämmernde Frühe
>
> hebt an, wo Licht und Laub
>
> ineinander wohnen
>
> und das Gesicht
>
> in einer Flamme vergeht.

Within the private sphere, the poet was able still to evoke a vision which, as we have seen in 'Das Zeichen', was no longer attainable in the daily round of working life in the GDR life.

The Stasi now sought to infiltrate Huchel's private sphere. A plan was drawn up, identifying people in the area who might be persuaded to provide information about the Huchels.[22] They included comrade Erdmann, the woman employed as regional secretary of the Kulturbund, who had earlier proposed Huchel for the Johannes R. Becher Prize. Another was Huchel's lawyer, Ingeborg Gentz, who was representing him in West Berlin, where Dora was seeking a share of the Fontane Prize money. The attempt was made to gain access through friends of Huchel's step-children. The aim of all this activity was to gather details of Huchel's hostility towards the GDR and of his links to West Germany and West Berlin, as well as abroad. It was proposed that Huchel's regular copy of *Die Zeit*, which was sent by post, should be confiscated. Huchel should be informed of this in person by an official. In this way, a Stasi informant or a post office manager might hear Huchel's response to the confiscation. The hope was that Huchel might be provoked into articulating his opposition to the GDR in front of witnesses. Through stage-managing things in this way, a legal basis might be established to act against him. Yet, none of these ploys was successful. There was little that could be found out about Huchel that was not already known. He was living quietly in the countryside. The Stasi's only 'success' was the recruitment of Herr Menle, a pensioner from the neighbourhood, who agreed to note down the details of the number plates of cars that stopped at Huchel's house. Huchel immortalised him in the poem 'Hubertus-weg', (i,222) which contains the lines, 'Dort unten steht,/ armselig wie abgestande-ner Tabakrauch,/ mein Nachbar, mein Schatten ...'

Yet, despite the efforts of Huchel's neighbour, on 14 August 1964 the Stasi in Potsdam decided that there was no point continuing with surveillance which was yielding nothing of interest to them.[23] Huchel received visitors, among them the Jankas, the Arendts and Christa Reinig, until she left the GDR later that year. There was, however, absolutely no evidence that Huchel was engaging in seditious activity. Huchel was not interested in joining any underground movement. For anyone like his neighbour on the outside looking in, his existence must have seemed quite uninteresting. The material gathered on Huchel was deposited in the Stasi archive.[24] The evidence at present available indicates that the Stasi re-activated intensive surveillance of Huchel only in 1968, following the Soviet invasion of Czechoslovakia on 20-21 August, when the GDR's security organs were instructed to keep a close watch on all potential dissidents. It is puzzling that recently published accounts of Huchel's surveillance by the Stasi should give the impression that it was uninterrupted in its very intensity.[25] It is surely of relevance to our understanding of Huchel's wretched situation to be aware that surveillance was stepped up at particular points and then relaxed.

A Marginal Literary Presence: Bobrowski's Final Failure

Walter Jens recounts how, in February 1964, Huchel came to attend a conference on contemporary writing in Weißensee that was organised by the Evangelical Academy Berlin-Brandenburg.[26] Jens' paper, in which he argued the case for the indivisibility of German literature, met with great hostility from the audience, for many of whom there was no contemporary poetry in the GDR worthy of the name. Jens rang Huchel, who agreed to come along and read from his verse that evening and, 'Die Menschen lauschten ergriffen, der Dissens war vergessen, einige ältere Menschen standen auf, "wir schämen uns, wir bitten Sie um Verzeihung dafür, daß wir Ihre Gedichte nicht beachtet haben"'. The occasion also brought Huchel back together with Bobrowski. Bobrowski was glad to be able to write to Elisabeth Borchers, 'Da haben wir zwei alten "Naturmagier" beieinander gesessen, auch in der Kneipe, und unsere Kümmernisse beredet wie früher. Jetzt ist mir besser, denn er hat ja eine Weile gegrollt: daß ich zur Gruppe fuhr usw'.[27] Bobrowski wrote, similarly, to Michael Hamburger, 'Im Februar war Walter Jens hier, und ich habe bei dieser Gelegenheit mit Peter Huchel Wiedersehen gefeiert, es war auch schon Zeit'.[28] Yet, as Hamburger writes, a decade later Huchel had not forgiven Bobrowski and refused to acknowledge any friendship. For his part, in early 1964 Bobrowski still hoped that some compromise could be brokered between Huchel and the SED. [29] Yet, as we have seen, Huchel refused to budge an inch when approached by the likes of Gysi, and the result was a stalemate.

Nonetheless, Huchel could at times be persuaded to relent by a fellow poet. Heinz Czechowski, who had sent Huchel his verse for comment in 1956, was commissioned by Mitteldeutscher Verlag in Halle to compile an anthology of German nature and landscape poetry over the past four centuries. The anthology appeared in 1965 entitled *Zwischen Wäldern und Flüssen*. Such an anthology was, for Czechowski, unthinkable without Huchel's verse. He approached Huchel but Huchel declined on the grounds that he had resolved not to publish again in the GDR.[30] Czechowski would not be put off. He phoned Huchel and, despite Huchel's insistence that he would not give permission for publication, Czechowski at least persuaded him to let him pay him a visit. He took his manuscript along and showed it to his host. Huchel carefully examined the selection that Czechowski had made and finally relented. Eight of his poems were included. The same number were included in 1966 in another anthology by the same publisher, *In diesem besseren Land: Gedichte der Deutschen Demokratischen Republik seit 1945*, which was edited by Adolf Endler and Karl Mickel. Mickel tells much the same story as Czechowski of a visit to Huchel and Huchel's initial refusal, followed after a number of hours' conversation by his granting of permission.[31] Indeed, in this way, Huchel's poems were finally included in a number of anthologies before he left in 1971.[32]

While he was still prepared to consider requests from fellow poets such as Czechowski and Mickel, Huchel had no interest in attending events at the Academy, of which he remained a member, let alone the meetings, to which he still received invitations. He maintained contact with Wagenbach in the West and Kundera in Czechoslovakia. He wrote to the latter on 13 May 1964, saying that the publication of Kundera's Czech translation of *Chausseen Chausseen* would give him fresh heart.[33] He informed him that he had been invited to read at the *Documenta* in Karlsruhe. (sic) He had been offered a fee of 1,000 marks but he was sure he would not be permitted to travel. He was right, of course. He received another invitation to attend the meeting of the Gruppe 47 at Sigtuna near Stockholm from 10 to 13 September 1964. He applied direct to Bentzien's office for visas on 3 August, but the application was rejected on 19 August.[34] Huchel reported the matter to Günter Eich on 3 September 1964, alluding to Eich's poem, 'Nicht geführte Gespräche', that he had dedicated to Huchel, 'Es wird wohl immer bei "nicht geführten Gesprächen" bleiben. Denn in Stockholm, worauf ich so sehr hoffte, werden wir uns nicht sehen. Seit drei Jahren Reiseverbot und anderes mehr; es ist absurd, brutal und skandalös, doch für diese Eisenkette am Fuss gibt es keinen Schlüssel und keine Feile'.[35]

Following their reconciliation, Bobrowski and Huchel had agreed that they would only travel to Sweden if all five GDR writers who had been invited were permitted to travel.[36] In the event, only Bobrowski was granted permission, and he elected to go to Sweden alone. He was not able to go to the meeting proper, only to the Gruppe 47 week that followed in Stockholm, when Susanne Huchel read from her father's verse in his absence. Bobrowski's final letter to Huchel was written some time after his return. He wrote rather lamely to 'Lieber Herr Huchel' on 5 November that he had travelled to Sweden 'nach längerer Bedenkzeit, auf Wunsch des Staatssekretariats für Kirchenfragen. Es war aber nicht gut'.[37] There is no record of further contact between Huchel and Bobrowski before the latter's death in September 1965.

The Eviction from Hubertusweg 35-39

The affair with the Wilhelmshorst council over the allocation of the rooms at Hubertusweg 35-39 dragged on through 1964. Huchel's step-son Roger moved into the rooms in 1963,[38] and Stasi reports suggest that Huchel was managing to keep the upper hand in the local propaganda war he was conducting on the basis of the mayor's dubious past. She was, however, replaced by a Herr Brüggemann, who was not constrained in the same way as his predecessor. The Stasi informant 'Ulrich' saw the matter as follows, 'Um das Ansehen der Gemeinde als örtl. Staatsmacht zu wahren und vor allen Dingen um den Fall Huchel nicht zum nachahmenswerten Beispiel für andere Bürger werden zu lassen, blieb dem Rat nur der Weg der Zwangsräumung offen'.[39]

Whatever one thinks of the 'Staatsmacht' and of Stasi informants, the logic of the situation in which Huchel had placed himself through his refusal to relinquish the rooms is very much as 'Ulrich' depicts it. 'Ulrich' reported that the council had deferred the eviction on one or two occasions after letters from Huchel. In December 1964, Brüggemann instructed that the long- threatened eviction should now finally take place. Things would have been little different in the West. A number of critics, some of whom should certainly know better, have followed Huchel in conveying the impression that the eviction was the first that he knew of the affair. The eviction on 18 December 1964 was overseen by Juhl and carried out by a Herr Schulze.[40]

Brüggemann then sent Huchel a letter on 18 January 1965, which reads as follows, 'Unter Bezugnahme auf die erfolgte Räumung teile ich Ihnen mit, daß die Gegenstände von uns auf Ihre Rechnung und Gefahr eingelagert wurden und stelle Ihnen gleichzeitig Termin bis *spätestens 30.1.65* darüber zu verfügen. Die Abrechnung erhalten Sie von uns im Anschluß'.[41] The Huchels did not respond to this letter, nor did they make any attempt to recover the material. The Wilhelmshorst council, following standard procedures, passed the matter on to the Potsdam judiciary for consideration.

Illness and New Poetry

In January 1965, Huchel went along to a reading by Eich in East Berlin. It was their first meeting since 1954. Their relationship was, though, by now destined to be marked by distance, and by the time Huchel left the GDR for the West in 1971, Eich was seriously ill. Shortly after their meeting in East Berlin, Huchel himself was admitted to hospital in Potsdam. As he informed Kundera on 14 February 1965, he was being examined due to bleeding from his kidneys. (ii,353) It was, it seems, a recurrence of his complaint during the war years, when he had visited a specialist whilst stationed at Greifswald. The problem would recur.

He informed Kundera that he had been visited by the Arendts, that S. Fischer were very pleased with Kundera's translation and that an Italian translation would be appearing in two years' time. Kundera had delivered a speech at the launch of the translation and Kurella had responded by spreading lies about Huchel. Huchel told Kundera that he had been so cheered by the publication of the Czech translation of *Chausseen Chausseen* that he had begun writing new poems. He sent Kundera a copy of a recent composition, 'Die Engel', (i,206) for a volume that Kundera was preparing in honour of Frantisek Halas. Huchel urged his friend, 'Lies bei Moses – kurz vor der Sintflut – nach, dann findest Du das Motiv'. (ii,353) He wrote again shortly afterwards. By this time, he was back at home in bed. He explained, 'Das Krankenhaus war zu kostspielig, eine Zystoskopie 240.– DM (im letzten Jahr hatte ich hier 80.– DM Einnahme)'. (ii,353) Huchel chose not to include the Academy sinecure in his calculation. He helped Kundera with the reference in his previous letter. It was to Genesis, 6, ii, 'Da sahen die Kinder Gottes nach den Töchtern der Erde, wie schön sie waren, und nahmen zu Weibern, welche sie wollten'.

Huchel's letter to Kundera demonstrates that, as he distanced himself from the intellectual confines of the GDR, he drew not just on the Bible but upon the learning and interpretations of myth that he had first been introduced to in the 1920s within the Goldberg Circle. He explained to Kundera, 'In den altjüdischen Legenden wird unverblümt von der Hurerei zwischen Engeln und schamlosen Menschentöchtern gesprochen'. (ii,353) As we saw much earlier, Huchel's library contained the

Insel-Bücherei edition of J.L.Perez's *Jüdische Geschichten* (No.204). As these references and Huchel's comments suggest, 'Die Engel' was much less readily accessible than other compositions such as 'April 63', 'Exil' and 'Hubertusweg'. Religious and metaphysical concerns come to the fore once again in Huchel's late verse. Conscious that a composition of this sort might well have taken his friend by surprise, Huchel offered to send 'Gezählte Tage' in its place. He added that he had written 'Gezählte Tage' in hospital and it was equally incomprehensible upon a first reading. Huchel had begun to immerse himself in myth and legend, in the esoteric, in a much more thorough manner than in the past. Yet he felt that the motif in 'Die Engel' was suitable for Halas, 'Die Greisin (einst schöne Menschentochter), die vom Spiegel (Welt) den Staub fegt ... Regen – Gefängnis der Toten – Sintflut – Zeit – Asche – Trauer'. (ii,353) The imagery of 'Die Engel' betrays, too, a renewed interest in Heym, as well as a sharing of Heym's conviction that Satanic, not divine powers presided over the earth. Hence, the angels 'die niederfahren hinter der dünnen Dämmerung,/ mit rußigen Schwingen zu den Töchtern Kains' are akin to Lucifer. Damnation, not redemption is the outcome of life on earth. With the chilling closing lines, 'Gedenke meiner,/ flüstert der Staub', the poem's final stanza echoes the message of the first.

Interpretation of 'Gezählte Tage' (i,184) did not rely on reference to biblical sources. Like 'Die Engel', though, it is constructed upon a framework of complementary opening and closing stanzas, which flesh out the motif of the poem's title, the poet's awareness that, now in his sixties, his days are numbered. The conditions under which he is forced to live mean that he has no real control over the time that is left for him. The final stanza reads,

> Zwei Schatten,
>
> Rücken an Rücken,
>
> zwei Männer warten im frostigen Gras.
>
> Stunde,
>
> die nicht mehr deine Stunde ist,
>
> Stimmen,
>
> vorausgesandt durch Nebel und Wind.

The opening and closing stanzas frame a section which begins, 'Vergiß die Stadt,/ wo unter den Hibiskusbäumen/ das Maultier morgens gesattelt wird'. A biographical reading lends itself here, the poem clearly referring to Huchel's wish to escape to Italy from the constraints of his life in the GDR. Yet the poem conveys his feelings of the very futility of that wish, given the bleak prospects of any change to his situation. The potential for life that he still felt within him was being wasted. This feeling that he was being robbed of the best of his late years fuelled the deep bitterness left by the *Sinn und Form* affair.

The pervading mood of futility and waste gave rise on 30 March 1965 to the composition of 'Ophelia', a poem which, unusually for Huchel, was written in a matter of minutes. (i,175) It was published the following year in the West. The poem evokes the aftermath of a failed attempt by the Ophelia figure to cross the German-German border, 'Später, am Morgen,/ gegen die weiße Dämmerung hin,/ das Waten von Stiefeln/ im seichten Gewässer'. Like 'Die Engel', it has echoes of Heym, who wrote his own 'Ophelia'. Yet, as Walter Hinck points out, Huchel's version goes back to Shakespeare with its darkly ironic references to 'Königreich' and 'Weidenblatt' in the final stanza,[42] which reads,

> Kein Königreich,
>
> Ophelia,
>
> wo ein Schrei
>
> das Wasser höhlt,
>
> ein Zauber
>
> die Kugel
>
> am Weidenblatt zersplittern läßt.

Equally, the 'schlammige Stacheldrahtreuse' at the end of the first stanza picks up on the 'Schlamm'gen Tod' of Schlegel's translation. This imagery is embedded in the Brandenburg landscape, which has become the site for Ophelia's murder by the border guards.

Summoned to Court

The Potsdam judiciary sent Huchel a letter on 16 March 1965, informing him that, due to his failure to make payment for the cost of the storage of the material that had been removed from Hubertusweg 35-39, a court action would be brought against him.[43] Huchel replied on 22 March, stating that the Wilhelmshorst council had not yet informed him what costs had been incurred through the eviction.[44] Only through the letter of 16 March had he discovered, after three months, where his archive material had been deposited. This was the first of ten points made by Huchel to support his contention that the court should not proceed with its action against him. Among other things, he claimed that he could not store the material in his own house due to design faults. He went on to allege that during the eviction Juhl had been very drunk and had called Huchel a 'Nuttendichter' in front of his wife. His final point was that during the past three months he had been ill and had therefore not been able to deal with the matter.

His letter was referred back to the Wilhelmshorst council, which discussed the matter on 22 April 1965. Brüggemann reported back to the court on 27 April that the council had agreed to proceed with the action against Huchel.[45] Brüggemann's letter pointed out that he had not received a reply to his letter of 18 January. He claimed that during the eviction Monica Huchel had said that they did not care where the material was taken. Juhl was outraged at Huchel's description of him. Huchel had claimed that some material had been lost during the eviction but Brüggemann disputed this. He concluded by saying that the council did not want Huchel's 'junk'.

Huchel later took the story up from that point, claiming first, 'Ich ließ es zum Prozeß kommen'. (i,380) According to Huchel, at the hearing on 28 May 1965, Judge Friedl had no idea what the affair was about. Huchel told him, 'Man hat meine Schränke aufgebrochen, meine Papiere weggenommen'. Friedl replied angrily, 'Sie beleidigen die Staatsorgane. Sie können doch keinen staatsfeindlichen Verlag gründen'. He had never heard of *Sinn und Form*. Huchel continued the story,

Eine Schöffin rettete die verworrene Lage, indem sie den Richter erinnerte, daß Exmittierungen in der DDR überhaupt verboten sind. Alle waren verdattert, der Richter diktierte wütend einen Vergleich: Ich sollte die Transport- und Gerichtskosten zahlen, die Gemeinde auf Miete verzichten. Die Gerichtskosten wurden – nach dem Altpapiergewicht! – auf neun Mark festgesetzt. Als ich darauf bestand, daß ich diese Summe mit drei Tagen Gefängnis absitzen wolle, war dies dem Richter höchst peinlich, er schloß die Sitzung, und ich hörte nie wieder etwas von der Sache. (ii,380-1)

As he later said, at least he now knew where his archive was; in an old shed. He went along there with Charlotte Narr. They found that some of the material was torn, and mould had begun to grow on it. Household effects of a recently deceased pensioner had been tipped over it. Huchel ended the story as follows, 'Ich ging zum Bürgermeister und hielt ihm ein Buch unter die Nase: Früher gab es Bücherverbrennung, heute Bücherverschimmelung'. (ii,380-1)

In the settlement ('Vergleich') which Brüggemann set out on 28 May 1965, Huchel was obliged to remove all his material deposited on council premises by 30 June 1965.[46] By the same date, he had to pay the council 53 marks to cover the costs of storage. Finally, he had to pay the court's costs of 120 marks. 'Ulrich', who attended the hearing, reported that 'H. kostenpflichtig zur Tragung aller durch die Räumung entstandenen Kosten an den Rat der Gemeinde verurteilt wurde'.[47] He continued,

Später erschien dann Huchel auf dem Rat der Gemeinde und sortierte seine Bücher, einen kleinen Teil schenkte er soviel ich noch weiß der Gemeindebücherei, während ein großer

Teil wohl als Altpapier abtransportiert wurde, bezw. er auch noch in seine Wohnung
nahm. Das kann ich nicht mehr genau sagen. Die Kosten wurden v. Huchel bezahlt.

Much material from the *Sinn und Form* archive survived in Huchel's house, which
Arendt took over when the Huchels left the GDR. As we have seen, it is now
deposited in the archives of the Berlin-Brandenburg Academy of Arts.

There are, as we have seen, significant omissions in Huchel's version of the
story. As he told it, it certainly served to confirm the worst western suspicions about
the GDR system of justice, as well as to foreground his own courage and integrity.
Huchel's story has, moreover, generally been read as the authentic backcloth to the
poem 'Das Gericht', which was later published in *Gezählte Tage*. It contains lines
such as the following, 'Wandanstarrend,/ nicht fähig,/ den blutigen Dunst/ noch
Morgenröte zu nennen,/ hörte ich den Richter/ das Urteil sprechen'.In truth, these
apocalyptic verses lend the affair a tragic grandeur that, as Huchel acknowledged
on the phone to Wagenbach far back in September 1963, in its petty and farcical
exchanges it did not merit.

Maintaining a Presence in the West

While he resisted Gysi's advances and relented with Czechowski and others, Huchel
placed some of his new compositions with West Berlin and West German outlets.
Wagenbach acted as his courier. 'Exil' appeared in 1965, 'Mittag in Succhivo' the
following year, together with a dedication to Bermann Fischer. 'Ophelia' also
appeared in 1966, 'Ankunft' in 1967, together with five other new poems, which
were published in *Neue Deutsche Hefte*. Others would soon follow.

Huchel had not been forgotten in the West. Jens chaired the jury for the 'Preis
der jungen Generation' (!) awarded by *Die Welt* in the autumn of 1965. Huchel
shared the prize of 15,000 marks with Carson McCullers. Jens re-worked his review
of *Chausseen Chausseen* for a piece, 'Das Dunkle gelassen anerkannt', which was
published in *Die Welt* on 9 October 1965. Jens engaged in breathtaking hyperbole,
concluding that Huchel ranked with the greatest German writers of the century. For
his part, Huchel entrusted the banker's son Jens with the investment of his prize
money in stocks and shares.[48]

Huchel had received official notification of the award in a telegram from
Italiaander, to whom he wrote on 21 October 1965.[49] He told Italiaander that in
addition to Hamburg, he had received invitations to go to Zurich, Venice, Tübingen
and Frankfurt, where he had now been offered the poetics lectureship for the winter
semester. He knew he would not be able to take up these invitations and added that
his wife, too, was suffering from the fact that they could no longer take their trips
to Italy. He ended, 'Ich habe mir vier Katzen zugelegt, diese respektieren weder
Mauer noch Stacheldraht, treue Gesellen, sie lassen mich nicht im Stich!' The cats

would figure repeatedly in Huchel's poetry written during the years of isolation, perhaps most notably in 'Meinungen'. (i,219) For Michael Hamburger,[50] this poem was a 'Bekenntnis gerade zu jener Verschwiegenheit' that was characteristic of Huchel's verse, as illustrated in the poem's final lines, 'Die Katzen,/ die hinter der Tür/ auf der Treppe dämmern,/ sind weise und schweigen'. Temperamentally, Huchel was inclined to keep his own counsel, a tendency which experience had served only to re-enforce as he sought now to preserve his private sphere against incursions.

'Willkommen sind Gäste, die Unkraut lieben'

Huchel did not become involved in the underground counter culture of readings at friends' flats in the manner of Wolf Biermann and others. His way remained as it had been in the early 1930s at the Artists' Colony, when he had received visitors rather than being the guest. Non-conformist GDR figures as well as visitors from the West were attracted to Hubertusweg. Among Huchel's regular visitors were the Arendts, Uwe Grüning, Walter and Lotte Janka, Franz Fühmann, Robert Havemann, Wolf Biermann, Reiner Kunze, Henryk Bereska, Günter Kunert and Rolf Schneider. Janka had been released from Bautzen prison in late 1960 and was working for DEFA. He got in touch in 1963, at a time when many people were reluctant to be seen in Huchel's company. He and Huchel overcame their differences of the early 1950s. Both now had their stories to tell about their treatment by the SED, and this served to cement a bond, as it would with others.

One night, the young Biermann turned up at the Huchels', claiming that he was being hounded by the SED. The Huchels gave him a bed for the night. That marked the beginning of a friendship, which saw Biermann staying for quite long periods, enjoying the Huchels' hospitality and composing his verse along with Huchel. Biermann commented on their relationship with typically sharp humour, 'Er war der Lehrer, ich war der Schüler. Er hat mir nichts beigebracht, aber abgelernt habe ich von Peter Huchel das Schweigen zwischen den Worten'.[51] Biermann had something of the young Brecht about him. He composed his famous 'Ermutigung' for Huchel, yet would later acknowledge that the encouragement to stay and act was really meant for himself rather than Huchel, who was by then 'verbraucht, verbittert, verhärtet'.[52] Huchel insisted on listening to one particular song, to a guitar accompaniment, which begins, 'Ich hab die ganze Nacht vertan/ Mit den alten Weibern am Küchenherd/ Ihre schönen Geschichten bis in die Früh/ Die waren nicht verkehrt'.[53] To Biermann's puzzlement, Huchel always responded to this song with just one word: Shakespeare. Such was their relationship that Biermann neither sought an explanation nor was he given one. Biermann concluded, not wholly flippantly, 'Was weiß ich schon von William Shakespeare, ich weiß ja nicht mal was von Peter Huchel, obwohl wir uns so oft sahn und uns so nah waren'.[54] The phlegmatic Huchel had no need for any greater degree of intimacy. What he derived from Biermann's good company was the stimulus for his own compositions such as 'Macbeth', (i,197) with its reference to 'die alten Frauen' who 'das Futter häckseln'.

Huchel still occasionally received visitors from abroad. Among them was the Bulgarian writer, Boris Deltshev, who was taken to Wilhelmshorst by Norbert Randow.[55] Huchel shared stories with Deltshev about Paris, where they had both studied. Huchel recalled Bulgarian students, whom he had known there in the 1920s, and Cheng Cheng. He talked about his trips to the Black Sea coast in the early 1930s and again in the late 1950s. He gave his visitor the recent compositions, 'Ophelia', 'Exil', 'Antwort' and 'Alkaios', encouraging him to publish them in Bulgaria. This Delshev did on 6 October 1966, together with an article about Huchel which happened to be placed beneath a headline referring to the GDR's national public holiday on 7 October. This juxtaposition so enraged the GDR embassy in Sofia that a protest was lodged and Dentshev was asked to account for his actions. Huchel would later cite the embassy's action as an example of the discrimination against him.

Further visitors from abroad were the Scandinavian teachers Jan Andrew Nilsen and his wife.[56] Following a first visit in 1964, they returned in March 1965 and on a number of other occasions, before in March 1966 they brought a group of 45 students. By chance, Biermann was staying, and the students were treated to readings by him as well by Huchel. They were aware that Huchel received occasional visitors from the Federal Republic, among them Heinrich Böll. Huchel came to view Böll and other similarly influential figures such as Jens as his only lifeline. A frequent guest from the GDR, Rolf Schneider, recalled, 'Unentwegt erschienen Neugierige aus dem deutschen Westen und suchten seine Begegnung. Er wurde ein wenig starrsinnig. Das Interesse an ihm jenseits der Grenze blieb seine Ermunterung, von dem er zuletzt abhängig war wie von einer Droge'.[57] For his wife, Huchel 'litt unter dem Eingeschlossensein und der andauernden Kontrolle'.[58] He was desperately unhappy in his situation. The only solution was to be found in the West, where he looked for help and support.

The Academy Attempts to Break the Deadlock

Between 1963 and late 1966, there was no movement in the SED hierarchy over the Huchel affair. Ulbricht had spoken, and there was nothing to add. In an act of solidarity, the West Berlin Academy made him a member in 1966. From now on, Huchel would receive regular invitations to attend meetings in West Berlin and would therefore have an opportunity to draw attention to his situation by applying for visas.

At the end of the year, Konrad Wolf, the new President of the East Berlin Academy, undertook an attempt to break the impasse after the repeated attempts by the Aufbau Verlag had failed to bear fruit. Aufbau's final effort was a letter of 17

November 1966. Hossinger discussed Huchel with Abusch on 2 December 1966.[59] It was agreed that final clarification of Huchel's financial situation had to be reached in terms of pension provision, the securing of a place for his son to study, provision of translation work for Monica Huchel and the issue of trips abroad.[60] Wolf wrote to Huchel on 19 December 1966, proposing that they should meet in order to clear the air.[61] Huchel replied on 6 January 1967.[62] He proposed that the Academy should first fulfil the promises that had been made to him in 1962-3. He questioned Wolf's reference merely to differences of opinion and misunderstandings, in the light of the official measures that had been taken against him in recent years, which had severely damaged him financially. He stated that his creativity had been crippled and he had been the victim of a petty vendetta conducted by local officials. Huchel suggested that not Wolf but Hossinger should be the person to resume the contact that had been broken off so abruptly in 1962. A conversation with Wolf might follow such a meeting.

Wolf passed the letter on to Hossinger, informing him that he had no objections to Hossinger's talking first to Huchel. Hossinger, no doubt mindful after his earlier experiences with Huchel, following which he declined to have any further dealings with him, went to see Baum in Abusch's office on 16 January.[63] Following the meeting, Huchel's letter was forwarded to Abusch. Meanwhile, shortly afterwards, Paul Dessau, a member of both the East and West Berlin Academies, attended a meeting at the latter, to which Huchel had also been invited. Huchel had sent a telegram, explaining that he could not attend because he was not permitted to travel. West Berlin Academy members urged Dessau to pay Huchel a visit in order to establish what could be done to help him. Dessau reported back to Eduard Claudius at the East Berlin Academy. Claudius, who was standing in for Konrad Wolf, wrote to Abusch on 17 April 1967, informing him of Dessau's findings.[64] Dessau had reported that Huchel was living 'unter unwürdigen Verhältnissen'. His house was badly in need of repairs. He had clearly given up on it. Dessau had contacted Gotsche and argued that Huchel should be permitted to leave. Gotsche had, however, rejected Dessau's plea on the grounds that it would simply harm the GDR. Claudius put forward his views on the matter. Firstly, it was necessary to resolve the issue of Huchel's pension. Huchel's claim seemed indisputable. Secondly, Huchel should be permitted some foreign travel, preferably abroad rather than to West Berlin. Finally, Hossinger should look into the question of repairs to Huchel's house.

The Literature Section discussed Huchel's relationship with the Academy on 26 April 1967.[65] Wieland Herzfelde, the Secretary of the Literature Section, was nominated to enter into a dialogue with Huchel, supported by Hossinger. Dessau followed up this initiative by urging Claudius in a letter of 2 May 1967 that steps must be taken to help Huchel.[66] Claudius responded the following day, informing Dessau of the action the Literature Section was going to take, which was in keeping with their own discussions of the matter. For Claudius, Huchel's own attitude was a decisive factor if negotiations were to be conducted successfully. Claudius knew that there was no point in his talking personally to Huchel, given the latter's attitude towards him. Herzfelde was a much more appropriate choice as a contact person.

Die Sternenreuse: from S.Fischer to Piper

At last, in the spring of 1967 the long-mooted new edition of *Gedichte* appeared, though under circumstances that Huchel could scarcely have imagined when in 1958 he was engaged on that same project for the Aufbau Verlag. Now the publisher was not the Aufbau Verlag, nor Rütten und Loening, nor, for that matter, S. Fischer. As we have seen, Gysi's repeated efforts on Ulbricht's behalf failed to elicit any response from Huchel, who had no doubt in his mind that he should again look to the West. Given the general contract with S. Fischer and the success of that partnership in the publication of *Chausseen Chausseen*, it is, on the face of it, surprising that Huchel signed a contract with the Munich publisher Piper for the re-issue of *Gedichte*. It was Piper, too, who the following year, after his 65th birthday, published *Hommage für Peter Huchel*, the first collection of critical essays, mémoirs and poems dedicated to him. *Chausseen Chausseen* remained the only fruits of Huchel's relationship with his Frankfurt publisher.

Huchel never commented in public on his break with S. Fischer, which was, however, regarded in the GDR as a particularly virulently anti-communist publishing house. Huchel's friend, the editor Klaus Wagenbach, who cultivated close ties with other GDR poets such as Bobrowski and Hermlin, was dismissed by S. Fischer in the autumn of 1963, just as *Chausseen Chausseen* appeared. The reason for Wagenbach's dismissal was that he had protested to the West German authorities over the arrest on 6 October 1963 of the East Berlin publisher Günter Hofé, who was on the way to the Frankfurt Book Fair.[67] That event cannot have encouraged Huchel to develop his relationship with S. Fischer, a continuing association with whom would also not have helped him in his efforts to leave the GDR.

In 1958, Huchel had been considering the inclusion of juvenilia in a new edition but had told Kundera that he felt it would be best to sit on this work for a few more years. By 1967, he had evidently come to feel that only a small number of his early poems should be added to the existing arrangement of *Gedichte*. Huchel's own involvement in the preparation of the new collection was, in any case, quite limited. Piper's editor Otto F. Best recalls that he himself chose the title and selected the poems, 'Ich habe das ganze als damaliger Cheflektor mit Huchel in Ostberlin diskutiert und sein Plazet zu beidem erhalten'.[68] The new collection's title was drawn from the title of the second section of *Gedichte*, which also included the poem of that same title. The titles of the three sections of *Gedichte* were dispensed with in favour of a simple numbering. Huchel made alterations to the cycles 'Deutschland' and 'Der Rückzug' in the third section, which was formerly entitled 'Zwölf Nächte'. The first section, formerly 'Herkunft', was extended by the inclusion of 'Damals', 'Caputher Heuweg' and 'Kinder im Herbst', all of which evoke the rural childhood. As we have seen, 'Damals' and 'Caputher Heuweg' also occupied a central position in *Chausseen Chausseen*. However, the most important addition to the second section was 'Lenz'. Written forty years earlier during the early stages of the period in France, it was placed between 'Cimetière' and 'Corenc'. The tragic mood of 'Lenz' had lost none of its relevance for Huchel since its first publication in *Sinn und Form* nearly a decade earlier.

The publication brought Huchel some welcome publicity in the West, as, belatedly, the poetry that he had written between the mid-1920s and the late 1940s became known to a wider West German reading public. Just as in the late 1940s in East Berlin these poems had appeared to many to be out of step with the politicised mood of the times due to their residual 'bourgeois' qualities, so too, ironically enough, the Federal Republic was now embarked on its own political revolution, which culminated in the denunciation of 'bourgeois' art. If the general public mood meant that many potential readers were not overly receptive to Huchel's early verse, nonetheless, reviewers who themselves were poets recognised the qualities of Huchel's early verse.

One of the most perceptive reviews was by Karl Krolow.[69] Huchel's views on Krolow's alleged plagiarism of his early poetry must surely have reached Krolow's ears. Yet he was unstinting in his praise of the magical qualities of Huchel's verse. He placed him at the forefront of the regeneration of German nature poetry that had begun in the in the later years of the Weimar Republic. A more critical edge was developed by Hans-Jürgen Heise, who was less inclined than most to take the Huchel image at face value.[70] Unlike almost all the other West German reviewers of Huchel's work in the 1960s and 1970s, not to mention the authors of those pieces that appeared in the GDR in the 1950s, Heise attempted a properly grounded, historical assessment of Huchel's development, including the Nazi period. Heise pointed out the curious manner in which Huchel's fame had been achieved in the West, after he had long been passed over as a poet. He wrote that, as the 1950s progressed, Huchel, as much in his capacity as the editor of *Sinn und Form* as a poet, advanced in the West 'zu einer fast mythischen Figur, einer Repräsentanzgestalt, die umso mehr in einen nebulosen Ruhm hineinwuchs, als man – außer wenigen Gedichten in Anthologien – überhaupt nichts Künstlerisches von ihm kannte'. Hence, the tone for the reception of *Chausseen Chausseen* had been set by his moral standing, following his struggle with SED cultural politicians. Heise expressed his clear preference for Huchel's early verse, writing that it was 'essentiell ein Protokoll archetypisch-erhabener Stimmungen und formal eine äusserst raffinierte, eine ästhetisch ausgereifte Artikulation'. He cited 'Havelnacht' in particular, in order to conclude – in words that demonstrate Heise's appreciation of Huchel's achievement –,

Das sind keine 'aktuellen' Strophen. Aber es sind Verse, die man, wenn man gerecht ist und sich nicht irreleiten lässt von dem Begriff Modernität oder von Vorstellungen der Ideologien, vom Kunstverstand her als gelungen und vom Gefühl, von der alten guten Seele her als wahr akzeptieren muss. Es sind Verse, die persönliches Erleben über das Ego und das Jetzt hinausgeleiten in jene grösseren Bereiche und tieferen Bezüge, an die jeder noch so aufgeklärte Dichter einfach glauben muss – sofern er in seinem Schaffen keine Tätigkeit sehen will, die nur noch mechanisch weiterklappert, längst jenseits von Anlass und Ziel.

Heise would develop his ideas about Huchel's development and achievements, and present them in reviews of *Gezählte Tage* in the early 1970s. Their critical acuity served further to polarise opinion – and caused Huchel himself considerable discomfort.

The Catalogue of Broken Promises

In a memo of 18 May 1967, Hossinger referred to Herzfelde's projected visit to Huchel.[71] There is no record of the visit itself, though it clearly took place in May and Huchel talked to Herzfelde about his request to leave the GDR for Italy. Hossinger himself visited Wilhelmshorst on 17 May in order to find out more about the affair surrounding Huchel's archive.[72] Hossinger was told that Huchel had lost the court case and had still only removed a portion of his books from the council's premises.

Huchel tried to get things moving again by phoning Hossinger on 31 August to enquire about his application to leave for Italy.[73] Hossinger queried Huchel's use of the term application, since to his knowledge no application as such had been lodged. Huchel followed up the call with a registered letter on 3 September.[74] It was clearly this letter to which Huchel was referring when in 1975 he wrote, 'Am 3. September 1967 stellte ich erneut den Antrag, mit meiner Familie nach Italien aussiedeln zu können. Trotz schriftlicher Nachfragen (1.August 1968, 23.September 1968) – keine Antwort'. (ii,329) In his letter of 3 September, Huchel referred back to their telephone conversation during which Hossinger had suggested that Huchel should make an official application. In Huchel's view, Herzfelde had already agreed that Huchel should travel to Italy; indeed, it was Herzfelde who had raised the matter. Yet Huchel, of course, knew full well that Herzfelde had no executive power in such matters. For Huchel, Hossinger's suggestion was only a further delaying tactic, consistent with his experiences over the past few years. Herzfelde must surely have been authorised to mention Italy in the first place? That being the case, there was no need for him to enter into time-consuming formalities. According to Huchel, Claudius had maintained to the Hamburg Academy that Huchel had never submitted any applications to travel to West Germany or anywhere else. Huchel challenged this assertion, picking at random a number of examples from recent years. He began with January and March 1963, when he had applied to go to Italy following Bermann Fischer's invitation and to the Hamburg Academy on the occasion when he was elected an honorary member. The latter application was, as we have seen, rejected by the East Berlin Academy in a letter signed by Hossinger on 8 April 1963. He then mentioned the application submitted to the Writers' Union in September 1963 to attend the meeting of the Gruppe 47 at Saalgau. As we have seen, the application was rejected on 25 September. He referred to the application he made in August 1964 to attend the 'documenta III' in Kassel and the Gruppe 47 in Stockholm. Professor Korlen had also invited him to read at Stockholm University. This application was rejected by the Ministry of Culture on 19 August 1964. In that letter, Huchel was informed that 'wir nicht in der Lage sind, Ihre Reisen nach Stockholm und Kassel gegenüber den Ministerien des Innern und für Auswärtige Angelegenheiten zu befürworten'. Huchel regarded this as evidence of total discrimination. He felt it was only understandable that, in the circumstances, he had not submitted any further applications for a long time, even though he had received invitations from Frankfurt University in 1965 and 1966, from Zurich radio in 1965, 1966 and 1967, from the Hamburg and West Berlin academies. He had also received invitations to read from his works in Cologne, Düsseldorf, Tübingen and other West German cities, as well as in Scandinavian countries.

Huchel went on to explain that, following an urgent request from the Austrian Society for Literature and the West Berlin Academy, he had decided in the autumn of 1966 to submit an application after all. He had talked on the phone to Bruno Haid, Deputy Minister of Culture, who, Huchel claimed, had promised a satisfactory outcome. On 15 October 1966, Haid asked him to visit him at his office. After a lengthy discussion, Haid promised he would write to let Huchel know the decision, but he had heard nothing. As far as Huchel was aware, the documents that he had submitted were still on Haid's desk.

Huchel recalled Dessau's visit that spring, when he had been assured of Dessau's support in his attempt to travel to the meeting of the West Berlin Academy. Dessau left, Huchel claimed, having promised final confirmation in a few days, yet again nothing happened. Huchel completed the story of his frustrated efforts to obtain a travel permit by returning to Herzfelde's visit in May. It was following that visit that he was now being encouraged to submit an application. Huchel wrote that in the light of all his experiences, he was no longer prepared to play this senseless and demeaning game. He went on to remind Hossinger that he was now 64 and was living in financially unacceptable circumstances. He referred to his letter to Wolf in which he had written that his creativity had been damaged by the total block placed on foreign travel. He refused to play the role of petitioner for the rest of his life. For Huchel, the only acceptable solution was for him and his family to be permitted to leave the GDR and to travel via West Germany to Italy or the South of France. He reminded Hossinger that Bredel had supported this idea.

He advanced a number of points in support of his application. He referred to his leading role in the development of radio after 1945 as well as his and his wife's engagement on *Sinn und Form* at Becher's express wish. He linked that with their decision to move from West Berlin to the GDR in 1950-1. The past few years had demonstrated, he wrote, that there was no reason for them to stay in the GDR. There was no point going into all the promises made and broken by Bredel and Hossinger. Huchel maintained that despite everything he and his wife had always remained loyal. It must be said, there were many in the SED hierarchy who would dispute that. Huchel closed his letter by asking Hossinger to forward it to the appropriate authorities, and on 9 September Hossinger informed Huchel that he had forwarded the letter to Abusch's office.[75] On 11 September, Hossinger noted that Abusch was thinking over whether Huchel should be allowed to leave the GDR for Italy for good.[76] Yet, once more there was no way forward through the SED hierarchy.

The Academy's Rebuff by the Council of Ministers

Huchel's 65th birthday was fast approaching and there was no sign of any resolution of the issue of his pension. Huchel alerted Hossinger to the urgency of the matter, and on 4 March 1968 Hossinger produced a document setting out the position as he saw it.[77] He made the, from a legal point of view, key point that Huchel had resigned and had declined further employment on the Academy's proposed almanac. The issue of his pension had not been resolved. Following the extreme antagonism of the final months of 1962 and the early months of 1963, negotiations with him had been discontinued. Hossinger put the question as to whether an application for a pension should still be made? He noted that as a National Prize winner Huchel had the right to an honorary pension. He noted, too, that Huchel's application to leave the GDR in his letter of 3 September 1967 had remained unanswered. Yet he did not mention the promises that he and Bredel had made to Huchel regarding both travel and the pension.

On 6 March 1968, Hossinger, on Wolf's behalf, contacted Reetz in Hager's office.[78] A draft containing two resolutions was produced for discussion at the meeting of the Academy's Presidium on 20 March.[79] The first resolution was that Huchel should be granted an honorary pension. The proposed monthly sum of 1,200 marks was the same as he would have received under the terms of his personal contract, which made provision for payment of 60% of his salary of 2,000 marks. The second resolution was that Hossinger should submit the first resolution to the Council of Ministers. The draft was approved unanimously at the Presidium on 20 March.[80] The draft was accompanied by an outline of Huchel's post-war career and a four-page sketch of his achievements. Fairly and intelligently written from an East Berlin perspective, the document concluded that as a 'linksbürgerlich' writer Huchel had his 'weltanschauliche Grenzen' but belonged politically in the East rather than the West. Hossinger then met with Abusch.[81] Abusch, however, went against the Academy's resolution, expressing his preference for a solution based on Huchel's personal contract rather than the award of an honorary pension. Another resolution was formulated for the Presidium of the Council of Ministers, according to which Huchel would at once receive 60% of his salary of 2,000 marks.[82] Abusch was evidently confident that he could secure support for his resolution in the Council of Ministers.

Huchel's 65th birthday came and went without any decision on the pension provision as set out in his contract. It should be pointed out that this provision was quite distinct from the standard state pension of 400 marks, which Huchel received as a matter of course from his 65th birthday.[83] Given that Huchel continued to receive his sinecure from the Academy, his monthly income was actually over 1,200 marks. By GDR standards, he remained financially quite comfortably off.

Friends and supporters in the West took the opportunity afforded by his birthday to draw attention to Huchel's plight and to express their solidarity with him. Peter Hamm, for example, concluded his article in *Süddeutsche Zeitung* with the words,

> Peter Huchel sollte heute wissen, daß er, auch ohne jedes Jahr einen neuen Gedichtband auf den Markt werfen zu müssen, ohne auf Gruppentagungen, Buchmessen oder Fernsehschirmen zu erscheinen, nicht im Ghetto, das ihm zugedacht wurde, lebt, sondern mitten unter uns – und nicht nur in seinen großen, genauen, unüberhörbaren Gedichten.[84]

The occasion was not mentioned in public in the GDR, though, as we have seen, organisations such as the Aufbau Verlag sent ritual congratulations. The Literature Section of the Academy sought to mark the occasion, but the manner in which this was done was utterly inept, as Huchel's sarcastic letter to Wieland Herzfelde of 8 April makes clear.[85] Huchel had made arrangements to celebrate at home with friends. Very late in the day, the Academy announced its intention to congratulate Huchel at the Academy, following the ceremony for the award of the F.C.Weiskopf Prize. Huchel remarked to Herzfelde that had he known early enough, he would, of course, have abandoned his twenty guests in order to have his hand shaken in the Academy! In the event, the Academy had arranged for Franz Fühmann, one of Huchel's guests, to take him some flowers on the Academy's behalf. Huchel took the opportunity of the letter to request of Herzfelde that he should, on his behalf, deal with the formalities so that he could attend the meeting of the West Berlin Academy on 27-29 April. Herzfelde replied on 18 April that permission had not been granted and went on to argue that Huchel should take the trouble to attend meetings of the East Berlin Academy![86]

On that same 18 April 1968 the Presidium of the Council of Ministers rejected Abusch's resolution concerning additional pension provision for Huchel.[87] Abusch was not present at the meeting on 18 April: he was taking the waters at Karlsbad. He was angry when he learned of the outcome. He wrote a letter of protest to Willi Stoph, the Chair of the Council of Ministers, and demanded that the resolution should be discussed again.[88] He tried, too, to enlist Hager's support, but to no avail.[89]

Another Approach to Hossinger

Unaware of this development, knowledge of which would come as a body blow later in the year, Huchel again bided his time. Occasionally, he travelled to East Berlin to meet up with visitors from the West. His favoured meeting place was the bookshop at Friedrichstraße station, where, for example, he arranged to meet Henry Beissel on 21 May. (ii,354) He also met up there on a monthly basis with Franz Tumler from the West Berlin Academy's Literature Section. When Hans Dieter Zimmermann went to work at the Academy with Tumler, they took it in turns with their supportive action. They discussed with Huchel what steps might be taken by Huchel himself or by the Academy in order to break the deadlock. In the absence of any action from the authorities, Huchel once again took it into his own hands to attempt to shame them into doing something.

On 1 August 1968 he sent a registered letter to Hossinger.[90] He drew attention to the fact that despite Hossinger's promises back in March nothing had happened. He referred back to Hossinger's letter of 21 December 1962 and to his own of 28 December 1962. He quoted the quite unambiguous promise about his pension made by Hossinger with Bredel's support. He reminded Hossinger that his letter of 28 December 1962 had been drafted specifically as a warning that he would take action if no pension should be forthcoming. He referred, too, to his letter to Konrad Wolf of 6 January 1967, in which he had demanded that the Academy should keep promises made by Hossinger and Bredel in 1962. He wrote that it was now only right and proper that the Academy should be confronted with his legal situation, from which all his difficulties as a writer stemmed. He listed the deprivation of liberty, permanent isolation, constant refusal to permit him to travel, the spreading of false information about him, and his financial situation, which, he claimed, had become extremely precarious. He accused Hossinger and others in the Academy of effectively preventing him and his wife from practising their chosen professions. All these facts were surely enough to persuade those in authority to approve the application to leave the GDR that Huchel had submitted on 3 September 1967. Yet that, too, had remained unanswered.

He now threatened to bring into play those institutions of which he was a prominent member, by which he meant the West Berlin and the Hamburg Academies. He drew attention to the fact that others such as Bloch, Mayer, Heinar

Kipphardt and Gustav Seitz had been permitted to leave and start a new life elsewhere. His reasons for wanting to leave for Italy were quite reasonable. Yet, in the eyes of the SED hierarchy Huchel had committed grave sins. This time, Huchel copied his letter to Konrad Wolf. Shortly after, Hossinger wrote to Huchel.[91] Although he did not refer to the ruling of the Council of Ministers, he informed him that the Academy had long since done all it could in order to set the wheels in motion. Nor did he now try to conceal from Huchel the fact that the legal basis for the pension had been removed by the termination of his contract on 31 December 1962. Hossinger lamely asked for Huchel's understanding that it would still take a while for the matter to be resolved!

Repression in Prague – and the GDR

Almost immediately the GDR, together with the rest of the Eastern Bloc was plunged into crisis by the Soviet invasion of Czechoslovakia on 20-21 August 1968. Soviet troops were supported by those from other Warsaw Pact countries, including the GDR. GDR security organs were placed on red alert and intense surveillance was undertaken of dissident intellectuals, among them Huchel. It did not escape the notice of the authorities that he was a close friend of Ludvík Kundera, who was active in the Prague Spring. From 22 August 1968 until 11 September, Huchel's house was observed by his neighbour, the pensioner Henle.[92] In the reports that Henle lodged, Huchel was given the nickname 'Reiter'. Henle went about his usual task of noting car number plates. Apparently, one day Huchel suggested to Henle that he could do the job for him!

The observation continued on a daily basis. Yet there was, in truth, little to be ascertained. The Huchels still employed a cleaner, and she – known as 'Besen' to the Stasi – came and went on a regular basis. There were visitors by car but 'Reiter' himself scarcely left the house, and then only to work in his garden. A report of 25 August noted that Wolf Biermann and Eva-Maria Hagen had long frequented Huchel's house.[93] A further report of 27 August noted that Huchel was very circumspect in his public comments on the invasion of Czechoslovakia.[94] An informant had, however, ascertained that in conversation he had described the situation as very serious and had tried to contact Biermann. The Stasi speculated that the Biermann circle was maybe planning something. By 9 September, the Stasi had come to the quite unremarkable conclusion that Huchel's attitude towards the invasion was extremely negative. He had seen the Prague Spring as an opportunity to enrich socialism by making it more humane, something, one might add, that he scarcely believed could be achieved in the GDR by the SED.[95] Yet there was little else to be gleaned from the observation. Indeed, the only pattern that emerged related to the frequency of the cleaning lady's visits. The observation was abandoned at 8 pm. on 11 September.

A Body Blow

On 23 September 1968, Huchel once again sent a registered letter to Hossinger, which he copied to Wolf.[96] He pointed out that the Academy had had from 1962 to deal with his pension. He therefore found it difficult to have much faith in Hossinger's statements, which Huchel saw merely as a delaying tactic. He reminded Hossinger that he had been due a pension of 1,200 marks a month since April and repeated his demand that his request to leave the GDR should be granted. Now he had reached his 65th birthday, there should be no legal obstacle to his leaving the country with his family. He was, though, aware that there were people who might still want to make an example of him. Hossinger passed the letter on to Abusch and to the Cultural Department of the Central Committee.

Huchel followed this up on 1 October, when he submitted an application to the local Potsdam police to undertake a pensioner's trip to the Federal Republic on 1 November.[97] Huchel claimed that he wished to visit his daughter in the Federal Republic. He had not had any contact with her for some two decades and, as we have seen, she was living in Sweden. It would appear that Huchel had received advance notice that he was about to be awarded a major literary prize in the West and was trying to use the cover of a pensioner's trip in order to accept the prize in person. His wife made an application at the same time and it was granted.[98] Huchel's request was, however, rejected by the Potsdam police on 15 October.[99] Reference was made to a resolution of the Council of Ministers of 15 September. Quite what the resolution consisted of, the letter did not divulge. Whatever the wording, the implication was clear. The legal exception that had been made for Huchel at the Council of Ministers related not to his personal pension but to a blanket restriction on the travel abroad that all GDR pensioners were permitted. This news must have come as a body blow to Huchel. On a legal level, it represented a degree of discrimination beyond anything he had experienced to date. Huchel was denied the freedom to travel which was granted by GDR law to all citizens of pensionable age. It is not without a certain grotesque irony that, like thousands of others, Hossinger would later take advantage of GDR pensioners' freedom to travel, electing to spend his retirement years in the Federal Republic.

Huchel was clearly shaken by this turn of events, which, as we have seen in his letter to Hossinger on 23 September, he had been fearing. The Stasi tapped into his telephone conversation with Reiner Kunze, with whom he shared this news, concluding that it meant he would never get out.[100] Kunze could not conceal his sense of shock that the law could be overridden in this way. He sought to offer some consolation by telling Huchel that he had dedicated a poem to him in his forthcoming collection.[101] Huchel also discussed the matter with his close friends, Arendt and Janka, with whom he came to the same conclusion as with Kunze that he would never escape.[102]

Meanwhile, on 23 October it was announced that he had won the 'Großer Kunstpreis' of the state of North-Rhine-Westfalia, although the official notification did not reach Huchel himself. The award of 25,000 marks would be made on 7 November 1968 in Düsseldorf. Further welcome publicity came when Piper published, somewhat belatedly, *Hommage für Peter Huchel*, the volume of essays, mémoirs and poems to mark Huchel's 65th birthday. It mattered little, in the circumstances, that much of the material contained in the volume was either not new or only of peripheral interest. However, in the Federal Republic's climate of a much more radical inquiry into recent German history and culture, the gaps in the presentation of Huchel's career began, for at least one critic, to look rather suspicious. In the *Berliner Morgenpost*, Wolfgang Maier referred to the editor Otto F. Best's 'verschörkeltes, uneindeutiges und mit merkwürdigen Ausweichungen befrachtetes Nachwort'.[103] Yet, in the circumstances, no one saw fit to explore matters further.

It is a measure of the gravity with which Huchel now viewed his situation that he elected to appeal direct to Abusch. In a registered letter of 31 October, he referred only to his proposed pensioner's trip and not to the Düsseldorf award.[104] The Ministry of Culture of the state of North-Rhine-Westfalia sent a telegram to the Academy, requesting Huchel's presence at the award ceremony.[105] The telegram was passed to Abusch, who made the obvious connection and on 5 November informed Hager of the action he had taken.[106] Haid had been instructed to tell Huchel that a trip was at present not possible because people were trying to use him in the Cold War against the GDR. Abusch concluded the letter to Hager, however, with the following, 'Ich wäre für eine baldige Aussprache zur Regelung der ganzen Angelegenheit Huchel dankbar'. In other words, it was necessary for the GDR to choose its moment to let Huchel go with minimum damage to its standing. Yet, so inherently defensive was the GDR leadership towards the West that such a moment could scarcely ever present itself.

Heinrich Böll accepted the Düsseldorf prize on Huchel's behalf and later saw to it that Huchel got at least some of the 25,000 marks. Böll was evidently under the impression that Huchel was in great need of the prize money. As Rolf Schneider recalls, at considerable personal risk Böll smuggled a large amount of money into the GDR for Huchel by concealing it about his person.[107] Schneider mediated a meeting between the two in the Karlshorst area of East Berlin. At the German-German border, GDR customs officials subjected Böll to a search and he collapsed. He none the less managed to make his way to the house as arranged. There, he revealed that he was carrying the large sum on him. Asked how he could countenance doing such a thing in his state of health, he replied that 'Er sei nun an einer Grenze aufgewachsen, und da gehöre eben der Schmuggel zum gewöhnlichen Leben, einfach so'. How did Huchel feel about this? As his wife points out, apart from his regular income and hers from translation work, they had 45,000 marks in a savings account. One could simply not spend sums of that order in the GDR. As usual, the humanitarian Böll sought to give practical help to a colleague in need. What Huchel actually needed, though, was permission to leave the GDR. It must be said that Böll showed a keener awareness of what might be of help to Huchel than did the North-Rhine-Westfalia Ministry of Culture, which encouraged Huchel to take a charter plane from Tempelhof airport to Düsseldorf in order to collect his prize![108]

Shortly afterwards, on 16 November 1968, Hossinger wrote to Abusch about Huchel's pension.[109] He had received confirmation of what he already knew to be the position, namely that Huchel had no legal right to a personal pension on the basis of his contract. There is no indication that Huchel received any official notification at this stage that there had been no progress whatsoever on the two key issues of pension rights and an exit visa. And there the matter rested yet again. Huchel clearly took the silence to mean that nothing would ever change. A memo written by Hossinger on 24 July 1969 states, in Kafkaesque fashion, that despite the rejection by the Council of Ministers of the resolution concerning Huchel's pension, no final decision had been reached.[110] Abusch and Hager were, Hossinger noted, continuing their discussions.

Bitter and Determined to Go

Huchel's 66th birthday was a sorry affair. The guests watched a T.V. film about Goya that had recently been completed by DEFA. Janka, one of Huchel's guests, had been involved in the production, yet such was his status in the GDR nearly a decade after his release that his name was not even mentioned in the credits. Another guest, Henryk Bereska, recalls that Huchel was in a depressed state.[111] He continued to depend on the West for support, which he received principally from the West Berlin Academy. His regular telephone calls with Hans Dieter Zimmermann and Franz Tumler and his meetings with them at the Friedrichstraße bookshop were a vital lifeline. Zimmermann recalls,

> Meist stand er schon da, wenn ich kam: in seinem abgetragenen Trenchcoat, groß, grauhaarig, müde lächelnd. Wir sahen uns verstohlen um wie zwei kleine Gauner und gingen dann ins Bahnhofrestaurant, wo wir bei einer Tasse Kaffee zwei Stunden zusammensaßen ... Literarische Neuerscheinungen konnte ich Huchel nicht mitbringen, sie wurden mir beim Eintritt in die Hauptstadt der DDR abgenommen. Einmal gab er mir fünf Gedichte, die ich nach Westen schmuggelte. Rudolf Hartung hat sie dann in der *Neuen Rundschau* veröffentlicht.[112]

As many as seven of Huchel's poems appeared in *Neue Rundschau* the following year. They were 'Die Gaukler sind fort', 'Schnee', 'Die Engel', 'Aristeas',

'Delphine', 'Gehölz' and 'Alkaois'. That year, 'Antwort' and 'Unterm Sternbild des Hercules' appeared in *Ensemble*. All would be collected in *Gezählte Tage*. 'Die Gaukler sind fort' (i,179) illustrates well how in Huchel's late verse the inherently rich potential of a natural world still conceived magically and mystically clashes with the deep pessimism born of experience which calls into question that very conception. The poem ends,

> Die Eiche, mächtig gegabelt,
>
> die den Donner barg –
>
> in morscher Kammer des Baums
>
> schlafen die Fledermäuse,
>
> drachenhäutig.
>
> Die hochberühmten Gaukler sind fort.

Following the exodus of the 'Gaukler', unreliable illusionists like poets themselves, there remains only the sinister presence of the dragon-skinned bats.

A Re-doubling of Efforts to Get Out

From October to December 1969, Huchel's telephone was tapped on a regular basis and conversations recorded as he maintained contact with the West Berlin Academy through Tumler and Zimmermann. By now, the situation for Huchel in the GDR could scarcely get worse. He resolved to use his western contacts for all they were worth. A source of some hope was the fact that Willy Brandt's initiatives with Moscow were beginning to bear fruit in creating a climate of détente between East and West over the head of the uncompromising Ulbricht. The Nilsens met Günter Grass in Bucharest and he agreed to intercede with his friend Brandt on Huchel's behalf.[113] Meanwhile, Huchel discussed tactics with Zimmermann and Tumler. Huchel had just been elected to the Bavarian Academy. Support was secured for a joint letter to the East Berlin Academy from presidents of the Bavarian, West Berlin and Hamburg academies, requesting that Huchel should be permitted to leave the GDR. Huchel suggested a number of formulations for the letter which Zimmermann drafted. The draft was approved at a meeting of the West Berlin Academy's Senate on 8 January 1970.[114]

Huchel's intention once more to tackle the authorities was signalled for the Stasi in their surveillance of his conversation with Janka on 4 January 1970, when, as they were arranging to meet, Huchel asked Janka if he knew Hager's office address.[115] Huchel decided now to engage the Pankow lawyer, Marie-Louise Münchhausen, to represent him in an action against the East Berlin Academy over the matter of his pension rights. She informed Hossinger of this in a letter of 6

February 1970, when she also requested of him a copy of 'eines etwa mit Herrn Huchel abgeschlossenen Aufhebungsvertrages'.[116]

Almost immediately afterwards, on 12 February 1970, the East Berlin Academy President, Konrad Wolf, received the letter from the western academies. It was signed by Friedhelm Kemp, President of the Bavarian Academy, Boris Blacher, President of the West Berlin Academy, and Wilhelm Maler, President of the Hamburg Academy.[117] Blacher was also a Corresponding Member of the East Berlin Academy. The three presidents pointed out that Huchel, a member of their academies as well as the East Berlin Academy and one of the outstanding poets in the medium of the German language, had for eight years not been permitted to attend any of their meetings. Huchel had drawn to their attention the fact that he had applied to leave the GDR on three occasions, on 3 September 1967, 1 August 1968 and 23 August 1968. On none of these occasions had he received a clear answer. Huchel, they wrote, wished very much to retire to Italy together with his wife and son. The climate there would be very beneficial to his and his wife's health. His son had been declared unfit for military service and was studying Theology at the Humboldt University. They pointed out that Huchel would soon be 67, which was beyond retirement age, and as such he should, under GDR law, be permitted to leave. They reported that Huchel himself wanted to draw to the Academy's attention that he wanted to retire to Italy, not to the Federal Republic. If permitted to leave, he would not go into print about the GDR. The letter concluded with the request for a fresh appraisal of the situation and for a satisfactory outcome without any great public fuss. In this way, the letter sought to assure the East Berlin authorities that no attempt would be made to make Cold War capital out of the affair. The letter was copied to Hager by Blacher.[118] The SED hierarchy elected not to respond at this stage. There was, in any case, the small matter of the resolution passed in September 1968 by the Council of Ministers, which preserved the facade of legality. Prussian socialism continued to operate through conventional bureaucratic procedures and did not descend into the naked lawlessness that had characterised the Third Reich and could be found in some other Eastern Bloc states, most notably Romania and the Soviet Union, however inhumane the operation of the GDR bureaucracy undoubtedly was.

Meanwhile, Hossinger grappled with Huchel's lawyer. He replied to Münchhausen on 24 February that no 'Aufhebungsvertrag' had been necessary, since Huchel had withdrawn from his personal contract *de facto*.[119] She countered that the personal contract had not been formally terminated in writing.[120] Consequently, it remained valid until 3 April 1968. She threatened the Academy with action through the employment court. ('Arbeitsgericht') Hossinger sought the advice of a legal expert, Münzer, at the Ministry of Culture.[121] Münzer replied in predictable fashion that normally things should be set down in writing, but in the present case agreement had been reached on both sides that the appointment was being terminated.[122] On 21 April, however, Klaus Wittkugel, the graphic artist and a Vice-President of the Academy, who was standing in for Konrad , wrote to Abusch, drawing attention to the letter from the West German academies and the unresolved issue of Huchel's pension.[123] He noted that in 1962 the Academy Director and President had agreed in writing that Huchel should be provided with a pension from the age of 65. Wittkugel concluded by proposing that Huchel should be permitted to leave the GDR. The pension would automatically cease to be an issue. Whatever else one might say, Wittkugel displayed a pragmatic attitude.

Signs of Movement

A memo produced by Hossinger the following day reveals that he had consulted an eminent lawyer, Kirschner, who had agreed with Münzer's assessment.[124] Unsurprisingly, Kirschner was of the opinion, on the basis of the evidence available to him, that Huchel would lose any case that he might bring against the Academy. The GDR judicial system was not going to find in Huchel's favour, as Huchel himself was well aware. His engagement of Münchhausen was surely designed to put the issue on the agenda from another angle, pressure thus brought to bear within the GDR complementing that of the western academies. However improbably, from his home in Wilhelmshorst, the resourceful Huchel was showing great skill in instigating efforts undertaken on his behalf in the West as well as in East Berlin.

Hossinger responded by arranging a meeting with Abusch.[125] Following Wittkugel's recommendation, they agreed that there was a choice to be made between the aim of providing a pension or of securing permission for Huchel to leave for Italy with his family. Abusch talked to Hager about the matter on 22 April and wrote to him two days later, setting out the points he had made in conversation.[126] He enclosed Huchel's application of 3 September 1967 to leave for Italy with his family and the original copy of the resolution of the Presidium of the Council of Ministers passed on 18 April 1968, which had rejected Abusch's proposal that Huchel should be granted additional pension provision. He reminded Hager of his efforts to have that resolution revoked and informed Hager that Huchel had engaged Münchhausen. In line with Wittkugel's view, he proposed that the Secretariat of the Central Committee should present Huchel with the clear alternative of an additional pension or permission to leave for Italy with his family. Abusch stated his clear preference for the latter solution. His reasons were that to grant the additional pension would mean a further financial burden of 800 marks a month and that they would repeatedly have to deal with Huchel's requests to travel outside the GDR to readings. Nonetheless, Abusch felt it was tactically better to give Huchel himself the choice. Abusch finally reminded Hager of the letter of 22 November 1963, in which he and Wagner had suggested that Huchel and his family should be granted a 'Sondererlaubnis' to leave. Hager and Abusch had subsequently agreed that it would be appropriate to defer the matter to a favourable point in time.

For Abusch, aware that pressure from the West was coinciding with the climate of détente, the time to act had clearly come.

Meanwhile, on 27 April Hossinger wrote to Münchhausen, encouraging her to persuade Huchel to talk to the chairperson of the Academy's 'conflict commission', Brigitte Bózelsack.[127] There is no doubt that Huchel would have regarded this suggestion as yet another delaying tactic. At a meeting with Zimmermann at Friedrichstraße station, Huchel suggested that Zimmermann should go in person to the East Berlin Academy and ask what had happened following receipt of the joint letter from the western academies. Zimmermann recalls,

> Das tat ich dann auch, kam aber nur bis zu einem kleinen, dicken Beamten in einem
> muffigen Büro, der sehr verwundert war über meinen Besuch; neben ihm saß einer, der
> nichts sagte, aber aufmerksam zuhörte. Ich trug mein Anliegen vor: die höfliche Bitte um
> Antwort auf ein Schreiben des Präsidenten.[128]

Hossinger's memo of the meeting reveals that he was the short, fat official and that his companion was Armin Zeißler, the deputy editor-in-chief of *Sinn und Form*.[129] Hossinger informed Zimmermann that Konrad Wolf would not be back in Berlin until September, when he would be notified of Zimmermann's visit. Zimmermann replied by saying that if there was no answer, the press would be informed. Hossinger passed his memo on to Wolf, Wittkugel, Abusch, Gysi, who was by now Minister of Culture, and Arno Hochmuth, head of the Culture Department of the Central Committee. Hossinger reminded Abusch that Gysi, Hochmuth and Abusch himself had agreed that the Academy would not answer the letter of the western academies.[130] Meanwhile, Zimmermann noted Huchel's suggestion that they wait until 10 September for a reply.[131] If it was not forthcoming, a second letter would be sent to Wolf, explaining that a reply within fourteen days was required. Otherwise the letter would be handed to the press.

The West Keeps Up the Pressure

When September came and nothing happened, Walther Huder, an old collaborator of Huchel's and head of the West Berlin Academy's archives, contacted the Academy with a request to discuss the matter with Hossinger.[132] Western pressure from other quarters was also stepped up. Susanne Michler, an old friend of George and Paul Tabori, rang the Huchels from West Berlin to enquire whether the Huchels still wished to leave the GDR.[133] It was felt that the right moment to act had come. Böll paid Huchel a visit.[134] On 22 September 1970, Max Frisch travelled to Wilhelmshorst on the pretext of a visit to the castles and gardens in Potsdam.[135] Huchel gave him a prepared statement that might be used in a press release. The Taboris arranged for an appeal to be sent to Ulbricht on behalf of the emigré

Hungarian PEN Club, but this was rejected. At a meeting in London, they passed the text on to David Carver, the General Secretary of the International PEN, whose President was Böll. The appeal, supported by, among others, Böll, Graham Greene and Arthur Miller, found its way into the hands of the press and was quoted copiously in the *Times* on 17 October. On two occasions, Böll appeared in person in East Berlin to lodge protests with the authorities. The PEN letter was widely reported in the western press.[136] Huchel himself (ii,381) and the editor of the 1984 edition (i,461) stated that this intervention was crucial. In April 1971, however, Huchel told Rolf Schneider that he simply did not know how the decision to let him go had come about. He knew only that it came suddenly from the top, as, indeed, it had to, given Ulbricht's pronouncement on the matter in late 1963.[137] Yet the evidence available in the archives suggests that the pressure from the western academies, principally the West Berlin Academy, was the decisive factor.[138] There is no reference to the PEN initiative in the East Berlin Academy's file on Huchel. What emerges instead is that the GDR authorities elected to negotiate with the West Berlin Academy through its East Berlin counterpart.

Blacher Pushes Open the Door

On 20 October, Hossinger reported to Wolf that no progress had been made in the Huchel affair.[139] After Zimmermann's and Huder's approaches had not borne fruit, it was agreed in the West Berlin Academy that Blacher should write a reminder to Wolf that no reply had yet been received to the letter of 13 February. In a letter of 10 November, Blacher gave voice to his concern over Huchel's fate.[140] He repeated his Academy's interest in alleviating the situation for Huchel without any great fuss. He went on to express his interest in improving relations between the two Berlin academies, with a view to possible future collaboration. Signs of good will on the East Berlin Academy's part would be most welcome, he said.

On 12 November, Konrad Wolf met with Hager to discuss Blacher's letter.[141] A memo in the former SED Central Archive, which was written shortly after confirms the outcome of their meeting. It contains the following, 'Angelegenheit Peter Huchel ... wurde Prüfung zugesagt'[142] Wolf and Hager agreed that Wolf now had to reply. Hager, as ever, did not want to be seen to be bowing to pressure, which had, however, become very real. Wolf sent Blacher a telegram on 20 November, proposing a meeting in West Berlin.[143] Blacher responded by messenger, suggesting 5 pm. on Sunday 13 December 1970. The meeting could take place either at Blacher's home or at the West Berlin Academy. Wolf sent Blacher a telegram on 10 December, agreeing on the date but suggesting 3 pm. His preferred location was the West Berlin Academy.

Zimmermann, who was present in an adjoining room, recalled that Blacher and Wolf, both fluent Russian speakers, elected to use not German but Russian for that meeting.[144] Despite the continuing intransigence of Ulbricht and his supporters, the political climate was quite favourable for a discussion about future collaboration in the light of the gesture of good will that the resolution of the Huchel affair would represent. Thus, it was in the final months of Ulbricht's increasingly insecure hold on power that the ground was laid for Huchel and his family finally to be allowed to go. Blacher was sufficiently confident of a favourable outcome that Max Frisch was now asked to put his parallel initiative on hold.[145]

The issue of Huchel's departure to Italy was item 8 on the agenda of the Secretariat of the Central Committee on 13 January 1971.[146] The issue of the pension had been shelved. The meeting was chaired by Erich Honecker. Gysi and Hochmuth were present for the item. The minute of the discussion reads, 'Das Sekretariat des ZK stimmt der Ausreise des Peter Huchel nach Italien zu'. Hochmuth and Gysi were requested to liaise with Abusch on the matter.

Arranging to Leave

As ever, it was Hossinger who was instructed to communicate with Huchel. He did this by letter on 18 January 1971.[147] The wholly unexpected and joyous news that Huchel could leave was couched in the usual bureaucratic jargon, 'Die Regierung der Deutschen Demokratischen Republik sich bereit erklärt hat, einen von Ihnen gestellten Antrag, mit Ihrer Familie nach Italien zu übersiedeln, zu genehmigen'. It was for Huchel, Hossinger explained, to submit such an application to Abusch. Hossinger's letter was delivered by hand by Meißner, who was also charged with the job of advising and supporting Huchel in order to ensure that the departure to Italy could be arranged as smoothly as possible. Huchel had surely not forgotten that, a decade earlier, it was Meißner, together with Dietzel, who had produced the report on the content of *Sinn und Form* requested by Abusch. Yet, this was not an occasion to bear grudges. Monica Huchel recalls her husband's reaction, 'Huchel war plötzlich wie umgewandelt und lud – was ich nun wieder übertrieben fand – die beiden Abgesandten mit erstaunlicher Courtoisie zum Sherry ein und ließ Tee servieren'.[148] Amidst their feelings of euphoria, it was not lost on Huchel and his wife that the GDR now wanted to see the back of them as soon as possible. It was imperative that they should state their conditions clearly and firmly.

Huchel replied to Hossinger on 30 January, asking him to forward to Abusch his application to leave, which he had drafted in the form of a letter accompanied by other documents.[149] Rather than formulating any new application, Huchel, having expressed his thanks to the government, simply enclosed for Abusch's attention a copy of the letter that he had addressed to the Academy on 3 September 1967. He went on to explain that he needed to travel via Munich. Academy colleagues in the West had promised him help in dealing with the necessary formalities for a lengthy stay and the temporary storage of his library and other items such as furniture, carpets and linen. He enclosed CVs, photos and application forms for himself, his wife and son. His wife's children from her first marriage were now adults and they elected to stay in the GDR. He pointed to the prominent positions that he had occupied in the GDR from 1945 to 1962 and to the fact that in 1951 (sic) he had moved to the GDR from Charlottenburg with his whole household. He thus expected a co-operative approach on the part of the authorities. He insisted that his step-daughter should be permitted to look after his house on his behalf and to live in it. His old friend Arendt would have the use of the three furnished rooms in the upper storey as a second home. Arendt suffered from chronic bronchitis and had been looking for a suitable second home outside the city for years. Arendt would have use of the rooms free of charge. He asked Abusch to arrange for the housing commission for the Potsdam area to be informed of these things. Finally, Huchel requested permission to travel to the West Berlin Academy for three days in order to deal with formalities such as visas. He had been attempting to contact the West Berlin Academy by phone for the past week but no connection had been made for him. Abusch responded to this request and Huchel was able to travel to West Berlin in early March.

Abusch notified Friedrich Dickel, the Interior Minister, of arrangements that had been agreed for the Huchels, asking him to put things in place at his end.[150] From 13 February onwards, the telephone tapping resumed, as the Huchels went about the business of procuring and filling in the appropriate forms.[151] Blacher wrote to Wolf, thanking him and the East Berlin Academy for their recent efforts, and to Huchel, expressing his pleasure at the good news.[152] Meanwhile, the Huchels maintained their links with the small circle of GDR non-conformists, including Biermann, Hagen, the Arendts, the Jankas and Rolf Schneider.

Huchel's trip to West Berlin, his first in a decade, was a great shock.[153] Zimmermann and another employee of the West Berlin Academy looked after him the whole day.[154] They went to the Italian consulate, where they discovered that the application would take three to four weeks to process. He would initially only be able to have a visa for a relatively short period of time. It would be necessary to extend the permit once they were in Italy. Erich Bendheim, a lawyer resident in Rome, who acted on behalf of the West Berlin Academy, managed to expedite matters.[155] The fact that the Academy would be supporting him financially strengthened his case. Huchel was shocked at the prices in the West. He was appalled to learn what it cost to rent a flat in West Berlin. They had lunch at the Giraffe restaurant in the Hansa quarter, near the West Berlin Academy, where they had to pay as much as 11 marks for a main course. His hosts had wanted him to see the Ku'damm but he had refused. Shortly afterwards, he told Rolf Schneider that he had not enjoyed West Berlin at all.[156] Wild horses would not drag him to live in West Germany. He was nonetheless looking forward to leaving for Italy, as he explained to Schneider,

> Mein Entschluß ist immer noch der alte, der steht fest. Für meinen Sohn ist es natürlich erfreulich, daß er in Rom zuende studieren kann bzw. endlich studieren kann, was er will.

Aber ich möchte sagen, eine Hochstimmung von Freude ist nicht vorhanden. Das wird aber noch kommen, denn dazu bin ich jetzt noch zu erschöpft.

On the day in West Berlin, Huchel and Zimmermann went with Hans Mayer and Jürgen Becker to visit Uwe Johnson in Friedenau. Johnson invited them to have dinner. Huchel was quiet, Johnson talked about a trip to Leipzig and advised Huchel to write down for the authorities everything that he wished to take with him. He returned home that evening. He would be able to go over twice more on the visa, which was valid until 22 March but he was afraid that two trips would not be enough. He was clear in his own mind that he wanted his removal to Italy to take place as quietly as possible, with a minimum of media involvement. In that respect, the East Berlin Academy was in agreement with him.

Meißner, meanwhile, performed his role on Huchel's behalf. He sent the Potsdam authorities a list of items that the Huchels wished to take with them.[157] They included ten pictures, among them drawings of Huchel by Meidner, Schwimmer and Stegemann; one wooden statue; Huchel's manuscripts; Monica Huchel's translation manuscripts; and 500 books from Huchel's library. Huchel later recalled,

Wir wollten einige Kisten, vor allem mit Korrespondenz, unkontrolliert mitnehmen. Ich hatte schon viertausend Briefe im Garten verbrannt, aber meine Frau kämpfte um diese Genehmigung mit dem Innenministerium, mit der Stadt Potsdam, mit der Akademie der Künste, und dann gelang auch das. (ii,381-2)

Monica Huchel looked after this and other matters, while Huchel travelled to West Berlin to arrange visas. She went to the Potsdam council offices, where she fired off a further list of items from their household that they wished to take.[158] She clearly felt that she had been left alone to deal with many matters. On one occasion, she complained that while she was getting on with things, he was sitting upstairs in his room, sifting through his past, old issues of *Sinn und Form*. He was, she said, filled with 'Wehmütigkeit und Erbitterung'.[159] That was not a bit of help to her. Huchel was considering his future as well as his past. Just before he left for the West he received an offer from Suhrkamp.[160] The general contract with S. Fischer had long been in abeyance, and Huchel now moved to Suhrkamp, who published his two final collections, *Gezählte Tage* in 1972 and *Die neunte Stunde* in 1979.

Having made good progress in procuring visas and in arranging the transport of their possessions, the Huchels were aiming to leave in late April or early May. One of the few outstanding issues was Huchel's membership of the East Berlin Academy. He told Meißner that he expected to remain a member and would be restating his old claims.[161] On 27 April, on schedule, the Huchels left a snow-bound Potsdam by train. He would later write,

Am Tage meines Fortgehns

entweichen die Dohlen

durchs glitzende Netz der Mücken.

Am Acker klebt

der Rauch des Güterzuges,

der Himmel regenzwirnig. (i,221)

He also depicted their 'exodus', as he called it, in a letter to Henry Beissel on 17 August 1971,

Meine Frau stand vom frühen Morgen an bis in den späten Nachmittag hinein im Schlamm des Güterbahnhofs Wildpark, um die paar Bücher- und Manuskriptkisten, die paar Klamotten von Möbeln, die wir mitnehmen durften, unter den Augen des Zolls verladen zu lassen. Ein Kreis von Freunden, es waren etwa dreißig, ließ es sich nicht nehmen, trotz meiner Warnungen, uns an den Zug Potsdam-Hauptbahnhof zu bringen; die Stasi gab Ehrengeleit, sie fuhr im Auto hinter der Kolonne der Aufrechten her. (ii,355)

Monica Huchel writes that Huchel won over the removal men with a 100 mark tip.[162] She travelled with them to the goods station and then returned to Wilhelmshorst for a farewell drink. From the circle of friends, it was Janka who spoke the words of farewell, which he confined to one sentence, 'Wenn ich hier in der DDR zu bestimmen hätte, so einen wie Huchel hätte ich nie gehen lassen'. No more needed to be said: the affair simply demonstrated the illegitimacy of the SED leadership's crass authoritarianism. A number of friends gathered at Potsdam station to see them off at dusk. They included the Hesses, who had driven them, Fritz Rudolf Fries, Franz Fühmann, Henryk Bereska and Uwe Grüning.[163] The Huchels left them behind on the platform, as they set off into the night on their trip to the South.

Three days later, Wolf met with Abusch. They agreed that, following his departure, Huchel's full membership of the Academy had come to an end.[164] It is a measure of the paternalistic self-delusion of those in positions of power in the GDR that Abusch and Wolf concluded that the possibility of corresponding membership depended on Huchel's behaviour in the West and whether he published in the GDR. On 20 May 1971, the Academy's Presidium invoked paragraph 6 of its statutes to declare that Huchel was no longer a member.[165] This was despite the fact that, as Hossinger had noted, Huchel had been very guarded in his comments since leaving.[166] With one exception, in 1977, Huchel maintained this reserve about the GDR state, although, quite understandably, he did give voice to his complaints at his own individual treatment. He never again sought to publish in the GDR. Only shortly after his death did his work appear there again, in the form of a small selection of his verse in *Sinn und Form*. Any thoughts that he might re-state his claims with the East Berlin Academy were soon forgotten. At the age of 68, he embarked on his new life in the West, not without great apprehension as to what life in the capitalist West might mean. He had almost exactly a decade left in which to make up for the time lost during the previous decade. Despite failing health and residual bitterness, he made great use of this late and wholly unexpected opportunity to live and work among people who had come to admire him for his resoluteness and artistic integrity.

The Struggle against Time Lost

Munich

The Huchels' train travelled into the night, crossing the German-German border into Bavaria and speeding on to Munich, where they arrived the following morning. They were picked up from the station by Clemens Podewils, Secretary of the Bavarian Academy, which looked after the procurement of West German passports. Monica Huchel shielded her husband from reporters, telling them that he would not give any interviews. Their first shock on arriving at their guesthouse in Schwabing was 'wie unsinnig teuer die billige Pension war'. (ii,355) The trip to West Berlin had not been sufficient to prepare Huchel for the shock, especially since, as he later claimed, he had 'sehr wenig Geld, denn ich fuhr nur mit zehn Westmark los. Mein Sohn bekam überhaupt kein Reisegeld'. (ii,389) In truth, everything was paid for and, as we have seen, the protestation of poverty had always been part of the Bohemian peasant poet's make-up. The Huchels were welcomed by Joachim Kaiser, Vice-President of the West German PEN Club and chief literary critic of the *Süddeutsche Zeitung*. Kaiser's report, 'Peter Huchel in München', appeared in the weekend edition of the paper.[1] It was a deliberately understated piece, in keeping with Huchel's own wishes. Among the welcoming party was Hans Mayer, who invited them to join him for a meal at the exclusive Vierjahreszeiten Hotel.[2]

Arrangements had been put in place by the Bavarian Academy, in conjunction with the Bonn Interior Ministry, for the Huchels to stay at the Villa Massimo in Rome. It had belonged to the Prussian state from 1910 and had been used as a residence for those artists awarded the Prussian Academy of Arts' Rome Prize. Since 1956, it had belonged to the Federal Republic. As the Deutsche Akademie Villa Massimo, part of the Stiftung Preußischer Kulturbesitz, it once again became a residence for twelve painters, sculptors, architects, writers and composers, who pursued their work there for up to a year. Before the Huchels set off for Rome, Podewils asked them where they would live when they returned from Italy. Despite Huchel's dream of settling in an Italian village, the Huchels certainly intended to return; it was a question of what part of West Germany they would settle in. Monica Huchel knew that Huchel would prefer North Germany, but for once she placed her own preferences above his, telling Podewils that she would prefer the South. Podewils promised to get in touch with Erhart Kästner, who lived in Staufen near Freiburg, and Monica Huchel left the matter in Podewils' capable hands.

Rome

The Huchels left most of their household goods and Huchel's manuscripts in storage in Munich and continued on their journey to Rome via the Tyrol and Venice. Huchel would later express his sense of gratitude to those individuals and institutions that helped to alleviate the difficulties of his translation from East to West so late in his life, when his family was – as he put it – without any visible means of support. Beyond the Bonn Interior Ministry's provision of the flat free of charge, Huchel pointed to Hermann Kesten's role. Kesten, a Rome resident of long standing and a bitter opponent of the GDR, who in the 1920s had worked for Kiepenheuer in Potsdam, took Huchel under his wing. He introduced him to Ignazio Silone and Benedetto Croce's daughter, Elena.[3] Together, they procured a small pension for Huchel from the Italian state. (ii,389) When he later met his daughter in Sweden, Huchel sported a leather jacket that Silone had given him. Kesten conveyed his impressions of Huchel to Hans Bender in a letter of 24 September 1971,

> Ich schreibe, und erwarte Peter Huchel, der zu uns kommen will, heute abend, ich las
> heute wieder einen großen Teil seiner Gedichte in der Piper-Auswahl, *Die Sternenreuse*.
> Es sind schöne Gedichte, kein reiches, aber ein strenges Talent ... Huchel kam und
> erzählte, teils von 1933, teils aus der DDR, erschreckende Erinnerungen, teils von 1971,
> und der BRD. Er ist voller Bitterkeit und Charme, voller Freundlichkeit und Ressentiment,
> man merkt ihm die abgesperrten Jahre in der DDR an.[4]

The melancholy that was always a presence in Huchel's charismatic features had hardened through experience into a bitterness that he made no effort to conceal. Kesten's characterisation captures well the mix of that bitterness and charm upon which many people remarked who met Huchel after he came to the West. Among them were his fellow German artists at the Villa Massimo and the permanent residents, the Wolkens. Initially, Huchel evidently enjoyed the attention that was paid to him by other residents, who included Rolf Haufs and Friedrich C. Delius. He talked about life at the Villa Massimo in an interview published in the summer of 1971, saying,

> Eigentlich bin ich recht dankbar, daß ich hier von den Stipendiaten der Deutschen
> Akademie überrannt worden bin. Sie besuchten mich jeden Tag, und so konnte ich mich
> mit den Problemen dieser Leute beschäftigen und erfahren, was auf dem kulturellen Sektor
> in Westdeutschland passiert. Gleichzeitig wurde damit eine gewisse Leere verdrängt, die
> wohl jeden anfällt, der seine Heimat verlassen mußte. (ii,385)

Radical left-wing politics were the fashion at the time among West German artists. Someone of Huchel's background and stature was bound to arouse great interest. He had after all been on the scene in the Weimar Republic, when he had known Bloch and Benjamin, and after the war he had collaborated with figures such as

Brecht. Yet, if they expected to encounter a sophisticated exponent of Marxist theory, they were bound to be disappointed. Huchel simply was not the person that many of them assumed him to be. Some were outraged, whilst others were charmed all the same. There are several accounts of Huchel's encounters with the New Left in Rome and later in West Germany. One of them is Ursual Bode's 'Beim Lesen eines Gedichts. Erinnerung an eine Begegnung mit Peter Huchel', which depicts the Villa Massimo scene just a month or so after Huchel's arrival.[5] He himself was usually dressed in cord trousers and a pullover, his grey hair combed forward, his manner both friendly and serious. Bode writes of the other residents,

'Wir treffen uns bei Huchel', sagten die jungen Stipendiaten. Sie kamen mit ihren Frauen, mit Freunden und Zufallsgästen. Huchels Teestunden waren beliebt. Man saß notfalls auf Mäuerchen. Huchels Frau beantragte bei der Direktion zusätzliche Sitzgelegenheiten ... Autofahrten in die Campagna, Besichtigungen, Empfänge. Huchels Ausflugsberichte waren amüsant. Sie klangen ironisch, im ganzen aber froher, als manche seiner kritischen Gäste wahrhaben wollten. Es war unausweichlich, daß man bald über Politik sprach. Bundesdeutsche Marxismustheorien gegen jahrzehntelange Erfahrungen mit der SED. Man redete aneinander vorbei. Nicht alle schienen es zu merken.

Huchel confided to Bode his disappointment that, having come to talk to him about his work, people talked about politics all the time. The message that Huchel had for the West German New Left was based on bitter experience of his life under actually existing socialism, which had little in common with the political theories then in fashion.

Looking back on these exchanges in the interview with Rudolph, he was forthright in his criticisms, speaking of these West German acquaintances as

linksradikale Elemente, junge Künstler, Maoisten, auch einige Stalinisten, und die Leute besuchten mich andauernd. Das begann schon um 9 Uhr morgens, und es kam immer ein Trupp und ein anderer Trupp, und es ging immer bis in die Nacht hinein. Ich muß ganz offen sagen, ich habe sehr viel von den Leuten gelernt. Aber ich habe da auch bittere Erfahrungen gemacht. Nämlich, daß man seine eigenen Erfahrungen wohl mitteilen kann, aber niemals vermitteln.

This final statement became Huchel's mantra in the early to mid-1970s when he travelled the length and breadth of the Federal Republic on reading tours, travelling, too, to a number of Western European countries. He could not conceal his exasperation that young West Germans showed so little willingness to comprehend what it had meant to live under the SED regime. He explained to Rudolph,

> Die Orthodoxie des politischen Apparats, der sich unvermeidbar früher oder später einstellt. Die Erfahrung der 'neuen Klasse', der Funktionärklasse, der Apparatschiks, die reich leben und die ihre Diktatur heuchlerisch als 'Diktatur des Proletariats' bezeichnen ... Und das wird einem nicht geglaubt, wenn man manchmal etwas darüber erzählt, oder es wird nicht ernstgenommen.

Huchel knew what he was talking about. He, too, had long been a member of a new class in the GDR, the intellectual elite of artists and technocrats that had been created on the model of the Soviet nomenclature, however unorthodox his behaviour and that of others in that class. That was all behind him now. There was a great gulf between Huchel and the New Left. Helmut Mader referred to 'dem pervertierten Idealistendorf Villa Massimo', where he got to know Huchel, of whom wrote, 'Huchel winkte ... müde ab, wenn ich das Thema Kunstpessimismus/Kunstskepsis zur Debatte brachte. Gut, was sollte er damit anfangen, der sein Leben lang sich selbst und die Welt nie anders als mittels Kunst begriff? Die jungen Progressisten wurden sauer oder aggressiv bei dem Thema'.[6] Huchel was by now somewhat world-weary. Mader recalls an excursion,

> Am Friedhof an der Cestinuspyramide in Rom wirkte er an den Gräbern von Keats und Shelley müde, fast gelangweilt ... saß er rauchend vor irgendeiner Lehmgrube für sanitäre Anlagen und stocherte in einem Loch in der Erde herum. Das Grab von Gramsci, für das er sich zunächst interessiert hatte, wollte er gar nicht mehr sehen.

Another young writer who met Huchel in Rome was Günter Herburger. Herburger was later awarded the Peter Huchel Prize for Poetry. Far from acknowledging any affinities or sense of allegiance, Herburger began his acceptance speech by stating the great distance between himself and Huchel, whose imagery he also criticised 'Huchel bleibt mir fremd. Er ist ein verschlossener Meister. Ich habe wenig von ihm gelesen'.[7] Herburger recalled Huchel in Rome,

> Ich sah Huchel einmal. Er stieg rauchend eine gewundene Steintreppe herauf, hinter sich seine Frau, die, glaube ich, blond war, beschützend, und dabei sollte es bleiben. Danach kam ein Sohn, der inzwischen Orientalist geworden ist. Damals war er verstört. Wir saßen im Söller eines alten Hauses in den Abruzzen zwischen den Dörfern Olévano und Bellegra. Huchel sah wie ein Indianer aus: viel graue Haare, große Lippen, im Gesicht längs- und

querverlaufende Runzeln. Es war faszinierend. Entweder stammte er aus Kanada oder aus Kamtschatka.

Huchel never lost the charisma attested to by Herburger, who refused to be won over by it for the poetry. It must be said that by the time Herburger spoke, Stephan Huchel was dead and a description of him simply as 'verstört' is brutally uncharitable. Stephan Huchel possessed a sharp intelligence and an outstanding memory, both of which were deployed in the study of ancient and modern languages. Certainly, physical problems were compounded by an extreme reticence in his dealings with others, yet the crude term 'verstört' does not begin adequately to capture his manner.

Huchel was more at home in Rome with figures of his own generation such as Kesten. At the time, an old friend, Ingeborg Bachmann, was living in Rome with Max Frisch, who had visited Huchel in Wilhelmshorst in 1970. Huchel later told Marie Luise Kaschnitz that in Rome he had bumped into Bachmann, 'als sie mit einem ihm unbekannten Mann auf einer Terrasse saß. Herbeigerufen, habe Ingeborg Bachmann lachend gesagt, gerade in diesem Augenblick habe Max Frisch ihr eine Liebeserklärung machen wollen'.[8] For his part, Frisch later wrote,

> In einem italienischen Restaurant kommt ein Deutscher an unseren Tisch, ich sehe eine Begrüßung voll Freude über den Zufall dieser Begegnung und höre eine halbe Stunde lang zu; sie stellt mich nicht vor und ich stelle mich nicht vor, weil ich weiß, daß sie es nicht möchte, und er, Peter Huchel, wagt sich auch nicht vorzustellen, obschon er mich erkannt hat.[9]

The dynamics of the relations between these three personalities were evidently such that Huchel could not even acknowledge Frisch, whose visit had been part of the sequence of events that had led to his departure from the GDR.

He had viewed Italy as providing a contrast with Germany. He wrote to Henry Beissel on 17 August 1971 of his enthusiasm for the Italian countryside and for its ancient culture,

> Auf jeden Fall sind wir recht munter, soweit die afrikanische Sonne des römischen Sommers es zuläßt, wir fahren mit Freunden durch die Campagna, nach Viterbo, nach Fregene, Tarquinia, Genzano, es gibt überall Wundervolles zu bestaunen, von dem schönen Umbrien ganz zu schweigen. Und hin und wieder haben wir doch Heimweh nach der Erde, in der ich mich nicht verscharren lassen wollte. (ii,355-6)

In this environment he wrote new poetry. He was able to achieve some distance from the struggles of the 1950s and 1960s, reflecting more deeply on experience. The poetry of the early 1970s is not only infused with the impressions of the Mediterranean world, but also foregrounds again the poetic self of the Brandenburg childhood. As we saw near the beginning of this study, in the poem 'Ölbaum und Weide' (i,187) the late juxtaposition of the two worlds yields a radically transformed version of the myth of the Brandenburg childhood. The poem was written in Argentario in September 1971. (i,422) As night descends on the Mediterranean world, 'Es ankern Schatten in der Bucht'. The shadows emerge as a threatening presence from the world he has left behind,

> Sie kommen wieder, verschwimmend im Nebel,
>
> durchtränkt
>
> vom Schilfdunst märkischer Wiesen,
>
> die wendischen Weidenmütter,
>
> die warzigen Alten
>
> mit klaffender Brust,
>
> am Rand der Teiche,
>
> der dunkeläugig verschlossenen Wasser,
>
> die Füße in die Erde grabend,
>
> die mein Gedächtnis ist.

The trauma of Huchel's origins is thus dramatically re-enacted in the Italian context. That context might provide an escape from the material constraints of Brandenburg life, but the deeper problems of his existence returned to haunt him in a classic demonstration of Freud's thesis of the vengeful return of the repressed. The terrifying 'wendischen Weidenmütter' are a counterpart of the earlier, beloved 'Klettenmarie'. Both images derive from compounds, which are formed through the merging of the botanical and the female. Marie Huchel takes her revenge as the threatening presence of the feared female swamps the 'Hof' of the obsessively cultivated memory of the rural idyll. Italy represented freedom not only from the restrictions of the 1960s in the GDR; in the Mediterranean world Huchel looked into the depths of his being in a way that he had never before dared to as an adult.

'Ölbaum und Weide' was not an isolated composition. During the year in Rome, Huchel wrote two other poems which reveal a truth hidden behind the accustomed mask. They are 'M.V.' and 'Unter der blanken Hacke des Monds', both of which were examined in the early stages of this study. The former treats his heavy-drinking father's death, which is described as ending an insignificant existence, the latter the impossibility of acquiring substantial knowledge about the world, and specifically about the childhood world of memory, which previously presented itself to his poetic imagination as the rich, rural world of Alt-Langerwisch. Like 'Ölbaum und Weide', 'M.V.' and 'Unter der blanken Hacke des Monds' were collected the following year in *Gezählte Tage*. The constitute perhaps the most remarkable of the late compositions, which were triggered by Huchel's removal to Italy.

Re-affirming the Poetic Persona and Socialist Credentials

In the first of the many interviews that he gave in the West, Huchel outlined basic biographical details that were quite familiar and would remain constant components in his routine interview manner. It is striking that at the time when he was writing verse such as 'Ölbaum und Weide' his comments included the following, 'Die Kindheit war für mich der Urgrund. Da meine Mutter lungenkrank war, hat eine Magd mich aufgezogen. Meine Welt war "heil". So wurde ich ein Märker'. (ii,370) That basic discourse was by now so firmly established in Huchel's self-image that any questioning of it in the late poetry could only take place from within the very terms of that discourse. He went on in that first interview to relate his conversion to left-wing politics through the Kapp Putsch. He referred to the danger for him as a nature poet of being appropriated by the Nazis and to the isolation and the insults, such as 'Arbeiterverräter' and 'Nuttendichter', to which he was subjected after 1962.

On various occasions, Huchel maintained that despite his disillusion with the GDR system and his disagreements with the New Left, he remained a socialist. He talked of the 'absolute Kleinbürgerlichkeit des DDR-Staates' and added, 'Ich bin heute immer noch Sozialist, wenn auch nicht im Sinne Ost-Berlins oder Moskaus, und wenn ich heute 20 Jahre alt wäre, wäre ich gewiß ein Linksstudent'.[10] In reply to Hansjakob Stehle's suggestion that with *Sinn und Form* Huchel had preferred to publish Marxist essays although he himself was not a Marxist, Huchel said, 'Das würde ich nicht so sagen. Natürlich konnte ich diese Art von Vulgär-Marxismus nicht übernehmen'. (ii,376) Maintaining the line established in the early 1950s in his statement in Zak's monograph, Huchel suggested further that 'Meine Lyrik hat sich doch stets mit dem landarmen Proletariat, mit Zigeunern, Schnittern, Mägden, Ziegelstreichern beschäftigt und war nie eine reine Naturlyrik. Natürlich war ihre Aussage nicht konform mit der damaligen Parteilinie'. (ii,376) In conversation with Rudolph, Huchel declared his support for Brandt's *Ostpolitik*, while warning agains 'Osteuphorie'. Asked where he stood politically, Huchel said, 'Ja, bei – in keiner Partei'. He went on to explain what for him was the core of socialism, 'Das Recht, das Maß persönlicher Freiheit in Anspruch zu nehmen, das, wie ich glaube, jedem Menschen zusteht, ist für mich das erste Recht, bedeutet eigentlich für mich Sozialismus'. He made exactly the same point in another interview. (ii,386) In the light of Huchel's own experience in the GDR, where his own personal freedom had been drastically curtailed, such an emphasis is more than understandable. Yet

Huchel's statement is surely more a classic definition of liberalism than any clear espousal of socialist values, with their fundamental belief in the need to temper individualism through action taken on behalf of the collective. With that, we are back with the discussion of Huchel's ethical idealism, the paradox of the apolitical socialist of the 1920s. Only a quite elastic definition of socialism could embrace Huchel's values, and Marxism certainly could not. Until 1977, when suddenly he described the Federal Republic as 'der freieste Staat, den es überhaupt auf der Welt gibt', by contrast with which the GDR was a 'Schrotthaufen', (ii,396) Huchel retained a guarded scepticism in his statements about the West's capacity to guarantee such freedom, since capitalism as a system was based on relatively unfettered exploitation. He was clearly concerned about the dominance of finance over everyday life in the West and about the way, as he said, that the market forced writers to publish before their work was actually ready to be released. Such pressure must have been most unwelcome for someone like himself who agonised greatly over publishers' deadlines.

Prizes

From his base in Italy, he undertook his first visits to the Federal Republic since 1961, apart from the short stop-over in Munich. He told Beissel of his plans on 17 August 1971,

> Wie lange wir hierbleiben werden, wissen wir nicht. Mitte September fahre ich ein paar Tage nach Wien, Ende Oktober nach Darmstadt und Anfang nächsten Jahres werden wir uns wohl in der Umgebung von Freiburg/Breisgau eine feste Bleibe suchen müssen, damit endlich Stephan sein Orientalistik-Studium beginnen kann. (ii,355)

In Darmstadt, Huchel was awarded the Johann-Heinrich-Merck-Preis für Literarische Kritik by the Deutsche Akademie für Sprache und Dichtung. He was also elected a member of the Darmstadt Academy. The prize was awarded primarily in recognition of his achievements with *Sinn und Form*.[11]

Back in Rome in December, Huchel sent his friend Kundera a card, in which he described his recent travel itinerary, which had taken in Berlin, Alsace, Frankfurt and Darmstadt.[12] The visit to Frankfurt had been to his new publisher, Suhrkamp. Erhart Kästner had been busy on his behalf in Staufen. Kästner's wife, Anita, knew Franz Armin Morat, a patron of the arts, who undertook to rent a house for the Huchels to live in on the Bötzen near Staufen. When Huchel's last collection, *Die neunte Stunde*, appeared in 1979, it was dedicated to Morat. Huchel later commented on the arrangement for accommodation, which he took up in preference to Marion Gräfin Dönhoff's offer to live in a draughty North German Wasserschloß,[13]

Ich konnte mir doch keine Wohnung leisten. Also trat ein Herr an mich heran, der in Freiburg lebt und ein Mäzen ist. Es war sehr schwierig. Ich wollte mich nicht unterstützen lassen. Schließlich haben wir uns geeinigt, und er zahlt mir für die nächsten Jahre das Haus, in dem ich wohne. Er hätte mich auch für die nächsten Jahre so unterztützt, daß ich davon hätte leben können. Das habe ich aber abgelehnt – vielleicht aus einer falschen Bescheidenheit heraus. (ii,390)

Huchel reported to Kundera that he had taken his manuscripts out of store in Munich and was preparing a collection for publication by Suhrkamp the following autumn. He would send his friend poems to translate in the New Year. As things turned out, no Czech edition of *Gezählte Tage* appeared.

It was also in December 1971, back in Rome, that Huchel wrote to his Caputh friends, the Hesses. He described the descent into Tegel airport, West Berlin, at the end of October, when he had seen Potsdam and the Havel lakes, 'vorbei, vorbei, und dort unten wohnen Freunde, für Dich unerreichbar'.[14] In early November, the press was reporting the award to Huchel of the West Berlin Academy's 'Arbeitsstipendium des Berliner Kunstpreises'. The jurors were Jürgen Becker, Joachim Günther and Uwe Johnson. The prize was worth 10,000 marks. This distinction, following the Darmstadt prize, was a further major show of support for a writer who by the late 1970s would, quite remarkably, become the most honoured of all writers in the history of the Federal Republic.[15]

Shortly after Christmas, Huchel was once again on his travels to receive a literary award, this time the Austrian State Prize for European Literature. Previous winners included W.H.Auden and Eugène Ionesco. The prize, worth as much as 18,000 marks, was awarded in Vienna on 26 January 1972. For Hilde Spiel, who accompanied Huchel during his stay, 'ging er immer noch umher wie Kaspar Hauser, trotz der vergangenen zehn Monate in Rom'.[16] Huchel would never adjust to the pace and pressures of city life in the West, which he clearly feared, principally due to the number of cars and their speed. When required to perform in public, Huchel adopted a manner which, whilst certainly friendly and gracious, preserved some great distance between himself and his audience. This was underscored by a quite monotonous delivery, which made no concessions. He had no desire to dispel the mystique of his 'otherness'. In his recollections of his first visit of 1925-6 to Vienna in his acceptance speech in January 1972, he cultivated the image, if not of Kaspar Hauser, then of the innocent farm boy abroad for the first time in the big city, 'Ich kam aus der preußischen Provinz, aus der Mark Brandenburg, es war meine erste Reise ins Ausland, ich kam vom Lande'. (ii,313) It goes without saying that no one could have recognised Potsdam in that description. He referred to his years of isolation in the GDR, yet did so not in order to attack the GDR but to excuse himself for not replying to the invitations from Austria that he had been sent during those years: they had simply not reached him. As he had in 1959 in Hamburg, he referred to the motto that he had adopted for his poetry from St Augustine, offering a similar gloss on it in the light of experience, 'Wir alle wissen, eine Bahn der Verwüstung ist durch diesen Hof gegangen'. (ii,314) In conclusion, he illustrated his message through reference to the bleak final lines of his poem 'Die Nachbarn', (i,203) which read,

> Keiner will Asche sein.
>
> Keinem gelingt es,
>
> die Münze zu prägen,
>
> die noch gilt
>
> in eisiger Nacht.

His audience might reflect that his poetry itself gave the lie to the message of those final lines.

Staufen: Marie Luise Kaschnitz

The Huchels' finances, which Jens continued to manage, were considerably boosted through the Darmstadt, Berlin and Vienna prizes. For the time being, they were able to continue their life in Rome. It was clear, though, that they would take up Morat's offer to move to Freiburg, which they did as the year in Rome came to an end. Shortly before they left, Huchel granted his most lengthy interview, to Hansjakob Stehle. It was published in *Die Zeit* on 2 May 1972. He talked at some length about *Sinn und Form*, the circumstances surrounding his resignation and the years of isolation.

The removal took place to Bötzenweg 51 in Staufen, where they lived for the next two years. Huchel was returning to the area where he had briefly studied in 1925 when he had got to know Joachim. Now, Stephan Huchel could look forward to a more settled period of study at the nearby Freiburg University. Erhart Kästner lived not far away from the Huchels, whose house was described as 'ein Terrassenhaus ... mit Vogesenblick und Swimming-pool. Die Kaschnitz kommt hier immer baden. Fünf Katzen streichen um Haus und Hosenbein'. (ii,395) Marie Luise Kaschnitz had two homes, one in Rome, the other in Bollschweil near Staufen. She was staying in Bollschweil just after the Huchels moved in. The two poets had been published together in *Die Dame* as long ago as the mid-1930s but had never actually come together. The closest they had come had been the planned reading in the late 1950s, when Kaschnitz had cried off. Their meeting finally took place in May 1972. Kästner took Huchel over to Bollschweil by car, and, as Kaschnitz's biographer, Dagmar von Gersdorff, puts it, 'gemeinsam saßen sie die halbe Nacht unter den Linden im Park bei nicht enden wollenden Gesprächen'.[17] Huchel and Kaschnitz fell for each other. Kaschnitz wrote to her daughter shortly afterwards,

Ich war glücklich, weil ich den Peter Huchel so liebe, er war auch zufrieden, aber still. Kästner führte mit seinen Gerhart-Hauptmann-Erinnerungen – er war sein Sekretär – das große Wort. Dann hat aber Huchel doch noch von *Sinn und Form* und seinen Erlebnissen erzählt.

As von Gersdorff writes, Huchel was quite different from the other men whom Kaschnitz had known, 'Weder verfügte er über die ubiquitäre Eloquenz des geistvollen Dolf Sternberger, noch über die bestechend scharfe analytische Intelligenz Adornos, er war vielmehr eher schweigsam, ein eigensinniger Mensch und grüblerischer Einzelgänger'. Yet they felt a great sense of affinity. They shared a similar taste: Bachmann and Eich were the living poets they most admired. Together, they would mourn the deaths of Eich in December 1972 and of Bachmann in October 1973, before Kaschnitz herself died in 1974. While Huchel had met Bachmann again in Rome, he had not seen Eich since his move to the West. As Huchel later told Hans Dieter Schmidt, he was deeply sorrowful over Eich's loss, 'In ihm sah er einen Dichter, der ähnliche Wege ging wie er selbst. Eichs Tod habe ihn 1972 schwer getroffen, tagelang habe er überhaupt nichts Sinnvolles unternehmen können'.[18]

Huchel's late poetry continues the poetic dialogue with Eich that informs 'Das Zeichen'. Like 'Das Zeichen', 'Unter der blanken Hacke des Monds' and 'Keine Antwort' (i,204) record the ageing poet's inability to decipher the signs and symbols in the world that earlier so readily gave up their secrets. Huchel also entered into a poetic dialogue with Kaschnitz. As von Gersdorff points out, Huchel dedicated 'Die Reise' (i,215) to her. The poem, which was collected in *Gezählte Tage*, evokes a walk between high reeds by a lake, 'Es wehte kühl an meine Schläfen,/ als ging ich/ zwischen den Mähnen zweier Pferde'. Kaschnitz replied with,

> In deinen Gedichten die Geisterpferde
> Streifen mit ihrem Atem mein Gesicht.
> Deine Flüsse drängen
> Sich mir an den Weg
> Dein riesiger Lebensbaum
> Wirft seinen Schatten.

In his old age, Huchel was, indeed, an imposing presence. When she was in Bollschweil, Kaschnitz met Huchel nearly every day. Monica Huchel accepted the situation, placing herself discreetly in the background as Kaschnitz came to use the pool and spend time with Huchel.

Preparing the Ground for *Gezählte Tage*

Huchel was in great demand for reading trips and was determined in his attempt to make up for the time he had lost in the 1960s. Monica Huchel has described his state of mind as follows,

> Während ich mich in dem Haus niederließ, blieb Huchel weiter auf Reisen. Es war, als ob er sich die neun Jahre aus dem Leib reisen müsse. Huchel war ein Gekränkter und hat diese Kränkung nie mehr überwunden. Er hat im wesentlichen nur in diesen letzten Jahren publizieren können und empfand die neun Jahre als gestohlene Zeit. Ich habe mir immer gewünscht, er könne sich auf seine gegenwärtige Situation einlassen, auf das, was jetzt war. Aber er war davon getrieben, sich etwas zurückholen zu müssen, was er aber nie bekam.[19]

What exactly was it that Huchel vainly sought to retrieve? For all the honours and late recognition in the Federal Republic, he had in the 1950s created with *Sinn und Form* a unique all-German institution for high-quality literature that was virtually synonymous with his name. The intellectual excitement generated through presiding over that project could never now be re-captured. In comparison, everything else was merely a consolation prize. He threw himself into his many reading tours as a means of trying to overcome the deep sense of regret and loss, from which, however, he could never free himself, as he confronted, too, the prospect of his death.

Among other places, he read at the Volkshochschule in Cologne in June 1972. He mentioned Trakl and Loerke as influences, adding pointedly, 'Daß ich auch von den Mystikern, vor allem Jakob Böhme herkomme, hat allerdings noch niemand bemerkt'.[20] In 'Alt-Seidenberg', (i,201) the name of the village in which Böhme was born, Huchel composed a poem for *Gezählte Tage*, in which he re-worked the Franckenberg legend of Böhme's youth.[21] Tending sheep with other youths on the Landeskrone hill near Görlitz, Böhme wandered off from the others. He discovered a vessel full of gold in a cave. Gripped by fear, he fled. Whenever he returned to the same spot with other youths, the entrance to the cave was sealed. Some years later, the gold was removed by a 'fremden Künstler', who subsequently suffered a wretched fate. In Huchel's poem, the young mystic Böhme is depicted as open to the revelations of God's presence through biblical imagery which is also referred to by Goldberg, 'sah er über der Stadt/ die glasige Kugel des Äthers,/ er hörte Stimmen in den Lüften,/ Posaunenstöße ...'. On discovering the gold, 'Er wich zurück und schlug/ das spukabwehrende Zeichen'. Resisting the temptation, Böhme is spared the later fate of the 'fremden Künstler'. The poem ends with the repetition of revelatory imagery, 'Der Hügel trug den Himmel/ auf steinigem Nacken'. Without becoming a late convert to Christianity, Huchel could use the Böhme story to illustrate the dangers in the artist's temptation to take the easy route by stealing the gold rather than to follow the hard path which might lead to genuine visionary insight. In that way, 'Alt-Seidenberg', like Huchel's statement in Cologne, re-affirms his position as the visionary poet of his beginnings in the 1920s. On a number of occasions in the final decade of his life, Huchel emphasised just how difficult that path leading to visionary insight had become for him.

In the autumn of 1972, Huchel returned to Berlin where he read to a packed audience one Sunday morning at the West Berlin Academy and attended a meeting of its Literature Section at which the election of members from the GDR was discussed.[22] Huchel's view in the discussion was that it was necessary to distinguish between authors who owed their reputation merely to their promotion by the SED and those who enjoyed a reputation despite the SED's enmity. As in Cologne, he read from older work as well as from his new collection, *Gezählte Tage*. He was, as he acknowledged, 'leider noch etwas sensationsumwittert'. (ii,390) As with *Chausseen Chausseen*, this was a factor in the reception of his new collection. He had worked on it in Rome, but, as usual, he made many changes at the proof stage. Nonetheless, it was ready for publication in the autumn of 1972, in time for the Frankfurt Book Fair.

Gezählte Tage

Nearly a decade had elapsed since the appearance of *Chausseen Chausseen*. Huchel's move to the West had aroused much attention, fuelling speculation as to what a fresh collection might contain. *Gezählte Tage* appeared some eighteen months after Huchel left Potsdam, the timing of its appearance confirming the rule that the poet needed to cross a threshold of some great moment in his life, which acted as a catalyst for his release of a whole collection.

Of all his book publications, *Gezählte Tage* was the one least plagued by his familiar indecision. Elisabeth Langgässer had feared for his talent shortly after the war, aware that even in the most propitious circumstances he would never be a prolific poet. Kesten's judgement had been not dissimilar. Since 1963, Huchel had lived without the professional commitments of radio or editorial work that, from the mid-1930s to the early 1960s, had generally had the first call on his energies. The conditions from 1963 to 1971 could not exactly be described as favourable, yet, as he approached his 70th birthday, Huchel summoned the creative energy to generate the distinctive strands of his late verse. Despite the upheaval of removal to Rome, then on to Staufen, he maintained a schedule which enabled him to fulfil his agreement with his publisher. He included poems already examined, such as those published in the West in the 1960s and early 1970s like 'Hubertusweg', in which he treated his biographical situation in quite direct terms, as well as other verse in which he made extensive use of biblical stories and other sources. The collection also contains a substantial number of poems that emerged from the surge of creativity that he experienced in Rome. These include a new group of Mediterranean poems and, as we have seen, fresh reflections upon his poetic re-casting of his family background and childhood.

Huchel's achievement was all the greater, given the fact that the years of struggle with the SED had taken their toll. Kesten was one of many who remarked upon how tired and embittered he was. His keen sense of irony had not left him and, as we have seen, some of the directly biographical verse of the 1960s is at points leavened by such a tone. That tone was, however, the exception in Huchel's poetry, which is distinguished throughout by a high seriousness from which he rarely deviated. *Gezählte Tage*, like *Chausseen Chausseen* before it and the later *Die neunte Stunde*, is permeated by a sense of the futility of the present world in the light of experience, and by a mood of finality, reflecting a well-nigh traumatic awareness of his own impending death. The dramatic tension of the Cold War struggle that informs *Chausseen Chausseen* is eclipsed in the last two collections by his preoccupation with the drama of death. The twilight of life is described amongst the debris of civilisation, in which shadowy, threatening figures torment the living, as in 'Im Gouvernement W.' (i,213),

> Taubstumme Boten
> besuchen dich nachts.
>
> ...
>
> Sie lachen lautlos
> und stechen mit eisernen Griffeln
> die Namen der Opfer
> in die Schläfe der Luft.

The ethical idealist's hope of earthly justice, which the early GDR briefly symbolised, has been brutally disabused. There is scant consolation to be had: little remains other than suffering and death, the final, awful enigma. In an absurd present, the truth which counts above all other things is the finality of death. The present is repeatedly evoked through wasteland imagery, in which death is all-pervasive. 'Antwort' (i,175) ends with the lines, 'Spinnen legen/ aufs Räderwerk/ die Schleier toter Bräute', (i,176) while 'Die Töpferinsel' (i,188) is described as a place 'wo tote Tage in den Kammern/ zerbrochener Öfen brennen' and where 'ein spitzer Rattenschädel/ liegt zwischen Scherben/ und schwarzer Spreu'.

Like the earlier collections, *Gezählte Tage* is characterised by careful architectural considerations. The editor's eye for the most telling juxtaposition of material remained sharp. Like *Chausseen Chausseen*, *Gezählte Tage* is divided into five sections. Huchel eschewed the obvious arrangement, which would have meant treating as a group poems such as those in which he reflected upon everyday life in Wilhelmshorst in the 1960s under what he described directly as the oppressive SED dictatorship. Yet, these poems have their place in each section, though less obviously in the third, unless one appreciates that his portrait of Richard III in 'Middleham Castle' was intended to allude to Ulbricht's rule. (i,423) The depiction of Huchel's everyday life in the 1960s is established as a recurrent theme for the reader, which runs alongside other concerns such as the Mediterranean and Brandenburg themes, which, too, are represented throughout the whole collection. Huchel's arrangement of material thus represents a refinement of the principle of juxtaposition as employed in *Chausseen Chausseen*, where thematically related groups of poems were placed in particular sections.

Gezählte Tage was passed over in silence in the GDR. In the West, there was little inclination to question the accepted wisdom that the collection was the work of a poet whose verse had been banned in the GDR. This image inevitably coloured the western reception. Once again, many reviews were cast in reverential tones, in acknowledgement of the poet's sufferings in the GDR. Once again, however, the critical reception was decidedly mixed. In his study of Huchel's poetry published in 1976, Vieregg maintained that the criticisms that were made actually derived from an inadequate understanding of the complex network of Huchel's imagery, which he set himself the task of elucidating. In that study and elsewhere Vieregg demonstrates an impressive grasp of interpretative issues. He explores elements of Huchel's 'private mythology' by means of an informed appreciation of literary allusions and references, which were deployed by a poet determined not to give up his secrets easily. Particularly in his interpretation of 'Ankunft', Vieregg shows how, through biblical allusion, Huchel created a vision of the impending destruction of a divided Germany as a punishment for the Holocaust.

We have commented upon the limitations of Vieregg's approach from a biographical point-of-view. Furthermore, by its own definition, Vieregg's approach could place only limited emphasis on stylistic matters, and it was precisely in that area that a number of critics voiced reservations. Some who had read his earlier work with enthusiasm made no secret of their growing perplexity. They did so in terms that moved the discussion on from Lehmann's and Holthusen's objections a decade earlier. Comparing Huchel with Eich and Krolow, Helmut Mader observed, 'Huchel hat sich verhältnismäßig zögernd und nie völlig von den formalen Techniken seiner ersten Veröffentlichungen gelöst'.[23] The fault lines showed in his stylistic development, and Huchel's verse was now subjected to a quite stringent examination by Hans-Jürgen Heise in his polemically-titled piece, 'Der Fall Peter Huchel'.[24] As in his earlier reviews of *Chausseen Chausseen* and *Die Sternenreuse*, Heise displayed a critical acuity absent from many others, revealing much greater knowledge than most of the historical complexities of Huchel's development and the way they had served to shape his poetic idiom. It is a pity that none of Heise's essays have been collected, since he identified some sources of unease felt by other readers.

Heise echoed Mader in arguing that Huchel occupied an earlier stage of stylistic development than Eich and Krolow. He wrote of Huchel's treatment of the Brandenburg Marches,

> die er nicht nur voller Nostalgie verklärte und mit archaischen Merkmalen versah, sondern der er auch Süd-, meist Italienmotive entgegenhielt, fast, als sei die mediterrane Welt imstande, jene Verheißungen zu erfüllen, die der karge und inzwischen auch verstandesdürre Norden nicht einmal mehr zu versprechen vermochte.

The Mediterranean 'wurde zu einem zeitlos-präsenten Synonym der Antike, aus deren stoizistischem Geist der Dichter Maßstäbe für die Gegenwart zu beziehen versuchte'. The mythical Brandenburg world of childhood and the Mediterranean acted as counterpoints in the moral condemnation of the present, in which the poet at times adopted a voice akin to that of a biblical prophet. Heise went on to argue that, for all Huchel's moral authority, 'sich hier ein Mann artikuliert, der niemals die – für die moderne Dichtung entscheidende – Auseinandersetzung mit dem Dadaismus und dem Surrealismus vollzogen hat'. Citing the Brandenburg imagery in 'Ölbaum und Weide', Heise suggested, provocatively, that Huchel's verse 'behält etwas Nornenhaftes, Nebelverhangenes'. We have seen how, for all Huchel's early contact with other cultures and his catholic tastes, his development was constrained by his emotional needs and by the political circumstances of the Third Reich and the GDR. The 'modernisation' of his idiom, beginning in the mid-1950s and accelerating in the early 1960s, remained only partially successful. Huchel's cultural conservatism, attested to by a number of critics, has its roots in his cloying attachment to the Alt-Langerwisch myth, the centrality of which the poet would continue to foreground throughout the 1970s.

Heise remarked upon the resulting crudity of some of Huchel's imagery which pleased more conservative readers, 'weil sie ihre Wirkung aus dem Repertoire überlieferter Vorstellungen und Metaphern bestreiten'. He cited the final section from 'Unterm Sternbild des Hercules', (i,176) which reads,

> Schon in die Nacht gebeugt,
> ins eisige Geschirr,
> schleppt Hercules
> die Kettenegge der Sterne
> den nördlichen Himmel hinauf.

One can also read lines such as 'Der Staat die Hacke,/ das Volk die Distel' in 'Hubertusweg', (i,222) while the ending of 'Winter' (i,193) reads, 'Zwei Frauen/ in schneeverkrusteten Schaffeljacken/ gehen nach Norden/ über das Eis'. Heise mentions, too, the middle section of 'Die Viper', (i,179) which contains the lines, 'Starren Hauptes,/ auf schartigem Schädel, wo Olegs Pferd/ in Fäulnis brennt,/ erwartest du die Nacht'.

Heise's polemic had the virtue of forcing into the open issues in need of discussion. Where there was crudity in some of Huchel's imagery, there was also still at times the tenderness of which Jens had spoken. 'Die Wasseramsel' (i,186) is a fine example of Huchel's great empathetic capacity, identifying his search for poetic language with the bird's dive into the water for its food. The poem ends, 'Goldwäscher, Fischer,/ stellt eure Geräte fort./ Der scheue Vogel/ will seine Arbeit lautlos verrichten'. A somewhat sardonic view of the poet is conveyed in another poem which projects human qualities onto a spider,

DIE FÄHIGKEIT

der Dichterspinnen,

aus eigener Substanz

das dünne Seil zu drehen,

auf dem sie dann geschickt

mit zwei Gesichtern

und einer Feder

durch alle Lüfte balancieren. (i,218)

This is a rare interruption of the accustomed tone, in which the inevitability of death blights the poetic vision, as in 'Abschied von den Hirten'. (i,209) It opens,

Nun da du gehst

vergiß die felsenkühle Nacht,

vergiß die Hirten,

sie bogen dem Widder den Hals zurück

und eine graubehaarte Hand

stieß ihm das Messer in die Kehle.

The drama of the poet's own sacrifice is symbolically enacted in the shepherds' killing of the ram, Huchel's birth sign Aries. The poem's second half rejects the alluring promises of the Creation myth, which encouraged the sublime vision of existence. The 'Zeichen' which the poet now heeds is the imperfect 'nicht zu Ende/ geschlagene Kreis aus Nadeln und Nässe'.

The terrifying enigma of death is *the* recurrent issue in the late verse, the subject upon which the poet engages in a sustained quarrel with himself. He gave some indication of his views on death in an interview shortly after coming to the West,

> Ich gehöre keiner Kirche an, bin aber im Grunde genommen gläubig – immer im Widerstand gegen die "Hofkirche". Ich glaube nicht an die Auferstehung des Fleisches, doch an eine höhere Ordnung. Und Sie werden auch bemerkt haben – vor allem in meinen neueren Gedichten – daß die Bibel zu meinen Lieblingsbüchern gehört. (ii,370)

Despite his rejection of the Christian message of the Resurrection, Huchel's poetry remained, to the end, suffused with the biblical imagery that he had assimilated in his childhood. 'November' (i,205) and 'Die Armut des Heiligen' (i,189) convey his rejection of Christianity. With its opening lines 'Wer du auch seist,/ geheiligtes Gebein,/ bleckender Kiefer', 'Die Armut des Heiligen' is reminiscent of the disputatious tone of the early composition 'Abraham'. The failure of Christianity is related to the unremitting suffering and injustice on earth, as illustrated in 'Lenz'. There is little solace to be gained from the present world, though the poet never gave up the view that through nature he could, as he put it in the 1970s, 'in die Transzendenz, in jede visionäre Landschaft vorstoßen'. (ii,332) As Goldberg had taught, despite the cultural decline everywhere in evidence, there was a residue of special places and special individuals with metaphysical powers. Though this is a quite isolated element in Huchel's late work, it is nonetheless significant.

Fritz J.Raddatz, who had known him in the GDR and had followed his development since the 1950s, saw in *Gezählte Tage* only Huchel's 'restlose(r) Bitterkeit. Die Klage ist nahezu stumm geworden, ein Schrei aus Stein. Diese Gedichte zeigen eine Verheerung, die an Celan und Beckett gemahnt: Passé défini'.[25] For Raddatz, (and there is much in this, if not the whole story) the collection represented the inversion of Huchel's earlier, dynamic perception of relations between man and nature. As a result, 'Es gibt kaum mehr Verbalkonstruktionen – und wenn, dann solche negativer Tätigkeit; die karsthafte Entwicklung von Mitleid zu Leid hat eine weitere Steigerung erfahren, von Tat zu Un-Tat'. Emptiness and barrenness had replaced the teeming plenitude of imagery in Huchel's early poetry. The self was left to contemplate the meaningless torment and suffering that characterised existence. With words that Huchel would echo in 1977 in one of his final poems 'Der Fremde geht davon', (i,258) Raddatz concluded, 'Peter Huchel klagt nicht einmal mehr an. Seine Gedichte haben eine geradezu maskenhafte Endgültigkeit, ziehen die Summe des Lebens von einem, der nie dazugehörte'.

The references to Celan and Beckett make sense to a degree, yet there is a key difference between them and Huchel in the treatment of the absurdity of existence. For them, the absurd is *the* condition of human existence. Any Utopian projection is, self-consciously, precisely that. In their post-Romantic sensibility, networks of imagery are drawn in the awareness of their artificiality. Something of this can be found in the late Huchel, but at bottom his poetic world is constituted differently. His temperament and emotional responses to his experiences served to determine his self-image as a poet who contributed to a Romantic regeneration of the German lyric, which throughout his life was remorselessly eroded. Other German poets of his generation had to confront the same problem. One can chart in their development a gradual acceptance of the absurd and the progressive abandonment of the Romantic attitude of their beginnings. Eich and Krolow are prime examples, not least in their ironic treatment of their early poetic practice. Again, Huchel's response was different. In contrast to them, Huchel could never free himself of the enormous emotional stake that he had in the mythical Alt-Langerwisch upbringing. His poetry was the expression of a deep existential bond, an autobiographical pact with that world, upon which he had based his very identity. His late poetry was, therefore, much more a struggle on a heroic plane than was Eich's. We have seen, and shall see further, how Huchel restated his personal myth in the 1970s. We have seen, too, how he tacitly acknowledged his awareness of the deep problems underlying the myth in poems such as 'M.V.', 'Ölbaum und Weide' and 'Brandenburg'. On an intensely personal level, Huchel was prisoner to a romantic attitude that he not only knew no longer held, but whose ostensible authenticity as an emotional anchor-point in the past part of him acknowledged to be a fiction.

The late poetry may not always be stylistically subtle, but in it Huchel sought to confront the problems that emerged from the logic of his position. The truth of Huchel's late poetry is located in a field of tension spanning an absurd present, in which death is imminent, and a mythologised past whose autobiographical authenticity is constantly reiterated, yet at points called into question in an act that undermines from within the very basis of his poetics and identity. He does this disarmingly in the few lines of 'Unter der blanken Hacke des Monds',(i,211) whose second section reads, 'Im Wasserzeichen der Nacht/ die Kindheit der Mythen,/ nicht zu entziffern'. The poet's very inability to gain substantial knowledge about his life is followed in the final section by a wretched death, 'Unwissend/ stürz' ich hinab,/ zu den Knochen der Füchse geworfen'.

At other points, the poetic myth is affirmed through the use of imagery which is often drastically pared back, in keeping with Huchel's late style. Echoes of 'Der Knabenteich', 'Am Beifußhang' and 'Sommerabend' can, for example, be heard in 'Auf den Tod von V.W', (i,189) ostensibly a treatment of Virginia Woolf's death,

Mit einem Teich begann es,

dann kam der steinige Weg,

der umgitterte Brunnen, von Beifuß bewachsen,

die löchrige Tränke unter der Ulme,

wo einst die Pferde standen.

Here, the 'remembered' imagery of childhood retains its celebratory quality. This supports Rudolf Hartung's comment on the late poetry, 'Das Bewußtsein des Todes fällt fast überall als Schatten auf die immer noch gewußte und nur manchmal noch empfundene Herrlichkeit der Welt'.[26] Something of the glory of the world is affirmed in the Mediterranean poem 'Delphine'. (i,208) Yet, Huchel's late poetry is at its most engaging when the poet summons the courage to challenge the very 'knowledge' of his own world and identity that he continued to disseminate in his public statements. At points in *Die neunte Stunde*, he would further pursue this theme.

In Demand: Driven by Financial Need?

In the 1960s, Huchel had conveyed the impression that he was in a difficult financial situation, though the reality was never as black as he painted it. Similarly, in the early 1970s he repeatedly made the point that he needed to accept many of the invitations that he received to give readings in order to keep his head above water. He pointed out that for many years he had been in a salaried position; he had not lived as a poet. Now, he had to 'mit meinen Versen hausieren gehen ... Nun mache ich aus der Not eine Tugend, fahre herum und knalle den Leuten manchmal ein paar Hundert Metaphern ins Gesicht. Aber sie ertragen es sehr geduldig'. (ii,391) Apart from the steady flow of prizes, which added to the money invested by Jens, other sources of income were the *Frankfurter Allgemeine Zeitung*, which published Huchel's new poems with some regularity throughout the 1970s, and periodicals such as *Jahresring*, which was edited by Rudolf de le Roi for the Kulturkreis im Bundesverband der Deutschen Industrie.[27] Huchel would be awarded that organisation's prize for literature in 1977. He told an interviewer that *Jahresring* paid him as much as 500 marks per poem. (ii,395) He placed eleven poems with the journal in the mid-1970s. In his acceptance speech for the Peter Huchel Prize, Herburger reported a story that had done the rounds in West German literary circles of how Huchel, 'am Fenster stehend und ins Breisgau blickend, einmal von einem Zeitschriftenverleger einen Tausendmarkschein zugesteckt erhalten habe, mit den Worten: "Sie können es doch brauchen?"'[28] Herburger went on, 'Huchel nahm das Geld wortlos, war schon zu erschöpft, zerschmetterte nicht das Fenster, den Geber, den ganzen, grünen Gau'. Huchel milked the sympathy of the West German literary establishment for all its was worth. His wife comments,

Huchel hatte in den letzten Jahren seines Lebens die Legende in die Welt gesetzt, er müsse Lesungen machen, um seine Rente aufzubessern. Wer Lyrik schreibt, hatte er immer gesagt, braucht einen Brotberuf. Da er diesen Brotberuf nicht mehr hatte, folgte er dem Bild des verarmten Dichters, und ich glaube, es gefiel ihm so. Aber Huchel hatte sich in unserem gemeinsamen Leben niemals um Geld gekümmert. Es interessierte ihn nicht. Alle Preise, die er bekommen hatte, waren gut angelegt, und das Geld vermehrte sich. Wir haben immer sehr wenig davon gebraucht.[29]

This story of his financial hardship in the West, following that in the East, was one of the final components in the myth-making, within which his life had become enveloped. Huchel's nonchalant manner belied just how much he was actually concerned with financial security. A measure of that concern – and of his ability to address it – is his very success in achieving financial security at each stage of his adult life. Even though he himself possessed no private means, throughout his adult life he spent only some seventeen years in full-time, paid employment, excluding his nearly four years as a soldier. In the 1970s, he exploited with consummate ease the great sympathy towards him in the West to secure a comfortable material base, which, as his wife writes, would have always been enough for their son to live off.[30] Yet he would only survive his father by nine years.

Huchel received support from circles in Switzerland. He received invitations to stay in the tower at Muzôt, where Rilke had completed his *Duineser Elegien*. He spent time in Switzerland in late 1972 and told Kaschnitz of his experiences at Muzôt, where, as she wrote to her daughter, 'eine meist betrunkene Dame ihn betreute und mit ihm entsetzliche gefährliche Autofahrten über die Schweizer Bergpässe machte'.[31] Huchel was preparing a selection of Kaschnitz's verse which appeared in the Bibliothek Suhrkamp series in 1973. His afterword might, in certain respects, have acted as a commentary on his own development, revealing as it does their close affinities, leaving aside Huchel's stylistic detour of the late 1940s and early 1950s. He explained that most of Kaschnitz's early poems had been excluded, since they 'meist noch im Herkömmlichen angesiedelt sind'. (ii,315) He continued,

Erst Mitte der fünfziger Jahre findet ein radikaler Stilwechsel statt, der Wuchs der Verse wird härter, ohne dabei die Transparenz zu verlieren, keine wiehernde Metaphorik mehr, die Verknappung der Sprache ist das poetische Element. Gerade durch das Aussparen von Metaphern und Wörtern, durch das Weglassen halber Sätze gewinnt sie die Sicherheit und Kühnheit des sprachlichen Ausdrucks. Das Weltwissen, das Visionäre, in wenigen Zeilen zusammengedrängt. (ii,315)

The process of condensation described here echoes Walter Jens' description of Huchel's work in *Chausseen Chausseen*, which had continued in *Gezählte Tage*.

Following the publication of *Gezählte Tage*, Huchel embarked on his first reading tour in the UK. It was his first trip to the UK since a PEN meeting in London in the mid-1950s. He could speak little English and his translator, Michael Hamburger, whom he now met for the first time, acted as a link person for the London leg of his one-month tour. Huchel had been nominated to represent the Federal Republic at the Fanfare for Europe reading, which was a celebration of the UK's entry into the European Community. During his stay in London, from 2-4 January, he lived at the Wilbraham Hotel in SW1. (ii,357) He then stayed with Hamburger, to whom he gave a copy of *Gedichte*, and discussed translation problems with him. Huchel's visit was reported in *The Guardian* on 12 January 1973 under the heading 'Berlin's Wandering Poet'. In the mid-1980s, Hamburger recorded his memories of their first and subsequent meetings. For Hamburger, Huchel remained an enigma, 'Mehrdeutigkeiten, Verschwiegenheiten, Geheimnisse gehören zum Wesen der Lyrik Huchels – wie auch zum Wesen des Mannes, den ich "kennenlernte"'.[32] From the outset, 'Ein Schweigen über vieles gehörte zu dem Einverständnis' of their relationship. Yet, for all that, Huchel was for Hamburger not 'verschlossen', 'Die Geselligkeit, wie das Essen und Trinken, schien er zu genießen, war auch für die Äußerlichkeiten der Umgebung und des Umgangs durchaus empfänglich'. Hamburger related a puzzling incident,

> Als Peter Huchel 1973 bei uns in London war, meldete sich ein Herr Guttmann, der dann auf Verabredung mit einem jungen Photographen ins Haus kam, um viele Porträts von Peter Huchel und mir aufzunehmen. An ein Gespräch zwischen Herrn Guttmann und Peter Huchel erinnere ich mich nicht, hatte aber das Gefühl, daß das Interesse Guttmanns an Huchel eine alte Bekanntschft voraussetzte, die Peter Huchel nicht anerkennen wollte oder vergessen hatte. Jedenfalls gingen die beiden wieder fort, ohne eine Adresse zu hinterlassen. Nie mehr haben wir von diesen Besuchern gehört, nie die Bilder zu sehen bekommen.

Herr Guttmann and Huchel did, indeed, go back a long way, to the Goldberg Circle in Berlin in the 1920s. Herr Guttmann was Simon Guttmann of the *Neuer Club*. He co-edited *Neopathos* and the posthumous edition of Georg Heym's *Umbra Vitae*. Portraits of him were drawn by Meidner, Kirchner and Erich Heckel. In 1913-4 he was associated with the group around *Der Anfang*, a journal of the Youth Movement. Walter Benjamin, who knew Guttmann from those days, wrote to Scholem in January 1921 that he had encountered the 'Kreis der Neo-pathetiker ... von seiner verrufensten und wirklich verderblichsten Seite zur Zeit der Jugendbewe-gung in einer für Dora und mich höchst eingreifenden Weise in der Gestalt des

Herren (sic) Simon Guttmann'.[33] Scholem recalls the following conversation with Benjamin, 'Thus he told me on one occasion when the conversation turned to Simon Guttmann and his destructive influence on him and Dora in the days of the Youth Movement, "Some day, when you and I are old people, I shall tell you about Simon Guttmann". But this never happened!'[34] Like Goldberg, Guttmann spent the First World War in Switzerland and the 1920s in Berlin. He fled Nazi Germany for France, before moving to London. There, he set up a photographic agency on Oxford Street, which was still in business in the early 1980s. Guttmann was, in fact, in possession of some of Goldberg's papers. From Benjamin's comments, it is clear that Guttmann had a reputation. Huchel's unwillingness to acknowledge Guttmann may be linked to Huchel's awareness of that reputation. Huchel, though, chose not to divulge anything whatsoever to Hamburger.

The trip to the UK was the first of three in the 1970s. The later ones were sponsored by the Goethe-Institut, which also invited Huchel to Oslo in 1973. He read there and to the Nilsens' students in Ringsaker.[35] The Nilsens took him to see the west coast of Norway, where they visited the fishing village of Bud. He was attracted by the rugged landscape, just as he was by Scotland and the North of England. The visit to the Norwegian coast gave rise later, on 17 October 1974, to the poem 'In Bud'. (i,240) It is one of a number of poems from the last, restless decade of Huchel's life, in which he contemplates the inevitability of death. The sea provides an appropriate setting for such thoughts, the poem ending, 'sei unterwegs/ auf Meeren mit stürzendem Himmelsstrich,/ wo jeder Name verlorengeht'.

Shaping the Scholarly Reception

Efforts were being made in the Federal Republic to develop a critical apparatus for scholarly work on Huchel. Hans Mayer agreed to edit *Über Peter Huchel* for Suhrkamp on his friend's behalf. The work was done in late 1972 and early 1973. The volume includes essays on Huchel's work as a poet and editor, poems dedicated to him, a table of his life and the first attempt at an authoritative bibliography, which was complied by Hartmut Kokott. Mayer's own essay on *Sinn und Form* was one of the most significant contributions, together with the section from Axel Vieregg's dissertation treating 'Ankunft', the inclusion of which Huchel had requested. Huchel offered his congratulations to Vieregg on his dissertation in a letter of 27 December 1972,

Meinen Dank, meine Freude, Ihre Arbeit hat mich tief beeindruckt, manchmal sogar betroffen gemacht. Ja, es stimmt, ich habe in machen Nächten meiner Isolation das Alte Testament gelesen, vor allem Jesaja; und die Entschlüsselung der 'Ankunft' ist für mich ja ein nahezu unheimlicher Vorgang, der sich mit der Handhabung des germanistischen Rüstzeugs allein kaum erklären läßt. (ii,357)

In a challenge to Vieregg's interpretive skills, Huchel later dedicated to him 'Der Ammoniter', which he completed on 28 December 1973.[36] After *Über Peter Huchel* had finally appeared, Huchel confided to Vieregg that he sometimes felt the publication to be a 'Staatsbegräbnis erster Klasse'. (ii,358) It must be said that the publication sidestepped thorny issues such as the controversies surrounding both *Chausseen Chausseen* and *Gezählte Tage*, not to mention Huchel's work as a radio author in the Third Reich and the lacunae in his biography.

Understandably, Huchel himself was now concerned to influence the way posterity would view him. Apart from his own public appearances, he had an obvious interest in guiding Vieregg down what he saw as the appropriate paths, while Vieregg was preparing his dissertation for publication. In the advice that he issued to Vieregg, Huchel was not concerned with the interpretation of specific poems, rather with changes of emphasis in the depiction of his relations with other poets and intellectuals. He made claims which we have already examined. He distanced himself from Lehmann, Bobrowski and Eich, not to mention the *Kolonne* Circle, writing, 'Ich kam aus einer ganz anderen Ecke her. Zur *Kolonne* habe ich niemals gehört, es war ein reiner Zufall, daß ich den Preis erhielt. Eich lernte ich erst 1934 kennen'. (ii,358) He stressed instead his relations with Ernst Bloch, 'mein väterlicher Freund' and with the Goldberg Circle, whose 'Schabbesgoi' he had been. The background in Marxism and mysticism should, Huchel indicated, differentiate him clearly from other nature poets, especially from those to whom he had, in actual fact, been close in the 1930s. As we have seen, the generally rather artificial distinctions that Huchel made have, for the most part, been perpetuated uncritically, despite the important revisions set in train during the mid-1970s and early 1980s by Hans Dieter Schäfer.

In a censorious letter of 5 April 1974, Huchel took issue with the draft of the foreword that Vieregg had written for his book. (ii,359) The poet was concerned that the reader might gain the impression that Vieregg's study had been conceived as a response to the attacks by Heise and Wondratschek. In Huchel's view, for Vieregg to write, on the basis of these attacks, that critics were divided over his work was to overstate Heise's and Wondratschek's importance. Huchel referred to a counter-attack on Heise in *Die Welt* and to articles in *Süddeutsche Zeitung* by Barbara Bondy and Peter Hamm. He stressed the overwhelmingly positive reception accorded to both his early and more recent work. Equally, he would not find it difficult to defend his poetry against the charges of Lehmann, of whom he wrote, 'so hege ich nach wie vor eine Art stiller Pietät für diesen erbitterten Querkopf'.[37] Around the same time, Huchel was questioned about Heise's attack in an interview conducted by Karl Corino, who took up Heise's claim that Huchel had not worked through the waves of stylistic innovation that had shaped the aesthetic understanding of poets in the Federal Republic. Huchel replied,

Für den jungen Lyriker mag es sie ja geben, das kann seine Meinung sein. Aber ich komme nicht aus der DDR-Literatur her, und ich bin ebensowenig, rein literarisch gesehen, in den Westen verpflanzt worden. Ich bin schon sehr früh entdeckt worden. Mitte der zwanziger Jahre z.B. von der *Literarischen Welt*. Ich war demnach schon vor 1933 da. Für mich gibt es als Voraussetzung nicht die DDR-Literatur und nicht die westdeutsche Literatur. Ich habe meinen kleinen Laden, den ich betreibe. (ii,391-2)

There is a good deal of truth in this statement, yet Huchel himself, of course, did much to obscure the actual lines of development that he had pursued since his 'discovery'. It is to Heise's credit that he was one of the few critics prepared to ask difficult questions about that development.

The Freemasons' Prize: the Poetics of Memory

Huchel seized a further opportunity to shape the interpretation of his life and work in his acceptance speech for the Freemasons' Literature Prize in 1974. He travelled to Frankfurt for the award of 5,000 marks and the Lessing Ring on Sunday 26 May, the last day of the freemasons' celebration of the 25th anniversary of the re-founding of the organisation after it had been banned by the Nazis. Previous winners of the Lessing Ring included Max Tau, Erich Kästner, Siegfried Lenz and Golo Mann. In his address, Wolfgang Kelch of Wolfenbüttel compared Huchel's poetry with Nelly Sachs'. He drew attention to their social conscience, which was 'keine blutleere Ideologie, sie ist spontan und damit glaubhaft, unmittelbar und immer wieder warnend, daß unsere Welt für lange Zeit keine humane Welt sein wird'.[38]

Huchel responded with a speech that was the fullest statement about his work since his radio talk of December 1932. He picked up on key issues from the early 1930s. He began by taking up the theme of childhood amnesia, which in 1931 he had described in the short prose piece, 'Frau', (ii,226) and of Proustian *mémoire involontaire*, the wholly unpredictable recovery from the subconscious of imagery relating to early experience. In this way, statements divided by forty years represent a remarkably unchanging continuity in poetic concerns and lend support to the view that Huchel's poetry remained anchored in the early 1930s in a manner unique among his contemporaries. Huchel went on to argue, in similar vein, that 'die Vergangenheit mit der Gegenwart und der Zukunft ein untrennbares Ganzes bildet. Gerade die Erlebnisse der Kindheit, etwa vom fünften bis zehnten Lebensjahr, sind es, die später einen entscheidenden Einfluß nehmen'.[39]

This statement is, of course, of a piece with the motto drawn from St Augustine, which, as we have seen, Huchel related to the Alt-Langerwisch childhood. Alt-Langerwisch was, he explained to his audience, the scene of those crucial early experiences. He maintained the following to the freemasons, in a way that only serves to emphasise Huchel's educated, urban background, as well as his later acquaintance with Marxist ideas,

> Die Natur war damals für mich, wie Kirche und Schule es lehrten, die Schöpfung Gottes, im Sinne der Bibel: Macht Euch die Erde untertan. Und sehr früh begriff ich, daß es keine absolute, keine heile Natur mehr gab, daß die Natur vielmehr durch den Menschen verändert und nutzbar gemacht worden war.... Die Idylle war durchlöchert, ich sah die grausame Seite der Natur, Fressen und Gefressenwerden, die Welt der Knechte, Mägde, Holzfäller, polnischer Schnitter, Stromer und Zigeuner, das Deputat, den kargen Brotkorb der Büdner und Kossäten. Die Landschaft des Kindes war nicht mehr allein ein geographischer, sie war auch ein sozialer Begriff.

We will recall that the emphasis on the social dimension of his art was one that Huchel had quite explicitly rejected in the speech of 1932. Though he had by the early 1950s come to interpret his early poetry as a contribution to the class struggle, by 1974 in the company of the freemasons in the Federal Republic Marxist discourse had given way to the much less controversial term, 'social'.

Huchel's interpretation of his development jumps from childhood to student years, a time of 'heftigen Diskussionen mit marxistischen Freunden', who objected to his use of metaphors drawn from nature. He found it impossible to heed their advice since whatever theme he chose,

> selbst in der Konfrontation mit der Gesellschaft, mit Hunger, Unterdrückung und Krieg, stets blieb in den jeweiligen Versuchen ein Metaphernrest zurück, ja, dieser Rest, ich mußte es mir eingestehen, war der eigentliche Urgrund des Schaffens. Ich kehrte durch das Gestrüpp marxistisch erhobener Zeigefinger immer wieder, oft mit schlechtem Gewissen, zu Augustinus zurück: '... im großen Hof meines Gedächtnisses. Daselbst sind mir Himmel, Erde und Meer gegenwärtig ...' Vielleicht nur deswegen, weil für mich der große Hof meines Gedächtnisses das alte Gehöft in Alt-Langerwisch war.

It is certainly true that Huchel's whole being as a poet drew upon sources of inspiration that had nothing in common with Marxism, within the discourse of the Leninist interpretation of which he, however, became caught up after the war, when, on occasion, he adopted its rhetoric.

He rightly pointed to the catholic taste in modern German literature that he developed as a young man. Among those works which he read as a student, he mentioned Trakl, Kafka, Freud and Bloch's *Spuren*. *Spuren* was, in fact, published only in 1930. He referred once again to the mystics, above all Böhme. This broadening of horizons was followed by 'Reisen in die Mittelmeerländer, Südfrankreich, Korsika, die Türkei, die ersten Versuche, Archaisch-Mythisches mit modernen Formen und Inhalten zu verbinden, den Stoff also nicht mythologisch zu vernebeln, sondern dialektisch zu erhellen'. Huchel's response to the Mediterranean and the Balkans in the 1920s and 1930s was, it must be said, much less mediated by classical mythology than he claimed here. Nor, as we have seen, was the visionary poet of 'Die Insel Aloe' driven in the late 1920s by the logic of the dialectic. His claims command much more credibility if applied to work produced from the mid-1950s onwards. He went on to defend his use of archetypes drawn from nature, myth and religion, which were deeply unfashionable on the left and susceptible to the charge of indifference to social reality. He offered his summary of the debates of the late 1960s and early 1970s and criticised the proponents of social and political commitment in art who 'entwerfen eine weithin durchschaubare Welt, bestreiten jede Magie, jede Metapher auch, da diese die Realität umgehe'. He sought to place himself above a controversy which, in his view, was being conducted with typical German intolerance on both sides. One side championed Jung, the other Marx. Huchel pleaded instead for a recognition of the limits of what scientific rationalism could achieve and for an acknowledgement of the specific quality, the aesthetic dimension, of poetry, which derived from the unplumbed and, indeed, unplumbable secrets of the poet's inspiration and the reader's openness in response.

In these ruminations upon the creative process, Huchel hinted at his awareness of the source of the complexities underlying his own creativity. He cast doubt on the capacity of Freudian analysis fully to understand these complexities, citing Freud himself as his witness,

> Freud deutet in seinem Essay über *Dostojewski und die Vatertötung* an, daß die Psychologie nicht das Lot besitze, bis zu den letzten Geheimnissen des dichterischen Geistes vorzudringen. Der Autor sublimiere seine Komplexe durch dichterisches Schaffen, der Prozeß geschehe unbewußt.

As we have seen, a conventional psychological analysis, centring on Huchel's emotional attachments and antipathies within the family group, does take us quite a long way. Towards the end of his speech, Huchel referred ominously to 'Versperrungen, tödliche Konstellationen', yet declined any further elucidation. Like poems in *Gezählte Tage* such as 'M.V.' and 'Ölbaum und Weide', these late statements hint at the deep emotional turmoil that lay behind the carefully constructed, seamless unity between experience and poetry that Huchel conveyed through his poetics of memory from the early 1930s to the 1970s.

It was not for him to do more than hint at that turmoil. There remained only the affirmation of the poet's unique visionary gift in a West German literary climate quite hostile to such a statement. He pointed out that scientists had not come fully to understand the nature of reality and, 'Die Natur bleibt geheimnisvoll. Wir können in die Transzendenz, in jede visionäre Landschaft vorstoßen'. Yet the role of poetry in exploring the world had been subjected to extreme doubts. Even though writers themselves knew well enough that 'Die Dichtung ihre eigene Dimension hat. Und ihre eigenen Erkenntnisse', the terms of public debate militated against the acceptance of that fundamental truth, for which Huchel stood in his poetry.

The Gryphius Prize, and Meeting Susanne in Stockholm

The following month, June, Huchel was in Düsseldorf to collect the Andreas Gryphius Prize awarded by the Künstlergilde Esslingen. This prize was worth 10,000 marks. It was awarded for literature about Eastern Europe; the venue was the 'Haus des Ostens'. The organisers departed from the usual format and invited Huchel to participate in a workshop discussion. He began by discussing *Sinn und Form*. He was reported as saying, 'Dieses Organ wurde sehr überschätzt'.[40] As the person principally responsible for promoting the journal and creating its legendary status, he certainly had the authority to make such a teasing statement. He added, 'Brecht war mein Schicksal', the full import of which has only begun to emerge in recent years. Turning to his poetry, he expressed his sense of affinity with Gryphius, explaining, 'er ist für uns heute wieder ganz aktuell nach all dem, was wir an Verfolgungen und Emigration erlebt haben. Gryphius gibt die leidende Antwort auf das, was geschah und noch heute geschieht in unserer Welt, die alles andere als eine Idylle ist'. Huchel's own experience had taught him the wisdom of Gryphius' phrase, 'Der Mensch – ein Spiel der Zeit'. In keeping with the self-image he had created in the West, Huchel went on to describe himself as a 'fahrender Sänger', who was obliged to travel throughout Europe 'um die notwendigen Zechinen zu verdienen'.

Though he did not need the money, Huchel continued his round of readings in Germany and abroad, travelling to Scandinavia in 1974, where, unexpectedly, he met his daughter in Stockholm. When he had overcome the shock of seeing Susanne for the first time in over 25 years, he assumed a charming, paternal manner, despite the fact that he was as ill at ease in the city as he had been in Vienna. He invited his daughter and her friend to eat with him at his hotel, but was most reluctant to use the hotel dining room. He finally made for the corner of the dining room, where he recovered his composure. After their meeting, Susanne Huchel wrote to her father and sent him photographs, showing him her life in central Sweden. Despite their agreement that they should stay in touch, she did not hear back from him.

Failing Health, and the Impossibility of Autobiography

Monica Huchel, meanwhile, was not happy in the house rented for them by Morat and in late 1974 she took it upon herself to purchase a smaller house on

Münstertälerstraße despite Huchel's objection, 'In dieser Hundehütte soll ich wohnen?'[41] When Hamburger visited him in the spring of 1975, he noticed that

> sich Peter gegen das Schreiben wehrte, daß er viele Stunden in wortloser Untätigkeit verbringen konnte – wie seine Katzen 'dämmernd' – und über fast alles lieber sprach als über das, was ihn als Lyriker anging und beschäftigte. Von seinen damaligen Arbeitsplänen erfuhr ich vor allem, daß er ein Erinnerungsbuch schreiben sollte, aber nicht wollte. In späteren Jahren beantwortete er auch keine Briefe mehr.[42]

Huchel was truly exhausted. His wife later suspected that he had suffered a stroke or strokes during this period, a suspicion shared by Hamburger. Huchel had signed a contract for his mémoirs with Suhrkamp, but such a task was certainly now beyond him. When in the best of health, Huchel's talent as a raconteur equipped him to produce dazzling vignettes for his listeners. Yet he was never really interested in, nor, indeed, capable of subjecting himself to the discipline of sequential narration that underlies conventional prose writing. That would also have involved addressing at least some of those 'wunde Stellen' identified by Hamburger. It is highly unlikely that Huchel could ever have completed such a project, let alone at that late stage in his life. In his interview with Corino, he set out the difficulties that he saw in writing his autobiography. He had clearly all but abandoned the idea. He referred to the difficulty in accessing material. Whilst acknowledging that, thanks to his wife, he had been able to bring correspondence out of the GDR, he pointed out that he needed GDR newspapers and periodicals from the 1940s until the 1970s. A further problem was the fact that he would have to criticise people who were still alive and 'ich möchte kein Buch schreiben, das von Haß erfüllt ist'. (ii,393) That was, indeed, not in his nature. He added that despite the criticism to which he had been subjected in the GDR 'möchte ich doch auch ein sehr selbstkritisches Buch schreiben'. That may have been Huchel's intention, yet his successfully established manner for dealing with issues which implied self-criticism was to find an elegant way out through anecdote or the adoption of a certain ironic distance.

Huchel responded to his publisher's encouragement by producing two short autobiographical pieces in the mid-1970s. The first was 'Der Fall von *Sinn und Form*', (ii,326-9) whilst the second was published in Suhrkamp's collection of writers' *Erste Lese-Erlebnisse* in 1975. 'Der Fall von *Sinn und Form*' has been referred to at appropriate points in this study. The latter is a mixture of fantasy and recollection, of gentle irony and authentic detail, similar to the much earlier 'Europa neunzehnhunderttraurig'. Like the 1931 piece, it supplies pointers to the attentive reader that all was not as it appeared to be in his presentation of his background and development. The setting is grandfather Zimmermann's farm 'in den frühen Januartagen 1913', (ii,317) that is to say shortly before the end of the school holidays. This authentic setting is also the site for the play of the child's imagination, stimulated by his reading in his grandfather's books. As we have already seen, however, on the level of basic biographical data, the story does not tally with what we know about Huchel's early years. Towards the end one can read, 'Am letzten Ferientag war ich bis zum Anbruch der Dunkelheit damit beschäftigt, lustlos die Mappe zu packen, morgen ging es nach Potsdam in die Schule zurück'. (ii,324) Yet, in January 1913 Huchel was attending not a Potsdam school but the Gemeindeschule 1 in Steglitz. Shortly afterwards, on his 10th birthday, he progressed to the Steglitz Oberrealschule. It was only in the autumn of 1915 that the Huchels moved to Potsdam where Helmut then attended the Oberrealschule.

Did Huchel no longer know these things in the final decade of his life? A reading of 'Erste Lese-Erlebnisse' suggests strongly that Huchel was keenly aware of the distinction between the attractive illusions created by the imagination and the insistent claims of reality. The Steglitz years simply had no place in the presentation of his public persona from the early 1930s onwards. He was surely sufficiently alert to the details of his family history to be aware of the significance of 1913. Friedrich Zimmermann, whom he adored, had died in the November of that year. His grandson thus chose to place his first reading adventure during what must have been one of his last stays in his grandfather's household.

Huchel's story centres on his discovery in his grandfather's gun-locker of the eleven-volume *Forst- und Jagd-Archiv von und zu Preußen*, which was, he assured his readers, still in his possession more than sixty years later. The nine-year-old boy admired on the front cover of each volume the picture of a young forester 'in grüner Uniform mit betreßten Epauletten'. (ii,318) Huchel himself would later, as Italiaander reported, assume a forester's persona, albeit with a more folksy rather than a military manner. The boy associated the uniformed figure with Georg Ludwig Hartig, 'Königl. Preußischer Ober-Landforstmeister, Staatsrath und Mitglied mehrerer deutschen und französischen gelehrten Gesellschaften'. (ii,318) What the boy assumed to be regular contributions by Hartwig were published under the rubric of miscellany. Hartig's articles amounted to the sort of popular wisdom which Huchel saw his grandfather and other members of the rural community as embodying with their 'Kuhbeschwörungen' and other folkloric practices. For the boy, Hartig thus also became a writer, just as the grandfather was a poet as well as, nominally at least, a farmer.

The boy imagined Hartig living in a house like his grandfather's, where, in his imagination, he visited him. Huchel's brief narrative of his adventures with Hartig is punctuated by his depictions of life in his grandfather's household. The boy's allegiance to Hartig is, however, called into question by Hartig's account of 'Holzhauerstiefel ganz eigener Art'. (ii,321) Hartig recommends combatting the snow and cold weather in the Prussian forests by 'Eisstiefel'. Yet the boy also recalls Hartig's advice 'jedesmal mit dem Holzschlag aufzuhören, wenn ein Schneesturm treibe'. (ii,319) These two pieces of advice simply do not tally, and the boy's image of the forester is irreparably damaged as he realises that Hartig's story of the manufacture of the 'Eisstiefel' is flawed. He withdraws his allegiance, concluding, 'H. wollte den Kopf des Lesers in einen Sack voll Unwissenheit stecken'. (ii,322). He looks instead to his grandfather, from whom he has learnt 'daß man den Gefühlen nicht trauen soll, überprüfe die Wirklichkeit, mit halben Maßnahmen ist nichts getan'. (ii,322-3) The grandfather is thus identified at this point as the true voice of authority, through whom illusions fostered through allegiance to Hartig can be dispelled.

The grandfather's position as a focus for the child's and poet's allegiance is thus re-affirmed. Near the beginning of the piece, Huchel writes, 'Der preußischen Strenge meines Großvaters, der mich aufzog, und den klaren Wassern meiner Heimat verdanke ich es, daß ich das lange Lineal fürchtete und das Schildrohr liebe'. (ii,317) Through his reference to his upbringing by his grandfather, Huchel was, though, quite knowingly putting the reader's head into another 'Sack voll Unwissenheit'. It comes as no surprise that certain phrases describing Hartig recur in Huchel's late poem 'Mein Großvater', who is depicted going about his country pastimes. Thus, one can read of Hartig, 'Er holte ein Gewehr aus der Ecke. "Die curiche Büchse", sagte er feierlich, "sie schießt ein kleines Blei, nicht stärker als ein Kirschkern, vortrefflich geeignet für die Auerhahnjagd"'. (ii,320) The second stanza of 'Mein Großvater' repeats this almost word for word, 'Für die Auerhahnjagd/ die curische Büchse./ Sie schoß ein Blei/ das nicht stärker als ein Kirschkern war'. (i,243-4) The parallel between the two male adult figures emerges, too, in the boy's question regarding his possible abandonment of his allegiance to them. In the prose passage, he writes of Hartig, 'Sollte ich von nun an ohne seine Führung durchs Revier streifen und allein Remisen anlegen?' (ii,322) In the poem we can read, 'Was wär, wenn ich fortliefe/ und ließe ihn mit seinen Netzen,/ Remisen und Fallen allein?/ Ich ging nicht über die sieben Seen'. The textual similarities, in fact, move beyond the person of Hartig, in that finally, near the end of 'Erste Lese-Erlebnisse' one can read, 'Die Magd kam ins Zimmer, füllte die Lampe, schraubte am Messingring'. (ii,324) In the poem, it is grandfather Zimmermann who 'drehte am Messingring der Lampe'. (i,244)

The myth of the Alt-Langerwisch world presided over by the grandfather is maintained to the end in both the prose piece and the poem. Yet, through the transfer of textual detail between ostensibly authentic figures from his biography and clearly signposted fictional creations, Huchel provided sufficient clues for the reader to pose the question as to the relationship between fact and fiction. Huchel could scarcely have been expected to go any further than to point up the problematic status of texts from which his biography, albeit with his encouragement, had been read off in a quite simplistic way. Viewed in this light, the prose piece complements poems from the early 1970s such as 'M.V.' and 'Ölbaum und Weide', as well as passages in the speech for the Freemasons' Prize, in which Huchel supplies the attentive reader with hints for the revision of the Huchel myth.

More Distinctions: *pour le mérite* and Bibliophile Editions

The public persona that Huchel cultivated was quite out of step with the politicisation and social commitment that continued to characterise much West German literature throughout the 1970s. This difference was not, one suspects, wholly unwelcome to Huchel: it served to foreground his distinctiveness in literary life, just as he was stylised by a number of critics as a figure akin to an institution, albeit one generally known only to insiders. Huchel corresponded with one such insider, Hans Bender, co-editor of *Jahresring* with de le Roi, on 26 May 1976.[43] He sent him a number of poems which Bender and de le Roi subsequently printed in their journal to coincide with Huchel's award of the Preis des Kulturkreises im Bundesverband der Deutschen Industrie. He told Bender that he was taking as many as 14 tablets a day, and added that the previous autumn and winter his health had been poor.

Following the steady stream of literary prizes, on 10 October 1976 Huchel travelled to Passau, where he was awarded the Federal Republic's most prestigious accolade, *Pour le mérite für Wissenschaft und Künste*. The award was made by Hans Erich Nossack, whom Huchel had won as an author for *Sinn und Form* through Jahnn back in the mid-1950s. Just a few days later, Huchel travelled to Duisburg, where, on 16 October 1976, he was awarded the Preis des Kulturkreises im Bundesverband der Deutschen Industrie, on the occasion of its 25th anniversary celebrations. Huchel was the recipient of the group's 'Ehrengabe' of 1,000 marks a month for the next two years.

That same autumn two bibliophile editions of Huchel's hand-written work were published by Erker Presse in St Gallen, which was owned by Franz Larese and Jürg Janett. One edition was devoted to the ballad 'Der Tod des Büdners', which, as he explained, had been written in Paris in 1928. 150 copies, each signed individually by Huchel, were printed on vellum after he had written his text on stone. He did the same thing with twenty-three of his recent compositions, which appeared in the volume *Unbewohnbar die Trauer*, whose title was a line from 'Schottischer Sommer'. The poems were accompanied by eight lithographs by Piero Dorazio. The limited edition of 200 was also produced on vellum and signed by Huchel and Dorazio. Measuring 39x29 cm., this collectors' item was republished in a miniature edition in 1978.

Wolfgang Heidenreich of Südwestfunk accompanied Huchel to St Gallen in November 1976. The stone upon which Huchel worked was 'der schwere Kalkblock mit den griffig muscheligen Kanten und der sorgsam geschliffenen Schreibfläche',[44] upon which already Ungaretti, Pound and Heidegger had worked. In awe of Huchel's execution of 'Enkidu', Heidenreich observed reverentially, 'Scriptorium. Kargheit und Sachlichkeit der Werkstatt und des Werkzeugs. Die Stille des Schreib-Hand-Werks, seine verschüttete Würde. Vergessene Heiligkeit des Schreibens und Wiederschreibens der Urtexte'. Asked about the title 'Aristeas', Huchel conveyed to Heidenreich 'Sparsam mitgeteilte Empfindungen beim Beladen eines Schiffes in

Frankreich; ein junger Jonas, vom Wale zum Einstieg in die Dunkelheit des Bauches aufgefordert. Wiedererwachen dieser Anderswonirgendwohin-Gedanken beim späteren Lesen des Herodot'. We see here how Huchel's imaginative re-casting of experience that lay as far back as the 1920s, which we have encountered in other versions as the self-stylisation as a docker in Marseilles, later blended with his reading of classical literature in the contemplation of the problem of death. Following Herodotus, who tells of Aristeas' death in a fulling-mill, Huchel ends the poem, later collected as 'Aristeas II', (i,234) with the lines,

> Noch stampft die Walkmühle nachts.
>
> Manchmal hocke ich als Krähe
>
> dort oben in der Pappel am Fluß,
>
> reglos in der untegehenden Sonne,
>
> den Tod erwartend,
>
> der auf vereisten Flößen wohnt.

A Final Trip to Italy

The process of physical decline was now accelerating. In 1977, Huchel undertook one last extensive reading tour abroad. Appropriately enough, he returned to Italy, travelling the length and breadth of the country. He did so in the company of an old friend from the GDR, Stefan Welzk, who went to a reading in Florence and then drove him around in his old Fiat for the rest of his itinerary. In Welzk's account we can read, 'Riesig, wie mir schien, und mit den Zügen einer römischen Charakterskulptur, war Peter Huchel eine imposantere Erscheinung als je zuvor, doch war er inzwischen 74 Jahre alt und hätte diese Tournee nicht mehr allein machen sollen'.[45]

Huchel could not speak much Italian and was vulnerable to the waiters and hoteliers who would have ruthlessly exploited him, had it not been for Welzk. Huchel wished to see the Capuchins' tombs near Palermo, but otherwise it was the Greek temples on Sicily, at Segesta, Syracuse, Agrigento and Selinunte that Huchel wished to visit, not Italy's cathedrals, 'Stumm saß er vor den ungeheuren Säulen bei Agrigent und rauchte Zigerettenschachteln leer, dieweil die Himmelskulisse von rot zu schwarz wechselte'. Huchel's poetry amply testifies to the deep spiritual affinity that he felt with that world, in which for the last time now he immersed himself.

Huchel and Welzk enjoyed each other's company hugely. They stayed in cheap, run-down hotels and visited bars, where they entered into conversation with locals. Welzk recalls, 'In einer Kneipe bei Syrakus fragte er die Männer am Tisch nach ihrem Beruf. "Camionist" – Peter vereiste zunächst, er hatte "Kommunist" verstanden. Sein Beruf? – die Rückfrage. Poet, Scrivatore, er malte schreibende Bewegungen in der Luft'. Returning north from Sicily, they stayed for a week at

Sorrento, on the tip of the Gulf of Naples. Huchel knew the area from the late 1950s, and, as Welzk writes, 'die Traumlandschaft schien selbst Peters Bitterkeit lösen zu können'. When they parted, Huchel made for Venice, before travelling to his final reading in Trieste, as he completed what he surely knew would be his last great tour of his beloved Italy.

Struggling On

From Trieste, he made his way home. Not long after, on 4 August, Ernst Bloch died. Huchel travelled to Bloch's funeral in Tübingen, where he read his verse dedicated to Bloch, as he had so often in the past twenty years. A photograph taken on that occasion shows a tired and ageing Huchel. That autumn, he became seriously ill. As Monica Huchel later wrote to Ludvík Kundera, it was a long time before the cause of the illness could be located.[46] As long as he could, Huchel remained active. Suhrkamp announced that a new collection, *Die neunte Stunde*, would appear that autumn but the announcement proved over-optimistic. As Monica Huchel writes, he found it impossible to conclude the collection. The main stumbling block was 'Im Kun-lun-Gebirge', which he re-worked time and again. Finally, that autumn his wife wrested a complete draft from him, an arrangement of six poems in each section followed by a blank page. Monica Huchel remembers him holding a blank page in front of him and saying to her, 'Das ist ja so schlecht getippt, daß man gar nichts mehr lesen kann'.[47] For her, that was the beginning of the end. Yet, even now, Huchel declined to be confined to his home.

Among his many awards, Huchel, together with Heinar Kipphardt, had been granted a stipend by the Hamburg Senate for six months starting in the autumn of 1977. The only condition was that Huchel should live in a flat provided by the city of Hamburg. His wife was concerned because he was in no state to fend for himself. Yet he set off, calling in on the way at Celle for the annual meeting of the Order *pour le mérite* and making a detour to Brussels to collect his most lucrative, perhaps also most prestigious literary award. He was the first recipient of the European Union's Europalia Prize for Literature, which was worth 33,000 marks. The award was made at a ceremony in Brussels on 19 October by King Baudouin of Belgium. In his acceptance speech Huchel essentially re-iterated aspects of the 1974 speech delivered before the freemasons. As Monica Huchel writes, just before he set off it emerged that Huchel had not actually composed a speech so she sat down and cobbled one together from the earlier text.[48]

In an interview in Brussels, he expressed himself about the GDR for the first time in a quite unguarded manner, comparing it wholly unfavourably with the Federal Republic, of which he said, 'Ich finde, es ist ein herrlicher Staat. Es ist der freieste Staat, den es überhaupt auf der Welt gibt'. (ii,396) He went on to say that some people in the West had defended the GDR but 'Jetzt merken sie selber, was das für ein Schrotthaufen ist'. (ii,397) This was not the discreet Huchel's normal public manner. His illness was evidently making itself felt. At this point in time, it was still being maintained that *Die neunte Stunde* would appear in November. Huchel said that he had no further literary plans, pointing to the fact that he was already 74. Shortly after, however, Huchel exasperated his publisher by withdrawing his manuscript.

From Brussels, Huchel travelled on to Hamburg. He had agreed with his wife that she would ring him every Sunday and Wednesday at 6 pm. During the second such call he said, 'Ich verstehe nicht, daß du mich morgens um sechs Uhr weckst'.[49] She contacted a neurologist friend from the Hamburg area, who went to Huchel's flat and tried for two days to gain access but Huchel did not answer the door. As things turned out, Monica Huchel's very worst fears were not confirmed. In mid-November, Huchel sent his wife first drafts of four poems to type, which were included in that form as the final four poems in *Die neunte Stunde* when it appeared two years later. They are: 'Im Kalmusgeruch dänischer Wiesen', 'Todtmoos', 'Der Fremde geht davon' and 'König Lear', Huchel's final poem. All four deal with the final enigma of life and death. Monica Huchel typed them and returned them to him for further drafting but he undertook no changes to them.

Huchel was quite unable to cope with the situation in Hamburg. He withdrew before Christmas and returned to Staufen. A report appeared in the press shortly afterwards of Huchel's demonstrative show of discontent before his departure. At a press conference he complained about draughty windows and the noise of traffic. It had disturbed him in his attempts to finish off 'Im Kun-lun-Gebirge'.[50] On his way home from Hamburg, Huchel took part in the 'Düsseldorfer Literaturgespräch 1977'. The motto was 'Gibt Literatur deutsche Zustände wieder?'[51] Three other poets attended, Nicolas Born, Sarah Kirsch and Elisabeth Plessen, together with the critics Hellmuth Karasek, Fritz J. Raddatz and Peter Wapnewski. A press report of the occasion foregrounds the mutual incomprehension of poets and critics.[52] The critics approached the poets' work not with sensitivity but their own pre-conceptions. Raddatz, apparently drawing upon his review of *Gezählte Tage*, categorised Huchel's poetry as an expression of resignation and passivity, drawing attention to the lack of verbs and the prevalence of nouns referring to fear, threats and death. Huchel, for his part, made familiar points. These concerned the poet's right to articulate his own feelings as things valuable in themselves and his memories of rural Brandenburg. When discussion turned to Prussia, Huchel mounted a spirited defence and took the part of the common reader against the professional critic,

Als schließlich auch noch Preußen mit jenem achselzuckenden Hochmut in das Gespräch eingeführt wurde, mit dem es gern als aller Übel Anfang verurteilt wird, mochte Peter Huchel nicht länger mehr zurückhaltender Zuhörer der Runde sein. Seiner kräftigen Erinnerung an das wahrhaft Preußische, an Tugenden, die hinter der gängigen Karikatur Preußens zu verschwinden drohen, folgte noch eine leise, aber sehr bestimmte Ehrenrettung für die Lyrik als Dichtung und für das Leben als individuelles Erlebnis. Huchel plädierte für den 'unmusischen Menschen', der Gedichte nicht von vornherein durch die professionelle Brille betrachtet, und gegen den Hang, alles 'philosophisch' zu untermauern.

The audience welcomed such an unstuffy, uncomplicated approach, especially when Huchel went on to conclude, 'Wir reden viel darüber, und dann stimmt es vorne und hinten nicht'. The eloquent critics were put in their place by the elderly poet, whose unfashionable views on Prussia appealed not least because they contained much commonsense. Their appeal was also to conservative values which had latterly been marginalised in West German critical discourse and which Huchel, invoking the authority of his experiences in the GDR, was in a position to legitimise.

The strokes

When Huchel returned home, he was diagnosed as having had a stroke, which, it was assumed, had happened in Hamburg.[53] His friends were by now prepared for the worst. One of his oldest admirers, Oda Schaefer, wrote to Bender, 'Peter Huchel ist ja schon seit langem herzkrank, sichtbar auftretend in den schweren Säcken unter den schönen dunklen Augen des wendischen Prinzen. Auch das geht mir sehr nah, obwohl wir den Kontakt zueinander ganz verloren haben'.[54]

From now on, Huchel's life was conducted in decidedly straitened circumstances. There was no question of travel. It helped little that, as a member of the Order *pour le mérite*, on his 75th birthday he had received congratulations from the Chancellor, Helmut Schmidt, and the President, Walter Scheel.There was a complication in his medical condition through the re-emergence of his old kidney complaint. As we know, he had undergone an examination of his kidneys at Greifswald during the war years and in the 1960s had been admitted to hospital in Potsdam with a kidney problem. Given this history, it is perhaps surprising that it took a year to identify the exact nature of Huchel's problem.[55] A kidney was infected by a malignant tumour and Huchel was suffering from chronic nephritis. The kidney was removed in the autumn of 1978. Huchel came through the operation, but an anaesthetic of nearly five hours proved extremely damaging. In early 1979, sporadic paralysis set in and he was admitted for observation to the neuro-physiological clinic in Freiburg. During examination, it was established that Huchel, unbeknown to anyone, had suffered a further massive stroke. The consultant predicted that the paralysis would spread and this duly happened after Huchel returned home. For the remaining two years of his life, Huchel was bed-ridden. The paralysis spread through both legs as well as his right hand and right arm. He could still use his left hand and did so for smoking, the only pleasure he had left in life. He had to be fed and cared for by his wife in every way. His son looked on in distress. His father's mind had been virtually destroyed.

The dying poet scarcely knew of the award in March 1979 of the Eichendorff Prize by the Wangen Circle of the 'Gesellschaft für Literatur und Kunst "Der Osten" e.V.'. The award was worth 3,000 marks. Shortly afterwards, Huchel's publisher Siegfried Unseld travelled to Basle, where on 8 June 1979 he accepted, on Huchel's behalf, the Jacob-Burckhardt Prize awarded by Alfred C. Toepfer's Johann-Wolfgang-von-Goethe-Stiftung. The address was delivered by the Strasbourg professor Gonthier Louis Fink. The award consisted of 20,000 Swiss francs and a gold medal. Stephan Huchel would be well provided for.

Die neunte Stunde

A decision had now to be made regarding the publication of *Die neunte Stunde*. Since November 1977, Huchel had been unable to undertake further work on the collection. The major areas of difficulty were 'Im Kun-lun-Gebirge' and the four poems composed in Hamburg. These were earmarked for sections five and six, which remained incomplete, in contrast to sections one to four, which had been arranged by Huchel according to a 'bewußten Anordnung'. (i,433) In the circumstances, there was no point in further delaying publication, and *Die neunte Stunde* appeared in time for the Frankfurt Book Fair in the autumn of 1979.

Sections one to four each have their own internal coherence in the established Huchel manner, while they share with sections five and six the overriding thematic pre-occupation with death within the debris of civilisation. As in *Gezählte Tage*, death is the great enigma, which the poet considers not with the calm born of faith but at points with horror at the prospect of its brutal finality. The theme of death's significance is signalled in the collection's title, which alludes to Christ's Passion. In Huchel's poem 'Die neunte Stunde', (i,241) the shepherd of the pastoral tradition becomes the executioner, 'in seiner Hirtentasche/ die neunte Stunde,/ den Nagel und den Hammer'. Similarly, the poet's warning not to enter the 'öde Kun-Lun-Gebirge' (i,254) is amply borne out by the poem's ending, 'es kamen zwei Knechte,/ sie legten die Säge an den Baum/ und töteten mich'.

Reviewers generally restricted themselves to pointing to such passages, greeting the collection 'mit der alten Hochschätzung, Bewunderung'.[56] Barbara Bondy spoke for many admirers when she wrote, 'Nun ist Huchel, der Große, Alte, ohnehin nicht mehr rezensierbar, soll man vor diesem geschlossenen, Bewunderung, ja, und Liebe abnötigenden Lebenswerk vielleicht etikettieren und benoten?'[57] None of those three critics, Jens, Mayer and Reich-Ranicki, who had contributed so much to Huchel's breakthrough in the West reviewed *Die neunte Stunde*, nor for that matter had they contributed to the debate over *Gezählte Tage*. In 1972, Heise was the one to insist on a more searching examination. In 1979, this role fell to Karl Corino.[58] Corino had evidently done his homework by reading Lehmann's and Heise's earlier reviews. In any case, he came to similar conclusions about the new collection and did so at the time as the first, abortive discussion took place in the

West German press concerning Huchel, Eich and others in the Third Reich.[59] Both
Jens and Reich-Ranicki contributed to that exchange, the former constructively, the
latter less so.

Corino found that Huchel persisted in the overuse of the rather hackneyed
genitive metaphor. There were no outstanding poems in the collection: the search for
originality on occasion resulted in preciosity, unintelligibility or trivial imagery,
'"Kopfweiden", die als "Besen ... den Nebel fegen", das sind alte Besen, die nicht
mehr gut kehren'. Referring to the lines, 'Die streifende Rotte,/ vereister Blätter/
fällte der Tag/ mit Drähten über der Feuergrube', Corino asked, 'Kann man etwas
in der Luft Treibendes überhaupt "fällen", und wenn ja, ist "der Tag" dann nicht eine
pseudopoetische, mythisierende "Hilfsgröße"?' He suggested that Huchel had
exhausted his store of imagery and pointed to the fact that one short poem
'Todtmoos' consisted entirely of expressions drawn from 'Im Kun-lun-Gebirge'. Not
inclined to spare the aged and infirm poet, Corino concluded that the collection
contained 'Zu viele Paraphrasen von Literatur, zu viele Verse, "die an nichts
erinnern" als an andere Verse in früheren Büchern Huchels oder seiner literarischen
Eidhelfer'.

Wolfgang Heidenreich leapt to Huchel's defence, polemicising against what
he saw as other reviewers' 'Leseschwierigkeiten', in other words taking a line
similar to Vieregg in response to earlier attacks.[60] Heidenreich took issue with
Corino's view that 'die Natur ist ihm so intakt geblieben', a view also represented
earlier by Heise. As we have seen, the poet's relationship to nature was much more
complex, and Heidenreich pointed out the obvious contradiction between Corino's
position and the silence up against which the poet repeatedly came in his late verse.
Heidenreich argued that for all the fact that Huchel's world had been drained of
meaning, he sought still to initiate a dialogue through his treatment of ancient myths
and legends. That is undoubtedly true. For the elderly Huchel, the subject that
dwarfed all others was death.

The immutable fact of death is treated in first section of the collection, by
means of a range of ancient myths and legends. 'Der Tod wird kommen', we read
in 'Melpomene'. (i,230) Through epic adventurers such as Odysseus and Enkidu of
the Gilgamesh story, the poet continues the interpretation of his own fate. Yet, by
now it is less their epic struggles than the fact of their deaths that is at issue. Enkidu
cannot return from the realm of the dead, about which he had dreamt as the house
of dust. The dust motif appears in 'Das Grab des Odysseus' (i,231) in the line 'Mein
ist alles, sagte der Staub', which echoes the earlier 'Die Engel'.

The second section contains compositions which related to Huchel's travels
in the 1970s, such as 'Wintermorgen in Irland', 'Schottischer Sommer' and 'In Bud'.
These poems have their place alongside others for named individuals. 'Begegnung',
(i,235) dedicated to Michael Hamburger, stands out as a finely drawn portrait of his
fellow poet and translator, 'Schleiereule ... Schnabelgesicht/ mit runden Augen,/
herzstarre Maske/ aus Federn weißen Feuers'. Huchel's sense of kinship with

Hamburger is attested to in the final lines, 'Laßt uns niederfahren/ in der Sprache der Engel/ zu den zerbrochenen Ziegeln Babels'. The poem acts, too, as a re-affirmation of the poet's calling.

'Jan-Felix Caerdal' is dedicated to another poet who had a special place in Huchel's heart, Günter Eich. It is followed by 'In memoriam Günter Eich'. (i,237) Both poems continue the theme of the poetic dialogue between poets who did not communicate and, indeed, could not anymore since Eich's death. The latter poem begins,

> Hinfließen wird der Himmel,
>
> aber wir werden dem Schnee,
>
> der ins schwarze Wasser sinkt,
>
> kein Tedeum mehr sprechen.

Caerdal, a Breton word meaning searcher for beauty and a pseudonym of the misanthropic French poet André Suares, was an appropriate choice for Huchel's title in the light of the poets' difficult relationship. The tragi-comic scene evoked in the opening lines featuring the dead man, who falls off the litter upon which he is being carried by the ragged procession 'am Ende der Öde', would surely have appealed to Eich's sense of humour. He was well aware of the seediness of the society in which he had been feted. The poem ends with lines which can be readily associated with Huchel's position after his friend's death,

> Ich, der Bretone,
>
> ...
>
> ich, der Nachzügler,
>
> der einst
>
> Geschmeide wie Ähren auflas,
>
> im Licht der Messe versank,
>
> ging nun voran
>
> mit leeren Händen
>
> und einer Rinne Salz im Gesicht.

The third section looks back to the Brandenburg world that Huchel had left behind. The section contains 'Mein Großvater' and 'Brandenburg', both of which were examined earlier in this study. The former constitutes an affirmation of the Langerwisch myth, while the latter, like 'Ölbaum und Weide', undermines it from within. These poems can profitably be read in conjunction with 'Östlicher Fluß', (i,242) another piece in the third section. It begins with the self-admonishment,

> Such nicht die Steine
>
> im Wasser über dem Schlamm,
>
> der Kahn ist fort,
>
> der Fluß
>
> nicht mehr mit Netzen
>
> und Reusen bestückt.

Like 'Auf den Tod von V.W.', 'Östlicher Fluß' deploys the vocabulary of the early Huchel, yet the message now is that it is a dangerous delusion to search for a world irrevocably lost. The knowledge of that world's earlier existence is not called into question, though 'proof' cannot be advanced beyond the presence of the willow, as the second part of the poem indicates,

> Nur die Weide gibt noch Rechenschaft,
>
> in ihren Wurzeln
>
> sind die Geheimnisse
>
> der Landstreichter verborgen,
>
> die kümmerlichen Schätze,
>
> der rostige Angelhaken,
>
> die Büchse ohne Boden
>
> zum Aufbewahren längst
>
> vergessener Gespräche.

The third section of the collection ends similarly with 'Entzauberung' (i,246) and its evoking of the mysterious 'verfemten König', Itau the gypsy. The setting is again the Langerwisch world 'am Mittelgraben hinter den Weiden'. Itau was reportedly seen practising his magic,

> Er ging im Kreis
>
> und schlug in die Luft das Zeichen,
>
> ein Feuer fuhr aus der Erde,
>
> das ohne Rauch
>
> mit finsterer Flamme versank.

Yet the story of magic which Huchel had first told in the 1920s cannot be sustained in a world from which the magician has taken his leave,

> In Wahrheit
>
> zog Itau der Zigeuner,
>
> im hellen Juli
>
> durchs Bischofslila der Disteln
>
> für immer fort.

A similar message is conveyed in 'Nichts zu berichten', (i,253) in which 'Das Einhorn ging fort/ und ruht im Gedächtnis der Wälder'. This poem, in turn, echoes the slightly earlier 'Die Gaukler sind fort' (i,179) of *Gezählte Tage*.

The fourth section returns to the Mediterranean. Yet here, too, we find the same emptiness and the imminence of death, as the poet conveys his awareness of the brittleness and futility of his life. In 'Rom', (i,249) we read of 'Verse, die an nichts erinnern', while 'Ein Toscaner' (i,248) contains the lines, 'Hinfällig/ wie der Staub auf vergilbten Manuskripten/ ist mein Leben geworden'. The poet is plagued by visions of his impending death, 'Der Tod, der mürrische Maultiertreiber,/ ich sah ihn gestern abend am Stall'. Similarly, 'Der Ketzer aus Padua' (i,251) is condemned, 'den alten Jammer/ bis zur Vernichtung der Sinne zu sehen'.

One of the group of Huchel's last four poems, 'Im Kalmusgeruch' (i,257), depicts the dead Hamlet, staring into the reflection of his while face in the 'Wassergraben', a grotesque rejoinder to the much earlier 'Der Knabenteich'. That celebration of the childhood world is in stark contrast to the message of 'Im Kalmusgeruch', whose final section reads,

> Das letzte Wort
>
> blieb ungesagt,
>
> es schwamm auf dem Rücken der Biber fort.
>
> Keiner weiß das Geheimnis.

For Huchel, too, the rest was silence, as he took to the grave with him the secrets of his life.

The End

In April 1980, Huchel received his final distinction, the Reinhold Schneider Prize, which was worth 7,500 marks. Appropriately, it was awarded by his adopted town of Freiburg, though Huchel can hardly have been aware of this honour. Michael

Hamburger recalls that during his final visit in November 1980 Huchel was, 'Fast völlig verstummt und konnte nur noch mit den Augen auf meine Mitteilungen über die Arbeit am zweiten englischen Gedichtband antworten. Die Antwort auf seine einzige wiederholte Frage an meine Frau und mich – wie es uns gehe – zerbrach auch schon an seinem Zustand'.[61] Monica Huchel felt that he was probably not aware of his situation. Though his death was long and drawn-out, he was not suffering. He remained very still, withdrawn, incommunicative, apathetic. His long-term memory had clearly been destroyed. On 3 April 1981, some of his poems were read on the radio. Monica Huchel recalls that he listened to them 'wie im Schlaf und sagte nur in einem kurzen Augenblick des Wachseins: "Schlecht gelesen"'.[62] She continues,

> Manchmal ruhten seine Augen auf mir. Ich war tagelang davon angerührt und dachte darüber nach, was in diesem Blick verborgen war. Ein wenig Trauer, ein wenig Verlorenheit – das blieb von ihm, als sonst nichts mehr war. Er war in ein tiefes Schweigen gefallen. Es war ein langer, zu langer Abschied.

Already in 1977 he had composed his own epitaph,

> Der Fremde geht davon
> und hat den Stempel
> aus Regen und Moos
> noch rasch der Mauer aufgedrückt.
> Eine Haselnuß im Geröll
> blickt ihm mit weißem Auge nach.
>
> Jahreszeiten, Mißgeschicke, Nekrologe –
> unbekümmert geht der Fremde davon. (i,258)

On 6 May 1981 it was announced in the press that Huchel had died at his home in Staufen on 30 April. He had directed that the news of his death should be announced only after his burial. He had died peacefully around ten o'clock in the evening, his cat Minouche next to him on his pillow.

Notes

Motto

1. Cheng Cheng wrote this dedication inside his new book of verse, *Ma mère*, which he gave to Huchel in 1928. The book remained in Dora Huchel's possession after she and Huchel separated in 1946. I took a photocopy of the title page, including the dedication, in 1981. It is unfortunate that the book was lost around the time of Dora Huchel's death in 1985.

Introduction

1. Letter of 20 February 1946 from Elisabeth Langgässer to Oda Schaefer, in *Elisabeth Langgässer. Briefe 1924-1950*, 2 vols., edited by Elisabeth Hoffmann, Hamburg, 1990, i, 529-30.

2. Willy Haas, 'Ein Mann namens Peter Huchel', in *Hommage für Peter Huchel*, edited by Otto F. Best, Munich, 1968, pp. 55-9 (55).

3. Rolf Italiaander, *Gedanken-Austausch. Erlebte Kulturgeschichte in Zeugnissen aus 6 Jahrzehnten*, edited by Harald Kohtz, Bernd M. Kraske and Stefan Zynda, Düsseldorf, 1988, p. 54.

4. Günter Herburger, 'Palimpsest', *Frankfurter Rundschau*, 6 April 1991.

5. Dagmar von Gersdorff, *Marie Luise Kaschnitz. Eine Biographie*, Frankfurt, 1992, pp. 316-7.

6. Peter Huchel, 'Der Preisträger dankt', in *Peter Huchel. Materialien*, edited by Axel Vieregg, Frankfurt, 1986, pp. 15-19 (17).

7. Walter Jens, 'Über Peter Huchel', in *Am Tage meines Fortgehns. Peter Huchel (1903-1981)*, edited by Peter Walther, Frankfurt, 1996, pp. 100-2 (100).

8. Joseph Strelka, 'Zum letzten Gedichtband Peter Huchels: *Die neunte Stunde*', in J.S., *Exilliteratur*, Berne, Frankfurt and New York, 1983, pp. 219-29 (220-1).

9. Hubert Ohl, '" ... im großen Hof meines Gedächtnisses ..." Aspekte der *memoria* in Peter Huchels Gedichtband *Gezählte Tage*', *Jahrbuch des Freien Deutschen Hochstifts*, 79 (1993), pp. 281-312 (282).

10. See Andreas Mytze's letter to Reiner Kunze in *europäische ideen*, no. 84 (1993), p. 86. Mytze was replying to Reiner Kunze's question, 'Was hätte Peter Huchel getan, hätte er erlebt, daß die Ost-Berliner Akademie *en bloc* in die West-Berliner Akademie einzieht?'. See, too, R.K., *Am Sonnenhang. Tagebuch eines Jahres*, Frankfurt, 1993, p. 161.

11. Michael Hamburger, 'Randbemerkungen zum Schweigen', in *Peter Huchel. Materialien*, pp. 282-287 (282)

12. Wolf Biermann, 'Über Peter Huchel', in *Am Tage meines Fortgehns*, pp. 29-32 (31).

13. Biermann in *Am Tage meines Fortgehns*, p. 29.

14. Ludvík Kundera, 'Fragmentarische Gespräche', in *Am Tage meines Fortgehns*, pp. 53-8 (53).

15. Kundera in *Am Tage meines Fortgehns*, p. 57.

16. Günter Kunert, 'Peter Huchels gedenkend', in *Am Tage meines Fortgehns*, p. 49.

17. Uwe Grüning, 'Motorradfahren nach Wilhelmshorst', in *Am Tage meines Fortgehns*, pp. 33-7 (33).

18. Grüning in *Am Tage meines Fortgehns*, p. 33.

19. Grüning in *Am Tage meines Fortgehns*, p. 33.

20. Grüning in *Am Tage meines Fortgehns*, p. 36.

21. I conducted a series of interviews with Dora Huchel at her home in Mora, Sweden in August/September 1981. Unless otherwise indicated, statements by Dora Huchel derive from those interviews.

22. Grüning in *Am Tage meines Fortgehns*, p. 35-6.

23. The piece from the mid-1970s was entitled 'Erste Lese-Erlebnisse', the one from 1931 'Europa neunzehnhunderttraurig'. Both were collected in Peter Huchel, *Gesammelte Werke*, edited by Axel Vieregg, 2 vols., Frankfurt, 1984. Hereafter references to the 1984 edition will be included in brackets in the main body of the text. The editor notes (ii,405) that Huchel explained that his friend Hans A. Joachim had revised and improved his prose work in the early 1930s.

24. Hans-Jürgen Heise, 'Der Fall Peter Huchel', *Die Welt*, 28 October 1972.

25. Grüning in *Am Tage meines Fortgehns*, p. 36.

26. Hamburger in *Peter Huchel. Materialien*, p. 286.

27. Hamburger in *Peter Huchel. Materialien*, p. 286.

28. See Frank Wend's account in *Die Welt*, 26 May 1995 of a conference recently devoted to Huchel at Rheinsberg near Berlin. Wend writes of 'eine starke Tendenz zur distanzlosen Intimität und zur Mythenbildung. Selbst in einem zwangsweise verfaßten Stalingedicht sahen Vieregg und der Huchel-Biograph Hub Nijssen noch einen Akt des Widerstands. Der Heros muß makellos bleiben ... So wurde Rheinsberg eher zur Weihestätte als zum Ort kritischer Auseinandersetzung'. Similarly, Dorothea von Törne wrote in *Der Tagespiegel* on 23 May 1995, 'blieben die Liebhaber unter sich und die Diskussion ohne größere Kontroversen'. Yet she noted, 'Wie ein Phantom geisterte der nicht eingeladene englische Literaturwissenschaftler Stephen Parker mit seinen bislang unbewiesenen Thesen über eine vermeintliche zeitweise Nähe Peter Huchels zu den Nationalsozialisten durch das Rheinsberger Schloß'. As we shall see in the course of the present study, such a characterisation of Huchel's literary development does not begin to engage seriously with the complexities of his position with regard to the German dictatorships.

29. Horst Piontek, 'Peter Huchel – siebzig Jahre', in H.P., *Schönheit: Partisanin. Schriften zur Literatur. Zu Person und Werk*, Munich, 1983, pp. 488-91 (491).

Part 1

Chapter 1

1. The record of Huchel's birth is deposited at the Standesamt Lichterfelde, number 176 for the year 1903. The spelling of his Christian name was Hellmut, though he generally used the spelling Helmut before he adopted the name Peter. Following Huchel's own preference, the spelling Helmut will be used in the present study.

2. Information relating to the Huchels' addresses has been extracted from the 'Adreßbücher' and 'Adreßkalender' for Berlin, Potsdam and Steglitz.

3. See Introduction, footnote 21 above.

4. Material from Dora Huchel's account was included in my essay, 'Recent additions to the Peter Huchel Collection in the John Rylands University Library of Manchester', *Bulletin of the John Rylands University Library of Manchester*, 74 (1992), No. 2, pp. 85-125. This piece was followed by 'Dora Huchel's account of her life with Peter Huchel: an edition and commentary', *Bulletin of the John Rylands University Library of Manchester*, 77 (1995), No. 2, pp. 59-84.

5. Huchel made this statement during an interview conducted by Ekkehart Rudolph in the series 'Autoren im Gespräch', broadcast by Süddeutscher Rundfunk on 31 August 1973. In 1974, Huchel stated, 'Nelly Sachs schrieb mir 1948 aus Schweden, ... ob ich mich denn nicht erinnere, sie wäre doch damals als junges Mädchen vom Nachbargut, dem Gut ihres Onkels, manchen Sonntagnachmittag nach Alt-Langerwisch zu Besuch gekommen und hätte mich als kleinen Jungen an der Hand durch den Garten geführt'. (Peter Huchel, 'Der Preisträger dankt', in *Peter Huchel. Materialien*, p.15) Huchel's early post-war correspondence from Sachs is extant and there is no reference to such a childhood meeting. This is hardly surprising, since, as Sachs' biographer Ruth Dinesen assures me, there was no landowner uncle in the vicinity of Alt-Langerwisch. I should like to thank Ruth Dinesen for the above information.

6. Kundera in *Am Tage meines Forgehns*, p. 55.

7. The fifth year is referred to in the same way in 'Europa neunzehnhunderttraurig' (ii,213), the autobiographical text of 1931, as well as in 'Frau', (ii,226) another autobiographical piece that appeared that year with Joachim's help.

8. Information relating to the Zimmermanns and Michendorf is taken from a village chronicle written by Alfred Schön in 1954. Material relating to the Zimmermanns and Alt-Langerwisch is

taken from a village chronicle written by Carla Krüger and Frank Nest in the mid-1980s. I should like to thank Carla Krüger for supplying me with details from the two chronicles.

9. In a questionnaire that he filled in for his employer on 31 May 1954, Huchel claimed that his father had been a 'Bauer'. The questionnaire is deposited in Huchel's personal file, marked A1, in the Central Archive of the Stiftung Archiv der Akademie der Künste Berlin-Brandenburg, hereafter in references CAA and SAdA.

10. This information as well as details of the Huchels in Wieglitz is taken from the 'Ariernach-weis', the document proving his Aryan descent, which Huchel filled in for the Reichsschrifttumskammer in 1939. The document is deposited at the Berlin Document Center.

11. Information about the Huchel family history in Wieglitz is taken from local records. It was kindly supplied by the Revd Hans Heidenreich.

12. Details of Carl Huchel's occupation and his family's address at Belziger Straße 58 in Schöneberg are contained in the Berlin 'Adreßbücher'. The same address can be found stamped in a number of books that Huchel acquired from his cousin, Erna Huchel. The books are now deposited in the Peter Huchel Collection in the John Rylands University Library of Manchester.

13. Details of Fritz Huchel's military and civil service career are taken from the archive of the 'Königl. Provinzial-Schulkollegium zu Berlin', reference Dr. Br. Rep. 34. Prov-Schulkollegium 27. The archive is deposited in the Brandenburgisches Landeshauptarchiv, which is located in Potsdam at Sanssouci (Orangery).

14. The photograph of Fritz Huchel in uniform is reproduced in *Am Tage meines Fortgehns*, p. 20.

15. A fragment of poetry treating Fritz Huchel's death with an immediacy suggesting a composition in the autumn of 1945 is among Huchel's papers in the Deutsches Literaturarchiv Marbach.

16. Dora Huchel imitates the Alt-Langerwisch vernacular on p. 1 of the second draft of her account.

17. Records of Fritz Huchel's marriage to Marie Zimmermann are deposited at the Stadtarchiv Potsdam, together with other records of the Zimmermann and Huchel families.

18. See Hartmut Harnisch, 'Peasants and markets', in *The German Peasantry*, edited by Richard J.Evans and W.R.Lee, London/ Sidney, 1986, pp. 37-70.

19. Harnisch, p. 46.

20. The photograph is reproduced in *Am Tage meines Fortgehns*, p. 19.

21. Peter Huchel, 'Preisträger dankt', in *Peter Huchel. Materialien*, p. 16.

22. Monica Huchel in conversation with Karl Corino, Hessischer Rundfunk, 8 September 1984.

23. A postcard sketch of the house is reproduced in *Am Tage meines Fortgehns*, p. 18.

24. It is unclear what Fritz Huchel did between the end of his army career and the commencement of his duties in the civil service.

25. Huchel used the term in a letter to his wife written on 1 and 4 November 1941 in Behrenhoff and Neubrandenburg. The letter is in the Peter Huchel Collection.

26. Michael Hamburger, 'The poetry of Peter Huchel', *Poetry Nation Review*, 18 (1980), 4, pp. 8-9 (8).

27. 'Peter Huchel anläßlich einer Gedichtlesung im Dorfkrug von Alt-Langerwisch (29.03.1962)', in *Am Tage meines Fortgehns*, pp. 21-22 (21).

28. Peter Huchel, 'Der Preisträger dankt', in *Peter Huchel. Materialien*, p. 17.

29. Walter Jens, 'Wo die Dunkelheit endet. Zu den Gedichten von Peter Huchel', *Die Zeit*, 6 December 1963.

30. Hebbel's influence on 'Herkunft' can be seen through a comparison with Hebbel's 'Das alte Haus', the penultimate stanza of which reads, 'Nun schweigt es still, das alte Haus,/ Mir aber ist's, als schritten/ Die toten Väter all' heraus,/ Um für ihr Haus zu bitten,/ Und auch in meiner eignen Brust,/ Wie ruft so manche Kinder-Lust:/ Laß stehn das Haus, laß stehen!' A version of the first stanza of 'Herkunft' appeared in the *Vossische Zeitung* on 14 May 1933 under the title 'Das Haus'. See below for reference to the significance of Hebbel's 'Herbstbild' for Huchel's composition of 'Oktoberlicht'.

31. Peter Huchel, 'Der Preisträger dankt', in *Peter Huchel. Materialien*, p. 15.

32. 'Marie' was published in the *Vossische Zeitung* on 14 July 1933, in *Der weiße Rabe*, 2 (1933), 5/6, p. 32 and in *Klingsor*, 11 (1934), 8, p. 314.

33. Axel Vieregg, *Die Lyrik Peter Huchels. Zeichensprache und Privatmythologie*, Berlin, 1976, p. 111.

34. Vieregg, *Die Lyrik Peter Huchels*, p. 134.

35. Vieregg, *Die Lyrik Peter Huchels*, p. 136.

36. Vieregg, *Die Lyrik Peter Huchels*, p. 129.

37. I should like to thanks the headmaster of the Hermann-Ehlers-Oberschule for permitting me to use the school's archive, from which the information below is taken, unless otherwise indicated. I should also like to thank Frau Fürstenberg of the Bezirksamt Steglitz for her help in identifying the archive.

38. Both elementary schools had only very recently been transferred to the new buildings at Ringstraße from the old elementary school in Schloßstraße. After extensive bomb damage in 1943, the school buildings were replaced by those of the present Freiherr-von-Hünefeld-Grundschule at Lauenburgerstraße 114, formerly Ringstraße.

39. Details of the curriculum at the elementary school are contained in the annual report, 1913-14, compiled by Dr Lüdecke, headmaster of the Oberrealschule. It is deposited in the school archive.

40. Details of Fritz Huchel's schooling in Oranienburg are deposited at the Geheimes Preußisches Staatsarchiv, Dahlem in the files marked Rep. 76. Seminare Präp.-Anstalt Oranienburg, Rep. 76. Seminare 11491, Rep. 76. Seminare 11502, Rep. 76. Seminare 11503, Rep. 76. Seminare 11505 and Rep. 76. Seminare 11538.

41. See *Über Peter Huchel*, edited by Hans Mayer, Frankfurt, 1973, p. 227.

42. See *Hermann-Ehlers-Oberschule, 1906-56*. The two unacknowledged quotations below are drawn from the same source.

43. This detail is contained on the school record card made out for Helmut Huchel.

44. Records were maintained in ledgers, which I was able to consult. Other details were provided in Dr Lüdecke's annual reports.

45. This information was provided by Dr Lüdecke in his annual report.

46. Taken from Dr Lüdecke's report, pp. 16-17. Further detail below comes from the same source.

47. In 1931, Huchel would publish his own 'Weihnachtslied'. (i,67)

48. Again, details were provided by Dr Lüdecke in his annual report.

49. Both *Deutsches Lesebuch für Quinta* and *Deutsches Lesebuch für Quarta* were edited by J. Hopf, K. Paulsiek and C. Muff. The books were published in Berlin by Grote.

50. The letter is deposited in the Peter Huchel Collection.

51. See Ulrike Edschmid, *Verletzte Grenzen. Zwei Frauen, zwei Lebensgeschichten*, Hamburg/Zurich, 1992, p. 129.

52. Peter Huchel, 'Sommerabend', *Ost und West*, 1 (1947) No. 1, p. 79.

53. The minister's words are quoted in Dr Lüdecke's annual report, 1914-15.

54. Dr Lüdecke's annual report of 1914-15, p. 24.

55. Both Huchel's record card and the class ledgers record this date, the former making it clear that this was the time when Huchel's parents moved to Potsdam. Puzzlingly, the 'Lebensdaten' in *Am Tage meines Fortgehns* (p. 310) have Huchel attending the Potsdam Oberrealschule from 1915, with his parents moving to Potsdam in 1916 or 1917. In his autobiographical piece 'Erste Lese-Erlebnisse', (ii,317-26) which he set in early January 1913, Huchel suggested that he was attending school in Potsdam at that time.

Chapter 2

1. Karl Voss, compiler of the *Potsdam-Führer für Literaturfreunde*, Berlin, 1993, refers (pp. 171-4) to Huchel's residence in Wilhelmshorst after the Second World War but, like other critics, is not aware that Huchel spent his adolescent years in the Teltower Vorstadt.

2. Huchel gave Teltowerstraße 8 as his address when he registered at the University of Berlin on 19 October 1923. I should like to thank Dr W. Schultze, archivist of the Humboldt University, for supplying me with the information relating to Huchel's registration and his subsequent dealings with the University authorities.

3. Details of the Potsdam Oberrealschule are taken from *Oberrealschule Potsdam. Festschrift 1822-1922. Zur Hundertjahrfeier*, by Geheimer Studienrat Schulz. A copy is deposited in the Potsdam municipal library.

4. Gerhard Heller, *In einem besetzten Land*, Hamburg, 1982, p. 31.

5. Heller made this point to me in a letter dated 8 June 1981.

6. A photograph of Huchel and Ewald Fritsch is reproduced in my essay, 'The Peter Huchel Collection of German literature in the John Rylands University Library of Manchester', *Bulletin of the John Rylands University Library of Manchester*, 72 (1990), No. 2, pp. 135-52.

7. Records are deposited in the archive of the successor school, the Humboldt Gymnasium in Potsdam.

8. The record is held at the Krankenbuchlager in Berlin.

9. Gertrud Zappe to Peter Huchel, 15 March 1955. The letter is deposited in the Teilbestand *Sinn und Form*, ref. no. 59 in SAdA.

10. The headmaster's annual report for 1923-4 is deposited at the Pädagogisches Zentrum in Berlin.

11. Karl Alfred Wolken, 'Zwiesprache mit der Wirklichkeit', in *Über Peter Huchel*, pp. 183-204 (187).

12. Huchel refers to the juvenilia that Erna Kretschmar had returned to him in a letter to his wife written on a Monday night in mid-November 1941 at Neubrandenburg. The letter is in the Peter Huchel Collection.

13. Huchel's library is the main focus of my essay, 'The Peter Huchel Collection'.

14. Peter Huchel, 'Der Preisträger dankt', in *Peter Huchel. Materialien*, p. 17.

15. For details of editions of Rilke and George in Huchel's library, see 'The Peter Huchel Collection', especially pp. 139-41. In conversation, Huchel much later played down any suggestion that Rilke might have been an important influence. See Hans Dieter Schmidt, '"Der Fremde geht

davon ..." Erinnerungen an den Dichter Peter Huchel', in *Peter Huchel. Materialien*, pp. 299-303 (301-2).

16. Hitherto, only one essay has been published on the juvenilia, Axel Vieregg's 'Der frühe Peter Huchel', in *Am Tage meines Fortgehns*, pp. 187-211.

17. Peter Huchel, 'Der Preisträger dankt', in *Peter Huchel. Materialien*, p. 17.

18. Huchel's poem 'Der Garten des Theophrast' is a famous later use of this conceit.

19. The dedication is written on Huchel's copy of *Das Kunstblatt* which is deposited in the Peter Huchel Collection.

20. The lines are among Huchel's papers deposited in the Deutsches Literaturarchiv, Marbach.

21. Erwin Könnemann and Hans-Joachim Krusch, *Aktionseinheit contra Kapp-Putsch*, Berlin, 1972, p. 193.

22. Von der Hardt's report is deposited in Pr. Br. 2A Regierung Potsdam, I Pol. Nr. 1063 at the Brandenburgisches Landeshauptarchiv Potsdam, Sanssouci (Orangery). Subsequent references to the report draw on the same source.

23. The detail is taken from Schulz's annual report of 1921-2, which is deposited at the Pädagogisches Zentrum Berlin.

24. Records are deposited at the Humboldt Gymnasium in Potsdam.

25. The photograph is reproduced in *Am Tage meines Fortgehns*, p. 199.

Chapter 3

1. See Chapter 2, footnote 2 for archival details.

2. Gerhard Schmidt-Henkel, '"Ein Traum, was sonst?" Zu Peter Huchels Gedicht "Brandenburg"', in *Gedichte und Interpretationen*, vol. 6 (= *Gegenwart*), edited by Walter Hinck, Stuttgart, 1982, pp. 50-8 (54). Also in *Peter Huchel. Materialien*, pp. 230-7.

3. Peter Huchel, 'Der jüdische Friedhof von Sulzburg', in *Peter Huchel. Materialien*, pp. 20-30 (20).

4. See Richard Sheppard, *Die Schriften des Neuen Clubs, 1908-1914*, 2 vols., Hildesheim, 1980-3.

5. Manfred Voigts, *Oskar Goldberg. Der mythische Experimentalwissenschaftler. Ein verdrängtes Kapitel jüdischer Geschichte*, Berlin, 1992.

6. Voigts, *Oskar Goldberg. Der mythische Experimentalwissenschaftler*, p. 157.

7. Gershom Scholem, *Walter Benjamin. The story of a friendship*, Philadelphia, 1981, p. 96.

8. Ibid.

9. Sheppard, vol. ii, p. 586.

10. Manfred Voigts, 'Oskar Goldberg. Ein Dossier', *Akzente*, 36 (1989), No. 2, pp. 158-91 (158).

11. Scholem, *Walter Benjamin*, p. 97.

12. Quoted in Voigts, *Akzente*, p. 172.

13. Quoted in Voigts, *Akzente*, p. 177.

14. Gershom Scholem, *From Berlin to Jerusalem*, New York, 1980, p. 131.

15. Voigts, *Akzente*, p. 163.

16. Scholem, *Walter Benjamin*, p. 98.

17. Thomas Mann to Jonas Lesser, 25 October 1948, quoted by Voigts in *Akzente*, p. 162.

18. Quoted by Voigts in *Akzente*, p. 163.

19. Quoted by Voigts in *Oskar Goldberg. Der mythische Experimentalwissenschaftler*, p. 157.

20. Voigts, *Oskar Goldberg. Der mythische Experimentalwissenschaftler*, p. 156.

21. Manfred Voigts, 'Metaphysische Politik und psychophysisches Problem. Das Verhältnis von Walter Benjamin und Erich Unger', *Neue Deutsche Hefte*, 35 (1988), No. 200, pp. 798-808 (806).

22. Peter Huchel, 'Der jüdische Friedhof von Sulzburg', in *Peter Huchel. Materialien*, p. 20.

23. Scholem, *Walter Benjamin*, p. 96-7.

24. Oskar Goldberg, *Die Wirklichkeit der Hebräer. Einleitung in das System des Pentateuch*, Berlin, 1925, p. 1.

25. Goldberg, *Die Wirklichkeit der Hebräer*, p. 16.

26. In a note, (i,444) the editor of the 1984 edition acknowledges that the archaic spelling 'Haide' was used for the poem's first publication in 1934, yet offers no explanation for his choice of the spelling 'Heide' in the 1934 version, which is rightly presented as a separate poem from the postwar 'Wendische Heide'. (i,50) The archaic spelling 'Haide' is quite in keeping with the effect Huchel was seeking to create with his poem.

27. Ludvík Kundera, 'Die wendische Mutter', in *Über Peter Huchel*, pp. 111-8 (112).

28. Vieregg, *Die Lyrik Peter Huchels*, p. 130.

29. Vieregg, *Die Lyrik Peter Huchels*, p. 133.

30. Goldberg, *Die Wirklichkeit der Hebräer*, p. 79.

31. Goldberg, *Die Wirklichkeit der Hebräer*, p. 299.

32. Kantorowicz recounted the episode in his essay 'Peter Huchel' in A.K., *Deutsche Schicksale. Intellektuelle unter Hitler und Stalin*, Vienna, Cologne, Stuttgart and Zurich, 1964, pp. 79-93 (81).

33. See Hans Arno Joachim, *Der Philosoph am Fenster. Essays, Prosa, Hörspiele*, edited by Wolfgang Menzel, Eggingen, 1990.

34. See *Peter Huchel. Materialien*, pp. 20-30. Subsequent quotations from the essay are from the same source.

35. Wulf Kirsten in his introduction to *Der Philosoph am Fenster*, pp. 5-7 (5).

36. I should like to thank Dr Dieter Speck, University Archivist of the University of Freiburg, for supplying me with details of Huchel's registration in Freiburg.

37. In 1973, he was accompanied by Michael Hamburger, whose poem 'In Staufen', which he dedicated to Huchel, includes reference to the visit.

38. Kantorowicz, *Deutsche Schicksale*, p. 81.

39. Alfred Kantorowicz, 'Das beredte Schweigen des Dichters Peter Huchel', *Zwanzig. Jahrbuch. Freie Akademie der Künste in Hamburg*, Hamburg, 1968, p. 159.

40. Ibid.

41. Wolfgang Heidenreich, 'Gespräche mit stummen Zonen unseres Lebens', *Badische Zeitung*, 18 July 1980.

42. Huchel's letter to his wife was sent from Neubrandenburg to Michendorf and written on a Monday night. Dora Huchel estimated that it had been written in mid-November 1941 on the basis of the dates of previous and subsequent letters.

43. Kundera, in fact, noted, 'Herbst 1924 Oberbayern; dann Wien', in *Am Tage meines Fortgehns*. p. 55.

44. Dora Huchel wrote the word Elmau at the beginning of her account of her life with Huchel. Beatrix Fankhauser kindly supplied me with a photocopy of the page in the guest book of Schloß Elmau which includes Huchel's and Joachim's entries. She also sent me Bernhard Müller-Elmau's *Vom Wesen der Elmau*, 9th edition, Schloß Elmau, 1993, from which information about Johannes Müller is drawn.

45. Eduard Zak, *Der Dichter Peter Huchel. Versuch einer Darstellung seines lyrischen Werkes*, Berlin, 1953, p. 32.

46. Peter Gay, *Weimar Culture. The Outsider as Insider*, London, 1988, p. 82.

47. I should like to thank Herbert Koch of the Vienna City Archive for supplying me with information concerning Huchel's and Dora Lassel's residence in Vienna.

48. This information was kindly supplied by Dr Kurt Mühlberger, University Achivist of the University of Vienna. A photograph of Huchel's 'Meldungsbuch', reproduced on p. 314 of *Am Tage meines Fortgehns* bears the date of 5 May 1926 for his registration at the University of Vienna.

49. For details of Hofmannsthal's works in Huchel's library, see my essay, 'The Peter Huchel Collection', pp. 138-40.

50. See Peter Huchel, 'Der Preisträger dankt', in *Peter Huchel. Materialien*, p. 17.

51. For details of Kafka's works in Huchel's library, see my essay, 'The Peter Huchel Collection', pp. 142-3. There are no works by Trakl in the Peter Huchel Collection.

52. Dora Huchel kindly provided me with a photocopy of Eugen Lassel's account of his life when I visited her in 1981. A photograph of Eugen Lassel and his wife Josefine together with Huchel and their daughter, taken on 22 April 1930, is reproduced in my essay, 'Recent Additions to the Peter Huchel Collection'.

53. Dora Lassel's address at the time was actually Reisnerstraße 25/9. (See footnote 47 above.) Zak, *Der Dichter Peter Huchel*, p. 22 gives 1922 as the year in which 'Die Kammer' was composed.

54. See footnote 48 above. Emil Reich's *Henrik Ibsens Dramen*, published in 1925 by Fischer in Berlin, is in the Peter Huchel Collection.

55. Huchel recalled the Wachau trip in a letter to his wife that he sent from a Franconian holiday which he spent with Günter Eich and A. Artur Kuhnert in the late autumn of 1937. The letter is in the Peter Huchel Collection.

56. *Mit allen Sinnen. Lyrik unserer Zeit* was edited for the Berlin Rembrandt Verlag in 1932 by Carl Dietrich Carls and Arno Ullmann. It contains five poems by Huchel. The copy in the Peter Huchel Collection includes annotations in Huchel's hand.

57. The letters exchanged by Huchel and Dora Lassel in the summer of 1926 have not survived.

58. Huchel's statement, dated 18 May 1948, is deposited in the Teilbestand *Sinn und Form*, ref. no. 59, SAdA. Kundera notes (*Am Tage meines Fortgehns*, p. 55), 'Frankreich 1926-28, drei Jahre. Größtenteils in Paris, ein Vierteljahr in der Bretagne. Nizza, Korsika, Grenoble, ein Vierteljahr in einem halbzerfallenen Haus Couronne (?)'.

59. Dora Huchel prefaces the section with the statement, 'Diese Aufzeichnungen sind ein Wettlauf mit der Krankheit. Es kann nur noch Stichworte geben'.

60. See Chapter 2, footnote 2 above.

61. Wolken in *Über Peter Huchel*, p. 187.

62. Horst Lommer, 'Das dichterische Wort Peter Huchels', *Tägliche Rundschau*, 4 June 1947. Now in *Peter Huchel. Materialien*, pp. 273-6 (274).

63. Huchel requested a leaving certificate on 26 November 1927. It was completed on 9 December 1927. See Chapter 2, footnote 2.

64. Joachim's two undated letters to Huchel are included in *Der Philosoph am Fenster*, p. 215.

65. Huchel's collection *Die Sternenreuse*, Munich, 1967, contains on p. 48 the reference 'Straßburg/ Paris 1927' regarding the composition of 'Lenz'.

66. Huchel made the statement in an undated letter from the late 1950s to Günther Caspar of the Aufbau Verlag. The letter is in Teilbestand *Sinn und Form*, ref. no. 58, SAdA.

67. The manuscript is among Huchel's papers in the Deutsches Literaturarchiv, Marbach. The information about the original title is not included in the 1984 edition.

68. In a letter of 8 October 1929, Joachim would encourage Huchel to send the publisher Pyler material for a 'Chansonbuch'. The letter is included in *Der Philosoph am Fenster*, pp. 216-7.

69. The letter is included in *Der Philosoph am Fenster*, p. 216.

70. Monica Huchel, *Fürst Myschkin und die anderen. Ein Katzen-Brevier*, Frankfurt, 1985, p. 96.

71. Joachim's postcard to Huchel, undated though evidently from the autumn of 1929, is in *Der Philosoph am Fenster*, p. 217.

72. It is of interest to note that in his *roman à clef Der Sohn eines Bürgers*, Alfred Kantorowicz – who got to know Huchel in Paris in 1928 and explored the city with him – makes a similar reference, 'Wir besuchten die Negerbälle in der rue Blomet in Paris'. See *Ost und West*, 2 (1948), No. 4, p. 71.

73. The pieces were recently collected in Wambly Bald, *On the Left Bank 1929-1933*, edited by Benjamin Franklin V, Athens, Ohio, London, 1985.

74. Alfred Kantorowicz, *Deutsches Tagebuch*, 2 vols., Berlin, 1980, i, 404.

75. Cheng Cheng's *Ma mère* remained in Dora Huchel's possession after she and Huchel separated in 1946. I took a photocopy of the title page, including the dedication, in 1981. It is unfortunate that the book was lost around the time of Dora Huchel's death in 1985.

76. Lommer, 'Das dichterische Wort Peter Huchels'.

77. See Gordon McVay, *Esenin. A life*, Michigan, 1976, p. 212 and p. 291.

78. Alfred Kantorowicz, *Der Sohn eines Bürgers*, *Ost und West*, 2 (1948), No. 4, p. 70.

79. Norbert Randow, 'Ein Besuch bei Peter Huchel und seine Folgen', in *Am Tage meines Fortgehns*, pp. 127-35.

80. In November 1960 Huchel wrote to August Closs, recalling the same trip to Brittany. (ii,346)

81. Kundera in *Am Tage meines Fortgehns*, p. 57.

82. Kantorowicz, *Deutsche Schicksale*, p. 82.

83. See footnote 58 above.

84. Franz Lennartz, *Deutsche Schriftsteller der Gegenwart*, 11th edition, Stuttgart, 1978, pp. 357-60 (357).

85. See *On the Left Bank* for sketched portraits of Foujita.

86. Kundera in *Am Tage meines Fortgehns*, p. 57.

87. Kantorowicz, *Deutsche Schicksale*, p. 82.

88. Karola Bloch, *Aus meinem Leben*, Pfullingen, 1981, p. 38.

89. Kantorowicz, *Zwanzig*, p. 163.

90. Kantorowicz, *Deutsche Schicksale*, p. 82.

91. Ibid.

92. Kundera in *Am Tage meines Fortgehns*, p. 55.

93. Joachim sent a card dated 8 October 1929 to Huchel at Corenc. See *Der Philosoph am Fenster*, pp. 216-7.

94. See *Der Philosoph am Fenster*, p. 216.

95. See, for example, Huchel's letter to his wife dated 22 December 1941, which is in the Peter Huchel Collection.

96. Monica Huchel acknowledges Huchel's abiding attachment to Dora in a passage of her mémoirs that reveals the intense rivalry, jealousy and bitterness between the two women in Huchel's life. Monica Huchel writes, 'Diese Ehe belastete ihn sehr, aber es war eben auch Huchel, der es nicht fertiggebracht hatte, sich einer Frau gegenüber eindeutig zu verhalten, mit der er nicht leben wollte'. (In Edschmid, pp. 126-7.)

97. Kundera in *Am Tage meines Fortgehns*, p. 57.

98. Seelbach's letter to Huchel is in Teilbestand *Sinn und Form*, ref. no. 56, SAdA.

99. Kundera in *Am Tage meines Fortgehns*, p. 57.

100. See footnote 93 above.

Chapter 4

1. See Chapter 3, footnote 46 above.

2. The account is dated 18 May 1948 and can be assumed to form part of his formal application for the editorship of *Sinn und Form*. It is deposited in the Teilbestand *Sinn und Form*, ref. no. 59, SAdA.

3. Rosen is described in a similar manner in correspondence between two other contributors to *Die literarische Welt*, Walter Benjamin and Ernst Bloch. See Ernst Bloch, *Briefe. 1903-1975*, 2 vols., edited by Karola Bloch, Frankfurt, 1985, ii, p. 666.

4. See Italiaander, *Gedanken-Austausch*, p. 55.

5. Haas in *Hommage für Peter Huchel*, p. 55.

6. Haas in *Hommage für Peter Huchel*, pp. 55-6.

7. Haas in *Hommage für Peter Huchel*, p. 55.

8. Italiaander, *Gedanken-Austausch*, p. 54.

9. He reported on the visit to Brecht and another to Döblin in a letter to Dora Lassel in December 1929. The letter, written in French, is in the Peter Huchel Collection.

10. Huchel's copy of the first edition of Brecht's *Hauspostille* is in the Peter Huchel Collection. It contains a sketched portrait of Brecht by Huchel.

11. Willy Haas, 'Restauration?', *Die literarische Welt*, 16 May 1930.

12. Anton Kaes, *Weimarer Republik. Manifeste und Dokumente zur deutschen Literatur 1918-1933*, Stuttgart, 1983, p. 45.

13. The letters are in the Peter Huchel Collection.

14. Huchel's second wife, Monica, presumably drawing upon her husband's account of his first marriage, states in her memoirs, 'Er war in diese Ehe regelrecht hiningeraten'. (See Edschmid, p. 126). Clearly, Eugen Lassel's role was decisive in determining that the couple should marry, an arrangement which neither Huchel nor Dora Lassel had actively sought. Monica Huchel's account overlooks the fact that Huchel and Dora Lassel had spent four years together before the intervention of Eugen Lassel and that their marriage lasted for sixteen years. Nor does it take into account the issue of Huchel's dependence, emotional as much as financial, on his female companion. His later reluctance to acknowledge his dependence translated, as was the raconteur's way, into stories of the sort we have already encountered in his presentation of his life in the 1920s.

15. The record of the marriage is deposited at the Stadtarchiv in Potsdam.

16. The photographs are reproduced in 'Recent additions to the Peter Huchel Collection'.

17. Lommer and Wolken are prime representatives of this tendency. See Chapter 3 above, footnotes 61 and 62.

18. A copy of Wilma Papst's doctorate, *Frege als Philosoph*, Berlin, 1932, is in the Peter Huchel Collection.

19. Kantorowicz, *Zwanzig*, p.163.

20. See Kundera in *Am Tage meines Fortgehns*, p. 58. By contrast, in a biographical piece for the Aufbau Verlag, which he wrote in the immediate post-war years, Huchel referred to his 'kritische und essayistische Arbeiten' in *Die literarische Welt*. The emphasis is in keeping with the orientation of his early post-war career. The piece, entitled 'Peter Huchel', is in the archive of the Aufbau Verlag.

21. Kantorowicz, *Zwanzig*, p. 163.

22. Huchel used the address in his correspondence with Martin Raschke, which is among Raschke's papers in the Sächsische Landesbibliothek in Dresden.

23. The photos of Huchel at Kladow are reproduced in my essay 'Recent additions to the Peter Huchel Collection'.The photo of Haas' car is in the Peter Huchel Collection.

24. See Kundera in *Am Tage meines Fortgehns*, p.55.

25. Huchel made these statements in the interview conducted by Rudolph.

26. Walter Benjamin, *Gesammelte Schriften*, 7 vols., edited by Rolf Tiedemann and Hermann Schweppenhäuser, Frankfurt, 1985, vi, p. 444.

27. Huchel's copy of Raschke's *Neue lyrische Anthologie* in the Peter Huchel Collection is particularly interesting due to its annotations in Huchel's hand. For details see 'The Peter Huchel Collection', p. 146.

28. Oda Schaefer, *Auch wenn du träumst, gehen die Uhren. Lebenserinnerungen*, Munich, 1970, p. 260.

29. Schaefer, *Auch wenn du träumst, gehen die Uhren*, p. 260.

30. See above all Hans Dieter Schäfer's essays collected in the volume *Das gespaltene Bewußtsein. Deutsche Kultur und Lebenswirklichkeit 1933-1945*, Munich and Vienna, 1981.

31. The article is reprinted in Kaes, p. 674.

32. Joseph P. Dolan, 'The politics of Peter Huchel's early verse', *The University of Dayton Review*, 13 (1978), No. 2, pp. 93-104 (93). It was re-printed as 'Die Politik in Peter Huchels früher Dichtung', in *Peter Huchel. Materialien*, pp. 92-119.

33. Huchel made this statement in the interview with Rudolph.

34. Dolan, p. 93.

35. The existence of Huchel's correspondence with Raschke in Dresden (see footnote 22 above) only became common knowledge after 1989.

36. In what was evidently a later, undated letter to Raschke, Huchel, to judge from the poems mentioned as well as the references to pagination, discussed the proofs of Raschke's *Neue lyrische Anthologie*.

37. Dolan, pp. 98-9.

38. Hans Dieter Schäfer writes, 'Das soziale Element freilich wurde in der Laudatio Martin Raschkes wegretuschiert'. See Hans Dieter Schäfer, 'Naturdichtung und Neue Sachlichkeit', in *Die deutsche Literatur in der Weimarer Republik*, edited by Wolfgang Rothe, Stuttgart, 1974, pp. 359-81 (368).

39. Martin Raschke, 'Zu den Gedichten Peter Huchels', now in *Über Peter Huchel*, pp. 157-9 (159). Subsequent quotations from Raschke's speech are taken from the same source.

40. Kantorowicz, in *Zwanzig*, p.164.

41. In a questionnaire that he filled in for the Reichsschrifttumskammer and signed on 10 March 1938, Huchel wrote that he had been a member of the SDS from 1932-3.

42. Kantorowicz, in *Zwanzig*, p.164.

43. Kantorowicz, in *Deutsche Schicksale*, p. 86.

44. Kantorowicz, *Deutsches Tagebuch*, i, p. 253.

45. Kantorowicz, *Deutsches Tagebuch*, i, p. 254.

46. Karola Bloch, p. 69.

47. Karola Bloch, p. 69.

48. Karola Bloch, pp. 69-70.

49. The questionnaire, which is dated 31 May 1954, is in CAA, A1, SAdA.

50. Willy Haas, 'Einleitung zu dieser Nummer', *Die literarische Welt*, 8 April 1932.

51. Langgässer's *Grenze: Besetztes Gebiet* and her *Triptychon des Teufels* are in the Peter Huchel Collection.

52. See Langgässer, *Briefe 1924-1950*, i, p. 150.

53. Huchel made the statement in the interview with Rudolph.

54. Huchel later acknowledged Haas' role in arranging the broadcast. (ii,299)

55. Peter Huchel, 'Der Preisträger dankt', in *Peter Huchel. Materialien*, p. 17.

56. Kurt Pinthus, *Menschheitsdämmerung*, Hamburg, 1959, p. 29.

57. In his essay 'Der frühe Peter Huchel' (in *Am Tage meines Fortgehns*, pp. 187-211 (191), Axel Vieregg quite misleadingly quotes from a statement from the 1970s, whilst claiming that it comes from 1931, in order to support his argument concerning the continuity of a dimension of social concern for the underprivileged in Huchel's poetry.

58. See Wilfrid Bade, *Kulturpolitische Aufgaben der deutschen Presse*, Berlin, 1933, p. 22.

59. Gotthard Böhm, 'Freiheit mein Stern', *Die Presse* (Vienna), 28 January 1972.

Chapter 5

1. Eberhard Haufe, 'Nachwort', in *Johannes Bobrowski. Peter Huchel. Briefwechsel*, Marbach, 1993, p. 46. See Chapter 6 below for further discussion of Huchel's early post-war relationship with Lommer.

2. The extract from Eberhard Meckel's diary was published by his son Christoph Meckel in *Suchbild: Über meinen Vater*, Düsseldorf, 1980, p. 40.

3. Karola Bloch, p. 81.

4. Huchel made this claim in his statement of 18 May 1948 that is deposited in Teilbestand *Sinn und Form*, ref. no. 59, SAdA.

5. See the questionnaire dated 24 May 1948 that is deposited in Teilbestand *Sinn und Form*, ref. no. 59, SAdA.

6. For a discussion of the use of the term non-Nazi, see Schäfer's essays in *Das gespaltene Bewußtsein*.

7. For details, see Chapter 4, footnote 58 above.

8. Haas, in *Hommage für Peter Huchel*, p. 56.

9. See Schäfer, *Das gespaltene Bewußtsein*, p. 7.

10. Huchel included this information in a questionnaire which he completed for the Reichsverband Deutscher Schriftsteller on 29 December 1933. The questionnaire is in the Berlin Document Center.

11. Schaefer, *Auch wenn Du träumst, gehen die Uhren*, p. 262.

12. Horst Lange, 'Bemerkungen zum Inhalt dieses Heftes', *Der weiße Rabe*, 2 (1933), No. 5/6. Links between Lehmann and the *Kolonne* Circle continued throughout the 1930s. Lehmann's collection *Antwort des Schweigens*, published in 1935, made a great impression on the group. See, for example, the reference to the postcard sent to Lehmann by Günter Eich, Eberhard Meckel and Martin Raschke on 5 October 1936, in *Günter Eich*, edited by Joachim Storck, Marbach, 1988, p. 23. In a letter to Lehmann dated 6 December 1939, Meckel referred to the collection, assuring Lehmann that he was loved by all Meckels friends, including Eich, Raschke, Huchel, Paul Alverdes and Georg Britting. The letter is deposited in the Deutsches Literaturarchiv, Marbach.

13. In his book *Der eigenen Fehlbarkeit begegnet: Günter Eichs Realitäten 1933-45*, Eggingen, 1993, p. 5, Axel Vieregg seeks to distance not only Huchel, but also Lange and Schaefer from Eich in the early period of Nazi rule.

14. Horst Lange, 'Landschaftliche Dichtung', *Der Weiße Rabe*, 2 (1933), No. 5/6, pp. 21-6. Subsequent references are taken from the same source.

15. Christoph Meckel, *Suchbild*, p. 38.

16. Ibid.

17. See Oskar Loerke, *Tagebücher 1903-1939*, edited by Hermann Kasack, Heidelberg and Darmstadt, 1956, p. 257 and p. 334.

18. Schaefer, *Auch wenn Du träumst, gehen die Uhren*, p. 264.

19. The statement is deposited in the Berlin Document Center.

20. Wolken in *Über Peter Huchel*, p. 188.

21. Heinrich Zillich, 'Peter Huchel und die Siebenbürger Sachsen', *Südostdeutsche Vierteljahresblätter*, 27 (1978), pp. 294-5.

22. See the introduction to *Das Innere Reich. 1934-1944. Eine Zeitschrift für Dichtung, Kunst und deutsches Leben*, edited by Werner Volke, Marbach, 1983.

23. The letter is quoted in Volke, p. 14.

24. The statement is reproduced in *Das Innere Reich. 1934-1944. Eine Zeitschrift für Dichtung, Kunst und deutsches Leben. Verzeichnis der Beiträge*, edited by Adelheid Westhoff, Marbach, 1983, p. 2.

25. See Glenn Cuomo, *Career at the cost of compromise: Günter Eich's life and work in the years 1933-1945*, Amsterdam and Altanta, 1989, pp. 24-5.

26. See Volke, p. 19.

27. The statement is made in a letter of 24 July 1940 from the Reichsschrifttumskammer to the Deutsche Schillerstiftung. The letter is in the Berlin Document Center.

28. See Wolfram Wessels, '"Die tauben Ohren der Geschlechter". Peter Huchel und der Rundfunk', broadcast by Südwestfunk on 16 January 1994. For an excellent general study see Wessels' book *Hörspiele im Dritten Reich. Zur Institutionen-, Theorie- und Literaturgeschichte*, Bonn, 1985.

29. See *verboten und verbrannt. Deutsche Literatur – 12 Jahre unterdrückt*, edited by Richard Drews and Alfred Kantorowicz, Munich, 1947, p. 77.

30. Vieregg, *Die Lyrik Peter Huchels*, p. 9.

31. Monica Huchel wrote to me in that vein on 9 November 1980.

32. Franz Schonauer, 'Peter Huchel: Porträt eines Lyrikers', in *Über Peter Huchel*, pp. 36-48 (41).

33. Bernhard Gajek, 'Dichter – Natur – Geschichte. Peter Huchels Weg in die deutsche Gegenwart', in *Die deutsche Teilung im Spiegel der Literatur. Beiträge zur Literatur und Germanistik der DDR*, edited by Karl Lamers, Stuttgart, 1978, pp. 121-44 (126-7).

34. Franz Lennartz, *Die Dichter unserer Zeit*, Stuttgart, 1938, p. 137.

35. Gajek, 'Dichter – Natur – Geschichte', p. 126.

36. For further details, see the 1984 edition. (ii,410)

37. See footnote 10 above.

38. For details of Hoffmann's career, see Vieregg, *Der eigenen Fehlbarkeit begegnet*, p. 66, footnote 15.

39. The lines are quoted by Wessels in '"Die tauben Ohren der Geschlechter"'.

40. See Mayer's afterword to Huchel's *Margarethe Minde*, Frankfurt, 1984, pp. 77-8.

41. See Vieregg's *Der eigenen Fehlbarkeit begegnet*. For criticism, see my essay '"Ein hoffnungsvoller Vertreter der Funkdichtung": Peter Huchel's radio work in Nazi Germany', in *Aliens – Uneingebürgerte*, edited by Ian Wallace, Amsterdam and Altanta, 1994, pp. 101-34.

42. Eich's letters to Huchel referred to here and below are deposited in the Deutsches Literaturarchiv, Marbach.

43. Christoph Meckel, *Suchbild*, p. 27.

44. See Lange's letter to Raschke of 4 April 1934, which is quoted by Vieregg in *Der eigenen Fehlbarkeit begegnet*, pp. 15-6.

45. Christoph Meckel, *Suchbild*, pp. 31-2.

46. The postcard is in the Peter Huchel Collection.

47. Susanne Huchel is quoted by Wessels in '"Die tauben Ohren der Geschlechter"'.

48. See Monica Huchel in Edschmid, p. 136.

49. The manuscript of 'Ballade im Eisfenster' is in the archive of Norddeutscher Rundfunk in Hamburg.

50. Schäfer, *Das gespaltene Bewußtsein*, p. 41.

51. Wessels, *Hörspiele im Dritten Reich*, p. 441.

52. Wessels, *Hörspiele im Dritten Reich*, p. 443.

53. Wessels, '"Die tauben Ohren der Geschlechter"'.

54. See 'Über hundert Originalmanuskripte', *Rundfunk und Fernsehen*, 7 (1959), No. 1/2, pp. 45-60 (51-2).

55. Ibid.

56. Schaefer, *Auch wenn Du träumst, gehen die Uhren*, p. 261.

57. For details see *Eugen Claassen. Von der Arbeit eines Verlegers*, edited by Reinhard Tgahrt, Marbach, 1981, p. 11.

58. Heinz Schwitzke, *Das Hörspiel. Dramaturgie und Geschichte*, Cologne and Berlin, 1963, p. 181.

59. See my essay 'The Peter Huchel Collection' pp. 147-8 for a discussion of the importance of Lenau's poetry for Huchel's cycle, as illustrated by Huchel's marginalia in the Lenau editions in the Peter Huchel Collection.

60. See Vieregg, *Der eigenen Fehlbarkeit begegnet*, p. 48 ff.

61. Gerd Eckert, 'Wo steht das Hörspiel?', *Die Literatur*, 39 (1936-7), pp. 298-300 (299).

62. Kundera kindly showed me the notes he made of his conversations with Huchel. This note remains unpublished.

63. Heribert Besch, *Dichtung zwischen Vision und Wirklichkeit. Eine Analyse des Werkes von Hermann Kasack mit Tagebuchedition (1930-1943)*, St. Ingbert, 1992, p. 496.

64. Besch, p. 500.

65. Lennartz, *Die Dichter unserer Zeit*, pp. 137-8.

66. Lennartz, *Die Dichter unserer Zeit*, p. 138.

67. Huchel's statement, dated 24 May 1948, is deposited in Teilbestand *Sinn und Form*, ref. no. 59, SAdA.

68. Lange's letter to Claassen of 4 June 1936 is quoted by Hans Dieter Schäfer in Horst Lange, *Tagebücher aus dem zweiten Weltkrieg*, edited by Hans Dieter Schäfer, Mainz, 1979, pp. 227-8.

69. The signed copy of Lange's *Schwarze Weide* is in the Peter Huchel Collection.

70. For a discussion, see Hub Nijssen, 'Peter Huchel als Propagandist? Über die Autorschaft des Hörspiels "Die Greuel von Denshawai"', *Neophilologus*, 77 (1993), No. 4, pp. 635-36.

71. Wessels, *Hörspiele im Dritten Reich*, p. 170

72. Huchel's letter to his wife is in the Peter Huchel Collection.

73. The name Itau crops up much later in Huchel's poem 'Entzauberung', (i,246) which ends with the lines, 'In Wahrheit/ zog Itau, der Zigeuner,/ im hellen Juli/ durchs Bischofslila der Disteln/ für immer fort'.

74. For further discussion of Huchel's relations with Eich and Kuhnert, see my essay 'Recent additions to the Peter Huchel Collection', p. 113 ff.

75. See Wessels, '"Die tauben Ohren der Geschlechter"'.

76. Ibid.

77. Papers in the Berlin Document Centre show that Heller joined the NSDAP on 1 February 1934.

78. Schäfer, *Das gespaltene Bewußtsein*, p. 41.

79. The manuscript is in the Deutsches Rundfunkarchiv, Frankfurt. The recording was recently discovered near Prague, among much other radio material from the Nazi period.

80. See Vieregg, *Der eigenen Fehlbarkeit begegnet*, p. 5.

81. Quoted in Schäfer, *Das gespaltene Bewußtsein*, p. 40.

82. See Wessels, '"Die tauben Ohren der Geschlechter"'.

83. Lennartz, *Die Dichter unserer Zeit*, p. 138.

84. Schäfer, *Das gespaltene Bewußtsein*, p. 40.

85. For details, see 'Recent additions to the Peter Huchel Collection', p. 115 ff.

86. The correspondence is in the Peter Huchel Collection.

87. See Desch, p. 514.

88. See Eich's letter to Ursula Kuhnert of 15 August 1938. The letters are in the possession of Kuhnert's son, Thomas.

89. See Wessels, '"Die tauben Ohren der Geschlechter"'.

90. Lange's letter to Kreuder of 27 February 1939 is deposited in the Deutsches Literaturarchiv, Marbach.

91. The letter is among the papers relating to Huchel in the Berlin Document Center.

92. Quoted in Wessels, *Hörspiele im Dritten Reich*, p. 295.

93. For details, see Wessels, *Hörspiele im Dritten Reich*, pp. 299-300.

94. For further details, see my essays, 'Peter Huchel als Propagandist. Huchels 1940 entstandene Adaption von George Bernard Shaws "Die Greuel von Denschawai"', *Rundfunk und Fernshen*, 39 (1991), No. 3, pp.343-53 and 'On Peter Huchel's adaptation of Shaw's "Denshawai Horror" and related matters', *Neophilologus*, 79 (1995), pp. 295-306.

95. See Cuomo, p. 63.

96. See Kundera, in *Am Tage meines Fortgehns*, p. 58.

97. See Wessels, '"Die tauben Ohren der Geschlechter"'.

98. Lange, *Tagebücher aus dem zweiten Weltkrieg*, p. 24.

99. Wessels, *Hörspiele im Dritten Reich*, p. 304.

100. Vieregg, *Der eigenen Fehlbarkeit begegnet*, pp. 57-8.

101. Monica Huchel in Edschmid, p. 118.

102. See Vieregg, *Der eigenen Fehlbarkeit begegnet*, p. 58.

103. This detail is not included among the notes of Huchel's conversations with Kundera in *Am Tage meines Fortgehns*.

104. See Koeppen's testimony in his interview with Manfred Durzak 'Überleben im Dritten Reich', *Neue Rundschau*, 95 (1984), No. 4, pp. 88-98 (97).

105. See Huchel's statement of 18 May 1948 in Teilbestand *Sinn und Form*, ref. no. 59, SAdA.

106. See footnote 103 above.

107. See Kantorowicz in *Zwanzig*, p. 167 and Bernhard Gajek, 'Tradition und Widerstand. Einführung in das Werk Peter Huchels', *Regensburger Universitätszeitung*, 10 (1974), No. 5, pp. 2-9 (3).

108. Michael Hamburger, 'The Poetry of Peter Huchel', *Poetry Nation Review*, 18 (1980), No. 4, pp. 8-9 (8).

109. Anon., 'Repräsentant deutscher Lyrik', *Nachtexpreß*, 2 April 1953.

110. Lommer, 'Das dichterische Wort Peter Huchels'. Huchel himself used the 1940 dating at least once. (ii,371)

111. The poem was first published under the title 'Im nassen Sand' in the second October issue of *Die Dame* in 1941, p. 34.

112. See my essay 'On Peter Huchel's adaptation of Shaw's "Denshawai Horror" and related matters', p. 306, footnote 28 for further discussion of Huchel's dating of 'Späte Zeit'.

113. See. Monica Huchel's statement in Edschmid, p. 116, 'Huchel hatte ziemliche Schwierigkeiten, weil er einen Offizierslehrgang nach dem anderen ablehnte'.

114. See Fritz Rudolf Fries, 'Das Senfkorn in einem Garten der Mark', *Der Tagesspiegel*, 12 March 1994 for Arendt's apparent dislike of Huchel's 'Seßhaftigkeit'.

115. Günther Birkenfeld, 'Peter Huchel. Porträt eines Dichters', *Ost und West*, 1 (1947), No. 1, pp. 77-8 (78).

116. The book is in the Peter Huchel Collection.

117. See Wessels, '"Die tauben Ohren der Geschlechter"'.

118. Huchel included this information in the questionnaire dated 31 May 1954. It is in CAA, ref. no. A1, SAdA.

119. Kantorowicz, *Deutsche Schicksale*, p. 84.

120. Monica Huchel in Edschmid, p. 126.

Part 2

Chapter 6

1. Monica Huchel in Edschmid, p. 126.

2. See Axel Vieregg, 'The truth about Peter Huchel?', *German Life and Letters*, 41 (1988), No. 2, pp. 159-83 (179).

3. This information was conveyed to me in a letter dated 15 February 1984 from the Polizeipräsident in Berlin.

4. Markus Wolf, *Die Troika*, Reinbek, 1991, p. 200.

5. See Wilfried Loth, *Stalins ungeliebtes Kind. Warum Moskau die DDR nicht wollte*, Berlin, 1994, p. 24. For a discussion of Stalin's German policy and GDR cultural politics of the early 1950s see Peter Davies, 'Ideology, resistance and complicity in the *Deutsche Akademie der Künste* in the context of Stalin's German policy 1945-53' (unpublished doctoral thesis, University of Manchester, 1997).

6. Werner Wilk, 'Peter Huchel', *Neue Deutsche Hefte*, 9 (1962), No. 90, pp. 81-96 (85).

7. The questionnaire is deposited in the Teilbestand *Sinn und Form*, ref. no. 59, SAdA.

8. See Heike Tauch, 'Der Hörspielautor Peter Huchel', in *Am Tage meines Fortgehns*, pp. 212-227 (224).

9. The notes of 26 August and 2 September 1945 are in the Peter Huchel Collection.

10. The Mayakovsky edition is in the Peter Huchel Collection.

11. Friedrich Huchel's death certificate, deposited at the Stadtarchiv in Potsdam, names natural causes as the reason for his death. The 1984 edition (i,422) mistakenly names December as the month in which Friedrich Huchel died.

12. Langgässer, *Briefe 1924-1950*, i, 509. For a photo of a rather gaunt Huchel taken at that time, see *Am Tage meines Fortgehns*, p. 234.

13. Max Seydewitz, *Es hat sich gelohnt zu leben*, 2 vols., Berlin, 1976-8, ii, 81.

14. Langgässer, *Briefe 1924-1950*, i, pp. 529-30.

15. Paula Steiner, 'Fünf Minuten Gedichte', *Nachtexpreß*, 16 February.1948.

16. Hedda Zinner, *Auf dem roten Teppich*, Berlin, 1978, p. 81.

17. Zinner, p. 115.

18. Zinner, pp. 81-2. Zinner's account is echoed in an article entitled 'Peter Huchel' and published on 29 February 1948 in *Sonntag*.

19. Rudi Elter's letter to Dora Huchel is in the Peter Huchel Collection.

20. Huchel provided this information in a questionnaire dated 29 June 1951, which is deposited in the Teilbestand *Sinn und Form*, ref. no. 59, SAdA.

21. A photograph of a meeting of Seydewitz's management team, including Huchel, is reproduced in *Am Tage meines Fortgehns*, p. 216.

22. See Axel Vieregg, *Der eigenen Fehlbarkeit begegnet*, p. 16.

23. The interview with Karl Corino was broadcast by Hessischer Rundfunk on 8 September 1984.

24. Monica Huchel in Edschmid, p. 125.

25. Monica Huchel in Edschmid, p. 124.

26. Monica Huchel in Edschmid, p. 125.

27. Monica Huchel in Edschmid, p. 129.

28. Monica Huchel in Edschmid, p. 126-7.

29. See Fritz Rudolf Fries, 'Das Senfkorn in einem Garten der Mark', *Der Tagesspiegel*, 12 March 1994.

30. The visitors' book is in the archive of the Kulturbund in Berlin.

31. Ruth Hoffmann's *Dunkler Engel*, Leipzig, 1946 is in the Peter Huchel Collection. It contains the dedication 'Für Dora Huchel Ruth Hoffmann'.

32. The minutes of the meeting of 24 August 1945 are in the archive of the Kulturbund, ref. no. 97/498.

33. The report of the evening at the Kulturbund in *Tägliche Rundschau* on 8 December 1946 indicates that the content of Huchel's paper was the same as his 'Rede über das Hörspiel' (ii,254-60), which is dated 1947 in the 1984 edition. It is likely that Huchel delivered the same paper to colleagues at Radio Berlin.

34. The memorandum is in the archive of the Kulturbund, ref. no. 16/223.

35. Kantorowicz, *Deutsches Tagebuch*, i, pp. 252-3.

36. Kantorowicz, *Deutsches Tagebuch*, i, p. 254.

37. See Monica Huchel in Edschmid, p. 202 for a correction of Kantorowicz's statement. See footnote 3 above for details of Huchel's registration.

38. See *Allein mit Lebensmittelkarten ist es nicht getan. Autoren- und Verlegerbriefe 1945-1949*, edited by Elmar Faber and Casten Wurm, Berlin, 1991, p. 116.

39. See the archive of the Kulturbund, ref. no. 16/218.

40. Lommer, 'Das dichterische Wort Peter Huchels'. Lommer's essay, first published in *Tägliche Rundschau* on 4 June 1946, was reprinted in *Peter Huchel. Materialien* and was recently referred to as an apparently authoritative source in *Johannes Bobrowski. Peter Huchel. Briefwechsel*, edited by Eberhard Haufe, Marbach, 1993, p. 46.

41. See footnote 7 above.

42. In his papers dealing with radio matters in the late 1940s, Wilhelm Pieck, for instance, describes Lommer as one of yesterday's men. See the Wilhelm Pieck Archive, ref. no. NL 36/750 in Stiftung Archiv der Parteien und Massenorganisationen der DDR im Bundesarchiv, Berlin (SAdP).

43. See Joseph Wulf, *Theater und Film im Dritten Reich*, Gütersloh, 1964, p. 397.

44. See footnote 20 above.

45. *verboten und verbrannt. Deutsche Literatur 12 Jahre unterdrückt*, edited by Richard Drews and Alfred Kantorowicz, Berlin and Munich, 1947, p. 77.

46. Dr K. Sch., 'Der Lyriker Peter Huchel', *Neues Deutschland*, 5 June 1947.

47. 'Lyrik der Natur gewidmet. Peter-Huchel-Stunde im Kulturbund', *Der Morgen*, 6 June 1947.

48. See footnote 30 above.

49. A copy of the report is in the archive of the Kulturbund, ref. no. 73.

50. The project is, for example, referred to by Becher in his correspondence with Wiegler on 3 May 1947. At that time, Becher was considering using the title *Die Tradition*. See Johannes R. Becher, *Briefe 1909-1958*, 2 vols., edited by Rolf Harder, Berlin and Weimar, 1993, i, 336.

51. Birkenfeld, *Ost und West*, p. 77.

52. The October issue of *Ost und West* was of especial importance: it contained the key speeches delivered at the First Writers' Conference, which was held at the Kulturbund's Klubhaus from 4 to 8 October. Invitations were issued by the Schutzverband Deutscher Autoren but the idea was originally discussed in the Kulturbund's literature commission.

53. The document recording the formal establishment of the department is in the Deutsches Rundfunkarchiv in Berlin, ref. no. 1946 (Justitiat).

54. The reference, dated 20 August 1952, is in the Teilbestand *Sinn und Form*, ref. no. 56, SAdA.

55. The document is among Huchel's papers in the Deutsches Literaturarchiv.

56. Monica Huchel in Edschmid, p. 132.

57. The document is in the Deutsches Rundfunkarchiv in Berlin.

58. Huchel made the same point two weeks earlier to Brandenburg writers in a paper 'Der Schriftsteller und der Funk', which he delivered in Potsdam.

59. Monica Huchel in Edschmid, pp. 132-3.

60. On 10 January 1950, Radio Berlin supplied Huchel with details of the repeat of 'Das alte Puppenspiel vom Dr. Faustus' on 1 January 1950 at 2-3 pm. on the medium wave. Huchel received 445 marks for the repeat. The same document reveals that the original post-war broadcast had been on 19 December 1947. Huchel was approached by Radio Berlin again on 9 June 1951, this time with the request to produce a new version. A meeting was proposed. It is

unclear if anything came of the initiative. Both letters are in Teilbestand *Sinn und Form*, ref. no. 57, SAdA.

61. The document is in the archive of the Kulturbund, ref. no. 16/223.

62. Bienek's correspondence with Frau Kelbe is in the archive of the Kulturbund, ref. no. 121.

63. Hans Mayer, 'Erinnerungen eines Mitarbeiters von *Sinn und Form*', in *Über Peter Huchel*, pp. 173-80 (173).

64. See footnote 7 above.

65. Becher's letter to the head of Radio Berlin dated 2 November 1949 is in the Becher Archive, ref no. 10188, SAdA.

66. Huchel's letter to the Aufbau Verlag is in *Allein mit Lebensmittelkarten ist es nicht getan*, p. 117.

67. A copy of the manuscript of Cläre Jung's mémoirs is in the Deutsches Rundfunkarchiv in Berlin. The original is in the Märkisches Museum, Berlin.

68. The documents are in the Deutsches Rundfunkarchiv in Berlin.

69. See footnote 54 above.

70. '"Säuberungs"aktion in der Masurenallee', *Tagesspiegel*, 29 October 1948.

71. See footnote 20 above.

72. Huchel made his demand in a letter of 12 November 1951 to Bruno Peterson of Verlag Volk und Welt that had assumed control of Rütten und Loening. The letter is in Teilbestand *Sinn und Form*, ref. no. 53, SAdA. It is reproduced in Carsten Wurm, *150 Jahre Rütten und Loening ... mehr als eine Verlagsgeschichte 1844-1994*, Berlin, 1994, p. 170.

73. See footnote 7 above.

74. Becher's letter to Mann is quoted in Uwe Schoor, *Das geheime Journal der Nation. Die Zeitschrift Sinn und Form. Chefredakteur: Peter Huchel 1949-62*, Berlin, 1992, pp. 20-1.

75. See footnote 50 above.

76. See Uwe Schoor, '*Sinn und Form*. Ort und Zeit einer redlichen Bemühung', in *Am Tage meines Fortgehns*, pp. 245-65 (246).

77. See Uwe Wittstock, 'Einsamer Hüter des Lichts. Peter Huchels *Sinn und Form* – ein Dichter und seine Zeitschrift', in U.W., *Von der Stalinallee zum Prenzlauer Berg*, Munich, 1989, pp. 17-32; Ian Hilton, '"Ein schlimmes Kapitel ..."', in *Peter Huchel. Materialien*, pp. 249-64; and Hans Dieter Zimmermann, 'Der Traum im Tellereisen. Peter Huchel in der DDR', in H.D.Z., *Der Wahnsinn des Jahrhunderts*, Stuttgart, Berlin and Cologne, 1992, pp. 119-25.

78. See the archive of the Schutzverband Deutscher Autoren (DSA), ref. no. 36/3, SAdA. Subsequent unacknowledged references are taken from the same archive.

79. Monica Huchel in Edschmid, pp. 128-9.

80. Monica Huchel in Edschmid, p. 129.

81. Huchel's letter to the Aufbau Verlag is in *Allein mit Lebensmittelkarten ist es nicht getan*, p. 118.

82. In his essay 'Tradition und Widerstand. Einführung in das Werk Peter Huchels', *Regensburger Universitätszeitung*, 10 (1974), pp. 2-8 (6), Bernhard Gajek gives 1929 as the date of composition for 'Die Hirtenstrophe' and Wulfern as the place, but provides no source for his information.

83. Gajek, p. 6, refers to 'dem wohl ebenfalls um 1930 geschriebenen Gedicht "Der polnische Schnitter"'.

84. Wilk, *Neue Deutsche Hefte*, p. 85.

85. Hans-Jürgen Heise, 'Peter Huchels neue Wege', *Neue Deutsche Hefte*, 11 (1964), No. 99, pp. 104-11 (104).

86. In Zak, pp. 17-8.

87. A radio version of 'Das Gesetz' was broadcast in October 1959 as Peter Huchel's contribution to the 10th anniversary of the founding of the GDR.

88. See Alexander Dimshitz's use of the term in his article 'Züge einer neuen Kunst', *Tägliche Rundschau*, 14 August 1946.

Chapter 7

1. Wilk, *Neue Deutsche Hefte*, p. 89.

2. Hans Mayer in *Über Peter Huchel*, p. 174.

3. Alfred Andersch, 'Marxisten in der Igelstellung', *Frankfurter Hefte*, 6 (1951), pp. 208-10 (208).

4. Huchel's letter of 14 June 1948 to Bergmüller is in Teilbestand *Sinn und Form*, ref. no. 57, SAdA. Bergmüller worked at the radio station in Strasbourg. Huchel's correspondence with Bergmüller shows that Huchel made a further effort to resume work as a radio author. Bergmüller wrote to Huchel on 28 April 1948 and 18 August 1949 with requests to broadcast Huchel's radio play 'Tartarin de Tarascon'. Both letters are in Teilbestand *Sinn und Form*, ref. no. 57, SAdA. In his first letter, Bergmüller wrote that a broadcast of Huchel's 'Tartarin de Tarascon' had actually been planned a decade earlier. He proposed some editing of Huchel's manuscript and that they should share the fee. In the second letter, Bergmüller informed Huchel that he was still trying to have the play broadcast. It is unclear if anything came of it. Similarly, on 18 May 1949 Karl Schwedhelm of Süddeutscher Rundfunk wrote to Huchel, 'An den Hörspielen, von denen Sie schreiben, ist unsere Dramaturgie (Herr Prager) interessiert, und ich bitte Sie, die Manuskripte unverbindlich doch dort hinzusenden'. On 8 September 1950, Gerhard Prager wrote to Huchel, 'Wir kennen Sie als einen bewährten Hörspielautor in den Anfängen des Rundfunks'. He invited

Huchel to send him his radio plays. Both letters are in Teilbestand *Sinn und Form*, ref. no. 57, SAdA. It is quite likely that Huchel was recommended by Eich, who was collaborating closely with Süddeutscher Rundfunk in the re-launch of his career as a radio author. Interest in 'Tartarin de Tarascon' was later shown by the GDR's Staatliches Rundfunkkomitee, from whom Huchel received a letter sent on 24 May 1954, in which he was invited to submit the manuscript for consideration. The letter is in Teilbestand *Sinn und Form*, ref. no. 57, SAdA.

5. Sabais' letter to Becher is in the Johannes R. Becher Archive, ref. no. 10172, SAdA. Becher replied on 21 September 1948, promising to discuss Sabais' offer with Huchel. The letter is in the Johannes R. Becher Archive, ref. no. 10173, SAdA.

6. Monica Huchel in Edschmid, p. 133. Monica Huchel states that at the same meeting Becher offered her an editorial post. Records show that she worked on *Sinn und Form* only from 1 August 1949. An agreement regarding her employment on a freelance basis for 600 marks per month was reached between Becher, Huchel and Riemerschmidt at a meeting in June 1949 at Saarow. Details are contained in Teilbestand *Sinn und Form*, ref. no. 57, SAdA. Until August 1949, she continued with freelance journalism for *Neues Deutschland*. In 1949-50, she worked occasionally for the Berlin newspaper *Friedenspost*. (See Central Academy Archive (CAA), ref. no. 81, SAdA.) From August 1949, *Sinn und Form* would resemble a family concern.

7. Monica Huchel in Edschmid, p. 133.

8. Ibid.

9. Riemerschmidt's letter to Huchel of 10 August 1948 is in Teilbestand *Sinn und Form*, ref. no. 53, SAdA.

10. The document is in the Johannes R. Becher Archive, ref. no. 10614, SAdA.

11. In *Das geheime Journal der Nation*, pp. 27-9, Schoor compares the published statement with the earlier draft, which contains an explicit reference to socialism.

12. The contract is in the Johannes R. Becher Archive, ref. no. 10174, SAdA.

13. The letter is in the Johannes R. Becher Archive, ref. no. 10188, SAdA.

14. See the telegram in the Johannes R. Becher Archive, ref. no. 10175, SAdA.

15. See the Wilhelm Pieck Archive, ref. no. NL 36/676, SAdP.

16. The letters are in the Johannes R. Becher Archive, ref. no. 10176-9, SAdA.

17. On 21 February 1949, Kasack wrote to Huchel, asking him to delay publication of Kolmar's poems in the light of the fact that he needed to secure Suhrkamp's permission. The poems, however, appeared in the second issue, together with Kasack's introductory essay. Kasack expressed his displeasure in a letter of 2 May 1949. Both letters are among Kasack's papers in the Deutsches Literaturarchiv, Marbach.

18. See Günther Wirth, 'Hermann Kasacks Wirken im geistigen Leben Potsdams', in *Hermann Kasack. Leben und Werk. Symposium 1993 in Potsdam*, edited by Helmut John and Lonny Neumann, Frankfurt am Main, 1994, pp. 119-39 (132).

19. 'Gespräch zwischen Hermann Kasack und Peter Huchel (gesendet im Januar 1949 vom Berliner Rundfunk und vom Deutschlandsender)', in *Am Tage meines Fortgehns*, pp. 22-8 (25).

20. Mann's letter is in the Johannes R. Becher Archive, ref. no. 10180, SAdA.

21. Andersch, 'Marxisten in der Igelstellung', p. 208.

22. Hans Paeschke to Kasack, 8 February 1949, in *'Als der Krieg zu Ende war': Literarisch-politische Publizistik 1945-1950*, edited by Bernhard Zeller, 3rd edition, Marbach, 1986, p. 516.

23. A distribution list is in the Johannes R. Becher Archive, ref. no. 10614, SAdA.

24. Paeschke to Kasack, 5 March 1949, in *'Als der Krieg zu Ende war'*, p. 517.

25. Wolfdietrich Schnurre, 'Das trojanische Panjepferd', *Berliner Montags-Echo*, 24 January 1949.

26. Schoor, *Das geheime Journal der Nation*, p. 54.

27. Schoor, *Das geheime Journal der Nation*, p. 69.

28. Brecht, *Briefe*, i, p. 613.

29. Brecht's letter to Huchel is in Bertolt Brecht, *Briefe*, edited by Günter Glaeser, 2 vols, Frankfurt, 1981, i, p. 577.

30. Werner Mittenzwei, *Das Leben des Bertolt Brecht oder Der Umgang mit den Welträtseln*, 2 vols, Berlin, 1986, ii, 379-80.

31. Uwe Schoor, 'Ein beharrlich verteidigtes Konzept. Die Zeitschrift *Sinn und Form* unter der Chefredaktion von Peter Huchel', in *Literatur in der DDR. Rückblicke* (*Text und Kritik. Sonderband*), edited by Heinz Ludwig Arnold, Munich, 1991, pp. 53-62 (59).

32. The minutes of the meeting of 25 April 1949 are in the Kulturbund Archive in Berlin in the file marked 'Büro Gysi. Kulturfonds. Berichte und Protokolle. Kommission Jugend und Studenten und andere Kommissionen, 1948-49'.

33. Huchel's letter to Becher of 26 January 1950 is in the Johannes R. Becher Archive, ref. no. 10190, SAdA.

34. *Briefe der Nelly Sachs*, p. 114.

35. Zweig's letter to Feuchtwanger of 5-10 December 1949 is in *Lion Feuchtwanger – Arnold Zweig. Briefwechsel 1933-1958*, edited by Harold von Hofe, 2 vols, Berlin and Weimar, 1984, ii, pp. 59-60 (60).

36. Arnold Zweig, 'Rede auf der Feuchtwanger-Gedenkstunde der Deutschen Akademie der Künste zu Berlin am 28. Januar 1959', in *Lion Feuchtwanger – Arnold Zweig. Briefwechsel 1933-1958*, ii, pp. 412-5 (415).

37. Zweig to Feuchtwanger, 20 October 1949, in *Lion Feuchtwanger – Arnold Zweig. Briefwechsel 1933-1958*, ii, pp. 51-4 (53).

38. Seitz's letter to Heinrich Mann is quoted by Schoor in *Das geheime Journal der Nation*, p. 69.

39. The minutes of the meeting of 3 April 1950 are in CAA, ref. no. 118, SAdA.

40. The minutes of the meeting of 24 May 1950 are in CAA, ref. no. 315, SAdA.

41. The minutes of the meeting of 13 July 1950 are in CAA, ref. no. 315, SAdA. As Zweig's entry in his pocket diary for that day shows, he met with Becher after the meeting to discuss *Sinn und Form*. (See Arnold Zweig Archive, ref. no. 2643, SAdA.) Zweig visited Becher in mid-September for a further meeting, which Zweig reported to Feuchtwanger. (See *Lion Feuchtwanger – Arnold Zweig. Briefwechsel 1933-1958*, ii, 85-7 (86-7)). Zweig noted a meeting with the Huchels in his pocket diary on 19 September. (See Arold Zweig Archive, ref. no. 2643, SAdA.)

42. CAA, ref. no. 118, SAdA.

43. Arnold Zweig, 'Zur Übernahme der Zeitschrift durch die Deutsche Akademie der Künste', *Sinn und Form*, 2 (1950), No. 5, p. 5.

44. Wilk, *Neue Deutsche Hefte*, p. 88.

45. Monica Huchel in Edschmid, p. 134.

46. Information about Huchel was supplied by the Polizeipräsident in Berlin. See Chapter 6, footnote 3 above.

47. On 4 February 1953 Huchel requested the extension for his employee Monica Melis. A copy of Huchel's letter is in Teilbestand *Sinn und Form*, ref. no. 56, SAdA.

48. See CAA, ref. no. 315, SAdA.

49. See CAA, ref. no. 323, SAdA.

50. See CAA, ref. no. 315, SAdA.

51. Among other material, Becher gave Huchel an essay by Fritz Usinger, which Huchel did not publish.

52. A copy of the letter is in the Johannes R. Becher Archive, ref. no. 10193, SAdA.

53. A copy is in the Johannes R. Becher Archive, ref. no. 10/2945, SAdA. The two poems by Kunert that appeared in the second issue in 1950, 'Gedicht' and 'Ein Mann sagt', were Kunert's only publications in *Sinn und Form* until 1961. For an amusing account of Kunert's dealings with Becher and Brecht, see Günter Kunert, 'Brecht und die Volkspolizei', *Neue Rundschau*, 107 (1996), No. 1, pp. 140-59.

54. See *Lion Feuchtwanger – Arnold Zweig. Briefwechsel 1933-1958*, ii, pp. 93-4.

55. A copy of the letter is in the Bertolt Brecht Archive, ref. no. 837/39, SAdA. On 3 January 1952 Brecht sent Huchel poems by Vera Skupin which Huchel published. See Bertolt Brecht Archive, ref. no. 837/41, SAdA.

56. See CAA, ref. no. 315, SAdA.

57. See CAA, ref. no. OM3, SAdA.

58. Brecht also nominated Kuba and Hermlin. Becher nominated Bredel and Renn, while Zweig proposed Bredel, Hermlin, Kantorowicz, Renn and Uhse. Uhse's name was at once dropped, while Bredel and Renn were accepted as members on 28 February 1951. See CAA, ref. no. 315, SAdA.

59. See CAA, ref. no. 605, SAdA.

60. Ibid.

61. Kantorowicz, *Deutsche Schicksale*, p. 92.

62. See CAA, ref. no. 315, SAdA.

63. The document is in CAA, ref. no. A1, SAdA.

64. Huchel's text is in CAA, ref. no. A1, SAdA. The text is not in the 1984 edition.

65. A record of the meeting is held in the archive of the Writers' Union, ref. no. 005/1, SAdA.

66. Ibid. The plan also included reference to correspondence with Weismann regarding support from GDR writers for his journal, which might be an instrument to bring together writers from East and West. Later that year, Weismann published *Worte wider Waffen*, which included contributions by writers from the East and the West.

67. Huchel sent the circular to, among others, Hans Henny Jahnn. It is included in *Hans Henny Jahnn – Peter Huchel. Ein Briefwechsel 1951-1959*, edited by Bernd Goldmann, Mainz, 1974, p. 13.

68. The letter is in the archive of the Writers' Union, ref. no. 006/2, SAdA.

69. The piece was published in *Wege zueinander*, 1 (1953), p. 2. It was reprinted in the 1984 edition under the title 'An die westdeutschen Kollegen und Freunde'. (ii,288-9)

70. Becher's letter of 15 January 1951 is in the Johannes R.Becher Archive, ref. no. 10616, SAdA. Huchel was, in fact, shortly afterwards admitted to the Charité hospital, where he was treated by Prof. Brugsch in March 1951. See the letter from the Literature Section to Huchel dated 9 March 1951, in CAA, ref. no. 58, SAdA.

71. Both letters are in CAA, ref. no. 323, SAdA.

72. See Zweig's pocket diary for 1951 in the Arnold Zweig Archive, ref. no. 2644, SAdA.

73. See the letter from Irene Gysi of Rütten und Loening to Rudolph Engel dated 2 May 1953, in CAA, ref. no. 81, SAdA.

74. See CAA, ref. no. 323, SAdA.

75. Caspar's letter to Huchel is in Teilbestand *Sinn und Form*, ref. no. 57, SAdA.

76. The memo is in the Aufbau Verlag Archive, ref. no. V204.

77. That and subsequent letters referring to 'Das Gesetz' are in the Aufbau Verlag Archive, ref. no. V204.

78. The letter was published in *...und leiser Jubel zöge ein ... Autoren- und Verlegerbriefe, 1950-1959*, edited by Elmar Faber and Carsten Wurm, Berlin, 1992, p. 169.

79. Janka's letter is in *... und leiser Jubel zöge ein ..., p. 170*.

80. Huchel's letter is in Teilbestand *Sinn und Form*, ref. no. 57, SAdA. Huchel signed a contract with the Aufbau Verlag on 23 June 1955. In the event, the cycle 'Bericht aus Malaya'(i,300) was published in *Neue Deutsche Literatur* in 1956. That year, the Aufbau Verlag published Paul Wiens' four-line 'Anruf', a gently satirical encouragement to Huchel that he should deliver what the Aufbau Verlag had agreed with him. Wiens' verse reads, 'Dein Dichterkris, nicht nur malaiisch wetz es!/ Wir harren auch – der Tafeln des Gesetzes!/ O Peter, o Schweigen im wendischen Walde,/ brich's balde!' The lines, accompanied by Elizabeth Shaw's caricature, are in *Zunftgenossen, Kunstgefährten*, Berlin, 1956, pp. 28-9.

81. Becher's letter is in the Johannes R. Becher Archive, ref. no. 10620, SAdA.

82. The document is in the Johannes R. Becher Archive, ref. no. 10623, SAdA.

83. Details of arrangements are in the Kulturbund Archive, ref. no. 24/370.

84. Kantorowicz, *Deutsches Tagebuch*, ii, 178-9.

85. For distribution details, see the Johannes R. Becher Archive, ref. no. 10624, SAdA.

86. Huchel's letter of 22 May 1951 to *Tägliche Rundschau* is in Teilbestand *Sinn und Form*, ref. no. 57, SAdA.

87. The initial correspondence about the issue is in CAA, ref. no. 58, SAdA.

88. Engel's letter to Huchel of 17 July 1951 is in CAA, ref. no. 81, SAdA.

89. Huchel's letter to Engel of 19 July 1951 is in CAA, ref. no. 81, SAdA.

90. Huchel's letter to Zweig of 19 July 1951 is in CAA, ref. no. 81, SAdA.

91. See the Arnold Zweig Archive, ref. no. 2645, SAdA.

92. Huchel's letter to Engel of 11 August 1951 is in CAA, ref. no. 81, SAdA.

93. The report of 28 September 1951 is in CAA, ref. no. 58, SAdA.

94. See *'Die Regierung ruft die Künstler'. Dokumente zur Gründung der 'Deutschen Akademie der Künste' (DDR), 1945-1953*, edited by Petra Uhlmann and Sabine Wolf, Berlin, 1993, p.169.

95. Wolf's letter to Becher of 10 July 1951 is in the Johannes R, Becher Archive, ref. no. 10625, SAdA.

96. Becher's reply to Wolf of 12 July 1951 is in the Johannes R. Becher Archive, ref. no. 10626, SAdA.

97. Zweig's entry in his pocket diary of 21 July 1951 refers to the issue. See the Arnold Zweig Archive, ref. no. 2645, SAdA.

98. The document is in CAA, ref. no. 81, SAdA.

99. Huchel's letter to Becher of 11 August 1951 is in the Johannes R. Becher Archive, ref. no. 10627, SAdA. Huchel is referring principally to the achievement of issue 5 in 1951.

100. Huchel's letter to Engel of 23 August 1952 is in CAA, ref. no. 81, SAdA.

101. Kantorowicz, *Deutsches Tagebuch*, ii, 227.

102. See the minutes of the Literature Section of 17 October 1951, in CAA, ref. no. 315, SAdA.

103. The report is in the archive of the Writers' Union, ref. no. 002/2, SAdA.

104. The report of their visit is in the archive of the Writers' Union, ref. no. 005/1.

105. See *Hans Henny Jahnn – Peter Huchel*, p.28.

106. See *Hans Henny Jahnn – Peter Huchel*, p.21.

107. See *Hans Henny Jahnn – Peter Huchel*, p. 40.

108. See *Hans Henny Jahnn – Peter Huchel*, p.42.

109. See the minutes of 6 November 1951 in CAA, ref. no. 315, SAdA.

110. See Ernst Bloch, *Briefe 1903-1975*, ii, 857.

111. Auer's letter to Huchel of 15 January 1952 is in CAA, ref. no. 323, SAdA.

112. See CAA, ref. no. 118, SAdA.

113. See CAA, ref. no. 315, SAdA.

114. Huchel's letter to Becher of 7 March 1952 is in the Johannes R. Becher Archive, ref. no. 10635, SAdA.

115. See *Hans Henny Jahnn – Peter Huchel*, p.39.

116. Huchel's letter to Engel of 15 March 1952 is in CAA, ref. no. 37, SAdA.

117. Huchel's letter to Schacht of 9 May 1952 is in Teilbestand *Sinn und Form*, ref. no. 56, SAdA.

118. Details are in the Kulturbund Archive, ref. no. 98.

119. Huchel's letter to Theuerkauf of 8 August 1952 is in Teilbestand *Sinn und Form*, ref. no. 57, SAdA.

120. See the minutes of the Literature Section of 11 June 1952 in CAA, ref. no. 315, SAdA.

121. Ibid. In this way, Huchel belatedly responded to the resolution of 12 December 1950 that a 'Spalte "Notizen" oder "Marginalien"' should be introduced.

122. Huchel's letters to Brecht and Becher of 14 June 1952 are in the Bertolt Brecht Archive, ref. no. 728/66, SAdA and the Johannes R. Becher Archive, ref. no. 10638, SAdA.

123. See *'Die Regierung ruft die Künstler'*, p. 217.

124. The document is in CAA, ref. no. A1, SAdA.

125. See the minutes of the meeting of 26 September 1952 in CAA, ref. no. 118, SAdA.

126. Kantorowicz, *Deutsches Tagebuch*, ii, 347.

127. Ibid.

128. See CAA, ref. no. 17, SAdA.

129. See *'Die Regierung ruft die Künstler'*, p. 218.

130. Huchel's letter to Engel of 30 September 1952 is in CAA, ref. no. A1, SAdA.

131. Engel's letter to Huchel of 1 November 1952 is in CAA, ref. no. A1, SAdA.

132. Huchel's letter to Baum of 9 October 1952 is quoted by Schoor in *Das geheime Journal der Nation*, pp. 237-8.

133. Auer's note to Huchel of 9 October 1952 is in CAA, ref. no. 58, SAdA.

134. See CAA, ref. no. 17, SAdA.

135. Ibid.

136. Weiskopf's letter to Bredel of 12 November 1952 is in the Willi Bredel Archive, ref. no. 3782, SAdA.

137. Both were scathing about Wieland Herzfelde's wish to write for *Sinn und Form*. See Bredel's letter to Weiskopf of 4 February 1952 and Weiskopf's to Bredel of 18 February 1952. Both letters are in the F.C. Weiskopf Archive, ref. no. 362, SAdA.

138. For details see *Wer war wer in der DDR*, edited by Bernd-Rainer Barth et al., Frankfurt, 1995, pp. 13-4. Abusch had used the pseudonym Ernst Reinhardt in his work for the KPD.

139. See *'Die Regierung ruft die Künstler'*, p. 229.

140. See Alexander Abusch, *Mit offenem Visier*, Berlin, 1986, p. 286.

141. See Zweig's pocket diary for 1953 in the Arnold Zweig Archive, ref. no. 2649, SAdA.

142. See CAA, ref. no. 17, SAdA.

143. See CAA, ref. no. 118, SAdA.

144. See CAA, ref. no. 17, SAdA.

145. Eisler's letter of 30 October 1953 is in *Die Debatte um Hanns Eislers 'Johann Faustus'*, edited by Hans Bunge, Berlin, 1991, pp. 263-4.

146. Engel's letter to Huchel of 13 January 1953 is in CAA, ref. no. 81, SAdA.

147. Kantorowicz, *Deutsche Schicksale*, p. 86.

148. See CAA, ref. no. 315, SAdA.

149. Wolf's letter to Abusch in his capacity as Secretary of the Literature Section is in CAA, ref. no. OM19, SAdA. The minutes of the meeting of the Plenary Session are in CAA, ref. no. 118, SAdA.

150. See minutes of the meeting of 2 July 1953 in CAA, ref. no. 323, SAdA.

151. See footnote 141 above.

152. Engel's letter to Huchel of 7 April 1953 is in CAA, ref. no. 81, SAdA.

153. See CAA, ref. no. 17, SAdA.

154. Becher's letter to Huchel of 1 April 1953 is in the Johannes R. Becher Archive, ref. no. 10645, SAdA.

155. Huchel's letter to Becher of 13 April 1953 is in the Johannes R. Becher Archive, ref. no. 10646, SAdA.

156. Huchel's letter to Becher of 17 April 1953 is in the Johannes R. Becher Archive, ref. no. 10647, SAdA.

157. The document, dated 8 April 1953, is in CAA, ref. no. 81, SAdA.

158. Wolf's letter of 12 April 1953 is in the file marked 'Dokumente zur Geschichte der Zeitschrift *Sinn und Form*', SAdA.

159. See Der Bundesbeauftragte für die Unterlagen des Staatssicherheitsdienstes der ehemaligen Deutschen Demokratischen Republik (BStU), Zentralarchiv (ZA), AP2237/64, vol. 1, p. 11.

160. See CAA, ref. no. 17, SAdA.

161. Auer's note to Brecht of 9 May 1953 is in the Bertolt Brecht Archive, ref. no. 799/50, SAdA.

162. See CAA, ref. no. 17, SAdA.

163. Marceli Ranicki, 'Erich Weinert. Ein Dichter des deutschen Volkes', *Sinn und Form*, 3 (1953), No. 2, pp. 138-42 (139).

164. Peter Huchel, 'Zum Tode J. W. Stalins', *Sinn und Form*, 5 (1953), No. 2, p. 12. Huchel sent a slightly longer version of the text to the head of the USSR's diplomatic mission in Berlin, Ilyitshov. It reads, 'Josef Wissarionowitsch Stalin ist tot. Aber wenn auch sein Herz aufgehört hat zu schlagen, er ist unsterblich. Denn an der Größe der Barbarei, wie sie noch in einem Teil der Welt herrscht und gegen die Stalin sein ganzes Leben lang und Sieg für Sieg erringend mit der Stimme der Wahrheit kämpfte, läßt sich für alle Zeiten die Größe seines Gewissens für die Menschheit, die Größe seines Genies ermessen'. The document is in CAA, ref. no. 27, SAdA.

165. Letters informing editorial staff and the publisher of what had been agreed were sent from the Academy on 15 May 1953. See CAA, ref. no. 81, SAdA.

166. Engel's letter to Huchel of 15 May 1953 is in CAA, ref. no. A1, SAdA. In keeping with the terms of his personal contract, Huchel's dismissal was with effect from 30 November. He later claimed that he had been summarily dismissed. (ii,375)

167. Engel's letter to Wandel of 16 May 1953 is in CAA, ref. no. 81, SAdA.

168. Monica Huchel in Edschmid, p. 139.

169. See footnote 150 above.

170. See Bredel's exchange of letters with Weiskopf (footnote 137 above) where *Sinn und Form* is described sarcastically as the competition. Not long afterwards, on 9 January 1954, Lestiboudois

would complain to Bredel about the treatment he had received from the GDR after he had acted publicly 'in eigener Sache', that is to say on the GDR's behalf. See Willi Bredel Archive, ref. no. 1170, SAdA. See, too, Lestiboudois' letter to Bredel of 9 December 1953 in the Willi Bredel Archive, ref. no. 3549, SAdA.

171. Herbert Lestiboudois, 'Offener Brief an den Schriftsteller Peter Huchel', *Neue Deutsche Literatur*, 1 (1953), No. 7, pp. 105-9.

172. Cwojdrak's letter to Huchel of 22 May 1953 is in Teilbestand *Sinn und Form*, ref. no. 57, SAdA.

173. Huchel's reply to Günter Deicke of 6 August 1953 is in Teilbestand *Sinn und Form*, ref. no. 57, SAdA.

174. Franz Fühmann, who accompanied Huchel on the trip to the Soviet Union, wrote a series of articles about it. They are collected in the Franz Fühmann Archive, ref. no. 11/1, SAdA. Huchel's letter of 11 November 1953 to Wloch of the Gesellschaft für Deutsch-Sowjetische Freundschaft indicates that Huchel gave a number of talks about the visit. See Teilbestand *Sinn und Form*, ref. no. 57, SAdA.

175. Monica Huchel's letter to Becher is in the Johannes R. Becher Archive, ref. no. 10649, SAdA.

176. See CAA, ref. no. 17, SAdA.

177. There was no mention of Huchel's name in a memo from the Literature Section of 12 June 1953 regarding a possible date for a meeting of the group. See CAA, ref. no. 323, SAdA.

178. See the minutes of the Plenary Session on 26 June 1953 in CAA, ref. no. 118, SAdA.

179. The minutes of the emergency meetings are in CAA, ref. no. 18, SAdA.

180. See footnote 178 above.

181. See Bertolt Brecht Archive, ref. no. 1518/06, SAdA.

182. Abusch, *Mit offenem Visier*, p. 290.

183. See footnote 141 above.

184. The fuller version of the minutes of the meeting of 2 July 1953 is in CAA, ref. no. 81, SAdA, the shorter version in CAA, ref. no. 315, SAdA.

185. Engel's letter of 11 July 1953 to the publisher is in CAA, ref. no. 81, SAdA.

186. Becher's poem was almost certainly his 'Dank dem Freunde', in Johannes R.Becher, *Gesammelte Werke*, Berlin, 1969, vi, 520.

187. The letter from the Academy to Huchel of 21 July 1953 is in CAA, ref. no. 323, SAdA.

188. Huchel's letter to Caspar of 31 July 1953 is in Teilbestand *Sinn und Form*, ref. no. 57, SAdA.

189. The minutes of the meeting of 29 September 1953 are in CAA, ref. no. 81, SAdA.

190. Huchel's letter to Engel of 30 September 1953 is in CAA, ref. no. 81, SAdA.

191. The minutes are in CAA, ref. no. 17, SAdA.

192. Engel's letter to Huchel of 29 October 1953 is in CAA, ref. no. 81, SAdA.

193. Huchel wrote to Engel on 5 January 1954, informing him of his discussions with Becher, who had agreed to his salary wishes. Yet Huchel and his wife wrote to Becher on 22 March 1954, pointing out that the agreement had not yet been fully implemented. Both letters are in CAA, ref. no. 81, SAdA. Huchel got his way.

Chapter 8

1. Huchel's letter to Thomas Mann of 20 September 1953 was published in *Sinn und Form*, 7 (1955), No. 5, pp. 673-4.

2. Thomas Mann's diary entry of 3 October 1953 includes 'Brief [an] den Redaktor von *Sinn und Form*' and the following day 'Fortsetzung des Briefes an den Mann von *Sinn und Form*'. See Thomas Mann, *Tagebücher 1953-1955*, edited by Inge Jens, Frankfurt, 1995, p. 123. Mann evidently had little idea who Huchel was.

3. Huchel's letter to Kantorowicz of 27 November 1953 is in CAA, ref. no. 81, SAdA.

4. Kantorowicz, *Deutsche Schicksale*, p. 90.

5. Kantorowicz, *Deutsche Schicksale*, p. 91.

6. The letter of 2 March 1954 from *Sinn und Form* to Kantorowicz is in CAA, ref. no. 81, SAdA.

7. Huchel's letter to Engel of 1 April 1954 is in CAA, ref. no. 81, SAdA.

8. BStU, ZA, AP2237/64, vol. 1, pp. 13-4.

9. See CAA, ref. no. 315, SAdA for Huchel's report to the Literature Section that he would be meeting Weisenborn, who was encouraged to visit the Academy.

10. BStU, ZA, AP2237/64, vol. 1, p. 12.

11. Jens in *Am Tage meines Fortgehns*, p. 100.

12. The decision was conveyed on 26 October 1955. See Teilbestand *Sinn und Form*, ref. no. 57, SAdA.

13. Huchel's letter of 7 September 1955 to the Wilhelmshorst housing commission is in Teilbestand *Sinn und Form*, ref. no. 57, SAdA.

14. Janka's letter to Huchel of 11 January 1954 is in *... und leiser Jubel zöge ein ...*, pp. 171-2.

15. Huchel's letter to Janka of 14 January 1954 is in *... und leiser Jubel zöge ein ...*, p. 172.

16. Janka's letter to Huchel of 25 January 1954 is in *... und leiser Jubel zöge ein ...*, p. 172.

17. See Teilbestand *Sinn und Form*, ref. no. 58, SAdA. Hünich visited Huchel in the spring of 1958. (See *Hans Henny Jahnn – Peter Huchel*, p. 88.) The project was revived when Insel sent

Huchel a contract on 2 December 1960 but, despite reminders in 1961, the contract was never signed. By then Huchel was in discussion with western publishers.

18. Huchel's letter of 31 July 1953 to Caspar is in Teilbestand *Sinn und Form*, ref. no. 57, SAdA.

19. Huchel's letter of 15 July 1954 to Theuerkauf of *Tägliche Rundschau* is in Teilbestand *Sinn und Form*, ref. no. 57, SAdA.

20. Theuerkauf's letter to Huchel of 20 July 1954 is in Teilbestand *Sinn und Form*, ref. no. 57, SAdA.

21. The letter to Huchel from Schroeder dated 26 July 1954 is in Teilbestand *Sinn und Form*, ref. no. 57, SAdA. Huchel's letter to Brecht of 30 July 1954 is in the Bertolt Brecht Archive, ref. no. 740/22, SAdA. There is no record of a reply from Brecht.

22. Nor, for that matter could Huchel move beyond the patently formulaic in his poem 'Moskau - Gedanken bei der Maidemonstration 1953 auf dem Roten Platz'. (i,351)

23. See the minutes of the Literature Section of 17 June 1954 in CAA, ref. no. 315, SAdA.

24. See Huchel's letter to Werner Krauss of 23 October 1956 in Teilbestand *Sinn und Form*, ref. no. 50, SAdA.

25. See *Der Briefwechsel zwischen Louis Fürnberg und Arnold Zweig*, edited by Rosemarie Poschmann and Gerhard Wolf, Berlin and Weimar, 1978, p. 206.

26. The commission's plan for February 1954 included the following, 'Zur Schaffung von Stützpunkten in Westdeutschland wird im Februar eine Dichterlesung in Hamburg durchgeführt (Peter Huchel)'. See the archive of the Writers' Union, ref. no. 005/4, SAdA.

27. See *Hans Henny Jahnn - Peter Huchel*, p. 50.

28. Kundera kindly supplied me with copies of Huchel's correspondence with him following a visit in September 1981. Some of the correspondence is included in the 1984 edition.

29. Huchel's letter to Erna Döblin of 16 September 1954 is among Döblin's papers in the Deutsches Literaturarchiv, Marbach.

30. Huchel's letter to Döblin of 27 September 1954 is in the Deutsches Literaturarchiv, Marbach. Huchel reported upon progress with Döblin to the Academy's Literature Section on 30 September 1954. See CAA, ref. no. 315, SAdA.

31. Huchel's letter to the publisher of 11 October 1954 is quoted by Schoor in *Das geheime Journal der Nation*, p. 174.

32. Ibid.

33. Ibid.

34. Ibid.

35. Ibid.

36. *Hans Henny Jahnn - Peter Huchel*, p. 72.

37. Christoph Meckel, *Suchbild*, pp. 123-4.

38. Schaefer's letters are in Teilbestand *Sinn und Form*, ref. no. 57, SAdA.

39. Heinz Friedrich, 'Gruppe 47 am herbstlichen Main', *Hessische Nachrichten*, 21 October 1954, now in *Die Gruppe 47*, edited by Reinhard Lettau, Neuwied and Berlin, 1967, pp. 104-5.

40. Hans Mayer, *Ein Deutscher auf Widerruf*, 2 vols., Frankfurt, 1984, ii, p. 230. Richter in fact invited Huchel to three meetings of the Gruppe 47 which took place after Huchel's resignation from *Sinn und Form*. On each occasion Huchel was not permitted to attend.

41. Two years later, Eberhard Meckel is reported as saying that at that meeting Huchel had been 'brüskiert' by Eich. See the archive of the Writers' Union, ref. no. 006/2, SAdA. See, too, Marcel Reich-Ranicki's report of Hans Werner Richter's report of the clash in *Am Tage meines Fortgehns*, p. 147.

42. Eich's card to Brambach is among Eich's papers in the Deutsches Literaturarchiv, Marbach.

43. Huchel's letter to Döblin of 15 November 1954 is among Döblin's papers in the Deutsches Literaturarchiv, Marbach.

44. Following Döblin's death in 1957, Huchel wrote to Erna Döblin on 17 July 1957 to offer his condolences and to express his interest in publishing items from Döblin's papers in *Sinn und Form*. On 7 August, he advised her that it would be in her interest not to sign away the rights to a collected edition of her husband's work now that, following his death, a number of publishers were interested in it. The letters are among Döblin's papers in the Deutsches Literaturarchiv, Marbach. In 1957, *Sinn und Form* published Döblin's 'Von Leben und Tod, die es beide nicht gibt. Aus nachgelassenen Diktaten'.

45. Huchel's letter to the publisher of 31 January 1955 is in *... und leiser Jubel zöge ein ...*, pp. 175-6.

46. Janka's letter to Huchel of 26 April 1955 is in *... und leiser Jubel zöge ein ...*, pp. 176-9.

47. Huchel's letter to Janka of 2 May 1955 is in *... und leiser Jubel zöge ein ...*, pp. 179-81.

48. See Vieregg, 'The truth about Peter Huchel?', p. 178.

49. Vieregg, 'The truth about Peter Huchel?', p. 177.

50. Janka's letter to Huchel of 23 May 1955 is in *... und leiser Jubel zöge ein ...*, pp. 181-2.

51. The contracts are deposited in the Aufbau Verlag Archive, ref. no. V204.

52. Huchel's letter to Caspar of 21 September 1955 is in Teilbestand *Sinn und Form*, ref. no. 57, SAdA.

53. See *Wilhelm Pieck*, Berlin, 1961, p. 17.

54. Janka's letter to Huchel of 1 July 1955 is in the Aufbau Verlag Archive, ref. no. 638.

55. Huchel referred to his plan of work for the second, extended edition of *Gedichte* in a letter to Kundera of 31 January 1958. (ii,340)

56. The text of Huchel's talk of 20 February 1955 is among his papers in the Deutsches Literaturarchiv, Marbach. Passages were published in *Konstellationen. Literatur um 1955*, edited by Bernhard Zeller, Marbach, 1995, p. 101.

57. Grotewohl's speech is quoted by Schoor in *Das geheime Journal der Nation*, p. 175.

58. Brecht's letter to Gilda Musa of 21 April 1955 is in the Bertolt Brecht Archive, ref. no. 688/70, SAdA.

59. Huchel's letter to Musa of 22 April 1956 is in Teilbestand *Sinn und Form*, ref. no. 58, SAdA.

60. Huchel's letter to Musa of 19 March 1958 is in Teilbestand *Sinn und Form*, ref. no. 58, SAdA.

61. Bobrowski's letter to Huchel of 1 June 1955 is in *Johannes Bobrowski. Peter Huchel. Briefwechsel*, p. 9.

62. Huchel's telegram of 16 June 1955 is in *Johannes Bobrowski. Peter Huchel. Briefwechsel*, p. 9.

63. See Eberhard Haufe's afterword to *Johannes Bobrowski. Peter Huchel. Briefwechsel*, p. 45.

64. Bobrowski's letter to Huchel of 5 August 1955 is in *Johannes Bobrowski. Peter Huchel. Briefwechsel*, p. 10.

65. See footnote 59 above.

66. Rülicke's letter to Huchel of 28 March 1956 is in the Bertolt Brecht Archive, ref. no. 764/99, SAdA.

67. Huchel's letter to Becher of 27 June 1955 is in the Johannes R. Becher Archive, ref. no. 10657, SAdA.

68. See *Johannes Bobrowski. Peter Huchel. Briefwechsel*, p. 59.

69. Huchel's letter to Engel of 27 September 1955 is in CAA, ref. no. A1, SAdA.

70. Engel's letter to Huchel of 29 September 1955 is in CAA, ref. no. A1, SAdA.

71. Huchel's letter to Engel of 23 October 1955 is in CAA, ref. no. A1, SAdA.

72. Ziesel's letter to Huchel of 17 October 1955 is in Teilbestand *Sinn und Form*, ref. no. 57, SAdA.

73. Huchel's letter to Ziesel of 25 October 1955 is in Teilbestand *Sinn und Form*, ref. no, 57, SAdA.

74. A copy of Huchel's talk is among Huchel's papers in the Deutsches Literaturarchiv, Marbach.

75. See CAA, ref. no. 619, SAdA.

76. Hauser's report is in the archive of the Writers' Union, ref. no. 006/2, SAdA.

77. See *Hans Henny Jahnn - Peter Huchel*, p. 79.

78. Huchel's letter to Höllerer of 12 June 1956 is in Teilbestand *Sinn und Form*, ref. no. 58, SAdA. At around the same time, Huchel edited a small selection of GDR poetry for the Hamburg almanac, *Das Gedicht*. For details, see *Konstellationen*, p. 385.

79. Huchel's letter to Koeppen of 20 July 1956 is in Teilbestand *Sinn und Form*, ref. no. 50, SAdA.

80. Monica Huchel in Edschmid, p. 141.

81. Marcel Reich-Ranicki in *Am Tage meines Fortgehns*, p. 147.

82. Huchel's telegram to Helene Weigel is in Teilbestand *Sinn und Form*, ref. no. 57, SAdA. It appears to have been sent only after Huchel returned to Wilhelmshorst and found Weigel's telegram there.

83. Huchel's letter to Schaefer of 5 November 1956 is in Teilbestand *Sinn und Form*, ref. no. 57, SAdA.

84. Hans Dieter Schmidt, '"Der Fremde geht davon ..." Erinnerungen an den Dichter Peter Huchel', in *Peter Huchel. Materialien*, pp. 299-303 (301).

85. Huchel's letter to Italiaander of 5 November 1956 is in *Gedanken-Austausch*, p. 55.

86. For details of the row that followed publication of Becher's 'Selbstzensur' in *Sinn und Form* in 1988, see Stephen Parker, 'Re-establishing an all-German identity. *Sinn und Form* and German unification', in *The New Germany. Literature and society after Unification*, edited by Osman Durrani et al., Sheffield, 1995, pp. 14-27 (18-9).

87. See 'Re-establishing an all-German identity', pp. 17-8 for a discussion of *Sinn und Form*'s re-introduction of Bloch and Lukács in the mid-1980s.

88. See *Lion Feuchtwanger – Arnold Zweig*, ii, 332.

Chapter 9

1. Hans Mayer in *Über Peter Huchel*, p. 180.

2. *Hans Henny Jahnn – Peter Huchel*, pp. 81-2.

3. Piana's 'Stellungnahme' of 18 April 1957 is in CAA, ref. no. 58, SAdA. In September 1956 Huchel did not yet have any estimates of fees.

4. *Hans Henny Jahnn – Peter Huchel*, p. 83.

5. Huchel's letter to Nagel of 23 February 1957 is in CAA, ref. no. A1, SAdA.

6. *Hans Henny Jahnn – Peter Huchel*, p. 86. An appreciation of Huchel's achievements, written by J.L. Döderlein, appeared that year in the Hamburg Academy's almanac.

7. Piana's memo of 28 February 1957 is in CAA, ref. no. 58, SAdA.

8. Piana's letter to Huchel of 4 March 1957 is in CAA, ref. no. 58, SAdA.

9. Huchel's letter to Piana of 16 April 1957 is in CAA, ref. no. 58, SAdA.

10. Quoted by Schoor in *Das geheime Journal der Nation*, pp. 149-50.

11. Huchel's letters to Schwimmer are in Teilbestand *Sinn und Form*, ref. no. 57, SAdA.

12. Huchel's letter to Hamm of 15 May 1957 is in Teilbestand *Sinn und Form*, ref. no. 49, SAdA.

13. Huchel's letter to Günther Deicke is in Teilbestand *Sinn und Form*, ref. no. 49, SAdA.

14. Zak, *Der Dichter Peter Huchel*, pp. 35-6.

15. Huchel's letters to Kundera of 27 June 1957 and 6 August 1957 are unpublished. Kundera kindly supplied me with copies.

16. For details of Huchel's trip to Bulgaria, see Norbert Randow in *Am Tage meines Fortgehns*, p. 133 ff.

17. See the document 'Angelegenheit von *Sinn und Form*', compiled by Karl Hossinger in 1963 and deposited in CAA, ref. no. A1, SAdA.

18. Hans Mayer, *Ein Deutscher auf Widerruf*, ii, p. 228.

19. Huchel wrote to Enzensberger on 3 January 1958, shortly after Enzensberger's visit. The letter is in Teilbestand *Sinn und Form*, ref. no. 49, SAdA. There is no record of any correspondence with Bachmann in Teilbestand *Sinn und Form*. Huchel wrote to Jens on 9 March 1959, inviting him to visit him in Wilhelmshorst. The letter is in Teilbestand *Sinn und Form*, ref. no. 50, SAdA. For Jens' account of a visit, see Jens in *Am Tage meines Fortgehns*, p. 100.

20. Kurt Hager, 'Den Dingen auf den Grund gehen', *Neues Deutschland*, 26 October 1957.

21. See Schoor, *Das geheime Journal der Nation*, p. 107. The document was recently published in *Konstellationen*, pp. 103-4.

22. Hans Mayer in *Über Peter Huchel*, p. 179.

23. See CAA, ref. no. 315, SAdA.

24. See footnote 17 above.

25. Huchel's letter to Caspar is in Teilbestand *Sinn und Form*, ref. no. 58, SAdA.

26. BStU, AP 2237/64, vol. 1, pp. 15-6.

27. See Ruth Römer, '"Und da kämen diese Gängster". Wie die Staatssicherheit Ernst Bloch abhörte', *Deutschland Archiv*, 27 (1994), No. 3, pp. 265-71.

28. See Ernst Bloch, *Briefe. 1903-1975*, ii, 881. Bloch was referring to 'Paradoxe und Pastorale bei Wagner', which was published in 1959 in *Merkur*.

29. *Hans Henny Jahnn – Peter Huchel*, p. 87.

30. See IV 2/2026/31, SAdP.

31. That integrity was recently called into question by Karl Corino in 'Dichtung in eigener Sache', *Die Zeit*, 4 October 1996, pp. 9-11. Hermlin replied in an interview published in *Der Spiegel* on 7 October 1996 and entitled 'Des Dichters "wahre Lügen"'.

32. *Hans Henny Jahnn – Peter Huchel*, p. 88.

33. Huchel's correspondence with the Tukan Circle is in Teilbestand *Sinn und Form*, ref. no. 57, SAdA.

34. Huchel's letter to the Academy of 15 October 1958 concerning the Becher special number is in CAA, ref. no. 81, SAdA.

35. See footnote 30 above.

36. *Hans Henny Jahnn – Peter Huchel*, p. 94.

37. *Hans Henny Jahnn – Peter Huchel*, p. 95.

38. *Hans Henny Jahnn – Peter Huchel*, p. 104.

39. BStU, ZA, AP 2237/64, vol. 5, p. 17.

40. See footnote 30 above.

41. BStU, ZA, AP 2237/64, vol. 1, p. 21.

42. Ibid. 'GI' = 'Geheimer Informator'.

43. *Hans Henny Jahnn – Peter Huchel*, pp. 100-1.

44. *Hans Henny Jahnn – Peter Huchel*, p. 102.

45. BStU, ZA, AP 2237/64, vol. 1, p. 22.

46. BStU, ZA, AP 2237/64, vol. 1, p. 23.

47. *Hans Henny Jahnn – Peter Huchel*, p. 103.

48. Jahnn's letter to Nagel is in CAA, ref. no. A1, SAdA. Invoking the importance of collaboration with the East Berlin Academy and stressing the significant achievement that *Sinn und Form* represented, Herbert von Buttlar wrote to Werner Hebebrand on 9 September 1959, asking him to represent the West Berlin Academy on Scharoun's behalf. The letter is in *"... und die Vergangenheit sitzt immer mit am Tisch"*. *Dokumente zur Geschichte der Akademie der Künste (West), 1945/54-1993*, edited by Christine Fischer-Defoy, Berlin, 1997, p. 454.

49. *Hans Henny Jahnn – Peter Huchel*, p. 104.

50. Huchel's 'Das Gesetz' was broadcast as part of the celebrations.

51. See the letter from *Sinn und Form* to Hans Mayer of 22 September 1959 in Teilbestand *Sinn und Form*, ref. no. 50, SAdA.

52. Nagel's telegram to Jahnn of 30 October 1959 is CAA, ref. no. A1, SAdA.

53. Uhse's letter to Huchel of 26 October 1959 is in CAA, ref. no. 320, SAdA.

54. Willy Haas in *Über Peter Huchel*, p. 160.

55. Willy Haas in *Über Peter Huchel*, p. 161.

56. Willy Haas in *Über Peter Huchel*, p. 162.

57. See Stefan Welzk's account 'Wilhelmshorst und anderswo', in *Am Tage meines Fortgehns*, pp. 116-25 (117).

58. Welzk in *Am Tage meines Fortgehns*, p. 117.

59. On 4 January 1960 Huchel agreed to Italiaander's request to join a group set up after Jahnn's death to administer his papers. See Italiaander, *Gedanken-Austausch*, p. 56.

60. The minutes of the meeting of the Literature Section on 18 December 1959 and of the later meetings referred to below are in IV 2/2026/31, SAdP. At the meeting on 28 January 1960, it was announced that the nomination would have to be held over because the prize would be awarded only from 1961, the year on which Becher would have been 70. Huchel's nomination was actually confirmed by the Presidium on 30 November 1960 but was note later acted upon.

61. BStU, ZA, AP 2237/64, vol. 5, p. 20. The information that the informant was Seeger is provided by Joachim Walther in *Sicherungsbereich Literatur*, Berlin, 1996, pp. 570-1.

62. See Mayer's account in *Ein Deutscher auf Widerruf*, ii, 232-5.

63. Mayer, *Ein Deutscher auf Widerruf*, ii, 235.

64. Huchel's letter to Bloch of 7 April 1960 is in Teilbestand *Sinn und Form*, ref. no. 57, SAdA. Bloch's letter of 3 April 1960 has not been located.

65. These matters will be dealt with at the appropriate point below.

66. See Schoor, *Das geheime Journal der Nation*, p. 88 and footnote 255, which refers to Huchel's memo of 23 June 1960. For details of the attempted *rapprochement* between the SED leadership and Bloch in 1960, including the role earmarked for *Sinn und Form*, see Anna-Sabine Ernst and Gerwin Klinger, 'Socialist Socrates: Ernst Bloch in the GDR', *Radical Philosophy*, 84 (1997), pp. 6-21, especially p. 17.

67. See Schoor, *Das geheime Journal der Nation*, p. 87, and footnote 252. On 19 December 1960 Huchel issued instructions that the printer should not proceed.

68. See Ernst Bloch, *Briefe. 1903-1975*, ii, 882.

69. Huchel's letter to Bloch of 8 July 1960 is in Teilbestand *Sinn und Form*, ref. no. 57, SAdA.

70. The copies are in BStU, ZA, AP 2237/64, vol. 1, pp. 24-5.

71. Huchel's letter to Dietzel of 12 May 1960 regarding the Becher Prize is in CAA, ref. no. 320, SAdA.

72. BStU, ZA, AP 2237/64, vol. 1, p. 27.

73. For the minutes see IV 2/2026/31, SAdP. Hermlin's official letter of invitation to the meeting of 23 June 1960 is in CAA, ref. no. 315, SAdA.

74. See 'Der Fall von Peter Huchel und *Sinn und Form*. Dokumente', *Sinn und Form*, 44 (1992), No. 5, pp. 739-822. Unless otherwise indicated, subsequent references to documents relating to the *Sinn und Form* affair of the early 1960s are drawn from the same source.

75. This was actually the rule in the journal's history after Huchel, too. See my essay 'The disloyalty of a loyal comrade. Wilhelm Girnus' conflict with the SED leadership over *Unvollendete Geschichte*', in *Volker Braun*, edited by Rolf Jucker, Cardiff, 1995, pp. 107-23.

76. Huchel's letter to Kundera of 17 August 1960 is unpublished. Kundera kindly supplied me with a copy.

77. BStU, ZA, AP 2237/64, vol. 1, p. 27.

78. BStU, ZA, AP 2237/64, vol. 1, pp. 48-9.

79. The Academy's open letter of 21 November 1960 is among Huchel's papers in the Deutsches Literaturarchiv, Marbach.

80. Haufs' poem is in *Am Tage meines Fortgehns*, p. 164.

81. 'Marion''s report is in BStU, ZA, AP 2237/64, vol. 1, p. 42.

82. See Klaus Völker's introduction to Roger Melis' *Berlin-Berlin. Porträts*, Marbach, 1992, p. 9.

83. The report is in BStU, ZA, AP 2237/64, vol. 1, p. 43.

84. See BStU, ZA, AP 2237/64, vol. 1, p. 44-7.

85. Huchel's contribution was at the meeting of the Literature Section on 19 May 1961. The minutes are deposited in IV 2/2026/31, SAdP.

86. See Walter Jens, *Deutsche Literatur der Gegenwart*, Munich, 1961, p. 29.

87. *Johannes Bobrowski. Peter Huchel. Briefwechsel*, p. 64.

88. Huchel told Livia Wittmann that Bachmann had inspired him to write 'Sibylle des Sommers'. (i,399)

89. Huchel's letter to Kundera of 17 August 1960 is unpublished. Kundera kindly supplied me with a copy.

90. Huchel's letter to Kundera of 14 July 1961 is unpublished. Kundera kindly supplied me with a copy.

91. *Johannes Bobrowski. Peter Huchel. Briefwechsel*, p. 68.

92. Huchel's letter to Caspar of 22 August 1961 is in *Das letzte Wort hat der Minister. Autoren- und Verlegerbriefe 1960-1969*, edited by Elmar Faber and Carsten Wurm, Berlin, 1994, p. 98.

93. Hesse's letter of 28 September 1962 to Stephan Huchel's school is in Teilbestand *Sinn und Form*, ref. no. 57, SAdA.

94. See Henryk Bereska, 'Die Welt kommt zu ihm', in *Am Tage meines Fortgehns*, pp. 77-84 (79).

95. The documents were collected in *Vaterland, Muttersprache*, edited by Klaus Wagenbach et al., Berlin, 1980, p. 183 ff.

96. Monica Huchel in Edschmid, p. 144. See, too, Welzk in *Am Tage meines Fortgehns*, p. 117.

97. Monica Huchel in Edschmid, p. 143.

98. *Johannes Bobrowski. Peter Huchel. Briefwechsel*, p. 24.

99. Völker in *Berlin - Berlin*, p. 9.

100. BStU, ZA, AP 2237/64, vol. 1, p. 50.

101. For details, see CAA, ref. no. 323, SAdA.

Chapter 10

1. Abusch's letter to Hossinger of 12 January 1962 is in CAA, ref. no. 81, SAdA.

2. See 'Angelegenheit von *Sinn und Form*' in CAA, ref. no. A1, SAdA.

3. The letter of 9 February 1962 from Hossinger and Nagel to Huchel is in CAA, ref. no. 323, SAdA.

4. The letter of 2 March 1962 from Hossinger and Nagel to Huchel is in CAA, ref. no. A1, SAdA.

5. Hossinger's letter to Huchel of 23 March 1962 is in CAA, ref. no. A1, SAdA.

6. See Monica Huchel in Edschmid, p. 144.

7. Huchel's letter to Kundera of 10 April 1962 is unpublished. In another unpublished letter of 14 July 1961, he had reported to Kundera that for nine months he had been suffering from painful arthritis in the right shoulder and had begun a fresh course of injections of Jenacain (Novokain), of which he had taken 20.

8. Willi Bredel, 'Die nationale Aufgabe der Deutschen Akademie der Künste zu Berlin als sozialistische Akademie der Deutschen Demokratischen Republik', in *Die nationale Aufgabe der Deutschen Akademie der Künste zu Berlin*, Berlin, 1962, pp. 13-34.

9. Bredel's diary is in the Willi Bredel Archive, ref. no. 1165, SAdA.

10. Huchel's letter to Bredel of 5 June 1962 and Bredel's reply of 8 June 1962 are in CAA, ref. no. 81, SAdA.

11. See footnote 9 above.

12. Hans Mayer, *Ein Deutscher auf Widerruf*, ii, p. 248.

13. The minutes of the meeting are in CAA, ref. No. 81, SAdA.

14. The agenda for the meeting on 25 June 1962 is in IV 2/2.026/31, SAdP. I have not traced a record of the meeting.

15. Bodo Uhse, *Reise- und Tagebücher*, 2 vols., Berlin and Weimar, 1981, ii, p. 493.

16. The record of the meeting of 27 July, completed on 8 August 1962, is in CAA, ref. no. A1, SAdA.

17. At the Presidium's meeting on 20 June 1962, Bredel actually proposed a new Academy journal which, like *Sinn und Form*, would appear every two months.

18. See footnote 9 above.

19. Ibid.

20. Hermlin's letter to Leonhard of 17 September 1962 is in CAA, ref. no. 81, SAdA.

21. Abusch's letter to Bredel of 24 September 1962 is in CAA, ref. no. 81, SAdA.

22. Hans Mayer, *Ein Deutscher auf Widerruf*, ii, p. 250.

23. Hossinger's memo of 27 September 1962 is in CAA, ref. no. A1, SAdA.

24. Huchel's letter to Raddatz is quoted by Schoor in *Das geheime Journal der Nation*, p. 240, footnote 470.

25. See Teilbestand *Sinn und Form*, ref. no. 46, SAdA.

26. See Teilbestand *Sinn und Form*, ref. no. 46, SAdA.

27. See Hossinger's memo of 29 December 1962 in CAA, ref. no. A1, SAdA.

28. See Uhse's letter to Hermlin of 5 October 1962 and Hermlin's reply of 6 October 1962, both in the file 'Sinn und Form Redaktionsbeirat' in CAA, SAdA. Uhse's correspondence with Felsenstein is in the same file.

29. See Stephan Hermlin, *Neue Deutsche Literatur*, 36 (1988), No. 423, pp. 35-40 (35-6).

30. See Mytze, Andreas, (ed.), 'Die Stasi-Akte Peter Huchel 1963', *europäische ideen*, No. 86 (1994), pp. 33-4 *(33)*.

31. See the document 'Angelegenheit von *Sinn und Form*'.

32. Ibid.

33. See Hossinger's memo of 18 October 1962 in CAA, ref. no. A1, SAdA.

34. See Hossinger's note to Bredel of 23 October 1962 in CAA, ref. no. A1, SAdA.

35. Hossinger noted the information from the insurance expert in a memo of 12 November 1962, which is in CAA, ref. no. A1, SAdA.

36. See Monica Huchel in Edschmid, p. 145.

37. Bermann Fischer's letter of 13 November 1962 is in CAA, ref. no. A1, SAdA.

38. Huchel's letter to Bender of 11 December 1962 is in *Briefe an Hans Bender*, edited by Volker Neuhaus, Frankfurt, 1984, p. 71.

39. Hossinger's memo of the call is in CAA, ref. no. A1, SAdA.

40. Hossinger's letter to Huchel of 22 December 1962 is in CAA, ref. no. A1, SAdA.

41. Hossinger's draft of 22 December 1962 is in CAA, ref. no. A1, SAdA.

42. Hossinger's memo of 29 December 1962 is in CAA, ref. no. A1, SAdA.

43. Hossinger's other memo of 29 December 1962 is in CAA, ref. no. A1, SAdA.

44. See 'Angelegenheit von *Sinn und Form*'.

45. Huchel's letter to Bredel of 3 January 1963 is in CAA, ref. no. A1, SAdA.

46. Hossinger's letter to Abusch of 7 January 1963 is in CAA, ref. no. A1, SAdA.

47. Hermlin's resignation letter of 13 January 1963 is in CAA, ref. no. OM 149, SAdA.

48. Monica Huchel in Edschmid, p. 149.

49. Much material was published for the first time in *Am Tage meines Fortgehns*.

50. See Eberhard Haufe, 'Huchel und Bobrowski/ Eine Erinnerung', in *Am Tage meines Fortgehns*, pp. 50-3 (53)

51. See Haufe in *Am Tage meines Fortgehns*, pp. 52-3.

52. See Monica Huchel's interview with Karl Corino, which was broadcast by Hessischer Rundfunk on 8 September 1984.

53. See *Johannes Bobrowski. Peter Huchel. Briefwechsel*, p. 67 for corroboration.

54. See *Johannes Bobrowski oder Landschaft mit Leuten*, edited by Reinhard Tgahrt and Ute Doster, Marbach, 1993, p. 226.

55. *Johannes Bobrowski. Peter Huchel. Briefwechsel*, p. 26.

56. *Johannes Bobrowski. Peter Huchel. Briefwechsel*, pp. 27-8.

57. *Johannes Bobrowski. Peter Huchel. Briefwechsel*, p. 29.

58. The letter of 28 February 1963 from the Hamburg Academy is in CAA, ref. no. A1, SAdA.

59. See *Johannes Bobrowski. Peter Huchel. Briefwechsel*, p. 28.

60. See Hossinger's memo of 6 March 1963 in CAA, ref. no. A1, SAdA.

61. Monica Huchel's letter to Hossinger of 18 March 1963 is in CAA, ref. no. A1, SAdA.

62. Hossinger's letter to Abusch of 21 March 1963 is in CAA, ref. no. A1, SAdA.

63. Hossinger's letter to Monica Huchel of 8 April 1963 is in CAA, ref. no. A1, SAdA.

64. Hans Mayer, 'Schneenarben, Schriftzeichen. Erinnerung an Peter Huchel, der am 3. April 81 Jahre alt gewesen wäre. Eine Rede zum neugestifteten Peter-Huchel-Preis für Lyrik', *Die Zeit*, 6 April 1984. Hermlin's presence at the party serves to qualify Hans Dieter Zimmermann's statement that after 1962 Huchel and Hermlin spoke again only on 12 September 1963. See Mytze, Andreas, (ed.), 'Die Stasi-Akte Peter Huchel 1963', *europäische ideen*, No. 86 (1994), pp. 33-4 (34)

65. Herwig Hesse, 'Zuflucht in Caputh', in *Am Tage meines Fortgehns*, pp. 38-42 (40).

66. See Hub Nijssen, 'Leben im abseits', in *Am Tage meines Fortgehns*, pp. 266-93 (271).

67. The report is in IV A2/2. 024/29, SAdP.

68. Huchel's letter to Eich is quoted by Nijssen in *Am Tage meines Fortgehns*, p. 272.

69. Hermlin's letter was published in *europäische ideen*, No. 86 (1994), p. 33.

70. See Hermlin's statement 'Bemerkungen zum Informationsbericht' in *Am Tage meines Fortgehns*, p. 47.

71. Monica Huchel in Edschmid, pp.147-8.

72. See Hesse in *Am Tage meines Fortgehns*, p. 39.

73. Huchel's letter to the West Berlin Academy was published in *"... und die Vergangenheit sitzt immer mit am Tisch". Dokumente zur Geschichte der Akademie der Künste (West), 1945/54-1993*, edited by Christine Fischer-Defoy, Berlin, 1997, p. 455. Much of the wording in the letter was taken over from Huchel's acceptance speech in Hamburg in 1959.

74. See Hesse in *Am Tage meines Fortgehns*, pp. 38-9.

75. BStU, ZA, AP 2237/64, vol. 5, p. 42.

76. BStU, ZA, AP 2237/64, vol. 1, p. 58. 'Martin's' report was subsequently published in *europäische ideen*, No. 84 (1993).

77. See Hermlin's statement in *europäische ideen*, No. 86 (1994), p. 33.

78. See *europäische ideen*, No. 76 (1991), p. 18.

79. BStU, ZA, AP 2237/64, vol. 5, p. 43 ff.

80. BStU, ZA, AP 2237/64, vol. 2, p. 14 ff.

81. The letter from Février is in CAA, ref. no. A1, SAdA.

82. Franz Schonauer, 'Peter Huchel. Porträt eines Lyrikers', in *Über Peter Huchel*, pp. 36-48 (38).

83. See Hossinger's memo of 13 June 1963 in CAA, ref. no. A1, SAdA.

84. BStU, ZA, AP 2237/64, vol. 1, p. 74.

85. Ibid.

86. See *europäische ideen*, No. 89 (1994), p. 21 for the reference to Völker.

87. The letter is reproduced in *Am Tage meines Fortgehns*, p. 268.

88. *Johannes Bobrowski. Peter Huchel. Briefwechsel*, p. 30.

89. BStU, AP 2237/64, vol. 2, p. 52.

90. The letter of 5 August 1963 is in the Aufbau Verlag Archive, ref. no. 638. The letter was not included in *Das letzte Wort hat der Minister*. It would appear that it is this has led to the erroneous assumption in *Johannes Bobrowski. Peter Huchel. Briefwechsel*, p. 68 that the first such contact was on 7 January 1964. The August 1963 letter pre-dates the merger of Rütten und Loening with the Aufbau Verlag in 1964.

91. BStU, ZA, AP 2237/64, vol. 2, p. 43.

92. BStU, ZA, AP 2237/64, vol. 1, p. 133.

93. See Hossinger's memo of 5 July 1963 in CAA, ref. no. A1, SAdA.

94. See Kurella's letter to Bredel of 20 July 1963 and Bredel's reply of 23 July 1963 in CAA, ref. no. A1, SAdA.

95. The letter was read by the Stasi before it reached Huchel. See BStU, ZA, AP 2237/64, vol. 2, p. 66.

96. BStU, ZA, AP 2237/64, vol. 2, p. 75.

97. BStU, ZA, AP 2237/64, vol. 2, p. 82.

98. For the most recent example, see Nijssen, in *Am Tage meines Fortgehns*, p. 275.

99. BStU, ZA, Po AOP 16578/89, vol. 1, p. 16.

100. BStU, ZA, Po AOP 16578/89, vol. 1, p. 18.

101. Huchel's letter of 21 August 1963 is in CAA, ref. no. A1, SAdA.

102. BStU, ZA, AP 2237/64, vol. 2, p. 104.

103. BStU, ZA, AP 2237/64, vol. 2, pp. 94-7.

104. Stephan Hermlin, 'Aber wir sind doch Brüder', *Die Zeit*, 15 May 1981.

105. See *Johannes Bobrowski oder Landschaft mit Leuten*, p. 131.

106. *Johannes Bobrowski. Peter Huchel. Briefwechsel*, p. 31.

107. See *Die Akte Kant*, edited by Karl Corino, Reinbek, 1995, p. 184.

108. Hossinger's letter to Abusch of 18 November 1963 is in CAA, ref. no. A1, SAdA.

109. Hossinger's letter to Abusch of 9 December 1963 is in CAA, ref. no. A1, SAdA.

110. See IV A2/2. 024/29, SAdP.

111. Ibid.

Chapter 11

1. Dieter Schlenstedt, 'Epimetheus – Prometheus. Positionen in der Lyrik', *Alternative*, 7 (1964), pp. 113-21.

2. *Johannes Bobrowski oder Landschaft mit Leuten*, p. 299.

3. *Johannes Bobrowski. Peter Huchel. Briefwechsel*, p. 32.

4. Hans Egon Holthusen, 'Heimat und Heimatsuchung', *Frankfurter Allgemeine Zeitung*, 29 February 1964.

5. Walter Jens, 'Wo die Dunkelheit endet. Zu den Gedichten von Peter Huchel', *Die Zeit*, 6 December 1963.

6. Peter Härtling, 'Der Zeuge tritt hervor. Zu dem neuen Gedichtband Peter Huchels: *Chausseen Chausseen*', *Deutsche Zeitung und Wirtschaftszeitung*, 22 December 1963.

7. *Briefe an Hans Bender*, p. 76. Schäfer's letter to Lehmann is among Lehmann's papers at the Deutsches Literaturarchiv, Marbach.

8. Wilhelm Lehmann, 'Maß des Lobes. Zur Kritik der Gedichte von Peter Huchel', *Deutsche Zeitung und Wirtschaftszeitung*, 8/9 February 1964.

9. Wolf Woldratschek, 'Maß und Unmaß des Lobes', *Text und Kritik*, 9 (1965), pp. 34-6.

10. Klaus V. Reinke, 'Pietät und Kunst haben nichts gemein', *Der Mittag*, 21 January 1964.

11. Kurt Hohoff, 'Mit einer Distel im Mund', *Süddeutsche Zeitung*, 11 January 1964 and Rino Sanders, 'Peter Huchel: Chausseen. Chausseen', *Neue Rundschau*, 75 (1964), pp. 324-9.

12. Gysi's letter to Huchel of 7 January 1964 is in *Das letzte Wort hat der Minister*, pp. 99-100.

13. The letter from the Ministry of Culture to Gysi of 21 January 1964 is in *Das letzte Wort hat der Minister*, p. 99.

14. In a review of *Das letzte Wort hat der Minister*, Hans-Georg Soldat took issue with the manner in which letters concerning Huchel were presented, asking, 'Will jemand 1994 ernsthaft

glauben machen, 1966 hätte der Dichter in der DDR noch – oder wiederum – verlegt werden können?'. Soldat's review, 'Das Elend der deutschen Literatur', appeared in *Berliner Zeitung* on 25/26 June 1994. One of the editors of the collection, Carsten Wurm, pointed out in reply (C.W., 'Unlautere Methode', *Berliner Zeitung*, 9/10 July 1994) that to publish the letters documenting the efforts of Gysi and others was not to suggest that the publication of a collection by Huchel was a real possibility in the mid-1960s. The correspondence, however, corrected the widespread view that Huchel was actually banned from publishing in the GDR.

15. For example, in a recent feature on Huchel in *Die Zeit Magazin*, 26 April 1996, one can read on page 21 that SED politicians 'verboten seine Gedichte'.

16. Hans Mayer in *Über Peter Huchel*, p. 180.

17. Wolfgang Maier, 'Peter Huchel. Lyriker hinter einem Vorhang des Schweigens', *Berliner Morgenpost*, 14 March 1969.

18. Vieregg, *Die Lyrik Peter Huchels*, p. 22.

19. Ibid.

20. Vieregg, *Die Lyrik Peter Huchels*, p. 21.

21. 'Exil' was first published in 1965 in *Atlas Berlin*.

22. See BStU, AP 2237/64, vol. 5, pp. 108-16. The document was published in *europäische ideen*, No. 89, (1994), pp. 20-6.

23. See BStU, AP 2237/64, vol. 5, p. 231.

24. Ibid.

25. See, for example, Hans Dieter Zimmermann's article 'Die Jagd auf einen Dichter' in *Frankfurter Allgemeine Zeitung*, 30 September 1992. Nijssen writes in *Am Tage meines Fortgehns*, p. 275 that, following the recruitment of the pensioner, 'Das Netz um Huchel war geschlossen'. Similar sentiments are expressed in *Die Zeit Magazin*. See footnote 15 above.

26. Jens in *Am Tage meines Fortgehns*, pp. 101-2.

27. *Johannes Bobrowski. Peter Huchel. Briefwechsel*, pp. 54-5.

28. Bobrowski's letter to Michael Hamburger of 11 March 1964 is quoted by Hamburger in *Peter Huchel. Materialien*, p. 284.

29. *Johannes Bobrowski. Peter Huchel. Briefwechsel*, p. 54.

30. Heinz Czechowski, 'Erinnerung an Peter Huchel', in *Peter Huchel. Materialien*, pp.278-81 (279).

31. Karl Mickel, 'Bei Huchel', in *Am Tage meines Fortgehns*, pp. 84-7.

32. See Anneli Hartmann, *Lyrik-Anthologien als Indikatoren des literarischen und gesellschaftlichen Prozesses in der DDR*, Frankfurt, 1983, p. 19. Hartmann is mistaken in her view on page 20 that the authorities would not have permitted publication of a collection of Huchel's verse.

33. Huchel's letter to Kundera of 13 May 1964 is unpublished.

34. See *Johannes Bobrowski oder Landschaft mit Leuten*, p. 136.

35. Ibid. Huchel sent a similar letter to Italiaander on 21 September 1964. It is in *Gedanken-Austausch*, pp. 58-9.

36. See *Johannes Bobrowski. Peter Huchel. Briefwechsel*, p. 70.

37. *Johannes Bobrowski. Peter Huchel. Briefwechsel*, p. 32.

38. See the letter from Lange to Hossinger of 7 December 1963 in CAA, ref. no. A1, SAdA.

39. See BStU, AP 2237/64, vol. 1, p. 18.

40. Details are taken from Huchel's letter of 22 March 1965 to the Kreisgericht Potsdam Land. The letter is in CAA, ref. no. A1, SAdA. Records of the affair deposited at what is now the Amtsgericht Potsdam were routinely destroyed well before 1989. I should like to thank Herr Ebert of the Amtsgericht Potsdam for this information in his letter of 14 November 1996.

41. Brüggemann's words are quoted by Huchel in his letter of 22 March 1965. See footnote 40 above.

42. See Walter Hinck, 'Integrationsfigur menschlicher Leiden. Zu Georg Heyms "Ophelia"', in *Gedichte und Interpretationen*, vol. 5, *Vom Naturalismus bis zur Jahrhundertmitte*, edited by Harald Hartung, Stuttgart, 1983, pp. 128-37 (136).

43. The letter of 16 March 1965 to Huchel from the Potsdam court is in CAA, ref. no. A1, SAdA.

44. See footnote 39 above.

45. Brüggemann's letter of 27 April 1965 is in CAA, ref. no. A1, SAdA.

46. The 'Vergleich' formulated by Brüggemann is in CAA, ref. no. A1, SAdA.

47. See BStU, AP 2237/64, vol. 1, p. 19.

48. Jens in *Am Tage meines Fortgehns*, p. 101.

49. Huchel's letter to Italiaander of 21 October 1965 is in *Gedanken-Austausch*, p. 59.

50. See Hamburger in *Peter Huchel. Materialien*, p. 283.

51. Biermann in *Am Tage meines Fortgehns*, p. 29.

52. Biermann in *Am Tage meines Fortgehns*, p. 31.

53. Biermann in *Am Tage meines Fortgehns*, p. 29.

54. Biermann in *Am Tage meines Fortgehns*, p. 31.

55. See Randow in *Am Tage meines Fortgehns*, p. 127 ff.

56. Jan Andrew Nilsen's account of their visits, 'Hubertusweg 43-45', is in *Am Tage meines Fortgehns*, pp. 67-75.

57. Rolf Schneider, 'Poet und Chefredakteur', *Süddeutsche Zeitung*, 19/20 November 1988.

58. Monica Huchel in Edschmid, p. 150.

59. Hossinger's memo of 5 December 1966 is in CAA, ref. no. A1, SAdA.

60. Stephan Huchel was awarded Abitur in 1968. Huchel actually made conflicting statements about what his son wanted to study, ranging from the sciences to oriental languages. With Heinrich Fink's help, Stephan Huchel secured a place to study theology at the Humboldt University.

61. Wolf's letter to Huchel of 19 December 1966 is in CAA, ref. no. A1, SAdA.

62. Huchel's letter to Wolf of 6 January 1967 is in CAA, ref. no. A1, SAdA.

63. Hossinger's memo of 17 January 1967 is in CAA, ref. no. A1, SAdA.

64. Claudius' letter to Abusch of 17 January 1967 is in CAA, ref. no. A1, SadA. Huchel's letter to Hans Scharoun of 18 April 1967, in which he reported Dessau's visit, is in *"... und die Vergangenheit sitzt immer mit am Tisch"*, p. 456.

65. See CAA, ref. no. 446, SAdA.

66. Dessau's letter to Claudius of 2 May 1967 is in CAA, ref. no. A1, SAdA.

67. See *Die Akte Kant*, pp. 182-3.

68. See Best's letter to Vieregg of 9 September 1983. (i,412) Details of changes from *Gedichte* are given on pp. 412-3 in volume one.

69. Karl Krolow, 'Brüchige Musik', *Stuttgarter Zeitung*, 20 May 1967.

70. Hans-Jürgen Heise, 'Peter Huchels frühe Lyrik', *Die Tat*, 6 May 1967.

71. Hossinger's memo of 18 May 1967 is in CAA, ref. no. A1, SAdA.

72. Ibid.

73. Hossinger's memo of 31 August 1967 is in CAA, ref. no. A1, SAdA.

74. Huchel's letter of 3 September 1967 is in CAA, ref. no. A1, SAdA.

75. Hossinger's letter to Huchel of 9 September 1967 is in CAA, ref. no. A1, SAdA.

76. Hossinger's memo of 11 September 1967 is in CAA, ref. no. A1, SAdA.

77. Hossinger's memo of 4 March 1968 is in CAA, ref. no. A1, SAdA.

78. Hossinger's letter to Reetz of 6 March 1968 is in CAA, ref. no. A1, SAdA.

79. The draft of 20 March 1968 is in CAA, ref. no.A1, SAdA.

80. See CAA, ref. no. 417, SAdA.

81. Hossinger's memo of 25 March 1968 is in CAA, ref. no. A1, SAdA.

82. A draft of the resolution is in CAA, ref. no. A1, SAdA.

83. In Edschmid, p. 149, Monica Huchel refers to a 'winzige Rente' that her husband received. In a letter to Hager of 24 April 1970, Abusch referred to an additional cost of 800 marks per month that would be incurred through the implementation of the pension provision set out in Huchel's contract. The letter is in IV A2/2. 024/29, SAdP. Despite Monica Huchel's testimony on page 287 of *Am Tage meines Fortgehns*, Nijssen maintains that Huchel was left with no pension provision whatsoever.

84. Peter Hamm, 'In der Mitte der Dinge die Trauer', *Süddeutsche Zeitung*, 3 April 1968.

85. Huchel's letter to Herzfelde of 8 April 1968 is in CAA, ref. no. A1, SAdA.

86. Herzfelde's letter to Huchel of 18 April 1968 is in CAA, ref. no. A1, SAdA.

87. See footnote 83 above for archival details of Abusch's letter to Hager of 24 April 1970.

88. Abusch's letter to Stoph of 4 July 1968 is referred to by Abusch in his letter to Hager of 24 April 1970. See footnote 83 above.

89. Abusch's letter to Hager of 3 July 1968 is in CAA, ref. no. A1, SAdA.

90. Huchel's letter to Hossinger of 1 August 1968 is in CAA, ref. no. A1, SAdA.

91. Hossinger's letter to Huchel of 23 August 1968 is in CAA, ref. no. A1, SAdA.

92. See BStU, Po AOP 16578/89, vol. 1, pp. 206-12.

93. See BStU, Po AOP 16578/89, vol. 1, p. 5.

94. See BStU, Po AOP 16578/89, vol. 1, p. 239.

95. See BStU, ZMA XX 728, p. 16. Biermann and Robert Havemann were named as Huchel's contacts.

96. Huchel's letter to Hossinger of 23 September 1968 is in CAA, ref. no. A1, SAdA.

97. The application is referred to by Huchel in his letter to Abusch of 31 October 1968. The letter is in IV A2/2.024/29, SAdP.

98. See Monica Huchel in Edschmid, p. 152.

99. The letter of 15 October 1968 from the Potsdam police to Huchel is reproduced in *Am Tage meines Fortgehns*, p. 321.

100. See *europäische ideen*, No. 76 (1991), p. 16.

101. The poem in question is 'Zuflucht noch hinter der Zuflucht'.

102. BStU, Po AOP 16578/89, vol. 1, p. 247.

103. See footnote 17 above.

104. See footnote 97 above.

105. The telegram is in CAA, A1, SAdA.

106. Abusch's letter to Hager of 5 November 1968 is in IV A2/2.024/29, SAdP.

107. See footnote 57 above.

108. See Henryk Bereska, 'Die Welt kommt zu ihm', in *Am Tage meines Fortgehns*, pp. 77 -84 (83).

109. Hossinger's letter to Abusch of 16 November 1968 is in CAA, ref. no. A1, SAdA.

110. Hossinger's memo of 24 July 1968 is in CAA, ref. no. A1, SAdA.

111. See Bereska in *Am Tage meines Fortgehns*, p. 83.

112. Hans Dieter Zimmermann, 'Der Traum im Tellereisen', *Die Zeit*, 2-4 January 1991.

113. See Nilsen in *Am Tage meines Fortgehns*, p. 74.

114. An extract from the minutes of the meeting on 8 January 1970 is in *"... und die Vergangenheit sitzt mit am Tisch"*, p. 457.

115. See BStU, Po AOP 16578/89, vol. 1, p. 149.

116. Münchhausen's letter to Hossinger of 6 February 1970 is in CAA, ref. no. A1, SAdA.

117. The letter to Wolf from the western academies is in CAA, ref. no. A1, SAdA.

118. The copy to Hager is in IV A2/2.024/29, SAdP.

119. Hossinger's letter to Münchhausen of 24 February 1970 is in CAA, ref. no. A1, SAdA.

120. Münchhausen's letter to Hossinger of 30 March 1970 is in CAA, ref. no. A1, SAdA.

121. Hossinger's letter to Münzer of 1 April 1970 is in CAA, ref. no. A1, SAdA.

122. Münzer's letter to Hossinger of 6 April 1970 is in CAA, ref. no. A1, SAdA.

123. Wittkugel's letter to Abusch of 21 April 1970 is in CAA, ref. no. A1, SAdA.

124. Hossinger's memo of 22 April 1970 is in CAA, ref. no. A1, SAdA.

125. Hossinger's memo of 23 April 1970 is in CAA, ref. no. A1, SAdA.

126. See footnote 83 above.

127. Hossinger's letter to Münchhausen of 27 April 1970 is in CAA, ref. no. A1, SAdA.

128. See footnote 112 above.

129. Hossinger's memo of 13 July 1970 is in CAA, ref. no. A1, SAdA.

130. Hossinger's letter to Abusch of 13 July 1970 is in IV A2/2.024/29, SAdP.

131. Zimmermann's memo of his conversation with Huchel is in *"... und die Vergangenheit sitzt immer mit am Tisch"*, p. 459.

132. The memo by Ulrich Dietzel of 18 September 1970, which records Huder's inquiry, is in CAA, ref. no. A1, SAdA.

133. See Monica Huchel in Edschmid, pp. 152-3.

134. See See *Am Tage meines Fortgehns*, p. 107 for a photograph of Böll with Huchel in Wilhelmshorst.

135. See Max Frisch, *Tagebuch 1966-71, in M.F., Gesammelte Werke*, 12 vols., Frankfurt, 1976, vi, p. 324.

136. The Stasi noted the report in *Die Welt* of 19 October 1970 in BStU, Po AOP 16578/89, vol. 1, p. 22.

137. Huchel's conversation with Schneider in April 1971, which was listened in to by the Stasi, is reproduced in *Am Tage meines Fortgehns*, pp. 108-111.

138. In 'Der Traum im Tellereisen', Zimmermann speculates that Böll's intervention in East Berlin was finally decisive. He corrects this view in *Am Tage meines Fortgehns*, p. 153.

139. Hossinger's letter to Wolf of 20 October 1970 is in CAA, ref. no. A1, SAdA.

140. Blacher's letter to Wolf of 10 November 1970 is in CAA, ref. no. A1, SAdA.

141. Wolf's memo of 19 November 1970 is in CAA, ref. no. A1, SAdA.

142. The memo of 30 November 1970 is in IV A2/2.024/29, SAdP.

143. Wolf's telegram to Blacher of 20 November 1970, as well as subsequent communications, is in CAA, A1, SAdA.

144. See Zimmermann, in *Am Tage meines Fortgehns*, p. 156.

145. Zimmermann wrote to Frisch on 17 December 1970, conveying Blacher's request. The letter is in *"... und die Vergangenheit sitzt immer mit am Tisch"*, p. 460.

146. See J IV 2/3 - 1706, SAdP.

147. Hossinger's letter to Huchel of 18 January 1971 is in CAA, ref. no. A1, SAdA.

148. Monica Huchel in Edschmid, p. 154.

149. Huchel's letter to Hossinger of 30 January 1971 is in CAA, ref. no. A1, SAdA.

150. Abusch's letter to Dickel of 5 February 1971 is in CAA, ref. no. A1, SAdA.

151. See BStU, Po AOP 16578/89, vol. 1, p. 119.

152. Blacher's letter to Wolf of 15 February 1971 is in CAA, ref. no. A1, SadA. It was recently published in *"... und die Vergangenheit sitzt immer mit am Tisch"*, p. 461, together with Blacher's letter to Huchel, p. 460.

153. A phone call that Huchel conducted on 9 March 1971 and in which he conveyed his impressions was tapped by the Stasi and recorded in BStU, Po AOP 16578/89, vol. 1, pp. 133-4.

154. See, too, Zimmermann's account in *Am Tage meines Fortgehns*, p. 157.

155. Tumler's memo of a conversation with Huchel on 15 April 1971 describes Bendheim's role. The memo is in *"... und die Vergangenheit sitzt immer mit am Tisch"*, p. 461.

156. See foonote 135 above.

157. Meißner's letter of 2 April 1971 to the Potsdam authorities is in CAA, ref. no. A1, SAdA.

158. See Monica Huchel in Edschmid, p. 155.

159. BStU, Po AOP 16578/89, vol. 1, p. 105.

160. BStU, Po AOP 16578/89, vol. 1, p. 102.

161. Meißner's memo of 22 April 1971 is in CAA, ref. no. A1, SAdA.

162. See Edschmid, pp. 156-7 for Monica Huchel's account of their departure.

163. See Fritz Rudolf Fries, 'Das Senfkorn in einem Garten der Mark', *Der Tagesspiegel*, 12 March 1994. It recently emerged that already at the time of Huchel's departure Fries was a Stasi informant.

164. The memo of the meeting of 30 April 1971 is in CAA, ref. no. A1, SAdA.

165. The Presidium's declaration is in CAA, ref. no. A1, SAdA.

166. Hossinger's memo of 18 May 1971 is in CAA, ref. no. A1, SAdA.

Chapter 12

1. Joachim Kaiser, 'Peter Huchel in München', _Süddeutsche Zeitung_, 30 April/ 1 May 1971.

2. See Monica Huchel's account of the brief stay in Munich in Edschmid, p. 157 ff.

3. Elena Croce wrote a short piece on Huchel, which was translated by Monica Huchel and published in _Über Peter Huchel_, pp. 101-4.

4. See _Briefe an Hans Bender_, pp. 126-7.

5. Ursula Bode, 'Beim Lesen eines Gedichts. Erinnerung an eine Begegnung mit Peter Huchel', _Hannoversche Allgemeine Zeitung_, 18 October 1972.

6. Helmut Mader, 'Motto zu einem Leben. Peter Huchel 70 Jahre alt', _Süddeutsche Zeitung_, 3 April 1973.

7. Günter Herburger, 'Palimpsest', _Frankfurter Rundschau_, 6 April 1991.

8. Dagmar von Gersdorff, _Marie Luise Kaschnitz_, p. 319.

9. Max Frisch, _Montauk_, in M. F., _Gesammelte Werke_, vi, p. 714.

10. lin, 'Dichter im Hotel', _Kölner Stadt-Anzeiger_, 17 June 1972.

11. anon., 'Kritik und Wissenschaft geehrt', _Darmstädter Tageblatt_, 22 October 1971.

12. Huchel's card to Kundera of 22 December 1971 is unpublished.

13. Monica Huchel in Edschmid, p. 159.

14. The words are quoted by Herwig Hesse in _Am Tage meines Fortgehns_, p. 42.

15. See _Handbuch der Kulturpreise und der individuellen Künstlerförderung in der Bundesrepublik Deutschland_, edited by Karla Fohrbeck and Andreas Johannes Wiesand, Cologne, 1978.

16. Hilde Spiel, 'Sanftmut und Zorn', _Frankfurter Allgemeine Zeitung_, 31 January 1972.

17. Dagmar von Gersdorff, _Marie Luise Kaschnitz_, p. 316. Unacknowledged references below are drawn from the same source.

18. Hans Dieter Schmidt, in _Peter Huchel. Materialien_, p. 302.

19. Monica Huchel in Edschmid, p. 160.

20. Helmut Stieler, 'Singen mit einer Distel im Mund. Peter Huchel las in Köln. Ein Gespräch mit dem Lyriker', _Kölnische Rundschau_, 16 June 1972.

21. See the 1984 edition (i,424-5) for details.

22. The reading was reported by M.C.K. in 'Lange hat seine Stimme geschwiegen', _Berliner Morgenpost_, 14 November 1972. An extract from the minutes of the meeting of the Literature Section is in _"... und die Vergangenheit sitzt immer mit am Tisch"_, pp. 463-4.

23. Helmut Mader, 'Abschied von den Hirten', _Stuttgarter Zeitung_, 28 September 1972. Also in _Über Peter Huchel_, pp. 125-31 (125).

24. Hans-Jürgen Heise, 'Der Fall Peter Huchel', _Die Welt_, 28 October 1972.

25. Fritz J. Raddatz, 'Passé défini', in Über Peter Huchel, pp. 139-44 (141). Unacknowledged references below are taken from the same source.

26. Rudolf Hartung, 'Keiner weiß das Geheimnis', *Frankfurter Allgemeine Zeitung*, 31 November 1979. Also in *Peter Huchel. Materialien*, pp. 199-202 (200).

27. Huchel dedicated the poem 'In der Verwitterung' to de le Roi for his 80th birthday on 13 April 1974. (i,353)

28. See footnote 7 above.

29. Monica Huchel in Edschmid, pp. 165-6.

30. Monica Huchel in Edschmid, p. 166.

31. Dagmar von Gersdorff, *Marie Luise Kaschnitz*, p. 318.

32. Michael Hamburger in *Peter Huchel. Materialien*, p. 282 ff. Unacknowledged references below are drawn from the same source.

33. Benjamin's letter to Scholem of January 1921 is in *Akzente*, 36 (1989), No. 2, p. 172.

34. Scholem, *Walter Benjamin*, p. 82

35. Nilsen in *Am Tage meines Fortgehns*, p. 74.

36. Vieregg offered his interpretation of 'Der Ammoniter' in an article, 'Ein Gedicht nach Auschwitz. Peter Huchels "Der Ammoniter"', which was collected *in Peter Huchel. Materialien*, pp. 216-29.

37. Huchel's words from a letter to Vieregg were published in *Peter Huchel. Materialien*, p. 30.

38. anon, 'Literaturpreis ging an Huchel', *Oberhessische Presse*, 27 May 1974.

39. Peter Huchel, 'Der Preisträger dankt', in *Peter Huchel. Materialien*, pp. 15-9 (15-6). Subsequent unacknowledged references are from the same source.

40. anon., 'Pläne – Projekte – Probleme bei den Schriftstellern der Künstlergilde', *Der Literat*, 15 August 1974.

41. Monica Huchel in Edschmid, p. 159.

42. Michael Hamburger in *Peter Huchel. Materialien*, p. 283.

43. See the 1984 edition (i,437) for a reference to the letter. Huchel sent Bender 'Wintermorgen in Irland', 'Entzauberung' (under the title 'Der verfemte König'), 'Rom', 'Persephone' and 'Die Rückkehr', all of which were subsequently collected in *Die neunte Stunde*.

44. Wolfgang Heidenreich, 'Deutzeichen. Begegnungen und Leseerfahrungen mit Peter Huchel', in *Peter Huchel. Materialien*, pp. 304-319. Subsequent unacknowledged references are drawn from the same source.

45. Stefan Welzk in *Am Tage meines Fortgehns*, p. 124 ff. Subsequent unacknowledged references are drawn from the same source.

46. Monica Huchel supplied Kundera with details in a letter of 14 November 1980. The unpublished letter is in Kundera's possession.

47. Monica Huchel in Edschmid, p. 162.

48. Monica Huchel in Edschmid, p. 161.

49. Monica Huchel in Edschmid, p. 162.

50. Mechthild Lange, 'Peter Huchel nahm Anstoß an zugigen Fenstern', *Frankfurter Rundschau*, 28 March 1978.

51. Monica Huchel appears to be mistaken when she writes, in Edschmid, p. 163, that the occasion was devoted to Heine.

52. Peter Dittar, 'Deutsche Zustände ohne Endzeitgefühl', *Die Welt*, 12 December 1977.

53. Monica Huchel, in Edschmid, p. 163.

54. Schaefer's letter to Bender of 22 November 1978 is in *Briefe an Hans Bender*, p. 192.

55. See footnote 46 above.

56. Manfred Dierks, 'Peter Huchel', in *Kritisches Lexikon zur deutschsprachigen Gegenwartsliteratur*, edited by Heinz Ludwig Arnold, Munich, 1982, pp. 1-10 (9).

57. Barbara Bondy, 'Tiefer ins Schweigen', *Süddeutsche Zeitung*, 10 October 1979.

58. Karl Corino, 'Seelenführer in die Unterwelt', *Hannoversche Allgemeine Zeitung*, 13/14 October 1979. Also in *Peter Huchel. Materialien*, pp. 191-3.

59. See Fritz J. Raddatz, 'Wir werden weiterdichten, wenn alles in Scherben fällt', *Die Zeit*, 12 October 1979. Raddatz's crude extrapolation of arguments deployed by Hans Dieter Schäfer drew a sharp reply from Marcel Reich-Ranicki, 'Verleumdung statt Aufklärung', *Frankfurter Allgemeine Zeitung*, 18 October 1979. Reich-Ranicki's article was followed by Walter Jens' astute piece 'Vom Geist der Zeit', which appeared in *Die Zeit* on 16 November 1979.

60. Wolfgang Heidenreich, '"Jahreszeiten, Mißgeschicke, Nekrologe"', *Badische Zeitung*, 5/6 April 1980. Also in *Peter Huchel. Materialien*, pp. 194-8.

61. Michael Hamburger in *Peter Huchel. Materialien*, pp. 283-4.

62. Monica Huchel in Edschmid, p. 163.

Bibliography

Apart from works of general reference, the bibliography lists only those published works by and concerning Peter Huchel which are referred to in the present study.

a) Works by Peter Huchel

The principal edition for reference is:
HUCHEL, Peter: *Gesammelte Werke*, ed. Axel Vieregg, 2 v., Frankfurt, 1984

Collections of poetry:
HUCHEL, Peter: *Gedichte*, Berlin, 1948
HUCHEL, Peter: *Chausseen. Chausseen*, Frankfurt, 1963
HUCHEL, Peter: *Die Sternenreuse*, Munich, 1967
HUCHEL, Peter: *Gezählte Tage*, Frankfurt, 1972
HUCHEL, Peter: *Ausgewählte Gedichte*, ed. Peter Wapnewski, Frankfurt, 1973
HUCHEL, Peter: *Der Tod des Büdners*, St. Gallen, 1976
HUCHEL, Peter: *Unbewohnbar die Trauer*, St. Gallen, 1976
HUCHEL, Peter: *Die neunte Stunde*, Frankfurt, 1979

Editions of correspondence:
GOLDMANN, Bernd, (ed.): *Hans Henny Jahnn – Peter Huchel. Ein Briefwechsel 1951-1959*, Mainz, 1974
HAUFE, Eberhard, (ed.): *Johannes Bobrowski. Peter Huchel. Briefwechsel*, Marbach, 1993

Radio play:
HUCHEL, Peter: *Margarethe Minde*, Frankfurt, 1984

Uncollected interview:
HUCHEL, Peter: Interview with Ekkehart Rudolph in the series 'Autoren im Gespräch', Süddeutscher Rundfunk, 31 August 1973

b) Works about Peter Huchel

ANON.: 'Kritik und Wissenschaft geehrt', *Darmstädter Tageblatt*, 22 October 1971

BEST, Otto F., (ed.): *Hommage für Peter Huchel*, Munich, 1968 (Individual contributions are not listed separately)

BIRKENFELD, Günther: 'Peter Huchel. Porträt eines Dichters', *Ost und West*, 1 (1947), No. 1, pp. 77-8

BODE, Ursula: 'Beim Lesen eines Gedichts. Erinnerung an eine Begegnung mit Peter Huchel', *Hannoversche Allgemeine Zeitung*, 18 October 1972

EDSCHMID, Ulrike: *Verletzte Grenzen. Zwei Frauen, zwei Lebensgeschichten*, Hamburg and Zurich, 1992

FRIES, Fritz Rudolf: 'Das Senfkorn in einem Garten der Mark', *Der Tagesspiegel*, 12 March 1994

GAJEK, Bernard: 'Tradition und Widerstand. Einführung in das Werk Peter Huchels', *Regensburger Universitätszeitung*, 10 (1974), No. 5, pp. 2-9

GAJEK, Bernhard: 'Dichter – Natur – Geschichte. Peter Huchels Weg in die deutsche Gegenwart', in *Die deutsche Teilung im Spiegel der Literatur. Beiträge zur Literatur und Germanistik der DDR*, ed. Karl Lamers, Stuttgart, 1978

HÄRTLING, Peter: 'Der Zeuge tritt hervor. Zu dem neuen Gedichtband von Peter Huchel', *Deutsche Zeitung und Wirtschaftszeitung*, 22 December 1963

HAMBURGER, Michael: 'The poetry of Peter Huchel', *Poetry Nation Review*, 18 (1980), No. 4, pp. 8-9

HAMM, Peter: 'In der Mitte der Dinge die Trauer', *Süddeutsche Zeitung*, 3 April 1968

HEIDENREICH, Wolfgang: 'Gespräche mit stummen Zonen unseres Lebens', *Badische Zeitung*, 18 July 1980

HEISE, Hans-Jürgen: 'Peter Huchels neue Wege', *Neue Deutsche Hefte*, 11 (1964), no. 99, pp. 104-11

HEISE, Hans-Jürgen: 'Peter Huchels frühe Lyrik', *Die Tat*, 6 May 1967

HEISE, Hans-Jürgen: 'Der Fall Peter Huchel', *Die Welt*, 28 October 1972

HERBURGER, Günter: 'Palimpsest', *Frankfurter Rundschau*, 6 April 1991

HOLTHUSEN, Hans Egon: 'Heimat und Heimatsuchung', *Frankfurter Allgemeine Zeitung*, 29 February 1964

HUCHEL, Monica: Interview with Karl Corino, Hessischer Rundfunk, 8 September 1984

JENS, Walter: 'Wo die Dunkelheit endet. Zu den Gedichten von Peter Huchel', *Die Zeit*, 6 December 1963

KAISER, Joachim: 'Peter Huchel in München', *Süddeutsche Zeitung*, 30 April/1 May 1971

KANTOROWICZ, Alfred: 'Peter Huchel', in A.K., *Deutsche Schicksale. Intellektuelle unter Hitler und Stalin*, Vienna, Cologne, Stuttgart and Zurich, pp. 79-93

KANTOROWICZ, Alfred: 'Das beredte Schweigen des Dichters Peter Huchel', *Zwanzig. Jahrbuch. Freie Akademie der Künste in Hamburg*, Hamburg, 1968, pp. 156-82

KLEINSCHMIDT, Sebastian, et al., (eds.): 'Der Fall von Peter Huchel und *Sinn und Form*. Dokumente', *Sinn und Form*, 44 (1992), No. 5, pp. 739-822

KROLOW, Karl: 'Brüchige Musik', *Stuttgarter Zeitung*, 20 May 1967

LIN.: 'Dichter im Hotel', *Kölner Stadt-Anzeiger*, 17 June 1972

MADER, Helmut: 'Motto zu einem Leben. Peter Huchel 70 Jahre alt', *Süddeutsche Zeitung*, 3 April 1973

MAIER, Wolfgang: 'Peter Huchel. Lyriker hinter einem Vorhang des Schweigens', *Berliner Morgenpost*, 14 March 1969

MAYER, Hans, (ed.): *Über Peter Huchel*, Frankfurt, 1973 (Individual contributions are not listed separately)

MAYER, Hans: 'Schneenarben, Schriftzeichen. Erinnerung an Peter Huchel, der am 3. April 81 Jahre alt gewesen wäre. Eine Rede zum neugestifteten Peter-Huchel-Preis für Lyrik', *Die Zeit*, 6 April 1984

M.C.K.: 'Lange hat seine Stimme geschwiegen', *Berliner Morgenpost*, 14 November 1972

MYTZE, Andreas, (ed.): 'Stasi-Lauschprotokoll Kunze/Huchel', *europäische ideen*, 76 (1991), p. 16

MYTZE, Andreas, (ed.): 'Die Stasi-Akte Peter Huchel 1963', *europäische ideen*, 86 (1994), pp. 33-4 (includes letters to the editor from Stephan Hermlin and Hermann Kant, followed by comments by Hans Dieter Zimmermann)

MYTZE, Andreas, (ed.): 'MfS contra Peter Huchel', *europäische ideen*, 89 (1994), pp. 20-6

NIJSSEN, Hub: 'Peter Huchel als Propagandist? Über die Autorschaft des Hörspiels "Die Greuel von Denshawai"', *Neophilologus*, 77 (1993), pp. 625-36

OHL, Hubert: '"... im grossen Hof meines Gedächtnisses ..." Aspekte der *memoria* in Peter Huchels Gedichtband *Gezählte Tage*', *Jahrbuch des Freien Deutschen Hochstifts*, 79 (1993), pp. 281-312 (282)

PARKER, Stephen: 'Collected – recollected – uncollected? Peter Huchel's *Gesammelte Werke*', *German Life and Letters*, 40 (1986), No. 1, pp. 49-70

PARKER, Stephen: 'Visions, revisions and divisions. The critical legacy of Peter Huchel', *German Life and Letters*, 41 (1988), No. 2, pp. 184-212

PARKER, Stephen: 'The Peter Huchel Collection of German Literature in the John Rylands University Library of Manchester', *Bulletin of the John Rylands University Library of Manchester*, 72 (1990), No. 2, pp. 135-52

PARKER, Stephen: 'The outsider as insider: Peter Huchel in the SBZ', *Internationales Archiv für Sozialgeschichte der deutschen Literatur*, 15 (1990), No. 2, pp. 169-92

PARKER, Stephen: 'Recent additions to the Peter Huchel Collection in the John Rylands University Library of Manchester', *Bulletin of the John Rylands University Library of Manchester*, 74 (1992), No. 2, pp. 85-125

PARKER, Stephen: 'Poetry and politics. Peter Huchel in Berlin literary life from the mid-1920s to the mid-1950s', *German Monitor*, 26 (1992), pp. 1-22

PARKER, Stephen: 'Peter Huchel als Propagandist. Huchels 1940 entstandene Adaption von George Bernard Shaws "Die Greuel von Denshawai"', *Rundfunk und Fernsehen*, 39 (1991), No. 3, pp. 343-53

PARKER, Stephen: 'Peter Huchel und *Sinn und Form*', *Sinn und Form*, 44 (1992), No. 5, pp. 724-38

PARKER, Stephen: '"Ein hoffnungsvoller Vertreter der Funkdichtung". Peter Huchel's radio work in Nazi Germany', in *Aliens – Uneingebürgerte*, ed. Ian Wallace, Amsterdam and Atlanta, 1994, pp. 101-34

PARKER, Stephen: '*Sinn und Form*, Peter Huchel und der 17. Juni: Bertolt Brechts Rettungsaktion', *Sinn und Form*, 46 (1994), No. 5, pp. 738-51

PARKER, Stephen, (ed.): 'Dora Huchel's account of her life with Peter Huchel: an edition and commentary', *Bulletin of the John Rylands University Library of Manchester*, 77 (1995), No. 2, pp. 59-84

PARKER, Stephen: 'On Peter Huchel's adaptation of Shaw's "Denshawai Horror" and related matters', *Neophilologus*, 79 (1995), pp. 295-306

PIONTEK, Horst: 'Peter Huchel – siebzig Jahre', in H.P., *Schönheit: Partisanin. Schriften zur Literatur. Zu Person und Werk*, Munich, 1983, pp. 488-91

REINKE, Klaus V.: 'Pietät und Kunst haben nichts gemein', *Der Mittag*, 21 January 1964

SCHMIDT-HENKEL, Gerhard: '"Ein Traum, was sonst?" Zu Peter Huchels Gedicht "Brandenburg"', in *Gedichte und Interpretationen*, 6 v., ed. Walter Hinck, Stuttgart, 1982, pp. 50-8

SCHNEIDER, Rolf: 'Poet und Chefredakteur', *Süddeutsche Zeitung*, 19/20 November 1988

SCHOOR, Uwe: 'Ein beharrlich verteidigtes Konzept. Die Zeitschrift *Sinn und Form* unter der Chefredaktion von Peter Huchel', in *Literatur in der DDR. Rückblicke (Text und Kritik. Sonderband)*, ed. Heinz Ludwig Arnold, Munich, 1991, pp. 53-62

SCHOOR, Uwe: *Das geheime Journal der Nation. Die Zeitschrift Sinn und Form. Chefredakteur: Peter Huchel 1949-1962*, Berlin, 1992

SPIEL, Hilde: 'Sanftmut und Zorn', *Frankfurter Allgemeine Zeitung*, 31 January 1972

STIELER, Helmut: 'Singen mit einer Distel im Mund. Peter Huchel las in Köln. Ein Gespräch mit dem Lyriker', *Kölnische Rundschau*, 16 June 1972

STRELKA, Joseph: 'Zum letzten Gedichtband Peter Huchels: *Die neunte Stunde*', in J.S., *Exilliteratur*, Berne, Frankfurt and New York, 1983, pp. 219-29

VIEREGG, Axel: *Die Lyrik Peter Huchels. Zeichensprache und Privatmythologie*, Berlin, 1976

VIEREGG, Axel, (ed.): *Peter Huchel. Materialien*, Frankfurt, 1986 (Individual contributions are not listed separately)

VIEREGG, Axel: 'The truth about Peter Huchel?', *German Life and Letters*, 41 (1988), No. 2, pp. 159-83

WALTHER, Peter, (ed.): *Am Tage meines Fortgehns. Peter Huchel (1903-1981)*, Frankfurt, 1996 (Individual contributions are not listed separately)

WESSELS, Wolfram: *Hörspiele im Dritten Reich. Zur Institutionen-, Theorie- und Literaturgeschichte*, Bonn, 1985

WESSELS, Wolfram: '"Die tauben Ohren der Geschlechter". Peter Huchel und der Rundfunk', broadcast by Südwestfunk, 16 January 1994

WILK, Werner: 'Peter Huchel', *Neue Deutsche Hefte*, 9 (1962), No. 90, pp. 81-96

WITTSTOCK, Uwe: 'Einsamer Hüter des Lichts. Peter Huchels *Sinn und Form* – ein Dichter und seine Zeitschrift', in U.W., *Von der Stalinallee zum Prenzlauer Berg*, Munich, 1989, pp. 17-32

WONDRATSCHEK, Wolf: 'Maß und Unmaß des Lobes', *Text und Kritik*, 9 (1965), pp. 34-6

ZAK, Eduard: *Der Dichter Peter Huchel. Versuch einer Darstellung seines lyrischen Werkes*, Berlin, 1953

ZILLICH, Heinrich: 'Peter Huchel und die Siebenbürger Sachsen', *Südostdeutsche Vierteljahresblätter*, 27 (1978), pp. 294-5

ZIMMERMANN, Hans Dieter: 'Der Traum im Tellereisen', *Die Zeit*, 2-4 January 1991

ZIMMERMANN, Hans Dieter: 'Die Jagd auf einen Dichter', *Frankfurter Allgemeine Zeitung*, 30 September 1992

ZIMMERMANN, Hans Dieter: 'Der Traum im Tellereisen. Peter Huchel in der DDR', in H.D.Z., *Der Wahnsinn des Jahrhunderts*, Stuttgart, Berlin and Cologne, 1992, pp. 119-25

c) Works containing references to Peter Huchel

ABUSCH, Alexander: *Mit offenem Visier*, Berlin, 1986

ANDERSCH, Alfred: 'Marxisten in der Igelstellung', *Frankfurter Hefte*, 6 (1951), pp. 208-10

ANON.: 'Über hundert Originalmanuskripte', *Rundfunk und Fernsehen*, 7 (1959), No. 1/2, pp. 45-60

BADE, Wilfrid: *Kulturpolitische Aufgaben der deutschen Presse*, Berlin, 1933

BECHER, Johannes R.: *Briefe 1909-1958*, 2 v., ed. Rolf Harder, Berlin and Weimar, 1993

BESCH, Heribert: *Dichtung zwischen Vision und Wirklichkeit. Eine Analyse des Werkes von Hermann Kasack mit Tagebuchedition (1930-1943)*, St. Ingbert, 1992

BLOCH, Ernst: *Briefe 1903-1975*, 2 v., ed. Karola Bloch, Frankfurt, 1985

BLOCH, Karola: *Aus meinem Leben*, Pfullingen, 1981

BRECHT, Bertolt: *Briefe*, 2 v., ed. Günter Glaeser, Frankfurt, 1981

CORINO, Karl, (ed.): *Die Akte Kant*, Reinbek, 1995

CUOMO, Glenn: *Career at the cost of compromise. Günter Eich's life and work 1933-1945*, Amsterdam and Atlanta, 1989

DIETZEL, Ulrich and Gudrun Geißler, (eds.): *Zwischen Diskussion und Disziplin. Dokumente zur Geschichte der Akademie der Künste (Ost)*, Berlin, 1997

DINESEN, Ruth and Helmut Müssener, (eds.): *Briefe der Nelly Sachs*, Frankfurt, 1984

DREWS, Richard, and Alfred Kantorowicz, (eds.): *verboten und verbrannt. Deutsche Literatur – 12 Jahre unterdrückt*, Munich, 1947

ECKERT, Gerd: 'Wo steht das Hörspiel?', *Die Literatur*, 39 (1936-7), pp. 298-300

FABER, Elmar and Carsten Wurm, (eds.): *Allein mit Lebensmittelkarten ist es nicht getan. Autoren- und Verlegerbriefe 1945-1949*, Berlin, 1991

FABER, Elmar and Carsten Wurm, (eds.): *... und leiser Jubel zöge ein ... Autoren- und Verlegerbriefe 1950-1959*, Berlin, 1992

FABER, Elmar and Carsten Wurm, (eds.): *Das letzte Wort hat der Minister. Autoren- und Verlegerbriefe 1960-1969*, Berlin, 1994

FISCHER-DEFOY, Christine, (ed.): *"... und die Vergangenheit sitzt immer mit am Tisch". Dokumente zur Geschichte der Akademie der Künste (West), 1945/54-1993*, Berlin 1997

FOHRBECK, Karla and Andreas Johannes Wiesand: *Handbuch der Kulturpreise und der individuellen Künstlerförderung in der Bundesrepublik Deutschland*, Cologne, 1978

FRIEDRICH, Heinz: 'Gruppe 47 am herbstlichen Main', in *Die Gruppe 47*, edited by Reinhard Lettau, Neuwied and Berlin, 1967

FRISCH, Max: *Gesammelte Werke*, 12 v., Frankfurt, 1976

GERSDORFF, Dagmar von: *Marie Luise Kaschnitz. Eine Biographie*, Frankfurt, 1992

HAGER, Kurt: 'Den Dingen auf den Grund gehen', *Neues Deutschland*, 26 October 1957

HARTMANN, Anneli: *Lyrik-Anthologien als Indikatoren des literarischen und gesellschaftlichen Prozesses in der DDR*, Frankfurt, 1983

HELLER, Gerhard: *In einem besetzten Land*, Hamburg, 1983

HOFE, Harold von, (ed.): *Lion Feuchtwanger – Arnold Zweig. Briefwechsel 1933-1958*, Berlin and Weimar, 1984

HUCHEL, Monica: *Fürst Myschkin und die anderen. Ein Katzen-Brevier*, Frankfurt, 1985

ITALIAANDER, Rolf: *Gedanken-Austausch. Erlebte Kulturgeschichte in Zeugnissen aus 6 Jahrzehnten*, ed. Harald Kohtz et al., Düsseldorf, 1988

JENS, Walter: *Deutsche Literatur der Gegenwart*, Munich, 1961

JOACHIM, Hans Arno: *Der Philosoph am Fenster. Essays, Prosa, Hörspiele*, ed. Wolfgang Menzel, Eggingen, 1990

KANTOROWICZ, Alfred: *Deutsches Tagebuch*, 2 v., Berlin, 1980

KUNZE, Reiner: *Am Sonnenhang. Tagebuch eines Jahres*, Frankfurt, 1993

LANGE, Horst: 'Bemerkungen zum Inhalt dieses Heftes', *Der weiße Rabe*, 2 (1933), No. 5-6

LANGE, Horst: *Tagebücher aus dem zweiten Weltkrieg*, ed. Hans Dieter Schäfer, Mainz, 1979

LANGGÄSSER, Elisabeth: *Briefe 1924-1950*, 2 v., ed. Elisabeth Hoffmann, Hamburg, 1990

LENNARTZ, Franz: *Die Dichter unserer Zeit*, Stuttgart, 1938

LENNARTZ, Franz: *Deutsche Schriftsteller der Gegenwart*, 11th ed., Stuttgart, 1978

MANN, Thomas: *Tagebücher 1953-1955*, ed. Inge Jens, Frankfurt, 1995

MAYER, Hans: *Ein Deutscher auf Widerruf*, 2 v., Frankfurt, 1982-4

MECKEL, Christoph: *Suchbild. Über meinen Vater*, Düsseldorf, 1980

MELIS, Roger: *Berlin-Berlin. Porträts*, Marbach, 1992

MITTENZWEI, Werner: *Das Leben des Bertolt Brecht oder der Umgang mit den Welträtseln*, 2 v., Berlin and Weimar, 1986

MYTZE, Andreas: Letter to Reiner Kunze, *europäische ideen*, 84 (1993), p. 86

NEUHAUS, Volker, (ed.): *Briefe an Hans Bender*, Frankfurt, 1984

RÖMER, Ruth: '"Und da kämen diese Gängster". Wie die Staatssicherheit Ernst Bloch abhörte', *Deutschland Archiv*, 27 (1994), No. 3, pp. 265-71

SCHÄFER, Hans Dieter: 'Naturdichtung und Neue Sachlichkeit', in *Die deutsche Literatur in der Weimarer Republik*, ed. Wolfgang Rothe, Stuttgart, 1974

SCHÄFER, Hans Dieter: *Das gespaltene Bewußtsein. Deutsche Kultur und Lebenswirklichkeit 1933-1945*, Munich and Vienna, 1981

SCHAEFER, Oda: *Auch wenn du träumst, gehen die Uhren. Lebenserinnerungen*, Munich, 1970

SCHLENSTEDT, Dieter: 'Epimetheus – Prometheus. Positionen in der Lyrik', *Alternative*, 7 (1964), pp. 113-21

SCHNURRE, Wolfdietrich: 'Das trojanische Panjepferd', *Berliner Montags-Echo*, 24 January 1949

SCHOLEM, Gershom: *From Berlin to Jerusalem*, New York, 1980

SCHOLEM, Gershom: *Walter Benjamin. The story of a friendship*, Philadelphia, 1981

SCHWITZKE, Heinz: *Das Hörspiel. Dramturgie und Geschichte*, Cologne and Berlin, 1963

STORCK, Joachim, (ed.): *Günter Eich*, Marbach, 1988

TGAHRT, Reinhard, (ed.): *Eugen Claassen. Von der Arbeit eines Verlegers*, Marbach, 1981

TGAHRT, Reinhard and Ute Doster, (eds.): *Johannes Bobrowski oder Landschaft mit Leuten*, Marbach, 1993

UHLMANN, Petra and Sabine Wolf, (eds.): *'Die Regierung ruft die Künstler'. Dokumente zur Gründung der 'Deutschen Akademie der Künste' (DDR) 1945-1953*, Berlin, 1993

UHSE, Bodo: *Reise- und Tagebücher*, 2 v., Berlin and Weimar, 1981

VIEREGG, Axel: *Der eigenen Fehlbarkeit begegnet: Günter Eichs Realitäten 1933-1945*, Eggingen, 1993

VOIGTS, Manfred: *Oskar Goldberg. Der mythische Experimentalwissenschaftler. Ein verdrängtes Kapitel jüdischer Geschichte*, Berlin, 1992

VOIGTS, Manfred: 'Oskar Goldberg. Ein Dossier', *Akzente*, 36 (1989) No. 2, pp. 158-91

VOLKE, Werner, (ed.): *Das Innere Reich. 1934-1944. Eine Zeitschrift für Dichtung, Kunst und deutsches Leben*, Marbach, 1983

VOSS, Karl: *Potsdam-Führer für Literaturfreunde*, Berlin, 1993

WAGENBACH, Klaus, et al. (eds.): *Vaterland, Muttersprache*, Berlin, 1980

WESTHOFF, Adelheid (ed.): *Das Innere Reich. 1934-1944. Eine Zeitschrift für Dichtung, Kunst und deutsches Leben. Verzeichnis der Beiträge*, Marbach, 1983

WIRTH, Günther: 'Hermann Kasacks Wirken im geistigen Leben Potsdams', in *Hermann Kasack. Leben und Werk. Symposium 1993 in Potsdam*, ed. Helmut John and Lonny Neumann, Frankfurt, 1994

WURM, Carsten: *150 Jahre Rütten und Loening ... mehr als eine Verlagsgeschichte 1844-1994*, Berlin, 1994

ZINNER, Hedda: *Auf dem roten Teppich*, Berlin, 1978

d) General reference

BALD, Wambly: *On the Left Bank 1929-1933*, ed. Benjamin Franklin V, Athens, Ohio and London, 1985

BARTH, Bernd-Rainer, (ed.): *Wer war wer in der DDR*, Frankfurt, 1995

BENJAMIN, Walter: *Gesammelte Schriften*, 7 v., ed. Rolf Tiedemann and Hermann Schweppenhäuser, Frankfurt, 1985

BREDEL, Willi: 'Die nationale Aufgabe der Deutschen Akademie der Künste zu Berlin als sozialistische Akademie der Deutschen Demokratischen Republik', in *Die nationale Aufgabe der Deutschen Akademie der Künste zu Berlin*, Berlin, 1962

BUNGE, Hans, (ed.): *Die Debatte um Hanns Eislers 'Johann Faustus'*, Berlin, 1991

CORINO, Karl: 'Dichtung in eigener Sache', *Die Zeit*, 4 October 1996

DAVIES, Peter: 'Ideology, resistance and complicity in the *Deutsche Akademie der Künste* in the context of Stalin's German policy 1945-1953' (unpublished doctoral thesis, University of Manchester, 1997)

GAY, Peter: *Weimar Culture. The outsider as insider*, London, 1988

GOLDBERG, Oskar: *Die Wirklichkeit der Hebräer. Einleitung in das System des Pentateuch*, Berlin, 1925

HARNISCH, Hartmut: 'Peasants and markets', in *The German Peasantry*, ed. Richard J.Evans and W.R.Lee, London and Sydney, 1986, pp. 37-70

HERMLIN, Stephan: 'Des Dichters "wahre Lügen"', *Der Spiegel*, 7 October 1996

KAES, Anton, (ed.): *Weimarer Republik. Manifeste und Dokumente zur deutschen Literatur 1918-1933*, Stuttgart, 1983

KÖNNEMANN, Erwin and Hans-Joachim Krusch: *Aktionseinheit contra Kapp-Putsch*, Berlin, 1972

KOEPPEN, Wolfgang: 'Überleben im Dritten Reich', *Neue Rundschau*, 95 (1984), No. 4, pp. 88-98

KUNERT, Günter: 'Brecht und die Volkspolizei', *Neue Rundschau*, 107 (1996), No. 1, pp. 140-59

LANGE, Horst: 'Landschaftliche Dichtung', *Der weiße Rabe*, 2 (1933), No. 5/6, pp. 21-6

LOERKE, Oskar: *Tagebücher 1903-1939*, ed. Hermann Kasack, Heidelberg and Darmstadt, 1956

LOTH, Wilfried: *Stalins ungeliebtes Kind. Warum Moskau die DDR nicht wollte*, Berlin, 1994

MCVAY, Gordon: *Esenin. A life*, Michigan, 1976

PARKER, Stephen: 'Re-establishing an all-German identity. *Sinn und Form* and German unification', in *The new Germany. Literature and society after unification*, ed. Osman Durrani et al., Sheffield, 1995, pp. 14-27

PARKER, Stephen: 'The disloyalty of a loyal comrade. Wilhelm Girnus' conflict with the SED leadership over *Unvollendete Geschichte*', in *Volker Braun*, ed. Rolf Jucker, Cardiff, 1995, pp. 107-23

PINTHUS, Kurt, (ed.): *Menschheitsdämmerung*, Hamburg, 1959

POSCHMANN, Rosemarie and Gerhard Wolf, (eds.): *Der Briefwechsel zwischen Louis Fürnberg und Arnold Zweig*, Berlin and Weimar, 1978

SEYDEWITZ, Max: *Es hat sich gelohnt zu leben*, 2 v., Berlin, 1976-8

SHEPPARD, Richard, *Die Schriften des Neuen Clubs, 1908-1914*, 2 v., Hildesheim, 1980-3

VOIGTS, Manfred: 'Metaphysische Politik und psychophysisches Problem. Das Verhältnis von Walter Benjamin und Erich Unger', *Neue Deutsche Hefte*, 35 (1988), No. 200, pp. 798-808

WOLF, Markus: *Die Troika*, Reinbek, 1991

ZELLER, Bernhard, (ed.): *'Als der Krieg zu Ende war': Literarisch-politische Publizistik 1945-1950*, 3rd ed., Marbach, 1986

ZELLER, Bernhard, (ed.): *Konstellationen. Literatur um 1955*, Marbach, 1995

Index

Britische und Irische Studien zur deutschen Sprache und Literatur

Nr. 1 Geoffrey Perkins: Contemporary Theory of Expressionism, 1974. 182 S.

Nr. 2 Paul Kussmaul: Bertolt Brecht und das englische Drama der Renaissance, 1974. 175 S.

Nr. 3 Eudo C. Mason: Hölderlin and Goethe, 1975. 145 S.

Nr. 4 W. E. Yates: Tradition in the German Sonnet, 1981. 98 S.

Nr. 5 Rhys W. Williams: Carl Sternheim. A Critical Study, 1982. 282 S.

Nr. 6 Roger H. Stephenson: Goethe's Wisdom Literature, 1983. 274 S.

Nr. 7 John Hennig: Goethe and the English Speaking World, 1983. 288 S.

Nr. 8 John R.P. McKenzie: Social Comedy in Austria and Germany 1890-1933, 1992. 262 S., 2nd Edition 1996.

Nr. 9 David Basker: Chaos, Control and Consistency: The Narrative Vision of Wolfgang Koeppen, 1993. 352 S.

Nr. 10 John Klapper: Stefan Andres. The Christian Humanist as a Critic of his Times, 1995. 188 S.

Nr. 11 Anthony Grenville: Cockpit of Ideologies. The Literature and Political History of the Weimar Republic, 1995. 394 S.

Nr. 12 T.M. Holmes: The Rehearsal of Revolution. Georg Büchner's Politics and his Drama *Dantons Tod,* 1995. 214 S.

Nr. 13 Andrew Plowman: The Radical Subject. Social Change and the Self in Recent German Autobiography, 1998. 168 S.

Nr. 14 David Barnett: Literature versus Theatre. Textual Problems and Theatrical Realization in the Later Plays of Heiner Müller, 1998. 293 S.

Nr. 15 Stephen Parker: Peter Huchel. A Literary Life in 20th-Century Germany, 1998. 617 S.